War Stories

Down on Stanford's Farm

By

Raoul K. Niemeyer

Stanford Police Captain

(Retired)

Printed by Create Space, an Amazon.com Company

Copyright ©2014 by Raoul K. Niemeyer. All rights reserved.

No part of this publication may be reproduced or transmitted in any form or by any means electronic or mechanical, including photocopy, recording, or any information storage and retrieval system now known or to be invented, without permission in writing from the author.

ISBN-13: 978-1492816393

ISBN-10: 1492816396

Because of the nature of the Internet, any web addresses or links contained in this book may have changed since publication, thus may no longer be valid. The views expressed in this work are solely those of the author and do not necessarily reflect the views of the publisher, so the publisher disclaims any responsibility of them.

This book is printed on acid free paper. And, Made in the United States of America!

For my dearly departed Dad,

Irving "Irv" Niemeyer,

Whose memoir and travelogues inspired me to write this book.

Contents

Introduction: About "The Farm" x

Foreward: About this Book xii

Chapter One: Mem Chu 1

Chapter Two: The Old Guard 12

Chapter Three: Captain Midnight 29

Chapter Four: The "A" Units 45

Chapter Five: Growing Pains/Communications 81

Chapter Six: A Cop's Rite of Passage 104

Chapter Seven: Hell Week: Stanford vs. Cal 120

Chapter Eight: Homicides 142

Chapter Nine: The Delts 178

Chapter Ten: Smile. You're on Candid Camera? 188

Chapter Eleven: The Other Shoe 209

Chapter Twelve: Sexual Misbehavior 217

Chapter Thirteen: *Dumb 'n Dumber* 241

Chapter Fourteen: Demonstrations 254

Chapter Fifteen: Sexual Assaults 276

Chapter Sixteen: DUs 287

Chapter Seventeen: Drugs at Stanford? 297

Chapter Eighteen: Art Thefts 310

Chapter Nineteen: Random Tales 321

Chapter Twenty: Dignitary Visits 336

Chapter Twenty One: O.R.E 382

Chapter Twenty Two: Really BIG Events 389

Chapter Twenty Three: Crash and Burn 422

Chapter Twenty Four: Zeta Psi aka Zetes 426

Chapter Twenty Five: Farm Funnies 442

Chapter Twenty Six: The Art of Conversation 471

Chapter Twenty Seven: Bad Boys 497

Chapter Twenty Eight: Typical Farm Crime 525

Chapter Twenty Nine: Some Good Pinches 543

Chapter Thirty: The Jogging Burglar 557

Chapter Thirty One: Angela...608

Chapter Thirty Two: Tales from the Cuckoo's Nest....623

Chapter Thirty Three: Pros and Cons..........................642

Chapter Thirty Four: Honorable Mention 664

Chapter Thirty Five: Bitter Rivals................................685

Chapter Thirty Six: Football/My Last Big Game.........705

Chapter Thirty Seven: Aloha 'Oe.................................730

Chapter Thirty Eight: Chief Marvin N. Moore 735

Post Script: Laura Wilson, DPS Director 741

Acknowledgements 742

About the Author...749

Cop Jargon...751

Introduction: About "The Farm"

Someone recently asked me why Stanford University was often called "The Farm." Since he was not a San Francisco Bay Area resident, I thought the man's inquiry was a fair question, so I gave him a succinct—something I often find difficult to do—historical purview:

Former California Governor Leland Stanford was not only a successful lawyer, politician and railroad magnate, but he also was a thoroughbred trotting horse enthusiast. In 1876, Stanford acquired 650 acres of land near Menlo Park, which is now the Stanford Shopping Center. The Governor later expanded his acquisition to encompass 8,000 acres, then known as Mayfield, in order to establish orchards, vineyards and many horse training facilities. Stanford dubbed his property as "The Palo Alto Stock Farm." His manager, Charles Marvin, an experienced trotting-horse trainer and driver, employed over 150 personnel; the complex included blacksmith and wheelwright shops, a feed mill, 50 paddocks, eight tracks, an office building with sleeping quarters for 40 men upstairs, a dining hall, harness shop, the superintendent's house, and a school. In its heyday, The Palo Alto Stock Farm housed over 600 of the best horses in the world. Mr. Eadweard Maybridge published a series of photographs which proved that while a trotting horse was at full gait all four hooves were actually off the ground. Maybridge accomplished this feat by utilizing 24 cameras spaced 12 inches apart, electrically tripped at rapid succession. This was the precursor of motion pictures.*

In 1884, after the untimely death of their 16 year old son due to typhoid fever (in Florence, Italy), Governor and Mrs. Jane Lathrop Stanford were committed to building a first rate university on the Palo Alto property in memory of their beloved son. And, indeed they did!

* A Chronology of Stanford University and its Founders.

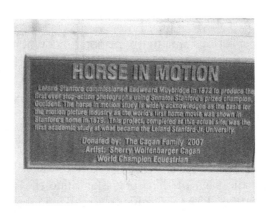

Trotting Horse: Horse in Motion at Stanford's Stock Farm

Photos by Nina L. Niemeyer, D.O.

FOREWARD

About this Book

Although I was a cop for nearly three and a half decades, I was also many other things: First and foremost, I was very dedicated to my family; I took the captain's position at Stanford, in part, to take advantage of the University's generous higher education benefit for my kids. My daughter graduated from Stanford and my son from the University of California at Davis. On the job, many thought of me as a hard-nosed cop, but in reality, I was just a big pussy cat with a bark. Throughout my life, I always tried to maintain a good sense of humor; I found early on that one shouldn't take him/herself too seriously. As you will see in this book, I always relished a good laugh and prank. Had I been a Frat Boy in college, I most likely would have been at the bottom of *some* of the trickery those devils exacted on their peers and others—save for brutal hazing, which you will read quite a bit about!

But, I also have a serious side to my personality: When it came to my job as a law enforcement official, I tried to put forth my very best effort, no matter how big or small the case might be. I was very methodical and strove to achieve excellence; I led by example and demanded no less from my team.

I have always been a history buff. I loved all forms of history, particularly World War II, the Civil War and the 19th Century West— especially the saga of the Lone Star State of Texas. Soon after arriving on the Farm, I quickly realized that Stanford University was rich in history and tradition. I began clipping articles from the Campus Report (now known as the Stanford Report, compiled by the Stanford Historical Society) which featured a weekly column, which briefly outlined significant occurrences on campus 100, 75, 50 and 25 years ago. One thing I noted, however, that there was virtually nothing written about the security/police department until the "Tumultuous Years" in the late 1960s and early 70s, when the Vietnam War was raging—not only "over there," but on hundreds of college campuses "over here!" I met Karen Bartholomew of the Historical Society in the mid-1970s; I told her that I loved the work they were doing and hoped to write an article (some day) about the origins of Stanford's security system, which later evolved into a campus police force. Karen encouraged me to do so, but due to the time constraints of my police duties, I was unable to do anything until I retired in 1999. By that time, I had amassed boxes of news clips about the Stanford University Department of Public Safety (SUDPS), as well as my University history file.

After hanging-up my gun and badge on January 29, 1999, my wife and I enjoyed several years of travel, goofing-off and setting-up new digs in the Sacramento area. In early 2000, I finally decided to get going on this "work in progress!" After much thought, I decided to "kill two birds with one stone?" *Why not write a memoir and weave-in some Stanford history?* I mused. This is what I have tried to do here. I'm not a New York Times Best Selling author nor am I a scholar or journalist, by any stretch of the imagination. But, I *have* been told that I *am* a pretty good raconteur. And, although I admit to some embellishment, the "War Stories"* herein are factual—not even *I* could make-up this stuff!

This book isn't for everyone: I tried to be apolitical, but some of the passages are brash and critical: I'm a lot like that mythical baseball umpire who once said (when an unhappy manager protested one of his calls) *"I calls 'em like I sees 'em!"* There's some cop jargon in this story (which I translate in the text or in the glossary) often coupled with jaded speech—typical of this breed. . . I have tried to tone down the invectives, however, a total cleansing would diminish the context and render the text to read like a children's book—I can assure you, this is NO children's book! As I previously indicated, you can expect large doses of humor when I described the zany events associated with students—especially the "Greeks." There also some disturbing chapters about the horrible murders and rapes which tragically occurred over the years. There is no levity in any of those cases!

Much of the historical data was gleaned from my news clips; however, Ms. Karen Bartholomew gave me a gem entitled "A Chronology of Stanford University and its Founders," created by Karen, her late husband, Claude Brinegar, and Roxanne Nilan. If you are a Stanford alumnus or just fan, their book is a must read.

Many of the historical works I've read over the years, although interesting, might cause an ice cream connoisseur to describe them as vanilla. I've added some chocolate, nuts and marshmallows to this serving, so I hope you will find my rendition to be more like "Rocky Road!" So, based on the historical resources, my memory and ability to spin a yarn, what follows is a chronicle of campus life from a perspective not always heard. I am exceedingly proud of my 25 years of service to the Stanford University community and greatly relished my position, as you will soon see. I hope that you will enjoy my sojourn and learn as much as I did about Stanford University—truly an incredible institution.

Raoul *Kalani* Niemeyer
Captain of Investigations, SUDPS (Ret.)

Note: Pseudonyms are used in this story in order to protect the true identities of victims, innocents and the stupid!

*My title, <u>War Stories—Down on Stanford's Farm</u>, is not intended to depict actual combat—although sometimes I thought we were damn close! Many of my Sheriff's colleagues, back in the day, were former military veterans and used to gather at shift's end and tell stories (often embellished) about what happened the previous night; they called those tales "War Stories." These are mine!

CHAPTER ONE

Mem Chu

Stanford University's Memorial Church

Photo by Douglas Theisen

That Dreaded Call: October 13, 1974

It was *O-Dark 30* when the phone rang and booted me out of a sound REM sleep. My wife handed me the phone and sleepily said something about Radio. *Damn, I thought, only 3 weeks on the job and they are already calling me in the middle of the night.*

"Hello" I said, groggily.

"Captain, this is Charley at Dispatch. I tried to get ahold of the Chief but he's not answering his phone."

"Yeah, I know," I interrupted, "He's up in Placerville with Cap'n Bill for the weekend; what's up?"

"They found a 'stiff' in the church."

"A what?" I barked.

"A dead body, Captain. They found some girl in the chapel; looks like an OD!"

"You've gotta be kidding me! Whaddya mean an OD?" I screamed.

"Maybe drugs or something. Q-7 and Q-9 are on the scene and they have already called for the S/O," the dispatcher advised.

"OK, so where exactly is this chapel or church? You know I'm new at Stanford and don't know the campus very well yet," I confessed.

"It's Mem Chu, aaah, Memorial Church— in the Quad! You can get there by taking Duena Street!"

"OK, I'll find it. I have a map," I asserted, trying not to seem too stupid. "I'll be there, travel time from Campbell. And, tell the officers NOT to touch anything and stay away from the victim and have them seal off the entire church. Above all, tell them NOT to let the media in, under any circumstances! OK?"

"10-4, Sir. Bye-Bye."

I quickly threw on some duds and jumped into my hot rod, a '70 Ford Torino Cobra, with 365 ponies under the hood. That thing would lay down a hundred feet of rubber and could pass almost anything on the road, save a gas station. . . On the white knuckle ride up I-280, at record breaking speeds, I wondered what was in store for this fledgling captain. . .

Using my official Stanford University and Vicinity parking map, I somehow found my way to Duena Street. As I passed the Old Firehouse, I recalled spending many hours of bivouac in the Courtyard where the old Stanford PD used to be:
****

This was during the tumultuous years of the Vietnam War. As a member of the *Mean Green Machine*—what the radicals had dubbed our Crowd Control Unit—we were literally holed-up in that Courtyard waiting for the *wimpy* administration to make a decision whether they wanted to stop the rioting or not. Like Nero before them, the previous administration literally fiddled while the place was being thrashed and burned! Every once in a while, they would put us on leashes and let us out of our cage in order to scare the kids—we felt like Dobermans. . . *Kicking Butt and Taking Names* was not in the game plan under that hierarchy.
****

As I entered the Memorial Church for the first time in my life, I'll never forget the chill and eerie feeling that came over me. I was immediately met by our newly hired Deputized Patrol Officers (DPOs), Art and Dolores. Both were very intelligent young charges, but green as grass. Art had spent some time as a Community Service Officer (CSO) before being deputized; he knew the campus like the back of his hand but had virtually no active police patrol experience. Dolores was one of the first female patrol officers in Northern California; she had worked as a cadet in another department and was as smart as she was stunning—a real head turner, she was.

"Whaddya think we got" I asked?

"Looks like a '10-56.'" Art revealed.

"A suicide? Charley from Dispatch said it was an OD." Both of them just shrugged.

"Where's the victim?" They both pointed toward the East Transept of this beautiful House of God. *Why would anybody OD or kill themselves in here,* I mused?

I had handled many awful death cases in my short 10-year law enforcement career, but something told me that this was going to be the worst.

As I approached the scene, I could see that the victim was a young, petite female in her early 20's. The first thing that sickened me, was the way this poor soul was *posed:* The sick SOB who did this wanted to shock God and everyone! Her jeans had been thrown over her legs, waist band facing her feet, which were spread apart. A large altar candle, perhaps 2.5 to 3 inches in diameter, had been inserted into her vagina. Part of the shaft had broken off. Another candle had been thrust through her bra and protruded through her top, alongside the poor woman's neck. (I later learned that these candles were equipped with solid brass caps on the wick end so as to collect and prevent melted wax from running down the shaft. I also discovered that the savage beast, who did this dastardly deed, had inserted the candle approximately 3 inches into the victim's body.) My attention shifted to the poor young lady's face; I noticed foam protruding from her lips and nose, and spittle was running down onto the floor. *Damn,* I thought, *this isn't suicide or OD. This is a fricking murder, for Chrissakes!* Out of the corner of my eye, I spotted an old buddy of mine, S/O Sergeant Jim Hart, dusting some altar candles for possible fingerprints. As I walked past him, I commented:

"This is the weirdest suicide I have ever seen!"

"Yeah, me too," he exhorted. I made a beeline for my deputies and ranted:

"This is not a 10-56 or an OD. This is a Murder, guys, 187 P.C.!" They just gave me the deer in the headlights look. . .

After my blood pressure returned to about 125/70, I asked the officers what had happened. Their synopsis was as follows: There had been a report of a missing girl called-in by an undergraduate student sometime before midnight. The man reported he and his wife, who had recently arrived on Campus, were walking around the Quad when they got into an argument. I later discovered that Arlis was somewhat despondent about being away from home, and felt that her husband, Bruce, was consumed with his studies, and wasn't taking care of issues he was responsible for, such as maintaining their only car. When things got a little heated, the wife departed his company and indicated she was going the church to cool off. Both were devout Christians; she absolutely loved Memorial Church (*Mem Chu,* as the students called it) for its beauty and serenity. She went there often. This chapel rivals many of the classic cathedrals and churches in Europe for its architecture and stained glass windows. It also has one of the biggest and most impressive pipe organs in existence.

When his bride didn't return by Midnight, Bruce Perry called Stanford Communications and told the dispatcher that he was worried about Arlis' welfare. Dispatcher Charlie Papp put out a BOL (Be on the Lookout) for the young lady and asked Q-7, Art, to check out the church. Upon acknowledging that he was en route, a CSO (an unarmed community security officer) came on the air and stated that he had already checked the church and had locked-it-up for the night. All units were cancelled. In the meantime, the worried husband called Radio a couple more times during the wee hours and said that his wife had *still* not come home.

Sometime around 4:00AM, the same CSO, who said he had locked-up the church, excitedly contacted Dispatch and advised:

"There's a 'Stiff' in the chapel." He was told to back off, whereupon DPOs and Sheriff's units were ordered to the scene.

Being a newbie in this department, I didn't know the CSO who had found the victim, but certainly wanted to talk to him. When asked where he was, I was told that he went back to the station.

"He *what*," I screamed? "Tell him to get his ass back here. This is a murder investigation for God's sakes! Investigators need to talk to him!"

My blood pressure was peaking and probably went off the charts when Radio replied that our R/P (Reporting Party) had already turned-in his keys and went home. You could have knocked me over with a feather. Clearly, it looked like I was going to have lot of training to do with this bunch.

When the Sheriff's Homicide Detectives arrived, I was happy to see they sent some of the best: Sergeants John Johnson and Dave Pascual, among others. Johnny had been my training officer 10 years before; Dave and I were beat partners frequently and pushed patrol cars around San Jose for many years. These men were top notch, so if anyone could solve this horrible crime, they would! Detective Johnny Johnson remained at the crime scene, while Dave and I went to our station to interview the victim's husband, Bruce Perry. We had the awful task of telling Bruce that his lovely bride, Arlis, had been savagely murdered in the church she loved so much. He was devastated. Bruce, a new student at Stanford, then recounted the last hours that he spent with his wife, and the agony of not knowing what had happened to her. They were relative newlyweds who had come to Stanford from a small town in North Dakota. This man seemed to very credible, in my mind. I just couldn't visualize this seemingly very gentle individual committing such a heinous crime—let alone on his beloved wife. However, first impressions are often wrong, so Dave and I decided to shelve our opinions until a polygraph examination could be administered.

CSO Stephen Crawdad—A Pseudonym

Back at the church, it was discovered that the assailant and the victim had apparently been locked inside prior to the murder: The chapel had a corridor between the Nave and the outer wall. There were huge oak doors that permitted egress; these doors were routinely locked from the exterior. There were also emergency exit doors with crash bars, which led to the outside. Examination revealed that the doors on the Westside of the Nave were broken open, and with a great deal of force, perhaps via body weight. Once out of the Nave, the suspect had to merely push on the outer door's crash-bar and he was gone. This, we surmised, is how the CSO Crawdad realized that something was amiss when he spotted the emergency door wide open during his last round. But, there was more: When finally tracked down by Sheriff's Investigators, the CSO admitted that he never *really* checked the interior of the chapel prior to locking-up the church. We later learned that he was afraid of going into the dark interior by himself because of all of the weirdos who used to hang-out there. Crazies and burned-out druggies used to flock to Mem Chu like it was a magnet. As I later discovered, officers had dozens of encounters with some of these people, many of whom were totally whacked out of their gourds—some violent, as well! The sign-in book at the entrance of the chapel also reflected this phenomenon: Some of the passages that were written must have been the work of folks who had flown from the Cuckoo Nest. . .

The security guards assigned to this beat were supposed to check every inch of the church, roust out any malingerers and call for a DPO if they encountered any resistance. Tragically, this procedure was not followed on the eve of October 12, 1974. CSO Crawdad walked part way into the Nave and merely announced that he was going to close-up for the night. Receiving no response, he secured the building and went on his way, presumably locking Arlis in with the killer! No one, except the murderer, will ever know if she was alive at that point or already slaughtered.

Questions

Subsequent inquiries revealed that the CSO Crawdad was actually in the church for most of that night: He had a habit of goofing-off in the Round Room, which was the Dean of the Chapel's office. We believe this is exactly what happened on the night in question. To think that a security officer was in the same structure, only a few feet away, while a cruel murder was taking place is beyond belief! Some of the detectives believed that this CSO could have been the killer: Despite the fact, that by all reports, Crawdad was a "Wuss"— always afraid to go into the depths of the church by himself at closing— why did he charge in there without first notifying radio of the suspicious open door? And, why did he mysteriously abandon the scene and go home without reporting the facts of his discovery to his superior? More troubling to me was why did Crawdad become so uncooperative with the S/O detectives by invoking his Miranda Rights when they finally tracked-him-down the next day? Initially, I rationalized these anomalies to inexperience, a lack of training, and perhaps consciousness of guilt for not properly doing his job by ensuring that the church was clear of interlopers. He might have saved Arlis' life; if she was already deceased, the deputies might have caught the killer. We continue to ponder these discrepancies to this very day because we original investigators have never given up. Needless to say, the CSO in question was the scorn of the department and *persona non grata* in most circles. Stephen Crawdad later resigned, but would pop-up again before my career was over. So, why have I maligned this CSO with such a moniker? As I learned more about this character over the years, I found him to be the ultimate bottom feeder. Stay tuned.

More Questions

If Crawdad didn't kill Arlis, then who did and why? The answer to this question is still a topic of debate. The most popular theory is that this was a satanic, ritualistic murder. Quite frankly, most of us had very little understanding of satanic cultism at that time. This pronouncement came soon after the Dean of the Chapel was allowed to view the crime scene: We initially thought that the victim was possibly a member of the church's staff, thus the Dean was asked to see if he could identify the deceased woman. That turned out to be a major mistake: Not only was she *not* part of Memorial Church's staff, but the Dean immediately trumpeted that this crime was clearly the work of *Devil Worshippers* performing the so-called *Black Mass*. We subsequently learned that the Dean had previously allowed a group of actors into the chapel, where they entertained an audience to their theatrical rendition of this ritual, which dated back to medieval times. This, coupled with the Satanic movement in San Francisco, under the tutelage of Anton Szandor LaVey, self proclaimed High Priest of the Church of Satan, made said theory quite plausible.

In addition, the California Department of Justice (DOJ) had been compiling information about a series of unsolved murders of young women in Northern California and put out a publication for Law Enforcement's eyes only: Most of these victims' bodies, perhaps as many as 20 or more, were discovered along the CA-101 corridor and the El Camino Real (ECR). The victims were all white females with fair complexions, 16 to 25 years old, slightly built, most being blonde or having light hair, parted in the middle; several of the victims wore glasses and almost all had small earrings. All were stabbed and/or strangled. Also, in some cases, there were suspected *satanic signs*, either drawn in the dirt or created with sticks and stones. Although the placement of Arlis' jeans was not immediately recognized as a satanic symbol at that time, speculation later surfaced that this could have signified a *Pentagram*—clearly a sign of the Devil! After recently viewing the painful post mortem photographs, I felt the Pentagram theory was a distinct possibility. My view is that the killer(s) had incredible disdain and anger toward women. After he strangled and killed this unsuspecting lamb, he (maybe "they" but most likely "he") displayed great animus toward women due to the extreme violation of the sexual areas of her anatomy. When he was through with his violent act of humiliation, he placed her jeans onto her body in a symbolic fashion. Recently, investigators have entertained the notion that the juxtaposed placement of the jeans over the victim's legs might well have been an attempt to replicate the ancient symbol of the Freemason's Fraternity, the mysterious secret society which dates back to the 16th Century in Scotland.

Many of the characteristics of DOJ's homicide analysis were present in our case. Another dot we connected was that almost all of these killings were committed along the El Camino Real, ranging from Santa Rosa to Stanford University. So, was this a group of Devil freaks—perhaps those who appeared in or attended the Black Mass performance in Mem Chu prior to the murder? Maybe it was a solitary killer of the same persuasion of that *Bay Area 666* crowd? Perhaps he was a sexed crazed maniac who just availed himself of an opportunity when it presented itself? And, let's not discount the possibility that the killer might have been a mental patient, who had just slipped through the cracks. How about Theodore Bundy? He was investigated and eliminated from the Perry homicide, as he was in custody during that time frame. Well, despite thousands of leads, untold man hours and years of investigation, this brutal crime remains unsolved. Why this killer never struck again in like fashion is truly a mystery. There will be more on this baffling case later on.

Reflection

And to think that only a few weeks before this horrific crime, I had some reservations about taking the job at Stanford because nothing ever happened there. Most of my friends and colleagues thought that I would be bored to tears policing a 5 square mile university campus after working some of the toughest venues in the county for nearly 10 years. What could possibly happen at a college, they said: "Some petty thefts? Weekend Frat parties? Perhaps a bike collision or two? Or, maybe even a fight at a football game?" Who would have thought that one of the most heinous crimes in the history of Santa Clara County would not only occur on a university campus, but in a church! *AND,* on my first watch, no less! Something told me that this gig was going to be anything but boring!

CHAPTER TWO

The Old Guard

The Days of Rage

During my short career in law enforcement (at that time), I had heard some pretty zany and downright goofy stories about that campus cop's group known as the Stanford Police, which I have dubbed the *Old Guard* (OG). Be it truth or exaggerated fiction, the thought of giving up my stripes at the S/O and to change horses in the middle of the stream, so to speak, gave me great pause. This ragtag outfit on the Farm was known in regional law enforcement circles as *Stanford's Keystone Cops!* Chief Herrington took over as top cop in early 1972, at the height of some the most violent confrontations between cops and Vietnam War protesters on any campus in the USA. The confrontations began in 1968 with peaceful sit-ins and building occupations. The situation accelerated like a locomotive—slowly at first but then, with the addition of more coal, the movement was full steam ahead!

Buildings were occupied for days, property thrashed, burned and defaced, and roof tiles were hurled at the Sheriff's deputies like Frisbees—cowardly riffraff torched President Wallace Sterling's office in the middle of the night destroying personal memorabilia, rare books, paintings from the Stanford collection and his own library—all of this just two months before his retirement. After this arson, S/O patrol deputies were hired to constantly patrol check the President's Office—what was left of it— as well as his residence high up on a hill, known as the Hoover House. I was one of the deputies working the graveyard watch after completing my swing shift in San Jose. This was the first time I had set foot on Stanford grounds since those crazy days when our gang used to raise hell on campus. Keep reading; those confessions will be forthcoming...

The dastardly *Rads* (radicals) even burned down the Naval ROTC building in May of 1968, after their initial arson attempt in

March failed! Pressure mounted via students and outside agitators to kick ROTC off campus. Finally, the ultra liberal Faculty Senate voted to disallow credit for military courses, thus the ROTC program evaporated. This unit was established in September of 1916 with the induction of 250 recruits. Enrollment later rose and the program flourished throughout WWII and Korea. There were over 500 students enrolled in the ROTC program before disruptions began; their numbers soon spiraled down to about 250. Dissident anarchists employed terror tactics, which intimidated the faculty and administration. The rabble-rousers simply got their way thus eradicated a very valuable curricula for future military officers. With the caliber of education at Stanford, the ROTC program clearly could have produced superior, clear thinking leaders who would have been instrumental in keeping our country safe in the future.

After the bombing of President Richard Lyman's office April 23, 1971 in Building 10, the University hired S/O patrol officers to constantly patrol check the President's Office—again— as well as his residence high up on a hill. The explosion resulted in over 25K in damage. Three days later, arsonist(s) struck a lounge in Wilbur Hall costing $50,000 to restore. I later learned that one of the old Stanford cops was upstairs sleeping at the switch, so to speak, when that huge explosive device went "KABOOM!" in President Lyman's office. That was one helluva wake-up-call! I heard that following that explosion, the guy, who was rudely awakened from his nap, often replied, "Whaaat??" when spoken to. . .

Unlike the demonstrators at UC Berkeley, who did their mischief in the afternoon and then rushed back to their dorms in time to view their handiwork on the 6 o'clock news, the Stanford rioters did their dirty work at dusk and throughout the night. The nucleus of the anti-war movement was the worst: Comprised of socialist and communist mobs, they were spurred-on by anarchists like *Weather Underground, Venceremos,* Angela Davis, some members of *The Black Guerilla Family,* (BGF), Students for a Democratic Society (SDS) and the driving force, Stanford Professor H. Bruce Franklin— and avowed Maoist, who spewed more venom than a pit of vipers. Also in the mix was Stanford Student Body President David Harris. He was a piece of work, too. But, he got his just desserts when a group of masked men conducted a classic ambush and shaved his head like a USMC boot. He cried like a baby and implored the group not to shave off his scraggly beard; being the considerate Stanford students they were, the self-appointed *barbers* gave Mr. Harris a free pass. . . There will be more on this award winning performance later on.

I took great interest in this conflict as I was a member of the Sheriff's Crowd Control Unit (CCU) aka, *The Mean Green Machine*. Unfortunately, I wasn't particularly "mean" at that point in my life, as I was confined to I.C.U. in Kaiser Permanente Hospital, having survived a grinding head-on-collision—me in a TR-6 and the idiot who spun out of control in a Pontiac GTO. Our S/O guys were getting their asses kicked on the Farm, as they simply didn't have enough troops. The Old Guard had very little police training and experience and zero riot control training, so their effectiveness in a riotous situation was minimal. Actually one of the OG guys, a real knucklehead, thought he'd lend a hand to the S/O crowd control unit by lobbing rocks back at the rioters—great in medieval warfare, but hardly appropriate in this venue. Needless to say this goofball was sent to the dog house, never to emerge with a gun and badge again. During the countless skirmishes, Chief Herrington immediately recognized that his team was overmatched and inadequate, at best, and set out to completely reorganize and rebuild this group into a bona fide police department. The details of the reorganization will be revealed in Chief Herrington's chapter.

I had been involved in the oral board selection procedure for the new Stanford Department of Safety; our panel had no difficulty in identifying the most of unqualified personnel from the Old Guard after interviewing them for about 30-40 minutes. Those who didn't make the grade to Deputized Police Officer (DPO) were given an opportunity to remain in the department as unarmed security officers. This was not received well by the have-nots, and a tremendous amount of dissension ensued amongst the rank and file for many years. I understood their plight: One minute these men had guns and badges and patrol cars, now all they were only allowed to carry on duty was a two-way radio, flash light and a ring of keys.

Back in the Day

Let me tell you about the Old Guard so you will have a better perspective of what Chief Herrington and his administration was dealing with: After research and consultation with the Stanford University Historical Society, I *initially* couldn't pin point exactly when the Stanford Campus Police force was formed. I interviewed numerous OG guys before they passed away, but no one could tell me when SPD was officially established: However, everyone I talked to were convinced that the first chief known to them was Gordon "Gordy" Davis. He was top cop for 27 years! However, there *were* other chiefs, so we need to go way, way back to the turn of the 20th Century...

Sam McDonald: Stanford's First "Mobile" Patrolman*

My research has led me to believe that Emanuel B. "Sam" McDonald was Stanford University's first mobile patrolman—stay tuned.

Mr. McDonald had an incredibly interesting life and his early contributions, in many ways, helped define the security program on the Farm. Born in Monroe, Louisiana on January 1, 1884, Sam's father was a Methodist minister, whose Dad was a freed slave. Incredibly, Grandfather McDonald purchased his wife for $500, a very tidy sum in those days. Sam's father relocated the family to Southern California in 1890 where Sam got his first schooling at age 12. The family worked on a sugar beet farm, and when the soil played out in 1897, they packed-up their horse drawn wagon and headed north to Gilroy in Santa Clara Valley, where sugar beet farming was a big money crop in those days. In 1900, the restless Rev. McDonald decided to make the long trek to Walla Walla, WA, where homesteads were open to eager beavers who wished to be their own bosses. This arduous journey took the McDonald clan through Sacramento, Redding, Alturas, and then into Lakeview and Canyon City, OR.

*Sam McDonald's Farm: Stanford Reminiscences. By: Emanuel B. "Sam" McDonald.

At this point, young Sam became very homesick for the Santa Clara Valley that he fell in love with and decided to "jump ship," so to speak. While his family continued northward, Sam took on various odd jobs and was literally living from hand to mouth. This big, strapping kid, at over 6 feet and weighing 200 pounds, bucked hay, cared for stock and enlisted himself in any back-breaking task he could find— earning a measly $.75 a day! He saved his pittance and bought two horses for fifty bucks. Sam later traded one of his mounts and his .32 caliber rifle (which he used to put small game on his campfire) for a little .32 revolver—undoubtedly for self protection, for living on the trail and being a young black man was certainly a high risk proposition. . . After the transaction, McDonald turned south and headed back to his adopted home.

En route, E.B. McDonald's first stop was San Francisco, where he tried to land a sailor's position on a U.S. Army transport ship: McDonald's interview at the Presidio seemed to be progressing well despite the fact that he fibbed about his age (the minimum age was 21, and although Sam looked older, he was only 19). Sam got over that hurdle OK but started to get into turbulent waters when he prevaricated that he had been a deck hand on a steamer in the Great Lakes. When asked what ports he had plied, McDonald enthusiastically replied: "Chicago and Liverpool, Sir!" The officer then looked the young applicant right in the eye and rejoined:

"To Liverpool, you say?"

"Yes, sir," Sam replied.

With a big grin on his face, the officer queried: "So, how did you go over or around Niagara Falls?"

With that, the misguided youth was quickly shown the door!

Sam eventually got on as a steamboat deckhand and "plied" between San Francisco and Sacramento—no treacherous falls to navigate in the Delta. . . McDonald later put into the Port of Alviso (now within the City of San Jose) and migrated to the Town of Mayfield—later known as South Palo Alto, which at that time encompassed College Terrace and Barron Park. Being a very congenial young man, Sam took up with a family of Scandinavian emigrants; they dubbed him *Svart Svensk* (the Black Swede). It was during this period that McDonald became very interested in law enforcement and enrolled in a number of detective correspondence courses. He eventually wanted to become a lawyer, but set his sights on being a U.S. Secret Service agent and enrolled in mail order courses for that position, as well.

Sam's First Job at Stanford

In 1903, a local contractor employed Mr. McDonald with a team of workers who were excavating and expanding the Stanford Museum. Sam, in effect, was the University's first "Affirmative Action" employee! When the museum project was completed, Sam seized an opportunity for more gainful employment on the Farm: He joined the Teamsters Union and became eligible to drive one of the many stock driven wagons used to haul rock and gravel out of the San Francisquito Creek and onto the campus' dirt roads during the resurfacing effort.

The Night Watchman

University Head Custodian, (that position later became known as Chief of Police) Mr. Phil Atkinson, hired Sam McDonald as one of two Night Watchmen at the Stanford Stock Farm in 1904. The former stock farm watchman, Mr. Nelson, was transferred to Old Roble Hall. The normal patrol schedule was from dusk to dawn. All night watchmen were under the direction of the Chief of Night Watchmen, Mr. Joseph Mathison, who later became Chief of the Palo Alto Police Department. His successor was Mr. Ed Fogarty. The Chief patrolled the campus on horseback; all of the watchmen were issued "billy clubs" and lanterns and patrolled their respective beats on foot. Do you remember that little .32 pistol Sam *horse-traded* for in Oregon? Knowing cops as I do, I'll bet you a dollar to a doughnut that Ol' Sam packed that baby! I know I would have: Years later, Sheriff George Burns, the lonely campus policeman said: "The campus was morgue-like at night, except for the fraternity hazing stunts during Hell Week." With the absence of lights, clearly, the Old Farm must have been a very spooky place!

Mobile Patrol

Sam McDonald's primary duty at Governor Stanford's stock farm was security. In addition, he was commissioned to care for the "blooded stock"—the Governor's prized collection of thoroughbred trotting horses: This task included feeding milk to the colts, and being vigilant for any sign of illness.

Sam was also charged with being the care taker of the distant and isolated Cedro Cottage, which was at least two miles away, on the other side of the San Francisquito Creek in San Mateo County. In order to make his commute a bit easier, McDonald was issued a bicycle. So, in essence, E.B. McDonald was Stanford's first mobile officer! This basic mode of transportation, you will soon see, became invaluable to Sam and the community that he was charged to protect.

Three Hots and a Cot

In that day and age, not many jobs afforded one with food, found and transportation. When in the Air Force, we were often reminded by our superiors that we were lucky to have such a deal, which was called "Three Hots and a Cot." I'm sure that Sam would have preferred better accommodations, but it was what it was. . . Cedro College was in a serious state of what realtors term, "deferred maintenance." This little bungalow was owned by Areil Lathrop, the brother of Mrs. Jane Lathrop Stanford. Mr. Lathrop was the classic absentee landlord as he traipsed all over the globe and almost never came home. Previous caretakers hated the place! It was way out in the boondocks and several custodians believed the cottage was haunted: Several folks complained about hearing weird noises during the night as well as seeing a ghost or two who made unscheduled and unwanted appearances. But, these reports didn't deter Sam. McDonald soon determined that the "unusual noises" were random critters that had taken up residence in the walls and attic: Flocks of woodpeckers had bored numerous holes all over the outer walls, thus allowing squirrels, rodents, birds—you name it—to set-up housekeeping within the confines of the dwelling.

Chaos

In mid April, 1906, Sam concluded his shift at the stock farm at 0430. He was supposed to meet his boss, Ed Fogarty, and some other employees for coffee at the old Power House. However, Sam told his chief that he was exhausted and desperately needed some shut eye so he could get in some serious studying before his next shift. So, Sam biked over to his pad and immediately hit the sheets. At about 0530, the attic came alive with animals scurrying about madly. Sam thought the critters were trying to exit the house all at once but didn't understand why. In a couple of minutes, the earth shook violently—the likes of which this kid from Louisiana had never experienced in his short lifetime. The date was April 18, 1906: The "Big One," an 8.2 magnitude earthquake had just struck San Francisco and the entire Bay Area!

"I remember being catapulted out of bed," Sam wrote in his memoir, "not comprehending what had given impetus to this acrobatic feat and finding myself on the floor, where I was in no spirit to be detained." Barely able to stand without falling over, Sam staggered from the cottage and tripped over bricks and debris, until he escaped. Once outside, the tremor began to subside. McDonald noticed that the 6,000 gallon water tank and windmill had, as Sam wrote: "been dashed to bits!"

Against better judgment, the young man re-entered the bungalow, retrieved some clothes and his bicycle, got dressed and lit-out for the campus. As he crossed the creek's wooden bridge, which amazingly was still intact, Sam immediately observed that the Power House's 125 foot smoke stack was no longer visible. As the distraught man continued to scan the campus' skyline, Sam also realized that the giant rotunda of Memorial Church had seemingly evaporated. At this point, McDonald instinctively felt a call to duty: He somehow knew that as a watchman, he must inspect the college for casualties and damage, so he raced over to his "beat," the stock farm. On arrival, Sam found many workers dazed but unhurt; most of the structures were still standing, although one of the carriage barns was leaning precariously. Feeling that he might be needed elsewhere, the diligent man pedaled to Roble Hall to check on the women students at that dormitory. Although the dorm was badly damaged, groups of dazed young ladies, most in their night gowns, were unhurt and just milling about. Roble's watchman, Mr. Nelson, feared that some women might be trapped inside but prevented anyone from going into the wreckage, due to the instability of the structure. A passerby told Sam that Encina Hall was really devastated so he speeded there for a firsthand look. Encina's men were fairly well composed despite being totally stunned. The sandstone chimney collapsed and many interior doors were reportedly jammed. Student leaders emerged and prevented others from re-entering the shambles until structural engineers could properly assess the damage.

From there, our mobile patrolman rode over to the Power House to see if he could be of assistance. In a passage of Sam's book, his description of the carnage caused me to visualize the destruction in today's world: The plant looked like it took a direct hit from a 500 pound guided bomb! The building imploded when the boiler blew-up. Sam's boss, Mr. Fogarty and a couple of other men were inside having coffee when the San Andreas Fault shifted. Everyone immediately bolted for the exits and got out unscathed. However, the 22 year old engineer, Otto Gerdes, ran back inside so he could turn-off the master power switch. After the tall stack came down, Mr. Gerdes was missing. When the shaking stopped, rescuers searched the interior of the plant but could not find the poor kid. Upon probing the wreckage of the chimney, the mangled remains of Mr. Gerdes was located. This man was later declared a hero: Fire officials and campus engineers surmised that if Gerdes had not turned-off the power, subsequent fires could have caused more devastation, similar to what occurred in San Francisco. Unbelievably, the only other fatality in the 1906 earthquake at Stanford was Junius R. Hanna, a student, who was killed in Encina Hall.

Sam's Last Job

In 1908, Emanuel B. McDonald was hired by the Board of Athletic Control (BAC) of Stanford University. This was a big promotion for the young man who had more than distinguished himself during the "Big One." Sam worked-his-way-up from entry level grounds keeper to the "Custodian" of BAC's Operations and Facilities.

In order to commemorate Sam's dedicated and stellar service to the University and campus community, President Ray Wilbur Lyman, in 1939, named and dedicated the roadway leading to the athletic facilities as "Sam McDonald Road." Mr. McDonald retired in 1954, moved into much nicer digs at Angell Field, now called the Track House, and published his book with the Stanford University Press that year. Sadly, Sam became ill and subsequently succumbed in 1957. He was truly a wonderful and extremely interesting man— And, an early pioneer in campus law enforcement! Finally, being the consummate humanitarian, Mr. McDonald bequeathed 400 acres of old growth redwoods and unspoiled land to the University when he passed away. Sam purchased this property near La Honda and Pescadero Road in 1917; he requested that his heirs utilize the land as a park for the benefit of young people. San Mateo County bought the piece of property in 1958 and in 1970, opened the parcel as Sam McDonald Park—for everyone's enjoyment.

P.S. Mel Nelson, Head of Athletics Grounds during my tenure, also a good guy, is memorialized on Sam's sign.

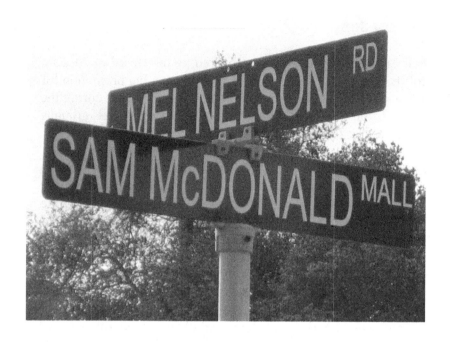

Sam McDonald Mall

Photo by Douglas Theisen

Original Stanford Police Sign (date unknown)

Photo by Author

Chief Fred Frehe, 1912-1940

According to Archivist, Pat White, of Stanford's Special Collection, the first official police chief was Mr. Fred Frehe. Chief Frehe first came to Stanford in 1912 and was employed by the farm. He soon became a member of the fire department and later was appointed both Fire and Police Chief. The original Fire/Police station was located at Santa Teresa and Duena Streets. The fire house now is home for the Gay and Lesbian Alliance at Stanford (GLAS). Although Chief Frehe intended to stay on the farm just a few months, he extended his stay until 1940—28 years! Mr. Frehe accepted a position on a large ranch off campus until he passed away in 1957.

Chief Gordon "Gordie" Davis, 1941-1968

My knowledge of Chief Davis was very limited, until I read the piece written by Pat White of Stanford's Special Collection for the Santa Clara County Sheriff's Office 150 Years of Service commemorative publication. According to Ms. White, Gordon "Gordy" Davis came to Santa Clara Valley from Tennessee as a youngster. He completed high school but had to provide for his family thus didn't pursue further education. Some of the OG told me that he had served in the military but it is unknown what branch or when he served. Mr. Davis began his Stanford career in 1931, as a time keeper at the Corporation Yard. Davis apparently became a patrolman sometime prior to 1941, exact date unknown, but in that year, he was appointed Chief of Police.

Chief Thomas "Tom" Bell, 1968-1971

As I wrote earlier, the campus was ablaze—literally—as mobs of anarchists made the Farm their rallying point. They did their dirty deeds under cover of darkness, which gave them a decided advantage over the police. Chief Bell certainly had his hands full. He not only didn't have personnel adequately trained and equipped to counter the radical onslaughts, but the Sheriff had recently rescinded Stanford Deputy Sheriff's status! Thus his officers had no peace officer authority—talk about going into a fist fight with one arm tied behind your back! But the Sheriff allowed SPD's personnel to continue to carry their weapons, and they were issued permits to do so. Bell was very knowledgeable about modern police practices; he was progressive and tried to get some contemporary training for his men.

Although there were some rallies and protests over the Vietnam War as early as 1965, the excrement really didn't start hitting the fan until 1968. Here are some excerpts from <u>A Chronology of Stanford University and its Founders</u> by the Stanford Historical Society:

<u>April 9, 1968</u>: ". . . protestors take over the Applied Electronics Laboratory, finally voting April 18 to end the occupation."

<u>May 6, 1968: Protests Against Student Suspensions</u>: "More than 200 students begin a three-day sit in at the Old Union. . ."

<u>May 7, 1968: Arson Destroys ROTC Building</u>: "A fire at 3:00 a.m. destroys Naval ROTC building. . ."

<u>April 30, 1969: Protesters Occupy Encina Hall</u>: "About 1 a.m. they (A3M—the April 3rd Movement) scuffle with 30 conservative students who are blocking the door, but about 200 break into the building through other entrances. The disrupters ransacked and removed files including payroll data. Provost Lyman summons sheriff's deputies and, under threat of arrest, the 100 students still there, leave before 7:30 a.m. on May 1."

<u>April 1, 1970: President Pitzer Doused with Paint</u>: An unidentified, masked *coward* (emphasis mine) dumped red water based paint on the President's back and shoulders as he talked to a group of students.

<u>April 23, 1970: ROTC Protest</u>: A crowd of over 300 students (high school kids, too) roam night after night smashing windows all over the campus. Anti-ROTC demonstrators take over the Old Union lobby. President Pitzer declares the building closed at 5:00 p.m. and warns the protestors to leave or be arrested. At 1 a.m. the

S/O arrives and arrest 22 people who refused to leave. Unruly, irate anarchists continued their rampage by breaking windows.

April 29, 1970: Cambodia Invasion Protested: About 250 protestors slug it out with police after a daylong sit-in at the Old Union. Tear gas and batons are used to disperse the mob. Sixteen anti-ROTC protestors are arrested. Thirty officers were injured by rocks and other flying objects. A dozen students were reported hurt.

May 1, 1970: Campus Turmoil: President Pitzer declares an "extreme emergency" in a special three-hour session of the Academic Council. Pitzer promises to defend the university by "whatever legal measures must be taken to preserve the integrity, the tranquility, and the academic viability of our university. . ." However, later that day, some idiot took a shotgun and fired a three shot fusillade into the campus home of the Army ROTC commander. Fortunately, no one was hurt; the sheriff's deputies were unable to nail the perpetrator.

I think you get the picture. Things were pretty nasty on the Stanford University campus, when Chief Bell took the helm. It's hard to believe that the situation could have gotten any worse, but it did!

Special Deputy

Because Stanford University and its adjacent property are unincorporated within the County of Santa Clara, law enforcement is the responsibility of the Sheriff. In addition, the University is private, thus is precluded from forming a police force that was legally recognized by law in the State of California. In those days, if a college or university needed a cop to investigate a crime or a arrest a violator, they were mandated to call the nearest official police department, such as Palo Alto, or in the case of U.C. Berkeley, that city's PD. Although the Palo Alto police had no jurisdiction on the Stanford campus, they were often called until the Sheriff's Office could be summoned. Being nearly 30 miles to the South, it might take a month of Sundays before a deputy actually showed up on a crime scene—as you will see later on in this book. (I often wondered how long it would to take to get a Sheriff's deputy on campus, before the telephone was invented. I imagine that a messenger on horseback would have been dispatched from the University to Sheriff's headquarters in San Jose, and then lead the deputy back to the scene? Not being an equine man, I have no idea how long it would have taken a mounted deputy to gallop or trot 30 some odd miles—Just asking. . .) In any event, Alexander Graham Bell and Henry Ford changed all of that!

At some point in time, although my research has failed to discern an approximate time period, University officials entered into an agreement—be it in writing, a hand shake or a wink and a nod—that the Sheriff would appoint Stanford policemen as "Special Deputy Sheriffs." Their mandate was basically to observe and report any crimes to the S/O: Stanford officers were allowed to make "on view" arrests and detentions, but had to turn over their collars to the deputies when they arrived on scene. SPD could also write reports on minor offenses, but had to defer all felonies to their parent department.

I first heard about the Special Deputy Sheriff status when I first joined the S/O in 1964. In those days, and reportedly since time in memoriam, Sheriffs conferred Special Deputy status to hundreds of citizens throughout the county, especially in rural districts. When I worked South County and the Mt. Hamilton areas, I can't tell you how many times I got "buzzed" by random guys who boasted "I know your boss!" Most of these individuals were often ranchers and farmers, who, "I heard," allowed various notables' access to their prime deer hunting property. . . Unfortunately, this was as common as it was long standing: Some S/O officials handed these tin stars out like flapjacks at a pancake breakfast, for God's sakes. In addition to land owners, every crony, such as: friends, friends of friends, relatives, friends of relatives, political campaign supporters and donors, lobbyists—you name them—had a Special Deputy Sheriff, County of Santa Clara star!

Even before I became a police trainer, I cringed at the thought of all these folks, most of whom were armed, running around with badges and I.D.s in their wallets. To my knowledge, none of these folks had been properly vetted, had no police training, no formal instruction on firearms training and marksmanship, let alone schooling on the moral and ethical use of weapons, laws of arrest and a myriad of other law enforcement subjects that cops had to go through, even back in the day.

With all due respect to the Old Guard, who never were afforded the opportunity to receive modern police training, save for firearms, the organization was clearly a step or two above the Special's classification: Since the mid-1930s, Stanford's officers wore recognizable police uniforms, were armed, and drove marked patrol units and motorcycles which were equipped with two way radios. The department had a command structure and generally performed as well as they could, given their lack of training. In retrospect, I believe that Stanford PD should have been designated as Reserves, after receiving some training from the S/O. But that will happen later on. . .

Stanford Police Department's Personnel 1966

Photo: Source Unknown

CHAPTER THREE

Captain Midnight

Stanford's Most Notable Cop

Carl N. Gielitz

Photo: Courtesy of the Stanford University News Service

First Oral Boards

It was the first oral board at the reorganized Stanford University Department of Public Safety. I was invited to be an applicant evaluator by Captain Frank Beasley, a very tall, dark and handsome dude, formerly a Sergeant motor cop at a nearby PD. In addition to his good looks, this man, was, as a buddy from the "Great Smokies" used to say:

Swa-*vay and Dee-boner*—a silver-tongued devil who could charm an agitated King Cobra. I met Frank through the California Association of Police Training Officers (CAPTO), soon after the Chief selected him as the department's first outside candidate for the Captain's position. I had been the S/O's Training Sergeant for a couple of years, and ram rodded the recruitment and selection of Deputy Sheriff Candidates. Being an adjunct wing of the Sheriff's Office, SUDPS was mandated to follow our selection protocol; in addition the Sheriff sent me in as a *shill* to ensure that the P.O.S T. hiring practices would be maintained, and that only the best qualified candidates would be chosen.

When I arrived at the Department, the cheerful staff invited me into their tiny coffee room, where *gut busters* and coffee were available. Attempting to make a good impression, I eschewed the tempting doughnuts—guaranteed to spike your blood sugar to 600, thereby causing you to acquire instantaneous Type I diabetes—after only one serving! And, besides, I was on my perennial diet. . . Captain Frank greeted me gratuitously with a double handshake and introduced me to the rest of the panel. This guy was good: I thought I was the master of *ho'omalimali,* but when it came to ingratiation and *blowing smoke,* I could barely qualify as a gun bearer in his company.

The University's Personnel Department enlisted a female panelist so as to ensure compliance with federal hiring practices; the Captain also had a patrol officer from the area on the panel, so all bases were covered.

We were led down the hallway past the Chief's Office and out into the fire apparatus bay, where a couple of 6-foot tables with chairs had been set-up; seeing folded cards with our names on them and the one chair—aka, The *Hot Seat* on the other side of the table, it was obvious to me this would be our conference room: *Hmmmmmm, strange place to hold an Oral Board,* I mused. *I hope the candidates don't evacuate themselves when the fire alarm goes off!* The Captain apologized for the interesting surroundings—about 6 huge fire rigs with fire laddies crawling in, under and around them, cleaning, polishing, checking equipment and whatever else they do when not fighting fires and rescuing folks. I couldn't help but get the feeling that some of them were taxing their auditory functions in an effort to figure out who would be chosen and who would be kicked to the curb!

Before convening, Captain Frank assured us that we would be in a more suitable environment for the remainder of the orals that week. He attributed this location to a scheduling screw-up; *Jeez*, I thought, *ya think they could have found a room somewhere in this vast learning emporium? I hope they don't serve us baloney sandwiches for lunch like when I was a member of Mean Green Machine during the Vietnam protests and riots.* Nonetheless, it was what it was. And, besides, I'd been in worse places.

One of our first *victims* was an emaciated old guy who had the shakes so bad I thought he had *St. Vitus Dance*. He was one of the original *door shakers* who had been relieved of their guns and badges when the new Chief took the helm. Most of the existing officers were in their 50's, former military guys, whom Chief Gordy Davis hired. There is absolutely nothing demeaning about foot patrol and rattling doors: As part of our duties in the Old S/O, my partner JJ and I were always on the prowl checking out large business and medical complexes on the Dog Watch—we caught a few burglars in the process, too. But, the poor men of the Farm were ill trained, not only in the rudiments of the law and modern police tactics, but, most importantly, in firearms procedures. I shuddered to think of Candidate #1 with a loaded pistol in his hand. He reminded me of an older gentleman, a Reserve Deputy, who I attempted to qualify at the DeAnza College pistol range during mandatory police basic training just a few months before:

****

He was the nicest man you'd ever want to meet—a WWII vet who saw considerable action during the South Pacific theatre. He was on an artillery battery: After untold weeks and months of pounding the enemy with incessant cannon fire from their 105mm Howitzers, the poor fellow developed severe shakes which he never got rid of. He told me that although he carried a .38 on duty, he really didn't like guns. I wouldn't either if I shook like a leaf every time I had a loaded pistol in my hand. Folks in the department dubbed the poor guy "Shaky Jake!"—certainly not funny anymore, since P.T.S.D. has been discovered in our vets.

Our Range Master was a crusty, no-nonsense retired army colonel, who wouldn't tolerate range rule violations. Being cognizant of this fact, my firearms instructors went over those rules chapter and verse with the shooters before they ever set foot inside the gallery. This was an indoor facility, constructed like Saddam Hussein's command and control bunker: The concrete walls were very thick. There was a steel trap at the end that would catch most semi-jacketed rounds—even 12-gauge shotgun rifled slugs. Full metal jackets were not permitted. There was an elaborate exhaust system overhead, which when activated, would evacuate most of the noxious gun smoke. There was a 25 yard range on one side and a 50 yarder on the other. There were 8 lanes, no dividers, so it was imperative that participants always kept the business end of their six-shooters pointed down range. If that gun strayed just a fraction to the left or right Ol' Col. Murphy would bellow over the loudspeaker:

"Hey, YOU on #4! If you ever point that firearm anywhere's but down range again, I'll have your Sergeant (me) put his #12 up your ass. YOU got that?"

So, when it was our jittery artilleryman's time to advance to the line, I kept a jaundiced eyeball on him and maintained a position of safety—behind and slightly to the right of his gun hand. When taught the two-handed hold, his nervousness subsided somewhat and he was actually able to hit the target at the 15 yard distance—his pattern looked like a couple rounds of buckshot, but at least he hit the paper. After my skittish pupil fired a few dozen rounds, I left him in order to work with another man, who was also struggling. When the line was ready, the colonel's commands blared:

"Ready on the left, ready on the right, commence firing."

A volley of shots rang out for about 30 seconds and then, all of a sudden, that dreaded authoritative voice blasted over the PA:

"**Cease Fire, Cease Fire** and holster your weapons! YOU, on #3, unload your weapon, holster and leave the range immediately! Sgt. Niemeyer, report to my office." *Holy shit, I thought, what in the Sam*

Hell happened? I hot-footed-it into the Colonel's control booth and asked him what was up.

"That old guy on #3 just put a couple rounds into **MY** overhead apparatus," he steamed.

"He whaaat?" I exclaimed. "How in the hell did he do that? I was watching him just a few minutes before and he was doing alright." The Range Master then explained that upon shooting the first round, the resultant recoil snapped the gun skyward, whereupon a second round went off. He did this twice, and when I viewed the equipment aloft, two tell-tale bullet holes were right above Shaky Jake's lane. Sadly, I was forced to relieve this gentleman of his firearm, and he was relegated to desk duty for the rest of his volunteer career.

****

After imparting this tale to my colleagues, we were all unanimous in our final assessment: A very nice man; dedicated, loyal, trustworthy, plus many more attributes of the Boy Scout oath. But, at his age and physical condition, clearly not DPO material—but, he would make a good CSO. And, thus it was with the next three candidates. So, we were 0 for 4. Boy, I was very disappointed and famished, too. I shouldn't have been so macho in restraining my urge to devour those *fat pills* this morning—but, like many progressive cops, we were trying desperately to shed that coffee and doughnut stereotype. So, I wondered what was for lunch.

I was pleasantly surprised when the Captain drove us to the Stanford View Inn (now the Sundance Mining Co.), a very nice restaurant on the El Camino right across from the campus. Many of the professors and higher level staff dined there. When handed the menu and viewing same, I choked quietly and hoped that this wasn't *Dutch Treat*. I initially decided on something *light* until our leader announced that anything on the pricey list was OK, whereupon he promptly ordered rack of lamb. . . *Whoa, this was turning out alright; I could get used to this duty,* I reflected. Best work-related luncheon I had ever had and I thanked our host profusely. Not a problem, he boasted, it's on old Leland. *I jealously thought our County would only pony-up with a paltry sum for our business meals. I definitely could work for an outfit like this*—little did I know. . .

Candidate # 4

Typically, the first candidate after lunch is a tough one, especially after that splendid meal we had gormandized. Even on the first day, this process of asking the same questions and hearing pretty much the same answers over and over again was somewhat trying. I was hoping for a surprise candidate and after talking with our next applicant for a few minutes, indeed, I thought we might have a keeper here. Candidate #4 was a 54 year old gentleman who had been with the Stanford Police Department for eons. His name was Carl Nelson Gielitz. His application and resume revealed that after serving as a Lieutenant in the U.S. Army Air Corps during WWII, he held a few short term jobs then joined the Stanford PD in 1948. After a brief stint patrolling the graduate student housing area, he was recalled to active duty with the Air Force during the Korean War. Upon resuming civilian life, he returned to the Farm where he matriculated from "Door Shaker", to mobile patrol, and then to motorcycle officer. He was later promoted to Sergeant. In addition, because of his apparent proficiency and expertise with firearms, he was given the assignment of Firearms Instructor and Armorer. Finally, Mr. Gielitz was one of the few applicants who had been to college and who had actually attended a police academy. He seemed to have a great sense of humor and also was a very good *conversationalist*: Like this writer, he got to the point, no matter how long it took. . . We all liked him, and despite his advancing age, Mr. Gielitz looked like he could still hang with the younger whipper snappers. At 6 foot and pushing the Toledo's at a Buck 90—save for a girth that many of us champions of culinary delights sport—I believed this man could get through the physical demands of the police academy and would be a viable deputy for a number of years to come.

Captain Midnight

Candidate #4 was unanimously given a thumbs-up by all oral board members. As he left the area, Captain Frank huddled us together and asked:

"You know who that guy is?" We all shook our heads in the negative.

"That my friends, is the infamous Captain Midnight!"

I silently began to nod in the affirmative, for I knew *exactly* who that man was.

The Captain went onto say that during the 50's, Gielitz rode rip-shod over the campus on his big Ol' Harley, handing out citations to violators as if they were free tickets to a police charity ball. Chapparal, aka. *Chappie,* a student magazine, began featuring a series of cartoons depicting hapless students in the clutches of this heartless, bigger-than-life motor cop astride his enormous Harley Davidson (*Hog*) glaring at the wrong-doer as he scratched the kid a ducat. The lampooners responded to the plight of their brethren with clever captions—all designed to demean the *Captain.* Believe me, it didn't work. How *Chappie* came up with the Captain Midnight handle is uncertain. Perhaps it was his dark lens aviator's glasses, black leather jacket, spit-shined motorcycle boots, gleaming white helmet with a white *Snoopy* scarf trailing in the breeze? Nonetheless, the handle stuck, and by the time I arrived in the Bay Area circa 1957, Captain Midnight was a legend—not in his own mind, but in the minds of every motorist who dared enter the Stanford University campus when he was on duty—He struck fear in those hearts. . .

****

Donut Land

It was another typical Friday night for our Happy Days Gang: We all met at "Pard's" (formerly in the apex of El Camino Real and El Camino Way) for the obligatory burger, fries and cherry coke. Then the round-table ensued as to what form of mischief we were going to get ourselves into over the weekend. It was the usual cast of characters I had met in Palo Alto when I was in the Air Force, stationed at Travis A.F.B. in Fairfield: Lee-Boy, Dick, George, Ken, Ed and Billy-Boy.

"Hey let's go to 'Donut Land,'" someone offered.

"How about tomorrow afternoon after I get off work," Dick suggested.

Great, so it was decided; the only thing was, I had absolutely no idea what they were talking about and was a bit sheepish about my ignorance, so I whispered in Geo's ear: "Where in the hell is 'Donut Land' and what kind of doughnuts do they have there?" Big mistake! Geo immediately guffawed and announced to the group: "Ha ha ha aha: Kalani thinks that he's going to get custard filled doughnuts at Donut Land!"

Everyone roared at my expense and when the din subsided, Dickie, probably feeling a little sorry for me, explained that Donut Land was actually a place on the Stanford campus where they took their mud runners—old beater cars they bought at the East Paly junk yards; they bobbed (cut down) the fenders so as not to collect too much turf in the wheel wells, and spun donuts in the dirt until Captain Midnight came on the scene. I later learned that this area was officially named Cactus Gardens, near the Mausoleum, where the Stanford family was interred. This was the Stanford family's Holy Land! And, I guess we were the irreverent punks who loved tearing it up. . . Although somewhat afraid to ask, I did anyway:

"So, who's Captain Midnight?"

"You'll see tomorrow," Dick said.

Dick wanted Geo and me to go to Eddie's grandpa's shop in San Jose to retrieve his mud runner, which they had been working on in preparation for another illegal foray on the campus. Naturally, we agreed.

Next morning, Geo and I were buzzing down the Bay Shore in his hot rod. The shop was right off the highway, so an easy in and out. I jumped behind the wheel of Dickie's beast and fired her up. The noise was deafening, so I hollered:

"Geo, I thought they said they were working on the tank; what happened to the muffler?"

"They cut it off—too many *pukas* and the fumes were killing us," he laughed.

Perfect, I thought. *Man I hope the CHP doesn't bag me—that's all I need.*

So, off we roared, all 8 cylinders of that 1948 Buick "Road Monster" humming. *Damn, wish I had brought my earplugs,* I lamented; *this toad sounded like one of the B-36's R-4350 engines I worked on.*

As I neared Moffett Field Naval Air Station, running at about 65, with Geo bringing up the rear, my feet and lower legs became increasingly warm. But, then I was wearing my traditional Hawaiian tuxedo: tee shirt, shorts and rubber slippers, so I wasn't too alarmed. *Must be the exhaust where they eliminated the muffler,* I figured. Then, all of a sudden my calves were on fire—literally, as flames were shooting out from under the seat. I immediately locked-up that old gangster ride, pulled-off the freeway and as soon as I dared, snapped open the door and bailed out of that ball of fire. Geo pulled up behind, looking as if he had seen a ghost; I motioned for him to back off as I beat feet until I was at least 50 yards away. By now the old Buick was history—totally involved with flames launching 30 feet in the air. That gas tank was sure to blow at any moment, so we took refuge behind Geo's car. Within minutes, the fire department (probably from Moffett) was on the scene and dousing the conflagration. Amazingly, they extinguished the blaze before the fuel cell exploded. We assured the police that we were en route to get the owner so the burnt-out hulk would be removed. Yeah right. . .

When we arrived at Dick's shop and told him what had happened, he just let out a big laugh, and exclaimed that he shoulda told me about the water.

"Water, what water?" I pressed.

"The water to put out the fire on the floor mats," he gleefully replied, and added:

"After I smashed the exhaust pipe up against the floorboard when I hit a big rock, that damn thing was always catching fire, so we used to carry several jugs of water with us," the Electric genius chuckled.

"That's OK," he continued, "we can ride with Lee-Boy and Fast Eddie," just as those boys zoomed into the parking lot. We were off in a matter of minutes, and after a short ride through Palo Alto—avoiding the cops at all possible cost—we were on the Stanford campus. Soon, we were hootin' and hollerin' as the cars emitted rooster tail showers of mud, turf and rocks, while spinning loops in moist sod of "Donut Land." However, our party was soon brought to a screeching halt upon hearing the distant sirens of Stanford's finest. Before we knew it, the fuzz was on us like a flock of ducks on June Bugs—two cop cars and a big guy on a Harley descending on our group like a swarm of angry hornets.

Following the pre-arranged escape plan (when encountered by the law, split-up and flee in opposite directions) the other two *mud-runners* boogied in juxtaposed directions with the patrol cars in hot pursuit. But, SPD's cop cars were no match for those big old straight-8 Buicks, as the cheapskates who held the University's purse strings would only provide their police force with gutless Chevy Biscayne's—powered by paltry straight-6 engines, hooked-up to "three on the tree" transmissions.

As luck would have it, the motor cop singled us out and was hot on our tail, siren screeching and all lit up like a Christmas tree. *Typical,* I silently cursed, *if I didn't have bad luck I'd have no luck at all!* Lee-Boy was a helluva driver, but all of his erratic, evasive maneuvers failed to shake our nemesis—that guy on that mount was relentless and I thought we were had:

"Jeez," I exclaimed, "he's gonna nail our asses!"

"Naaaa," Lee-Boy replied, as he cut through the eucalyptus groves and bounded onto Galvez Street. As we neared the El Camino Real, our luck changed: The light turned green in our favor. Lee started beeping the horn wildly and the other guys waved bye-bye to our tormentor, as he abruptly pulled-up at the intersection.

"That, Mr. Niemeyer, is Captain Midnight," Dick proclaimed, as he smiled broadly.

"But, how come he didn't come after us?" I queried.

"Cuz the El Camino is like the Rio Grande was for the Texas Rangers; they can't leave the campus!" Dick exclaimed while he chuckled.

Hmmmm, very interesting, as I recalled how my buddies in Hawaii successfully out-ran the Ft. Ruger MPs (Military Police), on more than one occasion, under the similar boundary constraints. *Glad I'm not a cop here, as that would really piss-me-off,* I concluded.

****

Little did I know at the time that not only would I *become* a cop, but that in 1974 I would be hired as Patrol Captain of the Stanford University Department of Public Safety, and soon to be Captain Midnight's boss...

Detective Gielitz

In 1977, when I was transferred to Investigations, I felt it was about time that Captain Midnight be semi-retired from police patrol work, so I had him moved upstairs and ordered a desk plate which read: Detective Carl N. Gielitz. In that position, I had him wear more hats than the NASCAR winners do after a race: He was my evidence officer, found property man—a miserable task, as that job is like shoveling sand against the tide, especially after football games and at the conclusion of the academic year. Carl also created the department's first crime prevention program. He conducted "safety first" seminars for students, staff and homeowners. The detective pioneered many of the safety-tip brochures, as well. He also served as bicycle program coordinator—perhaps even worse than found property, for in a community of a million bikes, just let your imagination run wild and guess how many stolen, recovered, and abandoned bikes might appear in his compound on any given week. Carl's biggest pinch came when he busted an enterprising young man who availed himself of in excess of one hundred bikes left by the students during summer break. The Russian immigrant, who perhaps had dabbled in the *Grey Market* in the old U.S.S.R.— refurbished some of the cycles and then ran a rental agency when the kids came back in the Fall. This was *verboten,* so Det. Gielitz had to school this budding entrepreneur in the lawful procedure of handling abandoned property. I later dubbed the kid's business: *Dragon's Rip 'n Rent a Bike!* Detective Gielitz was later named President of the California Bicycle Officer's Association. And, when Carl had a spare minute or two, I had him compile the department's crime statistics— another hair-puller. No wonder he decided to retire in 1981...

In an effort to create a unique tribute for Carl's retirement, I decided to assemble a slide show of his life. I secretly contacted his sister, Mary Dutton, who not only provided me with the precious family album, but also a plethora of inside scoop about his life, the highlights of which are chronicled below:

Born June 20, 1919, Carl Nelson Gielitz grew up and was schooled in Palo Alto; while in elementary school, his principal allegedly paddled him. When his parents asked why he was punished, the schoolmaster said he was merely trying to get Carl to talk; his teachers said he was too shy! I nearly fell out of my chair when I heard that tale, for this man was very, very *articulate.* On an elk hunting trip with Carl in Montana, I never once had to turn on the radio: I had a *radio talk show host* in the co-pilot's seat of my van for the entire 3,000 mile trek!

Many years after our first face-to-face meeting in the fire bay, I learned that Carl and I had a lot in common: CNG was quite the renegade hot-rodder in his youth. He performed a frame-off restoration of an old rattle-trap 1930 Model A Ford—mine was a '29 Model A pick-up. It was a frame-off, but the body never made it back on; however, tearing down the engine provided me with a lot of valuable lessons.

Carl "souped-up" his Model A in high school and was rather adept at running from, and ditching the Atherton cops. It seems, through trial and error, young Gielitz discovered that running over a particular manhole cover on a certain spot caused the heavy steel lid to pop-up and spin like a quarter on a bar top. So, this was the route of choice when fleeing from Johnny Law; when the manhole cover did its number, the police were forced to stop and remove this traffic hazard, which allowed our hero to make a clean get-away.

Master Gielitz graduated from Palo Alto High School in 1938. He then enrolled in San Mateo Junior College where he earned an Associate of Arts degree in engineering in 1941. He bummed around for a year or so until he enlisted in the U.S. Army Air Corps on December 7th 1942 as a *Ninety-Day Wonder*. After six months of training, he graduated from Yale University as an aviation cadet and received a 2nd Lieutenant's commission. Following his impressive learning regimen, he was assigned to a stateside duty station, much to his chagrin. Lt. Gielitz yearned for some action, but the only *action* he got was at the U.S.O. where all of the lonely ladies congregated—not bad duty, if you ask me...

When he finally got the green light for transfer to a combat zone, Imperial Japan had already signed the unconditional surrender aboard the USS Missouri in Tokyo Bay. After kicking around for a few years, Carl was hired by Stanford Police Chief, Gordon Davis, in 1948 thus beginning his 33 year sojourn on the Farm as a beat officer at the graduate student housing campus, then located at the U.S. Army Biddle Re-Habilitation Hospital in the Town of Atherton. The military used this facility for convalescence of wounded personnel during WWII. After the conflict, when all patients returned home, this facility was obtained by the University. I later learned that policing that complex was unorthodox at best: When beginning his swing shift, Officer Gielitz would don his uniform, strap on his gun belt and drive his personal vehicle to Menlo Park Police Department to clock-in.

Carl bought a spiffy 1940 Mercury in New Haven, Connecticut, circa 1946 and drove it cross country. This bomb was jet black, sported a white *rag-top*, and featured streamlined rear fender skirts, which accentuated the *dumped rear-end* look. This would make a perfect patrol car—and indeed it did!

After going 10-8 (in service) Officer Gielitz would proceed to the Biddle facility and cruise around until he got a call. When I referred to this operation as being unorthodox, I confess this is a bit of an understatement: For those of us who might remember, the car radios in the olden days had only one frequency—AM. No FM, no cassettes, no CDs, not even 8-Track. . . What many of you old geezers out there may know is that if you tuned in to the 1600 band, you just might receive police radio traffic from nearby agencies which had mobile two-way radios. Well, Officer Gielitz wasn't afforded the luxury of having a real cop radio in his hot rod, so he had to keep his ear tuned to 1600AM. You got it: Menlo Park PD would receive calls for service at their station and dispatch Carl via AM on his radio dial. How's that for American ingenuity? This was certainly a step-up from the semaphore system, but was certainly a far cry from the communications systems of today. When Officer Gielitz went 10-97 (arrived), he would get to the nearest landline (telephone) and 952 (report on conditions)—it's unknown to me what would have happened en route, or when he arrived and was unable to call in.

After a little more than two years, Officer G's police career was short-lived as he was called into active duty at the outbreak of the Korean War. An impressive photo and article appeared in the *Palo Alto Times Tribune* showing Lt. Carl Gielitz, in his smart Air Force duds, cleaning his police revolver and putting it away for the duration of the Korean *police action*. He flew in A-26 Marauder attack bombers and miraculously survived numerous dangerous bombing/strafing missions, while attacking heavily fortified enemy positions in the valleys and gorges of North Korea. Concentrated enemy fire almost took-off the aft end of his plane's fuselage on one mission, with pumpkin-size holes in the body, reminiscent of the films showing B-17s and B-24s limping back to England after suicide bomb runs over the flak-ridden skies over Germany.

In addition to his military service, Carl was recognized for his native intelligence. When back on the Farm, his savvy enabled him to move up the food chain and be promoted to Patrol Sergeant. As previously mentioned, Carl was one of the few Old Guard Stanford Officers who actually matriculated through a California Peace Officer's Academy. Carl's training was held at St. Mary's College where he finished near the top of his class. Prior to that, he was a motorcycle Traffic Officer and rode huge Harley Davidson police bikes. He mastered all of them: Pan Heads, Shovel Heads, three-wheelers—the man could ride anything on two or three wheels. In researching old photographs for the slide presentation at his retirement party, there was a nostalgic picture of Carl's partner, George Lester, on a three-wheel Harley, and Captain Midnight straddling his *Hog*. I later quipped that Hollywood actually patterned the hit TV series CHiPS after those two...

Officer Gielitz was also a firearms authority. He had received considerable training in the military and was also schooled in police firearms tactics. Sgt. Gielitz became the department's first bona-fide Range Master and Instructor. Although I didn't know it at the time, Carl Gieltz was also a consummate gun collector: He had firearms from the 18th, 19th and early 20th centuries. His expertise earned him an impressive reputation amongst gun aficionados in the region, which caught the eye of the ROTC program's Director, who featured him as guest lecturer during their firearms sessions. To liven up his lecturers, Carl often brought-in unique and rare specimens of his collection. Of special note was a .44 caliber rim-fire Pocket Pistol named the Hammond Bulldog, manufactured circa 1802. This particular pocket pistol gained fame in the Old West when it became the weapon of choice of the infamous Bordello Madame "Big Nose" Kate, consort of Doc Holiday, in Old Tombstone, AZ. She concealed this powerful and sizable equalizer in the cleavage of her ample bosom...

The R.O.T.C. students loved this man and often showered him with extravagant, unique weapons: An unknown member presented Carl with an incredible pair of encased dueling pistols—the origin of which is uncertain. This pair of octagon-barreled .36 caliber percussion duelers, possibly Belgian, is exquisite! The leather-covered case contains all the necessary accoutrements: powder measure, a ball and round-nose projectile swage, caps, a cap nipple removal tool—even a little compartment to store extra bullets and patches. This writer would love to locate the donor of this pair of pistols for further research, as Mr. Gielitz later passed this treasure onto me "for safekeeping," as he put it.

Another fantastic collectable was provided by a Stanford *Spring Breaker* who had traveled into the depths of Mexico. How this accomplished smuggler was able to cross the border with a gunfighter's pistol, purchased for 20 bucks in a pawn shop, is beyond me. At first sight, this old worn-out gun looks like a relic. But, on closer inspection,

I found that it clearly belonged to a killer—be he bandito or lawman: The weapon is a .45 caliber Colt Richards-Mason Conversion—a six-shooter which was formerly a cap-and-ball pistol later converted to metallic cartridges. The original 7 inch barrel was cut down to 4 inches, the ejector rod assembly totally eliminated, the hammer spur cut down, and blade front sight removed—with a BB in its place so as not to hang up in the holster when quick-drawing. The most telling characteristic of this collectable are the 15 notches carved in its well-worn grips. If only that gun could talk—like Carl . . .

Retiree Gielitz spent nearly 20 years hunting, fishing—he was an accomplished fly fisherman and taught fly tying at a local sports shop. He also traveled extensively: He drove to Alaska and back, visited Europe, and often lived the high life on Mediterranean cruise ships. Carl also embarked on a sensational photo safari to Africa and captured herds of exotic animals on film. He lived the good life as long as his health allowed, but sadly suffered a series of strokes in 2002; he was unable to live alone and had to be moved from his long time Santa Clara residence to a retirement home. I called him the other day and told him that I would be writing a chapter about his life, with emphasis on his role as *Captain Midnight* on the Stanford University campus. He liked that! On July 1, 2006, my wife and I traveled to Carl's rest home and shared the life of Carl Nelson Gielitz's life with other residents of the inn, via the slide show I created for his retirement, 25 years before.

Over the years, I can't tell you how many people who were alums, faculty or staff at Stanford in the 50s—60s asked me about Captain Midnight once they discovered I worked at SUDPS. He was truly an icon. Unfortunately, Carl passed away on November 18, 2006. *The Captain* is undoubtedly chasing violators on that immense campus in the sky, on his bigger than life Harley, with his Snoopy-like white scarf flowing in the breeze. God Bless!

CHAPTER FOUR

The A-Units

A-1: Chief Marvin L. Herrington

Marvin L. Herrington, Director of Public Safety

How I Got the Job!

I first met Chief Herrington, "Marv," as he was known by the University's senior staff and faculty members, when I was invited to participate on the SUDPS's Oral Board while the department was going through the throes of reorganization (circa early 1973) shortly after Herrington took over the helm. Initially, and throughout my tenure at Stanford, I almost always referred to the man as *The Chief* or A-1—a sign of respect for his position and persona.

My first impressions of Chief Herrington were that he was a very smart, straight laced, no-nonsense individual of very few words. My initial assessment of Stanford's new *Domo* was almost right-on; but when it came to being a soft-spoken individual of very few words, I couldn't have been more wrong. More on that later. . .

After completing the Stanford Oral Boards, I went back to my duties as Training Sergeant at the S/O. Having been in this position since I was promoted to sergeant nearly two years before and feeling that I had accomplished most of what I had set out to do, I became restless and desired another challenge. When I was a patrol deputy, I always admired the Patrol Sergeant's position, as it seemed like the best job in police work: During that period, there were only two Patrol Sergeants, one was in charge of San Jose's infamous Eastside, as well as South County (which was normally pretty tranquil), and the other supervisor was responsible for the Westside and North County. The caliber of deputies in those days was top-flight. The guys on the beat knew their jobs well and rarely needed supervision, save for dicey situations, wherein a questionable decision might grow teeth and come back for a chunk of flesh later on. This was about the only time a sergeant had to respond to an issue. Micromanagement was always looked upon with disdain by the rank and file. That signaled a lack of confidence by the field boss and would invariably drive a wedge between the troops and supervisors. I vowed that I wouldn't be over-bearing if I ever became a Patrol Sergeant. Sergeants of my era responded to all major incidents, took photos, helped with evidence collection (if necessary and requested), advised and counseled, but other than that, they just showed up, stood on the sidelines and let the deputies do their work. The Sergeant didn't have to stop cars or issue tickets and was even exempt from report writing, unless there was a major case in which the supervisor took part, then a supplemental report was required. What a job, eh? So, that's what I decided to apply for. And, within short order, I was transferred to the Patrol Division and put in charge of the Westside on the Second Watch (days). And, what a gig that was—best job I ever had, but you'll have to wait until my next book comes out—Tales from the Ol' S/O—"to read all about it. . ."

As I was just settling into my new, exciting position, I got a call from SUDPS's Captain, Frank Beasley. Frank told me he had just accepted a Chief's position in a small town near Pittsburg, CA and suggested I apply for the soon-to-be vacancy at SUDPS. After quizzing Frank for some time, the Stanford job sounded pretty interesting, so I told him I'd think about it. I then called my old friend and insider, Captain Bill Wullschleger, (who you will get to know later in this chapter) and asked him about the captaincy at the DPS. Capt. Bill was happy to hear that I was interested in the job and said he would love to have me as a colleague. That was encouraging and his enthusiasm inflated my ego. After a brief chat, I told the captain I'd throw my hat in the ring and asked him to let Chief Herrington know I was interested in the position and would stop by for an application.

After submitting my application and resume, Cap'n Bill caught me in the parking lot and we had a brief conversation. The Captain told me I had a lot of stiff competition for this coveted job and wondered if I would consider accepting a Lieutenant's position in lieu of being a "Skipper." I respectfully declined citing the fact that I loved being Patrol Sergeant, had a good reputation at the S/O having dedicated nearly 10 years in that organization, and was vested in the state retirement system. So, I really needed to take a big step upward with commensurate pay and benefits before I'd consider jumping ship. I also reminded the good captain that I had considerable field and training experience in the SUDPS' "parent organization" and knew the ropes there, thus would more than likely be a good fit. (I suspected that The Chief had commissioned Bill to feel-me-out on taking a lesser rank, but I had already made up my mind that I was either going to get the whole *enchilada* or *nada*!) Although I didn't articulate my thoughts in those exact terms, I think the good captain caught my drift.

About a week later, I was set up for an interview with the Director of Public Safety—his official title, but he was still "The Chief," as far as I was concerned. After exchanging pleasantries, I thanked him for affording me an opportunity to interview for the job and gave a brief spiel of what I could bring to the position. The Chief listened intently and then proceeded to destroy my initial assessment that "Marvin Herrington was a man of a few words" when he launched us into an hour and a half BS session. And, I thought I was a good conversationalist! Boy, his man could talk! He was very articulate, well read, and had an unlimited arsenal of "War Stories." The Chief told me his life story and how he had begun his law enforcement career in a small suburban town in the Detroit area. One of his best tales—and my favorite—concerned a salty old, grizzled cop who was a legend in the department. I can't remember his name but I'll call him Officer O'Reilly. This cop was, in my mind, a knuckle-dragging dinosaur reminiscent of the Clint Eastwood film character, "Dirty Harry." According to A-1, this old flatfoot absolutely hated smart mouth punks who defied authority. There was such a kid in their town who was always hot-rodding around burning rubber, speeding, busting stop signs, etc. One day, when Herrington was riding with Officer O'R, they spotted the town menace roaring around raising hell. Although they really didn't have PC (Probable Cause) to stop this hellion, Officer O'Reilly red-lighted him anyway. Once pulled over, the big burly cop approached the car and engaged the driver:

"License and registration!" (No please with this hard case.) So, the smart-ass caustically returned:

"So, Officer O'Reilly, what are you stopping me for this time? You got nothing on me; my car is in perfect condition; this is illegal!" the kid asserted.

"Oh yeah," the officer barked, "turn on your lights."

"What for?" the "Adam Henry" protested.

"So I can see if all of your lighting equipment is working," was the caustic retort.

After going through the light drill—all were functioning properly—the officer said:

"Hit your high beam switch, I wanna check your dashboard indicator," the frustrated cop ordered.

"See, it works, O'Reilly," the kid sing-songed in a teasing manner. With that, Officer O'R proclaimed:

"I'm gonna write you up for faulty head and tail lights, sonny boy!"

"But, they're all working," the punk sniveled. With that, the brutish officer of the law drew his nightstick and proceeded to smash-out all of the car's illumination. The totally stunned young man screamed:

"You can't do that! I'll report you to your chief!"

"I just did," O' Reilly snorted, "and who in the hell would ever believe a story like that from you. Wait 'til I finish your citation. . ."

So, not only was the Chief a superb raconteur, but he appeared to have a great sense of humor and a mischievous nature, much like myself. I figured that if I ever got this job A-1 and I would at least have a few things in common, which would make the task even more enjoyable. I left his office chuckling all the way to my car.

The Call

I was all suited-up and getting ready to head out the door and begin my Patrol Sergeant's duties on the Swing shift, when the phone rang. My wife answered the call and handed me the phone saying it was somebody from Stanford. I eagerly grabbed the wall device and discovered that it was Chief Herrington. After the "howdy do's," I kiddingly asked:

"So, Chief, are you calling to tell me thanks but no thanks?" Having suffered some hearing loss I wasn't quite sure what his response was so I asked him to repeat it.

"I want you," he said. "When can you start?" Totally stunned, I wasn't quite sure what to say.

When I finally recovered, I indicated that I was very interested in becoming one of his captains and would like to come up for a second interview. We set a date and I informed my spouse that I was going to meet with Stanford's Top Cop and we'd see about the package before I completely committed.

Decision Time

Although the position at SUDPS seemed awesome, I would be giving up a lot of seniority and job security at the S/O, in addition to a possible promotion to Lieutenant. But, the rumor was that the Sheriff's Staff was looking at me to head-up the Records Division, which would have been a huge nightmare, as I was a COP through and through: The thought of trading the red lights and sirens and zooming around the county to only the best calls, for an office gig supervising 40 women, was indeed daunting. . . I remember when I first got into Personnel and Training (P&T) and experienced some difficulty adjusting to working with the professional staff (women) after being used to bossing trustees and other inmates around in the Drunk Tank. I was clearly out of my element initially, but soon learned to adjust my temperament; however, we only had a handful of ladies (most of whom were delightful) in P&T, whereas in the Records Division, I would literally be "The Last Man Standing. . ." So, that gave me pause. Clearly, I wasn't ready for Records at that stage of my career! There was also a lot of dissension in the S/O at that time due to a hiring freeze and budgetary woes. Although many people were extremely frustrated and threatened to leave, I also knew that the perceived proverbial "green grass" wasn't always the delightful verdant pasture that it appeared to be. . .

Another troubling factor was I would be giving-up a full law enforcement commission and would have to accept a Reserve Deputy Sheriff status at Stanford due to existing law which precluded private institutions from having full peace officer status per Penal Code Section 832.1, which I will explain in short order. Finally, as I drove on the Farm for my secondary interview with the Chief, I drove around the 5 by 5 mile campus mulling over my concerns. I recall thinking: *Man this place is pretty small from what*

I am used to. I hope I don't get a huge case of claustrophobia if I take this job! But, I rationalized this fear by thinking that I was going to be an administrator—a desk jockey—not a patrolman. Little did I know what I was getting myself into. . .

But, there were a lot of positives about the captain's position at Stanford: Remuneration and the benefits package were excellent at that time. The University's medical plan was superior to the Kaiser plan I had at the S/O. The retirement plan offered to faculty and senior staff was touted as being one of the best private systems in the country. And, my kids would be able to attend the college/university of their choice as the University would pony up half of what Stanford's steep tuition was. That was a *biggee* for me as both of our offspring were very good students who aspired to receive college degrees.

After having another lengthy séance with Chief Herrington, I advised him that I would have an answer within a few days. My wife was supportive of the offer, so the final decision fell squarely on my shoulders. In the interim, and after talking to the existing players, I was confident I was up to the task. And, besides, we were going to bring-in a lot of fresh blood which I figured would revitalize the OG. This was every leader's dream: To build a new organization from the ground up, recruit, train, establish the rules, cross your fingers and turn them loose. After much soul searching I plunged head long into the abyss. . . What could possibly go wrong? Well, you shall see as this war story unfolds. . . Now, back to the Chief.

Background

Marvin Herrington moved his family to CA from frigid, crime-ridden (even then) Detroit's Motor City in the early '60s, and signed on as a patrolman with the University of California, Davis Police Department. This was way before the Vietnam upheaval so the only thing going on in those days was bike thefts, collisions and maybe a stray cow or two on the freeway. UCD was (and still is) primarily an agricultural research university and boasts one of the best Veterinary medical schools in the nation, if not the world, thus had a menagerie of animals on their expansive rural campus. Their scientists were on the cutting edge of agricultural and animal husbandry technology. One of their early achievements was a living see-through cut-away of a cow's gastrointestinal tract. Herrington didn't have anything to do with that, however. . .

While the academic and research of the University was humming away, Officer Herrington was quickly moving-up through the ranks. He soon became Top Cop about the time that all hell was breaking loose throughout the country, mainly over U.S. involvement in the Vietnam War. It was about this time that Herrington was recruited to become the Chief at Northwestern University, in Evanston, IL, a Chicago suburb. The benefits must have been extraordinary (although he never discussed this with me) for him to pack-up his family and trek back into one of the coldest places I had ever been to:
****

Way back in January 1957, I had the misfortune of being assigned to Chanute AFB, Rantoul, IL (about 60 miles south of Chi Town) for jet engine mechanic school. It was brutally cold that winter, with tons of the white stuff on the ground, three feet deep, and constant replenishment from the Big Guy in the sky—especially in the early AM when we had to march to the chow hall and remain in formation for up to 30 minutes at a time for our turn. Although it could have been worse if I was an Army ground pounder, I guess the Air Force wanted us to man-up, albeit scantily clothed in lightweight fatigues, without thermal liners in our jackets and gloves. Being the only "pineapple" in my group who had never, ever seen snow, let alone trudge though it at 0430, I had a tough time in that awful environment; more often than not, I hid out in the barracks or sneaked out of formation and headed for a warm hide. I paid for my non-compliance as the sergeants were soon onto my game and sought me out like heat seeking missiles. I spent a lot of time doing penance pulling extra duty washing nasty blacked pots in the kitchen and "policing" the area—not with a gun and badge, but with a stick equipped with a nail at the end. . . When I finally got my first off-base pass, I decided to visit my Grandfather, and Aunt and Uncle, who lived in Forrest Park, a Chicago suburb. This trek started with an hour train ride to Chicago's train terminal—an enormous structure located right on Lake Michigan. By this time, I wised up and bought a short furry jacket and a pair of insulated gloves. Once disembarked, all I had to do was walk across Michigan Avenue and go a few blocks to State Street where I could catch a southbound "El" (elevated railcar) and enjoy the ride to Forrest Park. However, when I stepped out of the building and began to cross the very wide street, I was almost blown away and felt as if someone had run-me-through with a frozen broad sword! I later learned that this 45 mile an hour breeze was called the "Hawk" by Chicago natives. Hawk my ass! This was a gale force arctic wind, which by a large thermometer on a nearby building registered a numbing minus 13 degrees! Of course, when I related this tale to the Chief, he just laughed, and in a nice way, which indicated I was a wimp. Indeed I was.

****

However, while the weather at Northwestern University was normally brutally cold and windy during the winter, happenings on campus and the surrounding area were always red hot during this period in American history, as the new Chief would soon realize.

Cutting Teeth

If one was to seek-out an advanced degree in political activism, Northwestern was the place to be. A host of social and political issues seemed to incubate and fester at this university during the 1960s and 1970s. Discourse ran the gamut from perceived structural racism within the institution, hatred of the Nixon administration, the Vietnam War and resultant draft, the massive bombing campaign in Southeast Asia, presence of NROTC in their midst (which mirrored the demise of Stanford's military student program), and the egregious slaughter at Kent State University which resulted in the death of four and caused serious injury to nine protesters. There was also considerable support for the Black Panther Party at the Evanston campus. What better place for the new Chief to cut his teeth!

Surprisingly, most of the civil-disobedience and protests at Northwestern were relatively peaceful. Although the campus and Evanston police had to ride herd on these disruptions, violence was minimal and only a few arrests had to be made. Like Stanford's leaders of that era, NW's administration was befuddled, quite malleable and they generally caved-in to student's demands. Several sit-ins and occupations took place for days until the hell raiser's demands were met, wherein the brats packed-up and went about their business. Chief Herrington learned a lot about negotiation at Northwestern, but he abhorred building occupations, strikes and obstruction of a university's primary mission—education.

After his "Basic Training" at Evanston, he and his family headed back to CA, as he had accepted a new and clearly much "nicer" position as the Law Enforcement Coordinator of the California State University system—by all accounts, a ripe plum! Herrington basically served as a police consultant for all of the state's university police departments. He traveled around the Golden State, parlayed with the chiefs, and offered advice on their particular problems. Then, he got the call that would change his life—forever!

"Don't Go to Stanford!"*

In 1971, Marvin Herrington got a phone call from Robert "Bob" Augsberger, then Stanford's VP of Business and Finance. The University was in dire need of a Chief and Mr. Herrington had been highly recommended by the Northwestern Dean of Students, who was Augsberger's brother-in-law. Herrington initially declined interest as nearly everyone in the world knew what a battleground Stanford was at that time. But, after some cajoling and *light arm twisting,* Augsberger convinced Herrington to at least make a visit. He was flown from Los Angeles to San Francisco on Stanford's dime, so the candidate figured it wouldn't be any skin off his nose. However, his first impression was not a favorable one, as his "chauffer" was a surly Old Guard malcontent who had the personality of a Cobra. In addition, he bad mouthed the University, "police" department, and administration with all of the vitriol of a dissident leader of the time. Talk about "first impressions."

*From an article in "Sandstone and Tile" Spring/Summer 2004 Stanford Historical Society, Volume 28, No.2, orchestrated and recorded by retired head of the Stanford Alumni Association, William E. Stone, when Chief Herrington retired on April 13, 2004.

Various luminaries gave their prospect the cook's tour and he met with several officials who acted as if they were selling a used car—a bad one at that! When Herrington returned to L.A., he talked with a number of friends and advisors and was strongly admonished: "Don't Go to Stanford!" He promptly declined Mr. Augsberger's offer, but agreed to just one more visit. This time, a chat with President Richard "Dick" Lyman, who William "Bill" Stone described in his article as: ". . . the gentleman who the *Stanford Daily* called the finest seventh president in Stanford's history. . ." (In this writer's opinion, President Lyman was one helluva leader, especially in those tumultuous times. He restored order out of absolute chaos! Most importantly, he got Stanford University back to its mandate of teaching and research. I felt privileged to have worked under his tutelage.)

After lengthy negotiations and some *heavy arm twisting*, Marvin L. Herrington agreed to accept the daunting position as Stanford University's fourth "official" Chief of Police. His experience in the college and university systems enabled him to exact some heretofore unheard of provisos in campus policing: First, he convinced the Legal Office (now known as General Counsel) not to allow protesters to occupy any structure during business hours—8AM to 5PM—and, if people insisted on occupying a building open to the public after they were ordered to leave, then those violators would be arrested per the mandates of CA penal law. Later on, and most importantly (in my view), the administration agreed they would not interfere in lawful arrests and prosecutions of ANY person within the University's jurisdiction! That included students, faculty, staff, donors, friends of friends, et. al.! This was huge, as so many other educational systems made the final call on who was and was not subject to the laws of the state, thereby allowing the "Old Boy/Old Girl Network," to flourish unchecked. This element later allayed my fears of engaging in law enforcement in a corrupt environment.

Into the Fray

As I described in the Old Guard chapter, Stanford was a virtual war zone when Chief Herrington took the tiller of the ship which was taking on water like the Titanic. The violent radicals skirmished once the sun set, and rearmed and planned for renewed guerilla tactics during daylight. This went on for months, with no end in sight. Chief Herrington received a rather rude welcome one night, when unknown missileers hurled bricks and huge rocks through the window of the Wilbur Hall dorm room he was temporarily squatting in, while his wife sold their home in Southern CA. That should have been a clue, but he persevered. As the story goes, the hellions basically did a "drive-by" on the good Director; however, this was a case of mistaken identity. The attackers were actually gunning for another university official, a Resident Fellow, who used to occupy the targeted room. But, I think this misguided effort might have been worse had they known that Stanford's new C.O.P. was in that room: They could have lobbed-in Molotov cocktails or hand grenades. . .

Be that as it may, the Stanford newbie had another task at hand which demanded immediate attention. The remnants of the Old Guard were, collectively, a sorry lot, especially among the night crew of so-called "Door Shakers." Right from the jump, the Chief was besieged with credible reports of theft, drinking on duty and general incompetence. Some of these clowns would go into the Faculty Club and avail themselves of copious amounts of high dollar, top-of-the-line booze. Several wannabe "Food Network Chefs" let themselves into various kitchens in the early morning and whipped-up four star breakfasts for their colleagues. Remember, these characters had keys to the whole joint! Theft of cash and other valuables abounded under the "watchful eye" of these scoundrels. They were literally getting paid to steal! You'll read about some of those antics later.

"You Don't Need No Stinkin' Badges—Or Guns!"

After a few weeks of experiencing some of this nonsense, Director Herrington was pretty fed-up with this wild bunch! In one instance, an OG guy, who somehow was living in an Escondido Village *student* apartment, heard a suspicious vehicle (11-54) late one night. There had been a rash of car burglaries in the area so he was sure these were the guys! He strapped on his Sam Brown belt, containing his loaded .38, and charged out into the darkness, wearing only a pair of BVDs. Stanford's finest "Rambo" then stealthily approached the vehicle in question. When the occupants of the 11-54 spotted the nearly naked guy pointing a pistol at them, they took off in a cloud of dust and burnt rubber. As I understand it, the scenario went something like this:

BAM, BAM, BAM! "Stop, Po-Lice!"

Luckily, no one was hit, but everyone in EV heard the gun fire and called communications. Once Rambo's action was verified, the Chief got the call, flew down to the station and relieved the errant gunman of his piece. It was then that he decided everyone in the department was going to be relieved of their hardware and deputization; the entire department would be vetted and go through the process of being real cops. And, so it was. That is one of the reasons I wound-up on the Farm.

Humor

At first glance, most folks would think Marv Herrington was a pretty serious man who really took his being and position with great reverence. That is all very true, but when you got to know him better, there was a whole other, often cantankerous side to this man. He knew that I was a consummate prankster, and often aided me in my scams. In one case, I spotted an article in the *Daily* that revealed a group was going to have a "Nude-In" at Lake Lagunita's Boat House "beach"—such as it was. I immediately seized this opportunity to spoof one of my youthful appearing new men, who even in his 30s, could pass for a student. I fired off a memo to him about this event and directed him to go check it out, in the buff, of course, just in case there might be some unlawful activity about. I initiated the "Nuremberg Defense" by pleading in my epistle that "I was just following orders," as Chief Herrington had made this call! I told the detective to put on a pair of shades, carry his credentials and radio in a tote bag, and that "He didn't need no stinkin' gun"—but we'd give him back-up... I sealed the directive in an envelope, tipped-off the rest of the crew and the Chief, and waited for the man to return from lunch. All hands were on deck in great anticipation. When our victim opened the envelope and read the memo, the guy went berserk and shouted:

"No Way! No FN Way," a mantra he continued as he flew into my office. I fought to keep a straight face and told the unhappy camper to take it up with the Chief.

"Well, I want to see him right away!" the reluctant would-be nudist shouted. I buzzed the boss and told him about my disgruntled employee and asked if we could come down to his office. Within minutes, we were bounding down the stairs. When we entered the Man's office, he put on his super serious face and asked the mark what his problem was. The kid incredulously screamed at the Chief that he just couldn't do this assignment as he was a very private man, and besides, it was against his religion—or a similarly bogus excuse. Herrington then broke out in a big grin and told the detective to relax because we were just messing with him. I heard a big sigh of relief from the pranked one, followed by a veiled threat that he'd get me for this... He never did!

Animal Rights

During the late 1980s through early 1990s, Animal Rights activists targeted Stanford University among many other entities in the Bay Area for performing medical research, in which a variety of lab animals were utilized. Initially, this research was carried out in a number of departments on campus. However, due to some violent protests and devastating firebomb attacks carried out by the radical group ALF (The Animal Liberation Front)—a huge laboratory was burned to the ground at UC Davis—Stanford got ahead of the game and built a virtual underground bunker—an animal research lab that could carry out experiments with some measure of security as the place was pretty hardened and tough to penetrate. Realizing that wreaking havoc on our facility would be difficult, lesser animal protest groups such as PETA (People for the Ethical Treatment of Animals), took a political tact and staged demonstrations at symposiums and other public venues. PETA's mission was to shame and scold the University, thereby pressuring it to cease all animal research. But, that wasn't going to happen anytime soon.

One of PETA's most impressive stunts was to picket the University President's Office at Building 10. Occupying the "Cat Bird's Seat," was the affable Donald "Don" Kennedy. Chief Herrington got to know President Kennedy quite well over the years, beginning when the "young" biology professor presided over the contentious Faculty Advisory Board hearings of radical Associate Professor H. Bruce Franklin. (Franklin was one of the dynamos who had been the spark plug in a number of violent demonstrations early in 1971. In the end, Franklin was given the boot and sent packing down Palm Drive. This was a serious blow to the radical movement.)

Approximately 200 folks showed-up at Building 10 one spring morning. The crowd was primarily comprised of middle-aged women and a mix of docile younger men and women; they marched around the President's Office with signs and chanted epitaphs such as: "Stop the Research. Stop the Murder!" This activity persisted despite SUDPS warnings that they were blocking ingress and egress, thus in violation of law, and were subject to arrest. As I will later describe in my piece on Demonstrations, after reading the group the so-called "riot act," we allowed them some time to disperse. Those who opted to be martyrs were arrested and taken to a processing area; prisoners were then transported by bus to our police compound where they were either cited and released, or taken to jail—their choice.

About half of the protesters decided to leave, so the remaining dissidents were put through the drill. Of particular concern was a middle-aged matronly lady who was apparently blind, as she was led by a gorgeous German Shepherd on a halter. Sensing that this would be a prize photo-op for the numerous media who were on the scene, Chief Herrington assigned one of our nicest deputies to arrest this die-hard, sightless woman. Deputy Al Blaisdell was a prince of a guy: He was tall, dark and handsome and as congenial as a man of the cloth. After Blaisdell advised the lady that she was under arrest, she took hold of his arm with one hand and held onto her comfort animal with the other and was led to the processing center. Talk about an epic shot! That photo was on the front page of every newspaper in the Bay Area.

The next day, as the Chief was out and about, he ran into President Don Kennedy. As I recall, the conversation went something like this:

Don: "So, Marv, I guess everything went pretty well with that animal rights protest yesterday; the newspaper articles looked fine and I especially like the photo of your man, arm in arm with the blind woman and her seeing-eye dog."

Chief: "Yeah, everything went OK but we did have a bit of a glitch."

Don: "Oh? What happened?"

Chief: "Well, when we booked the woman, Animal Control Officers took charge of her dog and the idiots put the darn thing to sleep!" With an ashen face, as if all of the blood drained from his head, President Kennedy exclaimed:

"You've got to be (bleeping) me! Are you (bleeping) serious?" The Chief tried to maintain his composure but broke out into an uncontrollable Cheshire cat grin and replied:

"Naaaa, Don, I'm just kidding!" With that, Stanford University's Eighth President did an abrupt about-face and scurried off muttering unprintable words. . . Don't kill this messenger. I'm just reporting what I heard. . .

Having given you this brief bio of Stanford's Director of Public Safety, I'll now proceed with the many stories I feel compelled to impart. . .

Chief Frank Andrew Jurian

Chief Frank Jurian, Stanford Fire Department

Photo: Courtesy of Mrs. Fred-a Jurian

Frank Jurian was a public safety icon in the annals of Stanford University. Born and raised in Portola Valley, just west in the lush foothills, Frank came to the Farm in 1946 when he was 20 years old and landed one of the four paid firefighter positions. Jurian was a U.S. Postal mailman at the time and apparently caught the eye of then Chief, John Marston, who invited the big lad (6'4" about 235) to sign-on. Stanford's fire protection program was augmented by a student volunteer force, which dates back to the 1880s, formed by Governor Stanford, to fight fires around his horse stock farm. The "official" Stanford Fire Department was established in 1904 and utilized hand-drawn firefighting apparatuses (hand pumpers) until

1913. I believe that Henry Ford's Model T chassis served as a platform for the new and improved motorized equipment.

When Fireman Jurian signed on January 1, 1946, he was awarded a whopping salary of $170 per month. Frank was not only smart, but he was extremely personable and likeable, so no wonder he was promoted to Captain just 2 years later. This promotion more than doubled his salary to 500 bucks a month, which was a pretty good chunk of change at that time. By comparison, when I took the oath at the S/O in 1964, my monthly stipend was a mere $535—and, no paid overtime!

After a decade, Captain Jurian was elevated to Assistant Chief (I believe this position was akin to what is now called Battalion Chief), but only got a paltry $20 raise. Frank was later promoted to First Assistant Chief in 1963, and finally took over the helm of the department in 1970.

Stanford's Finest Private Fire Department

I remember when our S/O Crowd Control Unit was bivouacked at Stanford during the "Days of Rage," and I had an occasion to visit the fire department. I was blown away by the volume and quality of firefighting equipment that was literally crammed into every inch of the fire bay. Even the older mainstays, Seagraves and Ford pumpers, looked like they just came out of a paint booth. The place was like an Operating Room: You could literally eat off the floors or any piece of equipment! My good buddy, Cecil Rhodes, then a Burbank District (San Jose) firefighter told me that without a doubt, Stanford's F.D. was the best equipped and trained private fire department anywhere. After seeing some of the antiques at the Burbank firehouse—and other Santa Clara County stations, I thought he was right. I later learned that most of the acquisition of state-of-the-art fire apparatus was due to the efforts of Chief Jurian. When I first began my watch in 1974, Frank had just purchased two Crown engines—arguably then the "Cadillac" of fire equipment, evidenced by the hefty price tag of over 90K each! After getting to know Frank better, I soon discovered the Chief had a penchant for the finest things money could buy, be it fire trucks, related equipment and supplies, or just dining out—no McDonald's for this guy!

Notable Campus Fires*

- In 1888, person(s) unknown apparently torched the Palo Alto Stock Farm's 12 stall stables. Nine Blue Ribbon horses perished in the blaze, but Governor Stanford's prize colt, "Palo Alto." was rescued. However, this famous equine died of pneumonia a few years later and joined his mates in a burial site nearby. The grave was later marked with a bigger than life bronze horse, which still stands today.

"Palo Alto:" Stanford's Finest Colt

Photo: By Nina L Niemeyer

- The vacant Phi Gamma Delta (Fiji House) fraternity burned to the ground in 1960. The loss of this beautiful antebellum-style structure spurred the University to acquire more resources to expand and improve campus fire protection services.

- During the Days of Rage (1968-1972), there were 30 suspicious fires and bombings—a few were unsuccessful—which I discuss in an upcoming chapter. This was certainly a very sad period in Stanford's unique history. But, the Grand Daddy of them all was the conflagration which severely damaged one of the University's most celebrated buildings, Encina Hall: In the late hours of June 7, 1972, a huge fire broke out in the upper floors of Encina Hall, which had been transformed from a men's dormitory back in the day, to the University's administrative offices. Although there had been some construction in progress during that time, the workmen weren't doing anything near the origin of the fire. This blaze soon raged out of control, despite the valiant efforts of Chief Jurian's firefighters; this catastrophe was more than they could possibly handle, so Frank called for "Mutual Aid." Within minutes after the call went out, fire apparatuses from nearly every jurisdiction in and around Santa Clara County began pouring-in. It was estimated that over 250 firefighters fought this raging inferno. After many laborious hours, the arson *(Author's personal belief)* was finally extinguished. Fortunately, the affected area was concentrated to the upper floors, so the rest of the structure remained relatively undamaged. Overall, the price tag for the Encina fire was over one million dollars. My research concludes that this incident went down as being the County's largest mutual aid effort. More importantly, there were NO injuries!

- Finally, I watched Chief Jurian and his crack firefighters in action when former Secretary of State George Shultz's residence caught fire sometime in the 1980s. Boy, I was impressed when they charged into that conflagration and knocked the flames down as if someone threw a huge asbestos blanket over the house. As a result of SUFD's quick response and fire suppression skill, this classic wooden home was saved and soon restored to better than new condition.

*Courtesy of the Internet

Notable Accomplishments

During his heyday, Chief Jurian commanded over 70 paid professionals, as well as a cadre of student volunteers. Frank is credited with greatly expanding and professionalizing the student firefighter program. When the new fire station was built on Serra Street in the late 1950s, one wing was designed to house the contingent of student volunteers. They were billeted in comfortable two-man rooms and had a communal bathroom and dayroom, which sported a TV and a regulation pool table. This table was donated by a professor, who was grateful to be alive as a result of heroic life saving efforts by the firemen, when the educator suffered a serious heart attack. During his tenure, Jurian's student fireman program enabled over 1,000 kids to defray their housing cost (free rent) and earn a stipend (over $200) for their services, as well. Equal opportunity happened in 1975, when the first female, Linda Bamman, '78, was admitted into the student firefighter program. Another graduate of the volunteer program, Bill Bamattre, '74, later ascended the fire career ladder by becoming Chief of the 3,500 strong Los Angeles Fire Department.*

Another feather in Chief Jurian's hat was the opening of a satellite fire station at SLAC (Stanford Linear Accelerator Center), which is located in San Mateo County. After bridging the politics of establishing a public safety facility in someone else's back yard, Frank convinced the hierarchy that it would be in the University's best interest to have on-site protection of the multi-billion dollar technology center. As I said before, Frank Jurian was a smart man and his wisdom ultimately prevailed.

*Stanford Magazine: "When Students Fought Fires," by Theresa Johnson, July/Aug. 2002

The Leland

The Leland Hand Pumper

Photo: Courtesy Mrs. Fred-a Jurian

One of the original pieces of firefighting equipment for the Farm was a little 1883 RUMSEY, manufactured by Rumsey and Co., Seneca Falls, NY. Governor Leland Stanford ordered this newfangled contraption in order to safeguard his stock farm and mansion. Students manned this apparatus before paid pros came on in 1904; sadly, "the little pumper that could," just couldn't when the stables went up in flames in '88! The below description explains why this machine was less than adequate, at best, to handle sizable conflagrations:

The hand drawn, hand powered 1883 was pulled and pushed to a fire by a team of robust individuals. Once on the scene, the "tub" or reservoir had to be hand-filled, either by a bucket brigade, or if a creek, well, or cistern was nearby, a sturdy suction hose could be immersed therein and water could be drawn into the pump by the vigorous pumping of an 8-man team. The pistons in this machine were rather small so the volume of water that left the hose nozzle wasn't much, by today's standards.

It is unknown to me when the 1883 Rumsey was retired, but at some point, Chief Jurian discovered that it was collecting dust in the basement of the Stanford Museum. Frank took possession of the hose cart, got it back into working order, and named it "The Leland."

After training several "robust" individuals, Chief Jurian began competing in a nostalgic firefighting event called "The Muster," which was held at various venues in CA and Oregon.

In the late '70s, I recall meeting some volunteer fire lads (from Prineville, OR) at an annual event I attended in Oregon for years and when they found out I was a Stanford cop, one guy asked:

"Hey, do you know Chief Frank Jurian?"

"As a matter of fact, I do," I replied.

"Man, those *ol' bouys* on that Leland rig kick our asses every year at the Muster," he sheepishly confessed.

Indeed they did: In the Class III hand-pumper competition, Frank's crews won nearly every event in their class during the 1970s and 1980s. I talked to my good friend, John Stafford, a member of the "robust" Leland crew (1970-1974) and he verified that those guys were damn good! In addition to Chief Jurian, the other "pumpers" included: Pat Cady, Ken Carlson, Dick Wilkerson, Lee Caudil, Mick McDonald, Dan Rhodes, Doug Williams and others. Stafford also recalled that the Leland came around Cape Horn on a sailing vessel in the early 1880s, which was contrary to my notion that the Governor had it freighted on one of his trains. However, in Ms. Johnson's article, "When Students Fought Fires," she mentioned that the hand pumper was ordered from Boston. The ocean voyage transportation of the Leland makes Stafford's recollection credible, as Boston was a major port during that era.

The Leland once suffered a near death experience when it parted company with its travel trailer after a Muster, and was thrashed when it came in violent contact with terra firma. Thanks to Chief Jurian's University network, and with the extraordinary skill of his Ace Mechanic, Al Rames, the Leland was renovated from stem to stern. The pump's mechanism was overhauled and nickel plated; the damaged wooden parts were repaired with period dated lumber by old timers from the Gold Country who had the expertise to fix 18th century wheels and wagon bodies. Leland's new body received a spiffy coat of high gloss varnish, but lost some of its antiquity as the original paint and trim couldn't be replicated. The Leland was often displayed in the fire bay during public events. It was not only a piece of art, but yet another example of Stanford's rich heritage.

Lights Out for Stanford's Glorious Fire Days

It was a sad day for Chief Frank Jurian and many of us who were close to him and his department when in 1976, the University decided to merge with the City of Palo Alto for fire services. I was heartbreaking to see the Stanford Fire Department's decals on the trucks being replaced with Palo Alto's logos. I'll never forget that day! I had lobbied hard to retain the autonomy of our fire department: Aside from cost, the real fly in the soup was the increasingly vocal firefighter's union and their demands. When the hard-liners started talking about striking, that did it for the administration. I optimistically argued that we could become a true public safety department like the City of Sunnyvale, who proved over the years that a small contingent of professional firefighters, augmented by police officers, was a viable alternative to giving up the Ghost, so to speak. I figured that we could cross-train a cadre of deputies and rotate them through the fire house. The great majority of fire runs on campus were not full blown 5-Alarmers—mostly injury accidents, resuscitation calls, minor fires, and a chemical spill or two in the labs—certainly, nothing major. And, if a serious fire or other incident occurred, then all hands could be mustered to handle the detail like Sunnyvale had done for years. When compared to other cities in the U.S., in so far as population and industrial base, Sunnyvale is always rated near top of the list for public safety. Nonetheless, the Palo Alto merger became an unfortunate reality, in my opinion. Fortunately, the SUDPS was able to retain the services of Chief Jurian and Doug Williams (Emergency Communications Supervisor), thanks to the efforts of Chief Herrington.

DPS Assistant Chief Jurian

Although a demotion of sorts for Frank, he seemed to take it in stride and maintained a positive attitude for as long as I knew him. Chief Jurian oversaw the fire and communications merger and ensured that the University's best interests were being fulfilled. In addition, Frank coordinated medical services at all sporting events, and ensured that the public's safety would be first and foremost at the Really Big Events (Chapter 22) like Super Bowl XIX, Olympic Soccer and World Cup, and major visits by V.I.P.s and Heads of State. If you ever had a problem with anything within his purview, Frank would be on it and have it rectified in a minute. He was quite a man.

The Man

I have trumpeted Chief Jurian's professional accomplishments during his 45 year stint at Stanford, but would now like to write a few words about the man. Although, by now you must already know that I'm inherently incapable of writing just a few words about anything! OK, I'll limit it to quite a few words. . .

Frank had a terrific family. He was married to a wonderful lady, Fred-a, who was a campus celebrity in her own right: Mrs. Jurian had a 30 year career at Stanford serving as the Physics Department's Executive Administrative Secretary. In that capacity, Fred-a assisted Nobel Laureate Arthur Schawlow as his faithful secretary. Fred-a bore the family two sons, Andy and Michael; they lived on the campus beginning in 1962.

As I indicated earlier, Frank seemed to know everything and everybody at Stanford. His gregarious and affable personality endeared him to nearly everyone! Frank's smile and hearty laugh was infectious. If you ever needed advice, he was the guy. If you needed to find out guarded secrets, Frank knew where all of the bones were buried. And, procurement was his forte: Prior to a raid on a suspected armed drug dealer, I asked Chief J. if there might be any surplus armored vests around; he not only knew where they were, but took me to the man who had them in his department! Jurian quickly persuaded the curator of surplus goods not to just loan them, but to give them to me. These were heavy WWII B-17 waist gunner's vests designed to protect the Flying Fortress' crew from the Lufwaffe's ME-109 and FW-190's machine gun fire, so these shields would surely stop a .45!

Not only did Frank Jurian know everybody on campus, but he was well known and respected in surrounding communities. Frank loved to eat, so every Friday at lunchtime, he would lead us to some of his favorite haunts in the region—and there were several, so we spread our charm around. In the early years, Frank, Cap'n Bill Wullschleger, and I were the "Three Amigos." Later, after being promoted to Captain, Marvin Moore made it a foursome. One of Frank's favorites was an Italian style family restaurant in Atherton called Fabbro's—famous for fresh cracked Dungeness crab on Fridays. San Francisco crab is usually always quite delightful, but the chef at Fabbro's developed a special marinade that was out of this world! When I asked how he made his killer sauce, he replied like a Mafioso hit-man: "If I told ya, I'd have to kill ya!" I never inquired again. . .

Frank and Fred-a were consummate epicureans: They often dined at the best eateries in the Bay Area, so they really knew their way around the restaurant scene. One of Frank's maxims or guidelines, in having positive dining experiences went something like this: "When you walk through the door of a restaurant and see a bunch of kids serving, turn around and head for the parking lot! Good places only hire waiters or "seasoned" waitresses!" Over the years of being a lover of good chow, too, I believe Frank Jurian was spot on—with a few exceptions, of course. My daughter, Nina, who lives in Las Vegas and frequently dines out, affirms the Ol' Chief's rule.

Fire Chief Emeritus

After 45 years of service to the Stanford University community, Chief Jurian retired in 1990. On the recommendation of Public Safety Director, Marvin Herrington, University President Donald Kennedy awarded Frank the prestigious title of "Fire Chief Emeritus." However, Jurian's much deserved retirement was cut short on July 10, 1995, when that tough old warrior succumbed to cancer, after a 15 month long battle.

I had the dubious distinction of helping to orchestrate Frank's funeral and interment arrangements as Chief Herrington was on assignment in the East. I was honored to do my part in seeing my good friend off to another life. I coordinated the event with Palo Alto Fire Chiefs Nick Marinaro and Mick McDonald, who worked under Jurian in the old Stanford F.D., and were similarly very close friends.

On July 15th, the funeral entourage left the funeral home in Palo Alto and we made our way to Chief Jurian's old "office," now Station #6, at 711 Serra Street. I was in the lead car as we pulled-up in front of the fire house. Two huge fire trucks elevated their telescoping ladders so they connected at the top and formed a "V." From the apex, a large American flag was suspended. Scores of uniformed fire and police personnel crowded around the station's apron and saluted "Old Glory" in honor of our beloved Chief. From there, we were off for our fallen friend's last ride around Campus Drive en route to Our Lady of the Wayside Catholic Church in Portola Valley for a Requiem Mass. Dozens of fire rigs from all over the region joined the motorcade during this journey. Frank was baptized and married in this little church, established in 1912, and now would complete his life's cycle there.

All told, over 200 folks were involved in Frank's last rite. The uniformed fire and police personnel formed-up in two columns at the church's entrance while the pall bearers carried the casket into the diminutive house of worship. There was standing room only and it was hotter than Hades. Nonetheless, all of the faithful stood tall and remained firm, the ultimate sign of unwavering respect.

After the Mass, we mounted-up again and headed for Chief Jurian's final resting place, Holy Cross Cemetery in Menlo Park. I don't know how we were able to get so many huge fire trucks and other vehicles into that burial ground, but we did. Before we realized it, the ritual was over and our dear friend was laid to rest. This recollection brings a tear to my eye after all of these years—18, I still miss that guy. But, his persona can be best summed-up in an excerpt from Chief Herrington's memo to the department:

"Frank was one of a kind. He was one of those people who spread laughter and good will to everyone he touched. He did a serious job in a light hearted way that made you happy to work with him. I shall miss his smiling face and laughing banter."

Cap'n Bill

Captain William Louis Wullschleger

Photo: Courtesy of Stanford University News Service

I first met Captain William Wullschleger circa 1973 when I was Training Sergeant at the S/O conducting 832 PC training: In an effort to upgrade training of peace officers who had never graduated from an accredited basic police academy, the State of CA mandated all sworn personnel must undergo classes in laws of arrest, search and seizure, use of force, firearms qualification and arrest techniques. I taught these subjects in the Santa Clara County Basic Peace Officer's Academy, thus was given the charge of crafting a 40 hour course of instruction. At the time, the Stanford DPS was going through reorganization under the command of the new Director of Public Safety, Marvin L. Herrington, who later hired me. In order to be in compliance, he sent Captain Wullschleger who, although a seasoned veteran of over 20 years in law enforcement, was never afforded the opportunity to attend an academy. So, that is how I met this fine individual.

Born in 1927 in San Francisco, Bill was the son of a self-made man, who later became a very successful printer. Bill attended Abraham Lincoln High School in the City by the Bay, and later, Mountain View High, when the family moved to Los Altos for a brief period of time. He went back to Abraham Lincoln when they moved back to S.F., but left school to join the Navy in 1945. Fresh out of boot camp, someone discovered that he could type—15 wpm on a manual machine—certainly no need for a standby bucket of water at that "blistering" speed—so, Uncle Sam sent him to typing school where he emerged knocking out 76 wpm—still no need for fire retardant—but, pretty darn respectable for a big man with fingers like a bunch of bananas. Before he knew it, WWII was over and he was a civilian again. Bill took a job as a warehouseman—so much for the typing skills he learned at our expense... After about 5 years of back-breaking work, his back *was indeed broke,* so his Doc advised him to seek another career; enter stage left, cop work.

Bill began his law enforcement career in the city of Menlo Park, which borders the Stanford Campus to the north. He was commissioned in 1951 and served as a patrolman until 1958. As things were in those days, organized training was a luxury: Occasionally, the FBI traveled around and put on dog-and-pony shows for the locals. But, other than that, most police training was acquired on the streets via the "school of hard knocks"—and there were a lot of those institutions all around the country.

Bill married and relocated to Las Vegas in order to pursue a business venture as proprietor of a cocktail lounge, located right outside of the main gate of Nellis Air Force Base. He named his establishment "The Flying Tigers" where he catered to USAF officers, as well as NCOs (non-commissioned officers). Although not prohibited, most grunts, who tended to be hand grenades when intoxicated, shied away from Bill's club. By all reports, the bar was a very successful venture, but the luster of "Glitter Gulch" soon faded and the Wullschlegers moved back to the Bay Area where Bill put in his application for Menlo Park PD. It was now 1960 and law enforcement was slowly evolving into a professional career with testing and vetting as part of the selection process. Relegated to a waiting list, Bill joined the reserves in an effort to enhance his chances of appointment to the *paid force*. Reserves had to buy their uniforms and all of their safety equipment—gun, cuffs, leather and billy club. Even then, the uniform suppliers were a ruthless bunch of racketeers—the officers were at their mercy and the haberdashers knew it and took full advantage of the situation.

It was April 1st, 1961. Bill, by virtue of his previous experience, was assigned to the "Dog Watch," patrolling the East Menlo area, known as Bell Haven—a pretty rough area, even in those days. While prowling the neighborhood shortly after midnight, an All Points Bulletin (APB) was broadcast—yes, they had those newfangled two-way radios then—to BOL (be on the lookout) for a group of extremely dangerous, violent criminals who had been on an unchecked crime spree on the Peninsula for several weeks. This gang preyed on lone motel clerks late in the evening and early mornings: Numbering 3 to 4, these "zeroes" robbed unsuspecting and defenseless victims at gunpoint—often pistol whipping their helpless prey and raping the females, leaving them bound and gagged. In this instance, the perpetrators were described as several black males in a large sedan: They had just committed a 211a/261 (armed robbery and rape) on a woman clerk at a motel in San Carlos. One of the assailants was described as being 6'7" tall. The witnesses described the suspect's vehicle as a GM product, possibly a Chevrolet. Bill was assigned to a Code 5 (surveillance post) at Willow and Cambridge roads.

At approximately 0400 hours, a Pontiac Bonneville 2 door suddenly appeared, heading eastbound. The vehicle looked like it was lowered—not from any suspension alterations, but from the sheer size of the occupants therein! Officer Wullschleger advised radio what he had and that he was going to effectuate a stop, near the beginning of the long approach to the Dumbarton drawbridge. Although not a Chevy, as originally put out on the air, Bill wanted to check out these four characters—just in case the vehicle description originally given was erroneous; he approached the suspect vehicle and asked the driver what they were doing. When the driver said that they were headed for Belmont—which was the other way—Officer Bill became suspicious and ordered the wheel man out of the car. As the driver complied, Officer Bill glanced to his right and saw that a subject in the rear seat had pushed the driver's seat forward, and had alighted with pistol in hand, aimed right at Bill's face! As Bill started to back-off, his head burst into a million shooting stars—much like the aerial fireworks displays on the Fourth of July! Although stunned, but not out, and bleeding like a stuck hog, he was able to keep his feet under him. The rat pack quickly surrounded him and one of the rodents tried desperately to yank his service revolver from the holster. But, the moron couldn't do it—he simply *could not* defeat that "trick" new holster Officer Bill had strapped on his side, so the punks jumped back into their ride and split!

When I asked how all of this went down, the Captain explained that while he reacted to the guy with the gun, he failed to see that the other scumbags had sneaked out of the right side of the car, out-flanked him, and then delivered an almost knock-out blow with a "sap". For those of you who are unfamiliar with the sap, aka "black jack"—a favorite gangster weapon during the 20s-30s, long outlawed and prohibited, even in police work—it's a hard leather pouch-like device, about 6 inches in length, shaped like a pregnant exclamation point, and filled with #8 shot lead BBs. Many saps had thongs that could be slipped over the sapper's wrist, and thus retained during an attack. Like it's more modern and deadlier Big Brother, the "Beaver Tail"—an appropriate and very descriptive moniker—those things could put a man's nose on the other side of his face! Worse, it could kill a person with a heavy blow to the head, as the Beaver Tail featured a flat, solid 8" long by 3"wide strip of lead, encased in very thick leather. Like its counterpart, it also had a leather thong. The cops of that era loved those things and they fit nicely in the slits of their trousers, originally designed for flash lights.

Having survived a near fatal attack on the Dumbarton causeway, Officer Bill was quickly able to advise radio of the assault; a corps of law officers from two counties promptly swooped down on the fleeing criminals and put them out of commission without incident. In this instance, that new holster contraption frustrated the potential cop killers and caused them to flee. This device, a rage among cops at the time, was called the "Clam Shell" holster. As the name implied—save for the grip and trigger guard—the revolver was totally encased within the shell. The gun could only be removed by depressing a small button inside of the trigger guard, which would cause the spring-loaded outer shell to flip open. Unfortunately, the crooks soon learned about this trick and guns would fly all over the place during down and dirty melees; in addition, as the holsters began to age, the locking pin was prone to release during foot pursuits—nothing worse than seeing your sidearm sliding down your leg while chasing an A&D (armed and dangerous) crook. . . So, departments outlawed them.

Bill went off to the ER, got about 10 stitches and went home with a big goose egg on his noggin. Like my dear old Dad used to say: "Never hit a German on the head; it just pisses them off. . ."

Cap'n One Liner

Cap'n Bill was a quiet, serious man, whose deep voice rivaled that of the late Levi Stubbs, bass singer in the R&B group—"The Four Tops:" Levi was the voice of the flesh eating plant in the movie "Little Shop of Horrors," who commanded his curator: "Feed Me, Seymour!" Although a man of few words, this trait actually belied Bill's incredible wit: He was the master of the one-liner, so much so that the likes of Henny Youngman and Rodney Dangerfield had nothing on the ol' Cap'n. First thing Monday mornings, the "brass" would file into the Cap'n's small office and discuss what went on over the weekend, current events, and of course, sports talk and critiques. The Chief was the master of what was happening in the world, as he was a voracious reader and was really on point when it came to world drama. Chief Jurian, a man of epicurean pedigree, usually had a meal or two in some of the Peninsula's fine dining emporiums, and always had a candid opinion of what was *hot* and what was *not*. Capt. Moore was the sports aficionado. We usually engaged in spirited discourse about any and all contests that were on the tube that weekend. Not to be outdone, I used to try to find some obscure trivia or an unusual occurrence that would give rise to a humorous reaction—especially from "Cap'n One Liner"—it was part of the plan! Although many of Bill's quips would be summarily censored from publication or airplay, here's one that is PG rated. During a Monday bull session, I related a recent news story that I figured might elicit a classic one-liner from the good captain:

"Hey, did you guys hear about the 62 year old woman up in Redding that just gave birth to her 12th child?"

I could read their minds: *OK, Niemeyer, what's the punch line?*

"And, not only that, this woman has been blind since birth!" I added.

So, there's Cap'n Bill, tilted back in his large chair, hands clasped behind his head looking slightly upward, and I can see the wheels just grinding away; he then retorted:

"And, she didn't even see it coming. . ." punctuated with his inimitable baritone guffaw, "Ho-Ho-Ho."

At this point, the Chief turned bright red and nearly fell out of his chair. Jurian guffawed loudly and immediately left the room. Marvin Moore doubled over with laughter. And, me? I just snickered quietly as the net result, although always predictable, was never the same and always more creative and hilarious than the previous quip. Captain Wullschleger clearly missed his calling—if only Jay Leno had known about this guy. . .

Walter S. Konar

"Walt" Konar, like me, came to SUDPS from the S/O. Not very many folks knew much about this man as he was a very private individual. He was a tall, handsome, well built young man with bright yellow hair and blue eyes. Walt was very smart. He was usually a man of few words, but could be very articulate when he chose to be. I first knew of him when he was appointed to the

Sheriff's Community Relations Unit during the early 1970s. It was through this position that Chief Herrington became acquainted with Konar during the waning days of the Vietnam days of rage down on the Farm because Walt was almost always on campus during disruptions. Herrington hired Walt as a Lieutenant early in 1973. In addition to administrative duties, Walt oversaw Investigations and monitored dissident activity, such as rallies and marches. After *Venceremos Domo* Professor H. Bruce Franklin was sacked by the University, violence on campus was nearly extinguished: In military lingo, this was basically a "mop-up" operation at that point.

Before taking the job at Stanford, I reached out to Konar in an effort to get to know him better and to pick his brain about the new Stanford PD which was on the drawing board. I met Konar one day and rode around with him for a few hours before and after lunch. Walt encouraged me to accept the challenge. He said that although there were a lot of problems to overcome at SUDPS, we could help out each other and lighten the load. Plus, the Chief was going to hire a couple of our S/O colleagues, Bob Coniglio and Steve Lawson, as sergeants, so the four of us would kick ass and turn this ship around.

My first experience working with Lt. Konar was during the Memorial Church murder inquiry of Arlis Perry, a mere three weeks after I came aboard in October 1974. Walt and I got on pretty well during that endeavor; he was congenial enough, but, sometimes, getting information out of him was like pulling eye teeth. Walt had apparently learned the "old school" detective trick of "hip-pocketing," e.g., not openly sharing secrets with teammates. I think Konar was a bit paranoid about leaks to the press, which was always a concern, especially in this extremely high profile case. But, in my view, Konar might have kept vital information he had gleaned very close to his vest. However, it seemed that he wasn't the only one. . . This was a very complex investigation with hundreds of leads and tips coming in, so, coordination was often difficult. Nonetheless, I believe most available information was checked-out to the best of the homicide team's ability, given the enormity of this investigation, plus the limited forensic technology available at the time.

After being promoted to Captain, Konar and I swapped positions in 1977. Initially, I didn't think Walt liked being Patrol Commander as he seemed to become more withdrawn. Sensing personal or domestic trouble, we all avoided broaching the subject of his dramatic behavior change. He suddenly resigned his position shortly thereafter. Sometime later, it was learned that Walt Konar was suffering from an early onset of MS (Multiple Sclerosis). Unfortunately, Walter S. Konar passed away several years thereafter. I regret not having a photo of him. R.I.P.

CHAPTER FIVE

Growing Pains

The New Guard

The fruits of my labor—12 hours a day, 7 days a week— was finally beginning to ripen: We just hired 8 FNGs and they were learning their trade at the Santa Clara County Peace Officer's Academy. There were 8 fledglings already on the streets, fresh out of the previous academy, trying to find their way around the campus and dealing with problems as best they could. They had been put through an accelerated ride-a-long program with S/O deputies prior to my arrival. One of my first tasks was to give this group a crash course in citation writing. I encouraged the new team to give me a call if they needed *anything*. They were a pretty astute bunch and when left to their own devices, found solutions amazingly well.

On the training front, things were definitely looking up: My *Field Training Officer's Manual* was coming together quite nicely, so when the recruits graduated from basic training they would be married up with our *vets*—most of whom would have approximately one year under their belts. I likened this venture to the *Blind Leading the Blind*, but with the pilot's check-list format of the FTO manual, "Nothing could go wrong, go wrong, gooo wrooooonnnggg"—a bold statement from that great 1973 Sci-Fi movie, <u>Westworld!</u>

When compared to the horror stories passed on by my S/O mentors, this system wasn't perfect, but would surely be a helluva lot better than what went on in the olden days at the Sheriff's Office:

****

When hired into the old Santa Clara County Sheriff's Office, prior to the sixties, many a recruit was sworn in, issued a badge and ID, given a CA Penal Code, a CA Vehicle Code, a County Radio code book, and a map book—uniform, gun and cuffs were on you! On your very first day, many of the crusty Sergeants simply handed you a set of patrol car keys, pointed to the parking lot and delivered this classic mantra:

"Stay on your beat, answer that damn radio, and don't screw up!" And, if a recruit had the temerity to ask:

"But Sarge, how do I know if I 'screw-up'?" The patented reply was:

"Listen, Buster! You'll know ya 'screwed-up' when ya feel my number 12 in your butt!"

"Yes sir, Sergeant. But, how do I know what to do if someone reports a crime or something?"

"Damn Boot—I gave you all of them there code books, so you figure it out; now get your sorry ass outta here!"

As legend has it, a deputy working the North County area encountered a complicated theft case at Stanford—that figures. He telephoned the good sergeant, explained the circumstances, and asked for advice. The ever helpful sergeant allegedly hollered:

"Listen, Buster. In my mind there are two kinds of stealin's—big stealin's and little stealin's, so you figger it out. . ." Click!

****

Back on the FARM: The new and improved New Guard was in its formative stages. We had come a long way during my first year but we still had a considerable distance to go. We were eager but untested—little did I know that said test would be right around the corner.

Final Exam

I called our new department's final exam "The Field Operations Course." In theory, the concept was based on a so-called survival course which was put on by a group of SWAT guys in the S/O during the late 60's, when cops were being *dry-gulched* all over the country. There were some good lessons to be learned by those experiences, but after going through the drill I came away dejected and paranoid as there was an un-winnable ambush at every turn:

****

The exercise was conducted from dusk to dawn at the Santa Clara Co. Fairgrounds, which was a good venue as it resembled a small town with paved roadways and building all over the place. We assembled in an auditorium, were relieved of all our ammo—so we couldn't shoot back—given a portable radio and waited to be called. When it was my turn, I got into my cruiser and went on the air:

"Control, 1-S-30, 10-8."

"10-4, S-30, 10-21 Radio, Code 2"

Now where in the hell am I going to find a phone in this labyrinth, I groaned to myself. *Everything is locked-up tighter than a drum.* But, as I turned where the directional arrow instructed, I saw a phone booth. We always carried a dime in those days so we could make an urgent call. But, we usually gave Radio the pay phone's number and waited for the ring. Of course, as soon as I entered the booth an overhead light came on followed by a fusillade of large caliber rifle fire. I was DOA!—figuratively as they fired blanks. I later learned the sniper had a BAR (Browning Automatic Rifle, which fired 30-06 rounds at a rate of about 550 rounds per minute!).There were only two more obstacles, and they ended the same way—so I had three chances: Slim, None and Non-existent! But, it got me to thinking that if I ever had a chance to create an officer's survival course the least I could do was give the participants a fighting chance. . .

****

The emphasis of my course was OFFICER SAFETY. There are numerous elements to this concept: 1) Observation—visual and audible; 2) Communications: Notify Radio and your beat partner when something doesn't look right, even when making a routine contact—if there is such a thing. 3) Stealth: Douse your lights, stow jingling keys, etc.; use concealment and cover. And, the most important element: 4) Good Ol' Horse Sense! Always keep your eyeballs and ears open when you're dealing with a person of interest. And, *never, ever,* turn your back on subject(s)! That's it. If the officers followed those basic tenants, which were drummed into their thick skulls during their arduous training, they'd pass with flying colors.

We utilized the Field Sites above the campus for the Field Ops course. The asphalt roadway was good and there were sufficient buildings along the way. I had street signs made at locations where events were to be staged. This exam would be run from dusk to dawn. I assembled a cast of role players from family and friends. I used my experienced sergeants, Lawson and Coniglio, and Lt. Walt Konar, as Safety Officers. I wanted the safety team to make sure no one would get hurt, and if events went haywire, the scenario would be called-off. The Safety Officers rode in the patrol units with the DPOs, and rated each and every move on a grading sheet we had brainstormed weeks before the drill. Each officer was issued 6 rounds of *primed* cartridges (no powder or bullets) so they wouldn't feel like they were going into a gun fight with empty revolvers. In actuality, there would be no reason for our deputies to fire their weapons—we didn't tell them that, however, because our theme was purely defensive: Due to the limited number of units we were able to field on any given day, we taught our deputies to back-off to a defensible position and call for assistance if a dangerous situation presented itself. The participants were checked and rechecked—no live rounds were to be anywhere on their person or in the vehicle. Finally, with the help of Communicators Doug Williams and Dave Rodriguez, each working separate frequencies, the stage was set to unleash our less than enthusiastic charges onto the course, spaced 30 minutes apart. I manned a white unmarked car flying a white flag on the antenna. The participants were briefed to ignore me as I was not part of the program. I roamed around the course to ensure smooth sailing with no jam-ups.

The Oregon Killers

Two nefarious characters were staged in a cab-over camper in a clearing about a half mile up the hill from the starting point at the Junipero Serra gate. These dudes were a crummy lot, my cousin Jerry Stram and his crime partner "Skip." They wore lumber-jack type clothing in which they concealed "Saturday Night Specials"—.38s with primed only empty cartridges. I loaded a box for them as I suspected that they might get an opportunity to blast a cop or two. . . The scenario was as follows: These two *dirt bags* were wanted for murders in Oregon, which could be ascertained if the deputy ran the OR license plate through Radio. To ensure they would be seen, the crooks turned-on their camper's inside light. The actors were instructed to go along with the program, present IDs and be polite. In order to make this duo really suspicious, there was a CA plate affixed to the front of the rig—only two of the participants checked out the front of the vehicle and noted the significant discrepancy. However, if an officer dropped his/her guard and turned their backs on the fugitives that was a green light for the killers to open fire. If the deputies radioed-in the truck's license number, Communications would immediately advise that these subjects were wanted for murder. The good guys were expected to draw their weapon, prone-out the suspects and call for assistance. The exercise was then terminated by the Safety Officer and the deputy resumed patrol. However, only about five of the fifteen participants made if this far with the Oregonians. It almost *killed me* to hear some of the radio traffic:

"Radio, I'm 10-55!" "Radio, I'm DOA!" "They got me!"—and, so on.

Many of the "victims" were former O/G guys who had irreversible attitudes that nothing like this could ever happen on a college campus—I guess they might have been in a barometric chamber when the "Texas Tower Massacre" took place in Austin eight years before.* The old adage about leading the horse to water was certainly prevalent with some of these folks, but I was sure they'd think about this exercise the next time they stopped a car. One of the officers didn't even see the huge camper—he obviously, didn't make the cut.

*On August 1, 1966, Charles Whitman, a former marine and then engineering student at the University of Texas in Austin, took up a firing position in the Bell Tower and systematically slaughtered 14 innocents and wounded another 32 people with a sniper rifle, for no apparent reason, other than he was undoubtedly nuts. Police finally gained access to the tower's platform and eliminated him. Source: Wikipedia.

Open Door

This problem was designed to bring the participants back to reality after the previous harrowing experience right out of the box. Once they received the 10-34 call at the Solar Lab on the hill, I calculated that everyone's B/P would be about 220/100. The Safety Officers later reported that after the Oregon Killer's episode, all of the troops were wired for 220 (volts)! This call was just a simple open door, which next to bogus alarm calls, is the most frequent response on The Farm. But, knowing my personality, the recruits were sure that bad guys would be hiding in the bushes armed with AK-47s. Not to be; it was what it was—an open door. And, that scenario worked as designed, for the group calmed down considerably after that.

Suspicious Vehicle

The 11-54 call came out next. Units were detailed to check out an old green station wagon parked off of the main road on a bluff. When they pulled up and lit up the vehicle, the garden hose leading from the exhaust pipe to the interior was unmistakable. Most officers cautiously inspected the area before approaching—good going! When they peered into the rear, they found *Resus-a-Annie* (a mannequin used in CPR instruction) with a note stating that she was DOA. Everyone knew to call the S/O for they were charged with handling death cases. Participants went 10-8 and resumed patrol.

Meet the Lady

"Q-1, meet a woman at the corner of Asphalt Road and Barn Way. She's hysterical and stated her sister is being battered by her husband. Code 2!"

When the unit arrived, they spoke to Ms. Fran Miller (a good friend), who was out of control. "Frannie" demanded the officer to arrest her brother-in-law as he was drunk and had been beating her sister all day. As a parting shot, Fran warned the deputy that the man is extremely violent and has a gun in the house. Most of the units reported this conversation to the dispatcher.

Once the patrol car arrived at the small cottage surrounded by a white farm fence with an entry gate, loud screams, shouts and banging could clearly be heard from up to 50 yards away. At this point, many, but not all, of the responders up-dated Communications about the screams for help. (The ruckus was actually a pre-recorded tape of my neighbor, Linda, screaming like a banshee—emulating Joanne Worley—in volume and pitch—from the old T.V. series "Laugh-In." While Linda screeched, I hollered for her to shut up and concurrently banged on a work bench with a large hammer.)

As the officer approached the gate, a large man with a sawed-off shotgun (played by another good friend, DA's Investigator Cecil Rhodes) appeared from the rear of the house and yelled:

"Hey, get the hell outta here or I'll shoot!"

Most of the deputies tried to negotiate with the suspect, however, the shot gun wielding fool was in no mind to be reasonable, so he fired off a round or two into the air. Although these were blanks, we put a lot of powder in the cases, so that really got one's attention in a hurry!

The majority of the participants quickly retreated for cover behind their patrol unit and called a Code 30—Emergency, officer under fire. At that point, the exercise was over.

Bush-Whacked

As the units proceeded along the course toward the next adventure, they came upon an obstacle in the road way, strategically located on a cattle guard. It was a small tree which was placed there in an area that was completely denuded. *Who did this and why, should have been the deputy's first thought*? I think you know the answer to that rhetorical question. . . When something looks fishy and smells fishy it most certainly won't be filet mignon! I was surprised that so many of our folks took the bait and got out of their vehicles to pull the obstruction away—most with the lights on high beam! All they heard was a big BANG! A sniper was perched way up on the hill armed with a 30-06 rifle, albeit firing blank rounds. Lesson learned: When you're a cop on patrol and you encounter a suspicious object blocking the roadway, do like the proverbial geese: "Get the Flock Out of There!"

The Hippie Dude

He was my brother-in-law: Reid G. Klatt, whom I had known since he was a teenager. When he completed high school, he enlisted in the US Army as a non-combatant and was stationed in South Korea for nearly 3 years. When he left to go overseas, Reid was a 98 pound weakling maybe 5'8"after hanging on a bar for an hour. . . When he returned he towered over me, now 6' 1"and nearly 180 pounds. He went back to college and became a Quality Control specialist in Silicon Valley. When the mid-70s rolled around, Reid was into the Hippie phase in his life. But, he was clean—no dope whatsoever! He sported a scraggily beard and long hair; he also had a dilapidated '60s Ford Falcon station wagon. He was perfect for the next exercise!

As Deputy Philip Love, aka, Philippe Crueseau, spotted Reid standing along his Falcon, he put out the following distress call in his inimitable British accent:"

"Radio, Q-2, I have a crazed man standing alongside a vehicle CA GFS 642, AND, he's holding a sword." (In reality, it was my machete.)

The actor was programmed to appear stoned out of his gourd—up there with the U-2s! However, he would be compliant if given authoritative commands. Reid wore a multi-colored knit cap pulled down over his ears and was draped with a *serape*. Boy, he really looked the part: Ominous! But, he obeyed directives to drop the weapon. When Philippe initiated a pat-search, he discovered bags and packets of simulated dope in every pocket, nook and cranny—pounds of it! Exercise completed.

After Action Report

The weary cast of role players and safety officers met for a working breakfast at the old Stickney's in Barron Park. That eatery had the best pecan pie ala mode on the planet. While there were considerable positive comments about the program as a whole, the same could not be said about many of the participants. Very few survived the Oregon Killers and Sniper scenarios—in my mind, the most important part of the exercise. Clearly, we as trainers had a lot more to do with this group before someone got hurt out there!

As in every exam process, the ones who excelled thought the challenge was realistic and fair. However, the under achievers thought it *sucked!* Sour grapes never made vintage wine, so I took that into account and pressed forward with more training; I utilized many great videos, provided by DOJ (CA Department of Justice), which were produced to enhance officer safety and to present other important legal issues. The majority of our cops were very smart (most were college graduates), thus they saw the hand writing on the wall. Improvement was clearly evident with each passing day.

Governor's Twenty

Competitive shooting among police agencies in CA was big. Almost every major, moderate, and even some small departments fielded shooting teams which strived to make the prestigious Governor's Twenty—the best 20 teams in the state at season's end. The Police Practical Course (PPC) was a derivative of the FBI's training regimen: At that time, nearly all departments shot .38 caliber 6-shot wheel guns. The matches consisted of timed fire exercises at ranges from 7 to 50 yards. <u>7 yards</u>: Fire 12 rounds (double action D/A—just pull the trigger as quickly as possible) within 15 seconds, which, obviously required a hasty reload. <u>15 yards</u>: Ditto within 25 seconds. <u>25 yards</u>: Fire 12 rounds D/A behind a vertical barricade within 30 seconds, using both right and left hands. <u>50 yards</u>: Fire 12 rounds, behind a barricade, D/A or S/A (single action: cocking the hammer back) with 50 seconds, using dominant, as well as off hand. The object was to score hits in the center of a silhouette target (center of mass) for 10 points each X 30 rounds. A "possible" was 300, which very few achieved during a high pressure match. I shot a couple of 300s in practice, but never reached that coveted 300 Club. Given my penchant for this sport and coupled with the absolute need for proficiency with a sidearm if you were a cop, little wonder I focused on a lot on firearms training. Most of the officers liked shooting, and several stepped up and became range instructors. In addition, we developed some dead-eye gunslingers. I organized two (four person) competitive pistol teams, both of which did very well on the firing line. We soon ran out of places to display all of the trophies we won in those shooting contests. Our A-Team comprised of Marvin Moore, Howard Ashcraft, Kris Henderson—yes, a lady—and I, placed 12th in the state during our first year, thereby making the Governor's 20. And the B-Team wasn't far behind. . . So, things were moving along rather nicely: The Chief was pleased and I was elated as to how far this fledgling department had progressed in such a short period of time. Our goal was to be the best that we could be, and by God we were on our way!

SUDPS Pistol Team A

The Last Lego

The last building block for Stanford's FNGs was designed to build character: What better place to test a new deputy's mettle than the Santa Clara County Main Jail in San Jose? So, off they went in groups of 2-4 for a week's stint in *the bucket,* aka *el carcel!* Here's where you had to work, up close and personal, with the people you would put in the slam during your career. There was no better place or opportunity in which to study aberrant human behavior than the Santa Clara County Jail! I specifically conveyed to my S/O liaison officer that all of the trainees needed to experience the section in the institution that would make or break them:

The Tank

Back in the Sixties and Seventies, the City of San Jose had a burgeoning homeless problem. There were thousands of derelicts roaming the streets, hanging out in the parks, and sleeping in doorways. A number of these folks lived in hobo jungles near the rail yards, or in the Guadalupe Creek—the latter were, and are still known as *Creek Dwellers.*

Nearly all of these lost souls were hopeless alcoholics who guzzled as much cheap wine as they could beg, borrow or steal. Sadly, ninety percent of these street urchins were WWII veterans, who mainly subsisted on Social Security, but panhandled and did odd jobs so they could purchase a jug of *vino* at day's end. Some of the younger men were Vietnam vets and were hooked on drugs, as well as alcohol.

Like most cities with a derelict problem, the police had to haul away the drunks in "Paddy Wagons" (see Cop Jargon in Glossary). When I was in the Air Force stationed in Sacramento, the cops had a couple of those wagons patrolling the Old Sacramento area like a regular bus route. When on liberty, a couple of my fellow airmen and I would periodically visit Old Town to watch the show. The boardwalks were lined shoulder-to-shoulder with hundreds of homeless folks, who literally took over the Second and L Street area before they were driven-off, once the historic restoration project began in the 1960s. Most, if not all of these characters were imbibing their beverage of choice, concealed in paper bags—drinking alcohol in public was unlawful... The Paddy Wagon crew consisted of four burly officers: two in the cab and two on the tailboard. Whenever they spotted an inebriate topple over, the guys on the tail board would jump off, pick-up the drunk and deposit him in the wagon. When they had a full load, the driver would head for their jail.

While San Jose's problem wasn't as severe as Sacramento's, SJPD employed at least one wagon during the day, and sometimes two or three on the evening shifts—more on weekends and days following the 15th of each month when the Social Security checks were issued.

The Santa Clara County Jail had a rather large section devoted to housing the drunken arrestees called the *Tank*. There were two general population cells for the drunks. All of these units had padded rubberized floors. D-2 and D-3 were very large facilities, perhaps 20' wide by 30' deep, which could comfortably house 30 to 40 guests. Unlike the Holiday Inn Express, there was no choice of beds... There were large break-proof windows at the front of each cell so that the inmates were always in view; steel sliding doors, controlled by the booking station kept them locked up. Our hotel was equipped with an adequate number of flush toilets as well as water fountains—clearly an upgrade from what our brave airmen were experiencing in the Hanoi Hilton at that time! These accoutrements were literally bullet proof, constructed of stainless steel and securely fastened to the walls so that disgruntled inhabitants couldn't tear-them-off and use them as weapons. After the arrestees had completed the booking process, all inmates received a set of clean white overalls, were issued a military style blanket and were encouraged to go *nigh-nigh*! Most did quite readily, for alcohol is a wonderful sedative...

The most interesting of the housing units was D-1. This little facility was located directly behind the booking desk, so that the deputies could keep an eye on inmates who were weak or infirm. Their abysmal living conditions caused a multitude of problems:

poor health, chronic diseases, some communicable such as TB, and often, severe mental issues. Needless to say, proper diet and hygiene was not a high priority among these people.

Although small, about 15'X 15', D-1 could accommodate about 8-10 men. Clearly, this cell was the Tank's suite, and many a malingerer tried to wrangle his way in because it was safer; in addition, we tended to mollycoddle our D-1 guys, more than the losers in GP (general population). D-1 residents enjoyed a form of room service: All they had to do was rap gently on the glass and talk nice. Banging and yelling was not tolerated so most in there knew the drill: Bad behavior meant a *time out* with the rest of the population, or the dreaded *Hole*: an isolated 5'X 8' padded cell.

In addition to being treated to the horrible jail coffee—which looked and tasted like 10,000 mile motor oil—a select few got to smoke the *real* cigarettes—hard rolls they called them. This was, of course, in the days long before it became unlawful to smoke in public buildings, restaurants and the like. Because of the danger of burning holes in the rubberized floor, commercial cigarettes were forbidden. As a result, all brand name cigarettes were confiscated and stored in a drawer of the booking desk. If a man wanted a smoke, we gave him a bag of Bull Durham and a packet of *Zig-Zag* papers—no matches, for obvious reasons; but our staff did the honor of lighting the cancer sticks, thus contributing to their declining health because that's what they chose to do. . .

While the Tank was often a bit smelly, we made sure that the trustees kept it as clean as humanly possible. I enjoyed my stint in the Tank because it was busy and most interesting. And, I liked most of our unfortunate guests; they weren't hardened criminals—just dejected and addicted poor souls. Most timed their arrests right after the Social Security checks were in the mail. The Judge would give them a thirty day sentence; they would be released, with good time, just a few days before the next gift from Uncle Sam arrived via the USPS. On that day, you could fire a shot in every cell and never hit a single person: they were en route to their mail drop for their precious gifts. Many would shout as they were released: "God Bless America!"

However, in an informal survey of our recruits who were ordered to experience jail duty, I learned that to the man and woman, they all hated the Drunk Tank. Call me nuts—I guess.

Humor in the Tank! (Amusing the Inebriates)

Communications: Or Lack Thereof...

The so-called Communications Operation at Stanford was, in my estimation, one of the biggest obstacles that our new DPS had to overcome if we were ever going to gain any respectability in the law enforcement community. The following story isn't pretty, but it was necessary...

The Players

Describing our communication's dispatchers as a motley crew would be a huge understatement. Save for a couple of individuals, this group collectively was the most incompetent, rude, unmanageable, recalcitrant, miserable bunch of human beings I had ever encountered in over 10 years on the job—and those were their good qualities...

The *Bobsie Twits* (as I dubbed them) were downright despicable and vile! Thelma *Lard-Ass*—you will hear about her when we were getting our butts re-arranged during the "Showdown at Lake Lag"—was a large, unattractive gal, with a big nasty mouth; she was an animal lover who at various times had the dispatch center looking like a menagerie: Apparently, she required caged birds, hamsters and the like to keep her company during her shift.

The other lady was a real gem, too: She was a belly dancer on the side. Unlike Thelma, the *Queen of Sheba* was a tall, buxom, attractive woman with long black hair. I heard that she performed at a number of Middle-Eastern establishments throughout the Bay Area. Rumor had it that she frequently titillated the firemen by performing her routines through the large picture windows which faced the engine bay—music and all! The only thing missing was the snake charmer. However, the most egregious stunt that *Sheba* pulled was waiting on a graduate student with a penis pacifier in her mouth! She was, indeed, a *professional*, but I think in the wrong line of work...

When I began my challenge, the Chief warned me about the Communications bunch and handed me a file of about 25 documented complaints from students, faculty, staff, and officers. Most of the gripes were police related: Rudeness, unprofessional demeanor, lack of knowledge, and in many instances, failure to send officers when requested to do so. The problem was that dispatch was totally focused on fire: In the old days, calls for police service were few and far between, so the group became ambivalent toward the Stanford PD. And, then when the *New Sheriff* came to town, they were not trained or used to handling the increased volume of radio traffic: Our deputies were actually stopping cars, running records checks on suspects, arresting crooks, so Radio resented the new and improved program. This wasn't like dispatching fire apparatus once in awhile, for the New Guard was out there shaking the bushes for mopes—trying to effectuate modern policing on a campus that had been a criminal's cherry patch for so many years.

Compounding the problem was the fact that Dispatch did not report to fire or police authorities: Communications was under the control of Telecommunications—the University's phone company, if you will. I was astounded that Dispatch was not within the Public Safety umbrella. Instead, their supervisors were former telephone operators who didn't know *didley squat* about Police and Fire Operations, which was our life's blood! And, to make things even worse, the dispatchers were in the Stanford Bargaining Unit (union), thus were almost untouchable. So, the complaints kept streaming in. The same old saw: arrogance (primarily from the Bobsies), smart mouth talk, hanging-up on callers, not answering the radio when the officers in the field called, and even blowing-off high ranking officials. In one instance, University President, Donald Kennedy called to report a loud, disruptive Frat party; Thelma basically pooh-poohed him and didn't respond any of our units until so many other annoyed neighbors forced her hand. That got the Chief's attention in a hurry. It seemed like almost every Monday, we called the Telecom supervisors, who were actually very nice women, and met with them about the latest laundry list of infractions. Most of the time, the poor supervisors just looked at the Chief and me like someone had blinded them with a spotlight. They seemed powerless to act, and had to refer the complaints to the union stewards, who did nothing!

One-upmanship

My Daddy taught me early on that there was always more than one way to skin a polecat. And, that's what I was about to do. I needed to turn the tables on this crew, primarily the *Bobsies*, who worked the busy 4PM to Midnight shift. The day crew was tolerable and they tended to avoid me at all costs, as I had the reputation in those days of being a somewhat nasty bull when ticked-off—now I'm just a lovable Ol' lap cat. With the Chief's approval, I pulled a page out of the S/O's Communications operation:

In the good Ol' days, the S/O, like most police departments of the day, utilized experienced officers on the Complaint Desk. I had an opportunity to work on that detail for some period of time while recuperating from a near-fatal collision in 1972. This was a key position; the deputies in the field depended on our sound judgment to obtain and relay potential life saving information to the dispatchers, who transmitted our orders to the field units from their center, high atop a hill in South San Jose. The Complaint Desk deputies were, in essence, the crucial link between the reporting party, the communicators and the patrol units—we ran the show, not like the rank amateurs I had inherited at Stanford. Decorum, field knowledge and a cool head were the prerequisites of the Desk Officer's position.

The Plan Unfolds

I had Telecommunications set-up 9-911 phones in our front office and assigned two experienced deputies to be SUDPS' *first* Desk Officers (DOs). One of the men originally hailed from England and was a real charmer. In addition to being civil and very cordial, he knew the campus geography and the mission. I assigned Ed Phillips to the Day Watch. Actually, the old timers in Dispatch liked it: All they had to do now was what Deputy Ed told them to do, which relieved them of a lot of pressure; they were really up against it as a result of all the complaints, and having *El Toro* on their tails! The DO monitored the radio traffic and was on top of any activity in the field. They could also communicate with the FC (Field Commander: Sergeant) and transmitted information to the dispatchers.

But, the swing shift was a horse of another color: The *Bobsie Twits* took great exception to this system: 1) Both women lamented they were nothing more than second class dispatchers—well, Duh! And, 2), the Twits hated taking orders from cops. I put a real good one on that shift, Deputy Bill Starbuck—you'll hear more about Bill as we weave through this saga. Right from the get-go, the *Bobsies* were not only antagonistic to the new program, but they were downright hostile and vicious to Bill. This gentleman was highly educated: He had a Master's Degree and was working on his PhD. In addition, he was a rough and tumble rugby player who wasn't about to take any cheap excrement from those two! Nonetheless, the girls kept pushing the envelope: hanging-up on Bill, not answering the phone in a timely fashion, giving him attitude in conversation, intentionally misstating orders to the field units, and occasionally flipping-him-off when he went to the dispatch center for a friendly *pow-wow*.

We carefully documented each and every indiscretion. I met with the Telecom "supervisors" on a weekly basis and tried to get compliance; the supervisors were sympathetic to our plight, but admitted that there was little they could do, given the union situation. I fumed; Bill fumed; everyone who had experienced this abuse fumed!

Gone Ballistic

It was about 4:30PM one day, and I was wrapping-up things getting ready to assault that parking lot on I-280 during my homeward commute. I made a final pass through the office and asked DO Bill Starbuck how things were going. Big mistake! Here's what he said:

"Captain, Thelma hung-up on me 3 times already and I have just started my shift. I didn't say anything to piss-her-off, so I don't what her problem is. I just don't know how much longer I can take this."

"Bill, maintain. I'm going to take care of this problem once and for all."

The hair stood-up on the back of my neck and my BP was off the scale. I then went to the nearest phone and called the Telecom Supervisors:

"Ernestine! You, Irma and the Union Steward need to get over to Dispatch immediately, as I'm about to arrest those belligerent women for obstructing and delaying a peace officer in the discharge of his duties—148 P.C.! Please get over here NOW!"

About 5 minutes later, the Telecom Trio arrived and I intercepted them in the hallway; Bill Starbuck was at my side. Ernestine tried to diffuse the situation by asking me what this was all about. But, I immediately burst into the dispatch room and confronted "Lard-Ass," who was in a fully reclined position, using her toe to activate the transmit switch on the console.

"You," I snarled. "If you ever hang-up on this deputy again, I will personally arrest you and take you forthwith to the Women's Detention Facility at Elmwood! Do you understand that?" I growled.

Thelma was so taken aback that she merely stared at me in disbelief. However, Sheba, who had spun around in her chair and fell butt-first on the floor popped-up and started screaming and gesticulating:

"You can't do this. Who in the hell do you think you are; we'll fight this and sue!"

"Go ahead lady, but if you get in my face again, you are history! And, as far as suing me, stand in line! Now, knock it off and get back to work. No more nonsense!"

As quickly as I entered, I made an exit. Ernestine and Irma were aghast and expressed their concern that these women may abandon their posts. The union representative was mute. I advised them if that happened, I would find a replacement until the situation could be rectified.

Sure enough, those twits walked out leaving Stanford University without public safety communication. Fortunately, the former communications supervisor, Doug Williams, who now worked for us, manned the console until the midnight dispatcher, Rod, arrived. Rod (and Doug, too) were super guys; Rod was a very capable man who wanted to improve his lot.

Suddenly, I'm on the Air

The phone jolted me out of REM sleep.

"Hello."

"Captain, this is Rod at Dispatch."

"Oh, hi Rod, what's up? What time is it?" I groggily mumbled.

"Captain, its 0420 hours and I just wanted to give you a heads-up that the dispatchers have staged a walk out and there will be nobody to man the center at 0600, when I get off."

"Those jerks; I figured this might happen. Tell ya what, Rod, gimme some time to get a cup of coffee and a shower, and I'll be there ASAP. I'll need you to show me the ropes but I'm going to be Stanford's *first* Captain Dispatcher!"

"OK, sir, I'll be here. . ."

And, indeed he was: Rod gave me a quick briefing and by God, after about 10 minutes, I had the mic all to myself. Being the consummate hambone, I actually enjoyed myself. My good buddy, Bob Leal, at County Communications, where I used to hang-out for coffee, allowed me to dispatch for a few minutes from time to time, but it had been so many years before, I was a little shaky at first. But, I soon got into sync and felt rather comfortable on the console.

About 0900, after being on the air for about 3 hours, I received a phone call from County Communications. *Man, I hope I'm not screwing-up,* I worried.

"Stanford Dispatch, can I help you?"

"Ahhh, Ahhh, are you a new dispatcher?"

"Well sort of," I replied. "The union idiots here staged a walk-out, so I'm it."

"Your voice sounds very familiar. Is this the old S-30, now called Captain Niemeyer?"

"Yes sir, it's me alright—in the flesh. Am I doing OK?"

"This is Paul Cosso, Chief dispatcher. I heard you dispatching and wanted to hire you!"

"Well Paul, your flattery will get you almost anywhere with me. You don't know what we have been through with this bunch of losers, who have been masquerading as dispatchers. I aim to get rid of these clowns."

"Yeah, I hear you, Raoul. That bunch has been a major thorn in our side for years. I hope you prevail. Let me know if there's anything we can do from our end."

"Boy, they have been my huckleberry ever since I took the job here. OK, thanks, Paul, I gotta go and I'll talk to you later."

Relief

At about 1100, Rod strolled into Dispatch and relieved me; this trooper with only a few hours of shut-eye took it upon himself to defy the union and spell the Ol' Captain. I must admit I was relieved—there's a lot of pressure on the console if you take the job seriously and realize that a lot of people depend on you!

I had envisioned developing our own Dispatch Center, but the City of Palo Alto offered us a deal we couldn't refuse. We were under their umbrella, but rid of that cancer that almost destroyed the department at the outset. And, by the way, my friend, Rod, the only dispatcher at Stanford who was worth anything, landed a job at Palo Alto Communications and did a wonderful job for many years.

The communications debacle is a piece I hated to write, for it brought back many terrible memories. However, it had to be told. I was excoriated by the Bobsie Twits and union bosses in the press for weeks! The Chief wasn't really thrilled about the negative articles. Nor I, but, in the end, the mission was completed. And, all's well that ends well, I always say!

The New Look

New Patrol Unit: 1976 Plymouth Gran Fury

Chapter Six

A Cop's Rite of Passage

The Old Guard's Rite

The O/G had a secret initiation for their FNGs: Once hired, a newbie Stanford patrolman was assigned to a senior trainer (T/O) on the Dog Watch. Ol' Captain Midnight related this tale to me years ago when I first began the research for this book. Once the Quad was secure, the T/O led the recruit to the Medical School's Anatomy building. The place was as dark as King Tut's tomb, I was told. Once inside, the T/O admonished the trainee not to turn on his flashlight so as not to wake the dead, so to speak. When their eyes adjusted to the pitch black darkness, the recruit could see about a dozen tables with white shrouded forms on them. This, my friends was the Gross Anatomy lab, where medical students honed their craft by dissecting cadavers until there was nothing left. And, many of the specimens were in various stages of dissection. So, to illustrate how *gross* this course could be, here is a little war story from my daughter, Dr. Nina's, "Journal of Gross:"

(Her med school scheduled their first year students to the anatomy course straight away. Nina's team drew a morbidly obese woman who weighed-in at nearly 250 pounds. While trying to clear away a mass of fat from the back muscle tissue, she lost the handle and the ooze went into reverse and virtually exploded in her face, showering her hair with huge lipid globules. That was the first and last time she ever approached a medical procedure without eye protection!)

Once the stage was set, the boss would lead the new man to a table, whip back the shroud, turn-on a pen light and announce: "Meet Your Cadaver!" After the FNG recovered from the initial shock, the T/O weaved throughout the lab until they reached the very end. At this point, the initiator suddenly pulled back another shroud causing the recruit to gasp. Suddenly, and without warning, the FNG let out a blood curdling scream and levitated 3 feet off the floor, all the while shouting:

"Aaarrrgggghhh, make it let go, make it let go, Aaaarrrggghhh!"

With that, and after rolling around on the ground with laughter, the T/O illuminated the area: The *gotcha* was an adult spider monkey who had a death grip on the new guy's wrist. The pesky critter stealthily occupied a cage way in the back of the lab and knew his task well, having performed this near death experience—on recruits—many times before. Having survived the O/G's Rite of Passage, the officer was sworn to secrecy and pledged never to tell any incoming officers of this prank. Hard to top that one!

****

Mine

I remember mine as if it happened yesterday: It was my first day as a Deputy Sheriff with the Santa Clara County Sheriff's Office, aka, S/O. I was 24 years old, and in tip-top shape as a result of years of weight training. I had been doing a lot of running also, while testing for this career in law enforcement upon which I was about to embark. Once I got the green light, they told me to go to San Jose Uniform—a police outfitter in the Burbank area of San Jose, where I was destined to patrol. The folks there knew the drill: They measured and made alterations so that my uniform fit like a glove; they even had brogans and leather accessories. I needed plain black, no basket weave. They called the rig a *Sam Browne belt,* absent the shoulder strap worn by *them thar Sheriffs in the Deep South*. In those days, you purchased all of your equipment, including the side arm. I was directed to Carroll and Bishop's pawn shop for my service revolver. This dump was located in a sleazy area of downtown San Jose. *Looking back, I can't imagine any law enforcement agency sending a recruit to a pawn shop for anything!* The folks there knew exactly what you needed: San Jose cops could have any pistol they wanted, but S/O newbies were relegated to a 4 or 6 inch .38 Special or .357 Magnum—Smith & Wesson or Colt. Being a gun enthusiast, and owning the "MOST powerful handgun known to man"—.44 Magnum, as articulated by Clint Eastwood in the movie, "Dirty Harry", I most naturally opted for a 4-inch S&W .357—possibly the second most powerful handgun...

The Patrol Captain, John Perusina, told me to report to the Squad Room at 0800 sharp! I woke up at O-Dark 30 and made sure that everything on my Sam Browne and uniform was in perfect order. I had spent many hours spit-shining my high tops, and I had even gotten a buzz cut! I was chompin' at the bit and eager to report for duty.

I got to the office about 0730 and, not wanting to appear too eager, sat in my car until about 0745. It was only a 5 minute walk to the Squad Room so I was dialed-in. Upon entering the room, I immediately realized that the meeting was already in progress. About 15 Deputies were seated at their desks and the Sergeant was briefing the troops at the podium, which was adorned with a huge six-point star insignia, superimposed over the County of Santa Clara seal. I tip-toed in and quickly took a seat—way in the back. All fifteen of those deputies turned around and glared at me.

The Sergeant, a big gnarly man who looked like a rodeo bulldogger, barked:

"Hey, Buster, what's your name?"

"Deputy Niemeyer, sir" I respectfully replied.

"OK, Deputy, I want to see you up in the parking lot after briefing!"

"Yes, sir," I snapped back!

Everyone turned around and smirked. My heart was pounding and my face flushed. How could I have been late? I had checked my watch via the phone recording, and the Captain explicitly told me to be here at 0800. Well, I thought, I'll just explain this to the Sergeant and surely he will understand that there was obviously some miscommunication between the Patrol Captain and me.

I was assigned to a really nice, low-key veteran, Deputy Richard "Dick" Hessenflow; we were going to patrol San Jose's infamous Eastside. I was excited. I asked what I could do; he handed me a shotgun and told me to carry it upstairs. We put the gear in the patrol car, gassed up, and waited for the Sergeant. I was extremely nervous, and began wondering if I was going to lose my job on the very first day. My partner said nothing. The silence was deafening! All of a sudden, the Sergeant rushed up to the passenger side of the unit, rapped on the window and motioned for me to roll it down.

He then lit into me with both barrels: "Listen, Buster. If you want to make it in this here outfit you'd better damn well be to MY squad meetings on time. I start at 15 before the hour, you understand that?"

"But, Sergeant," I protested, "The Captain told me to be sure to be here before 0800, and I was 10 minutes early!"

"Listen, Buster. If you wanna argue with me, I'll take your ass up to 'Johnny Two-Bar's' office right now."

"No, sir," I pleaded. "I must have been confused; I can assure you, Sir that it won't happen again."

As we pulled away, I asked my partner. "Jeez, who is THAT guy?"

"That, my friend, is Sergeant Everett York. We call him 'The Gunner' (so named after the WWI hero of the same name), but don't you dare call him that until he tells you that you can! Show up for the squad meetings on time, answer the radio, stay on your beat, advise him when you have a dead body, don't ask him any complicated questions, and he'll leave you alone."

I already had a name for that mean old bastard, I mused, *but Gunner wasn't it!*

Later in the shift, I got to thinking: *You know I might have been born at night, but not <u>last</u> night. I soon figured it out: This was a set-up. I had been had!* I mentioned my suspicions to my partner; he just clenched down on his stubby cigar, looked at me and just grinned...

Right then I vowed that if I was ever in a position of authority, I would never treat a Rookie like that. That mean ol' Sergeant scared the holy hell out of me! He was certainly someone I didn't *ever* want to cross swords with!! But, as it turned out, if you followed *his* rules Sergeant York was no problem.

After my inauspicious debut, I was always glued to a seat in the front row, at least 20 minutes before the hour. And, when Sergeant York came in for Squad meetings, I cheerfully greeted him with: "Good morning Sergeant!"

****

Deputy Niemeyer #246

Circa: 1966

Backfire

One of the Old Guard who had matriculated to the New Guard was a wily Ol' veteran, having retired from the U.S. Army after 30 years as a *Top Kick* (Master Sergeant); he also had served on SPD for several years as a door shaker. His name was Ted Hopgood; a more personable guy you will never meet. He also had a great sense of humor and loved to play tricks on people, as many of us vets were prone to do.

At that time, Francine *Penny* Patterson, was on campus doing research with her pet female gorilla, *Koko,* the famed talking ape. Well, Koko didn't really communicate vocally, but used American Sign Language (ASL) quite effectively. Ms. Patterson had an enclosure for the lowland gorilla and lived in an adjacent trailer. The place was alarmed and lit-up like Fort Knox, as this ape was invaluable. It seemed that this alarm had a habit of always activating in the middle of the night, and for no particular reason, so our guys had to respond and ensure that nothing was amiss. I had just hired a new sergeant, Bob Coniglio, formerly of the S/O; he was a green supervisor and could barely find his way to the bathroom, let alone around the Stanford campus in the wee hours. So Mr. Hopgood, *Hoppy* they called him, thought it would be great sport to introduce the new *Sarge* to the friendly and very curious Koko, who had a tendency to fall in love with new men. He called for Bob's assistance and awaited his arrival before making contact with Penny and Koko. When the sergeant got there, Ms. Patterson and Koko were in the compound. What usually happened is that whenever the gorilla saw a new face, she would make a beeline toward that unfortunate and glom onto him, with the force of 10 very strong men! But, in this instance, Koko latched onto Hoppy and refused to let go! She then marched off with the stunned prankster in tow. It took a helluva lot of ASL by Penny to finally get Hoppy extricated from Koko's death grip. The moral of this piece is sometimes pranks can go awry and backfire on the trickster...

CPR

It was a typical Monday morning. There had been several arrests during a football game, and the usual Frat parties that followed caused the Patrol deputies some grief; but other than that, nothing major. I was down in the Front Office looking for some reports and, as always, ended up in Captain Bill's office for our Monday morning BS session. As I left Bill's office, one of the Records' staff flagged me down, and advised that a family was out in the lobby wishing to speak to the Chief but that he was at the President's Staff meeting. She asked if I would speak to them about a missing person. Taking advantage of his absence, I met with two women in A-1's Office.

After introductions, I learned the women were very concerned about a missing relative, John D. One of the ladies was his sister and the other a psychic. *Uh-oh*, I thought—*this is going to be interesting.* My first question was where is he missing from? That was one of the first things my training officer, JJ, taught me, many years ago: It is imperative to ascertain where an event occurred so as to establish what agency has proper jurisdiction. And, a lot of times, you might be able *kiss it off* to another department. I hate missing person cases, as the reporting parties can drive you crazy, especially when a child or student was involved.

The sister said that he lived in a cottage with some other men over by the creek.

"What creek," I pressed?

"The one over by the golf course," she replied.

"The San Francisquito Creek," I hoped? (I knew we didn't have any houses on our side of the creek, in Santa Clara County, and, because this stream is dividing line between us and San Mateo County, it must be theirs.)

"Ma'am, I believe you should contact the San Mateo County Sheriff about this, as I think it's their jurisdiction," I asserted with relief.

"But sir, you don't understand, we already did that, and he's still missing. And, my friend, here, knows he's in a cave by the Stanford Golf Course, and he's hurt or something. The Sheriff over there took a report but won't send anyone out; they told us to call you. Please help me!"

So, I turned to the psychic and asked: "How did you determine that John is in a cave? Did you have a vision or something?" All the while, I was thinking: *Oh man, not another one of these deals!* I had some previous experience dealing with a psychic in the Church murder—one from the ionosphere—a total whacko, who was no help whatsoever! Also, a huge pain in the posterior, for she continually came up with *new and improved* theories which all proved to be a lot of hogwash. I know that some law enforcement people swear by *them,* and call me a *Doubting Thomas,* but I prefer to follow more credible leads.

This matronly lady related that she, indeed, had a vision last night: She visualized John struggling in a torrent of water in the SF Creek during Saturday night's storm. The violent current had dashed him on the rocks, but he was able to make it to the other side, where he crawled around until he found a cave by the golf course. I knew that the storm had been a bad one, judging from all of the downed tree limbs I saw on my way to the office. But, I just couldn't help wondering why in the hell any thinking human being would venture into a raging river during a major thunder and lightning storm—the guy must be nuts! I also knew the terrain there quite well, as a buddy of mine, Ken, used to live in the vicinity, on Homer Lane. As young adults, we used to crawl all over that creek and the surrounding area while hunting small game. We even found the old Stanford P.D. pistol range, which my now good friend, Captain Midnight, used to run when he was Range Master in the Old Guard. So, I was pretty darn sure that there were no caves in that area; nonetheless, I felt an obligation to help these poor ladies.

"OK," I acquiesced, "I'll put together a search party and see if we can find him. What does he look like, and do you have a photo?" No photo, but the sister described him as a male, white, 55 years old, blue eyes, balding grey hair, thin and about 5'10". After getting a call-back number, I saw the women out and went looking for troops!

The first person in my sights happened to be the patrol Sergeant, Sgt. Rick Enberg. He was a tall, very fit individual, and was used to taking orders, no matter how bizarre. Rick had come to us from another Sheriff's Office, thus had a considerable amount of field experience; he also could command troopers, as he was a Vietnam Vet, and currently a Lt. Colonel in the Army Reserve.

"Sergeant," I barked. "Are you busy?"

"No Sir, Captain. What can I help you with, Sir," he snapped back. This Sergeant was a very Gung Ho guy, thus had the highest regard for rank and chain of command decorum.

"Good. I need you to round up a couple of troops. We need to go search the golf course area for a 10-65 male, named John D. He went missing during that big storm Saturday night. His sister and a psychic were just here and the 'visionary' insists that he's holed up in a cave somewhere, injured. I know it's a long shot, but we have to make an effort—P.R., you know!"

"Captain, how did he happen to get on the golf course, way over there?"

"He lives by the creek on Wildwood Lane, off Alpine. They think he was in the fricking creek, for some unknown reason," I explained.

"Hey, wait a minute," the Sarge exclaimed. "Isn't that San Mateo's?"

"Yup, and they already made a report with the S/O, but you know how they are: if it ain't just shot and bleeding, they're not interested. Grab a couple of guys and let's go have a look-see. I'll meet you guys by the Annex."

"10-4," he saluted.

I went up to my office and put on my gym tennies—kinda goofy-looking with a coat and tie, but something told me that we were going to be crawling around in that nasty creek. I met the Sgt. out back and he had corralled two of our FNGs—fresh out of the academy, and as the fire lads say, *RFA* (Ready for Activity)—*Anything*, in this case!

We proceeded to the location in separate patrol units, Rick and I in one, and the rookies in the other. On arrival, I immediately noticed that the house in question was a real dump: Trash all over the front yard, a broken down rusty old barbeque, a semi-crushed metal garbage can that was overflowing with McDonalds's bags, hamburger wrappers, and beer cans—maybe a hundred of them strewn all over the yard, porch and into the entryway. The only thing missing was a car on blocks and a dilapidated fridge on the porch. . . And, it was no wonder that this yard hadn't *ever* been mowed: one could end up in the ER with all of the aluminum shards that would have been flying around!

The door stood wide open. I beat on it and announced: "Sheriff, anybody home? John, are you in there?" No response.

"OK, we are coming in." Kicking the beer cans out of the way, we searched the little cottage but couldn't find a living soul—not even a rat. What we did find, however, were literally hundreds of empties, mostly 16 ounce Rainier Ale cans, which my cousin, Jerry Stram, aptly named: *The Green Death!* Indeed. Although an absolute hovel, this trash heap was a recycler's dream.

After thoroughly checking-out the property, we were satisfied that no one was there, so I split the group up and directed the rookies to canvas the neighborhood. I took the place directly across the street and knocked on the door. A nice, elderly lady answered, and after I stated my purpose, she unleashed an avalanche of information about "those disruptive ruffians" across the street. She went on and on about the continual parties, loud music, periodic fights and just general chaos. When I asked her if she had seen John D. Saturday night, she replied:

"Yes, like I told the other Sheriff, they were having another raucous party, and after awhile, I heard some howling—like a coyote or something. So, I looked out of my window and saw that crazy man, up on his roof, arms out-stretched toward the heavens, howling like a werewolf!"

"Ma'am," I interrupted, "With all due respect, are you telling me that he was up on *that* roof (I pointed) during that thunder storm, howling like a wolf?"

"He most certainly was, lightning and all!" she asserted.

"So what happened after that? Did you see him later on?"

"Like I told that Deputy," she started, but I interrupted again.

"Are we talking about a San Mateo Sheriff, or one of my Stanford Deputies?"

"Yes," she continued, "San Mateo County; he came out Sunday afternoon, I think, looking for Mr. D, and I told him that when I last saw him during that storm he was heading down into the creek."

"Heading into the creek?" I repeated, "OK, and did you see if John ever came out or have you seen him since?"

"No sir, I certainly haven't."

"So, what did the San Mateo deputy do after you told him this?" I quizzed.

"Well, he just drove down the road to the dead end, got out and walked to the edge; then he looked left and looked right got back into his car, and drove off."

You've got to be kidding me, I thought. *What a turkey! That clown didn't even go down into the damn creek to find the poor guy. Stuff like this gives us all a bad name. Not only was John D. NUTS, but he was a drunk, too. Now, we're going to have to go down in there!*

I gathered up the troops and asked if they received any significant leads. The neighbors who were home, reiterated what my contact had revealed about the party house, but no one had seen John since Saturday. I briefed the crew on what I had learned and told them that we were going to search that damn creek. The Sergeant told the rookies, Q-6, Harry, and Q-7, Horace, to search the area to the left; Rick and I would go right.

Although they were brand spanking new, I had confidence in these men; both were well educated and seemed to have their heads screwed on right. After all, I had selected them for hire and oversaw their background investigations, so I knew they were solid, good prospects. I told Harry and Horace to switch their radios to Channel 2—our tactical frequency—and that if they saw anything, back away and advise me at once. I didn't know what we were going to encounter down there; this could very well turn into a homicide, so I damn sure didn't want any potential crime scene contaminated— especially if it would end up being a San Mateo case.

Sergeant Enberg and I cautiously descended into the San Francisquito Creek and moved slowly through the dense underbrush and rocks along the bank. I was in the lead and periodically glanced back at the Sergeant. He appeared to be somewhat nervous: He proceeded along as if he were in the jungles of South Vietnam, ever vigilant, on the lookout for booby-traps! There was a lot of downed timber, which made the going very tough. All of a sudden, about 20 yards ahead, on the other side of a large fallen tree, I spotted something. As I inched closer, I could make out a human form prostrate in a sandy area, adjacent to the now calm, gurgling brook.

I stopped and whispered: "Pssst, Rick. There he is!"

"Where?" he asked—while he rapidly scanned the area, in an attempt to focus on what I had called his attention to. I pointed to the form, and I impatiently asserted:

"Right *there*, Rick! About 15 yards ahead, over by those rocks."

Judging from the description that I had received from John's sister, this fellow appeared to be our 10-65. He was motionless; his arms, with fists tightly clenched, were rigidly protruding skyward— as if he were reaching for his *Creator*.

We crept forward, ever so slowly, with hands on our guns; I wondered if he had he heard us? Was this going to be another scene from the movie, *Friday the 13th* in which *Jason* would suddenly leap up at us while emitting a blood curdling scream? However, the closer we got, the more certain I was certain that this poor individual was a 10-55—a Coroner's case. Sure enough: He was in full rigor; his face was ghastly, horribly contorted, mouth wide open, as if he had been crying for help, while experiencing an excruciating death. And, that eye—I'll never forget that steely blue right eye—John was staring at me—actually more like giving me the *evil eye!*

Suddenly, a mischievous thought crossed my mind: I reached for my radio, keyed the mike, and shouted:

"Q-6 and Q-7, Code 3, Code 3!"

"A-3, this is Q-7, what is your traffic?"

"Q-7. Code-3!" I responded, "We found our 10-65 and need your help, on the double! We are about 30 yards west of where we entered. Hurry-up!"

"10-4, en route," the nervous-sounding rookie snapped back.

When I looked at the Sergeant, he was grinning; he clearly caught my drift.

"OK, Rick," get down on your knees and assume the chest compression position, but Do Not touch him or I'll have to arrest you, Sergeant!" He knew I wasn't kidding either, as I was a stickler for following the rules: California law clearly mandated that *only* the Coroner and Medical Examiner may touch a decedent.

You could hear them coming; they sounded like a herd of buffalo thrashing through the heavy underbrush. In a matter of minutes, they were 10-97, huffing and puffing as if they just ran a mile.

"Horace, get over here!" I commanded. He ran up, looked at the body, looked at the Sergeant, looked at his partner, and then looked at me. All the while, I was yelling: "CPR, Dammit! CPR!" He started to move downward and then pulled back suddenly and pleaded:

"But Captain, this man is dead!"

Damn, I thought; *"he must have seen the ants."* I just looked at him, and smiled:

"Well, rookie, that was YOUR 'Rite of Passage,' and I think you passed. What do you think, Sergeant?"

Sgt. Enberg smiled and nodded his head in the affirmative.

We posted the FNGs at the scene, advised Radio of our find and told the dispatcher to have San Mateo respond. We then trudged back to the roadway and awaited the Deputy. When he arrived, he blurted out that he had been *looking* for ol' John yesterday, but couldn't find him anywhere. Then he wanted to know why *we* were working *his* case in *his* jurisdiction? Initially, I was going to be polite, and let his comment slide; but his remark and attitude really ruffled my feathers, so I shot back:

"Well, deputy, John's sister came to our station today and asked us for our help as she believed her brother was hurt and stranded on the Stanford side of the creek. She also said that you guys weren't going to look for him. So, I followed my training and instincts and came to the last place John had been seen. And, sure enough, there he was, in the creek, just like that lady told you! Now, if you had gone down there and looked a mere 25 yards upstream, you would have found him, just like we did. Have a nice day!" Rick and I then got back in our vehicle and drove off.

To some, cop humor is strange, sometimes off-color and often macabre. Being around the dead was always very hard for me. I learned early on in my career, that a little frivolity can really take the edge off of stressful situations—as long as it isn't tasteless and disrespectful. Police work without a chuckle, would have been intolerable—for me, anyway. Pulling a fast one on FNGs was always in my bag of tricks, having been the target, myself, of a few good pranks while in the Air Force. But, *one-upmanship*, especially on an arrogant colleague, was the ultimate tension reliever! Without humor, I might have had a nervous breakdown long ago. Today, I can even write about some of these depressing events and still laugh.

CHAPTER SEVEN

Hell Week: Stanford vs. Cal

The Bonfire

It was Hell Week, November 1975, the prelude to the traditional Big Game between Stanford and Cal. This extravaganza had been going on since 1891, and from what little I knew about it at that time, this was *always* an interesting event.

Blue and gold bear paws were showing-up all over campus: The Weenies, as our students un-affectionately called their rivals, certainly didn't do Plant Services clean-up crews any favors by *tagging* the buildings, statuary and historic monuments with oil based paint! Some morons irreverently dumped blue and gold dye into Memorial Fountain. And, those pesky omnivores even left their scent on the 50 yard line of Stanford Stadium: the vandals indelibly marked their territory with acid on arguably the best natural grass football field on the planet at that time. Clearly, all 86,000 spectators and the rest of the free world would assuredly see that reviled moniker, *CAL*, throughout the gridiron battle Saturday afternoon. Stanford rooters would not be happy campers. . .

This was the New Guard's first Big Game. I briefed the troops, all *nine* of them—ten with me—before we deployed to Lake Lagunita where the program and subsequent bonfire would take place. Minions of Stanford students, staff and alums spent nearly a week assembling an enormous tower of wood, which would make Joan of Arc's pyre seem like a Boy Scout weenie roast. There were about 6-8 telephone poles, at least 50 feet tall, driven into the dry lake bed—how they accomplished that task is a mystery—forming a 15 foot diameter! The hundreds of worker bees then filled that void with pallets and lumber until it was jammed full. I later learned that volunteer guards, equipped with fire suppression equipment, manned this project 24-7, so that Cal interlopers wouldn't be able to ignite the fire prematurely: Old timers told me that there had been a number forays over the years, the most bizarre and dangerous occurred when a group of Cal archers unleashed a volley of flaming arrows from the Junipero Serra roadway, some 100 yards away. Luckily, nobody was impaled and the flames were quickly extinguished, thereby thwarting that medieval *Sneak Attack*. And, to add insult to injury, Stanford later won that game!

During the assembly of the bonfire, other artisans were busily creating a stuffed bear which would be hung over the stack just prior to ignition. Needless to say, this massive pile of fuel would ceremoniously reduce the effigy of "Oski," the Golden Bear mascot, to ash—in a nanosecond!

As my team approached the lake, the sour notes of LSJUMB (Leland Stanford Junior University Marching Band)—annoying to my ears—beckoned us to the Boat House. Although in full uniform, our mission was to blend into the shadows and to just observe, unless and until there was some trouble. The crowd was pouring in, thousands of Stanford students and supporters. As it got darker and more folks continued to stream in—more and more non-campus people, mostly high school kids and young adults (Paly Punks, we called them), a frightening flashback illuminated my mental screen:

****

Nearly the same time same station, only 16 years earlier, circa 1958: I was in the Air Force, stationed @ Mather AFB, Sacramento. I had recently hooked up with an old Hawaii buddy, George (Geo) Stickler, who then lived in Palo Alto; I spent many weekends with him and his crew. On this night in question, someone suggested that we go to Stanford for party-time at The Bonfire—lots of fine looking chicks and beer. When we got there, I had no-clue as to where I was, let alone that we were in going to whoop it up in a dried lake bed. There were thousands of kids milling and running around, most out of their gourds, blind drunk already! Once the fire was lit, the mob became more unruly, with fights breaking out all over the place. I saw a few cops in the crowd and recognized one as Officer Dick (good guy!), a full-time security officer at our favorite drive-in hang-out, Spivey's in Mountain View. He was also a Santa Clara County Sheriff's Reserve and there in full regalia. I went over to say Hi, whereupon he promptly advised us to get the hell out of there, as things were going to become downright dangerous. The Deputy pointed to his uniform trousers, which were splattered with green ink, apparently splashed on him by some malicious punk. He complained that those pants were brand new and cost him $50—a damn tidy sum in those days! Dick certainly wasn't kidding, for when I saw a 12' long X 3" diameter pole sailing through the air and into that mass of humanity, we were outta there! This was a full blown RIOT!! Geo and I had to literally battle our way through that sea of inebriated hoodlums: we dodged fists, feet, large rocks, beer bottles and other flak, and somehow made it to Geo's ride totally unscathed.

****

Back to the Here and Now...

The most memorable part of the program for me was ogling the new crop of Dollies (song girls) performing their routines—I regrettably missed that last time—to the accompaniment of LSJUMB: It was amazing to me how the quality of their tunes diminished as their collective BA's (blood alcohol levels) rose exponentially.

Suddenly and without warning, a *mummy* appeared on stage: *Someone must have raided the Mausoleum,* I quipped in my mind. *Was this none other than Governor Leland Stanford himself? If not, certainly an alumnus, from the Inaugural Class of 1894,* I chuckled silently.

As the Dollies closed in around our visitor from yesteryear, a large body of students and younger alums rushed onto the stage, led by a couple of guys who, save for their ethnicity, looked like Isaac Hayes in concert: Their bodies were draped in chains, which were affixed and padlocked to...The Axe!! The throng went ballistic. The Axe Committee held-up this coveted trophy for everyone to see. It was a huge fireman's pick axe, painted bright red, sporting a highly burnished business end and sawed-off handle; the prize was well secured to a large wooden plaque. I soon learned that this steel nugget was the property of last year's Big Game winner. While on the Farm, it was kept in an alarmed, see-through vault in the Tresidder Memorial Union (TMU) for the Stanford community to gloat over, while the "losers" hoped to get it back—if not on the field, by hook or by crook. However, armed SUDPS deputies escorted the Axe when it was not in the vault (see photo page 641).

As the din subsided, our Archaic Alum sprang forward with the vim and vigor of an 18 year old cheerleader: He exhorted the multitude, and led the body in the age old Stanford Axe cheer:

"Give 'em the axe, the axe, the axe. Give 'em the axe, the axe, the axe.

"Give 'em the axe, give 'em the axe, give' em the axe."

"Where?" He shouted. He then answered his rhetorical question:

"Right in the neck, in the neck, in the neck. Right in the neck, in the neck, in the neck; right in the neck, right in the neck, right in the neck!"

"Where?" He screamed again.

"There!" he exhorted, while pointing to his neck!

And, that was just the first chorus: The tempo accelerated until the crowd whipped itself into frenzy and became too hoarse to continue. As suddenly as the cadaver had arrived, he vanished—perhaps back into his sarcophagus until next year...

As quick as a lightning bolt, another group appeared and dashed through the major mob scene, led by a fleet-footed guy holding a lighted torch; the throng of onlookers sprinted wildly after the torch bearer and soon encircled that tower of building materials like a swarm of bees drawn to honey. The resultant WHOOOSH sounded like a 747 departing SFO; the blaze took-off like it had been primed with about 55 gallons of aviation fuel. The mass cheered loudly as the caricature of poor Oski became highlighted by the now raging inferno. As the enemy mascot disintegrated, the crowd screamed uncontrollably. Thick black smoke billowed into the sky, accompanied by a torrential shower of cinders—just what the EPA had ordered. And, once Oski was history, so were the Stanford faithful: Even in those days, we could spot a SU undergrad from up to 100 yards away. It was their uniforms: Red sweatshirt, white block S on the front, or white sweatshirt, red block S on the front. Most of the guys wore either a red baseball cap, block S on the front, or a white baseball cap, red block S on the *front*. Only the catchers on the baseball team were allowed to wear their caps with the bills backwards in those days. . .

Once the crowd thinned out to about 500, none of the uniformed students were visible; I knew that we were in trouble: We, all 10 of us, were the only ones in uniform—and it wasn't the type that would endear us to a bunch of drunken troublemakers! The only accoutrements I wished we had were riot helmets, full body armor and chest-high waders—especially the waders: I just had a feeling we were about to get into some very deep *Do-Do*. . .

Showdown at Lake Lag

The 1975 Bonfire show was over: The Stanford crowd, for whom this event was intended, had gone home. However, about 500 drunken, non-student adolescents pushed on with their wild party. Adhering to my marching orders, my squad of *Shock Troops,* all *TEN* of us, remained on the perimeter. *Surely, these idiots would tire or pass out anytime now,* I hoped. I damn sure didn't want to jeopardize our safety by mounting a charge on these morons—not just yet, anyway. And, besides, all of us needed to get some shut-eye before tomorrow's dreaded Big Game.

The fire was still burning; a couple of the charred poles collapsed, nearly taking out a bunch of kids. Unquestionably, this group was clearly bombed out of their minds and becoming increasingly violent. Moreover, I could easily differentiate the odor of burning wood from that green/brownish leafy material that was abundantly smoldering down there. . . Most of this wild bunch seemed to be acquainted: There was a lot of pushing and shoving and horsing around, but when one dude hip-threw another into the red hot coals, I knew enough was enough.

As if by cue, the radio started barking:

"26A-3, Radio." *Damn, it was that obnoxious dispatcher, Thelma Lard-Ass!*

"A-3, bye," I politely answered.

"A Professor reports unruly, drunken juveniles fighting and carrying-on at the Bonfire and he wants it stopped, immediately!"

"10-4, and be advised that I am well aware of the situation! Tell the R/P that we are about ready to move-in and disperse the group."

"A-3, Radio. Further, we are getting dozens of calls about this situation. Advise?"

"10-4. Again, we are on it! See if Palo Alto and the S/O can start a few units this way; looks like we are going to need lotsa help. . ."

A brilliant notion suddenly came to mind: *I'll just remove the attractive nuisance and this problem will go away.*

"Radio, 26A-3. Dispatch Stanford Fire to this 10-20, Code 2!"

"And, what is the nature of your request?" she snipped!

"*Boy, I hated this sassy twit! I was tempted to reply: "If your fat ass was out here the answer would be quite obvious!!"* But, being the gentleman I am, I bit my tongue and tepidly replied:

"Radio: We need to put this fire out NOW, before someone gets hurt or killed! Advise fire that I'll have FC-7 10-87 (meet) at the rim."

Assistant Chief John Barr (R.I.P.) quickly responded with two of Stanford's finest fire rigs and a team of seasoned fire fighters. After briefing Chief Barr, I directed my squad leader, Sgt. Lawson, to move his cruiser closer to the rioters and announce (via loudspeaker) that their party was over! *NOW!* The Sergeant's initial admonitions went mostly unheeded; FC-7's orders were met with boos, taunts and an untold number of universal salutes! Repeated orders to disperse caused a few kids to slowly drift off, but the bulk of the nasty critters refused to budge—these hardcore punks were obviously spoiling for a fight. As the fire trucks inched forward and put streams of water on the flames, a barrage of rocks, bottles, even chunks of concrete, peppered the fire rigs and the Sergeant's patrol car.

I immediately put out a Code 20 (HELP!) over the radio, but knew that the cavalry was probably too far off to do us any good. *Now I knew how Custer felt!!* I huddled-up the troops and hatched an impromptu game plan:

"Let's kick-ass and scatter these cowards," I barked, "On two; Ready, Break, Charge!" If we only had a bugler—Custer would have applauded our stupidity...

We quickly formed a skirmish line and like the troops at Bull Run, batons in hand, we charged forward like a herd of wild Mustangs. Several of our mainstays were immediately nailed with rocks and bottles—we got no respect. As we neared the extinguishing fire, one of our guys took a rock to the back of his head and momentarily lost consciousness. While the injured deputy was being attended to by a comrade, I urged the team forward and launched a savage banzai charge. Our squad chased the scoundrels out of that lake bed and into the surrounding boonies. Once all of the rabbits had scattered, we pulled back and got the hell out of there, lest the enemy get a second wind, mount a counter-attack and kick OUR asses.

We regrouped at the Annex and licked our wounds. Everyone was spent but damn thankful that we had prevailed, and without serious injuries, save for a few minor bumps, bruises and abrasions. And, just when I thought we were home free, Sgt. Lawson suddenly collapsed. Paramedics responded and later transported him to Stanford's E.R. Thankfully, Steve merely experienced an exhaustion/anxiety attack, so he was quickly released. I was also pleased that FC-7 would be available for the real challenge tomorrow at Stanford Stadium. Steve Lawson was one of my mainstays: He had been a top-notch deputy at the S/O and one of the best *Narcs* on Narcotics Task Force. I recruited him to Stanford as his training, experience, and street smarts would make him a good leader and mentor—and indeed he was! So, his clean bill of health was very good news!

When the dust cleared, five kids were nabbed for disorderly conduct, failure to disperse, and resisting arrest. We also collared a young adult for throwing a gallon wine bottle and a large chunk of concrete at Engine 95. Chief Barr, a 20 year veteran of Stanford Fire Department, later commented that the *Showdown at Lake Lag* was every bit as violent and chaotic as the campus riots during the

Vietnam War; I remember those days, but thought that era was history.

Big Game loomed as that big test our tiny, fledgling department needed to prove itself. Little did I know it would be as grueling as the Navy SEALs *Hell Week*: A challenge that those who persevered and survived would never forget!

The Battle for the AXE and Our Lives

When I crawled out of the sack, I felt like I had just played both ways on the gridiron myself. I was about 35 then and in pretty good condition due to my weight training and cardio regimen. However, I was never much of a runner, and the Showdown at Lake Lag, only a few hours before, really sapped me so, I was not looking forward to the challenge we were about to encounter.

Why in the hell are we doing this? I queried. *What was so damn important about this contest?* I continued to ponder. *All of this over a 10 pound lumberman's axe?* I ranted silently. *It's called Tradition,* Captain, that little voice way back in my head explained. And, what a tradition it is: Going on 113 years and still as wild as it was in yesteryear.

****

Moving back in time: On April 14, 1899, an over-exuberant Stanford cheerleader named Bill Erb did exactly what the rooting section exhorted him to do: At a massive bonfire on the Farm, the kid went berserk on a Golden Bear effigy with his huge lumberman's axe and reduced the mascot to confetti, all the while perfecting his "Axe Yell." The Stanford faithful roared with glee; however, the Cal crowd got wind of this spectacle and was not amused *at all*! As I have always said: "Don't get mad, get even." And get even they did: The Weenies soon pulled off one of the most historic rip-offs in the annals of this acrimonious co-existence. The following day, at a baseball series between the rivals, played in San Francisco, Mr. Erb went sideways, again, during the game and chopped up some blue and gold ribbon. While the cheerleader was doing his thing, Stanford's team was getting their posteriors handed to them by their rivals from across the Bay. (Stanford's football team had suffered a humiliating gridiron loss in the "Big Game," 22-zip, in the fall of 1898. This was the second consecutive Big Game loss in a row—a double whammy for sure.) After losing a close debate that week and now losing the baseball game, the fans were so dejected, they just left and headed back to the Farm. Someone forgot to secure Billy Erb's axe, so some crafty Weenies snagged it, cut off the handle, and smuggled the 10 pound instrument onto the ferry, secreted under a young Cal woman's dress. There were several forays to steal back the trophy, but all failed. Fearing Stanford resolve (and superior intellect—author's quip), the Cal bunch decided to stash the Axe in a Berkeley bank vault. Not even John Dillinger could get to that thing now! Or, so they thought...

The "Immortal 21"

In 1930, a group of twenty-one male students, mainly from Sequoia Hall, hatched a devious plot to recover the AXE from the Weenies in Berkeley. The Stanford marauders' plan was well thought out and apparently rehearsed. Cal held a rally every Spring, as they had for 31 years, since they purloined the trophy in 1899. The perps kept the prize in a bank vault, transported it to the rally site via armored car, displayed it to the Cal Faithful, and immediately returned the coveted trophy to the bank. On April 3rd, as the AXE was being removed from the security vehicle, our hero, Howard Avery Class of '31, dove from the roof of a nearby car, blind-sided the Weenie AXE custodian and relieved him of his responsibility. At that moment, another member of the team, Raymond Walsh '30, set-off a huge charge of magnesium flash powder which temporarily blinded a group of Cal students who were posing for a photo. During the pandemonium, Bob Loofbourow '29, acquired the prize, stashed it under his clothing and calmly sauntered-off to his get-away ride. As the car zoomed-off toward the Farm, Art Miller '31, lobbed a tear gas grenade into the discombobulated mob; this pretty much sealed the deal.

Hold on—it gets better yet: Several Stanford guys, who were dressed like Weenies (bumble bee rugby shirts, I suppose), calmed the group and suggested that they meet at the Campanile to form a recovery unit. In the meantime the "21's" wheelman was tearing up the road at speeds of up to 60 mph--they must have been in a Duesenberg, Caddie, or one of the hot roadsters built in Cleveland prior to the "Crash of '29"—I don't see a Model A reaching that speed...

Not even the "Mission Impossible Force" or a team of Navy SEALs could have pulled off an equivalent raid with such stealth and precision! Kudos to the "Immortal 21," and did they ever get the adulation they deserved when they returned to campus with THEIR AXE: Classes were canceled the next day for a gigantic rally of tribute to the Farm Heroes! In addition, the university presented the "21" with block S jerseys (heretofore awarded only to varsity athletes) and gold AXE charms.

Like the Cal thieves, Stanford stashed the trophy in a bank vault for 2 years fearing riots whenever the AXE was displayed in public. In 1933, both institutions agreed that the AXE would be awarded to the winner of that years' Big Game—But as we all know, those kids from Cal lie; they tried numerous times to reclaim the prize despite losing it. There will never be any equal to the mission of April 3, 1930. Clearly, Stanford ruled and the "Immortal 21's" effort will never be surpassed!

Postscript: There were many firsts in Stanford's history, especially when it came to the world of science: In 1952 Felix Bloch became the University's first Nobel Laureate winner for his efforts on nuclear magnetic resonance. Professor William Shockley received accolades for his work on semiconductors and the transistor, in 1956. Arthur Schawlow was a co-winner in physics for his contribution in creating the laser in 1981—and the list goes on. But for the purposes of this piece, and as an astute student of weaponology, I credit Raymond Walsh '30 with inventing and successfully employing what US troops and cops affectionately call, the Flash Bang! This extremely effective non-lethal device was developed by the British Special Forces group, called SAS, during the 1960s. The Brits called it a stun grenade, as it delivers a tremendous concussion blast which blinds and confuses the targets so they are unable to get their collective acts together in order to thwart an assault. The flash bang is a staple for SWAT and Special forces in the rescue of hostages. In the case of the Immortal 21, they need to receive a Stanford Atta-Boy, for developing and utilizing the non-lethal flash bang in repatriating the AXE in 1930...

****

Baptism of Fire!

When I entered the Annex Squad Room, most of the troops were milling around the coffee machine anxious to get their much needed caffeine fix. Once the group assembled and settled down, I opined that they all looked like a *remuda* of horses which had been ridden hard and put away wet! Quick witted Sgt. Lawson rejoined:

"Captain, you need to look into a mirror yourself and then you'll have some idea what we all have to look at..." *Touché'*

I ran over the game plan and beat responsibilities. We had 3 patrol units; one would handle urgent calls only on campus; the other 2 would patrol the exterior of that massive stadium and back up our deputies who were on foot. I had Sgts. Lawson and Coniglio in charge of the troops in the perimeter, evenly divided on the West and East sectors. They were to assist and supervise their respective 2 person teams; we had six teams, a total of 12 DPOs. The Chief, overall Commander, was in the Operations/Communications Center in the Press Box with Capt Bill, who was in charge of traffic and parking. I was designated as stadium Field Commander, on foot and charged with responding to trouble spots. So, how were 15 uniformed deputies possibly going to be able to keep the peace among 86,000 revved-up fans, you ask? Good question—I wondered myself, especially with the nature of this intense rivalry going back over one hundred years. Here's a journey to yesteryear, 1919, as recalled by Emanuel B. "Sam" McDonald from his autobiography Sam McDonald's Farm:

****

Mr. McDonald was now in charge of police and security operations of sporting events. With the first American style football Big Game between Stanford and Cal in four years scheduled for November 1919, Sam pulled out all stops and put out an SOS, as he termed it.

The rivals had ceased playing American football in 1915 as the game was determined to be too violent! Instead they went to Rugby, thought to be more civilized. I'm sure that the hammer heads who played that collision sport with no helmets or pads would have taken exception to that premise: Have you ever seen shirts worn by the Rugby set that proclaims: Ruggers Have Leather Balls..."

Because of the hiatus, Sam expected a horde of attendees, thus he called for a multitude of security and cops to manage this auspicious event. McDonald pioneered the process of hiring off duty officers and Pinkerton security to police the rowdy football games. Sam maintained great relationships with regional law enforcement agencies. He knew all of the top cops in the area: County of Santa Clara Sheriff Arthur B. Langford, Jack K. Albee, Constable and Marshal in Mayfield, his former boss, Stanford Chief of Night Watchmen, J.E. Jack Mathison, now Palo Alto's Police Chief. Then there was former SCCSO deputy, Ray Starbird, who became an Ace detective with the San Jose Police, under Chief Black. Starbird came to Sam's aid with some SJPD cops. He also received troops from the Sheriff's Office of San Mateo County's Under-Sheriff Meehan, as well as from Chief Mickey Collins of Redwood City PD. And, not to forget, Sam's good friend, D.A. White Esq. Chief of Police, San Francisco, CA who sent down a dozen or so uniformed cops—gratis. Sam had 15 mounted Stanford ROTC cavalrymen slated for the fray, but the Pony Soldiers canceled at the last minute due to another previously scheduled event. (*That's a likely story, but I don't blame them for not wanting to take on this detail!*) I don't know the final count of cops and security that Sam had amassed for this Big Game, but it was certainly adequate—perhaps overkill— to handle the "throng" of 23,000 fans... Well, better safe than sorry, and as you continue on, you will see how I would have loved to have had Sam's contingent at our first Big Game... By the way Cal won that 1919 contest 14-10, but as we all know they cheat: Cal had been secretly practicing the American style of football since 1917, but despite this advantage, the Cardinal hung-in there and made a credible showing.

****

During the 1960s-70s, the Sheriff's Office was contracted to provide gate and field security. We called them *Elton's Raiders*, named after Lt. Elton Heck, who assembled the group of sheriff's personnel, comprised of off-duty deputies, reserves, matrons and some civilians. They wore red jackets (also called *Red Coats*) with white lettering on the back that read: *Stanford Athletics Special Security*. In the old days, the Sheriff sent sworn deputies to Stanford's football games attired in full regalia. However, after a number of fights and resultant lawsuits against the County, the Sheriff would not permit any uniformed deputies to work pay jobs while off duty. The understanding was that the Red Coats would not take overt police action unless attacked, and would call for our DPOs if police action was required. After my initial experience with this group, many of them my friends, I was very dubious: During the 1974 football season, shortly after I was hired, a couple of instances occurred wherein Red Coats interacted with unruly fans, and being sworn deputies, they instinctively *badged* the troublemakers, which often made things worse. In many cases, fights would ensue and the R/Cs would dump the collars on our DPOs. Often, the R/Cs, who, in essence, effectuated a citizen's arrest, took off without identifying themselves or giving our officers information needed for a crime report, e.g.: They left our guys holding the bag! This was not a good situation and I intended to change it—but not at the moment.

Our contingent arrived at the stadium at about 8:00AM. On the way over, we saw that the parking lots were jam-packed with excited fans enjoying their tailgate parties. The air was thick with BBQ smoke and the aroma of hotdogs and hamburgers—the Chuck Taylor Grove crowd sizzled choice cuts of filet mignon. . .

While some people may disagree, my research indicated the tailgate phenomenon actually began at Stanford University once motor cars became vogue. From their inception, most vehicles of the first 3 decades of the 20th century were equipped with tailgates, which were designed to carry luggage. Cars of that era didn't have trunks, although many roadsters and coupes sported rumble seats. And, I can only imagine that while the Cal crowd was driving to their favorite tailgate locations in Model T Fords, our alums from yesteryear cruised-up in Duesenbergs, Cadillacs, and Packards.

Once on the Farm, they assembled their tables, clothed with red and white linen and magnificently set with the finest of China, exquisite silverware, Italian glassware, with French wine chilling in sterling silver buckets of ice... This was the original *Wine and Cheese set*, still in evidence today, only now, they haul their wares in shiny Escalades, Beemers and Mercedes SUVs!

Major Mob Scene

When we arrived at the stadium, the fans were jammed in like cord wood around the gates. Gate 2, the main entrance, was a nightmare but paled by comparison with the student gate. The kids were queued up 4-5 bodies wide along the fence for nearly 50-60 yards. Many of the early birds were sitting on their sleeping bags; most at the head of the line camped out. I was amazed!

The fence surrounding the perimeter was right out of *Stalag 13*: It was a sturdy wire mesh barrier, nearly 10 feet tall, with a couple of strands of wire at the top. It would have been nice to have some of that *razor wire* up there but I don't think it was in existence then. Each gate had numerous wickets with small hinged gates which were locked until the Athletic Department gave the order to open up. The wickets were very small—even a *runway model* might have difficulty passing through... These were cleverly designed so that ostensibly only one person could pass through at a time. But when it came to the students, that was quite another matter: When the gates were unlocked the kids fought and squirmed through the openings like a school of fish trying to escape a trap. Once in, the students dashed madly for their section, knocking over anyone or anything in their path—it was like the *Running of the Bulls*... Needless to say, I had no interest in being trampled so I got out of the way—way out of the way!

What's going on here? I asked myself. *Where in the hell did all this humanity come from? We sold out the University of Spoiled Children's game last year and I don't recall having so many more folks outside.* I continued to ponder that question. Then the radio chatter began:

"Control Gate 2, send a Stanford officer here. We are having a lot of fights going on."

"Gate 7. We need help!"

"Radio, this is Gate 4. We need the police over here right away."

So, our guys began running from gate to gate—like chickens with their heads cut-off—putting out fires. The R/C supervisor then called me to Gate 2. When I arrived, he excitedly thrust a handful of tickets at me (about a dozen or so) and said he thought they were bogus. The samples he displayed looked like the real McCoy to me until the *super* pointed at the serial numbers: They all read 40999. *Damn, I thought, that black cloud is still following me around. I wonder how many of these forgeries are out there? We are going to have our hands full dealing with a bunch of pissed-off people who bought these bogus tickets!*

I instructed the Gate supervisor to seize all phony tickets presented, and not to let those folks into the stadium. Further, I proclaimed: "If these people gave the ticket-takers any static, call us and we would gladly explain the facts of life to these so-called victims:" They were duped and bought a pig in a poke, which was unfortunate, but we would not let them in—period! My only consolation to those dumb enough to buy tickets from dubious sources was that our detectives would investigate the matter come Monday.

After the gate monitors turned away hundreds of ticked-off, would be spectators, the suckers began assaulting the fences in various spots—mostly between Gates 2 and 6. They were like *Spiderman* the way they went up and sometimes over the fence. Even with the limited personnel I had, we somehow staved off most of the onslaughts and were able to bag a few interlopers. This was like medieval warfare with the barbarians attempting to vault the castle walls. The difference was we didn't have any boiling oil or huge boulders to rain down on them—just kidding!

For nearly an hour, we ran around the perimeter fence like a pack of junk yard dogs trying to protect their property. As we nabbed more trespassers and sent them away in chrome bracelets, the word got around and the attempts appeared to subside—well, sort of: Groups of inebriated young men gathered outside and taunted us with jeers and invectives, but to us, that was just like the old *sticks and stones* ditty.

Super Weenie

After what seemed to be an eternity, I heard the roar of the crowd inside the arena, and Radio announced the game was on. *Good, maybe things will simmer down for a bit,* I hoped. I then called for a *pow wow* with Sgt. Lawson and his partner, Bill Starbuck, near Gate 6. The perimeter road was clear of pedestrians as most of them were in the stadium already—nobody wants to miss the initial kick-off. We shot the bull for a few minutes until I was called to meet a Sheriff's sergeant at Gate 2. As we parted company and I started to walk away, I suddenly heard some hollering. When I looked back, I saw Lawson and Starbuck were sparring with a short, burly, middle-aged man, who was wearing a blue and yellow rugby shirt—a UC Berkeley fan, no doubt.

It appeared that my pair of deputies were trying to grab his arms, but he parried and flailed wildly. I ran to their assistance and as I arrived, they were wrestling with a subject in the ice plant, adjacent to a stairway, trying to apply the handcuffs on this raging bull! I grabbed one of his arms and put him into an arm lock, so the bracelets could be secured.

"What in the hell happened here guys?" I implored.

All the while, the arrestee was protesting his incarceration by saying he didn't do anything and that he was going to sue us. Deputy Starbuck told me that the suspect in cuffs put a shoulder block into him for no apparent reason. When Starbuck asked the man why he did that, the subject said something to the effect that he was in a hurry and Bill was in the way. The Cal fan then started up the stairs. Deputy Starbuck told him to stop, whereupon the assailant told Starbuck to get fornicated! Starbuck then ascended the stairs and took the man by the arm in an effort to bring him down to ground level for an explanation of his behavior. The man, who exhibited symptoms of inebriation, resisted and was subsequently taken down to terra firma by the sergeant and deputy. Starbuck said that there were no other people on the roadway and, therefore, there was no reason for the suspect to forcibly bump into him like he did.

As we were getting ready to remove this individual to Gate 6 for transportation to jail, a middle-aged matronly lady approached me and asked why we had her husband in custody. She explained she was the man's wife and that they were late for the game due to a cocktail party, and he was very upset about that. She further stated she misdirected him to the location of their seats, and that really infuriated him. That, coupled with the fact that she couldn't keep up with his pace, really elevated his ire.

So, the truth was revealed: The Cal rooter, an alumnus I later learned, got bombed at a cocktail party, was late because his sweet wife made a geographic mistake, which caused him to miss the kick-off. He was apparently so angry that when a cop got in his way, he simply plowed through him. That got him, in my judgment, a free pass to North County Jail for assaulting a law enforcement officer and resisting arrest. This I explained to his poor bewildered spouse, as Steve and Bill started to walk the collar to the gate. Well, easier said than done. As I indicated, this guy was stout—about 5'8," and a solid 190 pounds; in addition, he was extremely agitated and refused to go along with the program. As my charges tried to walk the prisoner toward the gate, he dug his heels in and refused to move. He was too damn heavy to carry, so they had to muscle this jerk for approximately 30 yards. I had already called for a transportation unit so the patrol car was waiting for us at Gate 6.

When we reached the gate, my guys could not force this Adam Henry through the skinny wicket: He put his wide shoulders against the upright poles and locked his feet on them, too. I reminded Steve of the old Drunk Tank trick of introducing an inebriate into a cell when he didn't want in: You simply turned the drunk around, threw an arm around his neck and took him in head first. It worked like a charm; however, getting this chump into a '73 Plymouth with a cage was another story. Try as we might, and with four deputies, we simply could not get the obstinate SOB into tight confines of the rear seat. I next called for our Chevy station wagon, which was considerably bigger, and had a cage for this animal! In the meantime, several other deputies and I were holding the unruly, disgruntled mob at bay—the fools who bought forged tix from scalpers. Like the media who cover cop events, they often only see half of the story—a bunch of cops beating-up on an old man, but not what precipitated it.

When the station wagon arrived, our guys fought tooth and nail in an effort to get this maniac into the patrol car. The enraged arrestee thrust himself under the vehicle and locked his legs in the under carriage. When finally pulled free, they used the old Drunk Tank trick, again, to pull him into the cage and got his rear end out of there! There's nothing worse than having an unruly crowd of intoxicated people hanging around when you are trying to subdue a fighter. As the patrol vehicle pulled away, I knew in my mind that we had not heard the last of this caper. . .

Before I knew it, Communications summoned all hands to the field. The R/Cs and our DPOs ringed the perimeter of the playing field, in an effort to dissuade the fans from taking over the turf and pulling down the goal posts. I give huge kudos to Chief Herrington for insisting that the Athletic Department install a 6 foot cyclone fence on the short wall around the field. This was a very controversial move, as the spectators in the first 20 rows hated peering through the fence during the game. But, at game's end, it was a deterrent to fans bent on storming the field. In this game, however, no one ventured into no-man's-land as the Weenies prevailed 20-14. I don't recall seeing a single play, but took a huge sigh of relief when the spectators peacefully filed out of the stands.

Aftermath

When I returned to the station, I was actually surprised how few people had been incarcerated. Save for *Super Weenie*, the body count was less than a dozen—a few drunks, who had to be booked for at least 6 hours; the rest of the collars were gate crashers and fence jumpers who were released on citations. There was a ton of police reports but I would deal with them Monday. I learned that the person who had blasted Deputy Starbuck was apparently a big wig in Palo Alto. He lived in a very exclusive neighborhood so I guessed he certainly wasn't on welfare. . . Given the intensity of his actions and resistance, coupled with the fact that he committed a battery on a peace officer (243 P. C., a felony), I ordered our DPOs to have a technician draw blood prior to booking the intoxicated man. This would surely strengthen our case if his blood alcohol was above the legal limit, even though he wasn't driving. When I was convinced that all things were in order, I went 10-7 OD and headed home for a well deserved rest.

Monday morning, I called the North County Sheriff's Detective, Richard Min and asked him to accompany our Detective Don Lillie to the DA's Office to seek a complaint against the fighter. This man was well fortified with alcohol Saturday during our encounter. I learned his BA came back 0.15, clearly over the legal limit of 0.10. That afternoon both detectives returned with their hats in their hands: Complaint denied!

"What?" I screamed. "No complaint? How come?"

Lillie said that the DDA immediately commented about the residence the subject lived in and that he was an important man around town. I immediately figured this one out: Super Weenie was connected; I bet he had a good lawyer who had already dropped a dime on the DA's Office. This was BS, especially since the guy was high on booze and intentionally ran into one of our deputies for no good reason; he refused to explain his behavior and was totally unremorseful; he also fought like a cornered wildcat!

I briefed the Chief and told him that I was on my way to the DA's with Det. Lillie for another shot at getting this man charged with something. I figured that felony battery was totally out of the question at this DA's Office, especially since Starbuck had no visible injury, save for some sore ribs. I knew most of the attorneys at this office and thought perhaps I might be able to change their minds with some skillful debate. The DDA I talked to was a newbie, thus was assigned North County where things were a little more subdued than in San Jose. He was a very congenial man and told me that he was a Stanford alum, former football player and a member of the Delta Tau Delta fraternity—he could have gone all day without giving me that piece of information, for as you will see, the DPS and Delt's had a very checkered relationship. . . In any event, I argued magnificently but my talking points fell on deaf ears—No complaint! All of the issues I raised were like over-cooked spaghetti: They didn't stick to the wall. Clearly, in my mind, the fix was in, so we excused ourselves and went DA shopping in San Jose. I subsequently met with a female supervisor whom I knew pretty well from my days on the streets. She listened to my argument intently and said that she would talk to the man himself, the District Attorney of the County of Santa Clara. Several days had passed before I got the dreaded call from the Assistant DA. Sorry, but still no complaint. I couldn't even get him to go for a simple 647f (drunk in public, then a lowly misdemeanor). I ended our call by pointing out that their inaction was going to open us up for a major law suit—I could just smell it! The DDA commiserated with me, and parted by saying that Stanford would take care of us should a suit come forth. Boy, that was reassuring. So, I wondered: *When will that other shoe drop?*

The Counterfeiter

Our next focus was the culprit who printed all of those bogus Cal tickets: *Must have been a Weenie,* I figured. This was a very clever scam but the execution was lousy. I consulted with Det. Lillie, who had developed many contacts over the years and suggested that he get some past copies of the Daily Californian student publication as well as the Stanford Daily. About 20 minutes later, Don excitedly told me that checking-out the Cal paper was unnecessary. Lillie quickly identified a subject who had placed numerous ads in the Stanford Daily offering Cal Big Game tickets for sale—cheap, too, at 25 bucks a pop. Much to my surprise, the mastermind turned out to be an industrious Stanford graduate student residing in Escondido Village (EV)!

Don called the University telephone office and traced the number to an apartment in EV. It didn't take me long to strap on my piece and soon we were across the street knocking on the moron's door. After we IDed ourselves, I thought the kid was going to perform a bodily function right on the spot. When we told him why we were there and that we knew he sold the fake Big Game tickets, he rolled over like a big Golden Retriever. He copped-out to the caper and stated that he produced the counterfeits on a new, high dollar Canon color copier, available at the campus copy center at TMU. He admitted that he printed 1,000 bogus ducats and sold about 300 of them. He still had the paper, hundreds of unsold phonies, as well as the paper cutter; we confiscated all of this evidence and referred the case to the DA. He was later charged with a misdemeanor and received a slap on the wrist—hardly compensation for the all of the grief this young man caused us. Whoever said that justice was fair and balanced?

BUT WAIT! THERE'S MORE: Stay tuned. . .

CHAPTER EIGHT

Homicides

Overview

Given the size of the Stanford University campus—including the vast surrounding area—the sizeable population—Faculty, students, staff and researchers, drives the numbers to nearly 40,000 during weekdays, the homicide rate on The Farm is relatively low. According to the *A Chronology of Stanford. . .* publication I have referred to on many previous occasions, the first Stanford-related killing occurred in 1909 when a student, who had been imbibing way too much, stumbled into the wrong house and was shot and killed as a suspected burglar. This unfortunate and unnecessary event might have happened in Palo Alto; nonetheless, a life was wasted due to the excessive use of alcohol. This situation launched "The Liquor Rebellion," which caused the Academic Council to ban booze from the Encina Hall, fraternity, as well as other student residences on campus. Several hundred students staged a demonstration which resulted in the suspension of a dozen protestors. Then, in 1909, a CA state law was enacted and delineated an Alcohol Free Zone: A one and a half mile boundary was established around both Stanford and UC Berkeley campuses. Of course, students of both institutions adhered to the letter of law and became teetotalers. . .

When I first came to the Palo Alto area in the late 1950's, I often wondered why we had to buy our booze in Whiskey Gulch, East Palo Alto, or at Ernie's Liquors in Barron Park. Unlike the Stanford students, our group of hellions didn't choose to abstain.

The Lamson Case

When something happens at Stanford, people take notice. This event captured the interest of the country, if not the world. This incident came in the wake of the Lindbergh kidnapping, which dominated the eastern press; however, when the facts were revealed, newspapers all over the country had this story on page one—the first *really* big case in Stanford's history. And, a murder no less!

Initially, this incident, by all investigative accounts, was a slam-dunk for the People of the State of California: David Lamson, 31 years old, University Press Assistant Advertising Manger, Class of '25, found his wife, Allene Thorpe Lamson, Class of '25, dead in their bathtub in their residence on Salvatierra Street. The Lamsons were well known and very popular in the community.

The Lamsons had listed their home with a local realtor as a summer rental. On Memorial Day, 1933, a real estate agent showed up at the property with two clients, and found a shirtless Mr. Lamson tending a bon fire (brush and yard debris) in the back yard. After exchanging pleasantries, Lamson asked the agent and his clients to come to the front door so he could alert his wife that visitors were on the premises. According to a Time Magazine article, the agent and clients "...heard a peculiar sound. It may have been a hysterical cry." Lamson soon opened the door and said: "My God, my wife has been *murdered!*"

There are several versions of what the crime scene looked like: The Time article stated the realtor (Julia M. Place) and her two clients . . . "rushed to the bathroom. In the tub was the nude, dead body of the 28-year-old woman, her head and arms dangling over the edge, the back of her head crushed and bloody".

In a comprehensive and excellent piece of investigative journalism, "Was it Murder?" written by Mr. Bernard Butcher of Stanford Magazine, Butcher wrote that a neighbor, Buford Brown, saw David Lamson kneeling on the floor cradling Allene's head in his arms "sobbing hysterically and calling her," Buford reported the following day. "I induced him to leave and to go into the other room; he staggered and then fell to the floor in a faint," the neighbor said.

When Palo Alto officers arrived, they discovered the 28 year old victim's nude body draped face down over the edge of the tub, which was full of water. She had sustained a vicious blow to the back of her head and there was a considerable amount blood all over the floor and walls. Absent evidence of forced entry and the fact that nothing seemed to be missing from the residence (no evidence of a burglary or robbery), the PA cops concluded that this was a highly suspicious death, thus took Lamson into custody for questioning—they were allowed to do that in those days!

At some point in time, the S/O (Santa Clara County Sheriff's Office) took over the investigation as it was their jurisdiction. The detectives found a 10 inch length of water pipe in the fire, as well as blood evidence on a remnant of charred cloth believed to be a piece of Mr. Lamson's shirt. Sheriff William Emig and District Attorney Fred Thomas hardly shied from the spotlight. Their position never wavered: "Allene Lamson was killed," they said, "and Lamson is the only suspect," Butcher's article revealed. The big question was motive: Many friends and associates stated the Lamsons had a good loving relationship. However, others who knew them felt the couple's relationship seemed to be strained of late. Many people indicated Lamson's serene personality could turn into anger in a nanosecond: The night before the killing, David became amorous but was put off by Allene; she said she was menstruating. Lamson allegedly discovered she lied: The next morning, coincidently, just prior to the murder, Lamson found a sanitary napkin in the bathroom, used but unsoiled! Did that raise his ire? There were also rumors about David's infidelity, as well. First, there was the housekeeper, who became impregnated; a number of folks suspected Lamson planted the seed. However, when she delivered a red-headed bouncing baby boy, that theory went out of the window as her boyfriend was a carrot top!

Finally, there was talk of a blonde divorcee from Sacramento, Sara Kelley, whom Lamson had known for 10 years due to his and her involvement in the media.

With all due respect to our S/O detective pioneers, I wonder how thorough their homicide investigation was. Clearly, the crime scene was totally compromised due to all the people who had tramped in and out of the bathroom. Without benefit of the police reports or trial transcripts, I can only guess that it was a bit shoddy. From what I know of the scene, a blood spatter expert would have been handy as they are able read the droplets, determine trajectory, velocity and what type of blunt force trauma could have caused Allene's injuries. Criminal investigation was just starting to develop in the 1930s following the lead of London's Metropolitan Police, who arguably set the tone for modern detective work. Metro's efforts paved the way of forensic science, for they developed nearly every crime scene technique in use today: Latent fingerprint recovery, enhancement and analysis, the superglue process, reading and understanding blood spatter, inroads to DNA and countless other crime solving methods.

The David Lamson murder case began in San Jose on August 24, 1933 in Santa Clara County Superior Court, Honorable Robert Syer presiding. The jurors were chosen from all over the county. Deputy District Attorney Allan Lindsay was at the helm of the People's case. He reportedly was a hard charging, fiery prosecutor who was going to prove Allene's husband did the evil deed. A deputy sheriff testified that he overheard Lamson exclaim to his sister, Margaret:

"God, why did I marry her"—or something to that effect. Margaret, of course denied the statement. (*What motive would the deputy have to perjure himself? He didn't have a dog in this fight— he was just doing his job. Author's opinion.*)

The defense, on the other hand, argued that the victim merely slipped as she was leaving the tub and fell on the nearby sink thereby suffering the head wound. As Mr. Butcher put it, "The three-week trial settled into a battle of expert witnesses."

According to a September 11, 1933 Time Magazine article entitled Lamson Case, two doctors testified, one of whom was Blake Wilbur (son of Stanford President Ray Lyman Wilbur), a close friend of the accused and best man at the Lamson wedding. Dr. Wilbur testified for the defense and postulated that Allene's untimely death was the result of an accidental fall. Disputing the defense theory, Dr. Arthur William Meyer, head of the Stanford University Anatomy Department, opined: "Mrs. Lamson's scalp indicated that she had been seized and yanked forward," presumably before the killing blows were administered. I was especially intrigued by the bathroom experiment performed by Santa Clara County Pathologist Dr. Frederick Proescher, who testified he put himself in peril by stripping down (*to his birthday suit*) and intentionally slipping in the tub. The Pathologist testified that his head crashed on the rim of the tub and faucets. "I wasn't even hurt," Dr. Proescher boasted. He might have sustained a *pop knot* on his melon, but suffered no lacerations. . . Dr. Proescher also testified that although he found blood on the pipe and charred clothing, he could not determine whether it was animal or human. (Where was DNA when we needed it?) A neighbor testified she noticed heavy smoke coming from the fire and that it smelled like burning flesh. The aggressive and able prosecutor, ADA Lindsay maintained that Mr. Lamson had beaten his wife over the head with the pipe, and then sought to destroy all evidence in the fire. *Ya think?*

Back to the Lamson Matter:

On September 16, 1933, the jury of seven men and five women filed into the courtroom after eight hours of deliberation. "Defense attorney inferred the worst. 'Take it on the chin, kid,' he whispered in Lamson's ear," said journalist Butcher. The jury foreman read the unanimous verdict: Guilty of first degree murder. Lamson showed no emotion as the jury was polled. Judge Syer sentenced him to the gallows at San Quentin State Prison, and ordered the sentence be carried out within 90 days if no appeal was filed.

There was hue and cry among Stanford friends and colleagues. Driven by the English Department, a group formed and called themselves the "Lamson Defense Committee." Margaret Lamson ram-rodded her brother's appeal attempt by soliciting funds for the legal team. Defense attorney McKenzie prepared a 608-page appellate brief. Stanford English professors boiled the document down into a pamphlet entitled: "The Case of David Lamson." Twenty well-known professors, authors, doctors, as well as ministers and priests joined the protest. Momentum was building rather quickly for Mr. Lamson.

Life on the Row

Having visited San Quentin in the late 1990's with a group of law enforcement officials, I can assure you that life on Death Row is no picnic—undoubtedly worse in the1930's when the gallows was still in operation. When we toured the "Row," the place was very clean, perhaps the most sanitary section of the institution. The inmates were confined to their 5X10 foot cells, except for a weekly shower and some highly supervised exercise. The condemned prisoners were well fed and provided books, writing materials, and access to legal research. However, next to the guillotine, I personally believe that hanging a human being is cruel and unusual punishment. Somehow, the executioners at Q never learned the proper way to hang a man like they used to in Ol' Judge Roy Bean's days on his infamous Bench/Bar where, during recesses, the jury and spectators bellied-up-to said bar to quench their thirsts. . . San Quentin's prison museum displayed an array of photos of botched hangings:

When the old timers referred to hanging as "stretching one's neck," they weren't kidding. I saw some photographs of several poor souls who could have appeared in the Barnum and Bailey Freak Show! In many cases, the "Q's Noose" severed the condemned person's head like that French's contraption used during their Revolution. The worst example of debauchery was performed on a Chinese immigrant from San Francisco, who had committed some brutal murders. He was to receive the ultimate overkill: When the hangman pulled the lever, the poor guy dropped through the trap door, and when the Doc checked him out, the man was alive and well. Round Two: They added a little more weight in order to snap his neck, but when the physician put the stethoscope to the man's chest, his heart was pumping as if he had just run a 100 dash! Thrice is a charm? Not! They simply could not kill this guy, so they commuted his sentence—obviously, the prison officials didn't adhere to the "Three Strikes" and you're outta there rule...

In an article written by Kevin Roderick of the LA Times March 28, 1990 entitled *Last Steps and Last Words on Death Row*, the author described how Warden Holohan detested the gallows. He supervised every execution during his tenure (1930s) and was said to mutter angrily, "This has got to be changed." After leaving San Quentin, Holohan was elected to the CA State Senate and sponsored the 1937 law which discontinued hanging and authorized the use of lethal gas. Since the State of CA assumed the task of hangings from the Sheriff's Offices in 1893, over 300 convicts were executed by this barbaric method at San Quentin and Folsom Prisons.

The gas chamber went into operation in 1938. During our visit, I was the only one of our group who dared venture into that chamber of doom. Like the hanging tower which sported two trap doors, the there was a "two-seater" in the chamber. Our guide and longtime supervisor at the Q told us the "two-fer" was specially designed, so that crime partners could be euthanized together.

The Appeal

While David Lamson languished on Death Row, his legal team was hard at work whittling away at the prosecution's conviction. While on the Row, Lamson made good use of his idle time by compiling observations and views of his fellow inmates on the death penalty. In 1935, Lamson completed a Best Selling book, We Who Are About to Die. David astutely composed: "The men I knew on the Row, waiting to be hanged, were just people." He later wrote: "And not very smart people; for smart people don't get sentenced to the Row, no matter what their crimes. The smarty pulls the strings, the cons say; and the square-john stretches the rope." As in the old adage, "the squeaky wheel gets the grease:" Instead of *grease,* I think Lamson got the *"juice!"*

The CA Supremes

On October 13, 1934 the Supreme Court of CA overturned the Lamson verdict on the grounds that trial judge failed to require the prosecution to fully prove their case. The Court said, in Butcher's article: . . . "the prosecution must show not only circumstances consistent with guilt, but circumstances inconsistent with any reasonable theory of innocence." (A lot of legal mumbo-jumbo, if you ask me.) "When it comes to David Lamson, the court wrote, every statement tends to support his claims. It is true that he may be guilty, but the evidence thereof is no stronger than mere suspicion."

Although the court ordered a new trial, Chief Justice William Waste and two colleagues based their ruling on technical grounds only, and didn't dispute the fact a murder was committed. Honorable Waste further asserted they ordered a new trial even though, "a majority of the justices feel Lamson is guilty. . ." Whoa Nellie! So, you know the dude-did-it, and he gets to step-up to the plate for another "up?" As I say, "If you play a team often enough, you're bound to beat them once!"—Author, again!

And, They Did!

The second trial was convened in Judge Seyer's court. He also presided in the first trial. A panel of seven men and five women were impaneled. After three months of legal wrangling, the jurors were dead-locked: Nine for conviction and three for acquittal. In spite of a stronger showing by the prosecution's expert witnesses—key was the crime scene forensic scientists who addressed the blood evidence and described how the spatter on the walls was consistent with blunt force trauma—three hold-outs weren't convinced that David Lamson savagely battered his spouse with a lead pipe and then tried to incinerate the tell-tale evidence.

The third inning began in November 1935 but was declared a mistrial due to some problems with the jury list. The fourth and final inning began in January 1936. Again, after a three month trial and 36 hours of deliberation, the jury returned, once more, hung nine for and three against conviction. After these debacles, the District Attorney capitulated and after three years of incarceration, Mr. Lamson was free as a bird. He moved to Southern California, remarried and worked with Hollywood producers on a screen version of his book. He eventually moved back to the Bay Area and passed away at age 72.

Rehashing how and why Lamson beat the rap is fruitless, so I won't; this is how our system of jurisprudence sometimes works—like it or not. End of story. But, there will be more forthcoming. . .

The ROTC Murder

Thomas Wallace Cordry III had been an honor student in high school; little wonder that he was accepted straight-away to Stanford University: It probably didn't hurt that his parents were alums, both graduating in 1933, coincidently the year of the infamous Lamson murder. Mr. Cordry Jr. was considered a prominent alumnus by virtue of his position as CEO of a huge insurance company in San Francisco.

In 1958, Cordry III, 19, was a sophomore; he was a good looking athletic kid—a budding star on Stanford's formidable tennis team. Thomas seemed to have it all: He lived in a nice neighborhood in Palo Alto, just a few blocks from the campus, was doing very well academically, and had a brand new white 1957 Chevrolet Bel Air convertible—talk about a "chick magnet!" In comparison to my ol' "Nifty '50" Plymouth 4 door, Tom's ride was a car to die for. . .

On February 26, 1958, Thomas hopped-into his hot rod and cruised around looking to pick up a girl—any girl. After motoring around for about two hours, Cordry couldn't find any takers so he headed home. It was 10:00 PM. When he got there, he called his neighbor, a cute 17 year old, Deena Bonn. Deena was a Cubberly High School student and had been to a movie with Tom before. Nothing serious, for Deena already had a boyfriend, who was also a Stanford student. Thomas told Deena he was taking a train trip out of town and wondered if she would drive him to the California Street station, then bring his car back home. Deena jumped at the chance and was across the street in a flash—what teenager wouldn't want to zoom around in that powerful, new Chevy?

When they got to the El Camino Real, Thomas exclaimed:

"Oh, I almost forgot. I borrowed a rifle from the ROTC armory and I need to return it before I get into trouble!"

Somewhat confused the gullible young lady asked for directions. The ROTC building and indoor firing range was located in a eucalyptus grove, now known a Master's Grove, behind Sunken Diamond:

Subsequent research revealed that this facility was a converted horse barn, which was built during WWI for the cadre of ROTC "horse-soldiers." There were a couple of other smaller buildings at the complex, one of which was a power-lifting gym for the Stanford football team. I had been to both places in the 60's, but had no idea that this was the site of a murder.

When Deena pulled to a stop, Cordry got out of the passenger seat, retrieved a .22 caliber rifle from the rear seat and promptly shot her in the right temple. Death was instantaneous! Why in the world would this seemingly intelligent, charming young man with everything going for him, commit such an atrocious act?

The short answer is that Thomas Wallace Cordry III had a latent "Dark Side!" According to the numerous news articles and the original police report I researched, this guy had an uncontrollable "urge to kill!" Not only that, but after he killed this woman, he planned to do the unspeakable to the victim's lifeless body.

Upon shooting Deena, he pulled her over to the right seat and drove to the foothills; he headed up Sand Hill Road to the future site of the Stanford Linear Accelerator (SLAC), then open space. I knew the area very well as my buddy Ken Alley and I used to hunt small game there all the time. It was very isolated, but there were a few dirt roads that would enable one to drive way back into the boondocks:

****

As a matter of fact, my girlfriend of that era and I used to go up there quite often for star gazing—until one very eventful and, perhaps, the scariest nights in my young life: My companion and I were listening to rock 'n roll on KYA and minding our own business. Suddenly, there was a loud KABOOM on my hood, and my Plymouth shook violently. When we looked-up, there was TV ad's "Mercury Cougar," all 150 pounds of him, standing on my hood pressing his huge visage against my windshield. I seem to recall that he was licking his chops, too. . . In one panicked motion, I somehow managed to blow the horn, start the engine, throw it in reverse and peel outta there in a shower of dust and gravel.

****

When Thomas Cordry reached this desolate location, he prepared to commit necrophilia on the motionless girl. However, he ultimately decided against that despicable act. He also scratched phase three of his plan—to hide her body and then take-off for the Santa Cruz Mountains, where he planned to hide out. Cordry had packed survival gear, which he stashed in his trunk. He filled a suitcase with clean underwear, heavy clothing, food, cooking gear and a *BIBLE*. Can you believe that? Here's a calculated, cold blooded nut job, who just murdered a totally innocent young lady with whom he intended to commit the horrendous act of necrophilia, and then toss her remains away like garbage. As if reading passages from the Bible was going to cleanse his soul and make this savagery OK. Give me a break!

The killer then drove to the Palo Alto Police Department, pulled-up to the curb and went to the front desk. An expressionless Cordry related the following to the Desk Officer:

"I want to report a killing. I shot a girl and she's in the car."

The police officer was stunned: Judging from the demeanor of the young man, the officer thought Cordry was there to report a minor vehicle collision or something similar.

I recall seeing a Palo Alto Times front page photo of the car and the covered body of Deena, many years ago while I was going through a box of old Stanford cases. What piqued my interest was that I recognized some of the old Sheriff's detectives, who were still on the job when I began my career in 1964. Like the investigators seen in the old "True Detective" magazines, the S/O "Dicks" were similarly attired in "Columbo" trench coats and wide brim fedoras. That was the only humorous thing I found in this incident.

Sheriff's Inspectors Fred Goudy and J.C. Hooton, under the leadership of Detective Bureau Commander, Captain William Salt, wasted no time in establishing rapport with the stoic and remorseless Cordry. In those days, detectives had a decided advantage of not having to advise suspects of their Constitutional Rights, which was decided in the Arizona v. Miranda case in 1963. Those ol' Dicks were good—real good! No Good Guy-Bad Guy routine was needed in this case: Captain Salt realized that he could catch more bears with honey than vinegar, so he treated the youthful killer well, thereby gaining Cordry's confidence. Not only did they obtain a full confession of the murder, but Cordry laid-out his entire plan and confided that he had an uncontrollable "urge to kill:"

"I had an urge to do it. I've had the same urge before. I guess this is really a sex problem." Cordry admitted. He refused to speak with his parents at that point.

Thomas candidly advised he initially had intended to kill his victim with an ice pick (cops found one in his vehicle), but opted for a firearm instead. He purchased a .22 caliber scoped rifle and ammo at a local sporting goods store. Obviously, the story he told Deena about having to return a rifle to the ROTC was a ruse.

As we cops say these days, this case was a slam-dunk! On August 27, 1958, Thomas Wallace Cordry III pleaded guilty to first-degree murder with a mandatory life sentence to be imposed. The article from the Los Angeles Times entitled An Urge to Kill, ended by stating; "His (Cordry) name never again appeared in the Times."

Leslie Marie Perlov

Leslie was a shining star. She completed four years of a tough academic regimen in three years, and graduated with a Stanford University degree in 1972. Ms. Perlov had been admitted to several law schools and was working as a law librarian in the North County Municipal Court's library. By all accounts, she was attractive and well liked by her colleagues as well as clients. She was just 21—the brightest of the bright!

Sometime after 3:30PM, Tuesday, February 13, 1973, Leslie left her Los Altos Hills home and told her mother that she was going to photograph some scenery around the vicinity. She drove off in an orange '70's Chevy Nova. When Leslie failed to return home that evening, her concerned Mom called the Sheriff's Office. Shortly thereafter, a statewide APB (All Points Bulletin) was transmitted to all law enforcement agencies, describing the missing young lady as well as her distinctive car.

On February 15th, an alert officer spotted Leslie's vehicle parked near a gate off of Old Page Mill Road. Search parties failed to locate Ms. Perlov that day, but in combing a rock quarry in the general area, deputies located the body of Mark Rosvold 24, victim of an apparent shotgun blast to his chest. A sawed-off shotgun was found in close proximity to the deceased man. Initially, there was some excitement among investigator's thinking that Rosvold might have kidnapped and killed Leslie Perlov, then remorsefully ended his own life. Subsequent follow-up revealed the dead man had a checkered past—primarily with drugs—was on probation for substance violations, and was suffering from chronic depression. Rosvold's parents confirmed that Mark was in an extremely depressed state when they last saw him.

Searchers on foot were still unable to locate any sign of Leslie Marie Perlov, so they called-in the Sheriff's Posse. This move paid-off, for on the next day, February 16th, the lifeless body of Leslie was located in a depression approximately 400-500 yards uphill from where her Nova was found. Absent overt trauma to her body, a Medical Examiner later opined that Ms. Perlov died of asphyxia. Lead Detective Sergeant Howard DeSart and his crack-investigative partner, Robert "Bob" Malone (R.I.P.) worked tirelessly on this case. Howard, was one of the best forensic evidence collection trainers in the S/O when he was my Patrol Supervisor. DeSart still reviews his notes and news clips of this haunting homicide to this day. Countless individuals were interviewed; hundreds of Stanford DPS photos and FI cards of suspicious persons, many of whom were—*one can short of a six-pack*—were re-interviewed. Persons of initial interest were eliminated from further suspicion, one by one. The apparent suicide victim, Rosvold was reconsidered, however, no link or evidence could be connected to Perlov's murder and his demise.

Despite years of frustration and untold hours of follow-up investigation, the killer(s) of Leslie Perlov have yet to be identified. Lt. DeSart, recalled that Ms. Perlov was planning a special birthday present for her Mother: Leslie met an artist who was able to render magnificent oil paintings from photographs. The detectives, DeSart and Malone, opined that Ms. Perlov wanted to take some photos of fields with flowers in bloom, so she chose this normally serene location above the Stanford campus. Shockingly, amidst the peace and tranquility of these foothills, lurked an evil predator, who apparently had an uncontrollable urge to kill an innocent and unsuspecting young woman. It was like a Puma pouncing on a grazing fawn, for Chrissakes! All Leslie wanted to do was to create a special birthday surprise for her beloved Mother! And, in an instant, her precious life was snuffed-out? What a shame. In the minds of the cops who worked tirelessly on this senseless homicide, what a *Crying Shame* that we haven't caught the bastard who did this!

David S. Levine: Was He Slaughtered by the Death Angels?

The ratty 1968 Chevy Impala came off eastbound I-280 and headed north on Page Mill Road. It's a miracle that the CHP hadn't stopped this hunk of junk as it sounded like a B-25, and spewed more smoke that a WWII escort destroyer in the North Atlantic. . . Being unfamiliar with the area, the driver had to rely on directional signs; the four young men were looking for the Stanford University campus. As they approached Junipero Serra Boulevard, the guy riding shotgun excitedly shouted: "Turn left bro, turn left!"

This outfit had no idea where they were actually going: They just wanted to find an area where students might be out and about, but at 12:20AM, that might be problematic, for as we all know, most Stanford students were fast asleep after a hard evening of hitting the books, right?

After many zig-zags and running into some dead ends, the group finally pulled up near the Green and Undergraduate (UGLY) libraries. Three men got out of their rattle trap and started walking toward UGLY. They were on a mission.

A husband and wife janitor team was sitting in their vehicle, apparently on a break, when they espied these three guys, furtively lurking around. According to the Detectives I interviewed for this story, the man noted the trio's presence and said to his spouse: "I wonder what those dudes are up to around here—especially at this time of night?" Well, the short answer to that excellent observation is: No Damn Good! For within a few minutes, and when out of sight of the janitors, the three self-styled *commandos* attacked an unsuspecting young male student with a K-Bar USMC trench knife, and stabbed him fifteen times. David S. Levine, a 20 year old physics student from Ithaca, New York, was dead before he hit the deck. The killers stealthily vanished from the scene as quickly as they had appeared.

An early morning jogger discovered Levine, dead on the walkway in front of Meyer Library on September 11, 1973 at about 0300 hours; he immediately called campus police, who secured and protected the crime scene. When S/O homicide detectives Howard DeSart and Robert Malone arrived, they found the poor kid laying face down in a huge pool of blood. According to Sgt. DeSart, there was virtually no physical evidence or clues which could point to who was responsible for this savage slaughter—at least at that stage in their investigation. Clearly, this type of frenzied attack conjured-up all sorts of bizarre possibilities as to who would be capable of committing such a horrible crime? Motive was a huge consideration: Why was this student targeted and stabbed so viciously? Robbery was quickly eliminated, for Levine's personal effects, wallet, watch, and some cash were intact. Many crazed killers seem to have a perverted fetish of taking a souvenir from their kill so they may re-live the event later on. This did not seem to be the case here.

Homicide investigators often find that perpetrators who inflict multiple stabbing or slashing wounds harbor deep seeded hatred for their victims—this type of brutality is mostly found in relationships gone bad or in sexually sadistic homicides. However, in David Levine's case, who could have possibly had an axe to grind with this low key individual—a serious student who was merely returning to his dorm after hours of laboring in the computer lab?

The Levine murder was similar in concept to a couple of other strange homicides that DeSart had investigated. On Super Bowl weekend, January 16, 1972, Kenneth Holden's remains were found at the base of Almaden Dam in South San Jose. The 21 year old San Jose State art student was last seen hitchhiking from his home in Mountain View. The victim's body was shredded by numerous deep hacking wounds to his head, shoulders and arms. Clearly, he was the victim of person(s) who had great animus toward him. Once again, Sgt. DeSart got the call. This turned out to be another *who dunnit*: There was *No, Nada* evidence which could finger the brutal bastards who butchered this kid! During the post mortem examination conducted by Dr. John Hauser, Det. DeSart had the gruesome task of collecting tissue from underneath the deceased's fingernails. The detective recalled that it took the good doctor over an hour to count the chop wounds—twenty-three all told! The coroner had to use two anatomy sheets in order to accurately record the deep gashes in Holden's head! The people who slaughtered this kid meant business.

In addition to Keith Holden, DeSart investigated a somewhat similar crime in the early 1970s: The battered body of a young white male, Daniel Gruenberg, of San Carlos, CA was found at Stevens Creek Dam in Cupertino. Unlike the other victims of these senseless murders, Gruenberg had been bashed in the head with a blunt object, believed to be a 2X4; like the other killings, the kid had sustained brutal, repeated blows, reminiscent of the ferocity of a crazed assailant(s). Again, no physical evidence was found. Subsequent inquiry revealed that, like Keith Holden, Daniel Gruenberg had also been hitchhiking.

In May 1984, San Francisco Mayor Joseph Alioto announced that his homicide inspectors had arrested, charged, and identified seven Black Muslims as the "Death Angels" aka "The Zebra Killers." The Mayor proudly proclaimed that these men were responsible for at least 73 killings statewide. Included in that group was 17 year old

Jose Vallaroman of Pacifica, the coastal city in San Mateo County. Jose's body was discovered August 4, 1973 on Guadalupe Canyon Parkway on San Bruno Mountain. Detective Sergeant Brendan McGuire, who later became one of the best Sheriffs in our region, revealed that the young Vallaroman had been shot six times in his body and once in his head—perhaps the *coup de grace*—with a .32 caliber semi-automatic pistol. The victim still had his wallet with $33 in it; McGuire added that San Francisco inspectors maintained this was a clear indication the Death Angels were the perps, as they were forbidden by their demented code to rob their victims. The bullet's lands and grooves were a perfect match with the projectiles found in the bodies of other Zebra victims in the City. With the close proximity of the San Mateo homicide to Stanford's Levine murder, some sleuths attempted to link these killings, as well as the Holden massacre in south San Jose, to the Death Angels.

However, absent provable forensic and/or eyewitness corroborative evidence, Sergeant DeSart was initially skeptical that the Zebras were responsible for Levine and Holden's demise. Moreover, linking the entire 73 kills to this maniacal sect, DeSart opined, was a bit of a stretch.

In a well researched book entitled Zebra, written by Clark Howard, the author learned that in a six month period between 1973 and 1974, the Death Angels murdered 14 people and seriously wounded 7 others. Most of the unfortunates were shot with a .32 semi-auto pistol; the spent casings at the crime scenes spoke volumes. However, in the Angels' first known and perhaps one of their most savage attacks, the killers used a machete; they kidnapped a young married couple who was taking an after dinner stroll. Incidentally, these low-lifes, were always nattily attired and well groomed, sporting close cropped hair styles, thus didn't appear to be menacing at first glance.

The Death Angels' victims were male, female, young and old. The only common denominator was that all of their marks were *WHITE!*

San Francisco authorities held their cards very close to their vests and initially refused to give allied agency detectives any information on how they broke the Zebra murders. DeSart and Malone had, over the years, developed pretty good rapport with two SF's homicide detectives; the SF guys later admitted that a snitch had blown the Zebra plot wide open, but refused our investigators access to the informant so the Levine and Holden cases could be examined further—if indeed, the Angels were responsible for their deaths. Clearly, SFPD was babysitting their Angels' insider: This cat was deep underground—so to speak—under heavy police guard, so he wouldn't be bumped-off before the trial.

Money Talks. . .

And, BS walks, as the saying goes. Rewards offered for information leading to the arrest and conviction of evildoers, in my experience, is often spotty: Stanford University offered a $50,000 sum for the killer of Arlis Perry, but that incentive fell on deaf ears. An author named Maury Terry, in his book, The Ultimate Evil, espoused a theory that the "Son of Sam" killer, David Berkowitz, actually ordered the murder of Arlis from his New York prison cell: Terry believed that the Carr family, who owned the dog, Sam, who Berkowitz said directed him to brutally execute several innocents in New York, were complicit in the Memorial Church murder. One of the Carr brothers, John, was an airman stationed at Minot AFB, North Dakota, where Arlis and her husband Bruce came from. Arlis was very religious and supposedly worked in church groups who spoke-out against "Devil-Worship," which was rumored to have been going on in ND. As bizarre as we investigators thought this theory was, S/O Detectives Kenny Kahn and Tom Beck visited Berkowitz in prison and offered him the reward in exchange for the killer(s). The Son of Sam refused to cooperate in any way.

However, in the case of the Zebra Killers, SFPD's 30K in live bait was way too irresistible for Death Angel insider, Anthony Harris. Harris worked at the Black Self Help Moving and Storage Company on Market Street in San Francisco, making peanuts while trying to put food on the table for his wife and child. Thirty thousand bucks would buy a helluva lot of goods 'n stuff in his mind, so he reached-out via AT&T and told the cops he wanted to chat. While at SFPD's Dick Bureau, chatting turned out to be more like a canary's serenade. Anthony Harris laid-out the Death Angels' entire blueprint for murder on the table: This evil Black Muslim sect categorized whites as an inferior race created by a diabolic scientist called *Yacub*. Killing the "blue-eyed" devils or "grafted snakes" (the Angels' "N" word for Caucasians) would secure the participants a reserved seat in heaven! As Harris continued his diatribe, the detectives were all ears: When the informant recited a blow-by-blow account of the unimaginable murder of a sacrificial lamb, who the Angels had kidnapped from Ghirardelli Square, the cops knew they had the real deal, as this horrendous slaying had never been in the newspapers! Harris recounted that the group brought the unsuspecting man to the Black Self Help facility, stripped-off his clothes, trussed him to a column, and took turns dissecting and chopping up their captive with a knife, meat clever and machete. When these ghouls were done with their butchery, they scooped-up the remnants and dumped it in Baghdad (*by the*) Bay—an eerie interment site and akin to what happened to thousands of innocents 30 years later in the Iraq city of the same name: Saddam's hackers were a world away but the net result was identical and fueled by incomprehensible hatred!

After Harris provided homicide detectives with the names, ranks and horsepower of the Death Angels, arrest and search warrants were obtained. An army of over 100 cops quickly descended on an apartment in the Black Self Help building before first light and rounded-up the suspected killers. In the final analysis, only four of the gangsters were tried—three got off the hook for a lack of evidence. The trial went on for over a year, but the jury deliberated for just 18 hours and found J.C. X. Simon, Manuel Moore, Anthony Harris and Larry Green guilty of first-degree murder and conspiracy to commit first-degree murder; these heartless and brutal killers were all sentenced to life in prison. Larry Green, the monster who attempted to behead Quita Hague with the machete, merely laughed when his sentence was pronounced by Superior Court Judge Joseph Karesh. Two other killers, Leroy Doctor and Jessie Lee Cooks were also sent to prison. Doctor pled guilty to assault with a deadly weapon for trying to kill a PG&E (Pacific Gas & Electric) worker,

Robert Stoeckmann, who promptly turned the tables on this punk: The well-dressed would-be assassin, Leroy, approached Robert and asked for some directions. Suddenly, and without warning, Doctor fired a shot into the workman's neck. Stoeckmann wrestled the gun away and gave Leroy some of his own medicine! Police found the wounded "Angel" cowering under a railroad trestle with bullets in his arm, shoulder and gut. Ol' Leroy then had the audacity to tell the cops that Robert *was* the shooter!

Our other *hero*, Jessie Lee Cooks, tried to flag down Frances Rose at the UC Berkeley extension gate, but she thought something was up and stepped on the gas. Sadly, Cooks opened her passenger door and sprayed the interior with gunfire, hitting and killing the terrified woman. Cooks pled-out to that murder before the trial, and received a well deserved life sentence. So far, and after numerous appeals and appearances before the Parole Board, all of the Death Angels still languish behind bars!

The Bottom Line

Did the Zebra/Death Angels slaughter Stanford student David Levine? The jury is still out on that one, but given history and mission of this demonic cult, I would bet on it! Try as they might, Detectives DeSart and Malone could not get the janitors who saw the three assassins to even peek at a photo spread—they were simply scared straight. Our S/O's detectives later discovered from SF inspectors that informant Anthony Harris admitted that he and some cult members came to Stanford one night. Harris was most likely the individual who remained in the old '68 Impala while his cohorts stabbed Levine. SFPD refused to allow DeSart and Malone to interview the snitch, as they did not want to jeopardize their multiple murder cases. So, absent physical evidence and/or eyeball witnesses, our detectives were simply hamstrung! The same held for Keith Holden: The manner in which this person was hacked to death with a machete, I opine, was a harbinger of things to come in the City by the Bay. It might have been a "dress rehearsal" for the massacre of Robert and Quita Hague, which was the Angels debut in the City. But, the only people who know for sure are the maniacs who committed these crimes against humanity, and they "ain't talkin"...

Janet Ann Taylor

Ms. Taylor, 21, was also a Stanford alumnus. Her father was the very well liked Athletic Director, Charles "Chuck" Taylor. Janet had visited some friends in the faculty residential area, and was last seen hitchhiking on Junipero Serra Boulevard and Mayfied Avenue, near Lake Lagunita. Her body was found dumped in a ditch on March 25, 1974, off of Sand Hill Road, in San Mateo County. Like Ms. Leslie Perlov, Ms. Taylor had been strangled. Initial reports by the media alleged that the young lady *had not* been sexually violated; however, San Mateo Sheriff's investigators indicated that they have evidence which will not be disclosed until the killer is found. Santa Clara and San Mateo County homicide detectives conclude that there is clearly a link between these two murders.

Math Mayhem

The shrill of my whistle pierced the air!

"OK Falcons 'round the little red house; you guys on the 'Elephant Squad,' lap the field and no 'lollygagging.'"

My charges hopped to it, but those kids on the E-Squad were less than enthused: The little red house was about a ¼ mile round trip but the entire field was at least twice that distance. For once in my life, I was truly in charge: Head Coach of the Campbell Falcons Pee Wee full contact football team, under the auspices of the San Jose Police Activity League (PAL). When I hollered, those 9-10 year olds listened... The league had strict weight limits for each class: The Pee Wees had to be between 90 and 110 pounds, which was verified before every game. If a player tipped the Toledos, he was benched.

I vividly recall last year's regional championship game, where our star player—without whom we could have never won—came in 3 pounds over the limit 2 hours before kick-off! Running with a rubber sweatsuit, constantly perspiring, he only shed a mere pound.

Plus, the kid was exhausted. I remembered an old trick I read about in a wrestling book: Believe it or not, human hair is very oily and relatively heavy. This kid had a huge mop of hair, which he was very proud of, so getting him to agree to be "buzzed" would be a daunting challenge for this coach. Nonetheless, I met with Tommy one-on-one and proposed the unthinkable—in his mind for sure. . . At first he vehemently refused, but when I told him that the entire team was depending on him, not only as their leader, but as our star athlete, he reluctantly agreed. I rushed him to our home and my wife sheared him so close that his head was close to bleeding! We made it back to the locker room in record time, and Tom slowly stepped on the scale. The team and coaches held our breaths as the pointer hit the top bar, bounced back and forth, then ever so slightly, dropped just a hair so that about .002 clearance was evident. The roar from our team was deafening.

With the score tied 6-6 and only 2 minutes left in regulation play, our Head Coach pulled out the "hook and lateral" play from his bag of tricks, and Tommy was off to the races. We had just won the Northern California State Championship. At our awards banquet, I gave our hero a carefully gift wrapped box: Everyone howled when they discovered Tommy's shorn locks in there.

As I was looking at my clipboard for the next set of drills on the schedule, I saw my wife running toward me; she seemed upset.

"What's up, honey?" I anxiously asked.

"Communications called and they need you at Stanford right away; someone's been killed," she nervously said.

I sprinted to my old station wagon—the guys at the department called it "The Lebanese Tank" due to its OD (military green) paint and age, I suppose—and grabbed my police radio:

"Radio, 26-A3, 10-86?"

"Affirmative, A-3. We have a 10-55 in a Math Department office," Radio returned.

"Confirm a 10-55 and not a 10-56," I quipped.

"A-3, that would be affirmative; possible 187. The S/O and Coroner have been advised and are en route."

"Check. I'm en route from West San Jose. Confirm the crime scene is secure and that no one has been allowed into the office?" I barked.

"Q-7, did you copy 26-A-3s traffic re: the crime scene?" Communications differed.

"That's a 10-4, Q-7. The only person who has been into the office is the janitor who found the 10-55 and me," the deputy explained.

"Good, Q-7. Make sure the janitor remains on the scene until the homicide detectives arrive, and you make comprehensive notes on what you did, saw, heard and exactly where you walked, OK?" I ordered. *I damn sure didn't want a repeat performance of the Mem Chu murder wherein that idiot CSO who found Arlis took off before the homicide detectives arrived on the scene,* my memory sizzled.

"10-4, A-3, already done and we have the R/P here and he's not going anywhere!" the young officer replied.

Great, I thought, *these new kids heard my diatribe a million times about the Mem Chu debacle and it's finally sinking in.* I was proud!

I arrived about the same time as Assistant County Medical Examiner, Dr. Richard Mason. I was pleased that out guys had the area sealed like a tomb. I greeted the good doctor:

"Dr. Mason, I'm Captain Niemeyer of the Stanford DPS; you remember me?"

"Of course, Captain. You assisted me in that Cupertino murder where the low-life shot that store clerk in the face with a shotgun," Mason recalled.

"Yeah, Doc, that was a bad one; as I remember, there was something wrong with the trigger of that sawed-off 12 gauge express gun, so both barrels went off simultaneously?" I remarked.

"You're exactly right, sir. The robber said that it went-off accidentally while he was swinging it. As you remember, we tried that, but the only way it would fire was when the trigger was pulled; we sent that kid to prison for a long time; senseless killing for a measly few hundred bucks," the ME added.

"So, what do we have here?" the Coroner queried.

"Well it's not a suicide! Actually, I don't really know as I have been waiting for you before going in there."

The door to the professor's office was closed; there was a type written note taped to the door; it read: "No office hours today—family emergency."

Dr. Mason and I were horrified when we entered mathematics Professor Karel deLeeuw's office: He was seated behind a gigantic desk, leaning back in his chair against the wall. A green heavy duty garbage bag covered his head and upper torso. Despite the shroud, the Doc and I could plainly see that something really bad had happened to this man. There was a 3-4 foot fan of blood and brain matter spattered on the wall. *Man*, I thought, *the poor professor must have been blasted with the likes of that sawed-off the Doctor and I had just discussed.*

Per protocol—CA law mandates that the only official authorized to touch a deceased person is the Coroner—Dr. Mason removed the trash bag; I gulped; the man's face was barely recognizable: The were at least 4 large deep penetrating wounds on Dr. deLeeuw's face and head. It was plain to see that major impact caused the back of the victim's cranium to rupture! Ugly scene; very ugly!

"So, Captain, what do you think caused this?" the doctor asked.

"Boy, I don't know for sure; never seen anything like this. Maybe a very large caliber firearm—looks to be at least a .45 or even .50 cal," I guessed.

"Yes, this *is* a strange one; I'll just have to see more once I get him on the table," Mason offered.

About that time, the S/O homicide detectives arrived; they were briefed and I headed for my office to put my observations to paper.

August 18, 1978 at 1900: As I wrote my supplemental report, my thoughts couldn't help cringing: *Damn. Don't tell me that we are going to have yet another "who dunnit" in the annals of Stanford murders?* The evidence technicians were on the scene, but I heard from our officers that their results were less than remarkable. Not even a latent print on the note that the killer obviously taped to the professor's door was found; he must have worn gloves, I guessed. I dejectedly went home.

I had just watched coverage of Professor deLeeuw's murder on KTVU Fox Channel 2, when the phone rang. *Oh, don't tell me,* I panicked—*"Pa-leeeze,"don't tell me they found more victims. . .* (I pluralized my thought—knowing my luck!)

"Hello," I quietly answered.

"Captain, this is Q-7 (Deputy Harris Kuhn of CPR fame). Are you sitting down?"

"As a matter of fact, Harris, I am. So, how many more bodies do we have?"

"No Sir, not at all. The dude who killed the professor just turned himself in at North County Jail; he even brought a bag that contained a ton of evidence—even the bloody hammer!" Harris blurted.

"A hammer? What kind of hammer? The ME and I both figured it was a really big bore gun!" I rejoined.

"I heard that it was some kind of a sledge hammer—the kind they use for driving railroad spikes," Q-7 advised.

"Hmmm, no wonder those holes in his head were so deep—poor guy. So, who is this killer and what was the motive?"

"All I know is that his name is Ted Streleski; he was supposedly a graduate student, but why he targeted Professor deLeeuw is only a guess right now," Harris replied. "Oh, and by the way, I already advised A-1 and he is very relieved," he added.

"OK, Harris, thanks for the heads-up. I'll see ya tomorrow. Bye."

Wow, can you imagine that? Some things never cease to amaze me, I thought.

Over the next few days, this entire scenario began to unfold: Theodore Streleski, 42 years old at the time, had been a perennial Stanford grad student for 19 years while trying to earn his PhD in mathematics. Although he was a bright guy, he just couldn't seem to put his thesis to paper, I was told. In addition, Streleski was the classic "odd-ball:" At 6'4" and over 200 pounds, with thick shoulder length hair—often held in place with a Native American type head band—and a jet black flowing beard, Ted looked like a "Hells Angel." He presented himself as a disheveled, unkempt homeless guy—a major turn-off for most of the faculty and students. However, instead of motorcycle/engineer boots, Theodore sported a pair of scuffed-up wing-tip shoes, which obviously had never been polished. Streleski later commented that Professor deLeeuw, who had briefly been Ted's advisor more than 10 years before, had made an off-hand remark about his shoes, which ridiculed him in front of other students. Of course, had the good Professor known that Streleski was a head case, I'm sure he never would have made fun of him in any way, as nuts never let stuff like that go. Indeed. . .

After nearly two decades of frustration—self induced, most think, due to his inability to measure up to the high bar set for doctoral candidates of the Mathematics Department's demanding curricula—I think that Streleski snapped. Theodore Streleski blamed everyone but himself for his ineptitude, and hatched a savage, revengeful plan: He would simply "off" the impediments in his path. From his apartment in San Francisco, he created a hit list of Math department faculty members he thought should be eliminated. Virtually no one who had ever been involved with Streleski's program was excluded. He typed the "out of the office" signs and began to assemble a hit-man's bag: Ted went to a local hardware store and purchased a 3 pound railroad spike sledge hammer, a box of heavy-duty trash bags, duct tape, and gloves. He was all set. However, when H-hour arrived on August 18th, much to Theodore's surprise and chagrin, all of the professors and department heads on the top of his list were not there—except for the dedicated and beloved Professor Karel deLeeuw, whom Streleski hadn't been in contact with for over a decade! Sadly, deLeeuw became the killer's back-up target—just because he was there!

One can only imagine the surprise in the distinguished professor's mind when he set eyes on the hulking, disheveled figure filling his doorway. From what I ascertained from other faculty and friends, the affable deLeeuw probably greeted Ted warmly and invited him to sit down. Although it will never be known what sort of conversation might have taken place, if at all—unless Streleski writes a "tell all book"—but at some point, the monster attacked the unsuspecting educator with a barrage of heavy-handed blows with that deadly hammer. Dr. Mason believed that the professor was dead almost immediately. Whether the assassin's covering of his victim's head with the garbage bag was symbolic, or just a gesture of decency, we'll never know. But, judging from statements made to the press years later, there didn't seem to be much remorse in this maniac!

When he turned himself in to jail authorities in Palo Alto, Streleski merely said:

"I think you've been looking for me! Oh, and I think you might be needing these, too," as he handed the deputy a flight bag which contained the tools of his trade.

During his trial, shrinks for the defense argued Mr. Streleski was a paranoid psychotic at the time of the murder, thus suffered from diminished capacity. A jury found him guilty of second degree murder and sentenced him to a paltry eight years in the Correctional Medical Facility at Vacaville. Why "The Hammer," as he was dubbed, wasn't convicted of first-degree murder is beyond all comprehension: The killer had the presence of mind to plan his mission, obtain the implements needed to accomplish the task, then type note cards so that he either wouldn't be disturbed while carrying out the execution(s), and/or the victim(s) wouldn't be found for some period of time, thereby allowing him to escape—these elements certainly showed malice aforethought to me. . .

Moreover, the incredibly light sentence for committing such a horrific crime never made sense to any thinking human being in California, so the CA legislature finally got off their collective duffs and enacted new sentencing guidelines (up to 15 years) albeit a day late and a dollar short. Because the new sentencing mandate was passed after Prof. deLeeuw's murder, with credit for good behavior, Streleski would be back on the streets in 7 years or less.

The big issue on campus was how were we going to keep this predator off University property? Those faculty members who were on Theodore's hit-list were certainly upset, and rightly so, especially as that joker's parole hearings approached. Streleski poured a ton of coal into the boiler by making some well calculated and ominous statements just prior to his release date: Daily Senior staff writer Charlie Goffen (September 23, 1985) wrote an excellent article about this debacle entitled:

Freed Killer Draws Interest, Fear.

"Streleski said that his crime, and the media attention it received, succeeded in publicizing the plight of graduate students who have been treated unfairly at Stanford."

Here are some of the *outrageous quotes* the remorseless low-life made (Author's comment):

"I judged correctly that the notoriety would bring press coverage," he said. "People may make a value judgment about me, or the validity of my judgment, but still I think I'm getting some message out there. So it worked to that extent."

Streleski said that expressing remorse would undermine his cause.

"If I committed a murder to criticize Stanford, if I express remorse, I just throw my whole argument in the wastebasket," he said. "I feel regret. Not remorse. Regret as I see the tragic impact on people. I'm sorry. But if I had to do it all over again, I'd do it the same way."

Needless to say, the Chief and I spent many sessions with the Math faculty in an attempt to allay their fears. The only thing we had on our side was time: "The Hammer" refused to be governed by the conditions of parole, so he elected to remain behind bars until his sentence was completely satisfied. In the interim, Stanford's Legal Office was hard at work lobbying for legislation that would prohibit convicted felons from ever returning to the scene of the crime, although the CA Penal Code already empowered peace officers to arrest an unwanted "guest" if the person in charge gave law enforcement the green light. Stanford University President Donald Kennedy already threw that switch. . . Nonetheless, Ol' Teddy kept up his menacing diatribe by saying that he "probably" wouldn't come on campus, but if he changed his mind, he would make a public notice. In a glib moment, I recall telling the media that if Streleski set foot on our turf, I already had a special pair of "bracelets" with his name engraved on them. . .

Well, as it turned out, Senate Bill 677 passed with flying colors, so the merciless loser knew that we weren't fooling around. When that dirt-bag was released, the TV and print media were all over it like he was a celebrity rock-star! Despicable! I had a couple of under-covers on his tail, and he ultimately ended up in San

Francisco. Streleski was no dummy: He earned a BA in engineering physics from the University of Illinois, and planned to find a job in the electronics field in the City. He also took the civil service exam for a San Francisco *Muni* bus/rail driver, and according to reports, achieved the highest score in the history of that governmental entity. But, the big question was: If you were in Human Resources would you hire this hand grenade? Apparently not, for last I heard he was flipping burgers in some half-way house kitchen, in one of the less desirable sections of Baghdad by the Bay. Great job match! And, good riddance, Teddy!

The Ten Fifty-Six Syndrome—Again

It was April 25, 1981 at approximately 10:30PM when loud explosions rattled the windows of Faculty Ghetto homes on Pine Hill Road. The roar of a powerful engine and screeching of tires awoke the sleepy neighborhood. Most residents figured it was probably some frat boys just messing around and thought the reports were back fires. However, when a curious homeowner peered out his window, he saw what appeared to a human form sprawled on the roadway. Radio had received numerous calls about the pops, but when they received information from a resident about a possible body on the street, that changed the equation.

"Attention all Stanford and Palo Alto units, we have a report of possible gunshot and a body on Pine Hill just off Bowdoin; Units to respond?"

Total radio chaos ensued with every unit in the area "stepping on each other's" transmissions. Palo Alto Communications advised that Fire was responding from Station 6. They also broadcast that the suspect vehicle was believed to be traveling westbound, presumably into the residential maze—a system of circuitous winding streets, some coming to dead ends. At night, that area is like being in a black hole. Even our experienced officers often became turned around in that neighborhood. One alert PAPD Supervisor ordered his units to take up perimeter posts: Good move as perhaps one of the cops might espy the fleeing vehicle coming out the back door.

Deputy Mike "Da Shadow" Seamons sped to the scene and found the victim laying on the roadway with steam pouring from the massive impact wound to the back of his head; brain matter was splattered all over the street. Seamons surmised the victim was shot with a shotgun as he turned away from the vehicle, theorizing that the shooter fired from inside the car, thus explaining the upward trajectory.

Suddenly, a relatively green Stanford newbie keyed his mic and announced: "Code 4; 10-56!"

Somewhat stunned, Deputy Seamons looked at an equally shocked Fire Captain Patrick Cady and said: "Boy, this is the 'damndest' suicide I've ever seen. Where in the hell is the gun?"

"Maybe the guy (victim) threw it over the fence," Captain Cady quipped.

This faux pas was like receiving a phone call during torrid sex: All of the Paly units pulled their officers off the perimeter posts and resumed patrol. The shooter and company got away. Much like the Mem Chu murder, when the first responder rookie officers thought that the brutal slaying of Arlis Perry was a suicide, it seemed that the rookies in our fledgling department still had a mind-set that any dead body *must* be a suicide. After all, how many murders happened on our tranquil university campus? It took the Arlis murder and this case, plus years of training and experience to convince our deputies to treat ALL dead persons as a homicide until proven otherwise! Like my daughter's surgery professor, Dr. Michael Lodish, always *professed*: "Professors!—he called all the residents 'professors'— Remember, it's CANCER until proven otherwise!" Indeed.

The very capable Detective Sergeant Tom Beck was the lead in this murder investigation and acquired a snitch who was a member of the gang responsible for this murder. The deceased man was Horace McNair, 35, a serious "crack-head." His sister was the famed songstress of the time, Barbara McNair. Horace had a long history of petty crimes—mostly drug offenses. While out on furlough from the San Francisco County Jail, he was commissioned by some fellow dopers to score some crack for them. After receiving a sum of money, Horace bought some stuff, but instead of giving it to the folks who bank-rolled the deal, McNair stiffed them and used the drugs for his own euphoric enjoyment.

Double-crossing dopers certainly isn't a very wise or healthy thing to do. Bent on revenge, this crew set out to find the "dude who did them." In addition to not being too bright, Ol' Horace wasn't very difficult to find; after cruising around all of the usual hang-outs, they spotted their man strutting his stuff on the streets of San Francisco. These dopers invited McNair into their ride at the point of a sawed-off, side by side, 12 gauge scatter gun. The stiffed bunch wanted their dope, period! And, under no uncertain terms! A very nervous McNair told his unhappy friends that he knew where he could score some—at Stanford University, of all places...

Why Stanford you ask? Well, there was an entrepreneurial young man who was a prolific procurer and distributor of illicit substances in our region. This dealer was also the son of a well respected professor. The kid's dubious reputation apparently had spread throughout the Bay Area. Once on Pine Hill Road, Horace went up to the residence in question, knocked on the door and after receiving no answer returned to the car. Horace might have told the outfit that no one answered, but was directed to try again. So when he turned, the guy with the shotgun figured that they were being scammed again, so he nearly blew Horace's head clean off. During their frantic escape, these morons got lost and drove around the neighborhood for some period of time before finally finding their way off campus. But, not for the errant "Code-4; 10-56," the killers might have been nabbed. But who knows? The S/O's snitch IDed the shooter but there was no physical or direct evidence to prosecute the killer. Pity, but that's the way it goes a lot of the time in police work.

Angela Dee Arvidson:

Angela was found stabbed and nearly decapitated October 22, 1982 in a professor's home. This was one of the saddest and gory murders I had ever seen in my 18 year career. It was also one of the most gratifying cases that I had ever been part of. Read all about it in **Chapter 31.**

An Investigator's Dream

Imagine this: A shoots B in the head; B dies instantly. A flags down a cop, hands him the smoking gun and exclaims: I just shot my husband; he's in his truck over there—about 20 yards away. And, there are scores of eye-ball witnesses who saw it all happen! This only happens in the movies, right? However, every once in awhile stuff like this actually occurs:

I was just heading out the door for a luncheon meeting when I heard a G-Unit (CSO), scream over the Radio:

"Radio, send a police unit right away to Plant Services!!"

"G-unit what is the nature?"

"A woman just handed me a gun; she said she just shot her husband and he's in his truck in the Corp Yard—Hurry!"

"All units, Code 33, Code 33—a G-units reports a shooting, and he has the weapon and suspect in custody in the Corp Yard—Units to respond?"

The airways sound like a swarm of African Killer Bees. . . . Bzzzzzzzzzzzzzzzzz.

Finally, Sgt. Rick Enberg broke through the swarm and advised he had the suspect and gun in custody, and requested a unit for transportation to the Annex.

Another swarm erupts, so I eschewed my handi-talkie and drove over to the scene, which is just a stone's thrown away from the Office. When I arrived, the ever efficient Sgt. Enberg was having his team tape off and secure the crime scene area. About 20 Corp Yard employees, who were on their way to lunch, were milling around like a herd of cattle.

"So what's up Rick?" I query.

"Check-it-out, Cap—right through the eyeball!" he ghoulishly replied.

I walked over to the Plant Services pick-up and sure enough, dead center in his left eye. The round entered at an angle just below his glasses, which were askew on his forehead. The man never saw it coming!

Due to all of the extraneous air traffic, even after Communications had declared an emergency and admonished folks to hold their traffic, no one had an opportunity to declare that this was a 187, and that we needed the S/O Homicide team. And, that was a good thing as the number of media snoops might be less, so I went to the phone and handled all of the details via land line—so much better.

In less than two hours—which has got to be an S/O murder investigation record—the crime scene was cleared: The suspect, after providing detectives with a comprehensive, recorded confession, was en route to WDF (Elmwood Women's Detention Facility); the deceased was on his way to the ME, and reports were in the box. It seems that the Mrs. took issue with her ex-hubby's girlfriend, and ended the dispute with an early 1900s model Smith & Wesson .38 caliber 5 shot *Tip-Up* revolver. Only at Stanford...

Frozen Solid: The Arlis Perry Murder Investigation

It seems like only yesterday since I zoomed-up to Mem Chu in the early AM, October 13, 1974 and viewed the humiliated, deceased body of a lovely 19 year old young woman named Arlis Perry. But, alas, it's been nearly 39 years since we embarked on a crusade to find the cruel bastard who committed that crime, and to bring him to justice. It isn't as if "we" didn't try—and there have been many of us, mostly old retired cops—but that heartless individual simply didn't materialize—or at least, we didn't perceive him. As in most unsolved homicides, the investigators almost always have known of the culprit, investigated and perhaps even interviewed the suspect; but, in our case, we could never put a finger on the actual killer.

I talked about many of the theories and inquiries of that period in Chapter One. But, I would like to tell you about some of the "behind the scene leads" that were pursued—all of which ultimately ran smack-dab into brick walls.

Ted Bundy

Aside from the usual suspects—and there were hundreds of them who were interrogated, photographed and fingerprinted—celebrated serial killer, Theodore Robert "Ted" Bundy appeared on the radar screen in August 1975 after a Utah Highway patrolman arrested him for failure to yield when the officer initiated a car stop. Bundy was driving a beat-up 1968 VW Bug, which curiously was missing the right front seat. The cops thought that was odd, but even stranger yet were items found in the car: Burglars often assemble "Burglar Bags," consisting of gloves, tools, flashlights, and maybe, as is the case of the "Jogging Burglar," a rappelling rope. Well, Bundy's bag had all of the above, (save for the rappelling gear) and more! His kit sported hand cuffs, industrial cable ties, disguises, duct tape, and the items which really sparked my interest were a phony cop's badge AND, an ice pick! But not for a TV program which displayed Bundy's Bag, I would never have known this. Once again, I was on the phone talking with the lead Investigators on the Perry case, and was reminded that Theodore was in custody when Arlis was slaughtered. Nonetheless, many amateur crime sleuths continue to believe that Bundy was responsible. He's in Hades now so we'll never know for sure...

Sadly, the brutal murder of Arlis Perry remains unsolved and has gotten colder than Memorial Church was on October 13, 1974 when she was discovered in the early AM. After incalculable hours by the original S/O detectives during the first decade following her death, no suspect has ever been linked to, what undoubtedly is, the most heinous crime ever committed at Stanford University. In the early 2000s "Cold Case" Investigators and a Deputy DA resurrected the file and re-interviewed most of the original detectives (yours truly included), but their efforts went nowhere. A couple members of this team were fixated and convinced that the CSO who found Arlis, Stephen "Crawdad" committed the murder. All of us "dinosaurs," who worked this murder from day one insisted that although Steve was a weirdo, he was way too wimpy to perpetrate this horrendous crime. Well, after several years of being hounded for a DNA sample, their POI finally relented, gave up a saliva sample and was cleared. So, Arlis Perry's vicious killer remains a nameless individual— either incarcerated somewhere or dead and buried. I can't believe that anyone capable of engineering such a horrific event was a novice and would never strike again. . . Someone, somewhere, knows who killed Arlis and should do the right thing by calling the Santa Clara County Sheriff's Office (408)808-4900.

Finis

This concludes another difficult chapter for me in this book. No sane, civilized person would like to be in the midst of the ultimate crime perpetrated on a human being—least of all the cops who have to investigate these horrendous events. And for me, the more carnage I saw, the more I hated it! But, that's what we signed on for when we took the oath.

CHAPTER NINE

The Delts

Animal House

Sitting high on a hill, overlooking the campus, 650 San Juan Road was the residence of the Delta Tau Delta fraternity—affectionately known as "The Delts"—but, we called it "The Animal House." Although similar to the pad made famous in the movie of the same name, the guys in Stanford's frat, in all honesty, weren't that bad: A little wild on weekends, perhaps, with their raucous parties; however, they mainly stuck to themselves, didn't do a lot of mischief and generally obeyed the law. Their athletic careers depended on it. Being selected to attend one of the most prestigious universities on the planet is reason enough to be ecstatic; but, coupled with a full-ride scholarship to be a student-athlete was clearly a plum that every prospective student dreams about. It was probably for this reason that most of the guys minded their Ps and Qs, for losing a scholarship would be a death knell. But then, alcohol often clouds one's ability to make good choices. . .

The majority of these young men were recruited for one or more of Stanford's varsity teams, and to the man, most were large—in some cases, *very large*—and downright intimidating. The DPS' fledgling troops cringed whenever dispatched to calls at 650 San Juan. The fear of getting their deputized posteriors re-arranged was paramount, especially when Delta Tau Delta members were under the influence of untold volumes of alcohol and simply didn't want to go along with the program. The ignition source was always there, especially during those infamous parties; all that was needed was a spark, which could erupt in a nasty conflagration. And indeed, there were calls—lots of them—but diplomacy and cooler heads usually prevailed.

Like realtors profess—location, location, location: This situation was all about location and Delta Tau Delta's residence was simply in the wrong location! The house was right smack-dab in the middle of the "Old Faculty Ghetto." The homeowners there, mostly long time tenured professors, didn't much appreciate the ear-splitting music, masculine chants and cheers—they did a lot of competitive games in that domicile and cars roared in and out of there until the wee hours of the morning.

Another thorn in the side of the Delts was the presence of the Synergy House, right across the way. The Delts were snitched-off by their Synergy neighbors all the time—usually via anonymous, bogus 9-1-1 calls alleging fights, rapes, mayhem and the like. The Synergy dwellers were, as their house name implies, more socially sensitive? They regarded the unruly mob across the path as merely a wild bunch of pumped-up muscle-heads—devoid of any social graces or awareness. To the Delts, the Synergy folks were Marxist earthy tree huggers—the Birkenstock, granola and *Kum-Ba-Yah* crowd. Needless to say, there was no love lost between these factions. I often feared a Hatfields & McCoys type feud, although I doubted that any fray would have lasted very long—And, I would have put my money on the guys at 650 San Juan!

Shortly after the DPS began to function autonomously, the dog-watch got a call of a 415 party: loud music and B&P violations (minors drinking alcohol) at 650 San Juan. The entire force—two deputies—was responding and the Sergeant was en route from the station. When the first responder drove into the area, he could clearly hear the *music*—and I use the term loosely—reverberating all the way down to Mayfield and Dolores streets, over two blocks away. And, it was approximately 0200 hours. Upon reaching the house, there were cars and kids all over the place, but most started to scatter when they spotted the cop car prowling up the hill. The first deputy, although green, wasn't stupid, so he waited for his partner to arrive before approaching the pad. The door was wide open and they could see a crowd of young adults milling around inside—most with red cups in hand. The second deputy, an older fellow who had been around the block a time or two, took the point and beat on the door with his baton, announcing with authority: "Stanford Police, who's in charge here?"

Within a few seconds, the cops heard what sounded like a thunderous herd, but in reality it was a behemoth—a gargantuan creature bounding toward them. This giant humanoid was a 20 year old kid, all of 6'6" who easily tipped the *Toledos* at 295! He occupied the entire doorway and blocked out all light and sound from within. Clad only in shorts, his upper torso resembled a Michelangelo statue. With hands on hips, he bellowed:

"Whad Da F*** do YOU want?"

The lead deputy, who will from now on remain forever nameless, calmly inquired:

"Young man, are you a member of the Stanford football team?"

"Yeah, and Whad Da F*** is it to YOU?" the obviously inebriated/agitated youth growled. He then noticed the deputy staring at his legs and feet. "So, why ya looking at my legs like that? You got a foot fetish or something?" the athlete snarled.

"Nooo, I was just thinking that if you plan to continue your football career, it might be somewhat difficult if you suffered a freak accident, ah, like, ah, like getting your knees broken or something," the deputy replied, all the while smacking his 26 inch hard plastic baton into the palm of his gloved hand.

With that, the suddenly sober young gentleman stood erect and in a military-like voice snapped:

"Yes sir, and what is it you wanted me to do?"

The Fall

It was a typical Monday morning in the good Ol' SUDPS: A ton of reports from the weekend, in the aftermath of the Stanford vs. San Jose State football game. There were a million party ruckuses, a couple of fights, some drunk-in-public pinches, thefts and burglaries galore. There was also one very peculiar case: A supposed injury fall from an upstairs bedroom window at 650 San Juan. The female victim, a student, mysteriously fell out of bed through a window, and plummeted nearly 35 feet to the ground. She was found in a concrete entry way to a basement apartment, some four feet below ground level. The girl, although unconscious, was still alive when paramedics took her to the Stanford Hospital's E.R. When my detective called the E.R., he was informed that the young lady had been released and taken to Hoover Pavilion (The Old Palo Alto Hospital) for further evaluation. The Head Nurse advised that other than a few bumps and bruises, the victim was OK. When asked how could that possibly be, the nurse attributed the girl's good fortune to enhanced relaxation—the .21 blood alcohol level in her system—nearly three times above the legal driving limit—when she was tested at the E.R.! *Amazing,* I thought, and Detective Columbo (I dubbed him) and I headed out the door for Hoover Pavilion.

When Columbo and I visited the victim, we were both astonished at how well she looked, save for an obvious killer hangover, which she justly deserved for guzzling untold amounts of booze. When asked what happened, the student said that after partying (*hearty I surmised*), she made her way up to her boyfriend's room and got into bed, which was located up against the wall at the window. It had been a rather hot fall day, so the window was wide open. She said that she didn't remember a thing after that—until rudely awakened by the fall. She believed that she was pitched out of the window when her boyfriend got into bed. Boy, I wanted to check out this story, although I felt that the victim was being truthful with us. We then headed over to the Delt House.

When we arrived, we asked for the guy who lived in the room, where the female fell out. The house officer said that "Matt" was in class, and wouldn't be back until lunch—you could *always* find students at lunch time, especially these guys, who obviously *never* missed a meal. . . Although we didn't suspect any foul play, I wanted to err on the side of caution, so I asked if we could just look at the room. The extremely cooperative Delt led us to the room in question; I figured he wanted to be as forthcoming as possible so we wouldn't report the house to the University authorities—another beef was something they didn't need or want.

As we ascended the very steep stairs, I couldn't help wondering how in the world that woman ever made it up this flight, especially in her condition. Entering the room, we observed the bed, just as described, right up against the window, which was still open. When I pushed down on the bedspread, it was suddenly up to my elbow.

"No wonder," I exclaimed, "It's a damn waterbed!" About that time, I suddenly thought the San Andreas Fault was acting up again—at least a 4.8 on the Richter scale. No, it was just one of the Delts running up the stairs. . . And, as luck would have it, it was our boy, Matt, the victim's bunkmate. He was about the same size as the guy I described in the last story—*maybe they were brothers,* I thought. When asked what had happened with his girlfriend, the somewhat nervous kid related essentially the same story as she. He then spontaneously demonstrated how he plopped his enormous frame into the sack; immediately, it became plainly and painfully obvious what had occurred: The diminutive coed was passed-out cold on this waterbed, and when this 6' 6", 280 pound defensive tackle jumped into bed, the resultant *tsunami* vaulted the unsuspecting lady right out of the window, as if she had been ejected from a distressed F-16! Case closed.

Ice Sliding

It was another Monday morning, but no reports on the Delts. There were a lot of other events, but nothing major. I hadn't heard from Nina since last Thursday, so I thought I'd give her a call before she went to class. She was now a junior, majoring in Hum Bio, with a desired medical future in the offing. She had been an excellent student in high school, and was selected straightaway to attend Stanford.

****

I'll never forget how much she fretted and wrung her hands over whether she would be accepted to her dream university or not. Nina learned that if applicants received a thin envelope in the mail, then that was Stanford's equivalent of the "Dear John" letter. I had been monitoring the mail, so when a thick envelope arrived, from the Dean of Admissions, I was overcome with joy: My maternal ancestors emigrated from the Azores and Madera Islands to Hawaii in 1882. They were conscripted laborers, hired for 5 years of servitude by the Island's exploding sugar cane industry. Most of them had no formal education. I was the first to graduate from college after many years of part-time study. How proud our ancestors would have been to learn that a 6th generation youngster—a woman, no less—had been accepted to a prestigious 4 year university.

My mood quickly changed, however, when reality took hold of my emotions: Paying for this was going to be a challenge. One of the many perks of my employment was having the University pony up half the tuition; however, room, board and books were on us—still a tidy sum, *"but moa betta dan nuttin'"* as my ancestors would have said!

Being the cantankerous devil that I have always been, I steamed open the envelope, removed all of the admission and registration material, and re-sealed it with only the acceptance letter, and a note with the hurriedly scribbled taunt—an inside joke, based on the Johnny Cash hit, "The Rock Island Line," reading: "I fooled you, I fooled you, I got pig iron, I got pig iron, I got all pig iron." I conspicuously placed the letter on the coffee table in the living room, and beat it out the door, headed for *The Gym*, just couple of blocks from the house.

While struggling with some dumbbells, I suddenly heard an elevated voice that I recognized: "Daaaad, you turkey," Nina shrieked, as she zeroed in on me like a heat seeking missile. I burst into laughter, and got rid of the weights before she was able to rain a number of well placed and well deserved shots on my arm. Half-crying and laughing, we embraced and rejoiced at her achievement. After she left, I had to explain the outburst to the troupe of knuckle-draggers, including one of her heartthrobs, Steve A., a Cardinal football standout. They all thought it was funny, but then we all know how guys are. . .

Despite my cruel joke, our relationship became even closer, especially now that she was almost grown up and studying just a stone's throw from my office. Her brother, Kirk, who was my best buddy—also a good student and excellent high school athlete in football, baseball and league champ heavyweight wrestler—had just begun college, at U.C. Davis; so indeed, I was one very proud *Pappy*, as the kids called me. I picked up the phone, and dialed her dorm.

****

"Hey, Nina, what have you been up to?" I pried.

"I'm just getting ready to go my 'Sexually Transmitted Diseases??' class," she quipped. The inflection in her voice was yet another "Stanfordism:" Many of the female students had a peculiar manner of speaking in that they would end every sentence with an elevated pitch, punctuated by a question. Her STD's instructor was a classic example of this phenomenon, which Nina hilariously mimicked.

So, after a good belly laugh, I quizzed: "So, what did you guys do this weekend?" By guys, I was referring to her buddies, Helen and Theresa. They were thicker that thieves and stuck together like

Super Glue. Nina dubbed their clique, "The Three Musketeers"—must be a genetic thing, I figured.

"Dad, we went to the Ice Sliding Party."

"OK, I give; what in the hell is Ice Sliding?"

"Ice sliding at the Delts," she confessed.

"The Delts? I thought I warned you about those beer guzzling jocks? Jeez, Neen, that place can get you into trouble—not to mention the embarrassment for me. I can just see the Daily's headline: 'Police Captain's Daughter Busted!' So, what's the deal with the ice sliding?" I interrogated.

I wasn't too worried about her drinking, as she was now a confirmed teetotaler—after her 21st birthday blowout with the Musketeers, when she introduced herself to the perils of alcohol: It seems that Ms. Perfect Daughter got totally hammered, after throwing-down way too many Kamikazes. Needless to say, she paid homage to the Porcelain Goddess for several days thereafter.

"Awww, Dad, those Delt guys are just a bunch of big teddy bears. And, we were NOT drinking; you know what happened on Dec. 4th," she argued. "And, besides, *Pap,* we took Kirk as our bodyguard!" she continued. Although diminutive by Delt standards, Kirk was a pretty stout lad in his own right—dubbed "A Block of Flesh" by his teammates—so I felt a little more at ease.

Nina had always been a sports fan; she particularly loved football and actually understood the game. Obviously my youth league and high school coaching must have had something to do with her interest and expertise. In addition to the gridiron, she and her fellow Musketeers were avid basketball and baseball supporters; they never missed a game. So, it was no wonder that she liked to hang-out with the Big Boys.

After more back and forth about the perils of Frat boys, she told me about this Ice Sliding thing. The Delts had a beautiful 8-foot regulation pool table in their rather small living room. Whoever thought up this event must have been nuts or had a death wish—perhaps both. The boys protected their precious table with a sheet of plywood, and then covered it with a thick plastic tarp. They then poured several large bags of ice on the surface. The competitors then went up to the second floor and took their mark at the top of those very steep stairs. On the signal, those idiots would run down said stairs and dive head long onto the ice-covered table. This, of course, resulted in a subsequent short-lived airborne launch, followed by an uncontrolled crash landing. The object of this silly game was to see who could fly the farthest. Unlike Olympic long jumpers, where contestants landed in a sand pit, these schmoes slammed their bodies onto the rock hard wooden floor—some almost skidded out the side door, I was told. And, the field was open to all comers. Being at a non-discriminatory coeducational institution, many women were allowed, and encouraged to compete, as well. One of the top females, apparently a very tough young lady went to high school with Nina. This gutsy gal would slide time after time and out-distanced most of the jocks. I wondered what these crazy kid's bodies are going to feel like when they are into their golden years; based on my experience of body abuse, brought about by contact sports, fighting idiots on the streets and in jail—on duty of course—riding dirt bikes and experiencing frequent get-offs at break neck speeds. I can almost guarantee that those Ice Sliders will someday utter those infamous words, attributed to Bette Davis: "Aging ain't for sissies!"—if they live that long. . .

Bushwhacked

On the first day of classes in 1966, thirty masked desperadoes laid in wait until their quarry came into view. Suddenly, the group sprung from their lair and pounced onto their unsuspecting prey. Working with the precision of a Delta Force Unit, they taped the victim's legs and pinned his arms to the ground. One of the group produced a set of hair clippers and quickly buzzed the mark's nasty mop off—G.I. style! As they moved to his scraggily beard, the kid pleaded for mercy and implored the vigilantes not to shave-off his beard. The group decided to have compassion and let the man go. Darn!

The target of this exercise was none other than Stanford's Student Body President, dissident and chief dung-disturber, David Harris. The before and after photos featured in the 1991 Campus Report were hilarious, from my right-wing point of view: Harris went from looking like a Haight Ashbury Flower Child to Mahatma Gandhi...

A University's investigation immediately suspected that the "barbers" were members of the Delta Tau Delta fraternity. Witnesses described the group as being very large athletic-type males, most of whom were well 6 feet tall or better, and weighing in at 225 pounds or more. To put this in proper perspective, and if you do the math—225#s X 30 muscle-heads, equals 6,750 pounds of humanity holding down one average size hippie. Harris had no chance whatsoever! In any event, although the Delts initially denied any involvement in this stunt, they later copped-out, and were put on one year's probation by the Dean of Students, H. Donald Winbigler. The Dean should have given the team a Medal of Valor!

CHAPTER TEN

Smile. You're on Candid Camera!

Allen Funt

I always loved the Allen Funt TV show in which each vignette ended with: "Smile, You're on Candid Camera!" When I was Training Sergeant at the S/O I received some training in videography and small studio film production. Our equipment, although rudimentary by Hollywood standards, wasn't too bad. We had a pair of Sony reel-to-reel video porta-packs, which could operate on battery or AC power. We also had a brand new, high dollar Sony 360 reel-to-reel recorder, which allowed us to perform some basic editing. The porta-packs came in handy for crime scene investigation, crowd and riot observation and creating training programs. One of areas that especially piqued my interest was utilizing this medium as an evidentiary tool, particularly in criminal interviews and interrogations. Most law enforcement agencies were opposed to electronic documentation, apparently, on the theory that "if you live by the sword, you can die by the sword." My feeling was that if you played by the rules set forth by the Constitution and watched your Ps and Qs, you would have nothing to worry about. I was convinced, after talking to some of our Homicide Detectives that covert audio/video (AV) taping of interviews could provide powerful testimony in court: One of the investigators recalled a domestic homicide that he investigated once, wherein a disgruntled wife blasted her hubby with a .45! The choice of weapon, in my view, pretty well told a story of how she really felt about her dearly departed. . . During the interrogation, the woman coldly told investigators exactly how she had planned the event and once the deed was done, she was happy to be "rid of the no-good SOB."

Well, when the trial finally rolled around, she took the stand and had an entirely different version of the matter: She sobbed uncontrollably and maintained that she was merely defending herself from the brute who continually meted-out verbal and physical abuse. Furthermore, killing him was not in her mind. She cried, "I only wanted to scare him!" The judge was forced to take numerous recesses during her testimony so the bereaved widow could get ahold of herself. In the meantime, our Detective was flipping cheese burgers: *What a bold faced liar,* he thought, and wished that he would have recorded her confession, which would have dispelled this fallacious tale being spun before the Judge and Jury. But alas, he had no such thing; not even his partner's testimony could sway the Jury from coming to the verdict they ultimately reached: Not Guilty! After hearing this story, I convinced the Brass that we needed to bug the Bureau's Interview room with an audio/video system. While a picture is "worth a thousand words," I argued that a video might be worth a million!

A Model T

A year later, on The Farm, my lead Detective came into my office one Monday morning and reported that they had hit the Mitchell Building's gem and rock collection, again.

"What happened to the Varda Alarm you set-up?", I asked.

"They musta figured it out and aren't going in there," Don replied.

Don was one of the O/G who was retained from the original Stanford Police Department when the Public Safety Department was formed; he was clearly one of the best of the bunch. Although a bit crusty, he was very capable, had a lot of contacts and really knew his way around campus. He had also done some time in the trenches, having spent a number of years as a Public Safety Officer in Sunnyvale. One of Don's strongest suits was his technical skills: During his youth, he served as an aerial photographer in the Navy and was conversant in communications as well AV techniques.

The Varda alarm system was state of the art at the time. It was a portable device that transmitted a radio broadcast to the patrol units when tripped. The only problem was it sometimes didn't work very well in basements or buildings constructed with a lot of concrete and steel—which would be most of Stanford University! Therefore, Don would typically set-up the Varda and make test runs before deploying it. Although well hidden and a Top Secret operation, there obviously was a *Deep Throat* in that lab, for during the two week duration, the damn thing never made a peep! I even sent Don back over there to see if it was working. *So much for modern technology,* I thought. *Now, someone was pilfering gold dust that researchers used in their experiments.*

I had recently attended a *Techie* seminar hosted by the California Department of Justice (DOJ). The folks from DOJ put on a pretty sophisticated program which featured some really trick gadgets most law enforcement agencies could only dream about as they couldn't afford them. The best part of DOJ's spiel was they offered to assist the local cops by sending teams anywhere in the state to assist setting up their newfangled contraptions. So, I asked Don to call DOJ and see what they could offer so we could catch this gold thief in the act and put him out of commission. Don later reported that a crew from Sacramento was on their way and would be on campus after sundown. This cleared the way for a clandestine, FBI type operation. . .

The following morning, Don reported that everything was set and all we had to do was wait until the culprit pilfered some of that yellow metal. He assured me only the Dean and his Assistant knew about this trap. Being a gadget guy myself, I inquired how the DOJ gurus had set-up this *Eye in the Sky.* Don briefed me that the DOJ techies used an ordinary ceiling register (vent) and mounted our video cam at an angle so that it would capture anyone going into the drawer where the gold was kept. *Drawer,* I mused? *Why in the hell aren't they locking-up that gold in a safe, for God's sake—typical academic environment,* I thought; *they trust everyone, while we cops trust NO ONE!* Don continued to explain they hid the video recorder, our ol' tried and true Sony 360 reel-to-reel, in a locked closet next door and ran the camera feed over the top in the ceiling. More wizardry involved hooking-up a switch to the drawer so when it was opened the camera would roll. This was clearly a Model T, but by God, it worked! The only trouble was that the system never activated: Not by an unsuspecting janitor, student, lab-tech, mouse—no one! Boy, was I fuming. So much for: *"Only the Dean and his Assistant knew."* However, a concept was born. Now, all we had to do was to figure out how to keep people from shooting their mouths off while trying to conduct covert surveillance! No short order in this institution, I later discovered.

The Annex Lock-Up

When the Fire/Police building was built in 1958, accommodations for the Stanford Police Department were obviously not a very high priority. For years, the cops had been holed-up in a tiny building behind the Old Fire House at Santa Teresa and Duena Streets. While a Patrol Deputy in the 60's I responded there on assignment and I thought then that those poor officers must be stacked in there like cordwood—and indeed they were! After some radicals torched the late great Stanford President Wallace "Wally" Sterling's Building 10 Office, the Sheriff assumed the responsibility of guarding the University President's residence, the Hoover House.

When the Department of Public Safety was created in 1971, it became obvious that more space was needed. Following a concept developed in the 1950s when the old Manzanita Trailer Park was created for additional student housing, the powers-that-be just moved in a large "double-wide" and set-it-up behind the Fire Training Tower. It was known as "The Annex." So much for the high rent district. . . When I arrived on the scene, with my "Book 'em Danno!" attitude for bad guys, I knew immediately that we needed a temporary booking and detention center. With the blessings of the Boss, I took about half of the Squad Room and commissioned Plant Services to build a makeshift secure area. In retrospect, I guess it wasn't much of a Lock-Up as the ceiling tiles weren't secured, so a prisoner could crawl up into the attic and make his way out. I seem to recall one moron performed that feat but was nabbed coming down in the officer's locker room. "So much for watching your arrestee," I chided the thoroughly embarrassed rookies. After that episode, I had rings installed on the benches so that prisoners could be tethered. There were two rooms: One we used for fingerprinting and photographing, and the other for interviewing subjects. Utilizing the Model T technology we learned from DOJ, we employed the same trick. However, this application featured a video monitor and a VHS tape deck, which superseded the Sony reel-to-reel machine. Although, rudimentary, this system worked fairly well, save for the Venetian blind effect caused by the ceiling vent! I learned a long time ago that when you can't afford a Cadillac, you might just have to settle for a Chevy—in this case, this was a GEO, at best!

The Playboy Bandit

Fred, the owner and "Head Shears" Man at the Stanford Barber Shop, located in Tresidder Memorial Union (TMU), called and wanted to discuss a recurrent and very annoying problem. Fred had shorn many locks on campus over the years: I seem to recall that he once told me he used to have the old barber shop near the old bookstore, which was located somewhere near Alvarado Row and Campus Drive, before the new emporium was built on White Plaza.

"Hi Fred, so how's life treating you these days?" I cheerfully inquired as I knew something was up, for the man had never called me before.

"Well, Captain, I'm doing alright, but there's a sneaky thief who has been ripping-me-off for several weeks now. Quite frankly, I'm getting damn tired of it," he lamented.

"What exactly is being ripped-off?" I pressed.

"When I close the shop, I usually leave about 50-60 bucks in the till—'start-up' money for the early barber. So, about 2 to 3 times a week when we tally-up the daily receipts, we find we're consistently about 10 to 15 bucks short. At first I thought that maybe one of my barbers had sticky fingers. But, after a while, I started to keep track of how much I left in the till at night and had the start-up man call me to report how much was on hand when he arrived. Sure enough, at night, somebody is coming into the shop and tapping the till. Not only that, but the bastard is stealing my brand new Playboy magazines, too! And, that really pisses me off!" Fred exclaimed.

"Oh, yeah, he's figured out when I receive the new Playboy and the very next morning, it's gone! I don't see any pry marks on the door, so the guy must have a key," he concluded.

Must be the janitor, I thought, tongue-in cheek; it's always the janitor around this place—as far as the staff is concerned. However, if the truth were known, we never, ever caught a janitor stealing anything, as most of those folks were hard working individuals who were just trying to make a living—it almost always turned out be someone else. . . Case in point:

During the early 70's, we were beset with a rash of office burglaries—petty cash funds cleaned-out, plus anything of value that was concealable—these crimes occurred at night; there was no indication of forced entry and no physical evidence so we had no clues! Someone must have had a key, the victims asserted—"must be the janitors!" The trouble is, this was a campus-wide phenomenon and most of the janitors were assigned to specific areas and didn't have keys to every building on campus. *Could this be one or more of our night CSO's,* I pondered? Maybe, but again, the CSO's had keys to their beats, not to the whole joint, so we just put out orders to be ever vigilant. It was like trying to catch a wily bass with only one pole, so it took a month of Sundays before we got a strike and hooked the big fish:

One morning, at approximately 0400 hours, an intrusion alarm went off in the Business Office in Encina Hall. Most of our troops were pretty insensitive to tripped alarms, for dozens went off daily—99 percent were false alarms. It was a Stanford cop's nightmare as many people intentionally set-off the alarms because they either didn't have the code, or the key, or whatever excuse—actually many of the violators flat didn't give a damn! They just had to get to where they needed to be and couldn't really be bothered with silly alarms. . . But, in this case, one of our Old Guard, now Deputy Ted "Hoppy" Hopgood (RIP), had a gut feeling this was the Real McCoy so he shot-up to the front door, pistol in hand. When he spotted a guy who was in the process of leaving via the front door, Hoppy yelled, "Freeze MF'er!" Ted then "proned-out" the suspect and told him not to move a muscle. The guy, a Plant Service's night maintenance man, protested vehemently: He pleaded that he mistakenly set-off the alarm and was sorry:

"Officer Hopgood," he whined, "you know me, I had to fix a thermostat—I didn't do *nothing!*"

"Yeah, I know you," Ted rejoined, "but if you didn't do *nothing* why in the hell were you in the VP's Office (off-limits to everyone at night save for the police) setting-off the silent alarm???"

Marty, the maintenance guy, shut-up like *Tridacna gigas* (Google it). When Hoppy patted Marty down, he found gloves, a serious wad of dough, plus a huge ring of Stanford keys. After the cavalry arrived and got Marty in tow, Deputy Hopgood made a beeline for the Business Office, selected the correct key and entered. Sure enough, the place had been ransacked, and several empty cash boxes were found. I believe this was a "BINGO!" Suddenly, the janitors were vindicated and the real crook was busted! A subsequent searched of Marty's duty van, personal vehicle and residence yielded a treasure trove of very incriminating evidence: Piles of money, hundreds of University keys, and other valuables which were reported missing. He was toast, thanks to a cagey old veteran, a Door Shaker Emeritus, who took this alarm seriously!

"So, Fred, do you have any idea who might be committing these thefts?" I asked.

"Well I don't know for sure, but there's a new night janitor and I don't trust him."

"How come?" I pressed.

"I don't know, but every time I see him around closing time, he kinda avoids eye contact and seems suspicious, to me," he opined.

"OK, Fred, I'm going to send one of my detectives over here for a report; I also propose to install a covert video cam. Would you be OK with that?"

"No problem, Captain, I want to catch this thief and if you want to use a camera, that's fine with me," the barber replied.

"All right then, the sergeant will call you and set-up a meet—not in your shop though, as I don't want another soul, other than you, the investigator and me to know about this. We are going to want to borrow a key from you so that we can set-up our rig, in the early AM, when no one is around—not even the janitor. . ." I directed.

"Oh, by the way, when do you get your new Playboy?"

"Within a couple of days," Fred answered.

"Great. Perfect timing!" I exhorted.

By this time, we had acquired a newer, smaller camera and a time lapse video recorder for covert surveillance. The detective installed it in a corner of the barber shop. The trap was set. All we had to do was to wait. I figured not for long, as Hugh Hefner's latest publication was on the horizon. This was like fishing for Great White sharks at the Farallon Islands, with a huge Elephant Seal on the hook!

Two days later, Fred was on the line again:

"Captain, the bastard hit me again; he took $17 and my new Playboy. Can you send your sergeant over to check the video?" Fred excitedly blurted-out.

"He's on his way, my friend. We'll need you to come over to the station to view the tapes. See you in a few." I happily returned.

Within the hour, the tape was on the machine in my office. We all crowded around the 27" monitor. The sergeant already had the video set to where the time lapse tripped. We could see a shadow appear at the glass door at about 2210 hours (10:10PM). Suddenly, the door swung open and a figure appeared in the shop. The suspect went directly to the cash register, which was open; he quickly scooped up some cash and put it in his pocket. He then moved to the magazine rack, thumbed through some issues, then selected one and sat in a barber's chair. The intruder perused his choice with apparent great interest. He stroked his crotch a few times then abruptly got up, tucked the magazine under his arm and left the shop. The Playboy Bandit was a male Hispanic, medium build, dark hair standing about 5 foot 8 inches tall.

After viewing the video, I asked the barber if he recognized the man. He could scarcely contain himself:

"Thaaat's Him! That's him, the janitor I told you about!"

I silently ingested an enormous Black Crow—*Yeah, it's never the janitors eh?*

Needless to say, The Playboy Bandit was hooked and booked in short order and much to Fred's delight, we retrieved most of his Playboys...

Long Distance: 1(925)825-5378

Allen James, "AJ", had only been in Investigations for a few months when he came into my office to pick my brain about an unusual case he had been working on.

Allen was a middle-aged fellow who had learned his cop-trade on the streets of Alameda. It was busy little city during the heyday of the Alameda Naval Air Station. Drunken and combative *swabbies* (sailors) were the norm when ships from the Pacific fleet were in port. When coupled with the burgeoning homeless population and ladies of the night, who defiantly plied their trade on their streets, this town made for a very interesting place to learn one's craft. AJ had been out of police work for over 10 years, having jumped ship for an attractive business opportunity. However, when the economy began to wane, he decided to get back into steady employment, so he applied for a position with our department. He was one of the better candidates and had just completed a Peace Officer's Academy refresher course, so he was good to go; I snapped him right up. Like my Dad used to say: "Education is essential but experience is golden!" Indeed, AJ proved to be a very quick study.

"So what's up, AJ?", I asked.

"This is a weird one, Cap'n," he said.

"Welcome to the Farm, AJ! All of the cases around here are weird!", I asserted.

The detective went on to say that he was investigating a possible burglary/grand theft at the Stadium. He explained that the perp had racked-up over $2,500 in long distance phone calls from one of the first aid stations in the facility. Given that no evidence of forced entry could be found, he surmised that the suspect must have a key. Although this appeared to be the work of an insider, experience told me that it could be almost anyone, as key control in this institution was virtually non-existent. I couldn't count the times that our deputies found unauthorized keys on arrestees: It didn't matter if they were bona-fide bad guys, random students, staff members, janitors, crashers, or homeless guys, the officers would invariably find them in possession of official SU keys, with "Do Not Duplicate" stamped in the head. Where all of these passkeys originated from was always a mystery, but it surely explained why there were so darned many rip-offs on campus.

AJ stated that all of the illicit calls were placed either at night or over a weekend when the stadium was not in use. He assured me that the DAPER, (Department of Physical Education and Recreation) was currently obtaining phone records from Pac Bell, and that preliminary information indicated that most of the calls were being made to various locations in the Caribbean. When I asked if any of the Athletic Department employees were from that region, the detective said he didn't think so, but would confirm it. In the majority of the phantom phone caller cases we had investigated over the years, the cheat usually called family or friends, so those were no-brainers to solve. Something told me, however, that this one would be different.

"Maybe he's a dope dealer and is laundering funds in those banks down in Aruba, St. Lucia, or wherever," I postulated. But, at this stage of our inquiry, it was too early to speculate. Well, I thought, this is what makes detective work so interesting.

I wanted to check-out the scene to see if technology might aid us in identifying and apprehending the phone freak, so we buzzed over to Stanford's ancient sports arena. AJ and I discussed various options en route and decided we would try to catch the suspect on candid camera—that always seemed to work pretty well—especially since we acquired our state of the art time lapse video recorder.

The aid station was located in the stadium's concourse, about 80+ very steep stairs, straight up. Prior to 1992, I used to run up and down those stairs like a mad man—two or three times a week. But, that was "BH" (Before Hips)—before I had bilateral hip replacements. I grasped the guard rail firmly and pulled myself upward, one small step at a time. I felt like the Big Bad Wolf—huffing and puffing—until I finally made it to the top.

"Damn AJ," I wheezed, "I'm getting way too old for this stuff."

The dingy little room in question was one of two first aid stations in this archaic facility. It was crudely constructed under the grand stands above, and I quickly felt this operation was going to be a challenge: Even during the day, the lighting conditions were very poor; this coupled with a lack of readily available power and a secure location in which to conceal our equipment got us scratching our heads. However, the detective was a good gadget guy so I left this project up to his devices.

We concluded that in order to make this application work, we needed one of those trick new cameras with a low-light level lens. These "007" spy cams were typically disguised in a number of innocuous components such as, fire suppression sprinkler heads, night lights, and dummy switches or electrical receptacles. Before leaving, we noticed a riot-gear storage unit was conveniently located just outside of the room. *What a great place to hide the VCR*, we simultaneously thought—clear proof of the Great Minds theory. . . Patrol ordered these boxes to be constructed and placed at a number of strategic locations throughout the stadium. PC (political correctness) dictated that the troops must stow their helmets, gas masks, and riot batons in these bins, so as not to "frighten" or intimidate the thousands of football fans. I often wondered who scared who? 15 of us vs. 80K of them—go figure. . . However this gear was readily available in the "unlikely" event of a major mob scene. "Unlikely," my eye: The chaos and riotous behavior which ensued at the conclusion of nearly every stinking Big Game since the event began in the Gay '90's, made that a virtual certainty! Not even a hundred cops and a 10 foot wire fence topped with razor wire could keep those moronic Weenies from storming the field—win or lose. But, that's yet another story. . .

The next day, AJ reported the installation was up and running: He cleverly installed the stealthy camera, disguised in a small unobtrusive light up near the ceiling, zeroed-in on the wall telephone. Using a non-descript extension cord, he ran power to the recorder, which he secreted in the gear box, secured with a brand new bullet proof lock—And, he was the only person on the planet with a key! Perfect timing, I thought. TGIF so all we had to do was to wait and see what our candid camera would reveal.

After a meeting Monday morning, AJ retrieved the video and holed up in his office, while he painstakingly reviewed the tape, frame by frame. After about an hour or so, the detective burst out of his room like an agitated hornet and excitedly summoned me to his work space.

"You're just not going to believe this," he blurted out, while laughing hysterically.

He rolled the tape, and after a few minutes, I saw a male subject enter the aid station. Just as we suspected, the crook had keys. The detective told me that this fellow was the night watchman who worked weekends.

"Bingo. We gottem!" I high-fived. As I prepared to leave, AJ grabbed me by the arm:

"Hold on, Cap'n, the best is yet to come!" Here's what the video tape revealed:

The culprit suddenly closed and locked the door; he immediately picked up the phone and began frantically dialing—that's right, I said dialing! The only device that would have better fit the time period of our historic coliseum (built 1921-1922) would have been a crank phone... After about 5 minutes of apparent intent listening—it didn't appear as if he was doing any talking at all—the dude suddenly un-zipped his fly and brought *junior* into the mix.

"You've got to be kidding me; what's up with that?" I quizzed. I was stunned—totally shocked, even at this stage of my career, as I was cocksure I had seen it all. Obviously not...

"Cap'n, I called some of those numbers after I saw this, and they are all porn exchanges, you know, talk to me dirty phone sex sites," he snickered.

"Jeez, and I thought this guy was a major dope dealer or something," I mumbled.

"Bring that FW in here and toss him like a salad." I ordered.

It was the shortest interrogation I had ever seen: The detective brought the suspect in, sat him down in front of the TV and turned it on, so that just snow was visible on the screen. After allowing him to view the blizzard for a few minutes, AJ barked:

"Look, I know what you've been up to cuz I gotcha on tape. So, do you want to do the right thing and confess, or do I need to embarrass you some more by turning this damn thing on?"

The dejected phone freak, just hung his head and capitulated, by saying:

"No, Sir. No, don't turn it on! I'll confess!"

The video tape, and in living color, no less, was irrefutable! No other *evidence* was necessary...

Footsie

This is a tale of last minute desperation: The American Express Office at TMU reported person(s) unknown absconded with $25,000 in *just off the presses* AMEX traveler's checks. It didn't take a rocket scientist to conclude that this was more than likely an inside job, as the place was alarmed, and there were no signs of forced entry. But, who was the insider that pulled this off? So, I investigated the crime scene with a couple of my detectives—actually just showing the flag, for these office crimes are stubbornly tough to solve. We immediately entered the serial numbers of the checks into the FBI's WSP system (Wanted Stolen Property) and notified AMEX investigators, who could track when and where the checks were used.

After meeting with the AMEX brain trust, I convinced them I needed to interview every person who worked in the office. I drafted a letter to each and every person and asked them to contact me about coming into the department for an interview. I systematically talked with approximately four of the senior staff, using a list of talking points which included several sensitive questions intended to elicit certain reactions, often called body language. However, the phraseology of the response can provide important clues to an experienced interviewer. The initial part of the interview included an admonition, which alerted the "person of interest" that they were at the police department of their own volition, were not under arrest and were free to go at any time—take a break go to the restroom, and so forth. The so-called "boiler-plate Q's" were much like a standard application: "Name, rank, horsepower," place of residence, employment information—this information enables the investigator to get a baseline on the person's demeanor with questions which almost all normal people would have no reason to be deceptive. Following that block, I dove into some scenarios crafted especially for this type of crime. I quickly eliminated the supervisory staff as their responses were consistent with truthful persons. Here are a couple of scenarios which often gives the interviewer a heads-up as to the veracity of the subject in the hot seat:

Interviewer: "When we identify who committed this crime, should he/she be prosecuted to the fullest extent of the law?"

Person of Interest: (Innocent): "Absolutely! Anyone who would steal in our work place, thus bringing suspicion and the police on everyone in the office needs to be arrested and thrown into jail!"

Interviewer: "Should this person be given a second chance?"

Person of Interest: (Innocent): "If this was a small theft, like some office supplies, maybe. But, taking $25,000? No way!"

Interviewer: "Just to be clear, this crime is a burglary as well as a grand theft, both felonies, punishable by imprisonment in state prison from 2-6 years plus a fine to be determined by the Court. So, do you think the person who committed these offenses should go to prison?"

Most innocent people often respond like this: "You bet. If you commit the crime, you do the time!" "Hell yes! This theft took some aforethought and planning, so yes." The majority of truthful folks, in essence, respond like the juries in Ol' Judge Roy Bean's Court of yesteryear: "Hang the Bastard!" and then belly-up to the bar for some whiskey...

After assessing the interviews of the senior staff, more than one told me they suspected a cute new gal might have some involvement; no particular reason other than she was new and they didn't know much about her. The next thing I knew, this young lady was on the line wanting to be interviewed—NOW! She said she'd be at my office in 5 minutes. Then it hit me, our covert interview video cam wasn't in its usual place as the detectives had been using it for another purpose. The camera was on the floor of Sergeant's Office so I quickly plugged it in, tested the cam, and when I confirmed it worked, I quickly stuck it under the sergeant's desk—if nothing else, at least I'd get an audio recording. I arranged two chairs juxtaposed in front of the desk, to get up close and personal with whom I'm interviewing. Then came the rap on the door; just in time—my subject was here.

Christy's coworkers were right: She was young and very cute—charming, too. While reading the pre-interview admonition, I felt that this young lady seemed very nervous and seemed as if she just wanted to get the interview over with. I could understand her nervousness, as she said it was the first time she had ever been questioned by the police. Christy was diminutive—5 foot and weighing 110, tops. The office door was slightly ajar, so as not to get the subject paranoid and claustrophobic. Sitting across from her was a larger-than-life bear of a guy (some friends called me a 55 gallon drum with arms) armed with a big gun strapped to his side. I'd be nervous, too.

Turning on my charm, I attempted to allay her fears by making small talk and getting to know more about Christy and her family. She said she was a good Catholic and a recent graduate of a prestigious parochial school in West San Jose. By all appearances, she was a good kid, so I proceeded on with the interview. All went well until we got to the dreaded scenarios. When asked what she knew about the missing traveler's checks (at this point I minimized the incident by using euphemisms and avoided provocative words such as rip-off, purloined, burgled etc.). It was curious to me that she mirrored my tact by referring to the checks as *"stock."* Maybe *she's attended my interrogation class,* I mused. So, here's how it went:

A-2: "Christy, do you think the police should arrest the people who are involved in this incident?"

Christy: "Well, there should be a thorough investigation as to why this happened and maybe there might be some reason. I don't know. Maybe the **'stock'** was misplaced or something . . ."

After running down the crimes and punishment that could be meted out to the guilty party(s), I asked Christy:

"Once we catch the person(s) responsible, should they be prosecuted to the fullest extent of the law?"

Christy: "Well, ummm, well, that seems very harsh. Again, I think they should get a fine and 'strong probation'—very strong probation!"

A-2: "OK, Christy, did you know that ALL AMEX offices have secret cameras where they keep their *stock*? (Pause) So, is there any reason you would be seen removing this *stock* from the premises?"

Christy: (Visibly shaken) "I don't think so. Well, ummm. No, I don't believe... they... wouldn't..."

A-2: "Ahh, Just one more thing (ala Columbo, my hero!); you know, the AMEX investigators have been monitoring the *stock* and they have been showing-up all over Northern California; the people who are using them are heading south via I-5. When these people are captured, is there any way they might implicate you in this theft?"

Christy: "Well, ummm, I hope not. I mean why would they do that?"

Per the usual game plan, an investigator, who was monitoring the interview in my office, would buzz me on my pager at this point. But, in this case, they weren't there and the system wasn't hooked-up. However, as soon as I had completed the "Interview Phase" my beeper went-off. I read "10-21-2": Call your office Code 2—NOW!

I excused myself, retreated to my office, called the front desk and asked what was up? The clerk advised that Detective Sgt. Dave Stone of Milpitas PD was on the line and that it was important.

Perfect Timing

I had known Sgt. Dave Stone for a million years. That was the greatest thing about the old S/O as you often had the run of the entire county and got to know a lot of great people.

"Hey, Detective Dave Stone, how you been, buddy?", I exclaimed.

"I'm doing great, Raoul, and may have something for you. Are you working on a case where a bunch of traveler's checks slipped-out of your American Express Office?"

"You bet Dave! $25,000 in blank checks; they've been showing up in CA heading south on I-5."

"Well, they made a left turn on you and wound-up in Vegas. Harrah's Security bagged one of your perps, an 18 year old from our City, and they contacted me. He was caught trying to cash these checks and was figured to be under 21 in a casino, so they turned him over to METRO. The brains of the outfit beat feet and got clean away. But, Alejandro said that they got the checks from a chick, Christy, who works in the Stanford AMEX office. Here's the info on our kid; maybe it will help. Oh, by the way, the Security Office's number at Harrah's is (702)777-2222 ext. 911."

"Dave, I now believe in miracles as I have the gal in my interrogation room as we speak. I was just about to hammer her, but now with this info, that would be over-kill. She's really a sweet kid, but I think she's not the sharpest knife in the drawer!"

"Raoul, Alejandro has a great family—very cooperative and really upset about what their kid got himself into. I told them to call you, and they'll bring the knucklehead to your office for his confession. I told them you'd treat him right."

"Thanks, Dave I'll do the best I can as far as cutting him some slack. If he rolls, our DA is good and will likely do the right thing." I hoped.

I took down the pertinent information and collected my thoughts for the dreaded interrogation.

When I reentered the room, I could plainly see Christy was shaking like a leaf in a stiff breeze. I sat down and pulled my chair into her comfort zone; I had a file which was about 6 inches thick and began the monologue:

"Christy, here is the result of our investigation. So, now it becomes a matter of how we are going to work through this debacle as there is no question you took the checks and gave them to two of your friends." She began to refute my allegations, but I cut-off all of her denials. "Christy, I don't want to hear that. We both know you're guilty: That phone call I just took was from Sgt. Dave Stone of Milpitas PD. He was notified by Harrah's Hotel and Casino Security that they nabbed one of your friends, Alejandro, who was trying to cash a thousand dollars of those very checks that you ripped-off. He's copped-out that you provided those checks to your boyfriend, Benny. Benny's on the lamb now, but he'll be caught sooner or later. Now you are left holding the bag. You need to tell me all about this young lady."

It was like Chernobyl: A total meltdown! Her crying, sobs, and tears gushing forth were real. Christy knew she was in deep trouble and didn't receive a red cent for her foolish act. Luckily, I brought a big box of Kleenex with me. . . Being a big pussy cat in disguise, I became somewhat sorry for this kid as she was so naïve and in love with this big-time loser, Benny, thus would do anything for him. Before concluding, I told the young lady that I would go to the DA tomorrow and discuss the matter. Frankly, I advised her that she would have to be arrested and booked, but I would call and let her self-surrender and not have a marked unit pick her up.

I contacted the AMEX Office Manager and apprised her of the situation. Now the work began: Cop work was much like wild boar hunting, something I did a lot of in those days. As soon as you pull the trigger, the fun is over and the real work begins. In order to help me write a comprehensive report, I hooked-up the video-cam to my TV and ran the tape. Unbelievably, the camera shot was of the space where the two chairs had been set-up. And, when I answered the door, I soon learned our feet were on "Candid Camera." Unreal! Christy wore navy blue high heels; I sported big brown *gun-boats*, as my Dad called them—12 EEE. During the boiler-plate interview, Ms. Christy's feet were close together and flat on the floor.

However, when we proceeded to the scenarios, every time I asked her one of the questions about guilt, arresting the responsible(s) etc, she began to twist one of her toes as if she were grinding-out a cigarette. While I was concentrating on her facial reactions and other body language for indicators of deception, of which there were plenty, her Footsies were telling the real story. I had never seen anything like that in over 25 years of police work. Yet another element that good investigators needed to be aware of, so I included that tape in my Interview-Interrogation class which Sergeant John McMullen (one of my top detectives) and I put on for various investigative groups. But, all that did was cause me a lot of grief, as one wise guy accused me of having a foot fetish... Not!

Follow-up/Small World

After viewing the tape about a dozen times, not only for me, but for everybody in the department who wanted to see this phenomenon, I called the Harrah's Security Office to get a report from them.

"Harrah's Security, Sergeant Rivas."

"Your voice is very familiar to me Sergeant Rivas; is this Rivas as in Ralph Rivas?" I queried.

"Yes, it is Captain Niemeyer. After being your Range Instructor for several years at the S/O, how could I not recognize your voice?"

Unbelievable, after about 10 years, I finally located my long lost friend and the best Firearms Instructor who ever stepped onto the firing range. We subsequently renewed our friendship several times when I visited Las Vegas. Helluva guy!

Loose Ends

As promised by Detective Stone, co-conspirator, Alejandro, turned himself in for an interview and basically rolled over like a big lovable St. Bernard. He confirmed Benito, aka Benny, conjured up the whole deal and got his old girlfriend to provide them with the means for their sojourn. This information cast the die: All of these kids were guilty as sin. The DA concurred and arrest warrants were immediately issued.

As promised, I called Christy and her family and told her she had to be booked in WDF (Women's Detention Facility, Milpitas, CA). I knew some of the staff there and they advised me to have Christy booked in the early AM so she could be arraigned and probably released on her OR (Own Recognizance). So, I proposed that I would pick-up Christy at her home and get her into the system, thus avoiding incarceration for an extended period. I must admit, I felt this girl was duped and felt that she was not a Class A criminal. So, I went to her home, met her parents (really nice folks) and took her into custody, en route WDF. Yes, I radioed in my starting and ending mileage so the old man wouldn't be accused of molestation.

When I entered the booking area, several of the female deputies were astonished. One remarked:

"Sgt. Niemeyer, aren't you a Captain at Stanford now?"

"Yes, Ma'am, but when you are in a small department, it's 'All Roads—All Codes!'"

"Wow, I think this is a first; A Captain booking an arrestee."

"Well, it isn't the first for me and I doubt it will be the last. . ."

CHAPTER ELEVEN

The Other Shoe

Subpoenaed

The New Year of 1976 came in with a Bang! I was in the coffee room when one of the front office receptionists said there was a gentleman in the lobby who wished to see me about a case we had worked on. I strolled out there fat, dumb and happy; I didn't recognize the man and he just didn't look right to me—sort of goofy-like. He addressed me:

"Captain Niemeyer?" "I am." I replied.

"Well sir, I have some legal papers for you," whereupon he handed me "Greetings" from The Superior Court of the State of California in and for the County of Santa Clara! Damn! I had been dry-gulched by a process server who slapped me with a lawsuit by a high powered Palo Alto law firm on behalf of "Super Weenie," (of Chapter Seven infamy) Plaintiff v. THE BOARD OF TRUSTEES OF THE LELAND STANFORD JUNIOR UNIVERSITY, WILLIAM C. STARBUCK, DOE LAWSON, DOE NIEMEYER and DOE WARWICK, DOES ONE through FIFTY, DEFENDANTS.

We all knew that sooner or later, the ominous "Other Shoe" was going to drop. Well, sure enough, and with a very large thud! The defendant and his Chicago-type mouth piece wanted a pound of flesh from Starbuck, Lawson, and me (a.k.a. "The Three Amigos"): He only wanted a small slice from the University, a mere 25K in General Damages, but demanded our heads on a platter by calling for a whopping $75,000 in Punitive Damages from each of us ground pounders! I'd be lying if I said I wasn't scared: I was afraid that my whole life's work—my career, my job, my modest home, my family— would all go down the toilet in a heartbeat should this drunken rabble rouser prevail. And, given the general disdain for cops, especially in the wake of the Vietnam riots era and in Palo

Alto, which certainly is not a bastion of conservative ideology—Mom, apple pie and the Red, White and Blue—I was *very afraid* we would lose. Fortunately, with the handwriting on the wall, the University stepped-up early on and hired one of the best law firms in CA to defend us.

Our Hired Guns

I liken this upcoming battle to the Gunfight at the OK Corral: Given the potential damage this lawsuit might cause the University, as well as us *Three Amigos*—Vice President of Business and Finance, Robert "Bob" Augsburger, who in my mind, was the most straight shooting, stand-up individual I ever met in the Administration—reached-out and employed the best of the best gunslingers that money could buy. No two bit *shootists* like Billy the Kid would be considered in this fray! Instead, Mr. Augsburger employed "Wyatt Earp, Doc Holliday" *et.al.* to take on our determined adversaries: In reality, the prestigious San Francisco law firm of McCutchen, Doyle, Brown and Enersen* would face-off against our antagonists and represent the guys who stood to lose the most— Starbuck, Lawson and Niemeyer. Our litigation attorney was Richard C. Brautigam Esq., who did all of preparatory investigation, depositions and other legal work prior to the trial. He was superb and a damn nice guy, too! Our Big Gun was Mr. David Heilbron, who would actually argue the case in court should it go that far. In my heart, I knew that it would. . .

*I recently learned from the Santa Clara County Sheriff's Office Commemorative History Book that one of the principle founders of this law firm, Edward Johnson McCutchen, was the son of SCCo's third Sheriff, William McCutchen (1853-1855), who obviously eschewed his father's gun and badge for some law books. Had I known this at the time, perhaps I might have thought this tidbit to be a good omen. . .

Depositions

I had endured several depositions during my 35 year career, but never had I been subjected to such acrimony and vitriol as I experienced on March 5, 1976 in the Plaintiff's law office in Palo Alto. My tormentor was a lanky, pasty faced man with the disposition of a King Cobra. I hated his guts, but bit my tongue and answered his obnoxious questions, which were laced with venom. Fortunately, this wasn't my attorney's first gunfight so he effectively cut-off much of the interrogator's attacks and basically kicked his ass!

From what I later learned, my ordeal was like "Romper Room" when compared what Bill Starbuck and Steve Lawson went through. Deputy Starbuck was assaulted by "Super Weenie" in the Big Game of 1975, and Sgt. Lawson was hands-on in subduing the inebriated troublemaker. But, we all survived the depositions and hoped that truth and justice would prevail. We also prayed that the Plaintiff would see the error of his ways and drop this ridiculous lawsuit, as he was wealthy beyond belief and certainly didn't need the meager bucks. But, not this arrogant SOB: This man was bent on exacting revenge, primarily on the *Three Amigos*, and he would spare no amount to get even and ruin our lives. A trial date was set. Fortunately, our attorneys fought like hell and convinced the Presiding Judge that the matter should be heard before a more neutral jury at the County Seat, in a San Jose Superior Court.

And, that was where we were headed.

Anticipating the worse, I went through the legal process of homesteading our modest family residence in Campbell. If convicted and slapped with a 75k judgment, I was fully prepared to flee to Mexico, for I wasn't going to give that low-life one red cent of my hard earned, paltry resources. I had been to Baja B.C., Mexico several times and contemplated relocating to the *Cuidad de La Paz,* where I could open a motorcycle repair shop and perhaps do some deep sea fishing on the side. I was dead serious, and my wife was one hundred percent behind this desperate measure, should a jury find against me. Hell, I never laid a hand on the jerk! But, the Plaintiff's loudmouth said that I was in charge, should have known better and that the "Buck" stopped in my court. Bull! I was prepared to face the music and tell the truth, under oath, and hoped that perhaps a jury of my peers might have mercy on me???

The Trial

A diverse jury had been selected and our defense team seemed to be comfortable with the make-up. Most members were from 25-45 years of age, and of middle-class backgrounds. Their occupations ran the whole gamut: Machinist, middle school teacher, nurse, IBM employee, a female military veteran, caregiver and several other livelihoods that escape my memory. I believe there were four women, a couple of Hispanics, as well as one African American among the 12 member jury. I felt alright about the jury's make-up, but my opinion of citizen arbiters during my 12 year law enforcement career (at that point), having been through several jury trials, was that figuring out how a panel of 12 random folks might find on any given point was, at best, a crap shoot! My co-defendants held the same opinion but we were dealt the hand without an opportunity to discard and draw more cards, so we hoped our legal beagles would out-lawyer the other side and convince the panel to vote for us "good guys."

I was surprised how many spectators there were in our court room gallery—perhaps they were there to observe some cops squirm when in the hot seat. The historic, grand old courthouse is located at 191 North First Street, San Jose.*

****

*From an article "Murder of Brooke Hart" by Rick Sprain, Santa Clara County Sheriff's Office Commemorative History Book, 2010.

The complex was built in 1868 and once housed the Santa Clara County Jail. The lock-up and Sheriff's Office made worldwide news on November 26, 1933 when a crowd of over 2,500 angry rioters gathered at its steps in protest. Many of the enraged citizens stormed the bastion, overpowered and injured several Sheriff's personnel (including the Sheriff, himself, William J. Emig). The out of control mob *"rescued"* accused murderers (John M. Holmes, 29 and Thomas H. Thurmond, 28) and promptly strung-them-up on separate Elm trees across the street in St. James Park! Not even divine intervention from the venerated Saint could save these scoundrels from the clutches of the vigilantes!

The lynch mob was incensed over the kidnapping and brutal murder of 22 year old Brooke Hart (son of a prominent San Jose merchandiser): The handsome young man was ambushed by an armed thug, later bound with wire, hooded, weighted with concrete blocks and thrown off the San Mateo Bridge into San Francisco Bay!

The killers initially nabbed the victim as he was leaving work at his Dad's store, and were going to ransom him for $40,000. While momentarily stopped on the bridge to check on their bound hostage, the nefarious duo's plan went awry when the kid tried to hail a passing car; the desperados panicked and tossed their helpless victim into the Bay's frigid waters. For good measure, one of the cowards fired a pistol at him several times as the poor kid was thrashing around trying to stay afloat. The dummies returned to San Jose and the ringleader made an ill-advised phone call from a pay phone a couple of days later, which was traced. The Sheriff pounced on him within 7 minutes—clearly, a record response in the annals of the Old S/O. One of the scum bags escaped but was quickly tracked down and both were incarcerated for kidnapping.

When a couple of duck hunters found the badly decomposed body of Brooke Hart in the Bay on November 25th (two weeks later), the mood of the crowd suddenly changed from idly *talking* about lynching the cold blooded killers, to actually *doing it*! And, that is exactly what they did. Not a single hangman was ever arrested. The Governor, James "Sunny Jim" Rolf, quipped: "If anyone is arrested for the good job, I'll pardon them all!"

****

In any event, I didn't anticipate being rescued or lynched, but I surely was apprehensive about our ordeal and wished that Ol'

Governor Rolf was still around. . . . As per our defense team's instruction, my family was prominently presented to the judge and jury, seated in the front row, behind our lawyer's table. My wife was modestly attired, as were our children, Nina, then 12, and Kirk 9. I'll never forget viewing my stoic family from the stand and noting how spiffy they all looked; Kirk even sported a little long sleeved shirt, bow tie and vest!

Testimony

I was called to the stand first. My story had never deviated from day one. I studied my police report for days prior to my deposition—from Hell—months before, and spent countless hours perusing the transcript, so I felt all of my ducks were in a row. After my direct testimony, "Mr. Knucklehead," clearly a graduate of the School of the Spanish Inquisition, tried to shake my sworn story, but as in the deposition, he was out to lunch! When he finally "got it"—this was not my first rodeo, he sat down and shut up. I smiled at the judge and jury and made a hasty exit. We *Amigos* were admonished by our attorneys and the judge not to discuss our testimony, so I made sure that our guys were visibly separated in the court's hallways and told them not to speak or acknowledge one another. I once had a bad experience during a child abuse trial in which all witnesses were admonished not to talk about the case. Well, a self-appointed snoop eavesdropped on a conversation I was having with a deputy about hunting, and he snitched-us-off to the judge. I explained to His Honor that the man, himself a defendant, was totally wrong, so the judge suggested that we not talk about anything. Point well taken!

Obviously, I had no idea how Bill and Steve's testimony went but after an agonizing week of hanging around the court, both sides rested and the case was given to the jury.

Deliberations

As I recall, the jury was in deliberation for two days, although it seemed like two weeks. Just before lunch on day two, we *Amigos* were out in the hallway, and heard a loud commotion in the jury room. The outburst lasted for over 10 minutes, with shouting and banging which was audible through the thick walls of the building. *What in the hell's going on in there,* I thought, but was careful not to express myself verbally. However, several furtive looks were exchanged between the three of us. I later learned the big ruckus was a knock-down-drag-out reenactment of what occurred between the Plaintiff and Defendants at the Big Game of 1975. About 2 hours later, the Court Clerk advised our lawyers that the jury was back and had reached a verdict. Talk about having your heart in your throat! We solemnly filed into the court, took our positions behind the defense table and stood motionless while the Clerk read the verdict. It went something like this:

"In the matter of Case Number P29578, Plaintiff (*Super Weenie*) versus Defendants Starbuck, Lawson and Niemeyer, the jury finds the following:

1) As to William C. Starbuck, the jury finds the Defendant Not Guilty.
2) As to Stephen Lawson, the jury finds the Defendant Not Guilty.
3) As to Raoul K. Niemeyer, the jury finds the Defendant Not Guilty.

Being the consummate professionals we were, we merely nodded to the jury, shook our attorney's hands and congratulated them profusely. No high fives, no sneers or finger wagging in the face of the jerk and his mouth piece who brought on this ridiculous action, and lost—Big time! I hugged and kissed my family and thanked God and Stanford University for saving the *Three Amigos* from financial ruin and possibly a life of despair.

Kudos

I cannot say enough about the lawyers of McCutchen, Doyle, Brown and Enersen who put forth a super effort in righting this wrong. They faced a prominent member of the Palo Alto elite who had more money than God, and was bent on revenge against a trio of cops who were just doing their jobs. He was a victim of his own doing and paid the price. End of story.

Our point man, Richard Brautigam, was in the trenches with us from day one, performing journeyman's work. But, when it came to the trial, our heavy hitter, Mr. David Heilbron, was as smooth as silk when in front of the judge and jury. I knew that both men believed in us; it was evident in the passion of their presentation. Mr. Heilbron and Mr. Brautigam's skill as litigators was paramount, for our adversary was no lightweight, by any stretch of the imagination. The loser's attorney was committed and relentless, thus had a formidable reputation and thought to be one of the top lawyers in the region. He was skinned!

In the final analysis, I credit VP Bob Augsburger for saving our bacon. As I previously said, Mr. Augsburger was one of the finest gentlemen and stand-up guys I had ever met at the University! He knew that his officers, in this case, were lawfully engaged and didn't abuse the violator as was later claimed. The University had no obligation, whatsoever, to personally defend us—that's why the Plaintiff only sued Stanford for a meager $25,000, but went after the *Amigos,* individually, to the tune of 75k! Mr. Augsburger later said he would have never left us twisting in the wind to fend for ourselves. That could have been us dangling from those Elm trees just a stone's throw from the courthouse. . . I can't thank Robert Augsburger and Stanford University enough for their unwavering personal and financial support during this gut wrenching experience.

CHAPTER TWELVE

Sexual Misbehavior

Lake Lag

In order to get the flavor of the forthcoming episode, I feel compelled to conduct a brief historical interlude: Lake Lagunita, dubbed Lag, is situated on the southwest end of the campus, at the intersection of Junipero Serra Boulevard and Campus Drive; I referred to this location as the Back Door. During the winter months, seasonal rains filled-up the lake bed, which provided water recreation for the Stanford community: Sailing, wind surfing, canoeing, swimming and sunbathing were among the most popular forms of R&R at the lake. Holding true to environmental concerns, motorized craft were strictly prohibited. At night, especially on weekends, great volumes of beer suddenly appeared, along with legions of parched students, emerging from the cordon of Frat Houses and Dormitories that ringed the lake. This practice, more often than not, livened-up the program, especially for our men and women in uniform, who were charged with maintaining some semblance of order. Most of this activity took place around a small strip of sand near a ramshackle structure known as the "Boat House."

As Indian Summer approached and the temperature spiked, the water level quickly receded, resulting in a virtual quagmire—also, an irresistible allure for dare-devil 4-Wheeelers, who all seemed to have that "I can make it" attitude . . . Often, these tempters of fate would mire their rigs in the muck, and wind up on the end of a hook...And, after our gendarmes arrived, they were unceremoniously awarded a *paper trophy* for their accomplishment—a big fat citation! Motor vehicle use in CA's lakes, reservoirs, and wet lands, is a big-time No-No! Not only would the hero get a hefty tow bill, but the subsequent fine levied by the Court was usually a heart-stopper!

In addition to providing water sports, sun and fun, Lake Lag was a living laboratory for biology students: In the marshy areas, budding biologists studied the flora and fauna, with focus on Swamp Knot Weed, and the endangered Tiger Salamander! These little critters (approximately 5-7 inches in length) would hole-up in the foothills during the late summer and early fall, and then migrate to the lake when the rains came. Contrary to popular Farm folklore, there is NOT, nor has there ever *been*, a giant foot long amphibian known affectionately as *Laggie*—dwelling in the depths of Lake Lagunita! If you don't believe me, *check this out* with the Stanford Conservation Biology professors!

Once Lag began to dry-up, the salamanders would make the long trek back across Junipero Serra Blvd., and disappear into the hills. Their movement across the busy thoroughfare was always a concern for the environmentalists, as there were frequent encounters with vehicles—not a pretty sight! Students would often perform 11-84 (traffic control) by stopping cars, so that the creatures could traverse the highway with safety. There was even talk about building a subterranean viaduct in order to provide the species safe passage to and from Lake Lag.

Lag Berm Flasher

When Spring had sprung, the student population emerged from their dorms, donned in jogging attire, and would run their fool heads off around the five square mile campus and sprawling foothills. One of the favorite jogging loops was around the berm, which encircled Lake Lagunita. While the female students appeared on this circuit, most just clad in short-shorts and tube tops, the Bay Area FWs (freaking weirdos, as I call them) flocked to the Farm as if they had been drawn there by an MRI magnet! Most *flashers* were harmless exhibitionists, who, for some sick reason, obtained a rush by exposing their *junk*, however slight, while engaging in the manly art of masturbation. . . But, occasionally, physical assaults and rapes occurred. Continual warnings by our Department usually went unheeded, however. We implored the coeds to walk or jog in groups, or at least with a partner; but you know how it is when you are an 18 year old and have No Fear!

We had recently arrested a "serial flasher"—we dubbed him accordingly—who by self admission had committed over 200 such acts around the campus. But, as quickly as this man was hooked 'n booked, it seemed like many more exhibitionists queued-up, ready to fill-in, so to speak. One of these clowns fixated on Lake Lag's berm, performing his nasty craft on sleepy-eyed females as they were out for an early morning run.

After studying the unending supply of indecent exposure police reports that crossed my desk, it didn't take me long to conclude that this guy was an early riser! Most of his encounters with unsuspecting victims happened between 6:30 and 7:30AM; this pervert would typically walk or jog around on the berm in search of an appropriate target; he almost always sought the most attractive women in the area. In this case, it paid to be ordinary, I suppose...

Once he spotted a potential victim, he would either hide behind a bush or turn away as the student jogged by. Without warning, he simply jumped-out from behind his subterfuge or just turned around and shouted: "Hey! Check this out!" The stunned joggers then witnessed this psycho vigorously doing his thing. As quickly as he appeared, he'd be gone in a flash and vanish into the nearby eucalyptus forest.

Marshaling-up troops during this particular time frame proved somewhat difficult, for our "Lag Flasher" would usually strike right in the middle of our shift change. Somehow, I managed to corral some volunteers to stake-out the area. This operation would be a real crap-shoot with lousy odds, but we just had to try to locate this stealthy individual, either committing the offense, or in the process of fleeing the scene. I utilized all available assets in our limited arsenal: Plain clothes deputies on foot patrol and off-road bicycles, and the newly formed ORE (Off-Road-Enforcement) Squad, astride their spiffy red Honda 350cc motorcycles. We also employed our parking enforcers, CSOs, who maintained a loose perimeter on their Cushman 3-wheelers. After a couple of fruitless mornings, it was obvious to me that we needed some honey to attract that *bare*.

Kathy was a drop-dead-gorgeous FNG (G for gal): On a scale of 1 to 10, I gave her a solid 13! We asked her if she would volunteer as our decoy. Kathy eagerly accepted the challenge, so we outfitted her with a small backpack in which she secreted a hand held radio, a pair of handcuffs, her badge and ID, and just in case, a .38 caliber Smith and Wesson loaded with six 150 grain hollow-point bullets, charged with a magnum dose of +P powder—a round that could drop a 300 pound animal.

Kathy, call sign Q-13, was instructed to just walk or slowly jog around the lake and to immediately notify the team if she saw the suspect do his despicable deed. The Patrol Sergeant ram-rodded the detail and made sure that all hands were in place by 0600. I expected that the suspect would be in custody and going through the booking process when I arrived at the station that morning. How could we fail, given that irresistible lure? They were all still out there when I reached the station, and up to that point, there were no hits. At 0900, I called it quits for the day and awaited the detail to come in.

They were a very dejected bunch, I thought, as their long faces immediately revealed disappointment. A few deputies were certain that they were burned. My experience with stake-outs was similar: Ninety percent of the time when stake-out teams initially came-up empty handed, they immediately conclude that their cover was blown!

"Not so," I implored! "Cops *always* think they were 'made,' following an unsuccessful Code 5. This is almost *never* the case," I asserted. "People, don't see Dick! Y'all know that! When was the last time a witness actually saw a crook committing a crime?" I asked. The silence was deafening.

Using my one of PAL football coach halftime speeches—the one when we were getting the hell beat out of us—I pumped them-up, with some, "One for the Gipper," rhetoric: I *almost* guaranteed—something I seldom did as there are NO guarantees in life, let alone in cop work—this detail was going to bring-in big dividends—sooner or later! *Hopefully sooner,* I wished! Most seemed optimistic, but a few of the seasoned folks, gave me the, yeah, yeah, right look.

The next morning, I decided to leave the house a little earlier, so that I could monitor the radio traffic from our Lake Lag surveillance squad. I switched to Channel 3 and listened intently. At about 0720, I heard a female voice; it was Kathy:

"FC-3, Q-13. I'm 10-15, send me a fill!" The creep was busted!

"Q-13, FC-3, confirm, you got da guy?"

"Affirmative," she calmly replied!

Within a few minutes, I heard music to my ears:

"Radio, Q-13, we're 10-15 with one, en route the Annex."

"Q-13," Radio called, "Confirm the charge."

"314PC! Indecent exposure," Kathy boastfully proclaimed!

"Fantastic!" I shouted into the mic. "This is A-3."—as if they didn't know—Great JOB! All of you! I'll 10-87, you all in the Annex. ETA about 20."

So, I kicked that old Merc into *giddyup* and knifed my way through the usual heavy commute traffic; I soon arrived and didn't attract a single CHP along the way.

At our debriefing, I asked what had happened. The Sergeant chronologically related how the plan had been deployed, and described ancillary events that occurred during the stake-out.

"OK," I impatiently interrupted. Being a student of the TV "Dragnet's" Jack Friday School of Interviewing, I mimicked:

"Gimme the facts, Ma'am just the facts!" The Sergeant turned to Q-13 and said:

"Cat-lene, you tell A-tree what went down. . ."

Kathy related that she had been walking and jogging on the berm for about 40 minutes without seeing anything untoward. Numerous students, female as well as male, were running all over the place, but no suspect. All of a sudden, she saw a very 10-66 guy (suspicious person) in running garb, but he was just lurking around in the bushes ahead—seemingly waiting for her to come by. As she got closer, the young man (who definitely fit the profile and strongly resembled the description given by many prior victims), performed a classic pirouette. *This is him,* she thought and readied herself for action! When Kathleen was about 10 yards past the man, she looked back and observed the creep leap-out onto the path. He then yelled:

"Hey! Check this out!" And, there he was, shorts down to his knees, frantically . . . In front of God and everyone!

Deputy "Wonder Woman" immediately whipped out her badge and gun and declared:

"Freeze! You're under arrest!" However, this fellow didn't miss a beat—he carried on, and between pants pleaded:

"Please. . . Officer. . . Let me finish. . ." And, finish he did, whereupon, Q-13 put a wrist lock on this jerk-off and slapped-on the cuffs before he could even say "Thank you."

When the Sergeant arrived, he grabbed the terrified prisoner, and before whisking him away, barked:

"And, don't forget to collect da ebidence!"

All of this, in the days before we routinely carried latex gloves!

UGLY

Stanford University draws its undergraduate body from the upper reaches of the SAT scores. And, adolescents of that caliber can often be as irreverent as they are cerebral. Students on campus were forever devising abbreviated monikers and acronyms to identify familiar places and things: MemChu=Memorial Church;

MemAud = Memorial Auditorium; HumBio = Human Biology; LSJUMB = Leland Stanford Junior University Marching Band (such as it was. . .); and UGLY = Undergraduate Library, the paragon of study in any institution of higher learning! And, this was one of the finest libraries on any campus. *So, why were there so damn many perverts hanging around in that place,* I wondered?

In fact, I soon learned that an esteemed researcher was studying that very phenomenon. The Chief of Police at an Ivy League college called one day, at the behest of a library administrator at his school, to inquire what I knew about Stanford Professor X? Totally clueless at the time, I asked what he meant. The chief said their Head Librarian was really upset about the nature of questions that our renowned researcher was asking on his questionnaire: In essence, Professor X wanted to know how many incidents of masturbation were reported, were they finding any evidence of ejaculate on the books, stacks, floors, desks, and so forth. The chief wondered if this survey was on the level, or if maybe the Professor, himself, was a pervert. . . Having had some experience investigating sexual crimes on the campus, I was amused but not totally surprised. I told my caller that I would look into the matter and get back to him.

My preliminary investigation revealed that Professor X was somewhat controversial, but nonetheless, was an extremely bright published researcher and in very good standing with the Hoover Institution. I then called him and asked if he was really studying incidents of masturbation in libraries at other universities. Somewhat annoyed, the Professor said that this was a legitimate inquiry, and that he had already received hundreds of affirmative replies from colleges all over the United States. *What would possibly drive a man to masturbate in a library,* I thought? I guessed that's what Professor X was trying to figure out, too; so, I wondered some more and hoped that our taxes weren't paying for this. . .

I learned early on that the campus was crawling with FWs. One of the first cases of library masturbations during my watch was reported by two female students who were studying in one of the more isolated areas of the facility. These young ladies noticed that a distinguished looking middle-aged man, seated at the other end of the table, had been constantly leering at them; he also kept dropping items on the floor and after spending some time fishing around under the table, he began to lean back in his chair, all the while periodically looking under it—possibly trying to gaze up the girls' skirts. One of the students took a peek under the desk and observed that the guy's penis had emerged—it appeared as if he was playing with himself—in the library for Chrissakes! The interloper stared at them intensely, then suddenly got up and left. The young ladies went over and checked the area and espied some white viscous fluid on the chair and floor.

This was the perfect case for our brand new female detective. She established good rapport with the young ladies and learned that this guy had been frequently seen in the library. The detective decided to stake out the area the next time two girls had planned to study there. Good idea, but any cop will tell you that stake-outs are often very frustrating, as they seldom bear any fruit—especially the first time. I liken this police technique to *still hunting*, wherein the hunter picks a high ground location above a water hole and waits for the game to come and quench their thirst. Unless you are on the Serengeti Plain, results are usually spotty. In this case, however, Bingo! The suspect espied the two young ladies and homed-in on them like a heat-seeking missile. Now, how that is for beginner's luck?

My Detective was young, twenty-something, and wearing the ubiquitous red sweatshirt emblazoned with four-inch white letters boasting STANFORD; she blended right in—backpack and all. Our person of interest initiated the same MO as before: Dropping stuff on the floor, rummaging around under the table, slowly lounging back in his seat, almost in a reclined position. At this point, the detective gave the girls the previously arranged high sign, so they bundled up their books and left. A team of hidden Deputies then swooped down on the unsuspecting offender like a pair of hungry Red Tail hawks! They unceremoniously put the *habeas grabbus* on the creep and whisked him out the door in a pair of Peerless bracelets!

Unfortunately, the arrest was a bit premature since our FW was unable to complete his deed, thus depriving the investigation of tell-tale evidence. Fortunately, though, this individual had a prior history of sexual misbehavior. A criminal history search revealed that he had been arrested in southern California for exposing himself repeatedly to his neighbor: Like clockwork, our hero would come out to his driveway every morning, clad only in a terry cloth robe, ostensibly to retrieve his newspaper. However, the attractive woman across the street noticed that this man always appeared when she was at her sink which had a spectacular view of the neighborhood. The devious neighbor then would part his robe, shake his lily and return to his residence. She was not at all amused and notified the police.

The most amazing aspect of this situation was that our deviate was a well-respected member of the Palo Alto medical community—a Urologist, no less! Why a medical doctor would engage in this form of extracurricular activity is beyond me; I guess that's why *Shrinks* were invented. . .

Faux Pas

During my 25 years at Stanford I couldn't even give you a ball-park count on the number of flashings, masturbations, and other sexual activity reports we received from the library system. Clearly, the most egregious of sexual events ever committed on The Farm—to my knowledge—occurred at UGLY. I dubbed this demented serial offender "The Mad Masturbator." He was a very sick puppy who preyed on exhausted females after they had fallen asleep at their desks, usually around exam time. This guy was the ultimate FW: He would ejaculate on his unsuspecting victim's hair and quickly leave. Nobody ever saw him, thus identifying this *sicko* was next to impossible. Stake-outs, roving patrols, information bulletins—not even the *Stanford Daily,* could help us catch this moron. After about six or seven incidents, a *Daily* reporter interviewed me about the disgusting problem. I explained that we were doing everything in our power to apprehend this pervert, but so far, to no avail. He then asked me a perfectly legitimate question to which I gave him a perfectly honest answer. The dialogue went something like this:

Reporter: "So, Captain, why is it so difficult to catch these individuals?"

Captain: "Well, Andy, I guess it's because they just come and go!"

Next morning, as soon as the Chief returned from the President's staff meeting, he summoned me to his office. *This can't be good,* I thought, *what the hell did I do now, I agonized?* By the look on his face I knew something was up; he then whipped out the front page of the *Stanford Daily* and pointed to the lead column.

Chief: "What were you *thinking*? How could you possibly have made that 'come and go' comment? And, to a Daily reporter, at that, for crying out loud?"

Captain: "Chief, I, uh, really didn't mean it in *that* context..."

But, I knew immediately that he wasn't buying it, given my history of glib remarks to the media. Said misspeaks were coined affectionately as TDQs (Typical Dad Quotes) by my daughter, a Stanford student during this period. The Chief then broke out laughing, and admitted that at this morning's President's staff meeting, the members were falling out of their chairs over perhaps the biggest verbal *faux pas* of my career.

To this day, I maintain my innocence and insist that "no pun was intended." The entire episode was, indeed, UGLY . . .

The Cummings Tea Room

We were in the Projection Room of the Cummings Art Building's Auditorium monitoring a Fargo body transmitter that our officer had secreted on his person.

Our Rookie was the consummate wannabe: He used to be a Reserve Officer in another agency, had recently completed the Basic Peace Officer's Academy and was in our Field Training Program. By all reports, this kid was way too full of himself: He was rather short but well built; many of the women in the office thought he was very good looking—definitely not my type. He had a full head of jet black hair and would spend a considerable amount of time and energy primping and admiring himself in front of the full length mirror while in his uniform. Just prior to leaving the locker room, our hero would don a pair of black leather gloves, turn them down below the wrist, put on his mirrored glasses, take one last narcissistic look, and make a grand entrance to the squad meeting! I think that Byron was trying to emulate Erik Estrada, of TV's "CHiPS" fame.

The Sergeant had our undercover man staged in the Men's bathroom across the hallway: Our "plant" was wearing our brand new wire (Fargo transmitter), so any noises or conversations would be monitored and recorded by my lead Detective, Don Lillie, our gadget guy. The Rookie was instructed to just hang-out, and to report any overt sexual acts, by simply saying, "Oh WOW!" Once we heard the signal, our arrest team would quickly make entry and apprehend the involved parties.

So, why in the world would police officers have a men's bathroom under surveillance, you ask? Because, the Chairman of the Art Department, Professor Albert Elsen, called the Chief and complained about rampant sexual activity in that basement restroom, that's why! I immediately reported to the Professor's office for the straight story. Professor Elsen told me there were dozens of adult men, believed to be non-students, going in and out of the restroom all day long, and that a number of his faculty members had actually observed some illicit sex acts. The visibly irate Chairman continued by saying one of his colleagues rushed into the bathroom a few weeks ago, entered a stall only to find a pair of grown men engaging in a sex act! Needless to say he was not amused, especially since time was of the essence, and all the other stalls were occupied. The Chairman immediately ordered the removal of all the stall doors, believing that this would deter further sexual misbehavior in the restroom. However, Professor Elsen lamented that his bold action apparently had little or no effect, for this brazen activity was still ongoing, thereby preventing students and staff from using that bathroom for its intended purpose.

Not having experienced this type of investigation when I was a Deputy Sheriff, I reached out to a couple of my good friends at the S/O, who had actually worked this type of illicit behavior in many of the county's remote park bathrooms. Detectives Dave LaDuca and Dave Pascual had worked the Vice Detail for some period of time. So, I asked these fine detectives how I should proceed with this issue. They outlined what and what not to do:

- ❖ Find a young cop, preferably a rookie, wire-him-up, and just let him hang around the places in question. Oh, and make sure that those contraptions work for, in those days, the so-called "state of the art" equipment was less than state of the art: Malfunctions were frequent—especially with the crucial tape recordings, which have a tendency to go bzzzzzzzzzzzzzzzzz after an arrest is made. Then it's a "he said, cop said" case. Good luck in Court! Test the equipment frequently to ensure functionality.

- ❖ Have an arrest team hiding-out, close by.

- ❖ Develop a password so when the undercover sees illicit conduct, he can casually say the buzz word so the arrest team can deploy.

- ❖ Above all, instruct the officer never to make any solicitations, suggestive overtures, or begin any conversation until a possible suspect initiates the dialogue. Defense attorneys always cry "Entrapment" anyway, so don't give them any ammunition.

And, that's all there was to this, I was assured. Well, the detectives admitted that these were pretty boring details as you might go days—maybe weeks without a hit. Also, the plainclothesmen often complained that hanging around restrooms was less than inspiring!

Our man had been in there for at least 20 minutes and we hadn't heard a peep from him: We could heard the bathroom door opening and closing repeatedly; we also picked up some toilet flushes and some background talk, so I knew something was going on. *Damn, I thought, is this going to be yet another dry run?* I also wondered if our electronic gear was even working, although we had just tested it. I was just about ready to check on our guy, when we suddenly heard: BAM, BAM, BAM! Someone wanted into our room very badly, and when I opened up, there was our officer shaking like a leaf, ashen faced, clutching his abdomen and coughing, as if he was about to hurl.

"What in the Hell's the matter?" I hollered.

"God, Captain, where were YOU guys? I said the password THREE TIMES and nobody came. They're in there! One guy just performed .... Damn!"

We never heard the kid, as he said the magic words so softly—but, when we replayed the tape, there it was. Oooops. . .

The Sergeant and I rushed in and grabbed two suspects. Both were cuffed and removed to the processing center. The Sergeant, a tough burly man who spoke with heavy Eastern European accent ordered the sickened Rookie back into the bathroom. That did it for this novice, as he immediately went into gag reflex and up-chucked his breakfast burrito. . .

We had a saying in the Old S/O: "Once a Reserve, always a Reserve!" Indeed, this was surely the case. . .

This was the first of several "Tea Room Raids"—as The Stanford Daily trumpeted—that we conducted over Spring Break in 1980. A Cubberley Auditorium restroom was another popular location. In one attempted arrest, after sexual misbehavior was observed, our surveillance sergeant was brutally assaulted and the suspect made good his escape. We figured that this suspect might have been a cop as he knew several counter moves to avoid being wrestled into cuffs. Another individual was collared in the Sunken Diamond bathroom after we were tipped-off by the Athletic Department that it was also a hang-out. In all, ten men were arrested and subsequently charged with illegal sex acts in public restrooms on campus. Five other men were cited for loitering in and around bathrooms. As we suspected, which validated Chairman Albert Elsen's suspicions, 8 of the 10 arrestees had *no* affiliation with the University whatsoever! Two men, as I recall, were students, but contrary to news reports, they were not from Stanford. We had a nurse, a teacher, a man of the cloth and a foreign exchange student. These people came from all over the Peninsula—San Francisco to San Jose. I learned that notes were posted in the City's restrooms, as well as at Father Junipero Serra's rest stop on I-280 at Crystal Springs Reservoir. I verified that later when I checked-out the restroom, covertly armed with my trusty .45.

A Perfect Storm

Most of the media reported this incident in a straightforward manner. There was a hue and cry from gay groups and supporters, as well as a number of sympathizers. In an editorial on April 9, 1980 by the Stanford Daily entitled: <u>Random arrest is unfair,</u> the author asserted that "University officials had been aware of the activity in the restrooms for some time. Capt. Raoul Niemeyer of Stanford Police Services has been quoted as saying that the acts 'have been going on a long time' and 'have gotten out of control.'"

My admission was partially correct, as I was told by members of the Old Guard, specifically, Captain Midnight, that he used to have to work the bathrooms behind Bldg. 10 way back in the day—but only when they received complaints. To my recollection, Professor Elsen's volatile rebuke of "tea room" activity in his building was the first substantial complaint I ever received. In addition, before "I unleashed the dogs," I went into that restroom one noon time during Spring Break and found NINE, count them, NINE random men just hanging around in the bathroom—not in the hallway, not outside, but inside! That observation really piqued my curiosity, but I didn't stick around, for obvious reasons. That's when the plan was hatched.

The Daily journalist continued, "The non-enforcement on the pertinent laws by the University created an atmosphere of at least implied tolerance. Those who were randomly selected to be arrested had every reason to believe that this 'tolerance policy' would continue. They were given no prior warning that this policy was no longer operative."

"We think that those who were arrested in the Cummings and Cubberley were victims of capricious University action and ought to be released," the writer opined.

I have skipped several redundant paragraphs of diatribe, but the Daily article continued:

"In addition, the gay community has a stake in seeing that those who engage in such acts in public restrooms come to grips with their sexual feelings. Arrests in restrooms do little to enhance the image of gays."

Rebuttal

In the wake of The Daily editorial, there was a deluge of "Letters to the Editor." Surprisingly, to me anyway, there were quite a few opinions in support of our police action. In a letter, dated 5/16/80, signed by a host of professors and staffers of the Humanities Department, they pretty much echoed what the Daily article had articulated:

Arrests disturbing

Because of police inaction for many years, the community was lulled into a "'climate of at least implied tolerance.' Then suddenly, without warning and quite arbitrarily on a particular *'weekend,'* officers made the arrests that will lead to serious damage of 10 lives."

("Weekend" emphasis is mine: I especially chose a weekend so as not to inconvenience legitimate faculty, students and staff from carrying-out their lawful pursuits!)

"If the objective was to deter this kind of activity in the future, it could have been achieved in a much less destructive way by issuing warnings to those whose acts were observed and by posting warnings that, as of a certain date, these places would be under police surveillance and arrests made."

In retrospect, I guess we could have done that. . . Then, on the day after said date, as suggested by the esteemed professors who conceived of this plan, it is my opinion—based on my over three decades of law enforcement experience—it would just be business as usual in the *tea room* of choice! If military commanders subscribed to this dictum, they would never win a single battle. . .

Now, I'll let the late Professor Albert Elsen speak to this issue.

In Professor Elsen's piece to The Daily's "Letters to the Editor," 5/19/80, the good professor opined:

Pleased by arrests

"With regard to the group letter (*Daily*, May 16) that, in effect, complained about Captain Raoul Niemeyer having done his duty, I would like to share some information and views since none of the authors use our building on a regular basis.

For those who, over a very long period of time, repeatedly use one of our lavatories for illegal purposes, there was never any question about the Art Department being responsible for a 'climate of implied tolerance.' We made it clear over the years in a variety of ways that certain conduct was not wanted and that in other locations it had led to arrests.

Specifically, the stall doors were removed a few years ago. None but the most opaque or the most aggressive could ignore that signal.

Second, the lavatory was locked on weekends and during recess periods and signs were posted to that effect.

Third, even when the building was completely locked on weekends, we repeatedly found a side door propped open. We would close it and then find it propped open again within the hour.

Fourth, newspaper articles which recounted actual arrests for 'lewd and lascivious conduct' in public lavatories elsewhere were repeatedly posted in our own lavatory. They were torn down almost immediately.

People authorized to work in this building on weekends and at night were always uneasy about security. Those who use the building on a regular basis are frankly pleased to have it restored to us by Niemeyer's actions.

Albert Elsen

Acting Chairman
Art Department

Thank you, Dr. Elsen. You are a "stand-up guy!" God Rest your Soul!

The Aftermath

After emotions simmered, the Chief and I agreed that we should attempt to establish dialogue with the groups who were so vociferous about the traditional police methods of eradicating a serious community problem. Clearly, our covert and swift enforcement of illicit behavior in the *tea rooms* made a statement—loud and clear: The University was no longer going to turn a blind eye (if they ever did in the first place) and that lavatory dwellers were not welcome on the Farm—period! Having set this principle, I met with several concerned people, including the leadership of GLAS (The Gay and Lesbian Alliance at Stanford) on a number of occasions. After a bristling start, all agreed that we should develop an alliance—so to speak, and no homophobia is intended—to bring resolution to the restroom activity. It was agreed, that if the police received information about possible misbehavior in bathrooms, plainclothes officers would check-out the complaint for authenticity. If there was a likelihood that something was going on, GLAS would be responsible for posting warning signs at the location in question and follow-up to replace flyers, if indeed they were torn down. Chief Herrington and I felt that by having GLAS involvement, the interlopers would possibly take heed and cease and desist. However, the Chief proclaimed that if the situation wasn't alleviated, the arm of the law would reach-out and snag violators.

Following those parlays, the department rarely received any more complaints about the infamous Stanford *tea rooms*. So, in the final analysis, although our "Shock and Awe" tactic in 1980 was unpopular in some circles, it had its desired effect—All's well that ends well. . .

Man of the Cloth

The so-called tea rooms didn't have a monopoly on illegal bathroom activity: One late afternoon, patrol units received a call of a man possibly peeping in a women's restroom near the School of Education. Deputies John McMullen and Tony Beeman responded. When they arrived a few minutes later, an excited and shaken female student said there was a man in a ladies bathroom stall attempting to "spark" on her when she was using the facility. When asked exactly what happened, the poor victim related that while she was in her stall, she heard some shuffling; she then looked down and saw a big #12 (shiny black shoe) protruding into her compartment. What made this shoe so remarkable was a 3" by 2" mirror attached to the toe. She quickly got dressed, stood up on the toilet and peered over the divider. There seated on the commode was a 60's male, dressed in black, sporting a black full length beard.

About that time, the subject, whom the victim described to a tee, emerged from the building; the student exclaimed:

"That's him! That's him. I'm sure of it!"

With that, the deputies ran over and put the collar on this suspected pervert. When patting him down, Tony found the aforementioned mirror in the man's rear pocket.

"What's this for?" McMullen pressed.

"It is required by my religion, for trimming my beard," the suspect nervously rejoined.

"Boy, that's a good one," the suspicious deputy returned. "I never heard that one before. But, you're under arrest for loitering and peeping in a women's restroom."

The man's pleadings fell on deaf ears as he was hooked-up and taken to the processing center at the Police Annex.

It was there that the investigating officers learned that their *peeper* was a very high level cleric from a Middle-Eastern nation. The deputies got the man's name, rank and horsepower, had him smile for the camera and cut him loose. The incident report was referred to the District Attorney's Office for review. Given the station of the cleric and the sensitivity of relations with the Middle-East, I frankly was shocked when the DDA issued a complaint for loitering in a toilet area and for being a *peeping tom!* The DDA also issued a warrant for his arrest. Several attempts to locate the priest were unsuccessful, but our Dynamic Duo hadn't forgotten and vowed to track down this character. As luck would have it, Deputy Beeman spotted the wanted *man of the cloth* at the Stanford Shopping Center and quickly snapped his bracelets on him. McMullen heard the radio traffic and met his colleague at the Annex. The cleric sniveled like a main jail inmate and claimed that he had Diplomatic Immunity. He also pleaded that the deputies call his embassy. After verifying that the arrestee, in fact, *did not* have immunity, John dropped a dime on the embassy's Chief Counsel and explained the situation.

After relating exactly what had happened and the charges that were being brought forth (all misdemeanors), counsel inquired if there was anything they could do to make this case go away. She explained that this individual was a very important personage in their faith—a senior cleric, possibly of bishop's rank—and this incident would bring great embarrassment to their church and country. The astute deputy offered his condolences, but held firm as this charge was brought forth by an aggrieved third party, and that he would violate the law, as well as his Oath of Office, if he just cut the man loose.

Needless to say, the advocate was stunned: Here we have one of the leading religious figures in their church caught sneaking around in a woman's bathroom, trying to get a cheap thrill by using the old mirror on the foot trick. . . I thought that went out with the 50's. . . But, then again, *some* of these folks are several centuries behind, still living in the 5th Century A.D. . .

With that the counsel lamented:

"Oh, my God! Oh, my God. OMG, OMG, OMG."

The cleric was subsequently booked into North County Jail, and the DDA was advised following the cleric's incarceration.

Several months elapsed without receiving a court notice, so McMullen went to the DA's Office and inquired with the charging DDA. She was a real ball of fire and wondered, too, so she immediately checked CJIC (the County's Justice Computer System) and was aghast to learn that the entire file just went *Pooooffffff!* There was absolutely no record of the incident; nothing on the cleric's booking and brief incarceration. Magic! It simply vanished into thin air. And, of course, "Nobody knew nutting!" I guess when you're high and mighty, there's a different standard of justice. Like my Ol' Pard, Detective Jackie Waggoner (ret.) in Garland, TX always drawled: "Justice delayed is justice denied!" I'll say. But, at least we tried. . .

Sunken Diamond

This collegiate baseball field is not only the finest in all of the NCAA, but many experts argue that it rivals most MLB stadiums, anywhere in this country. The normally mild climate and relatively modest rainfall of the South San Francisco Bay area has a lot to do with this; however, geological aspects come into play: Like real estate, it's all about location, location, location. When the construction crews excavated the Stanford Stadium circa 1921, just a stone's throw away, they discovered that there had been an underground river in this region, at some point in time. Instead of bedrock, the crews found a subterranean layer of rock and gravel, which facilitated exceptional drainage. Percolation is a key element in growing healthy turf that can withstand the weather and rigors of athletes pulverizing the surface with their cleats. Even during monsoon-like rains, the water in these sports complexes quickly drains into that aquifer, thus averting a quagmire. When you add some refreshments, hotdogs, and the stands full of enthusiastic fans, you have the perfect ingredients for America's favorite pastime. What better place to enjoy a spring baseball game between Pac 10 rivals than Sunken Diamond?

Shortly after the Cummings Art Building *Tea Room Dragnet*, as our friends at The Daily called it, we continued to receive numerous complaints from intramural participants, as well as other athletes, suggesting that we still had a problem with illegal sexual conduct in public restrooms. In this case, the site was a huge public toilet/shower complex, located just outside of Sunken Diamond. I put the word out in the department that we needed an adventurous deputy to reconnoiter the reputed site, but volunteers were few and far between—especially after the Cummings Art debacle. But, one of the stand-up guys in our shop, Bill Starbuck, came to me and said that he would check-out that bathroom to ascertain if the reports were valid or not.

We employed the same drill: Bill was wired with the Fargo and I had an arrest team staged nearby. At the appointed hour, our decoy disappeared into the depths of this musty concrete structure and was in there for what seemed like an eternity, but in reality, only a few minutes. We heard nothing on the wire, and of course, I worried that the damn thing wasn't working. All of a sudden, we saw Deputy Bill emerge with a collar in tow. "Man, that didn't take very long—and he didn't even need a fill," I applauded.

Bill wasn't your run of the mill FNG: He had been with the DPS during those formative years in the early 70s and departed for a period of time for other pursuits. During that hiatus, he got a master's degree and was currently working on his PhD. In addition to being one smart cookie, this guy was a helluva athlete and was as tough as nails. Bill played rugby for years and was a member of a local team called the BATS (Bay Area Touring Squad). Between work, school, a wife and a part-time travel business, he somehow still found time for weight training, pumping as much iron as Arnold, CA's controversial "Goven-Nate-Ah!"

****

I'll never forget the time Bill and I took-on a very stout individual who had just broken into an EV (Escondido Village) apartment and sexually assaulted a young woman. This event happened one summer afternoon in 1975. Radio put out the urgent call and advised that the suspect was last seen running down Pampus Lane heading toward the soccer fields. When the call came out, I hailed Bill and told him to get into my car. He had been on the department only a few months, and although green as grass, I knew he was eager. I raced down Serra Street, hung a left on the ECR (El Camino Real) and made a *Uey* at Churchill, in an attempt to head-off the skell. Being at the right place at the right time is everything in police work. I immediately spotted the suspect out in the field walking toward the El Camino: He was a built like a fireplug—about 5'8" and weighing-in at over 225 pounds. It was obvious to me that this individual wasn't tightly wrapped, as he was bobbing and weaving and throwing wild punches at imaginary adversaries. As we approached, I knew we were in for a _beef_. I yelled:

"Hey stop, we need to talk to you!"

"Fuck you!" he shouted, and the fight was on.

My instincts told me that negotiation was not going to be an option with this psycho, so I whipped him into the *high chest hold*—a euphemism we used in the jail to describe the infamous carotid restraint, which was my weapon of choice when forced to subdue combative inmates.

Once I got the hold applied, I took him to the turf with a foot-sweep, and immediately realized that this kid was extremely strong: It was like having one of those 1,200 pound bucking bulls around the neck! In addition to raw strength, this guy was flying high on something, and knew no pain. Just when I thought he was going to break free, my young tough partner came in for the kill and we collectively pinned this sucker to terra firma. While we were struggling to get this dude into handcuffs, I noticed that there was a huddle around us: When I looked up, I realized that it was the Cardinal baseball team! Thinking they were going to jump into the fray and kick our butts, I *buzzed* them, and stated our purpose. As they backed off, a bit, I tried to catch my breath and gasped:

"Hey, [*huff*], where [*puff*] in the hell [*wheeze*] were you guys, [*whew*] when we needed you?" One of the young men stepped forward and replied, "Looked like you had everything under control, Sir!" *Yeah,* I thought, *easy for you to say. . .*

We later learned that our grappler had been a champion heavyweight high school wrestler a few years before. He also admitted to ingesting four (4) bottles of Romilar 44 cough medicine, which was loaded with Codeine! No wonder he was so out of his mind—soaring up there with the B-52s. . . Deputy Bill really saved my bacon on that one, and I had never forgotten it!

****

Once at our booking facility, I asked Bill what had happened in the restroom. He related that he entered a stall and closed the door. Almost immediately, someone came into the toilet next to him. Bill quickly noticed that an entire 3" panel of tongue and groove siding was missing from the wall between the stall, to his right. Our decoy could see the person next door was a young male. The neighbor flushed the toilet. Bill just quietly sat there. Quicker than lightning, the guy next door dropped his laundry and projected his appendage through the slot. That was enough probable cause for Deputy Starbuck; the transgressor was summarily arrested for lewd conduct and booked forthwith.

Spring Ball

It was nearly a year after Stanford's Finest had concluded the so-called Tea Room Raids, widely reported in The Daily, as well as in every other media source in the Greater Bay Area. It was a glorious day for intercollegiate baseball. Things were relatively quiet on the Front, so I decided to take in a few innings at Sunken Diamond. We were playing the Cal Weenies, and although not as intense as football or basketball—clearly because the Cardinal *always* had a top seeded team, and would regularly beat-up on the Bears—I thought the game might be worthwhile checking out, just in case some trouble brewed.

I arrived at the bottom of the 5th. True to form, the Stanford nine, was putting a major ass-whipping on the Golden Bears. All was quiet, so I went over to the snack bar for a coke and some popcorn. Before I knew it, the organ played America's traditional 7th inning stretch melody: "Take me out to the Ballgame." As soon as the music ceased, a group of about 30-40 male rooters suddenly stood up and began chanting something. They were all clad in blue and yellow polo shirts, so I immediately recognized them as the enemy—*probably one of those Frats who painted those stupid bear paws all over the place during Hell Week,* my suspicious mind told me! Once those clowns had everyone's undivided attention, they shouted in unison:

"We want to go to the bathroom, but we are afraid!"

Typical Weenies: They lost the game, but had to have the last laugh...

CHAPTER THIRTEEN

Dumb 'n *Dumber*

The Dean's Narcs

Soon after Fall Quarter 1981 commenced, rumors drifted around campus that there was a couple of covert operators who were preying on students for drugs and money. Obviously, not many of these victims wished to step up and make a formal complaint for fear of getting busted—and possibly kicked to the curb by the University. The pair had been working the weekend party scene, schmoozing their way in and demanding to know where they could score some drugs—primarily marijuana, hash and "shrooms." The male was an older, well-dressed black man with an intimidating manner. His companion was described as young—perhaps a teenager—but, dressing as if she was 20 something. This young female was attractive and described as having a light brown complexion.

When the pair found a mark willing to sell a small quantity of dope, they followed the student to his/her dorm room. Once the unsuspecting *schmo* showed the crooks the stash, the male simulated a firearm underneath his coat, claimed to be a member of the "Dean's Narcotics Task Force," and summarily relieved the frightened student of his leafy, vegetable material, any available cash (hush money), then quickly vanished. In more than one instance, the crooks marched their quarry down to the ATM at Tresidder Memorial Union (TMU) and forced the terrified student(s) to make maximum cash withdrawals. I'm sure that more than one student lamented: *How am I going to explain this to Dad?*

After a number of anonymous calls and conferences with the Dean of Students, who disavowed any university connection to the pseudo-Narcs, the Chief put some plain clothes officers into the party mix, in an effort to ferret out these heartless criminals—easier said than done. After several fruitless weeks, the detail had to be terminated due to many other pressing matters.

In early April 1982, a young woman called me and requested a meeting; she said she was aware of what was going on with these extortion/robbery cases and thought she might be able to identify the male suspect because she had just seen him on the Marguerite shuttle. Naturally, I asked her to come on down. In the meantime, I asked my detective, Don Lillie, who had been around the PD for eons, to pull all photos of black males, age 25-40, who had been questioned or arrested.

Our eager witness was led up to the conference room and I told her we were going to have her view a series of photographs of subjects who were similar in race, age, and physical build of the individual we were seeking. I admonished the young woman to take her time and to look at each picture very carefully; I advised the potential witness to remove the photo from the stack, if she recognized the perpetrator. I also cautioned that just because these pictures were of people who the police had encountered in the past, their photo, alone, did not necessarily mean they were guilty of any crimes.

Following the admonition, Detective Lillie brought in a huge stack of photographs. This was an impressive heap of pictures—about the size of the decks the 21 Dealers dispense in Las Vegas casinos. . . Having been through a million of these exercises, I was less than optimistic, because obtaining photo identifications of perpetrators, especially at Stanford, had always been problematic: Many of our victims and witnesses were scared—and, I didn't blame them, for some of the creeps who came to our attention were indeed frightening. In addition, there was also a liberal and compassionate component at work: Many students often shared their feelings that fingering a guy for a crime could ruin that person's life—especially if they were wrong! Moreover, the cumbersome criminal justice system often worked against victims and witnesses, in the sense that the rights of the accused, at times, seemed to trump those of the People of the State. Often, the criminal justice process revolved around the defendant—be it a speedy trial, or a litany of bogus continuances under the guise of needing more time to prepare a defense. Defense lawyers just love to stall. This unsavory tactic often worked very well for the accused, especially when the kids went home during the summer months and were generally unavailable to testify in court—especially on very short notice, for the DA's limited budget didn't allow payment for transportation, food and lodging for victims and witnesses. In addition, the students were at Stanford for an education; their parents were paying big bucks for their schooling, so missing classes, exams and study time was always an obstacle in getting victims to cooperate.

While the woman studied each picture and turned them over as if she was playing solitaire, I thought: *Naaaaa, she'll never pick anyone.* Suddenly, when the witness was one third of the way down the stack, she grabbed a photo, smacked it down on the table, as if she just *Canasta-ed*, and exclaimed: "That's him!"

"Are you sure?" I pressed, while retrieving the photo and looking at the information written on the back.

"Absolutely," she gleamed, "And, here he is again!"

I looked at the mug and sure enough it was the same dude: John Michael Allen, 28 years old! Now, that was impressive! Having nearly 20 years on the job at that time, I had never seen a victim or witness spy a suspect's mug shot with such certainty! And, to spot the character twice (each picture taken at different periods) in that huge pile of photos was truly amazing. This crook had been busted for similar offenses in 1971 by Detective Donald Lillie; Allen was convicted and sent to prison. He must have recently been released from the joint. *Damn, what are the odds?* I quietly mused and swallowed an imaginary canary...

Now that we knew who this so-called "Narc" from the Dean of Students Task Force was, all we had to do was convince the District Attorney that we could prove the allegations. We still didn't have any other witnesses or victims who would step up to the plate. Furthermore, photo arrays are always suspect at best. And, the unconventional method we employed would certainly be challenged, as the "Rogue's Gallery" (*Round up the Usual Suspects*) method of identifying criminals went out a long time ago. Photo identifications, even line-ups, are always attacked by the defense as patently unreliable—and, with good reason, for they often are!

In the case at hand, I charged my lead detective to pursue an arrest warrant for our charlatan, John Allen, and in the interim, an area wide BOL was put out for the dope stealing duo.

The weekend was virtually uneventful. No reports of any consequence, so I went up to my office to return calls and work on overdue projects. About 0930, I returned to the Front Office to get another cup of coffee and as I entered the rear door, I saw one of the Records Clerks escorting a man to the Chief's office. I nearly choked on that last gulp of coffee: *Holy Moly, that's the pseudo-Narc, John Michael Allen*, I realized. As he was being ushered into the Boss' office, I flew to the phone by the copy machine and buzzed Investigations:

"Get down here, guys! That phony narcotics suspect is in the Chief's office as we speak. He may be armed, so I'm going down there, NOW!"

I ambled down the hall and entered the Chief's office. Startled, the Chief said that he was just about to call me, as "this gentleman" wanted to work for us as an undercover investigator—the man said that he had been doing some covert surveillance for the Governor's Drug Task Force and had a lot of connections to the drug trafficking problem on the Stanford Campus. Still positioned behind the self proclaimed "Narco investigator," I put my hand on his shoulder and pronounced: "John Michael Allen. You are under arrest for robbery, kidnapping and extortion. Stand up and put your hands behind your back!" Click-Click and it was all over.

The Chief looked as if he had just had a séance with Leland Stanford Jr.—his eyes were as big as saucers, too! When the cavalry burst in, Mr. Allen was induced to make a hasty exit and was soon en route to North County Jail. His 15 year old gun moll was apprehended later and incarcerated in Juvenile Hall.

What can I say? This knuckle-head clearly ranks among the dumbest criminals I had ever seen.

The "Mervie's" Bandit

On entering the Records Office one fall Monday morning in 1984, I inquired if there had been any activity over the weekend. One of the newer clerks replied:

"Oh, the usual: Bike thefts, a couple of drunks and something called a 211?"

"My dear, do you know what a 211 is?" I quizzed.

"Not really," she answered, apparently embarrassed.

"That's an armed robbery! Remind me to give you one of my Ten Code cheat sheets so you'll know what some of this legalese means. Get me that report please," I said nicely.

"Yes sir!" the clerk snapped as she sprinted to the copy machine.

As I scanned the report, I couldn't believe my eyes, so I read it again—very slowly. It went something like this:

"Q-2 and I (Q-5) responded to the Servomation Office at Tresidder Union on a report of a 211, suspect armed with a knife. Before our arrival, Radio advised that the suspect had apparently fled on foot. As an officer safety measure, Q-2 and I searched the premises with negative results.

Upon meeting with the victim, Ms. Pascual, we ascertained she was an employee of Servomation Corporation, which operates most of the food concessions on campus. She was very upset and obviously shaken by the experience.

(V) Pascual stated that she was taking the day's receipts, a substantial sum of currency, to the office where she was going to secure the money in their safe. She said that when she entered the office, she was immediately accosted by a knife-wielding robber. She described the man as a black male, 6 feet tall, medium build, wearing a dark shirt and pants; he concealed his face by wearing a plastic Mervyn's shopping bag over his head, with holes cut-out for his eyes, nose and mouth. She then pointed to the bag on the floor, near a closet.

(V) Pascual continued by stating that the (S) demanded she give him the loot, which she immediately did, due to his highly agitated state. She described the weapon as a folding blade, similar to a Buck knife. Once the (V) gave the (S) the bag of cash, he ushered her into a closet, and as he was closing the door, the robber tore off the Mervie's bag and threw it on the floor. He then ran out of the office.

(V) Pascual said that she waited a few minutes, then immediately called 9-1-1. She then advised that she knew exactly who the bandit was. The (V) said that even with the bag over his head, she recognized the man's voice and stature, and verified her thoughts when she saw his face as he removed his subterfuge when stuffing her into the closet. His name was Donald Timothy Phillips, a former employee, who had recently been terminated for stealing food and other items.

Finally, Ms. Pascual said that we could obtain more information on the suspect the next day from the personnel manager. We collected the bag and booked it into evidence for possible fingerprints. We dusted the area of the closet, but could not locate any readable latent prints."

End of Report

Deputy Jim Ledbetter Badge #510/28/84 @ 2040 hours

I gleefully bolted into Sgt. Philip Love's (aka Philippe Crueseau's) office where I found Det. McMullen, feet up on the desk, drinking coffee and telling fallacious war stories. "Hey guys; you see that 211 report yet?" I tested.

"Yes, Boss," the sergeant replied in his inimitable British brogue.

Philippe's father was a World War II French Resistance Fighter who was exiled in London after the Dunkirk debacle. He married an English woman and they had several offspring, all of whom were educated in England. Sergeant Philippe, who spoke with a pronounced British accent, also had an excellent command of the French language, which surprised many a visiting student from the land of *beignets, cognac* and the Eiffel Tower. As an adult, he emigrated to Kamloops, Canada, became a cowboy for a few years, and then headed south for the US of A. He wound up as a driving instructor in San Jose and later became a Santa Clara County Sheriff's Reserve. I met Philippe when he attended one my training seminars. When I made the move to Stanford, he was one of my first recruits. Philippe graduated near the top of his academy class and was voted the "Most Outstanding Officer" by his classmates.

"Well, GOI lads and get that 'brain surgeon' in custody," I ordered.

"A-2 (my new call sign); you want us to run that Mervyn's bag up to DOJ and have them super glue it for latents?" the young Detective asked. *Damn sharp kid,* I reflected.

"Absolutely; but I don't want both of you up in Sacramento—how many detectives do you suppose it takes to drive a Mervie's shopping bag up there? John, you take the unmarked home tonight and take-off early so you can beat the traffic, OK?" Both men nodded.

Shortly after noon the following day, I got a call from John:

"Hey, A-2."

"Yeah, John. What's up, and please don't tell me they didn't develop any prints," I groaned.

"You got it pal; *NADA*, he dug.

"Typical," I lamented. "If we didn't have bad luck, we'd have no luck at all. Damn!"

"Heeeeeeee," that jokester guffawed. "They got a perfect match on that loser; that puppy is history. I'm headed for the DA's office right now for an arrest warrant."

"Alright! Great job, John. But, remember, payback's a bitch, young man. I'm gonna get ya for this, boy!"

Like Ol' Rodney Dangerfield used to say: "I get no respect"—especially from these young whippersnappers...

On October 31st, Stanford's finest investigators and uniforms, assisted by San Mateo S/O deputies, rousted Mr. Donald Timothy Phillips out of his sack at O-Dark 30. He was booked into North County Jail in lieu of $15,000 bail.

Sorry you won't be able to "Trick or Treat" tonight, loser. You are clearly the "dumbest of the dumb" criminals I have ever seen... I gleefully rejoiced to myself.

Taming Animal House II

Although the majority of stupid criminals I encountered during my career were uneducated street thugs, I must report that a few of them were among the 10% of the brightest minds in the world—you got it: Members of the Leland Stanford Junior University student body! This one is a classic:

In a March 1993 issue, the Peninsula Times Tribune ran a huge color spread on page one of their Peninsula Section entitled: "Taming 'Animal House.'" The sub-title read: "Fraternity parties becoming more 'responsible.'" An inset called, "Party Trends," featured a foamy beer mug within the universal "No" symbol, flanked with the following text:

"To combat pressure from insurance carriers and school administration, fraternity parties at Stanford often include:

No kegs, BYOB: You bring your beer and turn it in at the door. You are given a card, which is punched one-by-one as you bring back an empty can for a full one, by "sober monitors" mingling through the party. No mention of alcohol in the fliers about the party."

Page two of the detailed article contained a larger inset depicting a house with the Frat's signature on the cornice (albeit the Greek symbol for Theta was wrong!), and a more comprehensive description of the game plan:

"Hosting a college party used to be as simple as ordering enough kegs and spreading the word around campus about the time and place. Today, party preparation is far more complex as students seek ways to limit liability risks associated with drinking.

A social policy adopted by Stanford fraternities and sororities includes an extensive list of provisions. Among them:

Signs stating California law concerning alcohol consumption must be posted at the entrances to all parties. Door monitors or hired security guards must be stationed at the entrances to all parties. Only guests with a valid Stanford ID, who are not visibly intoxicated, can be admitted. An adequate number of 'sober monitors' shall be provided (i.e., three for a closed party hosted by two groups; 15 for an 'All Greek Tailgate').

Those of legal age must be identified, preferably with wristbands.

Emergency procedures should be determined in advance.

Social coordinators must be trained for responsible party planning. (Stanford provides a counseling program, known as the 'Party Pros,' which offers advice on organizing safe parties.) EANABS (equally attractive non-alcoholic beverages)—*Only at Stanford (author's comment)*—should be provided along with non-salty food. Sober rides home must be provided at the end of the party."

Wow, I thought, *Patrol will really like this, especially after football and basketball games*! Then, reality set in: Call me a "Doubting Thomas" but I've heard this kind of stuff before; it makes good press and has a lot of fluff that is very PC, but when it's party time on campus, it is party time! And, all the rules seem to just go out the window... So, let me tell you about the 5X7 color photo of the "party room." The caption read:

"The décor hasn't changed but the tenor of the parties has at Stanford's fraternities, including Phi Delta Theta, where senior Joe *Schmo*—true identity being withheld—reads a Sunday paper in the party room."

Well, Ol' Joe is sitting on a 20-foot long bar, which sported a 20 X 4 foot Heineken banner below, apparently "borrowed" from the Ice Hockey League... There were four huge kegs, one of which Joe had his feet on—presumably the ones that they were going to return, in lieu of the new and improved BYOB policy (ahem)... Then, on the rear wall was an enormous sign which read:

Youth Camp

GIRLS AND BOYSVILLE

Operated By
Optimist Volunteers Youth Inc.
Sponsored by Bay Area Optimist Club

Right above that endorsement was a 15 X 2 foot priceless hardwood piece of wood which was elegantly carved in relief:

Devil Mountain Brewery

These fine specimens were flanked by a gaggle of street, warning and directional signs, plus a dozen or so from Stanford Stadium; my favorite—always has been—and most appropriate one for this group: Pass-Out Gate! Stanford Stadium *used* to have signs like that at various portals...

What a bunch of circus clowns, I thought. Jeeezz, we recently busted another Frat for having a bunch of stolen signs, and The Daily was all over the story and chronicled our every move. What a pain in the posterior. Booking all that stuff into evidence, storage and abatement—something my Evidence Technician just loved. . . This looks like yet another and bigger sack of rattlesnakes to me, and I ain't going there unless I'm forced to, I silently hoped.

I had scarcely finished my second cup of coffee when that dreaded buzz jolted me from worry-land. Damn, the Front Office:

"Captain, there's a gentleman on the phone who needs to talk to the man-in-charge of Investigations."

"Well, my dear, that would be me; put him on.

"Captain Niemeyer, how can I help you?"

"My name is Jack Turner. Did you happen to see that article in this morning's Times Tribune about the fraternities and their new party policy?

"Yes, I did, Mr. Turner; interesting, yeah?"

"Yes; very interesting, indeed. Especially since my dearly departed sign from the Optimist Camp is prominently displayed on the back wall of their bar."

Choke—Cough.

"Sir, are you sure that's your sign?"

"Absolutely! That bunch of rowdies was up at our camp last summer and after they left, so did my sign. I figured it was them, but didn't have any proof," the man complained. He then added, "I called the Sheriff and they took a report, but you know how that goes."

"OK, sir, we'll get on this one, especially now that we have visual evidence. Looks like we are going to have to raid that place! I'll be in touch."

I no sooner got off the phone when I received another incoming call—the CEO of Devil Mountain Brewery. Uh, oh! "Yes sir, I know exactly what you are calling about. We are on the case as we speak, and we'll retrieve your sign as soon as we get a search warrant. I'll keep you posted, sir. Bye."

Damn, just what we need. Those idiots! What were they possibly thinking? How could they be so stupid as to have the Paly Times photograph their bar with those obviously hot signs all over the place? And, these are some of the brightest people on the planet? I lamented.

Buzzzz: "Sergeant, grab McMullen and come on in—got a great one for ya!"

And, so it was, with clear "PC"—the cop variety: Probable Cause!

Shortly thereafter, at about 0900:

"Bam, Bam, Bam. Stanford Po-Lice. Search Warrant. Open-up!"

After a few minutes, a couple of hung-over young men dragged their carcasses to the door. Despite a very clear explanation of our presence, these fellows just couldn't comprehend what brought the wrath of the New Mean Green Machine (our raiding party was attired in bright green windbreakers with SHERIFF emblazoned on the front and back) down on their on their posteriors at this ungodly hour—at least from their point of view. *Why in the hell weren't these guys in class, for God's sake,* I thought. Once inside, we were all over that Frat like ugly on ape! Just as I figured, the usual snivels came forth, now from a host of drowsy and bewildered fraternity members:

"But sir, we have had those signs in this house for years; they were given to us; we got them at garage sales," blah, blah, blah. But, they came up with a couple of really original ones: "But, sir, we got some of these at junk yards. Oh, and we found some at the waste management facility."

"Yeah, right," I retorted.

"Did ya get that huge Continental Divide sign from a junkie on Bay Road in East Palo Alto?" I asked.

"And, how about that one from the Inn at Martha's Vineyard? You know, son, I was born at night, but I can assure you it wasn't last night. . ."

With over 100 stolen signs recovered, my Evidence Technician, Sandy, was not a happy *camperette*; it took her over a year to return all of the goods to their rightful owners. I'm amazed that she still speaks to me.

Chapter Fourteen

Demonstrations

A Different Breed of Cat

Unlike the vicious, violent protesters of the 1960's, our Stanford students of the mid 1970s were rather benign. Whereas the crazies of the Vietnam War era would incite and goad the police into confrontations, the kids I encountered during my tenure were indeed a different breed of cat. We saw virtually none of the screaming "Pigs off campus," fusillades of rocks, bottles, roof tiles and anything that could send a stout copper clad in riot gear to the E.R. Nobody ever threw a bag of urine at us, let alone any punches! For the most part, our demonstrators were a well-mannered lot, often queing up to be arrested. Save for a few dung disturbers (mostly outsiders from far left fringe groups), our protesters were very well organized, willing to abide by the rules of decency, all the while making their voices heard. But, this preamble didn't go exactly as planned during our first encounter, which caught us totally flat-footed with no time to prepare or create a plan.

CCPC

I had only been on the job for a few years (April, 1977) when I got a panic call from the Chief that about 20-30 protesters were preventing a USMC Captain from entering the Career Counseling Placement Center for his scheduled recruitment session. A-1 told me to round-up as many guys as possible as we needed to get over there, *muy pronto*. I grabbed as many folks as I could and sped over to the scene, which was only a stone's throw away from the office. When we arrived, we met the Marine, a real specimen of a man: Tall, buffed and handsome; he sported a tailored uniform fresh out of the cleaners, with sewn-in military creases. The Captain, of course, had a fresh "buzz cut" and wore a splendid pair of mirror glass cordovan shoes. *God, I hope nobody steps on his footwear as that would really tick-him-off,* flashed through my mind.

"So, what's the plan Chief?" I asked. He looked at me like I was nuts and barked:

"We're going to get this man in there!" With that, we formed a wedge: The boss was the spear, me at his left flank and the Gyrene to my right. We were all in plain clothes, which I think was an advantage, as the protesters couldn't spot us in that mob. Their group was a rather wimpy lot, about 30 of them, reminiscent of the Haight Ashbury Flower crowd: Most of the obstructionists displayed signs decrying the "military industrial complex;" they locked their arms and formed a human chain. The boss zeroed in on the tall guy, who was blocking the door, as he appeared to be the *honcho* of this motley crew. The next thing I knew, there was a scuffle of sorts and someone in a beige striped sport jacket wearing a silver watch reached out and had the tall dude by the throat. Suddenly, the "Red Sea" parted and we were inside with the Leatherneck in tow. *Wow*, I thought, *that was impressive*. To this day, I wonder who that guy was who throttled the punk and broke the barrier. . . Wasn't me; I was wearing a long sleeve multi-colored Aloha shirt!

May 9, 1977: My Day of Infamy

So, what is a bona fide university without political debate and discourse? As Julia Child once said: ". . . that would be like serving hot pancakes with cold syrup!" Exactly! Following the CCPC incursion, we had dozens of rallies, demonstrations and even one occupation at the R and D building in the mid 1970s. As I outlined in the chapter about Chief Herrington, from the very outset of his career at Stanford, he got the University to buy into the policy that building occupations would not be tolerated at close of business—5:00PM, period! Non-compliant protesters would be warned they faced immediate arrest and incarceration if they chose to ignore our admonishment. In the R and D ruckus, we convinced the demonstrators to leave—and they did.

There was considerable concern in Bay Area law enforcement circles during the 1970s that we might be faced with similar circumstances of the 60s. So, in order to become better prepared, many agencies began to strategize and refine their protest/arrest policies and procedures. I belonged to several Intelligence groups and absorbed a myriad of plans like a sponge. At the time, there had been a number of pretty nasty confrontations at Moffett Field NAS, as well as at Sunnyvale's NASA facility over the nuclear energy program, which environmentalists wanted to shut down. Many people were arrested at both venues. I credit these agencies for coming-up with a very simple plan to deal with the offenders so as not to lose the cases in court later on down the line. I'll discuss that procedure shortly, but now I want to tell you about the *worst* birthday party I ever had. Yes, it was May 9, 1977.

Like a cyclone, hundreds of students and sympathizers swept into the Old Union (OU) and covered nearly every square inch of the floor with their posteriors. . . They allowed narrow pathways for the staffers to walk by, but for the most part, that place was wall to wall kids! I figured there were up to 500 boisterous protesters singing and chanting "Stanford out of South Africa."

This was a well organized, well thought-out plan by the student group who called themselves SOSA (Stanford out of South Africa). This organization was committed to forcing Stanford University to completely divest itself from South Africa, then dubbed the "Apartheid" nation. While the University was adamantly opposed to the racist policies of South Africa's ruling regime, Stanford's portfolio was simply too complex to simply walk away from billions in investments. I'm no economist and confess that I didn't thoroughly understand the issue, nonetheless, we had a whole bunch of pissed-off kids sitting on that floor of the OU.

Call to Arms

While I monitored the situation throughout the day, the Chief was in conference with administration as to what they wanted us (SUDPS) to do come 5:00PM. It was clear in our minds that these kids were going to stick to their guns and not leave when ordered to do so. They were committed! Misguided, in my view, but willing to impose their purpose, despite the consequences. I must admit, I admired that. . .

Although the mandate of no occupations beyond the close of business was established, we still needed the person in charge of the facility to order the demonstrators to leave. Peace Officers have no power to arrest anyone who is trespassing on private property, thus an elevated official, who is in control of the complex, has to say the *Magic Word*: "Get the hell out of here!"—or something to that effect.

Behind the scenes, the S/O's tactical squad was marshaling their forces. Their charge was to provide security and transportation; all else was left to us. They brought-up a 30 passenger security prisoner bus, which we staged nearby. Court Liaison Officer (CLO) Sandra Mize was in charge of processing all prisoners and ensuring that the chain would not be compromised. Sergeant Marvin Moore assembled three (3) two man arrest teams—admittedly, a paltry number of arrestors, but that's all we had! From a form I developed, another deputy would advise every person who chose incarceration that they were under arrest and recite the charges. I was given overall command of the arrest operation, should that occur—but there was no doubt in my mind we were going to have a very long night!

At 5:00PM, using a bullhorn and while being videotaped, I read a prepared admonition which, in effect, told the occupiers that the building was officially closed and that they needed to vacate the premises immediately or be subject to arrest. I then read a litany of possible Penal Code violations they could be charged with, and what potential sentences could be applied upon conviction. I called this "The Riot Act!" This warning scared the hell outta me, but to the kids on the floor, it seemed to run off like water on a duck's back. . . I knew then, we were in for it.

The so-called deadline clock continued to run; I later learned that the administration was having difficulty in appointing a person to order the protesters out: The issue was not one of *wimpdom*, but the administration didn't want the defense to be able to call the University President into each and every trial, should this situation come to that. It made sense, but it set-up an attackable precedent (in my view), that the building wasn't *really* closed at 5:00PM after all. *Oh, well,* I thought, *we'll let the lawyers duke-it-out.*

It was pretty close to 6:00PM before a mid-level administrator arrived to say the "Magic Words." I gave the man my bullhorn and he told the mob that the building was closed and that they were subject to arrest if they chose not to leave at once. Save for one or two students, the throng was mired in concrete...

Prepare to Arrest—Forever!

At this point, I went to our process center, which was in a little lounge near the rear door of OU, across from the Old Courtyard where the S/O bus and troops were staged. I advised my charges that we were about to embark on the biggest arrest operation in California to date. I told my crew we were very well prepared, had excellent personnel and that everyone knew their jobs, which would be executed accordingly. Finally, I reminded the troops that this situation was going to very tedious, but they shouldn't be discouraged. Most importantly, I implored the troops to stick to the game plan—no short-cuts! I felt like I was giving a half-time speech to my youth football team when we were down by three touchdowns...

At approximately 6:50PM, I went back to the lobby and re-read the riot act to the squatters; once again, there was no reaction and absolutely no movement—they were like statues! I radioed our HQ and advised them to commence the operation. The incarceration teams (T-Units) arrived in a column of twos—all six of them... *Boy*, I agonized, *this is going to take a month of Sundays!* After each protester was told s/he was under arrest by the "Arresting Officer" and what the charges were, the teams bound the prisoners with cable ties behind their backs and marched them off to the processing center.

The Process

We developed a simplistic "Field Arrest" card—a 4X6 inch piece of cardstock with a detachable NCR (kind of like carbon paper) form. The T-Units filled out their names and badge numbers, the arrestee's name, rank and horsepower, location of arrest, time and date, and charges. CLO Mize had previously written large sequential numbers on the rear of these cards; this number was the person's arrest number, which was also written on the subject's hand with an indelible felt tip pen. She then took a Polaroid photo of the arrestee and the T-Unit officers. The hard copy was retained at the HQ and the prisoner was handed-off to S/O deputies with the top sheet; this enabled a jail booking officer to record all of the necessary information. Nothing could go wrong. Actually, in this system, nothing did—up to this point—I was shocked and amazed!

Uh-oh

Just when I thought we were in the clear, CLO Mize informed me that she just processed a subject who had previously been arrested and released on citation. Despite the S/O cordon, this sucker somehow got back into the building! As a matter of fact, several other suckers got back in and were rearrested. This was not good. To say that I was rather displeased is a huge understatement: I was totally pissed! How these clowns were getting back into the Old Union was quickly solved by one of our alert CSOs (name forgotten due to time but kudos to him, nonetheless): He spotted some miscreants scaling the structure by way of a covered walkway adjacent to the OU. Once on the precious tile roof, they scampered up to the second story and were gaining entry through an open bathroom window. A couple of the S/O's finest knuckle draggers scurried upstairs, shooed the enablers away, and plugged that hole. We were back in operation and the arrests went on, and on and on. I felt like Pope Julius II (Rex Harrison) in the great movie, "The Agony and the Ecstasy" as he screamed at Michelangelo (Charlton Heston), who was laboriously painting the ceiling of the Sistine Chapel, "When will you make this end?"--my sentiments, exactly...

Enter Lt. Steve Kriss

Writing about my former Patrol Sergeant, Steve Kriss, might encompass another book in and of itself: He was clearly one the most colorful characters I ever worked for at the Old S/O. A retired USMC Captain, Steve was a classic! He was built like a lowland gorilla: He was huge; a thick block of flesh, he was, and there wasn't an ounce of fat on this man. His impeccable uniform bristled with hard muscle! Kriss was the kind of man you simply did not want to mess with! He was extremely funny and very outspoken. When fired up, he'd often mount the huge oak table in the Squad Room and pontificate freely about the administration and how screwed-up some of them were. Our squad would roll in the aisles with laughter. But, his real strength was the way he supervised men: If you had his confidence, he'd let you run the show; if you didn't, he'd "bird dog" your sorry ass until you got "squared away," as he termed it. Fortunately, I seemed to have acquired his confidence, so we got along famously.

Steve Kriss was promoted to Lieutenant and was in charge of the S/O contingent in the Old Union demonstration. It was about 0430 hours; we had been arresting kids hand-over-fist for almost nine hours—nearly 280 something and counting. There were about 10-12 left—sitting in a line, waiting for their turn to be incarcerated. Everyone was spent, especially the Arrest Teams who had been going non-stop for the duration.

Suddenly, a mischievous thought occurred to me. I approached the vaunted Lt. Steve Kriss and postulated a ploy:

"LT! How about you tell those remaining fools on the floor that we are done and they can go back to their dorms. Tell 'em we have exhausted all of our assets and we simply have no way to arrest and process the remaining protesters."

Lt. Kriss liked that—I could tell from the way he chomped down on the stub of his cigar and the sudden glint in his eyes. He nodded, smiled and said:

"Niemeyer, you are a cantankerous son-of-a-bitch, but I'll do it—just for you!"

Behind the scenes, the powers that be were aware of the prank. The Chief snickered and Stanford's top lawyer, John Swartz, chuckled quietly.

Lt. Kriss approached "The Last of the Mohicans," arms folded, cigar about chomped in two and declared:

"Okay, kids; time to go home. We are done here and can't arrest your sorry asses—as much as I wish we could. We are outta deputies, forms, film, and transportation. Good Night!"

As he began to leave, one of the more outspoken students, pleaded:

"But, sir, this isn't fair! We have been sitting here for over 20 hours! We demand to be arrested!"

About that time, I unleashed our near comatose Arrest Teams, who formed up in a column of twos and doubled-timed to the kids while chanting "Hut One-Hut Two-Hut Three-Hut-Four!"

The kid with the mouth complained to Lt. Kriss: "But, Sir, you just told us there were no more men available to arrest us!"

The good lieutenant just smiled and retorted: "I lied!" . . .

Tom Farenholtz, D.D.A.

After several days of assembling the massive amount of paperwork from this episode, my detectives and I went over to the North County District Attorney's Office. I approached the counter and slammed down the huge pile of paper, which would have made the 2,300 page Obama Care bill look like a comic book. I bellowed:

"We need to speak to a D.A. who knows about mass arrests; we have 294 cases here!"

The clerk gulped and just stared at me. But, from the back of the office someone said: "Give it to the new guy!"—I mused, *even these lawyers know about the FNG concept. . .*

Within a few minutes we were led to an office about the size of a closet. Behind the desk was a young man, slight of stature and soft spoken; he looked like a "Preppy" with his tweed jacket, nondescript tie and button down collar. When I plopped the huge pile of paper on his desk, I thought he was going to stroke. After exchanging pleasantries, he quickly delved into the pile as if he had been a student in the Evelyn Wood's speed reading course. In actuality, this was not a very complicated case on its merits; however, the sheer number of arrestees and the political ramifications was immense. I could read this in his eyes.

Within a few minutes, Mr. Farenholtz said that he needed to view the scene. I was shocked! In all the years that I had dealt with the D.A.'s Office, I had *never, ever* seen a prosecutor leave the office in order to survey a crime scene—I'm sure that others may have experienced this, but not me, especially on a misdemeanor beef.

After pouring over the Old Union for nearly an hour and explaining exactly how this thing went down, DDA Farenholtz made some profound observations:

- He lauded our painstaking efforts and the way we treated and processed the arrestees.
- He applauded our S/O support and the manner in which they transported prisoners to Elmwood in Milpitas. Those arrestees refused to be released on a citation.
- He liked the way we captured the admonitions on video tape and with photos.
- But, he hated the fact that several previous demonstrators made their way back into the fray only to be arrested again!

In retrospect, I liken our breech in perimeter security to our porous U.S./Mexico Border. Oh well, we were/are human, thus prone to make some mistakes from time to time! After learning this, I joked that the S/O should have taken those who wanted to be booked to Loma Prieta, in the Santa Cruz Mountains (about 25 miles away) and leave them to their own devices. . .At least they wouldn't beat the bus back to campus. Just kidding. . .

In the final analysis, Tom thought that this was going to be a difficult but interesting case to prosecute. But, how do we try 294 students? We were certain that the majority of the protesters were going to plead not guilty and demand jury trials, and this would put a terrific strain on our judicial system—especially since this case was politically motivated and the penalties would be slight, in terms of fines and/or incarceration. This situation was a real conundrum, but if the People didn't draw a line in the sand, our entire judicial system would be imperiled.

The Trials

As expected, the defense was going to take the prosecution to the mat: Surprisingly, a number of kids pled guilty or *nolo contendere* (no contest), but the majority wanted to play hard ball. Most of the defense attorneys knew that Palo Alto juries would generally be liberal and sympathetic to the students.

The big win for our camp was the judge blocking the "Necessity Clause"—a defense ploy tried in the 60's during the aftermath of the Vietnam riots, which purported that protesters had a moral right to disregard the law, stand firm on their beliefs for the "greater good." This maneuver didn't work then, and it went down in flames again in our cases. Both sides agreed that the defendants would be tried before a jury in groups of 10-12—if my aged memory is correct. I lamented: *Would these trials be concluded before I retired?*

When I sized-up the jury pool in the first trial, I realized they were kids themselves. I figured we were toast, despite the evidence. Although I didn't know it at the time, in aftermath of the infamous O.J. Simpson trial, observers would coin a term that might occur in our cases: "Jury Nullification!"

Barracuda

Although slight in stature and soft spoken, Mr. Tom Farenholtz was like the lead Barracuda working a school of fish once he crossed the bar! He never raised his voice, flailed his arms, pounded the desk, or any of those antics you see on T.V. lawyer shows. He was very respectful to everyone, but if a defendant took the stand, Tom's cross examination was like surgery—without anesthesia! Before the "patient" realized it, s/he had been dissected, sutured and sent to recovery! The jury thought so, too, and convicted the first batch; ditto on the second group. The third bunch decided they had enough and threw in the towel! All of the rest of the Old Union 294 pled guilty or *nolo* to misdemeanor counts and received probation and community service.

Whew, I exclaimed silently. *I hope this never happens again in my lifetime*. But, somehow I knew this wasn't going to be my last rodeo. . .

They're Baaack!

Civil unrest on campus diminished significantly over the next 10 years, save for the usual Noon rallies at White Plaza. Then, all of a sudden, The Stanford out of South Africa thing reared its ugly head again. Clearly, the cause was understandable, but for the University to totally divest in the African country was a financial dilemma of infinite proportions. Instead, the University's policy was "selective divestment," apparently dropping accounts who actively participated in Apartheid. The movement, however, demanded a complete severance of fiscal dealings with South Africa.

Circle the Wagons

On another gorgeous day in May, 1985—not my birthday, thank God—a group of 20-30 protesters prostrated their bodies on Serra Street around some of the Stanford Board of Trustee's cars. Board members were having a regularly scheduled meeting nearby. We rallied the troops, and despite heroic negotiation efforts by our fearless and competent leader, Chief Marvin Herrington, the demonstrators "circled the wagons"—so to speak. . . The Peninsula Times Tribune's front page color photo and caption of the Chief standing in their midst, said it all: "They Won't Budge." Eventually, the students picked-up their backpacks and departed after repeated promises that they would be arrested and transported to the Main Jail in San Jose, where they would be unceremoniously booked!

Open the Flood Gates

The May 15th stunt by SOSA opened the flood gates; we were inundated with civil disobedience events over the Apartheid issue for the next two years. Here are some of the Stanford Daily headlines:

May 29, 1985: Police arrest 9 at Old Union. Photos featured 1) A student is frisked before police escort him to a vehicle following yesterday afternoon's sit-in at the Bursar's Office in Old Union. 2) Stanford Police Captain Raoul Niemeyer warns protesters that they will be arrested if they do not leave the building. Dean of Student Affairs James Lyons* looks on. 3) Students wave (*cheer, high-five, and raised closed fists—author's comments*) to arrested protesters as police take them from the Old Union . . .

May 30, 1985: Two freed, seven stay in custody: Photo depicts a sheriff's deputy leading manacled protesters into court. *(I'll bet Mom and Dad were proud . . . Again, author's two cents.)*

* Jim Lyons was one of the nicest, kindest human beings I had the pleasure of working with at Stanford. He loved the University and the students. He labored to keep his kids safe and out of trouble. Nobody worked harder than Dean Lyons to keep these students from being arrested!

Friday, October 11, 1985: SUDPS' Day of Infamy

I must admit that we were fat, dumb and happy: We felt that student unrest over the divestment issue had run its course after 294 had been arrested and convicted in 1977. In addition, we hadn't experienced an incident since the end of the Summer Quarter. I should have known that old wounds fester over the summer break and often erupt with each new academic year.

Suddenly, 11 SOSA members sat their sorry *derrieres* down on the floor of the Old Union and refused to leave at the appointed hour— 5:00PM, close of business. Dean Lyons squatted down with the protesters and tried to infuse some common sense into these student's skulls and get them to go home. Dean Lyons had some luck, for two dissidents left. But, the rest of the bunch was committed to the cause and refused to budge. I learned later that the group's core had apparently installed a new leader, a guy who had a great deal of animus toward Stanford's refusal to totally divest—it seemed he had a particular axe to grind due to his ethnicity! His name was Bobby Beekins.

Based on the over 300 arrests we had initiated as a result of the SOSA movement, we had no expectation of resistance or violence, so we decided to proceed with our program after the admonitions. *This would be a piece of cake,* I thought, *there are only 9.* Right from the get-go, things went awry: These kids decided to be hard cases and went limp on the arresting officers. No problem—all of our officers had recently gone through arrest technique training sponsored by the FBI and California Highway Patrol; both agencies had vast experience in dealing with resisters during the nuclear plant protests. All you gotta do is apply the tried and proven wrist lock on the tough guys, and in a minute, they'd be up on their toes like a ballerina and would walk anywhere you wanted you want them to. The wrist lock, aka "Compliance-Pain" (CP) hold has been used by cops since time immemorial—the reverse wrist lock was taught to me by my Judo/Jujitsu mentor, Roy Kimura in 1965.

Roy Kimura was an S/O deputy whom you simply didn't ever want to mess with! This man held numerous Black Belts and won nearly every tournament he entered. Kimura schooled me in some basic judo holds and told me to practice them continually—I did so, often without warning, on anybody I could find. In any event, the wrist locks worked well, even on our most inebriated guests in the Ol' Drunk Tank. (R.I.P. Master Roy.)

The CP technique worked pretty well on most of the resisters despite some them going totally limp—most got the pain and complied by walking to the processing area. And, then there was Mr. Beekins. He was a tall (well over 6 foot), gangly kid, perhaps tipping the scale at nearly 200 pounds.

When the officers applied the wrist locks on Bobby, this guy was like that rubbery doll, Gumby—of Gumby and Pokey TV fame: Beekins appeared to be double jointed as they put his wrist back to his forearm without results. Of course, he played to the crowd by screaming like a wounded animal; I got the feeling he was faking—he simply didn't seem to feel any pain at all, thus refused to comply.

Stop Fighting Sir, You're Hurting Yourself!

In 1984, the United States Secret Service sent me to Washington D.C. to attend their "Dignitary Protection School." Needless to say, this was an experience I'll never forget; however, there's a point to this digression: One of the training sessions involved a demonstration of arrest techniques. The arresting officer (instructor) was armed with only a rubber truncheon, similar to what the French Police use. The instructor's adversary was a huge helmeted man clad in a red padded rubber suit. The San Jose cops call it "The Red Man." The instructor stressed that when arresting a resister, yell at the top of your lungs: "Sir, Stop Fighting! You're hurting yourself!" "Say this over and over," he said; "witnesses will hear you and later testify that the cops told the suspect to stop fighting." With that, the instructor attacked the Red Man and pummeled the *bejesus* out of the dude, all the while shouting: "Stop fighting Sir, you're hurting yourself, you're hurting yourself. . ."

So, when it was Bobby's turn, he refused to walk thus was dragged like a sack of potatoes. This entire episode was being recorded with a video-cam; suddenly, a bolt of intelligence occurred to me. I remembered my USSS training so, live and on video-cam, I shouted:

"Sir, stop fighting, you're hurting yourself." It was a mantra and I repeated it a dozen times.

Mr. Beekins reminded me of the violent crazies from the Vietnam War days: He refused to cooperate with the pre-booking process; he would not stand up for photographs and answer pertinent questions. All he did was remain limp on the floor and stage a temper tantrum like a spoiled, 3 year old brat. It took 4 deputies--all beefy cops—to literally drag him to the transportation unit. This ugly scene was captured on videotape with me chanting the "Stop fighting" refrain until I was hoarse. As the vehicle pulled away en route North County Jail, I instructed Communications to give the Detention staff a heads-up that a fighter was coming their way. And, a fighter he was...

I later learned that Bobby Boy made the little "Green Room," aka "The Hole" due to his reticence to go along with the program. Bobby made a big mistake: He kicked the Jail Sergeant in the shins, which I'm sure didn't hurt that much, for this sergeant was as tall and as wide as a redwood tree! That stupid act didn't do this angry young man any favors, for he was stripped of his clothing, issued a pair of "whites" (coveralls) and deposited into the little padded cell where he would remain until he appeared before a judge the Monday morning, October 14th. Four SOSA supporters were cited and released on campus, while the other four, who put up some resistance, were released on their OR after being booked. I later learned that while going through Beekins' personal affects, the detention staff found a bottle of Darvon. No wonder he felt no pain!

When will this end?

That was my question to the "Higher Authority!" Our guys were exhausted and the Stanford Daily was pummeling the department over the Beekins incident—more sit-ins were to come. The Daily reported:

October 16, 1985: Six Arrested in Apartheid Sit-in. That demonstration occurred on Monday, Oct. 14th in the Old Union. Apparently, this was the protesters' venue of choice. A Stanford Professor (a first) and a Grad student offered no resistance so they were released on a citation. The other four went to the bucket on a variety of charges: Two fools wouldn't stand-up and identify themselves and walk to the pre-processing center; one stupidly possessed a controlled substance—and I've always bragged how smart Stanford students are?? The other clowns were "repeat offenders" and were booked for being knuckleheads!

October 17, 1985: Police Arrest 33 More Protesters. This event was more about alleged police brutality, especially involving Bobby Beekins: The crowd, originally numbering 100, marched into the Old Union from the Quad, sat down and conducted a "teach-in" on apartheid and civil disobedience. The group drafted a statement condemning Stanford Police brutality against all of the students, as well as "racist violence throughout America and the world security forces." "In the light of this brutality, similar to the violence in South Africa, we call on the University to divest from (companies that do business in) South Africa. We see its investments there as another sign of its insensitivity and racism."

Twenty-one of those arrested were immediately released with a citation and their promise to appear in court on the appointed date and time. Six men were booked into the North county Jail, while six women were carted-off to the Women's Detention Facility in Milpitas, CA.

Marvin's Magic Carpet Ride

After the Compliance-Pain hold debacle, Chief Herrington concluded that there must be a better way to move recalcitrant protesters who refused to "man-up" and face the consequences they had chosen. Fighting these limp rag dolls was no fun for the arresting officers, either. Many of our troops hurt their backs trying to lug dead weight back to our pre-processing center. Plus, it didn't look good and we played right into the hands of the biased liberal media. We needed an alternative.

During a pre-arrest briefing prior to the October 16th sit-in, the Chief unveiled his "secret weapon:" It was a 4X6 foot piece of canvas with four sturdy handles attached to each corner. When a demonstrator decided to be an Adam Henry and resist arrest by going limp, the officers would roll the subject over on his/her stomach, secure their hands and legs with industrial strength cable ties, and roll them onto the canvas. Four deputies would then tote the resister off. "Perfect," I exclaimed! "Chief, how did you come up with that idea?" A-1 replied that he had recently watched a Vietnam

War film and sadly saw our brave troops carrying their casualties out of the bush on these canvas stretchers.

Well, when a couple of the *first to be incarcerated* decided to go the hard way, an arrest team introduced the jerks to our new secret weapon. The deputies trussed them up like a rolled roast, and bundled them into the bag—they looked like big burritos! When the other protesters saw the humiliation their cohorts put themselves through, they hauled up the white flag and capitulated, opting for anything but what the troops called, "Marvin's Magic Carpet Ride!" Marvin Herrington didn't ascend to and maintain his position as Director of Public Safety at Stanford University for 3 decades by being dim-witted . . .

The Race Card

Following the difficult incarceration of Bobby Beekins, a ground swell of condemnation of police brutality and racist attitudes emerged in the media—primarily from The Stanford Daily. The reporters tried to convince the readers that the police and S/O singled-out Bobby because he was black. That proved to be totally false! The man chose to violently resist arrest efforts and assaulted an S/O Sergeant in the jail. He had plied himself with a narcotic substance, Darvon, which made him almost impervious to pain. This dangerous drug has recently been banned after causing untimely deaths of numerous people, including a Pro-Bowl Oakland Raider football player. We were damn lucky that this kid didn't croak on us!

One of SOSA's frequent flyer arrestees admitted in a Daily article that the Stanford Police treated the demonstrators well, but barbed: "But, then, I'm not black." This thing with Bobby Beekins had absolutely nothing to do about his ethnicity. In numerous public appearances and follow-up interviews with Daily and Campus Report reporters, Bobby stated: "I wanted to be arrested, but I didn't want the pain." Well, duh, he had the choice and chose the pain! After the alleged "brutality," he was taken to the Stanford Medical Center's E.R. where he was examined, photographed and cleared for custody. In a Campus Report article (October 25, 1985), which was based on a rally at the President's Office, Beekins admitted publicly to urinating on the Jail's Sergeant. Nonetheless, he promised to pursue his brutality case all the way to court. Good luck, Pal!

Dry Gulched

As most of you know by this time, my daughter was a Stanford student during this period and resided that year at Murray House, a quaint dorm in Governor's Corner. Nina's RA asked if I would be amenable to coming to the residence for a meal and chat with the students. I kind of suspected that I was being led into an ambush over the Anti-Apartheid issue, but figured I could handle the Q and A session. Moreover, I didn't want to disappoint my daughter. The meal was fantastic! Murray House had some of the best cooks in the university. I enjoyed chatting with the kids during and after dinner. But, then I was led into a lounge area and prepared to receive the fire.

Almost immediately, I noticed a group of about 10-12 young people huddled together in the shadows at the rear of the room. I recognized some of them, especially the gangly kid with a Cheshire Cat grin! I had a notion to go back there and wipe that smirk off his face, but common sense trumped my impulse. Much to my surprise, the audience was quite respectful, posed thoughtful questions and concerns, and listened intently to my address. I knew there would be some Daily reporters out there, so I chose my words very carefully, as I was worried what the paper's article would say the next morning. As it turned out, I credit senior staff writer, Stephen Kasierski for his fair and balanced piece of October 23, 1985. Although Kasierski's focus was on the Beekins incident, he correctly reported that all of the protesters were given the option to leave; however, if they chose arrest, they all had the opportunity to go peacefully. Only one of the October 11th arrestees elected to go out *the hard way* and he chose to accept pain over compliance. I pointed-out that we altered our resister policy with the inception of the canvas sling. Finally, I told the group that we were going to carry-out our sworn duties fairly and objectively. I added that none of our officers enjoyed harassing or hurting people, and many of us didn't like arresting protesters in this situation due to personal feelings about the issue. *Maybe this speech would put this issue to rest for awhile*, I hoped. Well, the peace held for nearly two years.

Building 10, May 15, 1989

At approximately 7:30 AM, the alarm went off at the President's Office. Ninety-nine percent of the time, the alarms at Building 10 were mistakes due to staffers failing to deactivate the darn thing before entering. Nonetheless, this alarm signaled "Battle Stations—all hands on deck," so all cops and CSO's immediately responded. Within minutes, our deputies cleared the radio channel and declared an emergency.

What in the hell now, I questioned myself, as I copied the transmissions over my police radio. The first responders reported that the President's Office was completely encircled with students. I tromped down on the gas and tried to dodge in and out of I-280 commute traffic as best I could. *Damn! This could be really bad.* And, it was, according to the initial reports: Fifty or more apparent protesters intercepted two office employees and forced them to unlock the front door; the pirates then shoved the ladies inside and barricaded the doors; their cohorts, hundreds of them, blocked both front and rear doors and windows with a phalanx of bodies, three and four deep!

"Looks like we are going to have to fight our way in," I told the Chief when I arrived at the scene. He agreed, but both of us didn't like the odds: This situation required back-up—lots of back-up, so I proposed an S/O call-up. We needed the "Mean Green Machine" (MGM) here, and that's who they sent. In the meantime, we pulled back and kept an eye on the scene. The S/O Tactical Squad Commander advised me that the troops would be mustered and should be on the scene within ninety minutes. That was fine with me; we had a lot of organizing to do, and as in the big sit-ins of the past, our department handled all of the arrests and processing. In this case, the occupiers were going into detention—no *get out of jail free* passes for this group, as they forcibly made entry into an alarmed building (burglary) and . . . All of sudden, it was like I was hit by a big brick: These idiots used force and took hostages (still locked inside), which took this crime to a whole other level. We are talking felony kidnapping and false imprisonment here! After conferring with the Chief, I approached the group and requested to speak with the leader. I was told the so-called "leader" refused to parlay with me but I could use one of his "stooges" (*adjective mine*) to relay the message.

"OK," I told the messenger pigeon, "you guys want to play hardball, then catch this 95 MPH fast-ball: When the riot squad arrives, we *WILL* make entry and arrest each and everyone inside on the following charges: 1) 459 P.C. Burglary, a felony. 2) 207 P.C. Kidnapping, a felony. 3) 236 P.C. False Imprisonment, a felony. 4) 148 P.C. Resisting Arrest, a serious misdemeanor. If you want, I can go on with additional charges for the next half hour but I think you get my drift. . . And, oh, by the way, those felonies I told you about all carry heavy prison time. So, you tell the dummy in there who is heading-up this group of marauders that he best release those women and think about surrendering peacefully before the 'Mean Green Machine' arrives." Within a matter of minutes, the front door opened and the women hostages were set free.

Here Comes the Cavalry

The arrival of the S/O "Cavalry" was not only a relief to us at President Donald Kennedy's Office, but it was also a spectacular show of "Shock and Awe," as well! The crowd control unit roared into the Quad, nose to tail, in 15 spiffy green and white cruisers. The pilots went through a perfectly choreographed staging maneuver as they parked their squad cars diagonally. Once the troops dismounted, they donned their protective gear: Chest, arm, elbow, knee pads and fully visored riot helmets. The squad formed-up and ceremoniously inserted their ominous black *Bokken* sticks into their baton rings. The S/O's *Bokken* (a curved 3 ½ foot hardwood weapon that closely resembled the wooden swords the Samurai utilized in practice) were brought into service at the S/O by a very skilled martial artist by the name of Sergeant Richard Min. Dick, a longtime friend and associate, previously schooled this 30 man force, and turned them into a very formidable unit. The squad's mere presence caused rioters to yield and give them a wide berth. Most of the people blocking Building 10 really took notice: They were probably thinking, *Uh-oh, I think we are about to get a serious ass whuppin'*. . . I know I wouldn't have wanted to be in their place.

Once assembled, I conferred with the commander and asked him to hold-off until our arrest and processing operation was in place. I also hoped that the group of dissidents would wise-up and give up the fight—no such luck. At the appointed time, I asked the MGM to clear the kids away from the front of the office so we could break-in and commence arresting the interlopers. With that, the MGM's boss formed a column of twos and double timed to the building. One of the columns broke into an oblique line and worked their way into the kids who were glued to the wall. Using their *Bokkens* like a scraper, the team peeled those demonstrators off that wall like barnacles on a ship's hull. It was a piece of work! The MGM then created a corridor so our arrest teams could make entry and begin their work.

Thwarted

Realizing that I wasn't going to be on the job forever, Patrol Captain Moore assigned the arrest and processing detail to some of the "up and coming" personnel in the department. When I learned they had staged the transportation bus in the alley adjacent to Building 10, I opined to the OIC (Officer in Charge) that I didn't think that was a good idea, as the outside protesters might sit-down in the narrow passage and mire the vehicle in a "sea of humanity." However, my suggestion was ignored. No sooner than when they had their first load and were ready to pull-out en route the compound (where the large S/O prisoner bus was located) did the "sea of humanity" flow into that alley! Not even Moses could have parted this ocean. . . Furthermore, we didn't need, nor want, any more arrestees! We had President Kennedy's Office back in our control so we just wanted to mop this thing up. So, how were we going to get the incarcerated folks over to the compound in light of this *foreseeable* development? This time, I approached the Chief and suggested that we utilize the MGM's personnel and vehicles to pick-up the arrestees at the head of the Palm Oval. The boss concurred and we started removing our prisoners from the trapped bus and literally ran our arrestees to the pick-up point. This really took the squatters by surprise; they couldn't understand what we were doing. The S/O sent a back-up squad there, and one or two at a time, patrol cars, un-marked vehicles and anything that had four wheels on it, transported the group to the compound. A handful of dissidents abandoned the blockade and attempted to rescue their buddies, to no avail—the tide had turned and they were no match whatsoever for the *Bokken* wielding MGM!

Epilogue

The best thing in all of the demonstrations we handled during the mid 1970s though the 1990's is that I can't recall one person, be it a cop, a protester or bystander, ever getting hurt. Well, except Mr. Bobby Beekins, who "claimed injury" in the October 11, 1985 Old Union sit-in and filed a lawsuit against Stanford University. However, U.S. Federal District Court Judge Spencer Williams in San Jose didn't quite see it that way. This ruling came nearly three years after the incident, wherein Beekins charged that the police violated his civil rights by using the "compliance-pain" hold to remove him from the building. The Honorable Judge Spencer ruled that compliance holds are not inappropriate for handling passive resisters. He also stated that Stanford was not responsible for the events that happened at North county jail. Case closed!

CHAPTER FIFTEEN

Sexual Assaults

Our Worst Nightmare

Sexual assaults, in any community, are something that police and sheriff's departments dread—especially if they are serial in nature. But, when they occur at a college or university, the hue and cry is ear-splitting! Parents, administration officials, women's groups and the campus at large—fueled by the media—demand immediate action, and rightly so. However, catching or even identifying the jackals who attack women indiscriminately is extremely difficult.

The geography at Stanford made apprehension of serial rapists very problematic for us. The five square miles of our campus, much of it vast open space on which hundreds of females jog at all hours of the day and night, has heavily foliated travel routes used by students, especially at night, and untold cubbies where predators could and often did hide. Policing this campus is a virtual nightmare, especially when there is a sexual predator around. Couple this with an independent mind-set: "I can walk or run anyplace I choose," made many a victim an easy target. Despite our media and kiosk advisories: "Please, ladies, don't go it alone," our warnings fell on deaf ears, even when bad guys were on the prowl.

The Trend

We began seeing the trend in the late 1970s through 1982. And, it certainly didn't go unnoticed by the community as reported by the Stanford Daily as well as other news organizations:

Female student flees from male assailants (November 6, 1978)

A female student here escaped from three white male assailants near Lake Lagunita at 9:45PM Thursday night when a car stopped—

the student was jogging—she made an attempt to fight off her assailants, kicking one in the groin. The other two dragged her into a culvert where she was molested—she escaped, suffering only minor cuts and bruises.

Stanford Women increasingly jittery as rapes increase. (March 5, 1978)

Woman raped on foothills jogging trail (April 18, 1979):

Another woman has been raped on a jogging trail in the Stanford foothills. The 25-year- old Mountain View woman said she was sitting on a trail enjoying the view when a man approached from behind. "You shouldn't be up here alone. It could be dangerous," he said . . .

Wilbur attack not by Terrace Rapist (March 12, 1980):

The composite sketch of an attacker *(an attempted rape)* at Wilbur Hall looks like the *(infamous)* College Terrace Rapist, but police are almost certain that the two incidents are unrelated. . . *(A look-alike was detained several times but the victims were unable to ID him)*

The College Terrace Rapist is credited for four attacks in 1979 and seven others between 1971 and 1976, the latest in early November. *(None of these attacks occurred on the Stanford campus. Melvin A. Carter was arrested by Palo Alto PD in 1980; he was convicted of multiple rapes on Dec.21, 1981 and sentenced to 25 years. Carter is suspected of committing nearly 100 assaults on women in the Bay Area over the past decade. He was released in 1996 and currently resides in Leicester New York.)*

Student fights off would-be rapist (April 30, 1982):

. . . The woman was walking along the west side of Kresge Auditorium on campus about 9:05 PM when a man stepped out from behind some bushes. He grabbed her from behind and tried to overcome her.

But, the woman fought back and managed to hit him with her backpack. She pulled free of him and ran away. Her assailant was described as a black male, 25-26 years old, 5'11" tall and weighing about 170 pounds.

The Blind-Side Rapist

For lack of a better name, The Daily attributed most of the attacks during the 70s and 80s to the "Campus Rapist." I since have dubbed him the "Blind-Side Rapist" based on his MO. Save for the Field Site attacks, which will be addressed later on in this chapter, the majority of the campus assaults happened either in open spaces during the day or in dark areas at night. The victims were blitzed from the rear, swiftly, and quickly overpowered by a very strong black male, who stood nearly 6' tall and weighed from 175 to 190 pounds; he sported a short Afro. Few of the unfortunates ever got a glimpse of his facial features, as he prevented them from doing so, by various means: I recall in one of the first attacks near the Stanford Stadium, the brute pulled the woman's shirt over her head and then dragged her into a foliated area where he consummated the rape. He continually admonished his prey that he would kill them if they looked at his face. He repeated a few weeks later, when he brutally overpowered a young lady who was enjoying a picnic near Cactus Gardens—certainly not a pleasant experience which would probably nix the thought of any picnics for the rest of her life!

During his evening attacks, this loser would use darkness, stealth and surprise to his advantage. I applauded the lady who clobbered this jerk with her backpack and made good her escape. Over this period, we ran a series of covert operations in an effort to nab this criminal, or if nothing else, to identify him. All attempts were fruitless, despite using wired-up SUDPS decoys, who were closely monitored by nearby armed plain clothes officers. In retrospect, it was like trying to find a needle in a haystack. Moreover, the frequency of attacks was sporadic: There might be a string of two or three assaults within a month, then nothing for up to six months or so. I believe if we had a hundred cops out there, the perp would have still remained invisible.

"Aarrgghhh, Aarrgghhh"

Well, that's what the guy said when the Marines at the front gate of Alameda Naval Air Station asked why he was covered with blood. Upon a closer look, they found the man bleeding profusely from his mouth, so the sentries called for an ambulance and sent him to the dispensary. Although almost unintelligible, the severely wounded man told the ER Doc that a couple of guys jumped him in Oakland, and he bit off his tongue during the fight. However, an area wide All Points Bulletin (APB) announced that University of California Berkeley police were seeking a rapist who got part of his tongue severed when he attacked a student near the library within the hour—so much for going *French* with an unwilling partner! Police at the scene immediately collected the evidence and packed it in ice. UCB officers soon learned their possible suspect was being treated at Alameda NAS's Dispensary, so they sped over there with the remnant of the man's tongue. When the police gave the appendage to the physician, he examined it briefly and forcefully threw it into a garbage can and said: "We won't need this—medically speaking!"

The man with his newly acquired speech impediment was Petty Officer Second Class Kenneth Dwayne Bailey, 25, of East Palo Alto. He was charged by UCB investigators with rape, oral copulation, aggravated assault and kidnapping; the predator was incarcerated in Alameda County jail on $75,000 bail. Bailey had been out of custody in lieu of $10,000 bond on two other rape charges at the time; one of the victims was a 15 year old high school student.

My investigators were very interested in Bailey, as his ethnicity, height and weight fit our rape suspect to a tee. We also learned that he had been transferred back and forth from Alameda to Moffett Field NAS in Mountain View on several occasions. In my mind, this accounted for the lapses in attacks. In addition to the fact that his home was in East Palo Alto, we ascertained that Bailey had been employed at the Stanford Medical Center as a security guard. Perfect! This effectively put the fox right in our chicken coop; this predator most likely knew our jurisdiction like the back of his hand.

My detectives obtained a mug shot of Bailey, created a photo spread and showed it to four of the five victims we knew about; one of the students would not participate for personal reasons. Unfortunately, none of the other women could positively ID the suspect, so we were unable to build any viable cases against this criminal. Palo Alto PD, however, was able to charge Bailey with burglary and attempted rape when their victim identified him straight away. As I said earlier, this brutal rapist carefully hid his facial features when committing his crimes at Stanford so his victims wouldn't be able to point the finger at him later on. Fortunately for all women in the Bay Area, Kenneth Dwayne Bailey went to the *slam* for many years and was forever branded as a Sexual Predator. These serial rapes reminded me of the Atlanta Child Murders: Once the perpetrator was incarcerated the attacks ceased.

The Field Site Rapist

The California Department of Justice (DOJ), Bureau of Organized Crime and Criminal Intelligence (BOCCI) produced a videotape 1992, which in part, chronicled a series of sexual assaults which had occurred between June 1989 and June 1991. The rash of vicious sexual attacks was being perpetrated on female joggers in the foothills above the Stanford Campus; the suspect was described as an unknown male white subject in his late 20s. The specific property, known as the Field Site, featured a number of research facilities scattered around the vast open space of grazing land and scrub oak; it had a single lane asphalt roadway which ran from the north and east gates and was crisscrossed with dozens of cow trails, which joggers and hikers from all over the region utilized. The purpose of the DOJ video production was to publicize their newly developed automated systems, then on the cutting edge of technology, designed to assist law enforcement in the apprehension of violent criminals. The producer of the video was a DOJ investigator who heard that one of BOCCI's analysts, Carol Hoffman, assisted the Stanford Department of Public Safety in solving these brutal attacks. This very astute lady was assigned to the Sexual Habitual Offender Program (SHOP); she routinely received and analyzed sexual criminal offender information from law enforcement agencies statewide. More of how this unfolded, later on.

The perpetrator was a brutal bastard: He stood about 6 feet tall and weighed close to 200 pounds. He began his crime spree on the north side of the property, near the San Francisquito Creek. On a Saturday in the summer of 1989, and in broad daylight, he sneaked up on his first unsuspecting female and bashed her in the head with a huge rock; but not for her toughness and determination, she clearly would have been murdered. Miraculously, she survived the onslaught and head trauma, and outran him to safety. This savage assault was a harbinger of the evil which this serial offender would soon unleash.

The second victim was kidnapped at knifepoint and dragged into the brush. The miserable loser bound her with duct tape, but gave up the assault when he discovered that the terrified Ms. was having her period. This guy was real good: After releasing his prey, he tidied-up the crime scene and took the used duct tape with him.

The next attack happened just before dark. A lady was jogging down a path toward the Campus when the punk blind-sided her from the rear with a bear hug; he was also armed with a knife. Our victim didn't hear him coming as she was wearing head phones while listening to tunes on her Sony Walkman. Mr. Macho apparently didn't realize who he was messing with, as this young lady was about to put "55 gallons of Whoop-Ass" on him: She rained a series of blows on this creep's head, neck and shoulders, which caused his eyeglasses to fly off! The perp clearly had a wildcat by the tail and had to let go when she knocked the knife out of his hand. She then sprinted toward the roadway below while screaming like a banshee! Fortunately, a group of people was walking up the path and came to her rescue. Our suspect then disappeared into the darkness, leaving his glasses and knife behind, hidden in the grass. Luckily, my responding deputy, a very meticulous individual, combed the crime scene, and found the knife and glasses. This knife was a very rare import, fancied by yuppie backpackers.

After a number of inquires, our Detectives found a specialty outdoorsman store in the Stanford Shopping Center that sold the same model knife; however, none of the clerks could ID the suspect from the sketch we had drawn by San Jose PD's finest police artist, Tom Macris. We later had the eyeglasses analyzed and learned the wearer had a very unique and rare astigmatism. Flyers were created: All information about the glasses, as well as the artist's sketch and suspect description was sent to every eye doctor and optician in the Bay Area—no easy task! I even put an ad for the glasses in the Lost and Found columns of *The Stanford Daily* and other regional newspapers. I hoped the suspect might take the bait and call our Tip-Line's voice mailbox. I also wrote a script and trained one of our Records' clerks, just in case he called. We carefully selected the dialogue so as not to spook the predator. We even reconnoitered some potential apprehension sites and my detectives rehearsed their roles should this low-life ever show up. But, like so many potentially great fishing expeditions I had been on, we got skunked! Not even a nibble. . . I've often said: "If I didn't have bad luck, I'd have no luck at all!" And, so it was—up to that point, anyway.

Shortly thereafter, the sadistic creep struck again—this time at gunpoint. He accosted a beautiful 18 year old hiker and forced her off the beaten path to a very secluded spot. She was bound, raped and subsequently released, otherwise unharmed. This young lady was completely devastated and unable to positively identify the suspect as being the guy in our sketch. She was also very lucky that he didn't shoot her with the blue steel automatic pistol he was packing. I personally went up to the crime scene with a detective and we poured over that place looking for clues, but to no avail. Once again, this clever serial rapist sanitized the scene and left us with nothing! The lack of breaks in this investigation was really irritating, for we all really wanted this guy—very badly!

I hired a retired DA's Investigator to assist with following-up on leads. Shortly after the first attacks began, we asked Patrol to stop and FI (field interrogate) every male who even remotely resembled the description of this assailant—Yes, we "profiled" suspects, even in those days. . . We were pretty sure this individual was not a jogger himself, as a number of folks had seen him wearing street clothes and hiking boots, just wandering around the main road and trails.

One sharp-eyed deputy, Mark Swineford, spotted a suspicious guy fitting this bill, so he stopped the man, FI'ed and photographed him. His name was Robert Michael Christy. When asked what he was doing, the suspect told the deputy he was a "nature lover" and was just walking around. The deputy then asked him where his car was parked; the man said it was parked on the main road below—pointing to Junipero Serra Blvd. Our cop cut-him-loose and buzzed back around to the area where Christy said his car would be. When the deputy got to where the ride was *supposed* to be parked, there were NO vehicles in sight! *Hmmmm,* Swineford thought. *That lying SOB just BS'ed me.*

Somewhat miffed, Mark went around to the north side of the property, a location where many joggers parked their vehicles, and as he approached, Mark spotted the suspect "sneaking out of the back door." Preferring not raise too much suspicion, our cop took down the license plate number and made a beeline for Investigations.

Upon hearing the story from our eagle-eye, I instantly felt the suspicious person Mark stopped was potentially a very viable suspect. So, I subsequently gave the information to my hired gun detective and asked him to run with it. Due to miscommunication, about a week or so passed before my investigator was able to get to Redwood City, where Christy was supposedly living. Unfortunately, Christy had already split to parts unknown—we were about "A Day Late and a Dollar Short. . ." And, to add insult to injury, we later learned Christy had previously been living with a graduate student in Escondido Village, right across the street from our Department, no less!

My Detective Sergeant attempted to make every lead we had work, but without much success. Then, by a stroke of good luck which had eluded us thus far, Ms. Hoffman from DOJ called me. She reported that a male subject had murdered an 18 year old girl in Rocklin, CA, and that his photo in the newspaper strongly resembled the composite sketch of our wanted rapist. The cold blooded killer apparently stalked this beautiful young lady, a popular cheerleader, after she had been dropped-off by her boyfriend following a date. The suspect used his vehicle to force hers to the curb, and then shot her several times—perhaps when she resisted his kidnap attempt. Upon hearing the shots, Rocklin PD sped to the scene and observed a pickup truck fleeing at a high rate of speed. They pursued the vehicle to a dead-end road where it suddenly stopped. As the officers cautiously approached the truck, they heard a loud pop from within and saw the coward keel over—DOA. This heartless bottom feeder was truly a "Dead Ender:" He took the easy way out and put a 9mm slug in his demented brain!

I originally thought this information from DOJ would probably be a long shot, until my Sergeant showed me the photo that appeared in a Sacramento paper: I especially liked the resemblance to our sketch and told the investigator I REALLY liked the fact the news photo showed the suspect wearing eyeglasses. I then had my detective call Rocklin PD to ascertain if Christy had any glasses in his possession. We quickly learned, that not only did the decedent have glasses in his possession, but also a case which bore the name of an optometrist in Mountain View, CA (just a few miles away from us) who had prescribed the optics to the killer! That clue cinched it for us, as the doctor's office immediately confirmed Robert Michael Christy was one of their patients, and the pair of glasses he lost while getting his ass re-arranged by our *Wild Cat* was indeed his. They sheepishly admitted that they had received our flyer but failed to check it out—so much for creative police work. . .

We also believe that the weapon Christy used in our final Field Sites assault was the very same Sig Sauer 9mm that he had used to kill the poor Rocklin cheerleader. I sent a team to search Christy's new residence in Reno. There, they recovered a lot of interesting and very incriminating evidence which connected the late Robert Michael Christy to the Field Sites rapes. I personally felt very disheartened that Christy slipped through our hands and was able to commit the ultimate crime on another innocent human being. But, on the other hand, I was pleased this cowardly scumbag did himself in and would menace society no more! Not only had Justice been swift and proper, but this Dead Ender saved us all a lot of time, not to mention a pile of tax dollars! When the victim of the brutal rape that Christy had committed at gunpoint identified his mug shot, I vigorously pounded my red stamp on the file: CASE CLOSED!

Falsely Accused

On November 3, 1998, I received a faxed copy of an article from Deputy Rich McOber of the Sonoma County Sheriff's Department, written by their local rag, The Press Democrat. Here it is:

Stanford woman attacked

San Jose—Stanford Police are searching for an aggressive, clean shaven young man who apparently ambushed a woman on campus, wrestled her to the ground and demanded she surrender her pants and underwear.

A 21-year old female student was working in a trailer near Roble Field on the Stanford campus at 1:30 a.m., Tuesday, said Police Capt. Raoul Niemeyer. When she left the trailer to walk to her bike nearby, the man grabbed her in a bear hug from behind, he said.

Niemeyer (emphasis mine) then dragged her into a dark corner of the field where he demanded that the student give him her pants and underwear. When the woman resisted, he tugged off her pants and underwear and fled with the clothing.

On first reading, I didn't get it; I asked myself, *why did a Deputy Sheriff whom I had never met, send me this article?* Then, it hit me like a lightning strike and I realized that perhaps the piece should have been entitled:

Stanford Police Captain is a Pervert!

Here I am, on the eve of retirement after nearly 35 years of faithful, honest service to the folks of Santa Clara County, and my reputation has been sullied by a reporter I didn't even know. I admit that I was a somewhat controversial figure from time to time, but this was over the top—way over the top...

Needless to say, the Editor of The Democrat got an earful from a "Republican!" And, I thought that some of the Stanford Daily's reporters' work was suspect???

CHAPTER SIXTEEN

DUs

Adios Amigos

Well, at the conclusion of the academic year '85-'86, Delta Upsilon's *Bad Boys* were banished from their choice residence for at least four years, due to the crazy stunts and bad deeds they had committed over the past five years or so. Now, it was up to the *Row Warriors* to make this hovel fit for human habitation after years of abuse. Son, Kirk, was a member of the clean-up and utility crew who shoveled out the mounds of rubble left by the Frats—they also repaired some of the damage, apparently done by the fraternal brothers. I'll never forget the time I visited Kirk and his unfortunate buddies who cleaned these pig sties. The site was the DU house at 553 Mayfield, after they had been invited to leave the campus. In addition to numerous punch holes in the walls on all three levels of the house, there was more trash in the hallways than I ever saw in the Santa Clara County jail, where the inmates just chucked everything out of their cells—well, I guess that afforded equal opportunity employment for the trustees. . .Once I entered the DU dump, the smell of stale beer, vomit and urine overpowered me.

"Damn, Kirk," I complained, "How in the hell can you guys stand it in here? Man, you guys need some Scott air packs like the firemen have. This is awful!"

He laughed and said, "Dad, come check this out." He then took off upstairs to the third floor. I labored behind. When I entered the room at the end of the hallway, the stench of beer and hurl nearly floored me. The kid then led me into a small sleeping compartment that was separated from the main room with a wall.

Kirk then smiled and pointed to a 2X2 foot hole that had been hacked into the sheetrock. Over the hole in large letters read: PUKE HERE! To the left was piece of plywood nailed over a hole in the adjacent area between the joists. Apparently, these morons would vomit in the hole until it filled up. Then, they would bust-out another section and throw-up in that one until it was filled, and so on, and so on. Clever kids, these DUs. . .

"Man you've got to be kidding me," I barked in disgust. "I'm glad those jerks are outta here." Maintenance folks estimated that the damage exceeded $20, 000!

So, what could these guys have done to get kicked to the curb, you may ask. Lots. . .

Erika's Palm

As I knocked on the Chief's door, I could hear he was on the phone; nonetheless, he beckoned me in. Then, I picked-up on his part of the conversation:

"Well, as a matter of fact, my Investigation's captain is in my office so I'll send him right over. OK, Erika, we'll take a report and put the word out; maybe we can find some of the stuff. Bye-Bye."

"That was Erika at the Law School. You know Erika, she's the Dean's Admin," the boss said.

I shook my head in the negative and said: "But I guess I'm going to meet her in a few minutes, eh?"

"Yeah, somebody stole a bunch of their new furniture; but what really ticked-her-off is they also stole *Erika's Palm!"* the boss chuckled.

"Darn it," I commented, "Those fricking frat boys rip-off furniture at the start of every Fall quarter. They know that the university crews don't go into the houses during the school year, but maybe they'll find some of the stuff during the Christmas and Spring breaks. I'll grab one of my guys and we'll take a report and notify the Row Office of what's been stolen, OK?" I said as I departed. It was October 1981.

After taking a comprehensive police report, I sent a copy of the stolen property to all of the university's building maintenance offices. *Boy, the thieves in this caper took enough furniture to outfit the Hoover House, for crying out loud—brand new high dollar stuff, too—estimated loss, $5,000! Man, I hope those culprits water Erika's palm...*

The campus was quiet. It was Christmas Break. On December 29th during a routine maintenance inspection, the crew's *straw boss* espied some furniture in the Delta Upsilon house that looked like the items that were purloined from the Law School. The Row Director dropped a dime on me and within minutes, the crew chief was in my office giving me a detailed statement of what he saw. The man also indicated that all of the suspicious items he saw were in individual rooms—not in common areas, which was very important in preparing an affidavit for a search warrant. After completing my affidavit, I was off to the DA's Office for the anticipated knock-down-drag-out dog fight to get that piece of paper that would legally enable our investigators to enter and inspect the DU's pad. I had all of my ducks in a row, so the DDA was fairly easy to convince. I sensed that he might bear some animus for the spoiled rotten kids in that fraternity, but I couldn't swear to it.

The next morning, I assembled our hit-squad and met the Row Warriors at the DU house. It was a pretty quick process as the stolen furniture was easily identified. We also found a couple of random couches, one from the Medical Center and the other from Terman Engineering. One of my hawk-eyed detectives spotted a small quantity of grass and hash so we bagged and tagged that, before the owner came back to school and got himself goofy! In all, we recovered 21 pieces of furniture—And, yes, Erika's palm was thriving—maybe they gave it a shot of cannabis from time to time.

After making my usual Bad Cop Quotes to the Daily—"This is serious stuff! A felony punishable by imprisonment in the penitentiary and a heavy fine; they'll put these guys so far underground they'll have to pump O2 to 'em"—Just kidding. At the request of the Dean of Students, Row Director and others, I agreed to have a sit-down, up close and personal parley with the DU leadership. They were actually pretty nice kids—dumb, but nice. Some of the group questioned the legality and scope of authority of the search. For example, we confiscated other items not named in the warrant and I explained that if suspected illegal contraband was in plain view, the police had the authority to seize it until subsequent investigation proved otherwise. Of particular note was the fact that we took a piece of mail, a bill or other identifier, to establish who lived in the 10 rooms where the stolen property was located. The DU president was a pretty smart guy—perhaps a *gonna be* lawyer for he generally agreed with my assessment. And, as usual with most of the students we busted, if they went along with the program, I'd speak to the DA on their behalf. Let the truth be known, after being long retired from law enforcement, that beneath the gruff bulldog façade, I was a big pussycat...

Rush

The 1982-83 Rush Book featured the following advertisement:

Delta Upsilon
553 Mayfield

Good times. How do you define them? Buttered popcorn? A medium Domino's? No, not at the D.U.'s. We like to party. Screams and urges and yes, the Energy. It's called a fraternity. A label. Anyway you look at it, it's still a party.

Life in the D.U. house. A residential education. Reptiles basking on the deck. Quad raging. Atomic drops. Wipe the sweat off your brow. Yes, of course, the Energy.

Edna. The newest Energy. Great cooks are hard to find. D.U. steaks. Taco salad and everyone's grinning. No more *buru*.

"I would have been a D.U.," said Stanford Police Captain Raoul Niemeyer, "but there was no place to sit."

The famous words of Facilities Manager Heloisa Edwards: "It may be crooked but it's the only game in town."

Pretty funny, but after several years of the same spiel, I suggested they update their draft warning with something that might captivate prospective pledges—like, when one or more of their clowns were doing pull-ups on the fire suppression water pipes and broke them! It must have been like the Titanic in there with high pressure water gushing out of the 2 inch pipe. . . So, a few years later, I wrote the DUs this letter:

Gentlemen:

I see once again your fraternity was unable to Rush-Me because. . . "There was no place to sit!" That line brings back interesting memories but don't you think it's a bit dated?

How about something more contemporary such as: "I would have been a D.U. but they didn't give me an aqua lung!" or. . . "But, all of the boats were full!" or. . . "They put too much water in their drinks!" Catch my drift?

Oh, by the way, feel free to call on me if there's any illicit property in your house—then maybe you can use that old line more appropriately!

Cheers,

Raoul K. Niemeyer
Captain of Investigations

The Fire

April 12, 1986 at 0130 hours: While on routine patrol in the area of the Law School, Deputy Harris Kuhn suddenly spotted a huge fireball belch from the third story porch of a dorm. Kuhn later identified the dorm as the Delta Upsilon fraternity at 553 Mayfield. Within a *nano*second, this enormous object plummeted to the ground like a meteor! Deputy Kuhn "Q-16" called for a Code 3 fire response. Rigs from Station 6 arrived within a few minutes and extinguished the blaze, which turned out to be a large couch. Quick detective work on the part of Deputy Kuhn ID'ed two inebriated DUs as the firebugs. They were subsequently charged, arrested and adjudicated in the North County Municipal Court. But, the real question is why would these highly educated young men put their house members in jeopardy—not to mention their well being and their future careers—by pulling such a brainless stunt? Alcohol? Obviously! But, I suspect there's more: Macho bravado? One-upmanship? "Hey Dudes. Check this out!" And, without any regard for human life as this conflagration could have burned out the entire Row, for Chrissakes! Enough said. This moronic act coupled with the below incidents of *Boys Behaving Badly* offered the University no alternative but expulsion. On June 11, 1986, The Campus Report succinctly outlined the high/low lights of the DU organization:

- Damage of about $2,500 to Sigma Chi fraternity when an individual believed to be a DU pledge threw a beer keg into a large window, cracking the frame, on May 30th. The following night, several rocks were thrown through other windows.
- A small arson fire at DU on May 19th when a member put a bunch of newspapers under a chair and burned it in the parking lot. A suspect has been identified.
- An arrest May 14th for drunk and disorderly conduct by a DU member who three months earlier had been taken to the hospital with a blood alcohol reading of 0.40. *(four times over the legal limit!)*
- A recent incident in which several DUs screamed at police as they responded to a possible burglary in progress at the Law School. Captain Niemeyer said the action "created a hazard for police."
- An April 11th attack on a 300-pound, 6-foot-6 member of Delta Kappa Epsilon (Deke). The individual, an IFC member, is blamed by the DUs for their problems with University officials. *(The victim, a Freshman, suffered broken ribs and a collapsed lung, when two DU assailants put the*

"boots" to him after the kid had been knocked to the ground. This was clearly a case of heavy alcohol abuse!)
- False emergency calls in which fire and police respond only to find a party in progress.

"These kinds of cases are very annoying to University officials and police because they are so senseless," Niemeyer said. "Trying to solve them is difficult because often there are no witnesses, or if there are, they are unable or unwilling to identify suspects."

Pi (Beta) Phi Prank

The Pi Phi sorority was the third woman's group to form at Stanford, way back in the day—October 1893! However, on April 30, 1944, the Board of Trustees voted to ban sororities and to utilize their housing for general female housing. There had been complaints, according to "A Chronology of Stanford University and it's Founders," that the *rush* process, in many cases, was undemocratic. A fallacious published story circulated that the real reason the sororities were booted was that two young ladies killed themselves after being rejected.

The Board of Trustees reversed the ban on sororities December 13, 1977, with following conditions: The selection process would be fair, and that the groups controlled their membership and adhered to university policies against discrimination. In January of 1981, Delta Gamma became the first recognized sorority in 37 years. Others soon followed suit.

I never met a Pi Phi, but from what I hear, while most men loved them, many ordinary Stanford women despised them: Most Pi Phis came from wealthy families; most were gorgeous, dainty misses who were in to cheerleading, dance, theater and arts. They were also very *cliquey*: Unlike, say the Delts, where all you had to do to get in was play any of the *manly sports*, drink beer and party—sororities like the Pi Phis were very picky who they admitted into their little society. One alum described the typical Pi Phi as "a high maintenance babe who enjoyed the high life in the fast lane—a potential 'Trophy Wife,'" she rejoined!

In any event, someone around campus apparently disliked this group, for a devilish plot was hatched: During a Pi Phi sorority rush social in a tent on Wilbur Field, April 15, 1991, a small device exploded in the canopy. The blast ignited the tent fabric which was supposed to be fire resistant. The fire was quickly extinguished by bystanders. Students checked the other five tents and discovered two more unexploded devices. Investigators found that the bombs were filled with a small charge of gun powder, as well as white talcum powder. They were fused with model rocket motors which were wired to small battery alarm clocks. Aside from this evidence, there were no clues or motives other than this was a typical frat prank; however, this fool hearty stunt could have injured or killed a bunch of kids, and I was determined to get to the bottom of it!

I met with my senior detectives, John McMullen and Sergeant Rick Tipton. After examining the remnants of the exploded bomb and closely inspecting the two that weren't fired, Rick opined that the clocks and batteries were similar to those sold at Radio Shack. However, after dropping into the Radio Shack store in Palo Alto, Tipton announced they had no record of selling any of those clocks and batteries.

"Well, gentlemen, how many other Radio Shacks do you think there are within a 20 mile radius?" I pontificated. "We need to think outside of the box on this one. Get out the phone book and start checking. Go *Detect*, detectives. Bye!"

It didn't take them long to report back that they found a store in Mountain View. The guy who purchased said items did so with a credit card! He just happened to be a Stanford student. Not only that, but he was a DU! Can you imagine that? He should have watched some crime stories on TV, for not even the dumbest of criminals would leave such an obvious paper trail. This was like tracking a wounded polar bear— in spite of global warming. . .

When they brought in *The Mad Bomber,* I walked into the interview room, introduced myself and said:

"Young man, I only have one question for you. What's up with the white talcum powder?"

He hung his head down for a moment, looked up and articulated:

"Well, the Pi Phi girls always wear long black satin gowns to their events, so I thought it would be neat if they got a white powder shower!"

"I must admit that would have been a pretty funny stunt, but your method of delivery and execution sucked! Why in the hell didn't you rig-up sacks in the canopy that could discharge your surprise via mechanical means, like a string or something. I hope you aren't going into engineering, I quipped," as I left the room shaking my head.

This was a Pi Phi prank that went terribly wrong. The kid picked up a pair of felony beefs on his rap sheet, and although later reduced to misdemeanors, it's like getting a tattoo!

Salt in the Wound!

Leave it to the Stanford Daily to come-up with a couple of satirist/cartoonists like Sam and Nalu. Funny guys, they were: Their piece was called The Farm Side. When the University started putting the DU's feet to the fire, not a week went by when that frat didn't get lampooned—perhaps harpooned would be more apropos. One of the first cartoons that caught my eye was a caricature of Row Director, Diana Conklin, (Bless her heart!) who rode herd on this mob like a Texas drover. It featured a smiling Diana flashing the DU sign. The caption read:

Diana Conklin: DU Little Sister.

Not!

After the DU's were given the boot, Sam and Nalu came up with this gem:

Top Ten Ways to Get Kicked Off Campus

10. When asking Diana Conklin if she agrees with you, ask "D'you?"
9. Say the letters DU
8. Say you once went to a DU party.
7. Say you think you know a DU.
6. Say you know a DU.zz
5. Say you wish you were friends with a DU.
4. Say you are friends with a DU.
3. Say you went out with a DU.
2. Say you wish you were a DU.
1. Become a DU.

And, the kicker: A cartoon of one of the Fraternal Affairs Directors, Joe Pisano, with a beer in his hand socializing with some young men, one wearing a Greek DU symbol on his shirt. The bubble out of Joe's mouth read: "You know, guys—it's too bad you lost your house. Throwing a burning couch is just WILD! I wanna PARTY with you guys!"

The caption below read:

Joe Pisano secretly rushes the DUs.

No offense, Joe. . . *Adios Amigos*. . .

CHAPTER SEVENTEEN

Drugs at Stanford?

Maui Wowie

The young lad had just completed his field training program, but there was no assignment for him due to a logistical SNAFU. The FTO Sergeant said that the kid had good skills in the field: He communicated well with the public, knew his way around campus, had excellent officer safety habits and was eager to learn. Only one problem: His command of the written word was somewhat below what we expected of our deputies, especially since they represented one of the most prestigious universities on this earth. I convinced the Chief that I could use him upstairs to help clear-up a backload of minor follow-ups and general housekeeping. That would also give me an opportunity to assess his report writing and perhaps give him a few pointers here and there. I taught report writing while I was at the S/O, and in my Patrol Procedures class at both San Jose and West Valley community colleges. I earned the reputation of being a real "stickler" when it came to penning clear, concise and complete reports—just ask my kids. I do believe, that on more than one occasion, my offspring had contemplated patricide on their ol' Pappy whenever I had them re-write their high school essays over and over again until they were perfect.

The kid reported to my office at 0800. His name was Iran White—an incredibly handsome young black man, 20 something, who although not tall, made up for his lack of stature with an incredible physique which was quite evident, even through his bulky clothing. This guy was no stranger to the gym, so we immediately had something in common for I had been "pumping iron" since I was 15.

Iran was a very mild mannered, soft spoken individual who I later learned was very righteous—no smoking, joking and drinking with the boys, which can be a death knell for all police officers. I felt that he'd work out fine.

I put him under the tutelage of my Detective Sergeant and suggested that he work some of the *Mickey Mouse* cases: Follow-ups on collisions, misdemeanor complaints and the like. I required that all of White's reports cross my desk for perusal.

Out of the blue, I got a call from Maxine at University Food Services. She was a very sweet lady but was exorcised about something very "hush-hush," and wanted to see me ASAP. So, off I went to Pampas Lane—having no clue as to what was in store. When I arrived, I was hurriedly ushered into a back office by Maxine's trusted assistant. Maxine was on her coattails. There was none of the usual chit-chat at this meeting, as Maxine got straight to the point. She confided that rumors were flying around the cafeterias that some Food Service employees were selling drugs to the students—it sounded to me that the kids could get a side of marijuana with their meat loaf, mashed potatoes and gravy...

So, having let the cat out of the bag, Maxine worried that if this situation went unchecked, it could cause serious damage to her operation and the University. While contemplating this dilemma, I asked the age old question: "Maxine, how many people know about this?" That was a very important question around this place. As I learned early on, trying to keep the lid on any secret was virtually impossible in this environment. Maxine was straight up, I believed, as she said she didn't know for sure. But, only one of her supervisors had confided about her suspicions and the students weren't breaking down her door with any corroborative information. *If true,* I mused, *perhaps I could hire an outside investigator to go undercover as a "hasher" or something and sniff around. I knew that ANNET (Joint Narcotics Task Force) wouldn't be interested in small potatoes as they were always working pounds not ounces.* So, I excused myself and told Maxine I wanted to run some ideas by the Chief and I would get back to her, pronto.

On the short drive back to the station, I got to thinking: *Wait a minute, why should I hire an undercover who more than likely couldn't find his way to the Alpha Drug House when I got a brand new kid, not yet known as a cop on campus? Hell yeah, I'll put Iran in there and see what he can do. All I gotta do is to convince the Boss about this hairbrained idea.*

After a considerable amount of convincing, I got the green light and called Iran. After running down the detail, I asked him if he would be willing to go in "deep:" No gun—damn sure no badge—no cover, no radio, no nada—and investigate this situation. I predicated my request by saying that this was probably a BS deal as most rumors about dope on campus usually never amounted to anything: Such allegations were usually a figment of someone's imagination or the result of watching too much Miami Vice! I also advised Iran that I would send him down to the Narco Squad in San Jose for a crash course on what NOT to do when rubbing elbows with dopers. Like the FTO Sergeant said, the kid was eager and willing to learn, so off he went—all by his lonesome.

I called Maxine and unveiled my plan. I told her that it was imperative that not a living soul, other than herself, knew about this operation as there could be dire consequences if Iran got burned due to "loose tongues." She agreed to zip her lips and instructed me that my man needed come to her office to apply for a job like anyone else. He even got credentials! I later learned that Iran was hired on as a pot washer on the afternoon shift at Lagunita Court dining hall, making a whopping $5.50 an hour. Before starting his assignment, I told White that he needed to call me nightly after he got off work, and that he needed to use a pay phone—you see, I watched Miami Vice, too....

Two days elapsed and no word from my Man. *Typical Narc,* I thought, *they are just like their counterparts—totally unreliable!* Then, on the third night at about 0030 my phone rang.

"Hello," I groggily answered.

"Mornin' Cap'n, it's Iran.

"Hey, man I was worried about you. Where in the hell have you been?"

"I'm dyin' Cap'n! I have never worked so hard in my life. Them big ol' pots and pans never stop comin'—and they are a bitch to clean."

"Ha Ha Ha, I hear ya son, but I used to carry hod for a miserly contractor back in Hawaii for $.75 an hour, so we all gotta start somewhere. So, are ya buyin' any dope?"

"Well, Cap'n, as a matter of fact I scored a lid tonight! The dude said it came from Maui."

"Oh, no kidding? Well, great. They call that grass "Maui Wowie." I've heard that it's some of the best MJ on the planet! Good job, man. Any more stuff available from your source?"

"Possibly, Cap'n; I think the dude is feelin' me out. He said he 'might' be able to score me some shrooms (psilocybin mushrooms) and coke, but I don't want to push him too hard."

"Yeah, Roger that. Hey, make sure you log-in the dope you got tonight—like ASAP, and account for the photocopied money that you gave the dude. Sounds like you're hot on the track. Just keep me informed, buddy.

"OK, I'll talk to ya later, Cap'n—Good night."

In order not to blow Iran's cover, I set up a rendezvous out of town to talk shop. When White walked in, I took a double take: This guy was really into his role as the sharp dressing, fast talking operator. By this time, his afro had grown several inches, he sported a huge stud in one of his ear lobes, allowed his pinky nail to grow very long (like many of the coke freaks of that era) and was awash in gold chains.

"Holy Christ." I exclaimed, "If you put on any more gold, I'm going to have to re-name you Isaac Hayes!" No offense intended—none received, as we both had a good laugh.

"So, how ya doing on your Search Warrant Affidavit?" I asked.

"Here's what I got so far, Cap'n"

After a slow and deliberate reading, I couldn't believe the progress this man had made in his writing skills. I smiled and nodded affirmatively:

"Man, I couldn't have done better myself. Good job, Iran!"

"It musta been that Ol' preacher you told me about; he must have reached out to the Lord and guided my hand," he proudly asserted.

(Years before, I took a "Bone Head" English class at Foothill College. My instructor was a cross between a USMC Drill Instructor and a Lowland Gorilla! But, he was one of the best teachers I ever had; he drummed the basics into his student's heads with a huge mallet, continually relating this parable about an old Baptist Preacher, down in Louisiana, who was the master at rendering powerful, impressive sermons. One day after meeting, a learned professor of English asked the orator how he managed to give such inspiring and well organized speeches every single Sunday. "Well Suh," the Ol' Reverend replied: "It's quite simple. You see, I tells 'um what I'm gonna tell 'um, I tell 'um, then I tell 'um what I tole 'um. . .")

"OK, once you get the deal set, gimme me a heads-up so we can orchestrate the logistics. We've got the S/O on tap and have to include Paly (PD), as the pad is in their jurisdiction."

"Will do sir. I'll call ya later."

Let's Get Ready to Rumble!

It was Wednesday evening March 26, 1981; we were all set and good to go. I coordinated the briefing at our station. There were about 15 of us. The S/O Narcs were going to handle the "buy/bust," Palo Alto PD would establish a perimeter and Stanford deputies would execute the search warrant with Detective White in the lead.

The game plan was to take down the principle with the coke once the dope and money had changed hands—the Narcs negotiated a purchase of ½ ounce for $1,200. When the suspect was under control, we would hit the house—the Judge issued a night service "No-Knock Warrant" as these dealers supposedly had some guns in the home, as most do. Once the door came down, we would effectuate a Banzai charge, take everybody to the ground, handcuff them and perform an orderly and systematic search of every nook and cranny in that place. I always liked to have two person finder teams move clockwise through the premises, locate contraband, notify the Affiant, have our photographer memorialize the stuff, and then our Evidence Officer would bag, tag and record the items to be seized. I also would have another team re-search the premises—you would be amazed at what fresh eyeballs can find that was missed during the first pass.

We caravanned to the area in question, set-up in the darkness and waited for the Narcs to give us the green light. It was about 7:00PM; for some unknown reason, the "mark" wanted to meet the undercovers right around the corner from the residence in question. This had its advantages, but the proximity made it difficult to hide our cars, so most were dispersed a few blocks away. I found a heavily foliated spot with a good vantage point, hunkered down in my silver 'n black Mercury Monarch and settled-in. The Narcs and Iran waited in their non-descript vehicle, a 60 something Chevy, piece of crap that I leased from a "Rent a Wreck" lot in East Paly. Now all we had to do was wait--the worst part of these operations because the crooks are never on time and often don't show. At exactly 1930 hours, a white male came out of the targeted house and walked down the street; he was met simultaneously by a couple of burly dudes and Iran, certainly no midget himself. It was like watching a COPS episode: Once the deal was done, the guns came out quicker than a flash, and the bad dude was prostrate on the pavement with cuffs on!

Then we were off to the races: Plainclothes cops in bullet proof vests and over a dozen uniforms descended on that domicile like a swarm of angry African bees. The big Narc, who looked like Grizzly Adams with flaming "Carrot Top" hair, kicked-in the door and everyone poured through the portal with large caliber guns drawn, all the while shouting: "Police, Search Warrant, get on the ground!" The swarm went through the house like a tornado, searching under beds, in closets, bathrooms, under piles of dirty laundry, and any cubby where someone might hide. Four losers were present and accounted for—two "local dudes," a "dudette"—all from Maui, and a chick from Mountain View, whose beau was somewhat tied-up on the street. . .

After the adrenaline and high-fives had subsided, Ol' "Grizz," the lead Narc who beat down the door, "gave me the business:"

"Hey Niemeyer, you must be getting old! I can remember when you'd be the first guy through the door. . ."

"With age comes wisdom, son," I proclaimed. "Besides you are a much bigger and better target than I. . ."

Everyone had a good laugh over this exchange, but no one knew that the Grizz and I went way back: He was a young whipper-snapper in one of my Academy defensive tactics classes; despite many full-on assaults, the kid could never control the old man on the mat—as a very competitive former high school wrestler, not being able to whip his elder didn't sit well. But, it was all in good fun.

Although this bust wasn't the pinch of the century, we took several pounds of marijuana off the street, as well as a small quantity of coke, speed, peyote, scales, and packaging materials. Of particular value was a tell-all log book which chronicled every transaction that was consummated: Date, time, location, purchaser, what, quantity, price and so on. It never ceases to amaze me how illicit business folks are compelled to set-up accounting records, either in ledgers or computers, making conviction a sure thing if law enforcement gets their hands on this incriminating evidence.

Alpha Drugs

Ah, it was Friday, September of 1982. Another week on the Farm had passed without any consequence, except for the variety of beautiful colors on campus as the leaves on a million trees began to turn. My mind began wandering as to what I was going to do over the weekend, when that dreaded "buzz" interrupted my thoughts. *What now*, I pessimistically wondered? I hit the com line, picked up the phone, and made a sarcastic remark like, "For God sakes, it's Friday!" The clerk giggled and announced that Inspector William Halonen (R.I.P.) of U.S. Postal Inspection was here to see me, so I invited him on up.

Bill was a distinguished looking gentleman who was well attired in a sport coat and tie; his graying temples announced that he'd been around the block a time or two! After exchanging pleasantries, I told him I had worked pretty closely over the years with Postal Inspector, Tom Brasher, from the San Jose Office and that we always had a great working relationship. That broke the ice as Halonen had good things to say about Inspector Brasher, as well. Inspector Halonen said that he was assigned to the Oakland office and was working a dope case with U. S. Customs out of San Francisco International Airport. This kind of took me aback as I was hoping that the Inspector was here about the infamous Unabomber investigation:

Some members of the Unabomber Task Force, made up of virtually every federal law enforcement agency known to man, as well as a myriad of local police agencies, contacted me some months before about one of the victims, a U.S. Air Force Captain, who had attended some post graduate courses at Stanford. This man later got part of a hand blown off when he moved a parcel that was at his work station in one of UC Berkeley's laboratories.

The Inspector explained that one of Custom's drug sniffing dogs, "Lightfoot," had made a hit on a package that originated in Beijing,

People's Republic of China, which was slated to be delivered to a location on the Stanford University campus. Inspector Halonen continued that the sender had tried to camouflage the little block of high grade hashish within several packages of Chinese tea.

At this point I called in *our* "drug sniffing expert," Detective Iran White. . .

The addressee was Nelson McVey, 375 Campus Drive, Stanford, CA. In the meantime, I called a trusted source in Res. Ed. (Residential Education) in an effort to ascertain if they had that individual living at the given address, and if so, exactly what room he occupied. I soon learned that the suspect was Nelson David McVey and he resided in room #114. Alpha Delts was formerly a fraternity house, now considered a Co-Op, but still named Alpha Delta Phi—dubbed "Alpha Drugs" by the students—and for good reason, as we were about to learn.

Inspector Halonen indicated that if we would obtain a search warrant, he would be willing to make a "controlled delivery" to the subject and then we could proceed with the bust. Sounded like a plan to me, so I had Iran reconnoiter the house and procure a search warrant from the North County District Attorney's Office—no easy task, even under the best of circumstances. It had been my experience that many of the Deputy DAs at North County were often inexperienced and thus, were very cautious: Search warrants out of that office were about as hard to obtain as gasoline vouchers in WWII! But, I believed that this was a viable case and that we would prevail, even if we had to go downtown (San Jose). Before leaving, Inspector Halonen asked me to give him a heads-up a few days before we desired to execute the operation. He said that he would don his mailman's garb and personally deliver the package. Good guy!

After learning that the Co-Op was a large two-story dormitory with numerous points of in/egress, near the rim of Lake Lagunita with wide open spaces, it was quite obvious to me that we were going to need sufficient personnel to cover the perimeter when we hit the place. I subsequently met with the Chief and Captain Moore and gave them the low-down. We devised a manpower plan that, in my view, should cover the bases: We had 3 patrol cars, a couple of dirt bikes (motors), 2 or 3 cops on bicycles and several CSOs on scooters—no one was going get through this dragnet! In addition, I got several gorillas from the County's Narco Task Force—if nothing else they'd scare the daylights out of these kids, as they made Hells Angels look like Boy Scouts!

The Postman Cometh

It was October 6, 1982. All players were present and accounted for, except Inspector Halonen. We were gathered in our upstairs conference room and when I heard the downstairs entry door slam, I knew the "Postman Hath Cometh." When the Inspector entered the room, the place erupted into applause. It was hilarious. He was perfect in his mailman's suit, Safari-like pith hat, leather bag and all. The Sergeant briefed the troops and sent them to their posts. The plan was to wait until lunch was being served. You could always find any given person in the chow halls as the quality of food around campus was generally excellent, and students, especially the guys, were always famished. Before departing, we wired the Inspector with our Fargo unit so we could capture this event on tape.

When lunch was underway, the Postman entered the dining hall and announced:

"Package for Mr. Nelson McVey; is he here?"

"Yeah, yeah that's me," was the reply of a tall young man who was knocking chairs and students out of the way as he dashed over to where the Postman was standing.

"OK, sir, sign here," Halonen required before he handed over the parcel.

As the Inspector was leaving, someone in the hall shouted: "Columbia?" McVey held the package high in the air and exclaimed: "No. China!" At this point, the place erupted into a deafening roar. The suspect made a quick exit and apparently headed for his room. After one of our spotters verified that our target had entered his room, Detective White, Narc Agent "Grizz" (same guy from the Maui Wowie bust) and I charged over to the suspect's room. I pounded on the door with my fist and shouted: "Stanford Police, Search Warrant, Open Up!" After no response, Grizz and I took turns kicking-in the door. Once open, soon to be "Agent" White flew inside and Mr. McVey found himself looking down the barrels of three very large caliber handguns. He apparently was trying to conceal his stash in a vinyl record album, which he clumsily held between his knees, all the while reaching for the rafters. Detective White quickly took him into custody and relieved the young man of his treasure.

In addition to the hash, we found some coke, small amounts of weed and assorted paraphernalia (pipes, papers, roach clips, etc.) and seized the Mercedes of scales—A Mettler! Boy, it didn't take the Crime Lab long to reach out to me and request that fine piece of apparatus once the case was adjudicated, as they didn't have anything close to it! The case proceeded to court and despite having benefit of high dollar "mouthpieces," Nelson David McVey was convicted of possession of concentrated cannabis and possession of cocaine for sale. He was sentenced to 50 days county jail time, 200 hours of community service work and a fine. Looking back on this case, it was hardly worth the effort and expense given the sentence. Oh well; at least we closed down the criminal enterprise in that house—maybe. . .

The Aftermath

Not only did we subsequently learn that Mr. McVey was the main distributor of dope from Alpha Drugs, but he was a descendant and heir to a very wealthy family of internationally renowned entrepreneurs. So, did his lineage spirit him on to another lucrative endeavor, without Mom and Pop's dough? Who knows, but in any event, McVey's lawyers challenged his conviction in the California Court of Appeals in 1984. As in almost all drugs cases, the defendants challenged the search warrant and how it was executed. Although the Court declared that our warrant did not specify the place to be searched, it concluded that this error was covered by the "good faith" exception articulated in several U.S. Supreme Court cases, so the appeal was denied. To this day, I can't understand that line of thought, and take exception that the CA Court opined our warrant was defective. We described the area to be searched with great specificity: The Affiant, Detective White, identified the premises, not only by street address, but by name of the frat (he described the sign and size of the letters), geographic location, color and construction characteristics of the building, number of stories and, most importantly, the exact room we intended to search—Room # 114. So, Duhhh. . . . But, I guess a win is a win.

Epilogue

Next time you walk, bike or drive around campus and expect to see an Alpha Delta Phi sign at 375 Campus, you won't find it. Perhaps, in order to erase this caper forever from the annals of Stanford history, the premises was given a new and exciting name: EBF—translated it means "Enchanted Broccoli Forest." Who would have thought? I can't even eat broccoli let alone smoke it. . . Only at Stanford!

Post Script

Iran White went on to a very successful career with the California Department of Justice as a Special Agent. He performed a myriad of tasks from drug enforcement—Iran was a Drug Recognition Expert—to recruitment and training of agents. White received many awards and accolades for his expertise in narcotics, high technology crime investigation, as well as Israeli Military style defensive tactics training. Agent White retired in 2006 due to medical reasons. Although the "loan to the S/O" turned out to be a long term assignment and we lost a good man, the County and later the CA Department of Justice acquired one helluva dope cop. Nobody said that "Narcing" was an easy gig. The pressure can manifest itself in many ways: Health issues—often resulting in long term illness or death, alcoholism/substance abuse, psychological effects, marital discourse, and often suicide—although none of these symptoms apply in Iran's case. The recent TV hit, "The Shield," although greatly exaggerated, provides insight into the seamy world of narcotics, and the toll it can take on our men and women behind the badge. I thank God that my request to transfer to the Narcotics Task Force in the 70's was turned down. The powers that be had other plans for me: Training Sergeant, which ultimately opened many incredibly interesting and challenging doors for me.

CHAPTER EIGHTEEN

Art Thefts

The Museum Burglary

I had only been on the job a few months when I was informed of a major burglary at the Leland Stanford Junior Memorial Museum in the early AM. Because of countless false alarms over the years, many of the old timers became desensitized when a 10-33 came into the communications center. For the most part, the crew that worked in communications was a sorry lot: They were ill-trained, ill-mannered, and the laughing stock of the other police agencies on the shared frequency due to their surly and unprofessional demeanor (documented in Chapter 10).

The first alarm came in shortly after 0100 hours. Q-1, Officer Carl Gielitz, aka "Captain Midnight," was dispatched to the front, while Q-9, Officer Nugent, covered the rear. How only two units were expected to cover this huge building baffles me to this day; but that's all we had then. Many of our sergeants in that era were former Old Guard guys—decent, well meaning individuals, but short on contemporary supervision methods of being in the field with their troops—especially on the Dog Watch! As Cap'n Bill used to say: "Nice guys, but they're Annex sitters." And, although you could get to almost any location on campus within 5-10 minutes, the "Sarge" often didn't show-up when he was needed—like Now! Palo Alto Police was only called in the event of an emergency; but, who knew when an "emergency" would suddenly occur? Often, when something hairy went down on the Farm, our guys were like the Lone Ranger and Tonto!

When Carl went 10-97, he radioed-in that he was going to enter the front door, which would trigger a perimeter alarm—the beat units had keys to the University's sensitive buildings—this place was indeed sensitive: Opened in 1884, M/M Stanford dedicated this monument to their beloved son, as he was an avid collector of historical memorabilia, as well as classical art. Mrs. Stanford later flooded the building with sculptures, jewelry, precious gems, gold and silver. The famous golden

"Last Spike," which Governor Leland Stanford drove in at Promontory Point, Utah in 1869, was displayed in an alarmed, see-through safe. By 1902, two additional wings had to be commissioned to hold all of the antiquities; obviously, the place was very, very large!

As Q-1 began his search of this Winchester Mystery House-like building—comprised of dozens of galleries, dead ends and cubbies—with only his flashlight penetrating the pitch black darkness, Carl was totally unaware that burglars were in the house, too, setting off alarms as they retreated into the basement. There's an old maxim police trainers often use as an object lesson that goes something like this: "When you A-S-S-U-M-E, you make an ASS out of U and ME! And, this is exactly what happened—a major SNAFU that could have been fateful to our "hero!" The moron on the communication's console apparently "assumed" that Deputy Gielitz was tripping the sonic alarms while he was checking out the galleries; had the dispatcher *not* been asleep at the switch, he would have noticed the interior alarms were already alerting before Carl *even* entered the museum's foyer! After shining his light around as best he could, Carl concluded the series of false signals was probably due to a malfunction. Little did he know that a gang of outlaw motorcycle thugs was hiding in the museum's basement.

Within minutes of Carl's departure, the bad guys busted out a rear door and took off. This breakout triggered yet another alarm, so Dispatch "assumed" that the system was malfunctioning *again*, thus nonchalantly reported, in essence: "Those darn alarms are going off again!" By the time our coppers returned to the scene, the crooks were long gone. Captain MN was damn lucky that he didn't get seriously hurt on that caper, as we later learned that the burglars were Hell's Angels affiliates and were reportedly "loaded for bear!"

Subsequent investigation revealed that this gang of thieves had been conscripted to steal some of the museum's very valuable Navajo silver, precious stones, jewelry, beads and related artifacts—worth a helluva lot in my estimation, although curators would almost never affix an actual value to the loot for fear of suffering repeat losses, if made known to the public. Also purloined were glass facsimiles of the 19th Century's finest gems (including the 280 carat Great Mogul diamond found in India circa 1650), all encased in a large velvet blue heart, presented to Jane

Lathrop Stanford by Tiffany & Company. I dubbed this collection "Stanford's Family Jewels..."

The Geriatric Squad

Nearly four years had elapsed since the 1974 museum intrusion, yet we received nary a tip or clue. The FBI, who actually had an art theft detail, even way back in the day, routinely sent out descriptive information to various auction houses and art dealers. But, in this case, the phone remained silent until one Friday morning: I got a call from a senior museum curator who advised me that a young woman had called the museum and wanted to discuss the repatriation of the Tiffany & Company's gift to Mrs. Stanford. The woman caller said that her recently deceased mother bought the collection in an estate sale many years ago, and that when she looked at the set more closely, she found an inscribed plate identifying the pieces as belonging to Mrs. Stanford. The disingenuous female stated she wanted to return the gem set to the University—for a price, that is... So, bring on the "Geriatric Squad!"

Well, that's what the troops called the Investigations Unit in those days: When I was assigned as Investigation's Commander in 1977, I had Detective Don Lillie, who had over 25 years of experience under his belt; he was a valuable asset to our fledgling unit because of his contacts and technical expertise. But, Don was nearing his sixties and sometimes needed a little motivation, which I often threatened to provide with a blow torch! I also took Capt. Midnight out of Patrol as he was in his sixties and planning to retire in a few years. My other detective was Ted Hopgood, neat ol' man, retired Army sergeant and a veteran of the Old Guard. Ted spent many years in the field and needed to let the young "whipper-snappers" do some of the heavy lifting. I was only 39 then, but you know how little respect anyone nearing 40 gets—even in those days.

So, after powering-up our wheelchairs, we zoomed to the museum for a pow-wow with the curators, and to reconnoiter the place where this parley was going to be. We took our then state-of-the art Sony 360 reel-to-reel video recorder, as I was determined to capture this event in living black and white... The place chosen by museum staff was a rather large room—I think they used it for framing. But, it was to our advantage.

Our new camera didn't have a peephole lens or anything like that, so Don decided to use a large art frame to disguise the sizeable camera and telephoto lens. He set the camera in a corner, and unless one really studied the room, you'd never spot that big eye; nonetheless, it was obvious to me, so I was rather nervous that we'd be burned.

While Don and crew set-up the equipment, I coached the principles of what to say and what not to say. Museum staffers had good photos of the items and were very familiar with the collection. So, if the unknown woman brought in the real deal for ransom, the head curator would signal me, whereupon us old guys would swoop in for the kill— well, maybe not "swoop," but we'd get into the mix one way or another. The exchange was tentatively scheduled for mid-morning on the following Monday. We were all set.

Enter Stage Left

Once we were in our proper places, a staff member led an attractive young woman and a 30 something gentleman into the meeting room. After they exchanged pleasantries, I observed the woman retrieve a case out of a large handbag and put it on the table. The curators examined it carefully and after a few minutes, the lead lady gave me the high sign. At that point, the Geriatric Squad with yours truly in the lead literally entered stage left, whereupon I bellowed:

"Good morning, folks. I'm Captain Niemeyer of the Stanford Police and these are my detectives. The Stanford Museum curators have identified this gem set as property stolen in a previous burglary, so you are both under arrest for possession of stolen property!"

The woman looked like the cat who had swallowed the canary and the guy appeared like he was ready to stroke! After I shut down the gal's denials, the man jumped-up and identified himself as the woman's friend, and, oh, by the way, he was also an attorney. *Good,* I thought, *I always wanted to bust a lawyer—came close several times. Maybe this would be a first, I hoped.* But, at the same time, I knew that this caper was going to be a huge sack of rattlesnakes: I had planned to hammer (interrogate, that is) this chick and find out who did the burglary, but she brought a damn lawyer with her! *Fat chance of getting her name, rank and horsepower, let alone the whole story,* I winced. My guys bundled-up the suspects and hauled them off to the Annex lock-up. In the meantime, I showed the video to the Chief; he loved it, having done something similar before I came on board. However, the boss was a little tentative on this one. A-1 directed me to "Run it by the DA." (I hated that because my experience with the North County Office was that most of the attorneys were a wimpy lot and would make you jump through so many hoops, you'd think you were a Barnum and Bailey Circus dog. In San Jose, we'd just hook 'em and book 'em, write a report and let the Dicks handle it. But, guess what? I "ARE" the Dicks now, so the buck stopped with me, and I knew it.). Damn. So, off I went.

The DDA was a really nice, smart guy, but he was as nervous about this case as a prostitute in church. And, because the "co-defendant" was a lawyer, that fact apparently raised the hackles on the back of his neck. During my career, I found relationships among lawyers are almost genetic, proving, in my mind anyway, that blood is, indeed, thicker than water! So, the DDA followed me back to our station to discuss the matter with the arrestees. The session was more like arbitration than a police interrogation: The woman stuck to her original story that her mother got the gems from her Mom, who had them for years. I basically told her, in a nice way, that "she was so full of *it* her eyes were turning brown. . ." And, of course, her mouthpiece "didn't know 'nuttin!'" In desperation, I told the DA that I wanted a search warrant, thinking we could find more evidence of the burglary in the woman's home. However, upon hearing how long the process would take, the lady relented and agreed to allow us to search her premises. I had our secretary prepare a Consent to Search Affidavit and we were off on our wild goose chase—arrestees and all.

Just as I figured, after a very exhaustive and thorough search, we got *NADA!* OK, maybe she wasn't involved with the actual burglary, but surely she must have known whom she got Stanford's Family Jewels from. The answer to that mystery would never be known. We were forced to drop all charges against the dynamic-duo. Oh well, you can't win them all, but at least we recovered a neat piece of Leland Stanford

Junior Memorial Museum memorabilia for future generations to view and enjoy.

The Geriatric Squad also demonstrated that one should never underestimate their seniors: We might have had some geriatric tendencies and moved a little slower than the youngsters, but like the tortoise and hare story, by God, we got the job done—and pretty darn well, too!

Whistler

I was having my second cup of coffee and shooting the bull with Cap'n Bill in his office, when one of the Record's clerks tracked me down. She said that there was a rather rude, demanding man on the phone who wanted to talk to someone of authority about some possible stolen art. That would be me so, I picked-up the phone. As our clerk described, the caller was rather abrupt and anxious; he wanted to know if we had any recent art thefts at the Museum on campus. I told the caller that I heard of a theft, which happened yesterday, but hadn't reviewed the police report yet, but would do so, if he explained to me exactly what he knew about this case. The man identified himself as Paul R, a San Francisco art dealer. Mr. R said that he purchased a couple of pieces of artwork the day before from a young man he had done business with in the past. However, in this instance, the man seemed very nervous and needed some money right away. Mr. R continued that he gave the guy $200 and promised more later on. The skittish individual took the money and ran, so to speak.

Mr. R said that one of the pieces was an etching, which he believed could be an original by Whistler; he checked his source book and learned that the Stanford Museum had a Whistler work in their galleries. Although an Art History minor in college (I was into Greek and Renaissance), I had no clue who Whistler was. So, I told Mr. R that I would read the report and get back to him as soon as possible; I also admonished him not to release those works to anyone!

The incident report revealed that unknown person(s) apparently cut the paintings out of their frames with a sharp knife. During that process, the suspect must have cut himself, as there was a good amount of blood on the floor where the artwork had been displayed. The perp must have rolled up the canvases, secreted them under his/her clothing and simply walked out. One of the pieces was indeed by the famous 19th Century artist, James Abbott McNeill Whistler; it was called "Zaandam, the Netherlands, c. 1889" (an etching), extremely rare and obviously very, very valuable. Whistler (1834-1903) was born in Lowell, MA, the son of a prominent engineer. Even in his youth, James traveled extensively and lived in Russia for a time when his Dad was building a railroad. Whistler began studying art when he was 11. James and his mother moved to England while his father continued to work on the Russian railroad project. When his father died suddenly of cholera at age 49, Whistler and his mother moved back to her hometown in Connecticut. Mom wanted her son to become a minister, but he wasn't "man of the cloth" material and decided to apply to West Point, where his father had once taught drawing. Although very slight in stature and frequently in poor health, Whistler was granted admission—giving credence to the old adage: "It's not WHAT you know but WHO you know." James didn't fare well at West Point: His grades were substandard; his appearance and performance on the drill field was abysmal. Plus, he was a "wise-ass" (*author's assessment*), as historical accounts state that James was often sarcastic and disrespectful to his superiors. After three years, Whistler failed to make the cut and was shown the door. He later landed a job as a draftsman mapping the entire U. S. coast for military and maritime use. James was often late, absent or just plain goofing-off, so he was transferred to the U.S. Coast Survey where he learned etching—this art form would be Whistler's strong suit later on. The Survey sacked him after only two months. From there, he traveled to France, England and elsewhere where he bummed around, living from hand to mouth. James was often flat broke, imbibed gratuitously, smoked and caroused around a lot—all of which didn't do his chronically poor health any favors. Despite Whistler's vices, he continued to study and perfected his skill as a portrait artist. Some of his works are very impressive—Google him. . .

After perusing the police report, I called one of the Museum's curators and asked if she had photos of the stolen art pieces that we could copy. They did, so we obtained them. I explained that we had a lead and could possibly recover the purloined artwork—with a lot of good fortune, that is. In the meantime, my former S/O trainee and partner, Detective Bill Cordoni, was en route from San Jose to join-up with me and jet to the City by the Bay. After calling the "Art Dealer" (of dubious reputation— in my opinion), we told him we were on our way and to stand by.

Mr. R's little shop was located on a side street off the Embarcadero, near Pier 39. When we met him, I knew that this little guy was going to be trouble later down the line. I recognized his accent and pegged him as being a typical New Yorker: He would be a very difficult person to deal with, in my estimation. Once we confiscated the art, he began sniveling about who was going to reimburse him for the two hundred bucks he paid the thief. I told him that he bought stolen goods, and as an art dealer, who knew that this stuff was priceless and probably "hot," he should have known better! He then countered: "Well, Stanford should pay me a finder's fee!" I retorted: "Well, you'll have to take that up with Stanford; that is totally above my pay grade!"

After obtaining the suspect's address, Det. Cordoni and I made a hasty exit. As Bill and I were going out the door, I warned my purveyor of stolen art "friend" NOT to call the skell (I think he understood that New York term) or we would be back and arrest him for receiving stolen goods, in addition to obstruction of justice. Mr. R didn't like me—I could tell. . . We then called San Francisco P. D. and requested back up.

SFPD's black and white was already down the street from the sleazy flophouse where the suspect was thought to be residing. This flea bag hotel was smack-dab in the middle of the infamous Tenderloin District! I briefed the officer and he very seemed very eager to kick ass and take names; he was a big wily veteran—big is good, in these cases. We ran up the stairs and the SFPD officer wasted no time in beating on the door with his club and gruffly announcing: "Police! Open the Goddamn door or we'll kick-it-in!" So much for PC by Baghdad by the Bay's Finest. . .

Within a few seconds, the door opened-up and SFPD's bulldozer led the charge and barged in. I grabbed the tall, well built young man and thrust him up against the wall, while Bill and the SFPD officer checked out the small dingy hotel room. When I applied my cuffs on the suspect, I immediately noticed a huge gauze bandage on one of his fingers. *This is definitely our guy,* I rejoiced silently. In the meantime, my colleagues located an attractive female in the bathroom, clad only in skimpy lingerie. The SF cop told her to get dressed as she was going downtown, too. I then asked the male:

"So, what happened to your finger?"

"Ah, I cut it while cutting up a box," he stammered.

"You sure it wasn't when you were cutting out those pieces of art work at the Stanford Museum yesterday. You know— the ones you sold to your "fence?" I pressed.

"I want my rights, man. I ain't saying *shit!*" was his surly reply.

"No matter, pal, I ain't asking you *shit*. I already know the answers. You and your girlfriend are going downtown, unless you want to waive your right to be booked here and go with us to the Santa Clara County Jail."

He refused to waive, so we deposited both lowlifes in the San Francisco County Jail. During the booking process, I noticed that this guy had more tracks in his arms than Chicago's Belt Railway yard! I figured that the $200 Mr. R gave this loser had already been infused into his blood stream, as well as that of his addicted partner. To think, we almost lost two valuable pieces of historical art for a measly 200 bucks of heroin!

And the Beat Goes On

Our pre-trial meeting with the DDA, Investigators and Museum curators was interesting: It was agreed that the arrestees should be prosecuted for their crime. However, Museum officials refused to give a "guesstimate" of what the recovered art was worth—totally understandable as citing values might inspire even more thefts. Clearly, these works were in excess of $200 in value, so we had the corpus for grand theft, as well as burglary, on the duo. However, it was the parting shot by one of the sassy Museum curators that raised my ire: During this open meeting she lambasted me for defacing the art works! When I asked her what she meant, she attacked:

"Why would you write your initials and time and date on a priceless piece of art?

The DDA's jaw hit the table; I felt like some unknown weather phenomenon had suddenly sucked the wind out of my sails! Having a hair trigger tongue enabled me to regain my composure, so I retorted:

"Madam, first of all, I DID NOT deface this precious artwork. I merely put my initials, time and date on the back corner of the piece as required by the CA Code of Evidence. When I'm called to the witness stand, I have to show some proof that this particular piece of evidence is the very one I recovered!" The DDA nodded. "And, furthermore, my annotations should enhance the status of these works—if Detective Cordoni and I hadn't rescued them when we did, they wouldn't be worth much to the Stanford Museum now, would they?" She just glared.

The Finder's Fee

I was absolutely beside myself when General Counsel, dear friend, Jennifer Westerlind, called and advised that the nefarious "art dealer," Mr. R, had filed suit in San Francisco demanding a so-called "finder's fee" for recovering the stolen artwork. As I recall, he was asking the court for 10 percent of the estimated value of the pieces, plus the $200 he "lost," as well as court costs. Needless to say, my position on the issue, as well as the University's, was to give this weasel the universal salute!

This adventure actually turned out to be quite an experience: Accompanying Jennifer and me was the esteemed art historian and Chairman of the Art Department, Professor Albert Elsen. What a delightful and interesting man! In addition to his impeccable credentials in art, Professor Elsen titillated us with stories about his involvement in the Nuremburg Trials after World War II. The professor served as a translator during the adjudication of the Nazi war criminals.

Entering the monolith Superior Court house in San Francisco reminded me of when I visited the Old Bailey in London. Our courtroom was huge and the judge sat behind a bench that seemed to be about 6-7 feet above the floor. This gave a spectator the notion that the jurist was larger than life—pretty intimidating! Mr. R took the stand following Professor Elsen and me. The "dealer" seemed to be totally unprepared and disorganized. Although judge's thoughts are very difficult to read, Jennifer and I both had the impression that the jurist was thinking: *Are you out of your mind? You bought a pig in a poke and the contents were stolen. So, now you expect Stanford University to compensate you for your stupidity? Get outta here, you loser—you are just a low level fence!*

At the conclusion of the short trial, the judge dismissed us and said that he would take the matter under submission and issue his ruling by mail. Within a few weeks, Ms. Westerlind called me and gleefully confirmed that the judge ruled in Stanford University's favor, proving we were all on the same page: Case Dismissed! Let there be justice. . .

CHAPTER NINETEEN

Random Tales

Ba'b: The Bobster

But, you can call him "Bob." Bob Henderson came to us from a military police unit at Fort Ord, in Monterey, California. When applicant Henderson walked into the conference room for his oral interview, I was immediately impressed with his physique: He was nattily attired in a fine suit, tailored to accentuate his build—I envisioned that our candidate was chiseled from a block of obsidian by a student of Michelangelo. Given the chance, this young man could have played fullback on any NFL team! He was articulate, soft spoken and confident. We needed a kid like this. The oral board was unanimous and we sent him onto the final phase of the selection process. Mr. Henderson was subsequently sworn-in as a Deputized Patrol Officer and went off to the academy.

Following his successful completion of training, Bob was on his own keeping the campus safe—and, he was doing a helluva job, right out of the chute. Some thought that Henderson was a bit of a *hotdog* as he stopped a lot of cars (with good cause) and made many arrests. But, I liked that—he reminded me of myself some 30 years before—well, absent the physique and athleticism thing: I was a lumbering lineman; Bob a gifted, fleet-footed running back. . . But, when it came to being a good policeman and protecting the citizenry, Henderson had the right mind set: You can't effectively do the job unless you know who is moving around out there.

The "Gay Statues" Caper

In February 1984, the Gay Liberation Statues were installed on Lomita Mall near the Quad. The work of artist George Segal was, indeed, controversial: The life size bronze figures (painted white) depicted two males standing close to each other, while two females were seated on a park bench. Within weeks of their debut, a hammer wielding protester inflicted a number of strikes on the art work. A witness followed the vandal and showed us where he lived. We subsequently detained him, and he voluntarily gave me the instrumentality of the crime; he was arrested and later charged with felony vandalism, as the bronzes had to be removed and repaired at a considerable cost. Ten years later, the statues were hit again, but this time Bob Henderson was on the case.

Several members of the Stanford football team decided that painting the statues would be a neat trick. However, this group of marauders didn't plan on getting caught! They were spotted throwing paint on the Segal work. The only mitigating aspect of their nefarious deed was they were considerate enough to use the water soluble variety. . . The witnesses gave the 9-1-1 operator a description of the vehicle and culprits. As it turned out, Bob and his fill-units (Deputy Navarra being one of the first on the scene) were Johnny-on-the-Spot and immediately gave chase. When the deputies put the rubies on the perps, the gang pulled over and bailed out of their ride as if it was stolen. And, the chase was on. . . Bob went after the driver, who was beating feet. So, we had a tall, trim athlete in gym clothes versus a 225 pound cop who was laden down with heavy woolen trousers, bullet proof vest, leather gun belt and holster with a Glock .40 in it; In addition, there were two extra magazines, two pairs of handcuffs, a brick size radio, 26 inch police baton, and an aluminum 6 cell flashlight. That's about 25-30 extra pounds, folks! So, here's the scoop, according to our cops at the scene: Henderson quickly closed the 25 yard gap with his quarry and trailed a few yards behind. After about a minute or so, Deputy Bob pulled-up alongside the fleet footed rabbit and said: "Hey, dude. Let me know when you're tired!"

The astonished young man, gave Bob that "you've gotta be shitting me" look, put on the brakes and threw-up his arms. Chase over! The rest of our troops rounded-up the rest of the scoundrels and hauled them down to the station, where they were tagged and released. Deputy Navarra later related to me that as they were leaving the area with their arrestees, a group of students, two males with female companions, dashed out of the shadows in front of the patrol cars clad only in their birthday suits. . . The University later spanked the group of vandals and put them on probation. The streakers got away—*barely*—by the skin of their. . .

Backgrounds

During our department's formative years, I hired retired law enforcement officers to do background investigations (BGs) of prospective candidates. This is a very demanding and exhausting process, so the burn-out rate is high—especially how I wanted the background checks performed. I learned this arduous task when I was a sergeant in the S/O's Personnel and Training Division. I belonged to the California Association of Police Training Officers (CAPTO), which kept members abreast of contemporary selection and hiring procedures for police personnel. CAPTO held an annual conference in which new laws and techniques were addressed. I created a step-by-step how to manual which contained volumes of printed material and state forms that had to be completed with extreme accuracy. Our Background Investigators (BGIs) were thoroughly indoctrinated in our program; they were sworn and given a badge and credentials. The applicants were required to fill out a twenty-six page comprehensive PHQ (Personal History Questionnaire) which the investigator had to verify through criminal history checks, credit reports, work references and neighborhood canvasses. Any omission or deception was grounds for dismissal from the process. The BGIs wrote detailed after-action reports on all contacts and interviews. I reviewed their labors, line by line, and if the candidate was acceptable, the BGI then reported their findings directly to Chief Herrington. The chief and I were adamant about having the very best candidates available to police the Stanford community, so in essence, "many were called but few were chosen!"

The BGIs

Overall, the quality of work performed by our BGIs was very good. All of them worked for many years in established Police, Sheriff and District Attorney's Departments in the region. Almost all of the BGIs were senior staff members of their respective agencies, so they clearly had not just fallen off the proverbial turnip truck! We had a couple of very serious individuals, as well as a couple of characters. One of my favorite guys was the "Bear"—cantankerous and sometimes grouchy, but generally a good natured soul. I had worked with this Ol' codger at the S/O way back in the mid '60s. He was a training officer then, working the North County area (B-1) on the dog watch. This war story will convey why the troops called him the "Bear:"

****

The Bear was training a rookie, like me, who was green as grass—ditto... The North County beat (B-1) was often a graveyard: I mean, what happens in Los Altos Hills after midnight? Because the hierarchy was big on documenting "activity," they created an Activity Log,—affectionately known as the "Fink Sheet," on which the rookie had to log every minute of their 8 hour shift. Self initiated activity was a must, so we used to make car stops, patrol checks at professional buildings, bar checks, and FIs--stopping and talking to suspicious persons, etc. But, B-1 wasn't like where I trained, in the Burbank section of San Jose: After 0100 hours nothing moved on B-1's beat—absolutely nothing—not even a stray dog! So, at the beginning of the shift, the Bear would patrol the El Camino Real (ECR) looking for CS pinches, such as defective tail or license plate lights so they could justify their existence.

On the night in question, Bear had just given his rookie the keys (that was a biggie for recruits, as we now were able to drive a real patrol car and talk on the radio, too) and directed him to find something—anything that they could log. Bear's partner was a bit of a hotdog, just like the rest of us rookies.

After a couple of passes on the ECR, the Rookie spotted a violator—a guy in a brand new Mercedes ran a red light. Biggie! So, the rookie pulled the hotshot over and issued the High Roller a citation.

At approximately 0300, while parked in a secluded spot, the Bear began to examine the rookie's paper work. Suddenly, without warning, Vesuvius erupted:

"Jesus Christ!" Bear boomed. "Did you look at that guy's driver's license, for Chrissakes?"

"Yes, sir," the rookie timidly replied.

"Well, was his name George Washington?" Bear growled.

"No, I don't think so," the rook returned.

"Well, God dammit, that's how he signed the FN citation," Bear asserted. "We're going to get that miserable SOB!"

And, off they went, Xing the switch back roads as if they were running the Pike's Peak race. At approximately 0330, B-1 arrived at the hoity-toity mansion of "George Washington," high atop a knoll in prestigious Los Altos Hills. Both men rushed to the door and the Bear pounded on the ornate stain glass double doors with his night stick, all the while hollering: "Sheriff's Office, open the God damn door!" After several minutes, a groggy man in jammies and a night robe answered.

"That's him," the rookie shouted.

"Are you Mr. George Washington?" the Bear bellowed.

"No Sir," the pajama clad man said.

"Well, why in the hell did you sign this citation as George Washington?" Bear scowled.

All he got from the man was a deer in the headlights stare.

"Let me tell you something Adam Henry, if you don't sign this new cite with your true name, we are going to haul your pajama-ass down to the bucket in San Jose. You got that?"

"Yes, sir, where do I sign?"

Sadly, Richard "Dick" Salsman, aka "Bear" passed away in 2013 (R.I.P.)

****

Professor William Shockley

Let it not be said that I am not an equal opportunity writer: This book is about cops 'n robbers, students and staff, and even our most esteemed faculty. . .

My intercom buzzed:

"Captain Niemeyer," I chirped.

"Captain, there's an elderly gentleman on the phone who wishes to speak to you about a confidential matter," our cheerful clerk chimed.

"And, does this "confidential" gentleman have a name or is that confidential, too?" I teased.

"Well, of course; it's Professor Shockley," she replied.

"Hmmmm, I wonder what's up with him? Put him on."

"Professor Shockley, how are you, sir? Is there something I can help you with?" I asked.

"Oh yes, Captain, I'm fine, but I'm sort of concerned about this strange package that I received in the mail," he said.

"So, what kind of package is this and where is it now?" I implored.

"Well," he slowly continued, "you once sent me a letter about suspicious parcels and this package bears a lot of the elements that you outlined. It's crudely wrapped in shopping bag paper, there is excessive postage, the paper is stained, there are many misspelled words, and the person wrote everything first, in pencil, then went over it in red crayon," the professor astutely related. "Oh, and it came from Iowa and I have no idea who the person is," he added

Boy, this old guy's mind is as sharp as a tack—he remembered almost every tell-tale fact about a possible parcel bomb—Christ, no wonder he invented the transistor...

"Professor, yes we are definitely going to want to examine that item. Where is it now?" I quizzed.

"Well, it's in the trunk of my car; I meant to bring it down to you several weeks ago, but I guess it slipped my mind," he sheepishly answered.

"It's in your car? How long have you had it?" I asked.

"Captain, I don't actually remember. Perhaps a month ago, I put it in my garage for a while then I decided to bring it to the police department."

This is a potential script for "The Absent Minded Professor II," I chuckled to myself.

"OK, sir. Drive very carefully to the rear of the police station where the fire department's training yard is and I'll meet you there; say in about five minutes? Please sir, do not touch the package in any way, OK?" I confirmed.

"Yes, Captain Niemeyer, I'm on my way now," he assured.

Man, I hope this distinguished professor doesn't forget, I mused thoughtfully. *Hopefully he'll remember how to get here as I'd hate to see this gentleman driving around campus with a time-bomb on board...*

Although I had never met Professor William Shockley, the Chief had briefed me when I was first hired. Shockley had espoused a theory in the 1960s, that blacks were intellectually inferior to whites. Needless to say, this notion drew the ire of many on campus and beyond; several protests occurred as a result. In one instance, a group of militants invaded Shockley's classroom and disrupted his proceedings. The police were called and the protesters eventually dispersed. This incident gave rise to alarming his classroom and residence, as well as monitoring his mail; thousands of threats had been sent to the good professor. So, the question still loomed in my mind: *Is there still some nut out there who wants to do harm to this professor emeritus?*

Before going downstairs to meet Professor Shockley, I had our communications call-up the S/O Bomb Technician, as *I* damn sure wasn't going to mess with that thing...

About five minutes later, I espied a vintage and very cherry '64 Cadillac Coupe DeVille—2 door hard top—drive slowly into the fire training yard. There was a diminutive elder with the whitest of white hair driving; he could barely see over the steering wheel! I rushed up to the driver's door and opened it for the gentleman. He alighted, keys in hand and immediately bolted for the rear of the massive vehicle—this car looked like an Essex class WWII aircraft carrier, with a trunk so large that UH-1 Huey could land on it... I respectfully halted the excited man and directed him to the fire bay, while I took his keys.

Opening that massive trunk was a heart stopper! There it was: The nastiest 10-66 (suspicious package) I had ever laid eyes on. Just as the professor had described, this looked like something the Unabomber had concocted. I backed away from the potential weapon of *my* destruction and asked Radio to put out a Code 33 (no transmissions whatsoever) for fear that this thing might go off with an errant radio wave. Against better judgment—probably because the good professor had manhandled this package for over a month and it had been rattling around in that cavernous trunk for at least 2 weeks—I took a deep breath and gently lifted out the parcel and gingerly carried it to the fire training tower, and placed it in one of the concrete/steel reinforced compartments. *Whew,* I exhaled...

I ushered Professor Shockley along and told him that I would call him the minute the bomb technician got into this package and rendered it safe—if necessary. Surprisingly, my good friend Sergeant Leonard Anderson of the S/O arrived in quick order, with his bomb trailer in tow. When I led him to the package, I seem to recall him saying:

"Holy Shit! This looks bad—the worst I've seen!"

"My sentiments, exactly, Leonard."

When the *sapper* put the magnetometer on the parcel and it pegged positive for metal, I was outta there! Call me chicken, but this was beyond my expertise and knowledge, plus, although I was born at night, it wasn't last night. . .

After what seemed to be a week, Leonard emerged from the bunker and said:

"Captain, you gotta check this out!"

I warily made my way back into the enclave and saw that Sgt. Anderson had unwrapped the parcel exposing a crude plaque. It was weird, obviously put together by someone who was not tightly wrapped. It read something to this effect:

"To my hero professer Wm. Shuckley who give the wurl so much. We luv you fer al the good werk you did. Yur frien frum Ioway, Ben."

Pretty pathetic and so sad, that a challenged person from Iowa would reach out to the aging Professor William Shockley, and render adulation—however imperfect and threatening as it was. Sadly, William Shockley passed away in 1989 at age 79.

****

Boomerang

This was my first pre-academy class—my brainchild which I dubbed the "Forty Hour Indoctrination Class"—a week of interface for our deputy recruits from civilian life to the Santa Clara County Sheriff's Department. My lesson plan was based on the 40 hour training regimen set down by P.O.S.T., recently mandated for all reserve and auxiliary peace officers. The itinerary consisted of department tours, classroom instruction, as well as some practical experience in laws of arrest, search and seizure, arrest techniques and firearms training and safety. I yearned to depart from my experiences and frustration of the old days when the sergeant practically gave recruits a badge—you got the uniform and gun on your own hook—a beat map, a set of car keys, pointed you to the parking lot and said: "Answer the radio, stay on your beat and don't F-up!"—you know the drill as I have beat on this drum before. . .

During one of our arrest techniques sessions, one of the cadets posed a question that really piqued my interest—especially since I had such an experience in the early 70's:

Recruit: "Sgt. Niemeyer, what do you do if you arrest a guy who spits all over the place??"

Sergeant: "Great question, young man. What's your name?"

Recruit: "Sir, Deputy Johanson, Sir!"

Sergeant: "Here's an appropriate 'War Story' that might benefit you in the future. As a matter of fact, I wondered about the same thing when I was a recruit. Toward the end of my training, I was invited to join the seasoned FTOs in *their* sacred coffee room after shift. Boots, in those days, were like 19th early 20th Century children at the dinner table: Seen but not heard. Coincidentally, the "spitter" issue came up in one of those *"can you top this* war story?" A salty 'ol veteran took the floor and described a situation where he encountered and successfully thwarted a recalcitrant arrestee. With stogie tightly clenched in the corner of his mouth, the T/O described a knock-down drag-out fight in which a drunken subject fought, bit, and spit uncontrollably—all over the deputy and his patrol car. The solution was quite obvious, our mentor, continued: "We handcuffed that 'son-of-a-bitch,' and put a shopping paper bag over his head. That's what they do with wild animals and crazy bastards—the bag calms 'em down and the spit dribbles down their neck. . ."

Sounds like a helluva good idea to me, I thought. So, when I awoke from my afternoon slumber, I discussed this plan with my spouse, as I had some doubts as to how a shopping bag would stay on an unwilling suspect's head. We tried this technique by placing a Safeway paper bag on my head, and lo and behold, I found that this tale may be far-fetched: I could shake the bag off my head while seated and handcuffed behind my back, every time. However, being a curious student of invention, I rolled up the bag so it sat on the top of my head, with the bottom just below my jaw—Well, no matter how much I struggled and whipped my head around, I simply couldn't shake that bag off. So, after a simple modification, the old salt's concept actually worked. I immediately rolled-up a couple of shopping bags and put them in my beat box where they remained unused for several years.

Rewind, circa 1970:

It was a dark, balmy night in San Jose. Nothing was happening so I was cruising around the old Sunol area of San Jose. While at the intersection of Sunol and San Carlos streets, I spotted a white male subject suddenly jump out into busy San Carlos Street traffic and flag down a female, who was driving a yellow VW Bug. The gal tried to swerve around this nut, but he jumped right in front of her car so she was forced to stop—or run over the loon. The crazy man then opened the passenger door and hopped-in, all the while motioning for the girl to drive-on.

When I put the pedal to the metal of that MOPAR, it took-off like the Shuttle—I was behind that Beetle in a heartbeat. I saw a lot of gesticulating—mainly from the hitcher, so I figured that this moron may be an unwanted interloper. I advised Radio of my situation; suddenly, the V-Dubb made a quick left onto one of the Burbank's residential side-streets. I continued to stalk the VW, and when it made an abrupt pull-over, I flipped on the rubies and gave the siren a piercing blast. When I illuminated the interior of the Bug, I could see that clearly: "Something was *definitely* wrong here," so I "slapped leather" and rushed the Beetle.

"Are you alright ma'am?" I shouted.

Young Lady: Out of breath: "No! Please, Sir, get this crazy man out of my car."

"Ma'am, I saw this guy flag you down. You stopped and he got in. Is he an acquaintance? I quizzed.

"No! Absolutely NOT! I have never seen him before in my life. Please sir, get him out," she implored.

So, without further ado, I sprinted to the passenger side, threw open the door and "eased" the man out by the scruff of his neck while I re-holstered my pistol. The dude was wasted: He smelled like he had just inhaled a bundle of grass and whet his appetite with a gallon of rot-gut *vino*. I cuffed him without much difficulty and strapped him into the front seat (protocol for transporting a prisoner when you were solo) of the prize of our fleet, the incomparable Dodge 440 Magnum—with only 40 miles on it. For a brief moment, I wished I had my cage car, *but I'd only be a minute getting the girl's information for my report,* I thought, so I grabbed my clip board.

The minute I put pen to paper, I heard a sickening screeching sound—the roar of that motor revving way past the red-line. I dashed back to the cruiser and realized the idiot had reached over the tunnel and had the gas pedal buried. Not only that, but the bastard had spit huge *lungers* all over the dash and windshield! I gave the jerk a couple of friendly hacks, killed the engine and retrieved the keys. At that point, I was rather annoyed so I released the seatbelt and snatched him out of the car. *Man,* I was worried: *I hope that stunt didn't hurt the motor. How will I explain this to the Sergeant? Damn, I should have taken the car (piece of junk) that was assigned* to me. *See what happens when you cross the line? God will punish you!*

After depositing this dirt bag back in the unit, I admonished him to stop spitting, and sternly cautioned that if he ever stepped on that accelerator again, he would be going to VMC's ER via ambulance—And, in critical condition! This guy was so out of it, he obviously couldn't even comprehend my *friendly* warning and continued to spit and fight. Suddenly, the bell went off in my head: *Bag trick!* So, I went into my case, retrieved my trusty Safeway bag and covered the spitter's ugly mug. As I spirited this jerk to the Drunk Tank, I couldn't help but notice that motorists took a double take, as I zoomed by—wonder what they thought?

****

Fast-Forward: Circa 1980's

The Stanford Department of Public Safety's Front Office receptionist called one morning and said that a police offer was on the line and wanted to talk to me. When I asked who he was and what he wanted, our clerk replied he knew me from the Sheriff's Office, and that the nature of the call was "personal." Once put through, the conversation went something like this:

"Captain Niemeyer, can I help you?"

"Ah, yes, Captain. This is Officer Johanson. I used to be a Sheriff's deputy before moving to "X" P.D. I was one of the recruits in your 40 hour indoctrination class."

"Oh, yeah, I remember you. So, when did you jump ship to the PD?"

"About six years ago. Captain, I wanted to talk to you about a problem I got involved in. My partner and I arrested a belligerent guy who was high on PCP and he began spitting at us, so I employed that bag trick that you told us about in your class. Unfortunately, the guy died."

All of a sudden, this case hit me like a thunderbolt! I remember reading about it in the papers and commented to our A-Units one morning that I couldn't believe the stupidity of those clowns (the cops)! Those dummies actually taped the bag around the arrestee's neck with FINGERPRINT (lifting) TAPE! According to news accounts, the subject freaked out and suffered a massive heart attack.

"Boy," I lamented, "That's too bad. So, what can I do for you?"

"My attorney wanted me to contact you for corroboration that you taught this specific technique in your class," he boldly asserted.

"Yeah, I demonstrated that trick with the bag, but I damn sure NEVER told you guys to tape the FN thing on with tape! Look, I need to report this to my Chief and our attorney, so you can have your lawyer contact the General Counsel's Office here at Stanford, okay? I'll talk to you later." CLICK! *Much later,* I mused.

Deposition

It didn't take long for the dreaded subpoena to arrive at my office. After being duly served, I was directed to the law offices of "Curly, Shemp and Moe" for my testimony. But, I came prepared—not only with well rehearsed dialogue, but a Fry's shopping bag, carefully folded in my attaché case. After taking all of the lawyer's shots, I performed my "Dog 'n Pony Show:" I whipped out my trusty bag—on which I had written, "'AINTS Fan,"* which actually got a couple of restrained laughs—covered my head, thrust my hands behind my back and initiated gyrations consistent with a man who was trying to get that damn thing off. After about a minute, the bag remained on my *cabeza,* so I ripped it off and exclaimed:

"See, it works, and WITHOUT FINGERPRINT TAPE!"

The plaintiff's attorneys grinned; the defendant's mouthpiece looked like they wanted to eat a gun—as much as I was tempted to give them mine, I restrained myself. . .

*Before they started winning, the New Orleans Saints were awful—So much so that many fans wore paper shopping bags over their heads at the games, with various captions, the most popular being "AINTS!".

The Moral

The moral of this tale is quite obvious: Words and deeds will often come back on you like an Aboriginal Boomerang! So, be prepared to DUCK!

CHAPTER TWENTY

Dignitary Visits: Most Good, Some Bad, a Few Ugly!

Secret Service Class

After being promoted to Sergeant at the Santa Clara County S/O, they sent me to an academy—well, sort of. . . This was a multi-agency program with departments attending from all over the Western United States. Classes were held at Gavilan Community College in Gilroy, CA. Although in plainclothes, the students knew very well who we were. This was in early 1973, so many of the college kids hadn't gotten over the Vietnam War protests and viewed the cops as the enemy—"Pigs," they called us. While we were never accosted or threatened—they would have never dared as all of us were armed—but we got a lot of dirty looks and the campus, as a whole, was less than hospitable. Be that as it may, we plodded along with our 2 week program on how to be an effective police supervisor, mostly pretty boring boiler-plate stuff, but we had to endure as this training was mandated by our respective states.

One of the more interesting classes, I thought, was a one day "dog and pony show" put on by the U.S. Secret Service. Many of the yahoos from some of the Podunk PDs and S/Os pooh-poohed this block of instruction as a pure waste of time and something they would never use. I disagreed. I not only found the presentation very professional and interesting, but knew that because of Stanford University and many of the community colleges in our county, I might very well be called-up to assist on a dignitary visit from time to time. As a former member of the S/O's Tactical Team (Mean Green Machine) as you read in the Old Guard chapter, our team had been deployed on a couple visits during the tumultuous 60s and 70s:

Our first assignment was to provide security and to back-up the Secret Service on a speaking engagement by Vice President Hubert Humphrey at Stanford's Memorial Auditorium on February 20,

1967. The over-capacity crowd was a literal powder keg! While about half of the audience gave the VP a welcoming round of applause, the rest wore white arm bands in solidarity over their desire to stop the war. Mr. Humphrey tried to placate the group with platitudes about how well the war was going and that it was America's duty to help South Vietnam preserve their autonomy. He further stated that President Johnson's White House was simply following the policies set forth by the popular JFK administration. The dissidents weren't buying it! Many of the protesters silently filed-out during the Vice President's speech.

Once this happened, the brain trust figured-out that there could very well be a serious disturbance when the principle concluded his remarks and was set to leave. So, they re-deployed a couple of our squads, who were guarding the front, to the rear entrance of Mem Aud on Memorial Way, adjacent to Frost Amphitheater. USSS moved the motorcade and set-it-up there. My squad was lined-up on the stairs and sidewalk, which provided a cordon leading to the limos and support vehicles. When the dissidents saw the repositioning of the VP's package, the throng of protesters—by this time, perhaps a couple hundred or more—came flying around the building and began chanting "Shame, Shame, Shame"—plus many other unprintable invectives. We stoically held our ground with our batons at port arms. Many of these clowns were munching on garlic and came right up to our faces, not more than 3-4 inches away, shouting, "Pigs off Campus." Their breath smelled like the old *aku* heads (Charlie the Tuna variety) I used to put out in the blistering Hawaii sun for a day or two before using them as crab bait. . . These people were the hard-core dissidents and probably not Stanford students or faculty. We just let them carry-on and allowed these individuals to vent their rage and spew their vulgarity, as we were decoys—this was a subterfuge: While the group was barraging our deputies with hate filled speech and political theater, our friends on Mr. Humphrey's detail had slipped a back-up vehicle to the loading dock around the corner. At the appointed moment, the Secret Service sneaked the VP out the back door and he was gone. The punks went berserk as the detail mounted-up on the motorcade and powered out of there. In those days, the limos had running boards with hand holds on the roof, accommodating three agents on each side. As the package pulled away, we peeled many of the protesters off of the vehicles, while the agents kicked the rest to the curb as they sped off. Wow! That was impressive, but then, we never could have gotten away with that level of rough stuff. The Secret Service was commissioned to keep their principle safe so they could pretty much get away with almost anything in preserving the life of their *protectee*. Remember, President John F. Kennedy had just been assassinated only three years before. . .

Our next outing was to provide security for the controversial Vietnam General, William C. Westmoreland, at Foothill College, Los Altos Hills, CA. After being relieved of his battlefield duties (for being the General who never lost a battle but couldn't win the war), the General returned to the States where he embarked on many speaking engagements throughout the country. Although Foothill's student body was considered to be pale by comparison to other radical student venues, we figured that there would always be a knucklehead or two in the crowd. The speech was given in a small auditorium and most of the students were respectful, but there was one clown who decided to lob a balloon full of red paint at the embattled General. We took care of that Bozo and the rest of the performance was uneventful.

These two examples were bad—with VP Humphrey's debacle being *Very Bad!*

President Gerald Ford: Stanford Law School Dedication

It was in early September, 1975. I had been the Patrol Commander for nearly a year, and was just learning my way around the Farm when Chief Herrington dropped an "A-bomb" on his A-Units: United States President Gerald Ford was going to dedicate the new Law School on September 21st. This undoubtedly was going to be one the biggest events on campus since the University opened its doors October 1, 1891. Former U.S. President Theodore Roosevelt visited the Farm in early 1910 as the guest of University President David Starr Jordan and V.P., Professor Casper Branner—destined to become Stanford's second president in 1913. The entourage cruised around the campus in an open motor coach, and by all accounts, this was a very low-key event. The Ford visit was going to be anything but low key, I feared.

Our first parlay with the Secret Service in our conference room seemed like a full board meeting; there was standing room only! I detected that the agents in charge were very nervous about this gig: Seventeen days earlier, a Charles Manson disciple, Lynette "Squeaky" Fromme, pointed a gun at President Ford when he visited the Sacramento Capitol. In addition, I think the USSS was concerned because we were new kids on the block. Even though the S/O would play a major role in site security and SWAT capabilities, our fledgling DPS would provide logistics and manpower assets, which included extensive site security and plainclothes support with the Secret Service. The California Highway Patrol would head-up the motorcade escort, but would give up the reigns once on campus. This, indeed, was going to be very big!

Right from the get-go, the USSS dug into our deep pockets: They wanted dozens of brand new 55 gallon drums and thousands of yards of 2 inch white nylon rope. They then ordered the barrels to be painted red, white and blue. These stanchions (filled with water) were positioned around the North face of the new and beautiful School of Law, leaving a void between the speaker's stage and the anticipated throng of attendees. The excited guests would be prevented from getting too close to the President of the United States once the rope fence was put together. All seemed to be going as planned. Our CP was located on the roof of the CERAS building (Center for Educational Research); S/O and Secret Service counter sniper teams commanded all of the high ground around the site—nothing could go wrong!

I'll never forget the incredible sight of my first presidential motorcade as it proceeded past our vantage point: It looked like there were at least 40 vehicles is this parade, with dozens of police cars and motorcycles giving us an early preview of Christmas. . . Once the President and entourage emerged from the Law School, the throng surged against the rope barrier. Suddenly, it seemed like the bursting of a levee, as a torrent of humanity surged forward and was within arm's reach of the President. The PPD (Presidential Protection Detail) pulled the President back to a safe area until our troops could re-establish a safe barrier. We learned, almost immediately, that person(s) unknown slashed the 2 inch rope like a hot knife through butter. I'll bet that was the last time the USSS utilized this method of barricades...

As exciting as this visit was, we were all relieved when we espied the last motorcade vehicle leave the Farm, en route San Francisco.

A Close Call

On the very next day, September 22, 1975, President Gerald Ford literally dodged a bullet while in front of the St. Francis Hotel in San Francisco: A gunshot rang out from a crowd of folks about 40 feet away from Ford; the bullet zipped over his head by a mere six inches and struck a wall. Fortunately for the President, a brave Marine grabbed the shooter's arm and disarmed the would-be assassin before a second round could be fired. A bystander was slightly injured by the ricochet. The miscreant was quickly taken into custody and whisked away by police and FBI agents.

The shooter was a recently radicalized 41 year old bookkeeper and former FBI snitch named Sara Jane Moore. Investigation revealed that Moore was fascinated by the kidnapping of Patty Hearst by the *Symbionese Liberation Army* (SLA), and adopted their anarchist point of view—hence her beef with President Ford's conservative philosophy. Moore came to the attention of the Secret Service earlier in 1975 and was interviewed by two very well respected and seasoned agents. One of my contacts said that although Ms. Moore "was as whippy as a 10 foot fly rod," she didn't exhibit enough bizarre behavior to certify she was a danger to others or herself, thus they were forced to do nothing, save write a report. Even if she had been committed for 72 hours, it would have taken an act of Congress to keep Moore hospitalized for any period of time back in those days.

Another fact that saved the President's life was that law enforcement had recently arrested Sara for illegally possessing a concealable weapon: The officers confiscated a .44 caliber pistol and over 100 rounds of ammunition, and apparently released her on her own recognizance the very day that Gerald Ford was dedicating our law school. A credible Secret Service agent later told me that Sara Jane Moore's Plan A was to hit the President at Stanford! She later admitted that she was near the law school but scrubbed her mission when she saw the intense security and the throng of people that would have made it almost impossible for her to get within range.

After the cops seized Sara's arsenal, she simply went down to the nearest gun shop, purchased and took delivery on a .38 caliber revolver and a box of ammo. This was obviously before laws prohibited firearms dealers from selling a pistol and making it available to the customer without first going through an FBI record's check. Fortunately, the dealer and Sara Jane didn't know that this weapon's sights weren't properly adjusted: FBI firearms experts subsequently discovered that the piece shot 6 inches high!

Lady Luck smiled on all of us during that potentially deadly visit from Hell!

Sara Jane Moore pled guilty to attempted assassination and was sentenced to life in Alderson Federal Prison Camp, in West Virginia. She tried to shorten her sentence by escaping in 1979; however, the "hounds" tracked her down within a few hours and Moore was relocated to a more secure facility in Dublin, CA, where she remained until paroled in 2007— a full year after President Ford passed away. All told, Sara Jane spent 32 years in stir; she was 77 years old when released and later openly expressed remorse.

Governor Ronald Reagan

It was 1977 and former California Governor, Ronald Reagan, was invited to the Hoover Institution to become inducted as a Hoover Fellow. This is a big deal as the Hoover Institution of War, Revolution and Peace is one of the most prestigious "think tanks" in the universe. Founded by Stanford Alum and U.S. President Herbert

Hoover '95 (ah, that would be 1895) in 1919, the institution is a public policy research center with focus on the study of politics, international relations, economics, and political economy—both at home and abroad. Over the years, Hoover assembled world-class scholars and other renowned personages to this *think tank*. Given Governor Reagan's transition from Hollywood to the Capitol in Sacramento as a result of his great political acumen and aplomb, it was little wonder that the Institution's Fellows invited the Governor to join their prestigious group.

Being between jobs, so to speak—although we didn't know it at the time—the Governor did not have an organized protection detail, so we were commissioned to ensure Ronald Reagan's visit to Stanford would be enjoyable and secure. This was to be our first solo flight: The DPS had gained some valuable knowledge and experience in assisting the U.S. Secret Service in President Gerald Ford's 1975 dedication of the law school, as well as the visit of German Chancellor Helmut Schmidt in 1976. We met Governor Reagan's limo at the Hoover Tower oval. I had a contingent of CSOs to provide traffic control and vehicle security.

When the Governor got out of his car, I approached and introduced myself as well as my team of four plainclothes officers. I was taken aback by Reagan's cordiality: He warmly shook all of our hands and commenced to titillate us with jokes and quips. We escorted the Governor into *HooTow* (Hoover Tower) where he was greeted by an enthusiastic staff who promptly gave him an accelerated "cook's tour" of President Hoover's office and wife, Lou Henry Hoover's wing. Reagan was impressed as the displays are indeed interesting and grand. From there we escorted him to a conference room where the official indoctrination to Fellowship took place. From there, we drove him to the auditorium at GSB (Graduate School of Business) where he was to address a group of students.

I have never been known as a shrinking violet, but I must confess I was a bit nervous about this gig: This was not only our "First Rodeo," but my guys were a tad bit on the green side, never having had to provide dignitary protection all by their lonesome—and being the detail leader, this was to be my first "Bull Ride" so I didn't want to screw it up. I was very concerned about the student audience: Were we going to have some Reagan-haters in there? Were we going to have a disturbance? What would the Daily say if my officers had to drag protester(s) out in handcuffs? Would the good Governor be harassed with jeers and chants? Worse, would some clowns pelt him with rotten fruit? Talk about anxiety! I needed a *Paxil* or two, although I didn't even know what that was in those days. . .

Once the Governor took the stage, the crowd gave him a standing ovation! They absolutely loved him! Whew! The "Great Communicator's" address was awesome! The students were engaged and showed their interest by presenting interesting dialogue during the Q and A session, which I thought would never end. But, true to form, the good governor fielded all questions and comments until the last man/woman was standing. Then, the surprise. . . .

After the speech, one of the Governor's staffers told me the *Man* wanted to walk to the Faculty Club for the scheduled luncheon. I'm sure my silent groan was audible: That wasn't in the original plan. Whenever a principle is out of a motorcade and on foot in an unscheduled move, this causes hair loss and graying to the leader. . . Still being a neophyte on campus geography, I deferred to my team who knew the place like the back of their hands. We adopted the classic diamond formation, with me in "drag"—not "drag queen," for heaven's sake: That's the guy who brings-up the rear—like in the old cattle drives on the ol' Texas Chisholm Trail. . .

As we were proceeding down Duena Street heading for the Faculty Club, it was hilarious watching people's facial reactions-- folks stared at our principle with quizzical expressions on their faces, as if to say: "I know that guy." Then, bingo: "Ohhhhh, that's Ronald Reagan!" Huge smiles of recognition would follow. All of a sudden, a pick-up truck emerged and was heading our way, with a huge guy behind the wheel. If looks could kill, the Governor would have been assassinated on the spot! That fellow gave us and the principle the major *stink-eye* as he slowly cruised by. I told my wing-man: "Watch that guy." Then, without warning, the dude slammed on his brakes, jammed the truck into reverse and smoked the tires as he backed-up to our formation. At that point, I cleared leather and had my piece hidden along the rear of my leg. The man pulled abreast to the Governor and shouted: "Governor Reagan, I want to shake your hand!" A broad smile replaced the grim looks. The *Man* approached the pick-up and robustly pressed the flesh with the driver. I let out another big "Whew."

Needless to say, I was very relieved to see our charge safe and sound with friends at the Faculty Club. Before the Governor departed the Farm, he took the time to shake the hands of all of the CSOs who guarded his motorcade. That was impressive, in my view. In the over 250 major visits I headed-up during my tenure at Stanford, only one other dignitary ever did this—And, I'll tell you about him later.

Ronald Reagan was a very humble and a personally engaging man; I shall never forget him! I learned more about this wonderful human being via a 2011 televised tribute of the Reagan Library, which had recently been refurbished. I also viewed a two hour documentary about Ronald W. Reagan's life; I am truly humbled and honored to have headed-up Ronald Wilson Reagan's security detail when he was admitted to the Hoover Institution. He was better than Good—He was Great!

Queen Elizabeth II and Prince Phillip, of Great Britain

The Queen of England was a big hit when she arrived in San Francisco on the Royal Yacht H. M. S. Britannia* in 1983. Queen Elizabeth and Prince Phillip's visit was a major concern for the U.S. Secret Service and her Royal Security detail. Because of raging discontent and animosity toward the British in Northern Ireland, extraordinary measures were taken to make certain the Royal pair and their entourage would remain safe and sound during the visit. Mission One was to keep the Royal vessel secure and impervious to an underwater attack while moored in San Francisco Bay. Like in WWII, anti-submarine nets were deployed around the ship. Navy SEALs were in the water and on patrol 24-7, while scores of aircraft covered the air space like a huge spider web!

Queen Elizabeth's visit to Stanford's Lou Henry Hoover House for an elegant luncheon was steeped with pomp and circumstance. Stanford University President, Donald Kennedy, hosted the gala event in which nearly 100 dignitaries, in their own right, attended. Hundreds of curious gawkers pressed the barricades and rope lines for a glimpse of the elegant Queen of England. Even the LSJUMB (The BAND) showed-up, properly attired in snappy red tunics and pressed black slacks. And, much to my surprise, they played as I had never heard them perform before: They were on key and uttered nary a sour note! Do you know why? This group, made-up of some pretty good musicians, was stone sober! The strongest adult beverage served at this affair was "High Tea"—and crumpets, of course. At this gig, doing the *Mariachi* thing of hitting dozens of football tailgate parties and playing tunes for libations and food was <u>verboten</u>—I'm sure President Don Kennedy made that perfectly clear when he issued an invitation to the Band. . .

*The Royal Yacht H. M. S. Britannia is quite a historic vessel. It was built in 1953 and served the Royals for 44 years. This exquisite 400 foot, 5 deck ship, was powered by twin steam engines which developed 12,000 shaft horsepower. She could motor along at 20 knots and had a top speed of nearly 22. The Britannia traveled over a million nautical miles, plying 600 ports in 135 countries. She was retired in 1994 and is moored at a historic port of Leith, Edinburgh Scotland, where she serves as a huge tourist attraction. This certainly was no "yacht"—like what comes to mind during America's Cup races—H. M. S. Britannia is a full blown cruise ship crewed by minions of seamen/women, epicurean chefs, a medical staff, as well as the 15 member H. M. S. Royal Marines Band. . .

Crown Prince Harald of Norway

While on a technology tour of Stanford's innovative laboratories in 1985, Prince Harald's lead security man approached me and asked, in beautiful English:

"Captain, the Prince wondered if it would be convenient for him to have a look at your stadium. He is a very big football fan—both soccer and American, and would like to see your field, which is supposed to be one of the best in the world."

"Absolutely," I fired back. "As a matter of fact," I continued, "they are putting the finishing touches on the field and stands in preparation for Super Bowl XIX."

"Yes, he knows all about that and perhaps you could tell him about your security plans and how you liked the Olympic Soccer games last year," the agent remarked.

"I'd love to do that, sir. I have never addressed a royal figure before and would be delighted to do so! Follow me." And with that, we got into our respective vehicles and zoomed over to Gate 2.

On arrival, the Prince's security chief introduced me to Prince Harald, we shook hands and I led him to a good vantage point at the south end zone. The NFL's excellent groundskeepers were decoratively painting the end zones: FORTY NINERS, including San Francisco's logo, and DOLPHINS, with Miami's logo, as well. The NFL had built two state-of-the-art locker rooms and installed sturdy aluminum bleachers, replacing the rickety, splintered originals circa 1921. The Apple computer company donated padded cushions for each and every seat—nearly 86,000 white pads with the Apple logo prominently displayed really spruced up the old joint. The Prince was impressed and quizzed me about the history of Stanford Stadium, which I eagerly related as I did in a previous chapter. I also explained the high crown on the turf for our football, and how our ground's personnel agonized over having to shave it level for the Olympic Soccer games. It was quite an honor and privilege to chat one-on-one with the leader of Norway, and I went away with the impression that Prince Harald was an OK guy! Definitely one of the Good!

Dignitary Protection Seminar

It was early spring in 1985 when I received a phone call from the RAC (Resident Agent in Charge) of the U.S. Secret Service office in San Jose:

"Hey Raoul, how ya doing?'

"Hi Bill. I'm doing well. Please don't tell me that you have another VIP coming our way!" I hoped.

"Naaww, we don't have anything on the horizon that I know of. Actually, we are looking for someone to send to our Dignitary Protection Seminar back in D.C. Are you interested?" the boss said.

"You bet I am; I'm very flattered that you'd consider me. All I have to do is to convince my Chief to pay for it," I replied.

"No, Raoul, this one's on Uncle Sam; we pay for everything! How's that for your tax dollars at work?" Bill chided. "All of us thought you'd already been to the class as you seemed to know the U.S.S.S. drill pretty well, but Marty (Haskell) said that he'd worked with you since the President Ford visit in '75 and didn't think you ever attended the seminar. We put this program on for command level police and sheriff's officers from all over the country, in an effort to foster good will and show our appreciation for the local's assistance on these visits. This is a great school—ten days of training put on by our instructors, including a day at our Academy in VA, where you'll experience what the PPD (Presidential Protection Detail) goes through at our mock village."

"Wow, that sounds awesome," I beamed. "When do I leave?"

"Unfortunately, not until mid July, the hottest time in Washington. But, we could always schedule you for next January," he teased.

"Yeah, yeah, the coldest period on the planet," I rejoined. "Sign me up for July. I'll see if the Chief will let me go. Being that he's not paying for it, I'm sure he'll be glad to get rid of me for a couple of weeks."

Washington D.C.

This was my first excursion to anywhere east of Rantoul, IL, where I was trained as a jet engine mechanic at Chanute AFB. At least I wouldn't have to be marching to the chow hall at 0430 during virtual white-outs! However, Bill wasn't kidding about D.C.'s weather in July: I took a week of vacation prior to the seminar so I could visit some of the incredible museums and sights in the Capitol city, and had to ring-out my shirts each evening when I returned to the hotel. It was about as hot and humid as Hilo, on the Big Island, after the daily 1:00PM deluge.

I quickly learned how to navigate on the Metro rail system, which enabled me to experience about five or six of the fantastic museums. My favorite was the Smithsonian Air and Space Museum. I was there when the doors opened and was booted-out at day's end.

Another highlight was an escorted tour of the Capitol and White House, orchestrated by a former Honolulu Liquor Inspector, Henry Junie, who worked for my Dad way back when. Mr. Junie became the Sergeant of Arms for Hawaii's Senator, Daniel Inouye, a highly decorated WWII survivor of the famed all Japanese 442nd Regimental Combat Team.

The International Hotel

Our class was billeted in a pretty luxurious hotel, in my humble opinion. Save for the location, or lack thereof, our digs were four star. The biggest problem for the attendees was fighting our way through the gaggle of hookers who hung out around the pharmacy/store—People's Drugs—you could score that there, too. . . The Secret Service Headquarters, where classes were held, was about two long blocks away. Making the trek unmolested in the morning was usually no problem, but when the sun set, that's when things got ugly. Being we were cops from all over the USA, we noticed how the ladies plied their trade. We also quickly realized that the D.C. police were working the area with decoys and plainclothes vice cops—not that any of us would take a chance of getting busted for solicitation while guests of the U.S. Secret Service.

One evening, when a bunch of us were heading out for dinner at one of the many fine restaurants in the neighborhood, we noticed a couple of gals chatting with a pair of young men in a non-descript vehicle. We stopped momentarily and immediately figured this was a sting team: The car was a plain, dark Chrysler product with soup-bowl hubcaps. The guys sported buzz cuts and the women were trying to look like ladies of the night, but didn't quite make the cut, in our collective view. When one of the women spotted us looking at them, she drawled: "Wa'll, we best be movin' along, 'afore them Po-Lice come!" Yeah, right. They *were* the "Po-Lice!" As we were walking away from the poorest piece of vice work that any of us had ever seen, a *real* street walker approached one of our guys and asked if he wanted a date. Our quick witted buddy, a command officer from Detroit asked:

"How do I know **you're** not a cop?" With that, the woman reached in her purse and whipped out a sting of prophylactics and declared: "Does this looks like a cop's badge to you?" We all buckled over in laughter...

A Visit to the White House

During one of our breaks, the class was offered a first-cabin tour of President Ronald Reagan's residence. Having already seen that beautiful historical home, I passed and decided to do more D.C. sightseeing. Big mistake! Although I thoroughly enjoyed my excursion, the guys were stoked when we met for dinner that night.

"Hey Raoul, how come you weren't on the White House tour?" one of my classmates asked.

"I already visited the place last week and went downtown instead," I responded.

"Well, you missed a once in a lifetime event," the man chided. "President Reagan came home from the hospital (he had been admitted for minor surgery) aboard Marine One and we got to meet him. He shook all of our hands!"

Damn, I lamented, *I would have loved to have seen him again.*

The Training Center

The Secret Service Training Center is located outside of Alexandria, VA in a rural area. This huge plot of ground houses the Academy/Administrative complex, which had a full-blown gym with more weights and strength training equipment than most Gold's Gyms. There are also miles of jogging trails and an enormous shooting range for pistol, shotgun, sniper rifles and machine gun firing. The CAT (Counter Assault Team) guys live there: Most of their workdays involve vigorous weight training, running marathons, and countless hours at the range. These snipers have to show proficiency at distances up to 1,000 yards! They have to shoot at superimposed targets, which feature a bad guy hiding behind a hostage, with only half of the criminal's head being exposed. Try to score a hit on the bad guy at 1,000 yards *every time!* Well, by God, they do it!

The Store Front

Our visit coincided with scheduled training of the PPD (Presidential Protection Detail), at the mock village. The actual President's team was to be tested in a series of scenarios they might encounter on any visit. The detail used an abbreviated motorcade consisting of a lead vehicle, the Presidential armored limousine, a follow-up car, a CAT SUV, and a spare limo. Unlike their usual Brooks Brother's tailored suits, the team was permitted to dress-down into casual attire. The *principle* (the poor guy who played the part of the President) wore black slacks and a *zebra* shirt—like football referees wear. My "poor guy" remark will become crystal clear as I proceed.

The first drill occurred at the store front's rope line. There was a short-block façade of shops, stores, restaurants and a hotel—much like you would see on a Hollywood movie set. Our class was playing the part of exuberant well wishers, who were hemmed-in by a rope line, anchored by stanchions. We all were eager to press the flesh with the Prez when he arrived. Within minutes, the motorcade appeared with red lights flashing. The detail guided the principle out of the limo and cautiously moved him along the rope line, while we all surged forward to shake the *Man's* hand. Suddenly, there was a commotion at the front of the detail's cordon: Some moron ducked under the rope and was trying to get to the "President." While this was happening, I felt someone trying to push his way past me and my buddies, who were all on the front line. The harder he pushed, the more determined we were not to let this rude sucker past us. Out of the corner of my eye, I saw a small pistol in the idiot's hand. Another cop and I grabbed the would-be-assassin's arm, but not before he snapped-off a round—blank, of course. The agents yelled "Gun" and they literally pitched the "poor guy" headlong into the rear of the armored vehicle. The limo then sped-off like a dragster! Those cagy Secret Service evaluators had bad guys infiltrate our group. Damn, that was way too real!

The Picnic

After the surreal Store Front scenario, the coordinators directed us to a grove about 100 yards away from the mock village. There was BBQ going on and we were treated to grilled hotdogs, potato salad and baked beans. Without warning, the Presidential motorcade rolled-up. The *Man* popped-out of his vehicle waved and *gripped 'n grinned* on his way to a short stump. *Hmmmm,* I figured, *so that's where the political term "stumping" came from. . .* The Prez mounted said stump and gave an inspiring speech explaining why we should vote for him for a second term; we all cheered and gave him a standing ovation. Just as I was finishing my frank, machine gun fire broke-out from the second story of the village's hotel. Two of the PPD guys tackled the principle and dragged him behind the stone BBQ pit. The PPD gunman immediately opened-up with his Uzi, which he carried in a canvas computer-like shoulder bag. After a lot of "rat-a-tat-tat," other agents tossed out some yellow smoke screen bombs; under the cover of the smoke screen, they low-crawled the *Man* to his limo and roared away. Mission accomplished! I think they got a pass...

Last Night

I took a cab to historic Georgetown for a dinner and show. The food was excellent as was the Colorado group, who sounded as good as the Manhattan Transfer. On the return trip to the International Hotel, my cab driver was from the Caribbean. He was a very friendly man and I delighted in telling him stories about a 1977 cruise that I had taken to his neighborhood. We pulled up to a stoplight on the side street right around the hotel's entrance—smack dab across from the People's Drugs. It was a very humid night, and even at midnight, it was hot so all windows were down. Suddenly, a lady of the night stuck her head into the rear of the cab and said:

"You want a date, honey?"

"No thank you ma'am, I can't," I rejoined sternly.

"Whaddya mean you *can't?*" she forcefully asked. "You gay or somethin'?"

"No, my dear. You see, I have AIDS!" I falsely asserted.

"I'm outta here," she exclaimed and virtually disappeared into thin air...

I thought my Jamaican driver was going to stroke; he was laughing uncontrollably, but managed to choke-out:

"Ah, Mon, that's a good way to get rid of them." Indeed.

So, the next morning I was winging my way back to the Farm where I could apply the lessons I learned in D.C.—save for hooker control—I hoped...

President Francois Mitterrand of France

In March 1984, U.S. Secret Service Agent, Marty Haskell, popped-in from out of nowhere.

"Oh no! Not you again, Marty," I joshed. "I thought we were done with you guys after the King Gustaf of Sweden visit a few days ago."

"Raoul, unlike the King's breakfast gig at the Hanna House with your 10 Nobel laureates, this one is going to be BIG," Agent Haskell returned.

"Whaddya mean BIG, Marty?

"Ah, how about three UH-1 Hueys and two CH-47 Chinooks landing on Roble Field—that BIG enough for ya?" Marty boasted.

"Holy Christ, who in the hell is coming and with all of that airpower?" I quizzed.

"Francois Mitterrand, President of France and his arrogant 80 person press corps—that's why we need the Chinooks," the agent said. "You got time to check-out the field with me?"

"Marty, I have a meeting with the Chief in a few minutes, but I'll have Sergeant Philip Love advance the site with you. By the way, has the University okayed this massive air assault?" I asked. "The Chief is going to flip cheeseburgers when he hears about this one. And, why is the entire population of France visiting our beautiful campus?"

"The President and his entoura,ge are going to visit some new integrated circuit lab or something; I'll need to see that, too. Also, the entire mob is going to have a luncheon at your University President's home."

Women's Soccer Practice

About an hour later, Sergeant Philip Love came into my office in total hysterics. When I asked him what was so funny, he related the following:

"When Marty and I arrived at Roble Field, the Stanford Women's Soccer team was having a full-blown scrimmage. Marty strolled up to the coach and told him that they were going to have to leave the field at once. The coach looked at Marty as if he was nuts. You know what Marty looks like to the average bloke: He was wearing a plaid sports jacket, a wide pin-striped shirt, a bright red tie, tan trousers, and was sporting his ornate lizard skin cowboy boots. So, I guess the coach didn't believe he was a *real* Secret Service Agent, except for his dark shades. Then, Marty says, as he displays his credentials:"

"Look, sir, if you don't get those young ladies off the field within the next few minutes, it's going to be 'Apocalypse Now,' and they are going to have 3 Huey helicopters land on top of them!"

"The coach gave Marty that 'yeah right' look until he heard that distinctive 'wop-wop-wop' sound of huge rotor blades getting louder and louder," Philip continued. "Then, over the rooftops came the three choppers that Agent Haskell promised. I'd never seen women run so damn fast. . ."

"Typical Marty," I laughed. "But, ya just gotta love that guy; nothing phony about him!"

Nam Re-Visited

If the women's soccer coach thought the trial run was spectacular, he was in for a real show on March 26[th.] A huge motorcade was positioned on the West end of Roble Field and awaited the arrival of France's leader and his entourage. As the choppers descended over Roble Gym and settled onto the grass—there were no soccer players or anyone else in the LZ (Landing Zone), and as Marty had previously alluded to, this *was* like a scene from the Vietnam War film "Apocalypse Now." Frightening! And, very noisy, too! We got Mitterrand into the motorcade and visited the new Center for Integrated Systems, which was funded and built by the heavyweights of Silicon Valley such as Hewlett Packard, Varian Associates, Intel, and numerous other semiconductor giants. As Marty predicted, the real pain in the posterior was the pushy French press. Watching them get on and off the luxurious motor coaches reminded me of when I visited France in 1972 and used the Paris Metro to get around. Getting on and off those trains during the Parisian rush hour was like being at the Stanford student's gate trying to get through the wickets for the Big Game!

After the lavish luncheon at the Hoover House, we herded the press onto their buses and proceeded back to the LZ. As the air armada ascended over the red tile roofs and disappeared from sight, I bid them *au revoir* and hoped they wouldn't come back anytime soon. This visit was Good from an organizational and spectacular view point, but Bad because of the rude and obnoxious French press. Well, at least they weren't Ugly...

Bishop Desmond Tutu, South Africa

Bishop Tutu was invited to address an eager audience at Memorial Auditorium in 1986 during a worldwind tour of the United States. Because the Bishop was not a head of state or held any office that would qualify him for governmental protection, this responsibility fell into our hands. Bishop Tutu's visit would be our first experience in picking-up a principle at an airport, establishing a motorcade to the campus, providing close-up personal protection, then returning him to the next destination. The Bishop was to fly from South Africa to Los Angeles and from there to San Jose International General Aviation Airport on a private jet. In order to consummate this task, I needed the best guys in our department for a small motorcade and protection detail. My plan was to have a marked patrol unit in the lead, a rented Lincoln Town Car for the dignitary, and a marked patrol car as the tail. I assigned Detective Mark Swineford (in uniform) as the lead unit, Detective Sergeant Philip Love (aka., Philippe Crueseau) as my limo wheelman, with yours truly riding "shotgun," with Detective John McMullen (in uniform) bringing-up the rear. But, the name of the game is practice, practice, practice. You don't just form-up a motorcade package, however small, jump on the freeway in traffic, however slight, and proceed to your destination. People often marvel how organized and smooth the Secret Service is in moving huge motorcades around congested cities (Washington D.C., for instance). But, let me assure you that when USSS agents aren't on a security detail, they are practicing and choreographing their moves.

On our first trial run, we ran several routes: Our primary choice was Oregon Expressway to southbound CA-101, turn off at De la Cruz (Santa Clara) and then merge onto Coleman Avenue, where the General Aviation terminal is located. We met with San Jose Airport Police, discussed our plan and requested their assistance when the Bishop arrived later on that week. We also picked some alternate escape routes, just in case we ran into trouble with traffic or any other unforeseen difficulty. On the way back to the Farm via 101, we practiced numerous lane changes, which even with a 3 to 4 car package, can be troublesome to execute. Here's how it works: When the lead unit spots a jam-up ahead, he radios to the detail leader (me) and suggests a lane change of choice. At that point, I would advise all units: "Prepare to move left (or right)." When the coast was clear, the tail car would announce: "Lane clear, moving NOW!" At that moment, the package would move as one, nose to tail, so no moron could take a spot and get into our pack. And, so it was all the way back home and the CHP didn't pinch us for any "unsafe lane changes," either! We performed another trial run the day before the event, and in my estimation, we were good to go.

On D-Day, we arrived at SJC General Aviation Terminal and were escorted out on the ramp by airport police. University staffers brought a 9 passenger van which we lined up behind the tail unit as I didn't want them in our motorcade without a properly trained driver: In the event something happened and we had to get the Hell gone in a hurry, I would never put our *principle* in harm's way because of a neophyte driver. When the Bishop's plane arrived, staffers escorted him and his nephew to our Town Car where we exchanged pleasantries and seated them in the rear. All of a sudden, I heard a high pitched wail—*definitely not a jet engine*, I mused—but the shrill of a hysterical woman who was fast approaching on the run.

"Oh, Yoo-Hoo, I'm in charge here and I'm riding 'shotgun,'" she declared. *The hell you say*, I pondered, *what is this woman thinking? This is a police operation and I'm in charge! And besides, she wouldn't know to operate a damn shotgun if it hit her in the ass!*

"Ah, Ma'am, I'm Captain Niemeyer of the Stanford Police. And, *I'm* 'In Charge' of the Bishop's security detail and *I'm* riding shot gun and will call all the shots relating to his safety. So, you need to go to the rear of our police motorcade and get into the follow-up vehicle—that van back there," I pointed.

"Well," she retorted as she stomped her foot, "I'm Mrs._____ (Although she didn't say, she was a San Francisco *wannabe* socialite, the wife of a prominent and well-known attorney—think "Dream Team," folks, ala the O.J. Simpson murder debacle), and I am in charge of protocol for the Bishop's visit while in the Bay Area, so I demand to be with Bishop Tutu."

"Well, with all due respect Ma'am," I drawled like a Georgia Sheriff, "I'm sorry but I can't coordinate this move from the rear of this motorcade, so I'm afraid that you best get (*your sorry ass*, I thought but didn't say) into that vehicle as we are leaving *with* or *without* you!" With that, I keyed my mic and stated emphatically: "All units, from A-3. Head 'em up-and move- 'em out!" And, we were outta there, en route Stanford University, as Ms. "in charge" dashed back to the van. . .

As I got into the car, I noticed Bishop Tutu had a big grin on his face and that his nephew had broken out into laughter. The nephew couldn't contain himself and burst out:

"That was great. You sure told her off. She has been very pushy and obnoxious ever since we landed in the States."

"Well, Sirs, I'm sorry about that. I don't normally lose my temper like that (I lied, Big Time), but there was no way I could permit that woman to run this operation and jeopardize your safety while you are in our hands. So, how was your flight to LA?" I asked, trying to change the subject.

"Oh, the flight was very long but nice," the Bishop returned in his inimitable South African accent. "But, I was quite concerned when we were coming in for a landing because of all the fog."

"Actually, Bishop, that wasn't fog like we have in San Francisco. We call that stuff in LA SMOG—a combination of carbon emissions and fog. And, did you know that LA is one of the safest cities in the U.S. in the event of a nuclear attack?" I asked. They both nodded in the negative.

"The enemy (the Russians in that era) could never hit the mark with that continual blanket of SMOG over it," I joshed. The Bishop and his kin both had a good belly laugh over that corn ball joke—but it broke the ice and we got along famously, exchanging funny stories and clean jokes, of course. I'll never forget being in close proximity with Mrs. Prissy at Med Aud and enduring her vicious stink-eye. A couple of times Bishop Tutu's nephew saw her antics and snickered. The Bishop was a huge hit. Everybody loved him—especially our detail who had the privilege and pleasure of keeping him secure. He was not only a great, impassionate orator, but I found him to be a humble, kind man with a great sense of humor—his nephew, too, although I can't recall his name. For our first real solo visit, motorcade and all, I thought we deserved an "A" on that deal. We all were sorry to hand-off the Bishop to San Francisco's finest, but I'll bet Mrs. Prissy didn't try to muscle her way into the shotgun seat with the SFPD guys. . .

Admiral Isaac Kidd Jr., U.S. Navy Ret.

Admiral Isaac Kidd Jr., former Atlantic fleet Chief, was one of many high ranking military and intelligence officers, global planners and scholars who attended a symposium hosted by the Hoover Institution. When I saw the roster of conferees, this Admiral's name immediately stuck-out in my mind. Later that night, the bell rung and I recalled seeing a photo of him and his Dad, Admiral Isaac

Kidd, Commander of the Pacific fleet at Pearl Harbor, in a commemorative booklet about the U.S.S. Arizona BB-39, destroyed when the Japanese attacked the fleet on that "Day that will live in Infamy," December 7, 1941.

****

I was a mere lad of 3½, but I remember that morning as if it were yesterday: We had just finished a terrific Sunday breakfast of bacon and my Dad's world famous waffles. He was the master of this craft, as his waffles were always so light and golden brown; when asked how he made them so scrumptious, he quipped that he stirred them with his elbow...

We lived with my widowed Step-Great Grand Mother, Virginia Gomes Pilares, in her grand old two-story home at the foot of Punchbowl Crater, an extinct volcano, later to be transformed into the National Cemetery of the Pacific (1948). Suddenly, air raid sirens wailed incessantly, followed by scores of fire apparatus and police cars, sirens blaring, speeding all over the place. My Dad turned on the radio then rushed out the front door. Deciding to get a better look, I ran upstairs and broke out onto the veranda. About that time, there was a tremendous explosion, followed by the roar of an airplane. As I looked up, I saw a plane zoom overhead, so low that I thought it was going to take-off the roof. Etched in my young brain were those huge red "meatballs" emblazoned on the wing tips. I later learned that a 500 pound bomb got hung-up on that aircraft's Pearl Harbor run and didn't salvo until it was in our neighborhood. Unfortunately, a family of five was incinerated when the bomb struck their house—they were Japanese immigrants who had nothing to do with the sneak attack...

A few years after the Arizona Memorial at Pearl Harbor was completed in 1962, I took my family on the tour. The huge audience was assembled in the auditorium where a docent of the National Parks Service ran a short film on the attack and resultant devastation. Before embarking to the launches, the Park Ranger asked if anyone was a "Pearl Harbor Survivor?" I was one of about five people who raised their hands—although I wasn't at ground zero, I consider myself a survivor of sorts, as we were damn lucky the Zero's errant bomb didn't fall on our home.

After the heartfelt tour, I bought a U.S.S. Arizona history book at the gift shop. Over the years, I read it several times as I have always been a WWII buff and student of the Pearl Harbor raid. Admiral Kidd Sr. chose the U.S.S. Arizona as his flagship in lieu of one of the carriers. A photographer snapped a photo of the Admiral and then midshipman, Isaac Kidd Jr., of the U.S. Naval Academy, shaking hands with his father during a summer cruise a just few months before that ill-fated day. Had the good Admiral chosen to be on an aircraft carrier, he would have avoided going down with his flagship while manning an anti-aircraft gun before the fatal blow was struck.

****

The very next day during a break, I approached Admiral Kidd Jr., and told him that I had a picture of him and his Dad on the Arizona. The Admiral looked bewildered and replied that he knew of no such photo as I described. I returned: "I'll tell you what Sir, I'll bring that book with the snapshot, if you'll give me an autograph." He readily agreed. I've never been much of an autograph hound but given the historical circumstances of this event, I made an exception to that rule.

Before the conference convened the next morning, I approached the good Admiral and opened the book to their photo page. He stared with almost a blank look, and then a small tear formed. Admiral Kidd Jr. then smiled and endorsed my find and thanked me. How often does that happen? He was truly a Good Guy, too.

The Dalai Lama, Tibet, April, 1994.

When the Chief assigned me to meet Dean Robert "Bob" Gregg of Memorial Chapel about a planned visit by the Dalai Lama, I was stoked! Being an avid TV news hound, I certainly had heard of the Dalai Lama but didn't know much else. You in the "X" generation must realize that this was before Al Gore "invented" the Internet so, research information was confined to libraries or learned individuals. . . And, Dean Bob Gregg was one of those! Not only that, but he was one of the nicest people I ever had the pleasure to work with on the Farm. Growing up Roman Catholic when most priests were a bit "stuffy," I was rather unaccustomed to the ease of interacting with Dean Gregg: He was extremely intelligent, affable and had my *kine* sense of humor! Great guy! Anyway, after being briefed on the basic game plan for the visit, I asked Dean Gregg to give me a few days to outline a plan and we would work out the details after the foundation was laid.

Perhaps the second best reason to rejoice with the Dalai Lama's protection assignment was that we could beg-off working with the Secret Service on Jean-Bertrand Aristide's detail: We all hated that sullen, deposed Haitian dictator—a Roman Catholic priest who had his thugs eliminate the opposition with "flaming necklaces"—burning tires hung around the necks of the condemned, and as the poor souls were being consumed, Aristide often exclaimed: "Ah, there's nothing like the smell of burning tires and flesh in the morning!" Why this mass murderer was ever granted asylum to the U.S. is beyond my comprehension. Moreover, why Aristide was being wined and dined at the Bechtel International Center on campus was and still is a mystery to me. My staff and I were elated when we parted company with that jerk and were off to serve a real honest to goodness soul, the 14th Dalai Lama, Tenzin Gyatso, winner of the 1984 Nobel Peace Prize!

The Game Plan

Because Tibet's leader had been sacked by the People's Republic of China (PRC) in 1959, the Dalai Lama, although revered and still considered the titular head of Tibet, was not technically considered a head of state. Thus, the U.S. Secret Service had no dog in this fight. So, the responsibility of this big time visit fell squarely on our shoulders, with the blessing of the State Department. Our protection detail had grown in stature and experience since Bishop Tutu's visit in 1986, so I was confident that our guys could do this! I eagerly accepted the challenge, as did my crew.

So, it was back to X's and O's, and practice, practice, practice. Like Bishop Tutu's visit, we set up a motorcade and ran the route to San Francisco International Airport (SFO) several times. The principle would be staying at St. Patrick's Roman Catholic Seminary and University* in Menlo Park, CA, so it would be our charge to pick-up the Dalai Lama when he arrived, transport him to the seminary and pick him up each morning for various meetings at Stanford.

On the final day of his two day tour, the Dalai Lama would be speaking to an expected overflow crowd at Memorial Church. I was a bit concerned about his exposure to an unscreened crowd, not because he wasn't overwhelming loved by the folks, but as a paranoid detail leader, you never, ever know when some whacko might try to harm your protectee—for whatever reason.

Show Time

It was April 17, 1994 and we were en route to SFO to pick-up the Dalai Lama. At the last minute, the Chief decided that he wanted to ride along with our entourage, which, of course, ratcheted-up my team's anxiety level. Although we had run the route twice and knew exactly where we needed to stage our motorcade, we made the trial runs during the day. Well, the *Man* was due to arrive after dusk, which proved to be a real game changer.

The boss made a couple of comments to the effect that he hoped we weren't lost—we weren't, and besides, I had made arrangements with the airport police to cordon-off an area for our vehicles, so we made it to the pick-up area without difficulty. But, I learned a valuable lesson in that you need to simulate your runs at the same time the principle is due to arrive—especially at a huge airport like SFO. Our SFO police representative got us through the security points and led the way to the Dalai Lama's arrival gate.

*Founded in 1898, this institution is one of the oldest seminaries in the Western Hemisphere. St. Patrick's has prepared over 2,000 priests during its one hundred year existence, most serving dioceses in the Western United States and the Pacific Rim.

Tibet's spiritual and political leader suddenly emerged from the plane's ramp flanked by several attendant monks. His red and yellow robes were unmistakable; he was an impressive sight! We escorted the "Ocean of Wisdom" to a VIP lounge where he held a short news conference. From there, it was to the motorcade and down CA 101 to St. Patrick's. We said our goodbyes and arranged to pick-up the high priest the next morning for a day of private meetings with Stanford faculty groups.

On the following day, our four car motorcade formed-up in the circular driveway at the entrance of the seminary/university. Our team, comprised of plainclothes, uniformed and Community Service officers, lined-up to greet our esteemed guest. When he appeared on the porch with a Catholic Bishop and his Buddhist monks at his side, he raised his arms and broke into a huge smile. The *Man* quickly descended the stairs and went down the line, warmly shaking each man's hand, bowing slightly, all the while profusely thanking the team for their service. I was pleasantly stunned! It was as if he knew each and every one of us, all of his life—being a reincarnate, maybe he did...

Before I knew it, we were headed through the Stanford University gates and down Palm Drive. We disembarked at a large GSB conference room where the Dalai Lama was to meet with faculty members. The topics of discussion ranged from physical and biological, to humanities and social sciences. The "Chief", as Tibetan's sometimes call their leader, was seated on an elevated platform while he fielded questions and engaged in dialogue like the consummate intellectual he is. Everything this plain speaking cleric said simply blew away the audience. He was truly amazing and to me, all that he articulated was very well organized and just made perfect sense!

At day's end, we took the Dalai Lama back to his residence, bid him farewell until tomorrow. The next morning, the pre-departure pleasantries were repeated. My team was flattered. This day would be a little unnerving for me, for as I said, the high priest was to address a throng of folks at Memorial Church. In his address, the

Dalai Lama called for a "global community and universal responsibility." Do you think he was trying to tell China something?

Following his speech, the *Man* insisted on mingling with the over exuberant audience. Needless to say, I wasn't particularly enamored with this move, but I was powerless to countermand this wonderful human being's wishes. People swarmed him! My close-up team covered him like a blanket, ever vigilant and focused on the crowd's hands and facial expressions: As I learned in the Dignitary Protection Seminar, the agents who surround a principle eye-ball hands, while the outer team looks at people's faces. As learned in the ill-fated assassination attempt of President Ronald Reagan, most of the crowd sported happy faces, whereas that coward John Hinckley had a nasty look on his mug.*

Fortunately, everyone pressing the flesh with the Dalai Lama loved him. Nonetheless, I couldn't wait to get him back in the limo.

We escorted the *Man* to a private suite in GSB so he could relax, meditate, and collect his thoughts for his next journey to U.C. Berkeley. *Damn*, I worried, *I hope those Weenies listened to me when I specified that their limos could be any color BUT **white**:* I recalled from my Secret Service mentors that when dealing with VIPs, especially religious personages, it behooved one to see if the principle had a color preference. When I first met with Dean Gregg, I inquired as to what color limo I should order: "Any shade except white," the Dean replied. "For some reason," Gregg continued, "Buddhist's have an aversion to white." As a result we rented a silver Lincoln Town Car.

*However, there are exceptions: In the assassination attempt of AL Governor George Wallace (May 15, 1972) in Laurel, MD, during a rally in his bid for the U.S. presidency, would-be killer, Arthur Bremer, was smiling and clapping enthusiastically as the Governor was pressing the flesh in the throng. Bremer suddenly produced a pistol and shot Wallace five times; Wallace was paralyzed from the waist down. Bremer fooled the protection detail as they were all looking for a minority with a not so happy face—not a 21 year old blonde haired, blue eyed kid...

While hanging out with my team, one of the Dalai Lama's representatives met me and said the *Boss* wished to see me in private. Needless to say, I snapped to. When I entered the room, the Tibetan leader sprung to his feet and gave me a warm welcome with a two handed shake. He was beaming from ear to ear. I was completely taken aback. This wonderful human being then gave me autographed copies of some of his mantras and sutras; he thanked me over and over again for not only taking care of his security needs, but for the warmth we all extended to him and his staff.

God! What could I do to reciprocate? Suddenly, a thought came to mind: I removed my Deputy Sheriff's pin from the lapel of my jacket, and pinned it on the Dalai Lama's robe. I then proclaimed our friend as an honorary Stanford Deputy Sheriff. I think, he too, was taken aback. And, then it was time to go.

Communications advised that the U.C. Berkeley PD's motorcade had arrived and they were ready to accept our dignitary. As I walked side by side with my spiritual hero and new found friend, the *Man* suddenly grasped my hand in a firm grip and we strolled hand in hand out to the pick-up point. Once we rounded the corner of the building and were exposed to dozens of people at curb side, I spotted *my* Chief: His jaw dropped as if it had an anvil attached to it! Other folks gasped, when they saw the tough Ol' Captain in tow with one of the most celebrated religious leaders in the world. . . This was the first and only time that a grown man (other than my father when I was a small kid), had grabbed and held my hand in a gesture of affection—And, I allowed it to happen! But, what was I to do?

Amazingly, not a single photo of that event ever surfaced. I actually regret that now, as it would have been neat to have such a photograph—if nothing else, for posterity. . . However, I'm still a card-carrying Dalai Lama fan: After all of these years, I still have a laminated credential of the "Ocean of Wisdom" in my wallet.

Oh, and as I figured, the Cal Weenies screwed-up their motorcade—all of their vehicles were *White!*

Dalai Lama & Protection Detail:

L/R: Stanford Marine ROTC student (memory lapse); Agent Victor Block, U.S. Dept. of State; SUDPS Det. John McMullen; The 14th Dalai Lama; Author; Deputy Mark Swineford; Deputy Tim Frecceri.

Dalai Lama Bids Farewell:

L/R: Det. John McMullen; Dean of Stanford's Memorial Church, Robert 'Bob" Gregg; Dalai Lama; Author; Unknown

The Grand Daddy of Them All: Gorby I

The Bay Area was abuzz. The leader of the U.S.S.R., Mikhail Gorbachev and his stately wife, Raisa, were soon to be on a whirlwind tour of San Francisco, which would include a visit to Stanford University. Next to the Monterey visit of Pope Paul II in 1987, my Secret Service liaison predicted that the Gorbachev visit would be the biggest challenge their agency had experienced in their 88 year history of Presidential protection.* Whereas Pope Paul's tour involved a multitude of people—which is always daunting from a security standpoint—most of the estimated crowd of 50-70,000 were screened and confined to the Laguna Seca Raceway, where the Catholic leader would celebrate an open air mass. The motorcade route wasn't too problematic, as the distance from the Monterey

Airport to Laguna Seca wasn't that great, and the Pontiff would be in an armored vehicle.

President Gorbachev's tour, on the other hand, presented a host of security and logistics problems: It was estimated that Mr. Gorbachev's motorcade would consist of at least 50 vehicles. Needless to say, moving a procession of that magnitude around a major city like San Francisco would present a whole range of headaches for law enforcement.

Couple that with the 35 mile trek to the Farm, and that move would keep dozens of police motorcycles and cars buzzing around like an agitated wasp's nest: Zooming ahead of the motorcade, blocking intersections and freeway on-ramps—not to mention the aerial surveillance of rotary and fixed wing aircraft which would maintain a no-fly-zone at all times.

However, the scariest element of this visit was the amount of time the principles would be on foot and in the open, touring the Quad, working the barricade line pressing the flesh with excited students and other well wishers. Although we knew that all 7,000 credentialed persons would have been "mag-checked" by the Secret Service's uniformed division, could some would-be-assassin slip through somehow?

Preparation for this monumental task began in early May, 1990. Former Secretary of State, George P. Schultz, a distinguished statesman, professor, and campus resident was the driving force behind this historic event. Mr. Schultz, working in concert with

*Although officially established by President Abraham Lincoln on April 14, 1865—a mere five days after the Civil War ended—the charge of the newly formed agency was to combat counterfeit currency, as about one third of the currency in circulation at the conclusion of the war was bogus. After the assassination of President William McKinley in 1901, Congress requested that the USSS become a full-time protection detail for U.S. presidents. They officially took on this assignment in 1902.

President Donald Kennedy and other high ranking University officials saw this as an opportunity to accelerate the thawing of the Cold War with the Soviet Union. The basic game plan was to make a grand entrance to the University via Palm Drive. President Gorbachev and his wife would alight from their "limo" (more on the Russian "limos" later) at the apex of the Quad, be greeted by Mr. and Mrs. Kennedy, as well as Secretary Schultz, his spouse and other University officials. The entourage would stroll through the Quad, exchange pleasantries with the crowd of nearly 3,500, and exit the Quad at the East side. The group would continue northbound on Lasuen Street to the Art Department and make a brief stop there to view a small selected collection of priceless art. Following that, the entourage would cross Serra Street and continue north along the brick walkway to the Graduate School of Business' Littlefield Center, where they would meet with five Stanford Nobel laureates and other distinguished scholars.

Following that meeting, Gorbachev and company would walk to Memorial Auditorium where the President would address a packed-house of 1,100 excited faculty, staff and students. It should be noted that "the chosen few" had been selected from a pool of 7,000 folks via a computerized lottery, run by the Stanford Daily. Curiously enough, one of the benefactors of the coveted seats in Mem Aud was none other than the chief architect, Mr. Secretary George P. Schultz! How's that for luck? He gave his ducat to a staffer as he already had a front row seat. . . After the address, the Gorbachevs would depart and motor back to the City by the Bay. A piece of cake, right? Well, not exactly.

The Advance

If I had a dime for every foot I walked of the Gorbachev visit route during the weeks prior to the June 4th event, I'd be a very rich man. It was not unusual for our DPS team of planners to do that trek 2 or 3 times a day. I got into pretty good condition during that period, but it surely raised hell with my deteriorating left hip, which had to be replaced in 1992. We knew that this was *the big one* when the Resident Agents-in-Charge from both the San Francisco and San Jose offices were frequently on site. We walked and eye-balled every nook and cranny on that trail, and left no stone unturned. All trash containers were removed; bike racks disappeared; trees, shrubs, and bushes got buzz cuts! Every office along the path was inspected; all surrounding rooftops were checked and plans were formulated to man any vantage point that could possibly be a sniper's lair. Designated press locations were established, much to the chagrin of the media; reporters were admonished to remain in their respective pods or lose their coveted press passes. Observation posts were set-up at strategic high points: The key post was at the observation platform high atop Hoover Tower. We assigned one of our best CSOs, Clifton Clark, who had eyes like an eagle. He would be teamed-up with Secret Service and FBI agents; Cliff knew the campus like the back of his hand, thus would be able to pin-point the exact location of any disturbance or threat. After dozens of trial runs, we all felt that the detail was ready for Showtime!

G-Day

We hauled our mobile command post to a secluded area near Memorial Auditorium. All ears were tuned into the console of radios, waiting to hear when the Gorbachev party departed their San Francisco hotel. The Secret Service communicators advised that they were running late. But, how late, we all wondered? This visit, like most, was on a rather tight schedule. University officials fretted that any delay could really upset the apple cart; not only that, but there would be a lot of ticked-off people: Promoter, George Schultz, would certainly get an earful from the five Nobel laureates, as well as from the GSB hierarchy. Faculty members and invited guests to the speech in Mem Aud certainly would not be pleased if Mr. Gorbachev was a late show—worse, if he was a NO show; and the students, many of whom slept out on the cold hard ground for as long as two days in advance in order to get through the magnetometers and establish themselves along the barricades so they might be able to *high five* the Soviet President, might riot.

But, alas, the word was transmitted that the motorcade was en route albeit about 35 minutes tardy; they'd be on campus within 30-40 minutes—without unforeseen difficulties, that is.

What a Motorcade!

Sergeant Philip Love was our motorcade liaison supervisor. He positioned his unit near the on-ramp of Page Mill Road and Interstate 280; he later commented that he thought the procession would never end—an estimated 75 vehicles, although he never actually counted them. Thousands of onlookers lined the route, especially on the El Camino Real leg between Page Mill and Palm Drive. Folks were shoulder to shoulder, 2 to 3 deep, along the entry roadway to the University, Palm Drive. From my vantage point at the apex of the Palm Oval, I noticed that the eastside area was jam-packed with spectators. To our surprise, there were hundreds of anti-Gorby protesters; we knew there would be some dissidents, but not to this degree. The primary groups in the void between the Old Chemistry building and the Herrin Labs was made up of disgruntled Lithuanian, Estonian and Latvian patriots, who displayed numerous signs and huge banners; they were also quite vociferous. These Baltic States had declared their independence from the Soviet Union in early 1990, but the USSR wasn't going to let them go without a major serving of grief. We were all very concerned that this protest could become very ugly; CAT #1 (Counter Assault Team), who was set-up at the top of the Oval, literally had their sights on the demonstrators. The sniper's spotter espied a clown who had scaled a large tree over by Herrin Lab, and told me to have one of our officers relay the following message: "Get the hell outta that tree or we'll shoot you out!" Once the word was delivered, the man descended the tree like a Navy SEAL fast roping from a Blackhawk!

Many dignitaries bunched-up on the Quad's landing. Out of the corner of my eye, I saw one of our uniformed deputies chatting with a very beautiful young woman. I then saw the guy pull out a pad and pen and give it to the lady, who promptly scribbled something on the pad and returned it. Did I just see what I thought I saw? I then recognized the gorgeous one: She was none other than the movie and TV starlet, Morgan Fairchild. She somehow got a backstage pass and was, quite frankly, a serious distraction as there were way too many guys taking double-takes, with libidos in over-drive. . . I then intercepted my deputy and asked him what in the hell he was doing. "I'm sorry, Captain, I just asked her for an autograph," he *mea culpaed* with head bowed.

"Damn man, we are on the biggest protection detail in the history of the Secret Service and Stanford University, and you are sniffing around a celebrity like a love sick puppy? I know you have a reputation of being a . . . hound, but you are not going to be an *autograph* hound on my watch. Get back to your post." I snorted. Ya think I was annoyed?

Here He Comes

The tension mounted as the motorcade pulled to a halt; greeters scurried down the stairs to welcome the Soviet President and his lovely wife to Stanford. Only one problem...Mr. Gorbachev and Raisa were not in this group of limos and Secret Service follow-up cars. It was a decoy! Very clever, those SS dudes! Once the VIPs ascended the Quad's stairs, the real Gorby entourage appeared on the Palm Oval. This *was* the real McCoy. The Gorbachevs were greeted and escorted into the Quad by President and Mrs. Kennedy, Secretary and Mrs. Schultz, and a host of other dignitaries. The throng of several thousand well-wishers went wild. Against the desires of the Secret Service and the KGB, Gorby broke away from his escorts and pressed the flesh with the super excited spectators. I thought he'd never leave the barricade line, but his security detail led him away like a bunch of experienced cattle drovers.

After a quick tour of the Art Department, we crossed Serra Street and proceeded along the limestone brickway toward GSB. Once again, President Gorbachev "gripped and grinned" with the estimated 1,500 screened onlookers. This time, two of the Soviet limos trailed behind Gorby's group. Now, about those Soviet limousines, called ZiLs: These heavily armored vehicles weighed-in at approximately 15,000 pounds, approximately 500 more than our Cadillac and Lincoln counterparts. The ZiLs were handmade and were supposedly impervious to heavy caliber rounds and RPGs (rocket propelled grenades.) The Secret Service offered their presidential limos but the KGB declined as they believed their tank-like vehicles were superior. I would argue that point...These

Russian monsters reminded me of the famed WWII Soviet T-34 battle tanks: And, they sounded like them, too, all the while smoking like coal fed locomotives and leaking more black oil than the Exxon Valdez! Not only that, but they were downright ugly. The two limos they brought to this event looked similar to the old Al Capone gangster cars—1937 Packards! I lamented for Stanford's poor maintenance crews who would have the arduous task of cleaning-up all of that nasty ooze from the recently steam cleaned walkway.

Exiting

That was the hard part. From the time Gorbachev & Company arrived on campus, the visit went along smoothly. The parlay with the Nobels, although a little abbreviated, went well. Mr. Gorbachev's speech was a rounding success, with exuberant standing ovations and cheering: "Gorby, Gorby, Gorby." But, outside, a tempest was brewing. Several hundred angry Ethiopian dissidents hurled invectives and vile comments at the Soviet regime. Banners and signs decried the USSR for providing bombs and rockets to their government's security forces who were trying to put down the rebellion. The crowd gathered and blocked the East exit of Serra Street at the Memorial Fountain's round-about—the motorcade's intended exit route. We had the Sheriff's Crowd Control Unit in reserve, and the Sheriff's Mounted unit formed a line with approximately 8 horses. Intelligence officers relayed to Chief Herrington that the KGB Chief intended to fight his way through this obstacle. The Chief assigned me to try to talk some sense into the Russian security boss. The motorcade was staged around the Mem Aud Fountain and ready for the entourage to depart from the auditorium. I contacted the KGB leader and told him that we didn't want to push the envelope by bullying our way through that mob. He looked at me as if I was a wimp, and said in heavily accented English:

"Hmmph. In Soviet Union we eliminate these people. You have riot police and horseman. Why not you ride horses into crowd and use police to make way for my President?"

"Sir, I respect your point of view, but we are not in Russia and this is a highly respected university in the free world; we don't operate that way. But, how about this: You get everyone in the motorcade (abbreviated at this point, with only about 15 security vehicles) and we faint as if we are going to drive right through them," I opined.

"What faint mean?" the General asked.

"That's a boxing term: We throw a jab (I demonstrated) as if we are going to strike one way, then we fool them with a countermove; I think you military guys call it a 'diversion,'" I proposed. He nodded as if he was catching my drift.

"We'll move up the horses and riot police to that opening in the bollards. You then drive around the circle, with red lights and sirens, stop momentarily at the opening, then speed around the fountain and go out the back door, West on Serra Street. We can hook-you-up with the rest of your vehicles and lead you out the back way. What do you think?" I offered.

At this point, the tough Ol' Soviet warrior slapped me on the back and said: "I like that plan—we get last laugh." *And, save face*, I mused. After consulting with the Secret Service team leader, he too thought that this was preferable to leaving a bunch of bodies in the wake. . . And, it worked like a charm. The biggest visit in our history went off without a hitch.

The Clintons

I about had a stroke when the Chief informed me that the First Lady and her daughter, Chelsea, were going to visit Stanford University as a possible choice of where the Presidential family would send their only child for a higher education. But, the good news was that it would only be a one day, low-key visit. . . *Yeah right*, I figured, *there ain't no such thing as "low key" when a sitting President's wife and daughter visit anything!*

When I met with my Secret Service counterparts, I learned that this whirlwind tour might be problematic: The Monica Lewinski scandal had recently been discovered and Mrs. Clinton was less than thrilled, as you might well guess. Scuttlebutt had it that the First Lady was very paranoid and suspected that her personal Secret Service protection detail was leaking tidbits about Bill and Hillary's "rocky" relationship. So, the First Lady fired her experienced all male detail, save for her Detail Leader, and replaced them with "greenhorn" female agents. Many of the replacements had virtually no experience with up-close and personal protection, so they might be a bit tentative, I figured. Well, sure enough.

Mrs. Clinton was very adamant about her marching orders: She didn't want any marked patrol units anywhere near her—and absolutely NO uniformed cops in her vicinity. She and Chelsea would be escorted in an unmarked USSS vehicle to various spots on campus by her Detail Leader (who would remain in the shadows), and would be accompanied by her two newbie female agents. I was with my Secret Service counterpart in his unmarked, and served as a mobile CP. The radio traffic from Mrs. Clinton's agents was unbelievable: This sounded like stuff from the Keystone Cops, often like the Abbott and Costello Classic: "Who's on First?" We all shook our heads in disbelief! With all due respect, this "protection crew" had NO clue—mainly due to a lack of hands-on experience. The most incredible incident occurred when an agent with our guests stated that she wanted one of our detectives to arrest a photographer. (It should be noted that the USSS has no arrest powers unless a principle is in eminent danger. After an incarceration, the agents must then turn the arrestee over to local law enforcement until a determination can be made as to what agency will handle the matter.)

When asked what the problem was, the agent relayed that Mrs. Clinton was annoyed by a photographer who was taking pictures of them. As it turned out, the guy in question worked for the Associated Press; I knew him well, and he was, indeed, a "pain in the arse"—he often tried to sneak into restricted areas to get a shot. However, in this case, the man was a good 25 yards away from the Clintons, taking photos with a high powered lens in an open area—

hardly cause for arrest! When my counterpart asked me what we should do, I replied: "Tell your agent we have a thing here called the First Amendment, and unless the photographer is in their face and/or is abusive or threatening, there is little we could or would do!"

Curve Balls

Just as the Noon hour approached, Clinton's detail announced that their luncheon plans had changed: One of Chelsea's sponsors suggested they go to Mac's Opera House, a yuppie eatery in the Stanford Shopping Center; we were to join-up with the First Lady's cars and lead them to the restaurant. The only trouble was that I didn't know *exactly* where the place was—and *exact* is imperative in this line of work! Luckily, a P.A. Communicator knew *exactly* where it was and talked us in. Whew...

Just when we thought we were going to bid the party farewell, the "pitcher" let go with another "curve ball:" She wanted to spend some time in the Stanford Museum's Rodin Garden, while Chelsea hung out with her friends at the bistro. Mrs. C. departed with her Detail Leader and her crew while we kept an eye on her daughter; The First Lady was expected to spend approximately 30-40 minutes in the garden, whereupon her motorcade of non-descript cars would pick-her up and would head back to San Francisco.

Incurring the Wrath

Once it was time to leave, I dispatched a marked unit to the general location so the package could be led off campus to I-280 via the back way. This area is very tricky to navigate so I didn't want them to get lost. Besides, our motorcade protocol called for a marked unit (equipped with emergency lights and siren, of course) as the lead car in the event of an *emergency!* I was later told that the First Lady flipped-out when she spotted the police cruiser. In fact, I later heard she was furious that her order had been countermanded and really let her Detail Leader have it. I told my counterpart to blame me: If something bad happened to the President's wife and daughter on this visit, the heat I would incur would be like a cool breeze when compared to the wrath of Mrs. Clinton. . . *Good Lord,* I prayed, *please let that nice young lady choose a school closer to Washington D.C.* Alas, as we would soon learn, Chelsea Clinton loved Stanford. What's not to love? But, I often wondered if her choice was all about geography.

Freshman Parents Day, September 1997

Chelsea Clinton chose Stanford as the institution where she wanted to pursue her higher education. Most in the department secretly wished she would have picked another school because of our limited resources. The next four years of having the offspring of a sitting President of the United States in our midst would certainly pose some huge challenges for our small organization—many clearly unforeseen.

The first order of business was to coordinate the Presidential visit with the USSS and University officials. The Secret Service was very concerned about the personal security of the President and his family: There would be thousands of parents and incoming freshmen, faculty, staff, other students, in addition to an unknown number of curious onlookers—none of whom would be "magged" like we did in the other major head-of state visits. This was going to be an open venue, so it was going to be up to the inner ring of the PPD to keep the Clintons out of harm's way. Our officers teamed-up with other agents and formed an outer ring with all eyes and ears wide open.

The Presidential family and staff set-up housekeeping at Rickey's, an aged hotel in South Palo Alto. While the digs weren't five star, the facility was ideal for security as the grounds were expansive, thus facilitating the 20 plus vehicles that would be needed for the motorcade. I was teamed-up with the motorcade lead agent; we chose to take a circuitous route to the campus, which would require less congestion and headaches for Palo Alto PD. Instead of going straight down the ECR, we elected to go up Arastradero and then to Junipero Serra and enter the Farm through the back door. That worked very well!

When we arrived on campus, surprisingly, everyone seemed to give the entourage a wide berth. When Chelsea decided to enroll in Stanford, the Administration beseeched the media and general public to respect her privacy; and, by God, they did! The family went to a number of events and were cordially received but not overwhelmed. The last event was orchestrated by my good friend, Dean Gregg, of the Memorial Church, where he hosted a small soiree. The President mingled with the guests and was extremely social. When it was time to go, the PPD arranged an individual "photo-op" for key University officials and my team of plainclothes deputies. When it was my turn, I introduced myself and received a firm handshake and a Clintonesque comment: "Take care of my daughter, Cap'n.'" "I sure will Mr. President." I later received an autographed colored photo of that moment. I really appreciated this memento, but what I really treasured is the pair of Secret Service Presidential Cuff Links given to me by the Lead Agent of the Presidential Protection Detail. I don't know of many campus cops who have a pair of those jewels. . .

To Captain Raoul Niemeyer
With Appreciation,
Bill Clinton

Some Good, Some Bad, and Some Ugly

During my tenure from 1974 to 1999, the SUDPS managed over 200 major visits of Kings, Queens, Princes/Princesses, U.S. Presidents, foreign Heads-of-State, members of the U.S. Supreme Court, Attorney Generals, et al. You name them, we hosted them and provided security, often in concert with the USSS, State Department, Department of Defense and other police agencies. Needless to say, I can't write about all of these adventures as this book would read like a Russian novel—but will mention a few of the more interesting ones.

Vice Premier Fang Yi of the People's Republic of China: According to my FBI counterparts, this was the first time anyone from the PRC visited our region and although the delegation was there ostensibly to visit the Stanford Linear Accelerator (SLAC), the Bureau's super sleuths were convinced they were all spies. . . Probably so, but the luncheon at the Buck Estate was grand. I rate this one as Good!

President Roh Tae Woo, Republic of South Korea*: The controversial 13th President of the ROK visited the campus for meetings which would culminate with a lavish dinner among twenty luminaries at Secretary George Schultz's residence. The former General was not popular amongst many of his countrymen, who showed up by the dozens to protest his presence. We cordoned them off a block away from Hoover Tower, where the first meeting took place. Our personnel put up yellow "Sheriff's Barricade—Do Not Cross" tape around the front of Hoo Tow. We maintained the perimeter with USSS agents, our plainclothes officers, as well as a contingent of Korean body guards. One of our oblivious University staffers, an avid jogger, apparently didn't understand that he shouldn't vault the barricade tape without consequences: When the man breached the safety zone, a swarm of ROK security guys introduced the jogger to the bosom of Mother Earth! We intervened, dusted the interloper off and sent him on his way, after he assured us that he would never do *that* again. This was BAD!

*In 1996, Roh Tae Woo and his cohort, former president Chun Doo-hwan, were convicted of treason, mutiny, and corruption. Chun was sentenced to death, but the ultimate penalty was later commuted to life imprisonment. Roh initially received a sentence of 22 and ½ years in prison, but it was soon reduced to 17. However, both men were pardoned by then President Kim Young-sam in 1997.

U.S. Secretary of Defense Casper Weinberger: This little panel discussion at Kresge Auditorium went to Hell in a handbasket. We anticipated that some anti-military dissidents would probably show up, but certainly not in the numbers they brought to the forum. Over 200 boisterous RCYB (Revolutionary Communist Youth Brigade) protesters swarmed around the building, shouted and beat on the windows so forcibly I believed the panes would disintegrate. Fortunately, we stashed an unmarked unit at the rear of the building and were able to get the Secretary out the back door and into the car—all the while, scraping several agitators off the vehicle so that our wheelman, Sgt. Love, could speed through the inner campus to a safe house. UGLY!

More on Chelsea

Contrary to our worst fears, Chelsea Clinton was absolutely no problem for us or the Secret Service. After a short indoctrination by a former Stanford student turned SUDPS deputy, (and now Stanford's first female Chief of Police) Laura Wilson, a team of young SS agents blended-in well and made sure that the President's daughter was able to go to classes, attend sporting events, parties and other activities without any form of harassment. Well, there was one exception: Although her dormitory was always under surveillance, somehow, a pair of students from the University of California at Santa Cruz managed to slip onto her floor and capture Chelsea on videotape as she was leaving the shower en route to her room—clad only in a large towel. A couple of agents spotted these interlopers and pounced on them just as they were trying to make a getaway. One of the agents snatched the camera out of the culprit's hands, opened it up and shredded the tape.

"You can't do that!" implored the "Banana Slug" (UCSC's mascot—kinda like a Cal Weenie).

"The hell I can't" the agent barked back. "I already did! Now, get the hell out of here before we have you arrested!"

End of story!

CHAPTER TWENTY ONE

O.R.E.

In the Beginning

SUDPS' Off-Road-Enforcement team was formulated in 1982, after considerable haggling over the pros and cons of utilizing lightweight dirt bikes as an additional law enforcement tool on campus. The Chief, like most top police administrators, was initially cool to this concept for many good reasons, and understandably so. Being an avid dirt bike rider myself, I approached the boss about organizing and training riders for the program in the late 1970s. But, at that time, he believed that the risks for injury, liability, and complaints outweighed the benefits of such a unit. Not being one to give up on what I believed was a pregnant idea, I lobbied some of the department's street riders to investigate this notion by consulting other departments in the area who had pioneered similar programs.

San Francisco P.D. had started out with a few Honda 200 cc motors, primarily to police the crime-ridden Golden Gate Park, where no sensible human being would dare venture. In just a matter of weeks, SFPD had the drug dealers, addicts, prostitutes and the homeless packing. As a measure of their initial success, SFPD bought a gaggle of those little scooters and expanded the program to ferret out criminals all over Baghdad-by-the-Bay. Those things were so stealthy and quiet that the cops often putt-putted into major drug deals before the narcotic purveyors realized that *The Man* was on that red *rice rocket*. It got even better when they painted their fleet black, transforming those "red beacons" into virtual F-117A Nighthawks. . . In addition, the riders were often able to weave their way through congested traffic, arriving at serious crime scenes before the beat cars. We all felt that this type of mobility would be great for Stanford's special events: Football, marathons, VIP visits, and Olympic Soccer and Super Bowl, which were in the offing. The chief finally relented and authorized the purchase of two bikes.

The Knoll

When our brand spanking new, and very red, Honda 250s arrived, it was like kids seeing their very first bicycles on Christmas morning: Everyone in the building gathered in the parking lot to ogle the new toys. Those who could ride buzzed around the lot, amazingly, with no casualties. *Boy, those things were bright and shiny,* I thought. *Wonder how long they'll stay that way??*

When the excitement subsided, the Patrol Commander and O.R.E. team leader, Sgt. Philip Love, aka Philippe Crueseau, decided to take a shake-down cruise. I must admit, I was a bit jealous, but it was Captain Marvin Moore's unit, so he got first dibs. I later learned that Philippe, who had ridden a "Beezer" (BSA motorcycle) on the highways and byways of Jolly Old England, had an *interesting* loop in mind for his boss and put the good Captain through the paces: Philippe led him on a 3 hour trek over hill and dale until they somehow ended up at The Knoll. This stately Spanish-style mansion was once the university president's residence, built for Stanford's third boss, Ray Lyman Wilbur, in 1918. After President Wilbur retired in 1943, the incoming president, Donald Tresidder, chose not to live there, so the university allowed other tenants to occupy the home, until the Music Department moved in circa 1946.

The front entrance of this structure featured a pathway, which ascended from both sides of the edifice. There was also a set of concrete stairs, perhaps four feet wide with an 18 to 20 degree gradient. Sgt. Crueseau motored up the gradual path, with the Captain in hot pursuit. Once the sergeant aimed his cycle for downhill, scuttlebutt suggests that the scenario went something like this:

"Captain, just follow me!"

"Down them stairs?" Marvin gulped.

"Piece of cake, Cap'n," Philippe shot back, and he bumpity-bumped down the stairs. Once he accomplished this stunt, the sergeant straddled his bike, and with arms folded, he goaded his Captain to follow.

The Captain looked as if he had just seen a ghost, I am told, but Marvin's competitive nature clouded his normally good judgment, so he kicked his mount into gear and shot down the ominous obstacle at break-neck speed, while emitting a blood curdling "Shheeee-itttt," as he careened out of control—and *T-Boned* his mentor. The resultant collision caused both men to become one with terra firma. . . Fortunately, neither daredevil was severely injured, save for a busted lip and cracked front tooth sustained by the Captain.

Now, we will never know for sure whether compression caused the cycle to go askew, or violation of Rule Number One: When riding a motorcycle downhill, never, *NEVER*, under any circumstance, grab a handful of front brake, as this move will put the machine into a downward spiral and result in a major crash and burn. . . However, the answer to my previous query as to how long these bikes would remain pristine was now abundantly clear. . . Ah, nothing like a little road rash to properly break-in a dirt bike!

The dynamic duo limped back to the station and, as luck would have it, the Chief was pulling into the parking lot at the precise moment of their arrival—timing is everything, I always say. The boss was very relieved that his officers weren't seriously hurt, but he was not a happy camper. A-1 simply shook his head and walked into his office, no doubt thinking: *I should have never let those guys talk me into getting those damn "donor-cycles!"* Oh well, nothing that a new fender, pair of handle bars and a couple of levers wouldn't fix. Welcome to the world of off-road motorcycling. . .

Add Insult to Injury

After the bikes returned from the shop, I got my chance to ride the repaired scooter. Sgt. Philippe took me on the same loop that he and Marvin had taken a week or so before and, as if tempting fate, we ended up at the Knoll.

"So, is this where the Captain went down in flames?" I teased. With that, I buzzed down the stairs, being very careful not to violate Rule Number One—Never, ever grab a handful of front brake when flying downhill—been there, done that a few times when I was a fledgling and vowed to stay away from the ER as much as I could. I once had an ER "Orthopod" tell me: "I just love you dirt bikers and bull riders; I'll never, ever be unemployed. . ."

The Sergeant was still at the head of the stairway, when I slammed the *tranny* into first gear and powered back up the steps.

"Piece of cake," I bragged, as I revved the motor and took off back down to the roadway and back to the barn before we got into real trouble. I read the sergeant's thoughts: *What a show-off!* He was 100 percent right.

Dirt Biking 101

In an effort to improve the team's riding skills, I offered to take them up to the motorcycle club I belonged to. The property was located off Skyline Boulevard, above La Honda, and featured some of the roughest terrain in California. It was a huge parcel, perhaps 5-6 square miles through dense forest with deep gorges, fast running streams, a number of killer hills and gnarly crags that only the best riders could master. This was *Trials* country folks: The association was known as the Pacific International Trials Society—PITS for short, and indeed it was, especially the first couple of times one went up there. Trials riding originated in Europe; it has absolutely nothing to do with speed. Competitors are tested on every section of the course, which is always set-up by cruel, sadistic people. This sport is all about balance; the machines are very lightweight, and are geared so low that they can bounce up and over boulders, climb huge fallen timber, and navigate trails that would break a snake's back. The trails are extremely steep and narrow, so much so, that mountain goats would be challenged. The object is to traverse the course without putting your feet down; riders are penalized for touch downs and other screw-ups. Falling is the equivalent of being KOed in a boxing match. Needless to say, the guys who endeavor in this purest of motor bike competition are the best!

My first encounter with the dirt-biking on the PITS property was truly a very humbling experience. My mentor, Ken Alley, allowed me to *try* to stay on his volitale Husqvarna 400cc—no easy task for a 250 lb. 38 year old who, aside from riding only a few street machines, had never mounted one of these bucking broncos! It seemed like all I did that day was crash into the Manzanita and Madrone chaparral; I performed a few spectacular "get-offs," much to the amusement of Mr. Alley—the demented soul that he is—and I went home totally demoralized, with a sprained ankle. I swore I would never, ever sit astride of one of those beasts again. But, my obsession with getting back in the saddle was irresistible.

The Net-al Trail

My first *victim* in our impromptu training session was none other than the Captain killer, Sergeant Philippe Crueseau. I decided I would utilize my then 14 year old son, Kirk, as a peer instructor; he was a very patient young man and had pretty good riding skills, having ridden dirt bikes since he was about nine years old. I learned some time before that I wasn't the best driving teacher due to my impatience:

I painfully remember trying to teach Kirk how to ride his first mount, a Honda XR75. We went to a beginner's motorcycle track in South San Jose, and after about a dozen attempts to get him going, I simply failed—miserably: He had a good command of how to start the motor, but when he put it in gear, instead of feathering the clutch while increasing the RPMs, he would pop the clutch lever causing the bike to leap forward and die. That maneuver would often cause the engine to flood, so we were then forced to turn off the gas petcock and pump the kick starter a million times to clear the cylinder. So, after going through that procedure a dozen times, you might say we *both* were a bit exercised. Fortunately, a very nice young lady, who was the kid's track monitor, saw the frustration from both of us and offered to help. She seemed to have the patience of Job, so I roared-off in order to cool-off. I took a couple of circuits on the big guy's track, and when I got back, that damn kid was zooming around the track like he was born on that thing! I approached Kirk's teacher and asked her how she did it. I couldn't believe that he was riding so well, when just a few minutes ago, he wasn't able to get out of the parking lot. As I was complimenting my savior, I noticed that Kirk was flying around that little oval, passing other kids as if they were tied to trees—in fact, he was going way too fast: As he came roaring into turn 3 and became somewhat "tight," instead of turning left, he shot straight into a hay bale and ricocheted into the wire fence. I shuddered, but soon saw him pop-up, extricate his putt-putt from the hay and fence entanglement, start it up and zoom-off. From that point on, there was no stopping that kid.

The Sergeant's Rite of Passage

Because of his prior street riding experience, Philippe got going pretty well, with me in the lead, the sergeant next and Kirk bringing up the tail. I decided on an *easy* loop so as not to freak Philippe out—unlike my first trial by fire on this nasty piece of real estate—so I headed for the "Fence Line Trail," so named for a challenging narrow section that bordered fenced private property, with a 40 degree slope on the inboard side. The first 30 or 40 minutes was like fire-roading for experienced riders, but somewhat challenging for a novice; yet, the sergeant hung in there just fine. Prior to heading uphill to the fence line, we stopped for "a blow" at our "initiation site"—a grassy bog that contained about 4-6 inches of pungent black mud. Kirk knew the drill, so he quickly moved ahead of his pupil and when I asked: "You ready?", Kirk kicked his pony into gear, revved-it up and took-off leaving a rooster tail of slimy, putrid sludge which thoroughly plastered our unsuspecting rookie. No respect—but the good sergeant was now duly inculcated to the PITS culture...

After making a sharp left, we ascended up a slight grade and then down into a steep gully on a skinny trail festooned with jagged rocks, gnarly roots and downed timber. But, the best was yet to come—a 5 foot diameter downed redwood, as if some sadistic architect had purposely felled it there, thus forcing the rider to go over it—any way he could! This was a typical trials obstacle, doable for most seasoned pilots, but a heart stopper for a novice. I got on the gas and powered over the impediment, rode up a knoll to a vantage point from which I could enjoy the show. After a couple of failed attempts, Kirk helped the student muscle the Honda over the big log. The kid then climbed over the barricade like a tractor and we *high-fived*. What we didn't tell the sergeant was that there was an easy way around the tree, but that it was well camouflaged and not for novice use. Just prior to reaching the fence, I cautioned Philippe to go fast, point the bike straight forward and, above all, don't look down. With that, I buzzed forward to the next rendezvous. After waiting a few minutes and not hearing the engines, I figured that something was wrong, so I rode back to see what the trouble was. As I neared the site, I saw the sergeant's mount prostrate, dangling over the edge. Kirk was astride his bike shaking his head and chuckling softly. Suddenly, I observed Sergeant Philippe Crueseau, supervisor of the newly formed O.R.E., crawling up the bank and through the dense briar patch of wild mulberries. The poor guy was covered with stickers and berries; I couldn't help but thinking: *Now I know why that Ol' Br'er Fox would never pursue Br'er Rabbit into that briar patch...*

I felt it unnecessary to ask a rhetorical question, for what happened was painfully obvious; nonetheless I chided:

"Philippe, what in the hell happened?" He remained mute and simply glared menacingly!

"Hey sergeant, welcome to the Fence Line Trail."

"Fence Line my *Arss,*" he shot back in his distinctive British brogue. "This is the goddamn *Net-Al* (nettle) Trail!" And, so it became—at least in our circles.

CHAPTER TWENTY TWO

Really Big Events

Farm Special Events

What started out as fun runs and some bicycle races in the late 70s, turned into major events at Stanford University. We started out with 5 and 10K (kilometer) charitable footraces, but they soon developed into full blown marathons. These sanctioned events were taxing on our department's meager resources, but we were able to struggle through and provide safety and security for the participants by utilizing our invaluable Special Events Patrol. Before we knew it, The Farm was fast becoming an attractive site for event planners throughout the country due to our geography, as well as our accessibility to transportation hubs in San Francisco and San Jose. A huge factor was Stanford Stadium, which although archaic in style and accoutrements, offered one of the finest natural grass playing surfaces in the nation, in addition to having a seating capacity of over 86,000 spectators. The surrounding open space afforded great accessible parking, as well as sites for enormous corporate entertainment and support tents.

Track and Field

Olympic competition at Stanford can be traced back to 1932 when track and field trials were held at the Farm's stadium. I don't remember that one as it was way before my time... On July 1st and 2nd 1960, a two day Olympic trials program was conducted in the stadium—a precursor for the Summer XVII Olympiad, which would occur in Rome. But, a blockbuster event that would have international implications would happen at Stanford in 1962, and I would be there, along with over 150,000 spectators...

USA vs. USSR*

This track and field event was the brainchild of world class track/field veteran and Stanford's Track Coach, Payton Jordan. Coach Jordan and his long time colleague and friend, Gavriel Korobkov, the Soviet Track Coach, persuaded skeptics that this competition would not only be a moneymaker, but might possibly bridge nationalistic attitudes in the widening Cold War gap—not only among the populaces but with the politicians, as well.

This competition would be a huge crap shoot, given the brewing Cuban Missile Crisis and exacerbated further by the recent shoot down of our CIA U-2 spy plane (piloted by Gary Francis Powers) over Soviet bloc territory. However, cooler heads prevailed and set the stage for one of the most anticipated and fiercely partisan sporting events that the world would ever experience—way back then and even today!

I remember this extravaganza very well—as if it happened yesterday—for I was fortunate enough to have been invited to the meet by a good friend and former Stanford football player, Robert "Bob" Peters. Bob scored some choice seats on the 40 yard line for our quartet—my brother, Dennis, and good buddies Ken Alley and George Stickler. For all of us, this was a really big deal: While George and I had attended many track and field competitions back in Hawaii, none of us had ever been to an Olympic-like event, let alone an international bracing between the world's super powers at the zenith of the Cold War! And, no one would leave this venue disappointed, I'll tell you.

As predicted and expected, the Americans cleaned-up on the sprints and medium distance races. With the likes of Bob "Bullet" Hayes (later an NFL Dallas Cowboy great) and famed Wilma Rudolph, who both seemingly crossed the finish line before you heard the starting gun's report, team USA swept the dashes straight away!

*Facts borrowed from <u>USA vs. USSR 1962: The Greatest Track Meet of All Time.</u> By Track and Field Magazine writer, Red Shannon, February 9, 2010.

Bob Beatty held off the CCCP guys by winning the grueling 1500 meter run. But, when it came to the field events, the Soviet athletes were going be tough to beat: Their long jumper, Igor Ter-Ovanesyan, who had just bested our World Champion, Ralph Boston's world record, was ambushed by Boston when he inched-out Igor on the final leap. American, Al Oerter, won the discus event and a "washed-up" hammer thrower, Harold Connolly, proved that his poor performance in the 1960 Olympics was, indeed, a fluke when he set a new world record of 231 feet and 10 inches! As expected, the muscular and talented Russian woman shot put and hammer thrower, Tamara Press, swept her competition. I recall jesting that Ms. Press could bench press the four of us guys with ease... But, the best was yet to come:

One of the world's greatest high jumpers of all time, Valery Brumel, was about to give the crowd of 81,000 fans the show of a lifetime. Having disposed of his US competitor, former world record holder, John Thomas, at a height of 7 feet 2 inches, Brumel ordered the bar raised another inch. This tremendous athlete had titillated spectators and the press with his version of a reverse "slam dunk:" I saw a photo of Valery propelling his body skyward on a basketball court and touching the rim (10 feet above the floor) with his big toe! He was an old school straddle-type high jumper who launched from a dirt surface and landed in a sawdust filled pit. No rubberized pad or foam pit for this guy! There should have been a drum roll but even in that vast arena, you could hear your heart thumping as Brumel lined-up for his first attempt at 7'3"; he took off like an agile gazelle and cleared the bar with ease. We all figured that the Soviet coach might give him a shot at 7'4", but they went for all the marbles and moved the cross bar to 7 feet 5 inches. If Valery Brumel could clear this height, he would be the world record holder.

Once again, the stadium was as silent as a morgue. Everyone held their collective breaths as the angular athlete approached the formidable crossbar with deliberate long strides. Within a heartbeat, Brumel was airborne, over the bar and into the pit. I saw him brush the cross piece and it vibrated—a lot! I thought, *Oh well, nice try.* To the surprise of everyone, the bar held and the arena exploded into cheers and applause. He did it! Valery Brumel just set a new high jump record. The gracious superstar waved to the throng as we gave him a five minute "Standing O." At the conclusion of the event, the plan was for the teams to line up side by side and file out of the South end. However, John Thomas and his Soviet counterpart, Viktor Tsybulenko, huddled and made an impromptu decision: They then led their contingents on a final victory lap around the track, with banners and flags waving while they exhorted the crowd—and the USMC band played on and on—for over an hour! Was this a harbinger for the LSJUMB??? At the conclusion of that momentous track meet, USSR long jumper, Ter-Ovanesyan, proclaimed: "It was not two teams, it was one team." The Box Score was US men 128, USSR 107; the Soviet women bested the USA 66-41 but nobody really seemed to care. This was indeed "The Greatest Track Meet of All Time!"

Olympic Soccer 1984: Idaho One-Two

Undoubtedly, serving on the crew of Idaho 1-2 was the most exciting and challenging assignment I ever had in nearly 35 years of law enforcement. It was 1984. The United States had been selected to host the Summer Olympics in Los Angeles, CA. There were preliminary venues all over the country and Stanford University was chosen as one of the sites for the elimination soccer matches. The Department of Defense (DOD) controlled all police and security activities and deemed that all athletes would command full police/security protection in order to thwart any terrorist attack. One of the elements of this security was aerial surveillance. DOD made arrangements for fixed-wing and rotary aircraft for observation, as well as for escort. All of the soccer competitors would be under our watchful eye from the time they deplaned until they arrived at their billets.

DOD hired a Bell 500 helicopter from ARIS Helicopter Company, in San Jose. Our pilot was Dick Alford, a former San Mateo County Deputy Sheriff, who pioneered their county's fledgling helicopter program. In those days, they flew a dragonfly looking piston-motor chopper, the Bell 300—a far cry from our jet powered high-tech bird. The Chief assigned me to coordinate the operation. This would entail selecting flight and ground crews and interfacing with the Sheriff's Office for personnel and training.

One of my first tasks was to select an appropriate LZ (landing zone) that would be close enough to the department where it would be defensible should someone try to sabotage our craft. As luck would have it, there was a triangular piece of turf right across from the department at Serra St. and Campus Drive. I had the pad mowed, chalked and taped—I wanted the tape to say in big bold letters: "Caution, Top Security Area. Violators Will Be Shot On Sight!" However, my Boss thought that would be a bit ominous so we opted for the traditional yellow and black crime scene tape. We also assigned guards during operations and equipped them with large wheeled CO_2 fire extinguishers for take offs and landings.

Once our crew was selected, we met with our pilot, Dick Alford, who thoroughly briefed us on air operations. We then traveled to their hanger in San Jose for aircraft familiarity and training. One of the safety features in this program was that we were to sit on ballistic WWII B-17 door gunner's vests. Dick explained that one of the San Mateo S/O crew members once took a 30-06 round in the butt from ground fire—for no apparent reason. Captain Alford quipped: "So, if you guys want to keep your family jewels intact, I strongly urge you to sit on these, however uncomfortable! It seems that some people not only hate cops, but also abhor helicopters!" This made sense to all of us!

Our air crew was made up of Stanford Sergeant, Rick Enberg, and two Sheriff's deputies. As Chief Observer, I usually rode in the co-pilot's seat and got to bark out orders over the craft's very audible loud speaker. The deputy in the rear operated the ship's 1 million candlepower *Night Sun*. Every once in a while, I just couldn't resist getting my paws on that light: That thing would light up the night as if it were High Noon! At 800 feet, you could actually delineate faces and clothing color.

One of our first aerial exercises was to lead the pilot to wherever he chose. This was my first experience in a helicopter and I must admit that the initial take off took my breath away. Once up at about

1,000 feet, Capt. Alford said: "OK, Captain, take me to your home!" I looked around and saw the rail yards next to the San Jose Municipal Airport and directed him East, to I-880. Hell, this was my beat for 10 years, so I damn sure knew my way around, even at a couple thousand feet. I found Hamilton Ave., had the pilot take a right then a left on Darryl Drive, and Bingo, there was our home, easily seen because of the backyard pool. We made several low level but legal passes and got waves from my wife and kids.

"That's pretty darn good, Captain," the pilot said. "You'd be surprised how many guys can't find their homes from the air—you passed!"

Whew, I sighed. *Woulda been pretty pathetic if the Coordinator of this shootin' match couldn't find his own home. . .*

Hound and the Hare

Because the Sheriff's deputies didn't normally patrol our very complicated campus, I thought it would be a good idea that we familiarize them with key locations. I then created some scenarios wherein the crews would be dispatched on a call and have to lead the pilot to the location in question. Our first, and perhaps most challenging exercises were at night. I told one of our riders of the ORE (Off-Road-Enforcement) team to go up to the field sites above the campus and to just buzz around there between 9-10 PM. In the meantime, Capt. Alford took us on a mission to San Francisco International Airport (SFO) where we would be meeting and escorting the majority of our athletes once the games began. We took a little detour to Palo Alto and buzzed the home of my friends, Ken and Mel Alley. They were out on the patio having a BBQ. I scorched them with the Night Sun and my partner hollered over the helicopter's megaphone: "Stop, Police! You are all under arrest!"As we choppered away, I saw Ken give us the *Universal Salute*...

Then, there was the now defunct Redwood City Drive-In: I can remember in those days that there was always a bunch of *wisenheimers* who would play spotlight tag on the screen while the movie was in progress. Well, when we made our pass, I illuminated the screen and the movie just evaporated—Boy, that light was awesome! I know, boys will always be boys...

After proper clearance from SFO Tower, we were directed to cross the runways and land on the east side of the airport. I felt like an owl as I rotated my head a hundred times looking for that 747 the air traffic controllers might have missed. We put down on a pad across from the tower and after another walk around the ship, I got back into the front seat and we were off and headed for our turf and more location training.

On the way back to the Farm, we patrolled the foothills en route Stanford. When we circled Felt Lake, we lit-up a dozen or so illegal fishermen who beat feet out of there once the beam of death was on them. Their pace quickened when my partner barked over the loud speaker: "Sheriff's Department. You are all subject to arrest. Leave NOW!" Man, that really got their attention... Then, there was this van: At 500 hundred feet we could clearly see that the vehicle was violently oscillating—and this was in the days prior to the advent of *Low-Rider* hydraulics... After a couple of rotations, the van sped away in a cloud of dust...

First Drill

Dispatch: "Idaho 1-2, we have a report of a 415 motorcycle running around restricted areas in the field sites. Can you respond?"

"Idaho 1-2, Affirmative. We are over the Felt Lake area and are on it!"

On the intercom:

"Dick, my guess is the rider will be on the main road so we should patrol that first," I opined.

"Yeah, Captain, let's just do a complete rotation and see if we can pick him up," Alford replied.

After several passes, none of us could spot that sucker. I was thinking the rider must have killed his lights, and my guess was right. After about 10 minutes of searching, I spotted a faint red light going on and off. I directed the pilot to the location and notified my rear seat spotter to put the Sun on that guy. Sure enough, we got him. He should have disconnected his rear brake light, but like all crooks—even cops—they always screw-up! He was bagged!

Branner Hall

Frosh dorm, Branner Hall, is one of the nicest and most picturesque of the older student residences at Stanford. Originally designed for men, Branner Hall was built in 1923: The residence took the name of Stanford's second president, John Caspar Branner, professor, geologist and originator of Stanford's first comprehensive science library. Historians wrote that President Branner's personal collection of over 10,000 volumes filled up a railroad freight car. When he sold his collection to Stanford, these books became the nucleus of the Branner Earth Sciences Library. In addition to being named after one of Stanford's mainstays, one of the most celebrated residents of Branner Hall was Supreme Court Justice, Sandra Day O'Connor, the first woman to be appointed to the highest court in the land.

When Branner Hall was designated as the primary billet for the soccer athletes, we turned that peaceful dormitory into a virtual fortress! A 10 foot chain-link fence was erected around the premises; a magnetometer was set-up at the point of ingress and egress, and an unarmed security force swarmed around the place 24-7, backed-up by our gun toting deputies. In addition to packing their trusty Glock .40 caliber semiautomatic pistols, our guys carried Bushmaster AR-15s—and they knew how to use them, too. We also had "Bear," a 100 pound Rottweiler, aptly named because of his bigger than life size. Bear and his handler, Deputy Larry Layton, made sure that nothing of an explosive or euphoric nature ever made it into the compound. People, luggage, bags and all delivery vehicles were sniffed and systematically searched.

Finals

On our last day of training, I constructed a series of scenarios for the Sheriff's crew, who were on their own and had to direct our pilot to the scene of various locations on campus. We had a little Air Ops office in the station where we hung-out when not on assignment; when the radio crackled, the guys had to hustle across the street, fire-up the bird and get airborne. A number of people on campus were irritated with our operation—maybe the chop-chop-chop of the rotor blades reminded them of the movie "Apocalypse Now," although the Bell 500 was considerably quieter than the UH-1 Huey's used in Vietnam. Nonetheless, we received a couple of telephonic death threats indicting "they" were going to either blow us up or shoot us out of the sky, so I'm glad we sat on those ballistic shields...

Show-Time

Little did the players know, but I had an Ace up my sleeve. At about 0630, I loaded my blue Yamaha 400 dirt bike into my huge E-250 Ford van with the extended body—the motorcycle was also blue. This vehicle would hold 3 motorcycles and supporting gear. When I traveled all over Mexico, the locals dubbed it *Carro Grande*. I arrived at the Farm very early, slipped in the back way and drove into the vehicle repair shop; this was all pre-arranged and held in the strictest of confidence among the workers. At the appropriate time, I sneaked over to the shop and suited-up for a little ride. I had a hand-held radio and made the following dispatch:

"Idaho 1-2, we have a report of a 415 dirt biker doing doughnuts in the Sunken Diamond gravel. He's described as a large male on a blue motorcycle, wearing a silver helmet, yellow jersey and black leathers. What's your ETA?"

"Radio, Idaho 1-2, we'll be 10-8 in 10."

At this point, I fired-up my mount, sped out of the garage and headed to Sunken Diamond where I had about 10 minutes of unabated fun spinning around in the pea gravel, kicking up huge plumes of debris and dust in the process. Because I cheated and had a radio and earpiece, I heard the cavalry coming: Three patrol units were speeding my way from all directions, and judging from the inflection in their voices, they were all amped-up. *This was Déjà vu from the good ol' days when we used to run from Captain Midnight in our dirt runners,* I recalled. I then spotted Idaho 1-2 suddenly vault up above the trees and zoom toward me with great velocity. *Time to get outta Dodge and head for the trees,* I schemed. I quickly went through the gears and flew around the stadium headed for the eucalyptus groves at Galvez and Arboretum, with Idaho 1-2 hot on my tail. Just as I was crossing Galvez St., one of my trusted gendarmes tried to cut me off with his patrol car—Texas Rangers style! *Jeez, these guys are taking this little training exercise way too seriously,* I realized. Fortunately, I zipped though the bollards, down into a drainage ditch and disappeared into the forest. All the while, the radio chatter sounded like a tree full of monkeys who just spotted a leopard:

"Radio Idaho 1-2: We can't see him now, but he's in there! We see the smoke from his bike."

Damn 2-stroke, I thought, *but maybe I can fool 'em.*

Idaho 1-2 continued: "All patrol units, form a perimeter around the trees, he's gotta come out sooner or later."

With the chopper above and keying on my exhaust smoke, I hatched a desperate escape plan: I slowly putted through the dense forest toward the Northwest side of the grove. The chopper crew reported where I was heading and suggested the cars move that way. I then killed the engine and immediately heard Idaho 1-2 report that there was no smoke, so I must have cut my motor. Good thought. At that point, I slowly muscled the 300 pound beast back the way I came in, and when I was within visual range of Galvez St., I snapped down on the kick starter and was out of that grove like a scalded dog. I twisted the throttle as far as it would go—WFO (Wide FN Open), blasted around the stadium and headed back to the corporation yard. The guys in the patrol cars were fooled, but not

Idaho 1-2. That SOB was on me like a "Duck on a June Bug." Thinking the S/O deputies weren't really familiar with the maintenance area, I zipped into the garage and got a couple of guys to help me load my bike. I waited for a few minutes and stealthily slipped out the back door.

As I exited the garage, I heard the Idaho's observer report that a big blue van had just left a garage. The air was alive with: "That's probably A-2's blue Ford van." I was done. *Damn. I shoulda borrowed one of the Corp yard's white vans as there were a million of those things running all over the place.* As I tried to boogie out the back gate, they got me. I was forcibly removed from my vehicle, slammed up against the side, unceremoniously handcuffed and searched.

"Good job, guys," I sheepishly admitted. "But, not for Idaho 1-2, ya never would have bagged me!" There were a lot of "high fives" at my expense, but it was all worth it as I was confident we were up to the task! Our job was to keep the athletes safe at our venue and I knew that our cog in the wheel was solid!

First Mission

We reported to ARIS Helicopter Company at San Jose International Airport one morning at 0700. After a pre-flight inspection of the helicopter, we took off for the Farm's LZ; this was going to be our first dry-run to SFO in concert with a caravan of Sheriff's units and a transport bus. We would simulate a pick-up of soccer players and their transport to Branner Hall. We landed at our pad shortly thereafter for a much needed "refueling:" Coffee and doughnuts, aka, a sugar fix—we already filled Idaho 1-2 to the max with JP fuel at San Jose. Once the Sheriff's units radioed they were past Stanford, we sauntered over to the bird, performed another quick pre-flight check and climbed aboard. I was in the co-pilot's seat. My job was to watch for other aircraft, trees, power lines or anything that might ruin our day. During my training, I was also told to monitor the gauges, warning lights and other bells and whistles. The powerful jet motor fired and in a minute, the rotors were whirring. At this point, the craft began to vibrate and after a brief jolt, we were off the ground and slowly elevating to 800 feet. All of a sudden, I spotted a red light blinking and heard an ominous beeping. Something was not right here! I notified Capt. Alford on the intercom and he immediately radioed the airport tower that we were going to land, like now, due to an engine malfunction. Helicopter aficionados call this situation an "Autorotation." I call it a controlled crash! Needless to say, I experienced a serious spike in blood pressure and my buttocks had a firm grip on the armored vest I was sitting on.

That Dick Alford was some kind of pilot: He put that thing into a counterclockwise spiral, and before I knew it, we were safely on terra firma. Whew, that was scary; we both agreed on that. Now, what were we going to do? We needed to perform the mission, but how could we do it with a sick motor? Or, was it that sick? When I asked Dick about the warning light, he said it was probably a crankshaft indicator that monitored fine metal filings and alerted when there was a build-up on the magnetic plug. Alford indicated this was a common occurrence and that the mechanics would just pull the magnetic plug, clean-off the filings and we would be good to go.

"Dick, I can do that. I interjected. I worked on jet and reciprocating engines when I was in the Air Force. No big deal. I'll get a couple of tools and have us 10-8 in no time," I bragged.

Captain Alford agreed to let me give it a go, and if the engine warning light didn't re-alert, we would be airborne in a few minutes. If not, we would have to scrub the mission until a certified mechanic could make the necessary repairs.

After removing the magnetic plug and cleaning it, I re-safety wired the bolt, and made the sign of the Cross. Captain Alford fired-up the motor and *Voila,* no more problems. We piled back in the bird and were en route SFO. Without divulging our security procedures, suffice it to say that our aerial unit scanned all roof tops around the airport and ensured that no snipers would be able to take a pot shot at our precious cargo. On the way back down highway 101, we flew all around the motorcade and reported suspicious vehicles and persons along the way. Our mission would be concluded when the visiting teams were safely in the confines of Branner Hall. We would deploy on any movement of the competitors, be it for practice, sightseeing, to and from the stadium and so on.

And, this is how it went for the entire Soccer Preliminary games at Stanford Stadium. I believe we hosted 8 sold-out matches—approximately 80,000 fans each, and most of the contests were at night. We never encountered a single incident and I believe that patrol made only a handful of arrests, mostly for drunkenness. There were no massive fights or disputes often associated with *futbol*. The most exciting phase of this entire program was our training, especially the Autorotation deal. From that time on, Idaho 1-2 performed flawlessly. Needless to say, all's well that ends well and our security and policing was second to none—not bad for a little cop shop of only 35 sworn officers.

Idaho 1-2 Crew
L/R: Sgt. Rick Enberg; CSO Clifton Clarke; Capt. Dick Alford (ARIS Helicopters); Author

Epilogue

In 1986, Idaho 1-2 made the newspapers, once again. A career criminal, Ronald J. McIntosh, walked away (e.g. escaped) from a minimal security prison on October 28th. He later chartered our Olympic chopper from ARIS on November 5th, and once aloft, Ron produced a .45 and ordered the pilot (not Dick Alford, thank God) to fly to the Federal Correctional Facility in Dublin, CA for a passenger—McIntosh's girlfriend, Samantha Lopez, who was cooling her heels after receiving a 50 year sentence for sticking-up a bank in Georgia. This was a classic scene right out of Hollywood! The helicopter swooped down and landed in the yard. Samantha scrambled aboard and they simply flew out of sight while the guards were trying to decide whether to grab their butts or their guns!

About 10 hours following the escape, a motorist spotted Idaho 1-2, abandoned, on a canyon road several miles away. The plan obviously included a getaway car as there was no sign of the escapees or the pilot. Fortunately, the pilot was later released several miles away, unharmed; the chopper was also unscathed.

Because Ronald J. broke his lover out of a federal prison, the FBI was hot on the case. The Feds had been monitoring McIntosh's bank account and quickly learned that *Romeo* had purchased a set of wedding rings for his *Juliet* and was going to pick them up November 15th. What a dope! This was a *no brainer* for the Feds as the daring duo was quickly busted when they showed up for their bonds of matrimony. Although the judge gave the Love-Birds an "A for effort", he awarded Mr. McIntosh 25 years in a federal slammer and tacked-on 5 more to Ms. Lopez' account. As Samantha was spirited away by officers, Ron uttered a heartfelt: "I love you!" *Awwwwwww. . .*

Super Bowl XIX

When it was announced that the 19th Super Bowl would be played at Stanford Stadium, I thought *Uh-oh*. While the attitude around the department was that this would just be another "Big Game," I felt otherwise. If the Rose Bowl is known as the "Grand Daddy of Them All," then a Super Bowl event must be the Great Grand Daddy. The Super Bowl is not just the biggest of all NFL games, but the most watched television event, attracting tens of thousands of people from all over the world. Many of these folks are rich and famous, thus prime targets for thieves and grifters. In my opinion, this spectacle would be SUDPS' worst nightmare!

As the playoffs unfolded, it was almost certain that the San Francisco Forty-Niners would be in the fray. I had been to many 9er/Oakland Raider games in my lifetime and it was a toss-up as to which fan base was more rabid: Out of control drunkenness and numerous fist-fights were the order of the day at both venues. Although we had weathered many storms at the collegiate level, somehow, I knew this was going to be different—and it was.

The Niners, led by world beater quarterback, Joe Montana, met the Chicago Bears and their famed (future Hall of Famer) running back, Walter Payton, at Candlestick Park in the NFC Championship game on January 6, 1985, and thumped the "Monsters of the Midway" 23-zip. Fans went berserk following the victory and ripped-up huge pieces of the turf as souvenirs. In the aftermath, the field looked as if a herd of wild Texas hogs had torn-up the place! This was *not* a good omen. We were determined not to allow our precious gridiron to be rooted-up by crazed fans, so we hired a hundred or so extra security officers, who would ring the field during and after the battle. The NFL insisted that our perimeter fence be removed, as high-roller fans wouldn't appreciate paying 500 bucks and up for tickets, and having to peer through a cyclone mesh barrier.

SUDPS' Game Plan

Planning had been going on for months. Chief Herrington attended Super Bowl XVIII in Tampa, FL—a blockbuster event which pitted the vaunted Washington Redskins vs. the upstart Bad Boy L.A. Raiders (formerly from Oakland, CA), who surprised everyone with a 38-9 beating of Washington. (Former Stanford Heisman Trophy winner, QB Jim Plunkett, emerged from the "wash tub" and led his Raiders to the one-sided drubbing.) The Chief brought back a lot of interesting information about how police and security operated at that event; but our venue and operation was as dissimilar as oil and water: Tampa had recently refurbished "The Old Sombrero," so it was now a state-of-the-art facility, touted as being one of the better stadiums in the USA. They had an army of sworn law enforcement officers, as well as minions of special security personnel. The parking lots were vast and ingress and egress points were good!

Conversely, almost everything about our site was pale by comparison: Although our antiquated stadium seated more fans and the butt splintering wooden bleachers had been replaced with aluminum seats, they were backless and crowded. Movement around the narrow concourse (initially built to be just wide enough for a Model T pick-up to service the hot dog stands) was next to impossible, and the stairways were treacherous. There was ample open space around the facility, but most of the parking was on grass fields or in the dirty/muddy eucalyptus groves. This was ok for tailgating, unless a monsoon turned the place into a swamp. At this time of the year in Palo Alto, rain was a distinct possibility... *Get more tow trucks on tap,* I added to my mental notes.

Traffic and Parking

One of the things our department did pretty well was to manage traffic and parking. This process was always in a state of flux, as Stanford football fans weren't shrinking violets when it came to complaining. At the end of every football season, Captain Wullschleger (who was the traffic and parking boss) met with his CSOs and devised new methods in which to improve the flow of incoming and outgoing vehicles. There was that one-percent who bitched about it, but as everyone knows, you can't please everybody. As I've always said: "Some folks would piss and moan if you hung them with a new rope!"

Perhaps the most often heard complaint was that outside visitors couldn't find their way to the stadium, due to almost non-existent signage. With SB XIX in mind, I volunteered to look into this squawk and found it to be valid. So, for the months leading up to the 1984 Stanford football season, I drove the Athletic Grounds' staff absolutely bonkers. I instructed the sign shop to create and plaster the surrounding area with signs, so that even a moron could find the way to Stanford Stadium.

Knowing that we were going to have well over 100, 000 people attending the Super Bowl, University and NFL planners came up with a brilliant idea to handle transportation of the masses: They hired hundreds of Greyhound buses, which would bring fans from San Francisco (where most of the visitors would stay) to the campus. Instead of driving these buses right into the eye of the hurricane, so to speak, they were staged at alternate sites (The Stanford Shopping Center, Palm Oval and other satellite parking lots) and shuttle vehicles were utilized to get folks to the stadium. Despite that plan, we anticipated vehicular traffic was still going to be a massive migraine. Figuring that impatient fans would park their cars along the roadways where parking had always been prohibited, our crews put up hundreds of tow away signs. I hired several towing companies and staged them at a temporary impound yard at the Plant Services Corporation Yard, which was staffed with a contingent of SEPs (Special Event Patrol). Out of the goodness of my heart, I arbitrarily set the impound fee at $40, which was about half of what the going rate was in this area at that time. We needed to have a quick turnaround because I knew that people would willfully disregard the tow away zones, as they could afford to pay the freight. Little did I know...

The Match-up

Whereas most previous Super Bowls had been virtual "yawners"— either one sided wipeouts or boring soccer-like defensive games, this one, by all accounts, promised to be a barn burner! This game was going to be a dog fight between two of the best teams in the NFL: The AFC's Miami Dolphins in their fifth SB appearance, posting a 14-2 record, versus the NFC's San Francisco "Prospectors." The 49ers recorded 15 straight wins, just one shy of the Dolphins 16-0 mark in the 1978 season. The 9ers were trying to dig out their second World Title. Both teams were solid on both sides of the ball, having broken all sorts of previous records.

The Stars

Both teams were superbly coached. The Dolphins head mentor was the iconic Don Shula, who had been a proven winner by leading his team to two of the six Super Bowls they had competed in. Shula began his NFL career in 1951 playing for the Cleveland Browns and later, the Baltimore Colts. He retired in 1995 and later was named to Pro Football's Hall of Fame.

Shula's counterpart was the brainy former Stanford coach (twice), Bill Walsh. Walsh was dubbed the "Genius" for his unconventional scripted and unique offensive play calling, which later became known as the "West Coast Offense." Coach Walsh began his coaching career at his Alma mater, San Jose State College in 1955. He remained in the Bay Area coaching at a high school and matriculated to the "Big Boys," with Al Davis' Oakland Raiders in 1966. Bill Walsh was also selected to the vaunted Football Hall of Fame.

However, the real Superstars were Miami's Dan Marino and S.F's Joe Montana. Both gladiators had thrown for over 300 completions. The media swooned over Marino, as he had just set an NFL record of 362 pass completions that season, and was the first man to surpass the 5,000 yard passing mark in a season (with 5, 084 yards). Dan also eclipsed George Blanda and Y.A. Tittle's 36 career TD's, by registering a whopping 48!

But, Joe Montana was no slouch: The former Notre Dame All-American and NFL Pro Bowler impressed with 279 completions for 3,630 yards, 28 touchdowns, while only suffering 10 interceptions. These two, coupled with a bevy of Pro Bowl players on both sides, stacked-up to be one helluva gridiron battle *Down on the Farm*!

Fly in the Soup

About a week before the battle lines were to be drawn, the NFL officials brought forth some very disturbing news that would clearly exasperate our policing operation: The Secret Service had just busted a very sophisticated counterfeiting outfit in South San Francisco that was producing the very valuable and sought after Super Bowl XIX tickets. While they confiscated a bunch of the bogus ducats, the investigators suspected that there were hundreds, if not thousands, of the fakes out there. The USSS guys said that a network of crooks was selling these things in the paper to various outlets such as "Ticketmaster," as well as to hotel personnel and cabbies—you name it. When we actually got a look at the counterfeit tickets, the investigator had a legitimate specimen and a bogus one in transparent sheet protectors; most observers couldn't tell which was which. I remember that the ticket had an image of the Lombardi Trophy, with a clear blue sky and (I believe) the Golden Gate Bridge in the background. The giveaway was the darker color of the scene, especially the sky. This must have been an "inside job," for each ticket had individual seat assignments printed on them; whereas, those counterfeited Big Game tix back in 1975 had the same seat number on all of them. Man, this was going to be a massive Excedrin moment. Given all of the last minute arrivals at normal football games, I imagined this crowd was going to wait until the last possible cocktail was drained before they poured into their seats. And, what would we do to extricate interlopers who were duped into purchasing phony tickets? This was going to be one big dog fight!

Plan A

After numerous last minute conferences with the NFL and Stanford's great Athletic Department, it was decided that instead of fighting the folks who got duped, we'd mollycoddle them—even though they should have known better than to buy a pig in a poke, so to speak. Another hospitality tent was set-up near the main entrance next to my temporary command post. This tent was equipped with a large screen TV and refreshments would be available for the vanquished. Several teams of cops were assigned to respond to ticket issues. The folks who had the bad ducats were given the option of going to the "Duped Tent," or they could leave the venue all together. There were a lot of pissed off people, but as I intimated before, "Buyer Beware!" It seemed like most of the "have no real seats" enjoyed themselves, despite having to watch the game on TV. At least they got to watch the game. Yours truly and my golf cart driver, son Kirk, only managed to catch a few snaps in the 2nd quarter, as we were too damn busy running from crisis to crisis amongst the throng of inebriated folks outside of the arena.

Pseudo Star

Rosenthal James Simpson (O.J. aka, "Juice") was the featured sidelines reporter for ABC Sports' coverage of this Super Bowl. The real stars of the ABC broadcast team were Frank Gifford, "Dandy" Don Meredith, and Joe Theismann. O.J., the former USC Heisman Trophy winner and NFL MVP in 1973 (when he rushed for 2,000 yards as a Buffalo Bill), was the *only* member of the TV guys who *demanded* a police security detail! In my humble opinion, Simpson thought he was so beloved that fans would mob him; I think he was just way too full of himself! As you can deduce, I was no fan of this charlatan—and that was some 10 years before he was charged in the savage murders of his former wife, Nicole Brown Simpson, and Ronald Goldman. In any event, it galled us that this big, tough football star felt he required personal protection—for no apparent reason other than his sense of personal importance and entitlement due to his celebrity. When Simpson was a TV spokesman for Hertz making tons of commercials, he galloped through airports all the time without a squad of cops running interference. . .

Chief Herrington had a policy of not mollycoddling athletes and coaches unless there was some specific reason, such as a threat of physical harm. I couldn't have agreed with him more on that issue! We almost never put uniformed deputies on coach "protection"— like they do in the South where the coaches are always escorted by two or three behemoth Troopers wearing their "Smokey Da Bear" campaign hats. . . Hell, not even the iconic Alabama coach, Paul "Bear" Bryant, got a police detail when he came to Stanford as an honorary mentor during a Shrine game! Coach Bryant never asked for it and didn't need it. Even in his 70s, he walked around the stadium's field all by his lonesome. For this Super Bowl, the CHP provided a motorized escort for the team buses, but we never received any requests from the Forty-Niners or Dolphins to babysit their coaches or the *real* Superstars, Joe Montana and Dan Marino. Nonetheless, we did the drill and held O.J.'s hand while he traipsed around the joint for the duration.

Pre-Game

Things were already abuzz when I arrived at 0500 hours. Even at that ungodly hour, the parking lots were seeing a considerable amount of activity; many San Francisco fans had camped out in the groves, with tailgate parties already in progress. This was going to be a very long day, with kick-off slated for 3:00PM, P.S.T. The areas close to the stadium were like a beehive with vendors and staffers readying the thirteen corporate tents. The Ford Motor Company's massive tent encompassed most of the infield of Angell Field, with Sony's elaborate canvas structure taking up hundreds of square feet of space near Sunken Diamond. Later in the morning, the sponsors didn't disappoint their invited guests by offering lavish buffets, *hors d'oeuvres* and cocktails, served by gorgeous young ladies—all the while being entertained by live musicians. I managed to crash a few of these *soirées,* where they had super-sized martinis and exotic sushi samplings— courtesy of the Sony Corporation, but I respectfully passed on the liquid refreshments. By mid morning, the area outside of the stadium was packed with humanity. I had never seen so many people roaming around in all my life—I guesstimated that we had upwards of 200,000 folks milling around before they opened the gates. The stated capacity of the stadium was 84,059, but I know that with standing room only, that old coliseum would tolerate 100,000 sardines! And, when I went to the Indy 500 in the early 90's, there was an estimated crowd of 500,000 in attendance. I verified (in my mind) that we had about half that number at our venue on January 20, 1985.

Game On!

As I anticipated, despite all of the transportation options afforded the fans, traffic was a nightmare. The roadways were a virtual parking lot as all of the available parking areas were jam-packed. As the *witching hour* approached, frustrated people were not only leaving their rides in the Tow Away zones, but they were unbelievably abandoning their vehicles right in the middle of the traffic lanes! Thanks to a premonition, I hired about 15 big, tough kids from Kirk's Prospect High School football team to run the tow yard, which was in the secure Corporation yard; they were supervised by their football boss, Coach Dave Johnson. Once I realized what was happening, we contracted more tow rigs and doubled the impound fee from 40 to 80 bucks. I learned from our officers that after warning violators of the fine for impounding vehicles, many replied: "Hell, I'd pay 40 bucks to see a piss-ant fornicate. . ." After the game concluded, many scoff-laws were just too inebriated to snivel and not very many violators bitched about the sudden rate of inflation—most thought the fine was still a pretty good deal! Although doubling the freight fee paid for all of the help, it certainly didn't seem to deter willful violations among this crowd of high-rollers. . .

Being severely understaffed, we instructed the troops to refrain from making arrests unless a threat to public safety was imminent. But, once the herd started pouring into the stadium, all hell broke loose. Our teams of deputies were running from call to call of fights, ticket disputes, car burglaries and thefts—all kinds of thefts, especially forcible theft of person and stealthy pick-pocketing. There were organized gangs of crooks, from all over the the world, who descended on our venue to avail themselves of the "easy pickens'." For miscreants, the Super Bowl was a target rich environment!

Bump, Hook and Lateral

This technique is as old as humanity but still very effective. I'll use a football analogy to explain this ruse: There is usually a boss, a signal caller, if you will, which I'll designate as the quarterback (QB), who will select a "mark," usually a well dressed man or woman, who is moving along in the crowd. Once the QB flashes the signal, a "lineman," or two, will bump or jostle the victim, while another guy initiates the classic "pick maneuver," by either suddenly stopping in front of the mark, or actually going to the ground, thus making an impediment in the mark's path. While the mark is sufficiently distracted and usually very pissed-off, the "hook" (often a woman) comes into play, and lifts the victim's billfold or wallet, which is quickly handed-off or lateralled to a speedy "back"—a kid with a good set of wheels. And, off they go. If the mark realizes what has just occurred, there isn't much s/he can do other than holler for the police. Many don't know they have been had until they go for their wallet to pay for a beer or something. . . I know, as a variation of this scenario happened to me once at Oakland International Airport. The bump was using luggage at the carousel as a ploy, holding onto a suitcase and knocking me off balance, despite my protestation. When I got home and went to a store, I reached for my traveler's checks—they were MIA. Then, I thought, *Ohhhhh! That well dressed woman standing behind me must have lifted my stash, all the while backed-up by an enormous guy, who stood about 6'7" tall.* Pretty nifty! Another reason to carry only traveler's checks when you're on the road, but not in a loose pocket, even the front one! I was picked-clean and never felt a thing.

Tex

I went to our compound's processing trailer to see how things were going. The S/O provided a 40 passenger prisoner bus and a couple of paddy wagons with a crew to create a holding facility for arrestees. And, there were a slew of them—at the end of the day, I think we had 43 in custody—far more than we needed or wanted. When I entered the big single wide, I espied an impressive looking gentleman who was reporting the theft of his wallet, which he said contained $3,000! *Wow, I thought, who in the hell would come to a football game with that much cash on him?* Well, I soon found out: This man was right out of the soap, "Dallas." He was middle-aged, tall, dark and handsome. He sported a 5 gallon Stetson atop his 6'3" frame and was decked out in a high dollar Western suede jacket, fancy shirt with all of those pearl snap buttons, a classic Bolo tie, a silver buckle about the size of a kid's football, designer jeans and, of course, a pair of custom lizard skin cowboy boots. So, I approached the man, introduced myself and commiserated with him about his loss.

He replied: "Waall, aye appreciate that Cap'n and I wanna compliment your bouys for their good work."

"Well, thank you sir; we have some of the best deputies around *these here parts,*" I responded in language he would understand. "So, what part of Texas are you from?" I nosed.

"Well, Suh, I'm from a lil' town called Midland," he drawled.

"Midland, isn't that where Vice President Bush is from?"

"Shore is, and I know the man personal like. He wuz a great war hero, an' I've done some binezz with him before he went to Washin'ton."

"Oh, now I understand why you were carrying so much 'pocket change' on ya; you must be into oil," I guessed.

"Shore am; got me a well or two. Maa whyfe scolded me for carrin' so much pocket money 'roun, but I figgaed we'd be OK, bein' at a college 'n all," he admitted.

"Unfortunately, many people have that mistaken notion, Sir. We've got more snakes around here than you have in the whole state of Texas, especially when we have big events. This place can be one big viper pit."

About that time, I heard the back door slam (where they brought in the collars) and one of our folks telling someone to shut up and sit down. Within a minute or so, a deputy rushed around the wall and burst into the interview area with a huge billfold in his hand. He opened the wallet and it was as wide as a deck of cards—stuffed with a wad of cash, mostly 50s and 100s.

"Captain, look what we got here! We ran down that little bastard all the way to the El Camino and caught his ass just before he made it over the fence."

Ol' Tex jumped up and shouted: "Waall, I'll be Dog-Gone. That's ma billfold!" After the deputy handed it over, Tex remarked: Waall, it seems to be all hea; you ol' bouys are awright!"

Come to find out, a couple of guys on our pick-pocketing detail spotted this theft go down and gave chase of the fleet footed "half back," after Tex's bankroll was tossed to the runner. The kid beat feet and took-off like a shot out of a cannon! But, many of our young guns were as fast as *cheetahs,* so, after a half-mile pursuit, the *gazelle's* gas tank ran low and he was taken down—Big-time! When they tried to interview the thief, he *No Habla Ingles,* for he was a member of a Columbian pick-pocket crew the FBI warned us about. That Ol' Bouy from Midland was one happy camper, I'll tell ya— Damn nice dude, too, as are most of the Texans I've known in my life.

So, what about the Game?

I'm probably the last person to ask that question, as my chauffeur and I raced around like a mini-fire truck, putting out small conflagrations all day and night! But, I read that the Forty-Niners soundly trounced the Dolphins 38-16, during a cold, damp, foggy day in Farm Town. Most of the fans were elated as they were rooting for the home team. I think the guys from Miami just wanted to get back to sunshine and their sandy beaches. The cordon of over two hundred security and police personnel dissuaded exuberant fans from storming the field, and we didn't even have attack dogs or horses! Unlike previous Stanford-Cal Big Games, the goal posts remained erect, and the turf, although soggy and a bit torn-up by the 22 very large men stampeding around, was none the worse for wear. More importantly, although there were numerous arrests, violence was minimal and no one got hurt. In retrospect, it was the most taxing event that our department ever handled in a single day; and it was accomplished with professionalism and aplomb. Most cops never receive many accolades for the work they do; but, in this case, all of the people who made our police/security effort a rounding success need to give themselves a "Standing O!"

First & Last Trivia

There were many "Firsts" in Super Bowl XIX. I'll list them in the order of importance:

- This was the first time that a sitting President of the United States participated in the "coin toss" ritual. This was indeed an "Inaugural Event," for the ceremony was accomplished via TV satellite, while President Ronald Reagan flipped the coin in the White House.
- It was the first time that a Super Bowl fell on Inauguration Day (January 20th). President Reagan elected to be publicly sworn in for his second term the next day; however, he took the oath of office in a small private ceremony in the White House on this day.
- This was the first time that the World Championship game would be televised by ABC. In addition, it would be the first and last time that play-by-play announcer, Frank Gifford, would be behind the mic and spotlight. This would also be the last game that Don Meredith, aka "Turn out the lights, the party's over!" would be a commentator, as well.
- The 49ers would achieve immortality as the first team in a Super Bowl to win 15 games in a row since the NFL expanded the schedule to 16 games in 1978.

- By virtue of being within 30 miles of Stanford Stadium, San Francisco was designated the home team. Their decisive win would go down in the history books as being the first team to win a Super Bowl in their own region.

- This would be the first time that Stanford University hosted a Super Bowl in their nearly 100 year history. And, when they reduced the size of the stadium from 85,000 to 50,000 seats, this would more than likely be their last!

- Finally, this would be the first time that a University police department of only 35 sworn deputies ever pulled-off the unimaginable: Hosting one of the biggest sporting events in the world with such meager resources, albeit backed-up with a contingent of the Sheriff's Crowd Control Unit and a couple hundred civilian security personnel. And, I'm quite sure the current members of SUDPS are relieved to know that they'll *never* have to do that again!

*Thanks to Wikipedia for all of the stats!

World Cup '94

Like many red-blooded American football die-hards, I viewed the other *Futbol* as Eeehhhhhh! But, like it or not, FIFA (*F'ed'eration Internationale de Football Association*) World Cup was coming to the Farm, with the first of six matches to begin June 20, 1994. Faculty and staff naysayers feared that fan violence and monetary costs for the university would bring about negative consequences, thus making the endeavor not worth the effort. Proponents (mainly the World Cup (WC) representatives) countered that the financial rewards to the school and community—which they touted would bring in $338 million, coupled with the international prestige—would be a diamond in the rough. The WC crowd also pooh-poohed the notion of fan violence by "hooligans" because the European troublemakers, such as England, didn't make the cut, thus would be home watching the matches on TV!

Stanford Stadium would be the site of four first-round matches, one "Round of 16" contest, as well as a quarterfinal event. There were eight other major U.S. cities hosting preliminary games, with the world championship match to be fought out in the Rose Bowl, Pasadena, CA.

Police and Security

Needless to say, Stanford DPS was tasked to head-up the public safety effort, under the auspices of the Sheriff of Santa Clara County. We would also employ over 500 additional security personnel, including over 100 of our SEP force. In addition, the event would feature federal, state and local law enforcement officials—even a contingent from Interpol, who specialized in soccer violence and tracked the ringleaders worldwide. The venue would be divided into two components: The stadium proper and the rest of the property around the arena. Chief Herrington, Captain Marvin Moore, and Sheriff Charles "Chuck" Gillingham would manage the stadium, while yours truly and Undersheriff (now Sheriff) Laurie Smith would operate the JOC (Joint Operations Command center), which was located in a "double-wide" near our secured Operations Compound. With luminaries from the FBI, Interpol, Palo Alto PD and Fire, Alcohol Beverage Control (ABC), Sheriff's Office, U.S. State Department, Department of Defense (DOD) and many more who escape my memory, what could possible go wrong?

Training

Preparation for World Cup was underway nearly a year before the events were to begin. The Chief went to several matches in Ireland, Captain Moore and one of his supervisors went to Spain, and I was sent to the World University Games (WUGs) in Buffalo, NY. I was able to visit and be trained in one of the most secure venues for international sporting events that I had ever seen. Under the tutelage of DOD, the New York State Police was the overall boss of the operation. They spared no bucks or brainpower in setting up the main site: A 10' steel fence, topped with razor wire (I thought I was in Louisiana's Angola State Penitentiary) ringed the enormous property and every inch of that barrier was closely monitored by video cams. If you don't like TSA and airport security now, you would have hated trying to get into the WUGs way back in 1993. I had a steel prosthesis in my hip, which my Orthopod assured me wouldn't alert when going through a magnetometer—Well, I got through the San Jose International Airport's security check without a hitch, but when I passed through the portal at WUG, the bells and sirens went off and I was immediately surrounded by several heavily armed NY coppers. I was impressed, but I think they were disappointed that they didn't snag a bad guy.

Probably the most impressive part of the NY security plan was their vehicle screening. I wrote about our procedure during the '84 Stanford Olympic Soccer event at Branner Hall, wherein we utilized a bomb sniffing dog, and if he alerted on something under a vehicle, we scanned the undercarriage with a mirror on a stick. The boy/girls in NY took vehicle inspection to another level. All cars and trucks were systematically searched with dogs as well, but the vehicles were driven over a "grease pit" and scanned by a high tech video system. Any suspicious item or possible hidden compartment was physically checked out by a technician who crawled down into the pit for a closer look. Finally, another feature of the WUG's operation was their command center, which looked more like a NASA launch center. It was truly state of the art! Although I didn't see any soccer, I got to enjoy one of the most spectacular wonders of the world, Niagara Falls. And, the lessons I learned in this visit enabled me to set-up and manage the JOC, which turned out to be a rewarding experience.

The Knock-Off Police (KOPs)

It seemed to me that the biggest concern for the WC organizers was that their proprietary rights be preserved. They went to great lengths to keep their products protected so that counterfeiters could not sell bogus copies of apparel and souvenirs, a.k.a. "Knock-Offs." This had always been a serious problem at Stanford because the laws were not defined sufficiently for law enforcement intervention. Thus, at Stanford games, hawkers peddled the dreaded Lil' Injun tee shirts out of the trunks of their cars and drove the administration nuts—us too, for there was little we could legally do other than scare the illicit vendors away. This practice was especially prevalent during the Soccer Olympics and Super Bowl, where we literally had dozens of scammers peddling off-shore junk with official Olympic and NFL logos. When the WC officials were presented with the dilemma the University had faced historically in enforcing proprietary rights, WC put their legal beagles on the case. In short order, the lawyers obtained a Superior Court injunction that delineated an expanded boundary around Stanford Stadium, which included all points of ingress and egress, and banned sales of any item (food and beverage, too) not sanctioned by WC. The perimeter was lawfully posted. Signage admonished scofflaws that they would be subject to prosecution, as well as having their goods confiscated. The best part of this plan was that WC hired a private security group to enforce the moratorium and handle all incidents and bogus goods they might seize. A huge tent was erected to accommodate the "knock-offs," and our officers wouldn't be called unless there was an unruly dispute as a result of the KOP intervention. I was a bit skeptical at first, but as it turned out, there were very few calls for service as the KOPs were pretty darn professional and did a whale of a job. At game's end, they amassed a mountain of apparel and assorted memorabilia. And, the best of the rest was that SUDPS had virtually no involvement in that sack of rattlesnakes!

Game Operations

Thanks to the DOD, the old sports arena was as secure and safe as it could possibly be. All of the rickety wooden bleachers (circa 1922) had been replaced with anodized aluminum benches. Although the WC *powers that be* were really unhappy about the cyclone security fence, which as you may recall was temporarily taken down for Super Bowl XIX, the University stood fast with Chief Herrington and insisted that the barrier must remain. Given the degree of fan violence in Europe, there was no way that Stanford wanted to open itself up for a nasty international spectacle—not to mention vicarious liability if rabid fans poured over that short wall and engaged in a bloody riot on the 50 yard line. In fact, a second fence was added; it was equipped with electronic gates which could be remotely opened should a "crush" happen, such as was the case in numerous matches globally, when folks were literally squashed to death. In order to keep an eyeball on the crowd, with the ability to zoom in on hot spots, a number of high tech video cams were installed. Talk about "Big Brother!" But, sometimes our constitutional rights have to give way for the greater good of the majority of the nice people in this world; in our view, fan and player safety was paramount.

Using the tried and proven football policing plan, teams of deputies were able to quickly respond and resolve any issues that might occur. Surprisingly, during the six matches, the calls for service were less than we experienced during an Oregon State vs. Stanford football game way back when OSU was the Pac 8's doormat. . . The only significant skirmish I recall was due to a father and son who were bombed out of their gourds and abusive to other fans. Both inebriates had to be forcibly removed from the stadium. The elder should have known better: He was a retired cop but chose poorly when he elected to take on a couple of our big, strapping, young bucks. The drunken duo lost; badly, but were uninjured despite the furious struggle they put up.

Meanwhile, back in the Joint Operations Command Center, our members were fairly busy fielding undercover teams and putting out little fires in the periphery. Because the entire premises was as dry as the U.S. was *supposed to be* during Prohibition, the CA ABC fielded several teams and raided tailgate gatherings and confiscated the booze. These "Revenuers" often needed back-up—for obvious reasons—so our exterior deputies were constantly on the run. In retrospect, I firmly believe the booze ban was the reason that World Cup '94 was so quiet. However, once the Boys from Brazil won their quarter final game, all bets were off. The Brazilians were a very lively bunch and had hundreds of supporters. Once the match concluded, the colorfully attired crowd formed-up and marched around singing and dancing to the beat of drums and tambourines. Some of our law enforcement colleagues were concerned that things would spiral out of control and turn ugly. However, our sources from Interpol knew otherwise and calmed everyone down. While the Brazilians are a boisterous, party-hearty bunch, they generally don't get out of hand and cause trouble—especially when they win. The exuberance went on for an hour or so until they got on their buses and headed for the Town of Los Gatos, where the team was billeted.

I heard that the triumphant ones drove the Los Gatos Police nuts until they finally shooed them away after the bars closed. Whew, I'm certainly thankful they had somewhere else to party. We all packed-up and went home while closing another chapter.

CHAPTER TWENTY THREE

Crash and Burn

Major Crashes: On the Stanford Campus?

According to the Old Guard, very few serious vehicle accidents/collisions ever occurred on campus. Ol' Captain Midnight was the department's Traffic Officer and told me some idiot had run him over once while he was directing traffic at a fender bender accident. But, other than some bike vs. bike collisions, not many major vehicle crashes ever occurred. However, I later learned that there *was* a fatal head-on bike collision several years back on Campus Drive, where one cyclist was going the wrong way! One of the students subsequently died due to severe head injuries. And, because Stanford was unincorporated, the California Highway Patrol was responsible for investigating any major accident. Boy, was I in for a surprise!

****

Another Flashback: The Monta Vista Dip

There is a very dangerous dip on Stevens Creek Road in a little unincorporated town called Monta Vista. This place was infamous for its 40 degree downhill gradient that flattened out at the bottom. Daredevils used to see how fast they could go before bottoming out and going airborne. I once clocked a kid in a souped-up VW Bug at 75 MPH on my radar. He disputed the citation in court; the speed demon told the judge that his V-Dubb couldn't go 75 MPH even if it went over a cliff. The jurist replied: "Son, I believe the deputy because the radar doesn't lie! Guilty!"

When I was a rookie, my partner and I drove by the worst accident scene I ever saw in my 35 year career: A couple of guys in a Corvette decided to take on the "Dip" at an estimated 90 MPH. Big mistake: They bottomed out and I imagine they flew through the air like an FA-18 that had been catapulted from a carrier deck. Only, instead of the wild blue yonder, these two went head-on into a big power pole. The fiber glass 'Vette literally disintegrated into a million pieces and burst into flames. The occupants were incinerated beyond recognition. That ruined their night; ditto for the first responders and it also made a huge impression on me, I'll tell you! But, that only happens somewhere else, right? Something like this would never occur in or around a reasonably tranquil university campus, right? Wrong!

****

S-10 vs. California Oak

I copied the radio traffic while in my office: Menlo Park PD was in pursuit of a white Chevrolet S-10 pick-up on the ECR. *I hope they don't come on campus*! However, the very next transmission piqued my interest:

"Attention, all Stanford units! The suspect vehicle in now on Palm Drive heading toward Campus Drive." All of our patrol units were covering each other's transmissions, so it was difficult to determine what was going on. Suddenly, the picture became clear:

"Radio, Q-14; the pursuit just turned onto Campus Drive going the wrong way!" A few seconds later, the same unit advised Communications that the suspect had hit a tree and that Fire and Rescue was needed—Code 3. At this point, I figured that I had better get over there and hoped that none of our personnel was directly involved in this incident.

As I got in my car, the word one never wants to hear came over the airways:

"Palo Alto, Q-14, Code 4, the suspect appears to be DOA!"

As I pulled up to the scene, I saw what was left of that mid-sized pick-up truck when it collided broadside into an old growth CA oak tree. . . The mini truck looked as if a bomb went off inside its cab! The sole occupant, as reported, was indeed dead. Very dead! This poor kid was sitting upright against the tree trunk and his legs spread

180 degrees apart. How the victim wound-up in that position is something that only God will know. The impact obviously split his pelvis. It was a horrible sight, even for this old cop who had seen his share of blood and guts—I never liked and never looked forward to seeing death, especially when a human being was mangled like this! No one, not even a car thief, deserved such a horrendous end of life...

Mustang vs. Oak II

I told you that story about the Monta Vista dip as a prelude to what occurred on a beautiful morning on Junipero Serra Boulevard, which borders the west side of the Stanford campus: Another young man, who had a "need for speed," apparently wanted to see how fast he could go in his modified Ford 5.0L Mustang, equipped with Nitrous Oxide (NO2), which can provide an engine with up to an additional 50 horsepower! According to a CHP senior traffic investigator, he went *very* fast—over 100 MPH! The kid didn't realize there was a deep depression in the roadway. In effect, the unsuspecting driver was destined to launch his Mustang like that carrier aircraft I just mentioned! When he reached maximum velocity, the car went airborne, bottomed out and careened out of control into a huge oak tree alongside the highway. Needless to say, the youngster was killed instantly. WARNING: THE FOLLOWING DESCRIPTION IS NOT FOR THE FAINT OF HEART. IF YOU ARE SQUEAMISH OR A MINOR, STOP READING AND GO TO THE NEXT CHAPTER!

When I got to the scene, several of our deputies were ashen faced and some looked like they were going to be sick to their stomachs. On approaching what was left of the wreck, I saw that the victim had suffered a horrific head wound: A six inch diameter tree limb had pierced his face and protruded through poor soul's skull, with one of his eyeballs staring at me. That was eerie! Save for the two men I cut out of a small plane which had crashed into a house in the late 1960s, this was the second worst damage to a person I had ever experienced. I was done and couldn't wait to get the hell out of there.

There's an old saying among Crystal Meth users: "Speed kills slowly." However, in the crashes I have seen, I say: "Speed kills instantaneously!"

CHAPTER TWENTY FOUR

Zeta Psi aka"Zetes"

Strike One: The Pond Caper

B-4 THE PENINSULA TIMES TRIBUNE, Friday, October 9, 1981 ***

Woman Injured at campus party

STANFORD—A 20-year-old woman student from Mills College in Oakland was injured Thursday night when she was thrown into a hot tub (sic: it was actually a 3-4 foot deep pond in the patio) during a party at the Zeta Psi fraternity at 353 Campus Drive.

The Mills student was admitted to Stanford University Hospital for treatment of a possible concussion and neck and back injuries. However, she was found not to be seriously hurt and was released this morning to her home in Oakland, according to Capt. Raoul Niemeyer of the Stanford police.

The incident occurred about 11:30 p.m. Thursday during a large party at the Zeta Psi house. The Mills student was apparently talking to or arguing with a couple of men when another man threw her into the hot tub, Niemeyer said. She was fully clothed.

Niemeyer said that police are investigating to determine exactly how the incident occurred and who was involved in it.

This incident was the beginning of the end of the Zeta Psi fraternity's occupancy of the coveted residence at 353 Campus Drive—no more room with a view of Lake Lagunita for these boys! After an investigation, the university suspended the fraternity for three years on October 29th and ordered the house to be emptied by the end of fall quarter. Stay tuned, there's more. . .

Strike Two: The Paddock Caper

Dispatcher: "911, what is your emergency?"

Male Caller: "*Habla Espanol?*"

Dispatcher: "No Habla Espanol. Is there anyone there who can speak English?"

A conversation in Spanish between the male caller and a female in the background ensues.

Female: "*Hola, I speak poquito Ingles.*"

Dispatcher: "What is the emergency?"

Female: "Hombres cry for help."

Dispatcher: "Where?"

Female: "*Alli', en el caballo*—corral."

Dispatcher: "Do you mean where the horses are kept?"

Female: "Si, Si! Horse barn. You come, *muy rapido!*"

Dispatcher: "OK, stay on the phone; Q-16, Palo Alto; Code 2."

Deputy: "Q-16, bye; go ahead with your traffic."

Dispatcher: "An X reports a 10-67 in progress, somewhere near the horse barn; are you familiar with that 10-20?"

Deputy: "That would be 'affirm-a-tative!'—Responding."

Dispatcher: "Q-16, be advised that the X is Hispanic and speaks very limited English."

Deputy: "'Affirmatative.' I'm familiar with the caretaker, Mario, and his wife and speak a little Spanish, myself..."

****

This deputy was none other than Michael "Da Shadow" Seamons, a great friend whom I got to know well while at the old

S/O Personnel and Training. Mike had been an aspiring radio broadcaster while a teenager in the Midwest. God gave him a beautiful, melodious baritone voice that was captivating—the chicks really dug it! He had a program in which he featured the "Nifty 50s" tunes of the day. At the conclusion of each broadcast, he worked-in a clever piece, which went something like this:

"Who knows what evil lurks in the hearts of man?"

"Da Shadow Do!" (Sinister laugh)

Bingo: A handle was born. . .

At that time, I was heavily involved in making training video tapes for the department as well as for Community Relations programs. Once I learned of Mike's background in radio, he was a natural commentator for our upcoming projects. Because we planned to reach out to the Hispanic community, I selected Mike to accompany me to an intensive Spanish conversational course held in Ensenada, Baja, Mexico. We were able to wrangle an S/O unmarked car, A 70s model, American Motors, "Matador"—how appropriate—but it was just a "Matadog" to me. . .

Before leaving for Mexico, I jury-rigged an 8-track stereo system into our green bomb so we would have our tunes for the 14 hour trek. I realize that most of you contemporary readers might only have a vague recollection of the 8-track stereo system; however, it was state of the art in those days. . . Mike loved Neil Diamond, so we had a stack of his cartridges; me, being the R&B guy, I brought a bunch of Motown hits—my favorite being the newly released side by "War," which featured the smash hit, "Cisco Kid." The speakers crackled with "Ceesco Keed was a friend of mine, he drink whiskey Pancho drink the wine," as we cruised *Calle Primero, en El Centro, Ensenada*. We were the Norte Americano dudes, man!

It didn't take me long to realize that Da Shadow was going to be culturally challenged in this south of the border experience: As we were low-riding down the street trying to find our way to the Hotel *Montemar,* Mike commented:

"Jeez, these people sure seem to love their licorice down here!"

"Whaddya, mean," I asked, as I was truly befuddled.

"Well," he clarified, "I've counted over 6 licorice stores in just this block!"

Then, it hit me like a Mike Tyson left hook:

"Mike, those are not Licorice stores; they are *"LICORES"* stores—as in Booze, Tequila—LIQUOR, *Cerveza*?

We both had a good belly laugh, but I knew that speaking the *Espanol* was not going to be Da Shadow's forte. . . Indeed, for after 10 days of dawn to dusk schooling, Shadow could master but a couple of phrases, which we found were necessary in the nightclubs:

"Dos cervezas, por favor! (Two beers, please—and Mike didn't drink—glad he was our designated driver...).

"Quiero bailar?" (Do you wanna dance?)

****

And now, Da Shadow was responding to someone calling for help with Spanish speaking R/Ps? Frightening!

10-97

It was a brutally cold night. It was December 4th, 1981 at 1:00AM; it was 28 degrees Fahrenheit and damp when Q-16 arrived. Once he got out of the patrol car, Deputy Seamons could hear cries for help apparently coming from the paddock area. Mario came out of his bungalow and frantically pointed to the corral; Mike broke into a run and sloshed through the sludge that one would expect to find in an area where horses are trained. When he got to the source of distress, Shadow found two young men, clad only in their skivvies, face down in the muck, with their arms tightly trussed behind their backs with surgical tape. The brutal bastards who did this must have been into S&M or something, for they prevented their quarry from turning upright, by the inserting of a long piece of lumber in the small of the victims backs. It gets better: The clowns who engineered this form of torture scooped out basins in the excrement and filled them with beer and pee—the drill for the unfortunates was to keep their faces out of the disgusting cocktail, or drown—no easy task when the kids were bombed out of their gourds in below freezing weather! But not for Mario, clearly, this caper would have gone down as Stanford's first hazing murder!

Once extricated, our cops tried to elicit more information about this incident from the victims, but they became very uncooperative and would only give the investigators their names, ranks and horsepower: These Zeta Psi pledges didn't want this investigation going any further—period! Getting the story from this crew was like extracting molars—the typical Frat "stonewall." But, undaunted perseverance prevailed as the deputies ascertained that the paddock stunt was a culmination of an all night event of boozing and hazing—aptly dubbed *Pledge Hell Week*. At one point, these two initiates were forced to walk around on the roof of the house sporting only candles for illumination. One of the pledges was legally blind, so how they survived that ordeal in their drunken stupor is beyond comprehension! However, the "hazees" refused to divulge the names of the masochists who committed this crime—one of the most sadistic and bizarre stunts I had seen in my career, up to that point.

The Inquiry

I had known about the Zeta Psi fraternity long before I got into cop work: In the early 1960s I met a Stanford football player who was a Zete. At that time, a number of gridders belonged to that fraternity. These ruffians were the scourge on campus and earned the title of "Animal House." I heard of raucous toga parties—one in which urinals were ripped off the walls and tossed onto the dance floor—assaults (muggings and groping of females), brutal hazing such as "running the gauntlet," going through the "mill", which consisted of firm ass paddling. But, nothing that I had heard of even approached the level of this paddock stunt. Having this knowledge beforehand enabled me to conclude that the Zete house was a potential powder keg!

My research revealed that the Zeta Psi fraternity is the first of the Greek clubs at Stanford, organized in 1891. Like most campus groups in the "good ol' days," there was a considerable amount of partying—behind rivers of alcohol, but I couldn't find any record of blatant violence, or out-of-control antics in the historical documents I perused. Zeta Psi has been characterized by unnamed university officials as "a group of bright young men, most of whom were offspring of wealthy Southern California families." While this outfit was into "gentleman sports" such as tennis, soccer, and *lacrosse*— once described as a "silly FN college activity" by stand-up comedian, George Carlin—"Zetes tended to believe that they were above community standards."

It appears the Zetes' behavior began to go askew circa 1957 when the house was put on a one-year suspension for a series of indiscretions: Residential Education took a very dim view of the rascals who streaked through a library, and I suspect there were other matters never divulged to the public. This frat was disciplined again in 1959 and was given the boot for three years in 1964— probably in the wake of one of those wild toga parties I spoke of. Save for the ubiquitous wild campus parties, all seemed quiet on the Zete front from 1974 until October 8, 1981, when they lit the fuse to the powder keg in "The Pond Caper." This incident was deemed a simple battery, although it could have resulted in a fractured skull or worse! Three Zetes were identified as the perps and were subsequently charged; the DA's Office later dropped the case in "the interest of justice."

The University was really on the ball on this one, as they summarily announced that the Zetes would have to find other accommodations for the next 3 years! Undeterred by this expulsion, the group continued their nefarious ways by miring two of their own in the horse *ka-ka*. . . an incident I was determined to get to the bottom of.

The Inquisition

Backed-up by the biggest and toughest cops on our roster, we stormed the house a few days later, in an effort to elicit some admissions or other incriminating evidence from the president and his cabal. No such luck—even with our show of force. Although I wanted to beat these kids within an inch of their collective lives, the Zetes knew damn well we couldn't and wouldn't administer a course of street corner justice, so they basically gave us the finger! By this time, the collaborators had their ducks in a row, as Mommy and Daddy had retained counsel for their darlings. But, that was OK. I believed in the theory that there was always more than one way to "skin a Zete!" After exchanging un-pleasantries with our hostile friends, we stomped out of the place vowing: "We'll Be Baaaack!" As we exited the living room, I couldn't help but notice their ceiling decorations: About a million pencils that they had apparently thrown into the drywall. Can you imagine grown young men, members of Stanford's oldest fraternity at one of the most prestigious universities in the world, having so much time on their hands?

One of our sergeants, who had some contacts in the Zete's inner circle, confided that after our little séance, the culprits thought I was a "Big Adam Henry!" Furthermore, the Sarge said they *really* hated me! Awwww, now that really broke my heart, being the sensitive individual that I am. . .

Disposition

Dogged police work and "other methods" netted five individuals who were actively involved in the Paddock Caper. The "Zete Six," as I called them, were arrested and booked, albeit a year after the fact. Had the Paddock Pair been injured and cooperative with the investigation, the culprits could have been beefed with felonies. The "victims" opined that they weren't hurt, **so what was the big deal?** The Frat insisted that they left a monitor at the scene so the pledges wouldn't be in danger. So, where in the hell was he? Since the caretakers were awakened in the wee hours by the pair's cries for help, if a member of this elite group was truly at the scene, he certainly would have realized that the boys were in distress and relieved them of their bindings and suffering, right? But, then again, alcohol often works in mysterious ways...

Here's the Big Deal

During the 70's, fraternity hazing became very popular again on college campuses throughout the U.S. In 1978, three pledges were stuffed into the trunk of a brother's car, ordered to consume a pint of bourbon, a six-pack of beer, and a fifth of wine during a half hour ride back to their house. It was a frigid winter day in upstate New York. By the time they got to the Frat, one of the young men was unconscious and subsequently died of acute alcohol poisoning and exposure. The other two kids were rushed to the hospital in critical condition, but survived. Moreover, according to a San Francisco Examiner article by Scott Winokur (dated 12/20/1981), "at least 65 kids died (as a result of violent hazing) since the turn of the century (20th), and 21 more have died since" the 1978 tragedy.

There was another horrific example in 1984 at California State University at Chico. A group of guys from the Tau Gamma Theta fraternity commandeered a couple of pledges, blindfolded them, forced them to consume large quantities of hooch, and then kicked them out of their cars, way out in the boondocks. These kids were totally unfamiliar with the vast rural/agricultural area and were left to their own devices to get back to campus any way they could. It was pitch black out there, and the drunken kids had absolutely no idea where they were. One of the pair found a paved country road and trudged along in the darkness. All of a sudden, he heard the roar of engines and saw two pairs of headlights coming his way at a very high rate of speed. The pledge moved toward the pavement and attempted to flag down these vehicles, which were coming like bats out of hell! These idiots were engaged in a full-blown drag race at speeds estimated to be 100 mph! That, my friends, is the last thing their "sacrificial lamb" heard or saw, as he was struck by one of the cars and crushed like an egg. So, who were those morons in the hot rods? The dead kid's boozed-up frat brothers...

So, is there any question what the "Big Deal" is now? In fact, the California legislature thought that hazing was becoming such a "Big Deal" that they hardened-up the anti-hazing sections in the Education Code, from the paltry $500 fine and six month jail term, to a "bullet" (1 year) and a $5,000 fine! The statute prohibits "personal degradation and disgrace, resulting in physical and mental harm," with a proviso that fraternities and universities publish notices of the penalties. Unfortunately, for those of us who wanted severe prosecution in the Paddock case, the revised law didn't take effect until midnight, January 1st, 1982.

Zete's Farewell Message: "Bye-Bye and Up Yours!"

As I previously said, on October 29th, the Director of the Fraternity Row advised the Zeta Psi fraternity that the Zetes were persona *non grata* and were to vacate their premises at the end of Fall Quarter, December 19th, 1981. They were sternly invited seek other accommodations—OFF CAMPUS! But, our pals at 353 Campus Drive weren't about to go quietly—was I surprised?? When their sentence was announced by Diana Conklin, the incomparable Director of the Row, you might say that the boys were more than a little pissed-off. . .That night, a member's car tore up the turf and a large section of a nearby fence. As per the norm with these cats, the vehicle's owner vaguely remembered loaning his car to some dude at a party, but "honestly" had no clue as to who the person was. Yeah, ah-huh. Coincidentally, the Res. Ed. office was thrashed. Wonder who did that? In detective work, investigators tend to focus on suspects who have motive and opportunity. But, it takes three strikes before they are out, so without an eyeball on the sneaks or other credible evidence, you are basically SOL (Surely out of Luck). So, the bad boys who committed these juvenile antics avoided the justice system, at least for the time being—The Big Guy in the Sky will proctor the "scales" on "Judgment Day." But, one pinch out of three wasn't too bad: The good guys bagged two students stealing a sign that night, and one was a Zete—Go figure!

Then, on December 18th, day minus one to "K-Day" (Kicked to the Curb), the boys on the lake celebrated their demise in an almost ritualistic, Potlatch-like ceremony: They hauled their beautiful redwood bar and stools out to the site of their tailspin from grace—the dreaded "Dunking Pond"—and torched their prized possessions. Observers said they thought the Big Game bonfire at Lake Lag was back, as the flames and embers soared over 20 feet into the heavens. The next day, they were gone from campus. And, believe it or not, the house was the cleanest that Row maintenance had ever seen, save for redwood charcoal in the Pond from Hell.

Jurisprudence?

On June 14, 1982, the Zete Six were assembled into the chambers of a North County Municipal judge, where they pled guilty to misdemeanor hazing. The gracious jurist sentenced the men to 100 hours of supervised community service work. If any of the defendants failed to complete their sentences, the judge promised that he would order a trial for any malingerer. In addition, each defendant was ordered to report to the authorities at Stanford that "all hazing has been eliminated"...

Needless to say, the officials that were close to this case weren't enamored with this disposition. It was less than a slap on the wrist, in my view—an opinion shared by many others. The two North County Court judges were always honorable, decent men, who always attempted to hand down fair sentences, especially with kids who had never run afoul of the law. And, I applauded their judgment in most of the cases that we presented over my 25 year tenure. But, in this matter, I feel that the Bench really missed an important opportunity to send a clear and vital message that society would not tolerate dangerous stunts involving the hazing of our youth. 100 hours of volunteer work certainly didn't underscore that message, in the minds of many. This non-sentence also illustrated that if you are a member of the privileged class and can afford good lawyers, you're going to beat the rap! However, the University *upped the ante* and banished the Zetes from campus, forever.

Strike Three—You're Outta Here!

Despite being socially banished from the campus for life, this group of mavericks decided to hold a ruckus "Rush Party" anyway. The venue was the picnic grounds near the old Lake Lag Boathouse. These miscreants would do anything in their power to defy authority and stick it in your eye. I'll bet most of this crew went on to become lawyers or politicians, or both. . .

The first inkling we had of this event was that someone reported a potential "rushee" was missing. The reporting parties said they searched the area, but were unable to locate the young man. We began our search at first light, the day following the unauthorized Zete party. We had 15-20 people beating the bushes around Lake Lag. Later on, searchers got a boat and began dragging the lake, as we felt that he might have gone into the water and drowned. At first, this was hard to believe as the man was a big muscular kid with a strong swimming background. I seem to recall that he was on the Stanford Water Polo team—or, at least was a prospect. The missing man, I'll call David, was a sophomore from Oregon. He had competed in a number of sports in high school and was lean and mean. According to my sources, David was a damn good kid, as well.

As more information trickled in, I was afraid that this was going to be a recovery operation: Witnesses said that David was assigned to be the bartender at this bash. This was the bar from Hell, I was told: There were several kegs of beer and every variety of hard liquor known to man—and lots of "Te-Kill-Ya!" Observers said that the Zete hierarchy typically wanted to test the "metal" of potential inductees. Thus, they would encourage pledges to "Man-up" and throw volumes of alcohol down the hatch. In David's case, he was putting down shots of Jose Cuervo with a powerful "back" of Foster's Australian Lager (4.9% alcohol), like these cocktails were going out of style! With the "Jose" running anywhere from 86 to 90 Proof, you do the math. This combination could put down an African elephant in short order!

Despite an intensive search by the boat crew, the missing student was not found. Where could he have gone? Everyone hoped that he simply left the area in an intoxicated state, became disoriented and was unable to find his way back to campus. I didn't buy that theory; I figured he was somewhere in the lake.

The next day, we enlisted the assistance of the S/O's helicopter. After a few passes, they unfortunately spotted what appeared to be a body just below the surface. We dispatched a boat and recovered the young man. What a tragedy! Here was a big, good looking kid who would never celebrate his 21st birthday. I shed a silent tear and vowed to get the person(s) responsible for this senseless death!

When I saw David's lifeless form, I couldn't see any visible signs of foul play; however, that determination would be made by the Medical Examiner. I thought the young man probably knew he was very inebriated and waded into the lake to sober-up. He might have stepped in a hole or tripped on something and went under. Due to his condition, he was most likely disoriented and then drowned. Later interviews revealed that a few of the attendees saw David walk into the water, but no one had the foresight to keep an eye on him—like in the "Paddock Caper."

The Coroner later confirmed that our victim died of drowning, and that his blood alcohol level was .23. At that time, any BA over .18 was considered to cause impairment. Now, we had to set our sights on who furnished this student with the alcohol.

While I knew the Zetes were pretty "con-wise"—based on my previous dealings with that bunch—they really "flubbed-the-dub" on this one: I guess in their panic to find their missing "pledge," they failed to clean-up the crime scene. The area was littered with empty beer and liquor bottles; however, the most significant pieces of evidence were the beer kegs, which our deputies wisely seized. On the bottom of the two kegs we found seals identifying the store where the beer was purchased. Bingo! My detectives made a beeline for the liquor emporium in Atherton and obtained the name of the person who bought the booze, as he had to furnish a driver's license; the proprietor recorded the subject's information in his little black book. A check of the student directory matched the suspect's name and provided an off-campus address. More inquiry revealed that the

21 year old who got the "poison" was, indeed, a member of the Zeta Psi fraternity—again, why was I not surprised? Detectives then sped to his address, located the kid and brought him to the station for a little chat.

When I entered the interview room, the kid appeared to be shell-shocked; he shook like a street inebriate going through the D.T.s (delirium tremens). I told the young man to just listen! I immediately launched into a diatribe of what evidence we had tying him into the unfortunate and untimely death of a fellow student. Further, I said that I knew the Zete leaders directed him to get the booze, and that he was merely being a good soldier, but that didn't absolve him of culpability in this case. I urged the kid to give up the guys who told him to get the alcohol and furnished him with the money to do so. Lastly, I told the shaken young man that although I couldn't promise anything, if he cooperated with me, I would advise the DA and Presiding Judge of his willingness to make this awful tragedy right. I then read the Miranda Warnings to him. He wisely waived his rights and sang like a canary. I complimented him for his courage.

The ring leaders of this ill-fated party were quickly rounded-up and arrested. All of the defendants, who I am told were contrite, had top notch attorneys so they were able to get a negotiated plea agreement. The Zete officers spent a few days in custody, as I recall, and received substantial fines, as well as long probation terms. Once again, we were very disappointed in the judicial outcome. The Zeta Psi wild bunch was subsequently banished from the campus for life, but continued to thrive off campus. In the interim and until I retired in 1999, I can't remember a single instance where a Zete was involved in any serious wrongdoing. So, maybe they learned their lesson, after all.

Post Script

While the hazing related death of Stanford student, David, in 1987 was the first documented incident since the University was established in 1891, the publication Sandstone and Tile by Karen Bartholomew and Claude Brinegar (a Stanford Historical Society publication, Winter, 2000, Volume 24. No.1) casts doubt on my statement, as you will see. The authors wrote primarily about Encina Hall, Stanford's Grand Hotel, which I found to be more like a "Star Chamber." This was a men's dorm and the occupants were a bunch of hard cases! Wasn't the Zeta Psi bunch Stanford's first fraternity, formed in 1891? Hmmm? You need to realize that when Stanford University opened its doors, there was no tuition. The University welcomed all who could satisfy the entry requirements. While some of these students may have come from families of means, many did not. There were a lot of tough ol' boys from the Western United States, who had grown up on the frontier and were apparently as tough as nails. If you've ever read any Dime Novels or seen any old Western movies, you will understand that many of those characters had serious mean streaks in them. Those ruffians loved to prove how tough they were, often, by showing-up weaker folks by pulling pranks on an unsuspecting victim and getting good belly laughs from their cohorts!

And, pranks are what the "Encina Thugs" did; some of their antics were very brutal and dangerous. It seemed that almost everyone (including the administration) was intimidated by the core of these pranksters. One of the stunts these nut jobs pulled was hurling missiles—be they tiles, rocks, bricks, firecrackers, water balloons, chairs, even toilets—down from the upper floors on unsuspecting people who were merely entering the building. One idiot indiscriminately fired 25 pistol rounds out of a window, without regard for the safety of his fellow colleagues; his sobriety or lack thereof is unknown to me, but this sounded like a scene from Tombstone, AZ, circa 1862. . . How anyone wasn't killed or seriously injured is a mystery to me. The rowdies of that era made the mischievous DUs of the 1980s seem like well mannered choir boys. . .

One of the most egregious forms of harassment to lower classmen was "tubbing." This outrageous act made "Water Boarding" seem more like a Navy SEAL training exercise by comparison—especially since there was no medical team standing by. . . As the name implies, the purveyors of this form of cruelty would fill-up a bathtub and plunge the victim's head under the water until bubbles appeared, indicating that the poor kid was simply trying to breathe! While the controversial water boarding technique was designed to elicit intelligence information from high value al Qaeda operatives who killed nearly 3,000 innocents in the 9-11 attack of the World Trade Center, what in the hell would have possessed the Encina men of yesteryear to put fellow students through a near death experience? This practice came to a screeching halt when the University removed all tubs and replaced them with showers.

"Hazing is Un-American"

By 1907, Stanford's first president, David Starr Jordan, began to exercise more control over the renegades who had been running ripshod over underclassmen at Encina Hall. One of the most heartfelt passages of Bartholomew and Brinegar's work was a letter written to University President Jordan in 1911. It was from a grieving mother who had recently lost her son to illness. The bereaved lady wrote that her son had entered Stanford in the fall of 1910, and had endured repeated hazings, including numerous tubbing episodes. The freshman was chronically ill thereafter with continuous colds. He never complained, Mom wrote, and said that this "practice was common for newcomers." She finished the letter by writing:

"He broke down completely in April—with diabetes—and came home three weeks before the close of the year and died the 18th of June. The trouble began with hazing. Can you not prevent this treatment of newcomers this year?"

Mrs. Caroline A. Miller

For me, that said it all. However, further research revealed that this practice of hazing has been alive and well in colleges and universities since the 1838, for God's sake. In an Internet blog authored by Hank Nuwer, I was stunned to learn that between 1838 and 2008, there have been 148 documented deaths of pledges in suspected hazing incidents. Almost all of these cases involved excessive alcohol abuse; the causes of death of the students ranged from acute alcohol poisoning, drowning, stabbing, gunshot, vehicle collisions, freezing—you name it. This is insanity! University and

College administrators need to step-up and really ride herd on their fraternities and sororities—although most of the tragedies involved males. In addition, the police and sheriff's departments need to take these events seriously: They must initiate thorough investigations, collect all evidence, fully document the incidents, and present the cases to their District Attorney's Offices with vigor. Also, the District Attorneys must tirelessly pursue the ringleaders behind these tragedies and bring them to justice! I believe that taking a no-nonsense approach to hazing will turn this vicious cycle around.

CHAPTER TWENTY FIVE

Farm Funnies

415 Neighbors: As recalled by Sergeant Philip Love.

It was a typical weekday night on the Farm—dark and not much going on. At approximately 2300 hours, Radio called:

"FC-3, check-out a report of a noisy neighbor on Pampas Lane."

"Palo Alto, FC-3; *Confirm* Pampas Lane?"

"Affirmative, FC-3! The R/P states that his neighbor is playing his radio too loud and won't turn it down."

Hmmmm, Love mused, *that's strange: Save for the Stanford Federal Credit Union, the Food Service facility and the Bing Nursery School, there are no residences on that street; it's just a dead-end roadway in the midst of a eucalyptus grove!* But, the good sergeant proceeded anyway and upon turning onto the street, he began illuminating the area with his roof mounted spotlight. Just as he knew: *There are NO houses here; not even a stray cat was about.* However, as Love idled along, he espied two large dumpsters alongside the road. Sgt. Love radioed that he was 10-97; he got out of his unit and cautiously approached the trash containers, ever vigilant of a possible ambush, although in his experienced mind, figured this was probably a prank.

The Sergeant then rapped on the wall of the dumpster with his night stick:

"Come in," a voice from within replied.

"What? You kiddin'?" answered the Sergeant.

Love threw open the cover and discovered that a transient had setup housekeeping in this rancid, foul smelling dumpster!

"Did you call the police?" The sergeant quizzed.

"Yes I did, sir. My "neighbor" was playing his music so loudly that I couldn't sleep. I asked him several times to turn it down, but he wouldn't."

"I'll take care of it, go back to sleep," the good sergeant retorted.

With that, Love went next door and beat on the side with his baton and barked: "You, in there, keep the noise down or I'll be back and you will not like that a bit! Be gone by morning!"

With that, Sgt. Love got back into his patrol car, radioed-in that all was quiet and was off to the next activity. Never a dull moment while on patrol on the Farm. . .

Prunes

My door was open. John McMullen strode in like he owned the darn joint!

"Hey, A-tree. I got a good one for ya!"

"Yeah, so what's up John?" I inquired.

"Well, you used to work agricultural crimes when you were in the S/O," he reminded. "So, whaddya got when somebody rips-off prunes?"

"Prunes?" I asked. "Is this some kind of a test for your old Captain, or is this going to be on your Sergeant's exam?"

"You know Mario over at the Faculty Club?" I nodded in the affirmative. "He says that somebody, probably on his staff, is stealing prunes—hundreds of dollars worth," the detective declared.

"Why in the world would someone want that many prunes unless they were constipated or something," I quipped. "Let's have a look-see in my brand new unabridged Penal Code," I bragged, as I reached back to retrieve the source book from my bookcase. (The Chief always got the A Units the high dollar editions and we would pass the year-old books down to the grunts—that really ticked them off.)

"Used to be, when I worked South County, ya had to snag bushels of fruits, nuts, and vegetables—valued at fifty bucks or more—before it was a felony, but let's see what's up these days," I pontificated, as I thumbed my way to the theft section.

"Ah, here it is" I proffered, "Grand Theft (to wit a felony), 487 (1) (A):

When domestic fowls, avocados, citrus or deciduous fruits, or other fruits, vegetables, nuts, artichokes, or other farm crops are taken of a value exceeding one hundred dollars ($100)"

"Man, it's gone up to a hundred bucks! Now, that's inflation, but still a helluva lot of prunes; better check this out, John. And, if you can prove intent, you might be able to squeeze in a 4-5-9."

"Yeah, A-tree, I was thinking we might be able to work this as a burglary," this whiz kid replied.

The Prune Sleuth Returnith

After lunch, Detective John caught me in the hallway; he was nearly doubled over in hysterics! We called in Sgt. Love, filed into my office and closed the door. I had a feeling that this was NOT going to be a conversation that would be for public consumption!

John related that he went over to the Faculty Club and caught Mario just before the lunch crowd had arrived. Mario was of German descent, and spoke with a very heavy accent—almost like Colonel Klink, of the famed TV series "Hogan's Heroes"—But what he lacked in perfect enunciation of the English language, he made up for with his professionalism and charm. That's why he had been the Club's Manager/*Maitre d'hotel* for a million years. This facility was very hoity-toity, and considered one of the finest of the fine dining establishments in the Palo Alto area. You had to be a faculty or senior administrative staff member to belong. Getting an invite there was a rare privilege! However, it took a very special person to be able to deal with some of the patrons who dined in this emporium, especially when they were hungry and in a hurry. This attribute was definitely an art form, and Mario mastered it!

Now, my Detective, John, although sometimes a hand grenade behind the scenes, could be extremely serious and a real *pro* when it came to dealing with the public, especially VIPs. He also had a dead pan manner of speaking—unlike his volatile mentor—which made him an extremely effective interviewer: Like Sgt. Friday of the Hollywood Division, he wanted the facts, Ma'am, nothing but the facts... So, here's how this crime scene investigation went:

Detective: "Hi Mario, I'm Detective McMullen; I'd like to see what's being stolen from your kitchen."

Mario: "Oh zess, Zhon, followz me!" The manager took the lead, and proceeded to the galley's pantry.

Detective: "So, Mario why are they stealing so many prunes?"

Mario: "Prunes? Vhat are zoo speakin' zabout? I zaid 'PRUNZ,' 'PRUNZ'!!" Undoubtedly Mario thought: *Zoo dumkoff!*

Still confused, the detective asked the manager to show him exactly What, Why, and Where. With that, Mario led my man into a large walk-in cold box.

"Zee," He exclaimed while pointing to several large cardboard cartons: "PRUNZ, PRUNZ!"

Choking back laughter, John nodded and smiled:

"Ohhhh, I see, Mario, PRAWNS. Jumbo PRAWNS!" And, at 10 bucks a pound, it wouldn't take very many of these boxes to make this caper a big-time felony!

In a subsequent Code 5, my guys bagged the "Prune Bandit". They caught the fool red handed as he was loading cartons of those delicacies into his van, at O-Dark 30. It seems that this employee was augmenting his Faculty Club janitor's salary, with a day-job—selling purloined seafood!

Every time I attended a social function at the Faculty Club, these enormous *langostas* were served: They were arranged on ornate silver bowls, which were filled with crushed ice, dipping sauces and sliced lemons. The "PRUNZ" dangled from the lip of the bowls. After my 15th one—God those things were fantastic—I chuckled and applauded Detective John for solving the "Great Prune Caper!!"

Ivory's Revenge: From an anonymous source, who will forever remain so!

As I have written thoughout this work, Stanford University had more than their share of crazies, street urchins, and various folks who were "a can short;" these unkempt individuals continually wandered around the campus, pan handling, crashing anywhere they desired and mooching food, which made their presence unwanted. Obviously, our lads were always responding to complaints about these forsaken souls. One of our regulars was a transient I'll call Peter. Peter can best be described as a Dr. Frankenstein experiment gone horribly wrong! His eyes looked like the goofy doctor initially forgot them, then at the last minute, realized his omission and stuck them into the poor man's melon in a haphazard manner!

After many calls and cars had been dispatched to eradicate this pest and remove him forthwith, one of our "finest" agreed to give him a ride off campus to Highway 101 so that Peter could hitchhike to San Jose. It should be noted that this tactic was quite common among all law enforcement agencies back in the day: When I worked the mean streets in the Burbank District of San Jose, I'd dump as many drunks as I could in San Jose PD's jurisdiction. . .

Another SUDPS source revealed that on numerous occasions, he dumped Peter miles away from campus only to have him show-up again within the hour. The guy was like a homing pigeon, for God's sake! Well, when the cops—as far away as South San Francisco—found out that our troopers dumped Peter in their jurisdiction, they simply brought him back!

Following good police procedure, Deputy X searched Peter's meager belongings, patted him down and stuck him into the cage compartment. Peter was let out at Embarcadero and the 101 on-ramp. The deputy continued onto southbound 101 and as he rounded the corner, he heard some rattling around in the rear of the patrol car. He pulled over and found a brand new bar of Ivory soap, which had somehow fallen out of Peter's stuff. Being the good guy that he was, our mystery man got back onto Oregon Expressway and circled around to where he had left Peter. Deputy X spotted Peter standing by the roadway thumbing a ride. He lowered his passenger side window—yes, we had electric windows in those days—and as he rolled by the crazy dude he hollered: "Hey Peter, here's your soap; make sure you use it!" With that, the deputy tossed the bar out of the window toward the hitchhiker. Unbelievably, the man had no hands: He muffed the catch and the cake of Ivory smacked him in his gourd! The resultant impact sent poor Peter into the ice plant—down for the count! By the time Deputy X saw this *faux pas* in his rear view mirror, he was already on 101 with no opportunity to stop and back up. Oooooooops. . .

When Deputy X had reached San Antonio Road, CHP intercepted the itinerant—it's illegal to hitchhike on CA freeways. The CHP called Palo Alto Communications and advised that Peter reported a police officer had knocked him out with a bar of soap. The silence on the air was deafening until the mics began clicking repeatedly, amplified by numerous "pants rubs. . ." The CHP officer added: "But, then this guy is 51-50!" Indeed he was. Sometimes the best of intentions go horribly wrong!

Febreze, please!

Detective John McMullen had just returned from the Reid and Associates School of Interview and Interrogation. This is an excellent forum to re-train police investigators in the art of contemporary communication with "persons of interest"—formerly known as probable or possible suspects. In cop work, *everyone's a suspect*... But, on a more serious note, in the late 70s and 80s, the police community began to realize that the archaic methods of interrogation—good cop/bad cop doing their routine, or the "Sipowicz" model—the hard-ass detective on the TV show "NYPD Blue," slapping guys around and threatening them within an inch of their life—simply didn't work! A famous polygrapher, John Reid, of Chicago PD, figured this out. Granted, he had the benefit of some form of technology, the controversial lie detector, but it's what Reid gleaned in pre and post poly interviews that proved one could get more information from people with a bit of honey rather than a poke in the snoot. After Mr. Reid retired, he formed a consortium and created lists of questions and answers, and hypothetical scenarios which tended to separate the innocents from persons of interest, who might warrant a closer look by investigators.

After several years of trying to get skeptical law enforcement agencies to buy into the revolutionary system, most of the new guys who had been to the training thought that the system had a lot of possibilities—even some of the old hard-liners began to nod and admit this technique wasn't too bad after all. I took the course in the early '80s and was very impressed with some of the interesting methods an investigator could employ when interviewing people, so I mandated that all of my detectives—all three of them—take this course when it came to our area.

Detective McMullen was already a pretty good interviewer before taking the Reid Tech course; he had a calm and straightforward demeanor, and knew just how to talk to people as well as suspects without getting them all fired-up and uncooperative. So, I was confident that he'd be able to charm a viper after taking the Reid class. At our daily meeting, John announced that he wanted to talk to a violator about the theft of a license plate sticker: It seems that the person was stopped by patrol for improper placement of the registration sticker, which goes on the upper right corner of the license plate. This moron affixed it to the left hand side, thereby covering the month sticker that indicates when fees are due. The deputy checked further and learned that the sticker was reported stolen! Furthermore, the registration fees were nearly a year overdue. The kid steadfastly denied any knowledge of how that stolen sticker could have possibly have gotten onto his plate. So, the patrol deputy confiscated the plate, gave the driver a citation, and wrote a report which was forwarded upstairs for follow-up. No biggie, but certainly worth looking into as the violation is technically a felony.

It was my policy that before any interview of merit, all of our detectives had a roundtable discussion of the case and possible strategies that could be used by the investigator. We also brainstormed questions and scenarios so that the interviewer would have a written game plan, including an admonition to the person that he/she was at the police department of their own volition, could leave at any time, and that if he/she wanted a break or refreshments, we would gladly provide same. All of this "boilerplate stuff" was on our computers, so once the plan was devised, it only took a few minutes to crank out the material.

A lot of old timers had criticized the "structured" interview as they preferred to *shoot from the hip*. But, we crafted our interviews much like a pilot's check-list, so that no legal steps would be overlooked. It also helped our investigators (mostly inexperienced at that time in their careers) to keep on track and not lose their train of thought in the heat of battle, so to speak. This is exactly why the Courts required all law enforcement officers to *read* an arrestee's Miranda Warnings from a printed card—not because we cops are stupid—I heard that more than once during my tenure while reading a mope his "rights". . . Most importantly, the so-called structure of our system didn't preclude an interviewer from digression if it would lead to fruitful grounds.

I also insisted that all interviews be tape recorded—not only for our protection, but as an ever present reminder to the detective that he/she was "On Candid Camera, Baby!" As long as we played by the rules, we were in the blue; I never recall losing a case involving a tape recorded confession or admission once the defendant's attorney viewed the tapes! Albeit a "Mickey Mouse" video system, it worked. We had a camera rigged up in the Investigations Office, somewhat disguised in a big stereo speaker, which sat on the closets near the ceiling. We ran the wires over the hallway ceiling and into my office where the VCR and a 27" TV set were on a cart. We also had a covert microphone near the "love seat" (literally) were the subject would be placed.

Detective McMullen called his subject and asked him to come-on-down—and, he did! You could see on the screen that this young man was as nervous as a "lady of the night" in church. He was not a Stanford student for Stanford students would *never steal a license "stickee" then put it in the wrong place, now, would they??* John began with the boilerplate stuff in a very low key manner. The kid was twitching like a big red worm on a hook. During the interview phase, the detective asked basic questions such as name, rank and horsepower—stuff we already knew, but necessary to calm the subject and to establish a base, so the investigator would get an idea when the person might deviate from the truth. When John got into the nitty-gritty of the matter, the subject suddenly popped out of the chair and declared: "I'm Guilty, I'm Guilty. Can I please go to the bathroom?" John nodded and the kid shot out of the office and down to the head in a flash. At this point, I dashed into the interrogation room and said: "John, what happened?"

I figured it out in a nano-second:

"Jeez John, you scared the crap outta that kid. Damn, that's awful! Get some "Febreze, please! You're good, man, real good, and you didn't even get to the interrogation phase, for Chrissakes—Thank God for that or I might have had to call the Paramedics!"

Needless to say, McMullen spirited the soiled and humiliated person out of the building posthaste. Then, everybody on the second floor got into the act, opening all of the windows, spraying volumes of air freshener around, all the while cursing McMullen. Some brave soul took the love seat cushions out to the patio for a couple days of fresh air.

You Get Egg Roll with No. 3

Here's a story about foreign intrigue. . . An unnamed FBI agent, who I will dub "Secret Agent 001" called me and asked if I could help him locate a student, who was purportedly from the PRC (Peoples Republic of China). The Bureau was always on foreign students as they were heavy into counter intelligence then. Utilizing a source I had in the Registrar's Office, my friend quickly found the student named Zu Yangtze, indeed, from mainland China. He might have grown-up near one of the longest rivers on the planet as that's what his folks named him—but who knows. Zu was a graduate student majoring in physics (uh-oh), so that's why the "Feebs," as we local cops called them, were putting the jaundiced eyeball on this guy. Zu was living with another Asian grad-student in Escondido Village. It was no deep, dark secret that many of the PRC students, whom the university, and country, for that matter, welcomed with open arms, were master spies and soaked up propriety information like a "Sham Wow!" They weren't unlike our nation's chief law enforcement agency in that regard, as FBI agents would glean every bit of "intell" from us, then when we asked what the deal was all about, they came back with the old cloak 'n dagger reply: "If I told you, I'd have to kill you!" Oh, sorry I asked. But, I always made it perfectly clear if they were going to use our guys in an operation that might put our troops in jeopardy, I wanted a heads-up so I could brief the Chief for authorization. Don't get me wrong, I worked with several Federal agencies for decades and never got burned by them. I liked most of the agents whom I came in contact with. I worked-out in the gym with guys from the Palo Alto RA, and pitched for their softball team—somehow, although out-manned, we eeked out many wins against the powerful San Jose team. I trusted these folks and I believed the feelings were mutual.

After identifying where this Zu cat lived, we stepped back and let SA-001 do his thing. On a drizzly day, 001 called and asked if McMullen and I could give him some undercover back-up as he had set-up a rendezvous with this potential mole. 001 set up the meet for

12:00 Noon in front of a little library in Barron Park. John and I arrived a few minutes before, and immediately spotted SA-001 pacing back and forth; he was wearing the typical CIA "spook's" trench coat, dark, no-see-through glasses, and a funky rain hat which looked like the "boonie hats" our troops wore in Vietnam—absent the "camo," of course. After about 30 minutes of standing in the drizzle, 001 concluded that his "spy" was going to be a no-show (very typical), so he contacted us and wanted to have lunch. 001 loved Chinese and led us to a really good place on the ECR in Los Altos, then called China First.

After a great lunch, we departed and went our separate ways. Several days later, Detective McMullen burst into my office laughing his tail off;

"OK, John, share the joke with me, will ya!" I implored.

"You remember that PRC caper that 001 was working?" he quizzed.

"Of course. I may be getting old, but I don't have dementia yet! What's up?"

"You are not going to believe this," John excitedly prefaced. "Zu Yangtze borrowed his roommate's car and never brought it back; so the kid called SUDPS and reported it 10851. Get this: 001 called me and said that he set up another meeting with Zu, and the auto thief insisted on driving. I think they were going to eat somewhere, but after only a few minutes, 001 started freaking out 'cuz Zu was all over the road, running stop lights and stop signs, and didn't seem to know how to drive at all. At this point, 001 asked Zu if he had a valid driver's license. Of course, the answer was negative, so our agent ordered Zu to pull over; 001 then took the wheel. They went to dinner and drove all over the frickin' place in a stolen car! Can U imagine if Paly PD, CHP or our guys ran that license plate and it came back 6-F? A dozen units would fly to the scene red lights flashing and sirens a wailing. . ."

John continued his theatrics: "I can just see it now: The cops are shouting through the loud speaker: 'You, driver, throw the keys out of the vehicle. OK, now, slowly open the door from the outside with your right hand, and slowly exit the vehicle, with your hands high in the air—Dammit! Don't look back! Slowly walk backwards and listen to my commands—very carefully!"

"But, SA-001 meekly protests: 'Sir, I'm an FBI agent. I have my credentials in my coat,' as he begins to retrieve his shield and ID. The lead officer goes ballistic: 'Don't move your hand or I'll blow your FN head-off!'" I think you get the picture—especially if you have ever watched a "Cops" episode on the tube. . .

By this time, I could hardly breathe as I was laughing so hard. We were both in hysterics! Once we got a hold of ourselves, I admonished John to promise he would never reveal this major F-up to anyone, especially to any of the agents in the Palo Alto Office—they could be a cantankerous pack and just loved to needle 001, so this *faux pas* was going to be very 10-36! Agent 001 was a slightly built, very mild mannered individual, who was highly intelligent. He had a heavy educational background in Accounting and was a CPA. In the old days, the only persons who could qualify for the Bureau had to have a degree in either Accounting or law (JD). This tradition stemmed from the Al Capone era when the FBI realized that the only way they could bring down the mob was through financial investigations—most resulting in long prison terms for tax evasion. So, 001 wasn't from a cop background by any stretch of the imagination. But, he was great at analysis, thus was assigned to counter espionage.

Next, I asked John to have SA-001 set up another meeting with Zu, so we could recover the stolen car and put this dude in the slam. The very next day, Detective McMullen advised the sting was all set up—providing the PRC flake showed up. We were in position near the North County Court/Jail when our mark drove up, parked and got into 001's vehicle. As soon as he was settled in, the "Goon Squad" swooped-in, jerked this puppy out of the car and had him secured before he could say "wuz-up." The booking was uneventful, and the car was recovered, so once again, we went to China First for some *dim sum*. While we were having lunch and enjoying our accomplishments—although I rather doubt that 001 was able to extract any useful information from the Yangtze man—SA-001 became very serious and said:

"Captain Niemeyer and Detective McMullen; I really appreciate all of the assistance you rendered in this case, but as far as the state charges against Zu, I must inform you that I cannot bear witness against him."

Somewhat shocked, I pressed, "Whaddya mean? You were involved in the case!"

"I know," he lamented, "but I'm a federal agent and we are exempt from testifying in local matters—even if we are subpoenaed."

Hmmmmm, I conjured, *I'm going to have fun with this one...*

"OK, I really didn't know that, but this is a slam dunk case anyway. Once we file felony auto theft charges against Zu, the INS will revoke his visa and put him on that proverbial "Slow Boat to China..."

On the way back to the station, John bitched about the fact that the feds were immune from testifying in state matters. I told him to cool his jets, as I had something up my sleeve.

The Sting

It was all set: The guys at the RA were on board. John had previously called 001 and told him we wanted to take him to lunch; we'd pick him up at 1130 hours at the FBI office. Once we got through the security door, we were ushered into the main office where the agents had already formed a semi-circle. 001 knew something was up but didn't really know what. After we exchanged pleasantries with our fed colleagues, I suddenly whipped out a piece of paper from my coat pocket. It was the dreaded Subpoena, which I immediately began to read:

"The State of California sends greetings to FBI Agent (name redacted) aka., "Secret Agent 001" in the matter of the State of California vs. Zu Yangtze, charged with Vehicle code section 10851, to wit; Vehicle Theft, a felony."

At this point, Agent 001 began his vehement protestation:

"But Captain, I already told you that you cannot compel me to testify in a state court as I'm a federal agent, thus immune to your subpoena!"

"Bear with me, sir," as I continued: "Because of your position with the Federal Bureau of Investigations, and taking into account your clandestine investigations, the Court has granted a request by Captain Raoul K. Niemeyer that your identity be protected."

At this point, John pulled out a paper shopping bag, which had two eye holes cut out, as well as a nose and mouth aperture; there was an inscription on the forehead which read "Secret Agent 001". The cat was out of the bag, as our friend now realized this was a big spoof and he was the mark!

I continued: "Special Agent 001 is herby commanded to report to China First restaurant, in Los Altos, CA at 1200 Noon today. And, remember: *You get egg roll with number 3...*"

After the belly laughs were concluded, photos were taken with the bag on 001's head for posterity. We had way too much fun on this one.

Consummate Prankster and FBI Victim

The Boy Bitch

One of the most endearing characters in our group of Background Investigators was "Bernie," a retired investigative boss from an area department. He was referred to me by a great friend and colleague, George Hesse, who had worked with this man for many years. Bernie was very smart and had a great personality. He had been used to being in charge and although he deferred to my position, Bernie had a tendency to complain—a lot! After getting to know him a little better, I once commented:

"You know, Bernie, I think you would piss and moan if we hung you with a new rope!" That's when I dubbed him "The Boy Bitch!" (BB)

His affable personality made Bernie somewhat vulnerable to playful bullyragging. John McMullen and I did that on a frequent basis. One Friday at our weekly scheduled lunch, we took Bernie and a couple of other guys to "Chinese" at a local restaurant in downtown Palo Alto. I had never been to the joint but they advertised in the Stanford Daily and some folks in the office vouched for the food. We ordered "family style" wherein everyone gets to order their dish of choice. All of the crew seemed to enjoy the meal, but Bernie mentioned that there were some "crunchy" things in the Kung Pao Chicken. While drinking our tea, I noticed that a waiter was clearing a table next to us. When he picked-up the Lazy Susan there was a herd of huge cockroaches underneath. Not missing an opportunity I announced:

"Bernie, there's the relatives of the 'crunchies' in your Kung Pao Chicken!"

With eyes as big as saucers, Bernie clutched his belly and coughed:

"Niemeyer, if you mention that again, I'm going to puke!"

Our guffaws were deafening. Everyone in the little dive focused on us, wondering what in the hell was so damn funny. Even the waiters looked at us with perplexed expressions on their faces. If they only knew. . .

Lebanon

My office door was open. All of a sudden, Bernie darkened the portal with a BG packet in hand:

"Kalani," he addressed. "You want ME to go Oakland on this case?"

"Bernie," I replied softly—a first for me, I think. "Calm down, sir, I have a good friend on OPD who will be your protector when in his jurisdiction. Just take a deep breath, go get a cup of coffee, and let me give Doug a call. You'll be fine!"

Looking somewhat skeptical, he nodded and headed for the coffee room. I then picked up the phone and dialed one of the best trainees I ever had on the S/O; unfortunately for us, after a couple of years, he jumped ship and headed for the mean streets of Oakland to ply his trade. He was now Lt. Doug Wright, Patrol Watch Commander.

"Hey, Doug, it's me, your old FTO, Kalani. I have a huge favor to ask of you."

"OK, but I hope it's not going to cost me any money!"

"No, we have a candidate in Oakland and I need to send-up a background investigator to check out this kid."

I explained to Doug that Bernie was as nervous as a street walker at the Pearly Gates about coming to Oakland, and asked if he could get somebody to escort him to the candidate's home so he could do a face-to-face interview and neighborhood check—in the "hood." I also gave the Lt. a heads-up that we all loved to tease the old man, so drama would be good. Doug caught my drift. . . The time and date was set and I gave Bernie a map and instructions on how to get to OPD. The very next day, BB was off to one of the most dangerous cities on the planet!

Uh-Oh

I was just clearing my desk getting ready for the "5:00PM Indy 500 on I-280" when Bernie blew into my office like hurricane Katrina. Boy, I could tell that he was really ticked-off.

"Niemeyer," he shouted, if you ever try to send me to Oakland again, I quit!"

"Bernie, what in the hell's the matter, I had it all set up for you. What happened?" I implored.

"Damn, everything!" he snorted. "I met the Lt., who is actually a really nice guy, and he told me he had to 'suit-up.' He was already in uniform and had a pistol on his belt, so I couldn't figure out what he meant. I followed him to the locker room where he started pulling out all kinds of guns, vests and stuff. He asked me if I was armed and wanted to check out my revolver. The Lt. commented that my gun was a pretty paltry piece (S&W .38, Air Weight 5 shot "snubby"), and that I might need something more substantial; he handed me a .357 Magnum, but I declined his offer."

"So, then what happened?" I inquired, bursting at the seams with suppressed laughter.

"Well, he put on a big bullet proof vest with side panels, slipped a 9mm auto in the small of his back, put a .380 auto in a holster sewed into his boot and slapped on a Sam Browne belt with at least 3 double clip ammo pouches. Finally, the Lt. put a big hog leg into his holster—a Colt .45, I think—and we were out the door."

At this point, I didn't know how I was going to maintain my composure, but I let him continue on with his saga.

"Lt. Wright is a mad man behind the wheel, blowing stop signs and roaring around at break neck speed; I was holding on for dear life and asked him why he drove so fast," BB said.

"So I don't get hit with a stray bullet from a drive-by," the Lt. snorted!

"We then went down one of the worst streets in town—East 14th Ave., I think. He also commented that they don't need the headlights at night. When I asked the Lt. how come, he answered:"

"Because, the gun flashes light the way! We call this district 'Lebanon,'" he laughed out loud!

"Then, he pulled-up to a delapidated Mom and Pop store that had about a dozen mopes hanging out. "Why are you stopping here?" I asked.

"I need some gum," Lt. Doug matter of factually replied. "Want something?"

"I told him all I wanted to do was get the hell outta here! When he went inside, I made sure the doors were locked. But, as soon as the 'dealers' spotted the squad car, they scattered like rabbits. I was so relieved when we finally got under way. About two minutes later, the Lt. got a call to respond to a homicide. The acceleration pinned me to the seat back and within a few minutes, we skidded to a stop near a dumpster. Wright asked me if I wanted a look-see, but I declined. He was back in a few and finally, we were headed to my candidate's house. En route, the Lt. described a pretty gory scene back in the dumpster: A suspected drug dealer was shot-up pretty good, and had been in there for a couple of days. I almost threw up when he described the scene. I asked him how he could work in a place like this. He stoically replied: "It's all in a day's work and, it kinda grows on you..."

"Well, that's quite a tale Bernie. So, aren't you glad went?" I joshed.

"Hell NO! Never again!" The BB rejoined, as he headed out the door.

"Oh, by the way, Bern, how is the candidate?" I chuckled.

"I'll tell you later!" he barked. So, as quickly as the Boy Bitch blew in, he blew out.

Epilogue

Our dear friend, Bernie, passed away several years ago. So, if you're up there, Bernie, don't take these war stories about you personally, as it was all in good sport. You were a helluva nice guy and we loved working with you. We miss you, pal. R.I.P.

Another "Chucky" Faux Pas: As recalled by Deputy Anthony "Tone" Navarra

Several units were dispatched to former Secretary of State George Schultz's residence due to a burglar alarm sounding. Needless to say, this was a priority call due to the stature of the resident, as well as a known fact that Mr. Schultz often had high placed dignitaries visiting him. Deputy Navarra made a semi-stealthy advance on the home and noticed several men in suits milling around the side entrance. He recognized them as German Secret Service agents who were on Chancellor Helmut Kohl's protection detail. The Chancellor was also present. When Tony asked the lead agent what the matter was, he replied in heavily accented English that they were unable to enter the house, and apparently punched-in the wrong code. The Deputy was able to reset the alarm, which also alerted at the Pentagon, and he was clearing the scene when Deputy Chuck Hardy Kemper roared up. The "Chuckster," as the troops called him, bounced out of his cruiser and approached the Chancellor and his bodyguards, gave them a smirk and blurted out: "Ah Ha! You guys fucked-up, huh?" The Germans looked at each other, whispered something in their language and broke out in laughter. Only Hardy Kemper could have gotten away with that verbal blunder and not get reported. . . What a guy!

Do-Do in the Garden: As recalled by Deputy Anthony "Tone" Navarra

Deputy Navarra was sent on a suspicious circumstances call in the Faculty Ghetto, the home of a well known and respected surgeon. When "Tone" arrived, a very distressed woman, the wife of the Stanford Medical Center's surgeon, met him at the front door and immediately led him to the backyard where an extensive landscaping project was in progress. The woman then directed the deputy to a three foot square hole where an elaborate valve system was being installed. She related that every morning when the landscaping crew arrived at 7:00AM, the foreman found a huge pile of feces in the hole, all over the control box, valves and wiring; the boss was not happy about having to clean-up the nasty mess before they could proceed with their project; he postulated that it might be the work of raccoons.

When the woman's husband looked at some of the recent "leavings," the good doctor laughed and concluded that the do-do was, in fact, human feces. He jokingly told his wife, "I know human shit when I see it!" (Given the close proximity of fraternities, the Doc's conclusion was quite plausible! That was my first thought when Tony began to relate this tale to me.)

Deputy Navarra advised the woman to keep the rear lights on at night and he would urge his patrol colleagues to make spot checks during the night.

One week later, Deputy Navarra received a note from the lady who had complained about the unwanted deposits... It read:

"My husband and I put our heads together and came up with a surveillance plan to catch the villain(s) 'doing the infamous deed'! We left the patio lights on every night and my husband borrowed some low-light level video equipment from the hospital. He set up the camera in the bedroom window overlooking the entire backyard. Last night, we solved the big question. Along about 1:00AM Tuesday morning, a pack of four raccoons came into the backyard and appeared to be looking for food. After having a drink of water out of our new fountain, they casually looked into the new control box hole, turned around and put their furry butts over the edge of the hole. Then, they jumped the fence. Case closed."

Well, so much for a medical opinion from a renowned surgeon... Only at Stanford!

The Play

It was October 1, 1991, opening day of Stanford University's Centennial celebration. A stage was set-up at the east section of the Quad, bedazzled with decorative flags and pennants. A crowd of nearly 11,000 spectators assembled to hear an impressive array of keynote speakers and music. Among the luminaries was CA Governor Pete Wilson, who had just vetoed a bill that would have bolstered homosexual rights. A group of over two hundred gay rights advocates, The Queer Nation, (sponsored by GLAS—Gay and Lesbian Alliance at Stanford—and bused-in from San Francisco), breached our barricades and poured into the Quad.

We had anticipated trouble from this group, but simply didn't have sufficient manpower to effectively cover that huge Quadrangle. Fortunately, there was a construction project going on, so an 8 foot chain-link fence had been erected around the back of the east end; there were two gates, one to the north facing Serra Street, and the other at the opposite end. The Governor's protection detail brought him into the construction compound in a motor home, which served as their CP, as well as a down place for Pete Wilson. There were about a hundred or more activists swarming around the fence, displaying protest signs and hurling obscenities at us. A couple of brash kids crawled under the fence but were quickly extricated by one of our deputies, a rather large individual—a former offensive tackle at Chico State.

When Governor Wilson took the stage, the throng of gay protesters quickly massed in the aisle of chairs that was set-up for university faculty and dignitaries. Like Hitler's Brown Shirts of the 30's, they attempted to drown out the Governor's address by yelling invectives and blowing whistles. The faculty members and guests were not amused! Palo Alto PD sent us a squad of riot trained officers, which we deployed in front of the stage, as we were fearful that the unruly mob might rush the Governor. Instead, Governor Pete received a massive barrage of fruit: Several of those idiots attempted to pelt Pete Wilson and his bodyguards with peaches and oranges. Not to be intimidated or deterred from completing his speech, the Governor caught an errant peach and fired it back into the mob. That got him a standing ovation from the disgusted guests.

Once he finished speaking, we spirited the Governor off the stage and stashed him in the motor home. The livid dissidents raced out of the Quad and sat their sorry butts down in front of the north gate, which was to be our exit point. What to do?

Being the consummate football fan and coach, I hatched my version of *The Play*. One of my favorite and often very effective football plays was the "counter:" This is where the quarterback takes the ball from the center and stuffs it in the halfback's bread basket as the runner dives into the line. The QB then pulls the ball out of the dive back and pitches to a speedster, who is running in the opposite direction. Works almost every time!

I called-in our lead units, a motorcycle and cruiser, and they formed-up in front of Governor Wilson's motor home. In the meantime, we created a human shield, secreted the *Man* in one of our unmarked police cars and had him hunker down. We then fired-up the rigs, and with sirens wailing and emergency lights flashing, the motorcade slowly emerged from our enclave. As I said, most of the mob was blocking the north Serra St. gate, but there were several squatters at the south gate, as well. So, instead of turning right, the motorcade hung a left. The Queer Nation dissidents went berserk and sprinted toward the south access. When the entourage reached the gate, the throng pressed their bodies against the fence, which would have made it nearly impossible to get through. While some of our troopers feigned an exit, one of my detectives and the Governor sped out the backdoor and made a clean get away on Serra St.—unscathed... Boy, were those protesters pissed!

The "Chief's" House: As related to me by Ranger Doug Williams (Ret.)

The entire department was on a big protection detail with the Secret Service, save for our patrol units. Doug Williams was undoubtedly one of the most valuable members of our organization: In addition to being a good guy, Doug was our logistics man extraordinaire. He provided us with material assets such as: The mobile command center with everything including a kitchen sink and privy, communications, barricades, fencing, traffic control devices, generators, flood lights, evidence storage, crime scene tape, etc.—you name it, Doug got it! When managing prolonged details for cops and security personnel, food and liquid is paramount, for "Hungry troops is bitchin' troops!" Doug was the master at providing refreshment and sustenance for personnel who were on special operations; the Secret Service and S/O often commented that they loved to work at Stanford as they could always look forward to getting a first class meal—no peanut butter and jelly sandwiches like the jail farm provided us troops during the "Tumultuous Years" of the Vietnam riots. Of course, the Chief coughed-up the bucks from our budget for these amenities...

Doug made sure that all of our people got the sandwich of their choice: He always knew what I wanted—Turkey, Swiss and avocado on wheat! Once the orders were received, he phoned them into "The Cheese House," a deli at the Town and Country shopping center, just across the ECR. Williams would then call a CSO on the radio and dispatch him to the sandwich shop. In this case, something got lost in the transmission...

The CSO in question drove to the Chief's residence and rang the doorbell. The boss' friendly wife answered the door and when she saw the imposing figure in her portal, she was startled: Mrs. H probably feared that something had happened to her husband. Bewildered, she asked what was wrong. The man replied:

"Oh, I'm here to pick-up 25 sandwiches!"

Now, thoroughly confused, Mrs. H told the CSO that she had no idea what he was talking about. The equally clueless CSO immediately got on the radio and called Ranger Williams. The transmission went something like this:

"Ranger 1, G-34."

"G-34, this is Ranger 1, go ahead."

"I'm at the Chief's house and his wife knows nothing about sandwiches."

"G-34, confirm you're at the CHIEF'S residence?"

"Ten *Foa* G-34."

"G-34 you are at the wrong location; I said go to the CHEESE HOUSE! The Cheese House, in Town and Country Shopping Center!"

The poor guy never lived that one down as long as he was with our department.

Bloopers: Officer Knucklehead

Do you remember the Old Guard "officer" who threw rocks back at the protesters during the Days of Rage? Well, needless to say, he didn't make the first cut when the department was reorganized. He chose to stay on and accepted a position as CSO, walking the campus on the Dog Watch, shaking doors—just like he did in the old days. However, this young man was what we called in the Air

Force: A Habitual F-up! This kid couldn't do anything right if his life depended on it. I was elated when the Chief relieved him of his firearm...

Another example of this individual's tendency to screw-up was when, as a member of the OG, a Sergeant put Mr. SNAFU into a brand new 4X4 vehicle, which the department purchased in order to better patrol the vast open space areas on the campus. Our hero was out on patrol not more than an hour when Radio received this call:

"Radio, 26 L-44, send a tow rig to Lake Lagunita."

"L-44, what is the nature of your tow request?"

"Ahhh, Radio L-44, Ahhh we have a vehicle stuck in the mud out here. Ahhh make it Code 2!"

Being somewhat suspicious, motor Sgt. Carl "Captain Midnight" Gielitz cruised over to the rim on the lake which was nearly all dried-up except for one sizable mud hole. And, lo and behold, Officer Knucklehead was seated in his brand new 4X4—mired in the muck half way up the doors! God, I wish I had a photo of that!

First Company Picnic

In an effort to bring the newly reorganized department together, the Chief, with the concurrence and enthusiasm of the A-Units, planned a big spread for everyone and their families at Master's Grove. This was no hot dogs/hamburger BBQ, but the real deal: A New York strip steak feed with all of the trimmings—and on the "house," too! Assistant Chief Frank Jurian and Captain Bill Wullschleger tended the fire and put out the best NY strip that you ever sunk your teeth into. Frank was quite the connoisseur: He knew all of the best eating emporiums in the Bay Area, and also knew where to purchase the finest cuts of meat—bar none. Finally, Chief Frank challenged the rank and file (R&F) personnel to a friendly game of softball: A-Units and Sergeants vs. the DPOs and CSOs. Because of our lack of people, the A-Team would be allowed to let our kids play; the same opportunity was offered to the R&F.

There was still quite a bit of dissension in the department at that time, particularly among the members of the OG, who hadn't been selected for the sworn positions. Also, the Chief had brought in several members of the S/O for supervisory jobs: In addition to yours truly, A-1 hired former Community Services Sgt. Walt Konar as a Lieutenant, and Deputies Steve Lawson and Bob Coniglio as Patrol Sergeants.

After everyone gormandized ourselves on that King's feast, we began warming up for the softball game. When Chief Jurian took the mound and started chucking that huge ball at nearly 85 MPH, jaws dropped. He was a top underhand fast pitch ace in the area and despite his advancing age, he could really put some heat on that pumpkin! My son, Kirk, who was a catcher in Little League, was behind the plate in full regalia. Every time Frank fired a pitch, I swear you could see smoke come off of the kid's glove. The R&F protested wildly that we had a "ringer" on the mound and refused to take their first ups. We all had a good laugh and Jurian promised to "slow pitch."

During the contest, I noticed that Officer Knucklehead had moved in where my family was sitting on blankets. I think he was trying to hit on my mother-in-law, Edythe, who, at 58, was still an attractive woman. I later learned that Knucklehead was disparaging our A-Team, having very little nice to say about any of us. So, when I got up to bat, he went on a tear and scowled:

"You see that guy at bat? That's Captain Niemeyer; he's a big asshole—a real prick!"

"Listen here, young man!" Mom rejoined. "Captain Niemeyer is my son-in-law and he's a very kind, good man. So, don't you ever say anything bad about him again or I'll scratch your eyes out!"

With that, Officer "Foot in the Mouth" made a hasty exit stage left, holding his butt after that ass chewing! It pays to know who you are talking with. . .

Dottie

As I indicated earlier, the Special Event's Patrol (SEPs) were invaluable to us in staffing a myriad of special events. One of the loneliest and most boring details was pre-game stadium security. Except for The Big Game, where we flooded the place with dozens of SEPs in an effort to deter Cal-vandals, we normally had a small crew of 4-5 personnel guarding the stadium the night before football games. We typically utilized B and C level team members for this type of security assignment.

One of our office staff, a delightful young lady named "Dottie," joined the SEP force. Because of her lack of security/police experience, she was assigned to the C team, thus was put on the nighttime stadium patrol. This was her first mission.

The loneliest position on this detail was the stadium Press Box; it was a key post, however, for the guard had a bird's-eye view of the stands and field, and could report any infiltrators who often slipped though the outer perimeter patrol. Most of the interlopers were Stanford students who would hide their "stores" near where they were going to sit during the game. Most of this activity took place after we convinced the Athletic Department to enact Stanford's 18th Amendment . . . Once, an alert SEP bagged a couple of Frat boys actually burying a large cooler, filled with beer, wine, ice and tons of tequila. How in the hell they got that stash over the 10 foot cyclone fence is beyond me.

So, on this night in question, Dottie was assigned to the Press Box. The place must have been like the Stanford Family's Mausoleum, as the power for the stadium was routinely cut-off. Nothing was happening that night; the radio seemed to be on mute. Long about Midnight, a strange call for help shrieked over the airways:

"Help, Help! This is Dottie. I'm scared!"

The poor woman's partners charged-up the pitch black stairway thinking that she was being attacked and injured or something.

When they got there, they found Dottie shaking like a leaf in a gale wind. This was no place for her. . .

Actually, I can identify with lovable Dottie, as my S/O Sergeant, Ken Hart (R.I.P), and I had the daunting task of searching the Winchester Mystery House at 0100 hours for possible intruders back in the day. It, too, was pitch black and as quiet as a morgue. Even with my .357 in one hand and a 6 cell flashlight in the other, I was scared! That place was creepy, and Sarah Winchester was right on: The house was full of ghosts! But, that's another story. . .

Ooops

It was late 1983; I had just purchased a brand new Mercury Grand Marquis. It was a black 2 door with a vinyl coachmen's roof and was a beauty. Some of the guys teased that it looked like a *Mafioso* limo. The A-Units received an allowance from the department for our personal vehicles, which we used on duty. All of the cars had to be equipped with two-way radios and safety equipment such as flares, first-aid kits and a fire extinguisher. Our fire extinguisher man was Larry Mattix, a former CSO supervisor, who accepted a better position with the University's Fire Marshall's Office. Larry, a really nice, good man, contacted me one morning and asked if he could install an extinguisher in my new ride. He asked me to show him exactly where I wanted the thing placed. I looked in the huge trunk and decided that it would be out of the way in the left front corner. He said that it shouldn't take too long and that he'd return my keys when the job was completed.

About 30 minutes later, the Front Office called me and said that Larry wanted me to come down to the parking lot right away. As I opened the door to my office I knew immediately that there was a problem. The smell of raw gasoline was pungent and overpowering! I ran down the stairs and out into the rear parking lot. My Merc was jacked-up in the rear but it was leaking about as much gas as the Exxon Valdez leaked oil!

"Jeez, Larry, what in the hell happened?" I cried.

"Well Captain, I just drilled where you told me to and musta went through the gas tank," he sheepishly explained. "You told me where you wanted it installed."

"Yeah, Larry, I told you to put it here, but I didn't tell you to drill through my fuel tank," I implored. Mattix was totally flustered and apologetic so I backed-off of him—for the moment.

As it turned out, the bulkhead, where I wanted to affix the extinguisher, was very thin and the tank was only maybe an inch and a half forward of it. So, in all honesty, it would have been easy for the drill to bust through the thin wall and then into the gas tank. But, as I chided later, and do so to this day: "Larry, I can understand you drilling one hole, but two? That's out of the question!"

CHAPTER TWENTY SIX

The Art of Conversation

Good Cop—Bad Cop

If you watch old cop and robber films of the '30s and '40s, the street cops and detectives seemed to always employ this technique when interrogating suspects. I think Hollywood perpetuated this myth, which some dinosaurs in law enforcement still believe to this day. However, in reality the Good Cop—Bad Cop routine rarely works, especially with an educated public, like we have at Stanford.

Somewhere, back in my upbringing, my parents, especially my Dad, who was the Assistant Chief of the Honolulu Liquor Commission, taught me that a pleasant smile and demeanor would always triumph over being a grumpy sourpuss. It was then that I began to adopt a persona Hawaiians called *ho'omalimali*, which literally means "to make a bargain." Other interpretations include: "to compliment, ingratiate and compliment"—in effect, be personable in order to build rapport and make people feel comfortable with you. This characteristic became part of my personality, and although I had my detractors, I found it very effective when I began my law enforcement career.

Back then, most crooks were generally unsophisticated, so the old *Third Degree** technique followed-up with a nice talk by an empathetic officer sometimes worked. But, if a guy was "con-wise," forget it! My T/O, John "JJ" Johnson, was a great teacher and a super crime fighter: He had eyes like a Red Tail hawk and the hearing of my Bichon Frise pups. But, when it came to interviewing suspects, he often came across as a hard-ass, therefore, the *skells* wanted to talk to me—perhaps because I had a young, smiley face and talked nice—but, most likely because they knew I would be a gullible rookie. But, whatever the reason, I often seemed to ferret out valuable information. We had very little formal interview and interrogation training in those days. Most coppers back in the day just flew by the seat of their pants, or utilized information handed down from the older guys. I read a couple of books on interrogation but the information was old school. It actually wasn't until I was assigned to the SUDPS Investigation's Unit in 1977 that I had an opportunity to receive any formal training in police conversation. The third degree in my foot note was absolutely forbidden in most CA police and sheriff's departments by the late 1950s—I can assure you that no deputies I ever knew took that path.

*Believed to have been coined by Washington D.C. Police Chief Richard H. Sylvester (1898-1915): First Degree: Arrest; Second Degree: Transportation to jail or police station; Third Degree: Harsh interrogation using intimidation, sleep deprivation, hot lights and physical force, which often elicited false confessions. Apparently, no one thought of "Water Boarding" in those days. . .

Hostage Negotiation

During the 1970s and thereafter, a rash of hostage taking incidents occurred. Most of you have heard about them, but I will cite a few of the most significant cases:

1972: A team of eight Palestinian terrorists called "Black September" seized nine Israeli athletes from the Olympic Village in Munich, Germany. In a botched rescue attempt by West-German assault teams, all of the hostages were killed, as well as five of the terrorists.

1973: Robbers hit a big bank in Stockholm, Sweden and held the bank employees hostage from August 23-28th. In the aftermath, a peculiar psychological quirk emerged called the "Stockholm Syndrome," wherein the captives became emotionally attached to their captors and even defended them following their ordeal.

1979-81: After President Jimmy Carter agreed to allow the deposed Shah of Iran to be exiled in the U.S., a group of Iranian radicals stormed the American Embassy in Tehran and took 66 American diplomats and embassy staffers prisoner. Thirteen of the hostages were released shortly thereafter, but 53 persons were held until January 20, 1981, curiously just eight days after the inauguration of Ronald W. Reagan as the 40th President of the United States—the Iranians must have seen the handwriting on the wall, eh?

Although the chances of having a terrorist hostage-taking incident on the Stanford campus seemed pretty remote, I was concerned about a mentally-ill student or deranged person, with an axe to grind with the administration or faculty, doing something rash—like Charles Whitman, the infamous "Texas Tower Sniper," who indiscriminately shot and killed 16 innocents with a high power rifle at the University of Texas on August 1, 1966. Later, the Stanford community was shocked by the brutal murder of popular Math Professor, Karel deLeeuw. As you may recall from Chapter 8, the Professor was beaten to death in his office on August 18, 1978 with a 3 pound sledge hammer by Theodore Streleski, a disgruntled graduate student. Both of these events could have very well resulted in the killers seizing hostages!

With two financial institutions on campus, I was also fearful that a robbery gone wrong could result in a hostage stand-off when our troops surrounded the banks, preventing an avenue of escape for the suspect(s). I felt we needed a person trained in negotiation to calm potential hostage taker(s) until the S/O SWAT team and negotiators arrived. I talked to the Chief about my concerns and he agreed to send me to a Basic Hostage Negotiator's school that was to be held in San Jose.

The primary instructor was a NYPD detective who had been involved in the Chase Manhattan Bank take-over robbery attempt in Brooklyn, August 22, 1972*. Two amateur wannabe robbers, John Wojtowicz and his pal, Salvatore Naturale, stormed the bank armed with handguns. John, the primary crook, soon discovered there was only $1,100 cash in the vault. By this time, NY's finest had the place covered like a glove.

*Hollywood later made an Academy Award winning movie about this botched caper entitled, "Dog Day Afternoon," starring Al Pacino and John Cazale, which was based on an article, "Boys in the Bank," by P.F. Kluge. John refused to surrender and held the bank's personnel hostage for five days.

At first, the "master mind" demanded that a helicopter land on the roof and fly the duo and a few hostages to the airport so they could secure free passage out of the country. However, the NYPD negotiator convinced the robbers that the bank's roof wouldn't support a helicopter, so the stand-off went on and on. Those trapped were afforded food, water, and even medical attention when one of the captives suffered a seizure. Finally, the police and FBI agreed to take the bad guys and a couple of hostages to the airport in a limo. An FBI agent drove and John was in the co-pilot's seat, while Sal, the hostages and another FBI man were seated in the rear. The agent in the rear convinced Sal to point his weapon in the air so he wouldn't inadvertently shoot the agent who was behind the wheel. The agent in the rear subsequently controlled John's gun, which distracted Sal, thus allowing the driver to retrieve a hidden pistol from the console and shoot the dummy in the head. John was convicted and sentenced to 20 years in prison—he served 14 years of hard time.

After this incident, NYPD and the FBI realized that most departments throughout the nation, including theirs, weren't adequately prepared to handle a hostage dilemma of this magnitude. They collaborated and created an impressive road show program, which they put on all over the country. I was fortunate enough to attend the first class in our area.

Negotiation in Action

While the basic course was very informative and interesting, it was just that: Basic classroom instruction. When the advanced course came to San Jose within the year, I jumped at it. This phase of negotiation techniques would involve in the field, hands-on, practical exercises. On our first day, our class was instructed to report to the San Jose Fire Department's five-story training tower in gym attire. *What was this going to be all about?* I sweated. Once we assembled, our FBI instructor directed us to focus on the fifth story window. Suddenly, a nut job emerged on the sill and dove, head-first, into space. We soon realized that he was tethered to a rappelling rig and was coming down that rope at a frightening pace. *I damn sure ain't doing that,* I quietly said to myself. The guy was good—real good—a member of the Bureau's elite tactical response team. He would be our safety officer and make sure nobody would get hurt during this phase of the scenarios we were about to participate in.

At this point, none of us had the vaguest notion of what we would be up against. One by one, we were led to top floor for our first of several scenarios with role-players. When it was my turn, "Spider Man" rigged-me-up with rappelling gear. I protested: "Sir, I hope you don't expect me to dive out that window!"

"Oh, no. We have you secured to the crane's boom and the top so that when you 'walk the plank', you'll feel more secure," he calmly returned.

"Plank? What plank?" I shot back.

My question was soon answered when several role-players appeared in the small room with a 2" thick by 8"wide by 8 foot long plank—like painters use on scaffolding. They then positioned the thing on the window sill and invited me to step-up and move out of the window; they assured me they could support my 250 pounds by weighting down the opposite end with their body weight. I wasn't so sure: This was like a schoolyard teeter-totter, for crying out loud! But, not wanting to come across as a wimp, I climbed up on that plank and gingerly inched my way out of the aperture. I am terrified of heights, and even though I was tethered and had been briefed on the rig, I thought I would certainly soil my shorts. . .

I had a death grip on that rope as I slowly made it outside; I was pulling on that hemp with my right hand, while my left hand was locked onto the rappel ring. I thought I would bend that boom with the amount of force I was exerting. So, what was the purpose of this death defying exercise you ask? The instructor said that I was on the wing of an airliner that had been hijacked by a group of terrorists, and the plank trick was designed to induce stress. *Stress? How about a fricking heart attack?* I grumbled to myself.

Several role-players were shouting Islamic epitaphs like: *"Allahu Akbar, Allahu Akbar, Allahu Akbar!"* (God is great). All the while, I tried to convince these guys to release their hostages and I would assure them safe passage back to their homeland. Yeah right. . . All I wanted to do was get off that damn plank of doom! After a number of exchanges with these psychos, the instructor motioned me in after commenting that I did alright. I would have sold my soul to the Devil himself if it would get me out of that precarious predicament. After the scenarios were completed, Spider Man invited the class to rappel down the tower. A handful of the younger macho dudes stepped forward, were briefed, and came down that tower like Green Berets. Most of us old guys passed. But, not wanting to be shown-up by those young whippersnappers, I approached our instructor and asked him if I could go out the third story, first, as a confidence builder. He said "sure" and helped me. When I pushed off from the window I realized that I had made a mistake as the length of the rope from the boom to my body went slack for a moment and I dropped about three feet before the rope was taut. I descended the rest of the way without difficulty. It was kinda fun, despite my fear of heights. I intended to rappel from the top, but we ran out of time—probably a good thing. . .

Moffett Naval Air Station

On our final day of the Advanced Hostage Negotiation class, we assembled at Moffett NAS, which borders Mountain View to the Northwest and Sunnyvale, CA to the South. This base was built in 1931, initially to house the enormous airships of the era, which patrolled the CA coastline for potential enemy ships and submarines. We were directed to report to Hanger One, the world's largest hanger. This enormous structure (1,133 feet long, 308 feet high and 198 feet high) was constructed to house the gigantic blimp U.S.S. Macon. The hanger is an elongated dome building with huge motorized sliding doors at either end; the floor space can house 10 football fields!

It was a cold blustery morning and I'm glad I brought a warm jacket. Our class was broken-up into several teams: Command Post; Communications; Logistics; Negotiation; and SWAT (armed with blanks only!). I was assigned to the Negotiation Team and was nominated as "Chief Mouth Piece." *Why me, Lord?* I silently quizzed. Probably because of my Portuguese ancestry: "I get to the point no matter how long it takes. . ."

Hijacked

The scenario read like a Hollywood movie script: A distraught and heavily armed Navy airman was holding a crew and numerous dependants on board a P-3 Orion anti-submarine aircraft, which was on the tarmac. The hostage taker was a middle age Chief Petty Officer (CPO) whose wife had just dumped him for a younger man. I don't recall his name, so let's call him "Jeff." The FBI coordinator said that Jeff was prepared to kill all hostages and blow-up the plane. This was not good. Furthermore, he had disabled the aircraft's communication system, thus we had to establish some way to talk to this lunatic. At that point, the coordinator handed me a pair of WWII field phones* with several hundred feet of wire. This was obviously before the advent of cell phones! My team's mission was to somehow deliver one of the phones to the airplane so I could chat with the crazy man. After connecting the wires to the phones, my back-up and I went out on the ramp and positioned ourselves under the wing of another P-3, about 50 yards from the hijacked aircraft.

One of the Logistics guys affixed a big white flag to a stick and cautiously approached the stranded airplane with EE-8 phone in hand, all the while frantically waving the flag back and forth. He ascended the stairway, placed the phone on the platform and made a hasty withdrawal. Within a few minutes, the cabin door opened and a female quickly scooped up the phone and disappeared back inside. I waited a few minutes and cranked this archaic contraption several times; no response.

*EE-8 Field Telephones were used by the Signal Corps in WWII and even in Vietnam. They were powered by two D-cell batteries and the operator had to crank the apparatus to alert the operator at the other end.

I did it again and again and after about a minute, an agitated man picked-up:

"Yeah, what the f*** do you want?"

"Hi, I'm Raoul and just wanted to know how you are doing?" I offered.

"Are you an FN Navy stooge, or what?" Jeff screamed.

"No sir, I'm just a lowly Deputy Sheriff who would like to help you," I meekly replied.

"Well, whatever your real name is, I don't need or want your help. I'm fixin' to blow-up this FN airplane, so go tell that to the Base Commander and tell him to &^%*$ himself!" Click.

Great start, I lamented. *This guy is going to be a real hard case.* Nonetheless, I continued to crank on that damn phone, only to get in a few lines before the mad man would hang-up on me. *This was going to be a Dog Day Afternoon,* I feared. So, I decided to play his game and I ignored his calls to me; I knew this was a gamble, but I figured he might focus his frustrations on me rather than on his captives. After a couple of non-responses on my end, I decided to engage Jeff in dialogue again and see if they needed any food and water in that P-3. This tactic seemed to work; the hostage-taker wanted some sandwiches and water. Logistics was on top of that as the coordinators knew the drill and had the refreshments on hand. They sent several people out to the plane's ramp and set the food and water on the deck. Once they retreated, a young lady came down the ladder and began taking the stuff into the plane.

Jeff, gun in hand, cautiously peered out of the door but didn't offer much of a target for the sharpshooters. I also admonished the SWAT Commander *NOT* to engage the suspect at that time as I still hadn't determined whether he had a bomb on board. When the girl came back for the second trip, she suddenly bolted for the SWAT team, who was strategically staged behind large military vehicles.

The SWAT guys were armed with rifles with blanks and were of the mind-set to take a shot, if an opportunity presented itself. In my view, this exercise was all about getting the disturbed man to peacefully surrender, thereby saving lives.

Immediately after the hostage's break for freedom, Jeff was cranking on his phone; I picked-up:

"Dammit!" he shouted, "If any other person in this plane tries to escape, I will shoot them in the back. You understand that?"

"Jeff, calm down. We didn't have anything to do with that! Put me on with the pilot, and I will convey your message, OK?"

"No! That's not necessary; they all got my warning." He rejoined.

"So, where do we—you and I, Chief—go from here? I want to get this situation resolved without bloodshed. You're in control of what happens to you and those innocent people in the plane. Let's work this thing out, OK?" I pleaded.

After over two hours of commiserating, cajoling, pleading and every other adjective in Webster's dictionary describing *ho'omalimali* (bargaining), Jeff, the distraught and dejected man, finally agreed to surrender. I was elated. I radioed the Command Post and SWAT commander that Jeff would come to the door, hands in the air and capitulate. I was very proud of myself!

Within a minute or so, the hostage-taker darkened the doorway. I advised the SWAT team to send-in an arrest team. Suddenly, and without warning, a volley of shots rang out. Jeff fell over like a big sack of rice—DOA!

"Command Post, Negotiator 1. SWAT just killed my guy. What were they thinking? That really sucks!"

My transmission was followed by a volley of clicks and pant rubs—even a horse laugh or two. This was a set-up! My heroic effort was foiled by a bunch of idiots! Was this part of the plan that the instructors concocted, or was it the SWAT team's middle finger? To this day, I don't know. Despite high-fives from my team members and the instructors, I went home dejected and perturbed. *Maybe I'll hijack a bus or something,* I humorously lamented...

The Reid Technique

While attending a WSSBIA (Western States Safe and Burglary Investigator's Association) seminar in Santa Cruz, CA in the early 1980s, our conferees attended an 8 hour class on the Reid Technique of Interviews and Interrogation. This was a very polished presentation conducted by two very sharp, experienced private investigator/polygraphers, who knew more than a thing or two about "the art of conversation." Reid and Associates Inc. is a big operation based in Chicago and they put on classes all over the world. The CEO and founder, John E. Reid, was a long time polygrapher for the Chicago Police Department. During his tenure, Mr. Reid interviewed and interrogated thousands of people and discovered that he and law enforcement could benefit greatly from his experiences and theories on obtaining incriminating facts from suspects by using a well planned, systematic approach. Reid found that in pre-polygraph interviews, he could ascertain if subjects were, for the most part, truthful at the initial stages of the inquiry: Personal questions such as name, age, educational background, occupation, family etc., were always answered straight forwardly, with little or no emotion or "body language." During this phase of the "Interview," which is non-accusatory, others elements I call "what ifs" are tossed into the mix. For example, if a speculative question such as: "When the police catch the (suspect), do you think that person should be given a second chance?", innocent subjects would normally reply "No," while a guilty party might say something like: "Well, everybody makes mistakes, so yes, I think the person should be given a break." While not an absolute indication of innocence or guilt, this technique lays a foundation for further probing.

While police polygraphs have never been upheld in the courts, over the years they have become a very valuable investigative tool. But, so-called lie detector tests are time consuming and often very expensive, so the Reid brain trust came up with alternative methods that, in many cases, can solve crimes. When an investigator develops sufficient evidence to take-on a "person of interest"—we used to call them suspects, but the PC thing to do these days is to refer to an accused as a "POI"—the inquiry moves into the "Interrogation" or accusatory phase. This method requires an interrogator who is well prepared and is mentally quick on his/her feet: You basically tell the suspect that there's no question who committed the offense, but you want to know the motive and work toward an admission—better yet, a confession—all the while, cutting off denials while basically performing a monologue, something that is more often than not very difficult to achieve. I could hardly wait to try out this new technique, and it didn't take very long...

Captain Gold Finger

Just prior to my Reid Technique basic training, my Detective, Sgt. Philip Love, and I were working with the Palo Alto Fire Department in trying to catch a firehouse sneak thief—the worst possible thing that any organization can experience. This guy was stealing money from the coffee fund, to which everyone on "A" shift contributed five dollars a month. The scoundrel was believed to be a Captain at Stanford's Fire Station 6, the building that the police shared. In fact, my Investigations Unit shared the upper level with the firefighters, as our offices were the former dorm rooms of the Stanford student volunteer program which had been discontinued before I arrived in 1974. Two Battalion Chiefs met with Philip and me after they simply couldn't allow this thievery to continue; they asked us to set a trap in order to catch the rat.

I remember when I was in the Air Force, we once had a barracks' thief, and even back then, I was a wannabe cop and set-up a sting so that we could catch the sucker who was stealing us blind! It didn't take long to find out who the responsible party was, and justice was swift: The following night, a "group" grabbed the culprit out of his sound slumber, put a blanket over his head, dragged him off to the showers (no gas involvement) and administered a "Blanket Party!" The next morning when the battered guy couldn't make reveille, the Sergeant sent him to sickbay and never said a word. We never lost even a bar of soap out of our foot lockers from that time on! Needless to say, this rather harsh punishment was out of the question here...

To Catch a Thief

This caper was going to be tougher than originally thought. Although we had the video spy cam at our disposal, we could not deploy the camera as the thefts occurred in the men's locker room—a definite No-No! So, we had to resort to rudimentary techniques. The pilfering almost always happened the night after the keeper of the coffee fund collected $5.00 on the first of the month from the team members. He then put the cash in a coffee can, which he stowed in his locker, which was supposedly secured. Obviously, the crook knew the combination. Sgt. Love came up with the idea of wiping the can clean after the money was counted and written down; he further instructed the good fire Captain to draw a pencil line around the can, and to report if it was moved. Well, on the first attempt, we had a version of "Keystone Firemen:" Our well meaning colleague got so excited when he found that the can had indeed been moved, he brought the container to the Sergeant's Office, thereby contaminating any potential latent fingerprints. Upon checking the count, we found that the suspect had lifted 25 bucks. We also added another element to our plan: For next month's collection, we advised the curator to record all serial numbers of the collected money. Our intent was that when another theft was discovered, our man would call Sgt. Love and he would confiscate the can, take inventory and determine which bills were MIA; the sergeant would also dust the can for latent prints. Once we knew that our suspect had swiped some cash, our associate would approach the bad guy and ask him to make change for a 20 dollar bill. Hopefully, the suspect would give our man one or more of the stolen bills—Game over! We all watched the calendar and awaited the next collection...

Keystone Fire, Part II

Unfortunately, our "barracks thief" was on vacation when the collection occurred, so we had to wait several more days before he finally hit. All went according to plan except for a major screw-up: Our fire contact got a marked "Lincoln" (#L 742680280 A) from the culprit when he came back to the station and "paid his dues". Now all we needed to do was file a complaint with the DA, get an arrest warrant, and PAFD would be promoting a new fire captain, right? Wrong! After receiving the incriminating five dollar bill, our good guy inadvertently made change for another fireman and our evidence slipped away, but was hopefully at that man's home in East San Jose. Upon receiving this distressing news, I called the fireman, who now had the marked bill, and asked him if he still had that "five spot" in question; he did and I was off like a shot! I had to get that bill if I was going to be able to nail this despicable individual who had been ripping-off his fellow firefighters!

The next morning, I was beating down the door at the DA's Office. *This should be a slam dunk,* I thought: Hell, we had the crook's fingerprints and a marked bill in evidence; what more could the DA want, a video tape? Well, wouldn't you know the first thing out of the prosecutor's mouth was: "Raoul, you are big on covert video, how come you didn't get this one on tape?" I was fuming and retorted: "Counselor, the crime scene was in a locker room where men change their clothes. How do you think a jury would react to seeing a bunch of naked guys? Plus, it's against the law!" He hung his head and suggested that perhaps I should interrogate the man and get a confession. "OK, I said, we'll do that. Can I use your interview room?"

Reid Tech in Action

One of the things that the Reid instructors talked a lot about was office thefts or embezzlements, wherein a number of people could be suspect. They stressed that an investigation needed to include everyone! That included department supervisors, as well as persons who were "above suspicion." By interviewing everyone, a good inquirer can amass a plethora of information, which might bring focus on the actual culprit. In this case, I had previously interviewed several men on Capt. Gold Finger's (CGF) shift and learned that he had long been suspected of a variety of suspicious behavior: A couple of guys recalled that CGF had home sat for them when they were on vacation, and when they returned, some inconsequential items seemed to have grown legs. . . The Battalion Chief reminded me that our department had suspected this captain of stealing a $900 racing bike, a set of Porsche rims, and an oxyacetylene torch from our bike compound, where we stored some of the 1.5 million dollar cache purloined by the Jogging Burglar (Chapter 30). The Chief reiterated that CGF was a bicycle enthusiast and mentioned to others that he would really like to have that bike we had confiscated in one of many search warrants. We figured we might get lucky and see him riding the thing around, so I sent a surveillance team to the area where CGF lived in the Gold Country. Per professional protocol, our team leader went to the S/O in that county and told them what they were up to. After several unsuccessful days, they gave up the ghost. We later learned that our suspect's brother-in-law was a deputy sheriff at that office—so much for professional courtesy. . .

In this coffee cash caper, I sent out letters to every firefighter on the involved shift. I met with two men prior to CGF and went through the scripted basic (boiler-plate) questions. Both individuals felt that we were on the right track as far as who the thief was.

My meeting with our suspect was cordial and respectful. I obtained a good reaction base from his responses during the interview portion. He reacted to the "what if" questions as I anticipated: He exhibited defensive behavior and thought that perhaps the suspect might have some psychological issues.

As to what should happen to the guilty party when found, CGF thought that instead of being arrested and prosecuted, the party should be given amnesty, probation with a proviso of restitution. After hearing those thoughts, I dropped a classic "bait question" on him: "So, is there any reason that your fingerprints would be found on the coffee can which had been previously wiped clean and stored in a secured locker?" As he was humming and hawing, I set my pager off and excused myself—ostensibly to answer a phone call, but really so that my mark might have an opportunity to chew on that bone for awhile. . .

The Interrogation

After about 20 minutes, which probably seemed like an eternity to CGF, I re-entered the room, plopped down a huge file and declared: "Here's the results of our investigation, which clearly shows that you are involved in this incident." The man was visibly shaken and made some very weak denials. I cut those off, commiserated with him and told him that he needed to come to grips with the situation so the end result would be less painful to him and his family. The man became very emotional and suggested that he might have a marital and alcohol dependence problem, and really needed help. He was on the verge of confessing but couldn't take that final step. Instead, I elicited an admission, after I told him that I would work with the DA on his behalf, but being careful not to make any promises I might not be able to fulfill.

In the end, I promised not to humiliate him any further by physically placing him under arrest for burglary (a crime that presupposes intent, and given the number of thefts he committed, that would have been very probable to prove). Instead, I arranged to have him self-surrender for petty theft, which he later pleaded guilty to; CGF was ordered to pay restitution and was put on probation and ordered to undergo psychological counseling. The Fire Department asked and received his resignation in lieu of being terminated. The last I heard, the crooked captain was working as a security guard in a gold mine. . . Talk about putting the fox in the henhouse! I wonder if he lived up to the nickname I gave him?

Oh, and about that monetary tribute to President Abraham Lincoln... I'll bet you all think that I just made up the serial number from a random 5-Spot, right? Actually, it is the original piece of evidence I seized (and paid for), and still have today after all of these years. I kept it to commemorate my first successful interrogation using the Reid Technique of Interview and Interrogation.

Bizarre Beyond Belief

We had just left Garland, TX when my cell phone went off:

"Captain, I have a real weird case that I'd like to run by you," my rookie Investigations Sergeant (I'll call him Bryan) declared. *Unbelievable,* I thought. *Here I am, on an extended vacation, trucking my Med School daughter from Des Moines, IA to Tucson, AZ for her first rotation, and I'm doing detective work via a cell phone...*

"Lay it on me, Sarge," I invited. And, lay it on he did! All the way across the West Texas "moors," through El Paso, New Mexico and until we reached our destination at Tucson General Hospital, I got a daily earful of one of the most bizarre cases I had ever encountered: A sophomore female reported that she was being harassed and threatened by person(s) unknown. The young lady, whom I shall call "Princess" (P), initially said that she began getting phone threats from a female who disguised her voice. She offered that she believed the antagonist was possibly a jealous woman who had designs on a star basketball player, who had been seeking P's attention in a romantic way. She refused to identify the athlete, however, which raised questions in my mind. I suggested that the Sgt. give the victim (V) one of our telephone recorders so we could capture the harassment on tape. After a few days, the calls increased both in volume and intensity. The perpetrator, who according to Sgt. "B" was clearly altering his /her voice, would repeat the same mantra: "I'll get you; I'll kill you if you don't leave my lover alone!" Bryan played the recordings for me, and they sounded like a woman with a hoarse voice. In other instances, the caller whispered: "I love you, I'll get you, and I'll kill you." This simply didn't make any sense, so I was beginning to smell a big rat. I then opined that a trap should be installed on the V's phone in an effort to trace the caller.

After my investigator admonished the woman, "Do not go out alone at night," I got a call that our V had been accosted outside her dorm near midnight, by a big black man, who was wielding a huge knife. I went berserk:

"What in the hell is she doing out of her dorm at that hour after you told her NOT to go anywhere at night by herself?" I shrieked.

"I know, Captain. She said that she had to go to the laundry room and nobody was available to accompany her. But, it gets worse!" the sergeant said.

According to the police report, the V was en route to the laundry room when the assailant, dressed in black and wearing a "hoody," grabbed her from the rear, put a trench knife to her throat and told her not to look back. He then exclaimed: "I love you; you're mine, and I'll kill you!" Does this make any sense to you? But, wait, there's more: The responding deputies found that the V had a red heart drawn on her neck, which she said was put there by the suspect. While the officers were searching for clues, the V suggested they look in a storm drain, as her attacker "might" have hidden something there. Sure enough, the first responders found a red felt tip pen in the drain sump. How about that? I had to pull over at that point, for I couldn't contain myself.

"Sarge, I think this case is a bunch of B.S. This has all the earmarks of a False Allegation situation. Just keep that in mind 'cuz there is bound to be more." I proffered.

However, my poor investigator had the Chief, the Administration, the Dean of Student's Office and the woman's parents all over him like a pack of jackals, so he had to play the game. Everyone *demanded* to know what he, as lead detective, was doing—not only to protect this young lady, but to apprehend the culprit(s). Talk about being under the gun! In outlining what had been done on this matter, the sergeant had to divulge that a trap had just been placed on the V's phone. After the V became aware of the phone monitoring, all alleged telephonic threats ceased and there was no record at University communications of any random, harassing or threatening calls to the V. That set-off another bell in my suspicious mind. So, I advised the sergeant to tell the V that the phone company had to remove the trap after no hits, per their procedure. Well, that very day, Princess called Investigations and reported yet another threat, which she said that she just captured on our trusty little tape recorder. The only trouble with this assertion was that I instructed my investigator NOT to remove the line trap. And, when he checked the V's phone record through the University phone center, there was absolutely no incoming call corresponding with the time the alleged threat was received. I was convinced that this caper was indeed bogus, and Princess was scamming us all! It was obvious that this student was disguising her voice and simply talking into the recorder; however, I felt we needed more proof: The University was all over this case like a cheap suit, in part, due to the constant badgering of her parents, who were both influential medical doctors in their home state. Both parents were outraged and demanded immediate action, so we were forced to go along with P's little game. By this time, I was back on the Farm and took the bull by the horns—so to speak.

The Stalker

I no sooner got settled into my work routine when two Midnight Watch deputies excitedly barged into my office one morning. Both were in the process of completing their Incident Reports from last night's prowler call. Both men, really bright and astute, had been involved in the "knife wielding" caper, and said that they had been called to Princess' dorm shortly after they went on the air (in service). They said the V reported hearing some scratching on the screen of her window and heard some cat-like "meowing." When she opened the shade, she discovered a note on the window sill. She denied seeing the prowler, but when she opened the folded piece of white paper, she saw the all too familiar red heart and message: "I love you, I'll get you!" The inscriptions appeared to be written with a red felt tip pen. When I looked at the note, the writing was very shaky as if written with one's non-dominant hand. The deputies further related that when they examined the scene, they didn't find any footprints in the soft dirt below the window. In addition, the entire area was covered with wet, dewy grass, and save for the footsteps made by them, there were NO other footprints. So, how did the intruder get to the window? Did he just levitate, or "fast rope" down from a UFO? When the deputies confronted Princess with these irregularities, she simply shrugged and steadfastly stuck to her story. The deputies commented that the area around her room faced a street, but the illumination was very poor.

Let's get some light out here!

After hearing this saga, I picked-up the phone, called Plant Services, and put in an emergency work order for increased lighting. The sergeant and I met the Facilities Supervisor at the scene and showed him where we wanted high intensity lights to be installed. I also ordered that the bushes along the dorm's outer wall be given a haircut. The supervisor understood the gravity of this situation and said the project would be done ASAP. I stressed that we needed to do everything possible to keep the students safe in their residence. But, what I didn't tell him was that we believed this case was phony, and that we really wanted increased lighting so we could use a covert video system to "surveil" the area around P's dorm window.

We were in the process of purchasing a time lapse video recorder and a low light level camera with a high power lens. The sergeant was really into technology and figured he could set-up the system in his older car on the street, disguise the camera, and power the system with two 12 volt marine batteries, which would facilitate 48 hours of surveillance before recharging. That sounded like an excellent plan to me; the Chief was also very enthusiastic, gave us the thumbs-up and dragged-out his checkbook. . .

Not Again

The next morning, the same deputies busted into my space and were really steamed. It was a re-run of the previous night's prowler call: P called Communications in the wee hours of the morning and said the guy came back and left another note on her window sill. This time, the V met the officers outside and showed them the crime scene. Yup, there were footprints leading from the street, across the dewy grass and to her window. Unlike the first time, there were deep impressions in the soft dirt, which appeared to have been made by tennis shoes. The only problem was that the shoe prints were made with a size 8 shoe—hardly worn by a big man, unless he grew up in the Far East and had his feet bound. . . This caper was spiraling way out of control!

Valentine's Day

During the week before St.Valentine's Day, the Sergeant learned that P's mother was coming from Texas to be with her daughter for a few days. Prior to Mom's arrival, the girl reported yet another stalking incident, which she said happened in Green Library. In that instance, Princess said she was studying and fell asleep. When she awoke, she discovered the signature "love/threat" note stuck in one of her textbooks. As I said at the outset, these events were bizarre beyond belief...

While this nonsense was going on, my techie investigator's equipment was up and running; his first order of business was to retrieve and review the videotapes from the previous night. There had been no further reports of the phantom prowler, nor had anyone been seen, on the tape, anywhere near P's dorm window. However, on St. Valentine's Day, at approximately 11:30 PM, units were dispatched to P's dorm on another suspicious circumstances detail. They were met by the V and her mother. P stated that while her mother was in the bathroom, she once again heard some noises outside her window. As in the other cases, P found a note on her window sill. The officers checked outside and found only the size 8 shoe impressions from the last incident around the window. The grass was dry, so no footprints were seen. The troopers took another report, seized the note, and promised to advise Investigations of the latest development, first thing in the morning.

Upon hearing the news, the sergeant made a beeline for his hidden surveillance equipment and retrieved the tape. Shortly thereafter, he came running into my office acting as if he had just hit the Lottery.

"We got her, we got her!" Sgt. B rejoiced. "Come see," he beckoned, as he bolted back into his office. I was hot on his tail. The TV was fired-up and ready to go; Sgt. B ran the tape back about 30 seconds. The image on the screen was that of P's darkened dorm room window. The frames advanced slowly. Suddenly, a light came on in the room; the shade was drawn, but you could make out the silhouette of a person approaching the window. The shade was opened momentarily and quickly drawn. The next frame revealed a little white object on the window sill. "Damn," I shouted, "that's the fricking note; she slipped that note under the window screen! Bingo. Game over!" I said with relief and glee. When Sgt. B re-ran the tape in very slow motion, you could see the paper being advanced from inside under the screen, a half inch at a time. This was beautiful. "Now, we'll go for the jugular," I said.

The Game Plan

After some deep thought—something I seldom had the luxury to do, for many of my decisions were akin to "Fast Draw" and shoot from the hip—I decided to interview Princess under the guise of performing a "Victimology" study for the FBI, eg.: What kind of person would stalk and harass a young bright college woman like this? I got this idea after previously attending a class on "typing" criminals by FBI Special Agent Mary Ellen O'Toole. Agent O'Toole was one of the most impressive investigators I had ever met in my career: She was a pioneer in the FBI's new Behavioral Science Unit, which was developing Criminal Offender Profiles, in an effort to assist law enforcement, primarily, in solving serial murder cases, but in other crimes as well, wherein the suspect(s) was unknown. Mary Ellen had interviewed dozens of incarcerated murderers in order to discover what made these sadistic killers tick. The most intriguing of Agent O'Toole's subjects was the infamous "Co-ed Killer" Edmund Kemper:* I saw the videotape of that session and it made a nauseous impression on me, I'll tell you!—more about Kemper in a minute. I had previously talked to Mary Ellen about our alleged stalking case and opined that I believed it to be a False Allegation situation. The FBI was very interested in this phenomenon, as there had been a huge police effort to solve a series of bizarre stalking events in Vancouver, B.C. a few years before, which ended very badly. Agent O'Toole encouraged me to proceed with my charade and asked to be kept apprized, as she might possibly use what we gleaned in her research. I was encouraged.

*Edmund Emil Kemper III was one of California's most vicious and sadistic serial killers of all time. A giant of a man at 6'9" and over 300 pounds, he gained notoriety when he literally butchered 6 young college females who had the misfortune of being picked up by Kemper while they were hitchhiking in Santa Cruz County, CA from 1972-73. He also murdered his grandparents as a juvenile, and decapitated his Mom and her friend, which finally led to his arrest.

The Vancouver Debacle

A thirty something year old nurse complained to her friends that an unknown male had been calling, leaving death threat notes and, apparently, stalking her 24-7. Her friends invited the woman to stay in their home until the police caught the culprit; the good Samaritans allowed the V to reside in their basement apartment. The police were alerted of the V's change of address and said they would do frequent patrol checks of the residence. One morning, shortly after midnight, the homeowners were awakened by the smell of smoke. When they ran downstairs to the main level, they found the nurse bleeding and crying hysterically. In addition, the basement was on fire! After the fire department put out the blaze, police and fire investigators deemed that the conflagration was purposely set with an accelerant. The nurse said that her assailant broke-in through a small widow and slashed her with a knife; however, she managed to escape. Within a few minutes, she heard a loud "swoosh" and smelled smoke. When investigators examined the scene, they found that the window at the so-called point-of-entry was broken-out, NOT in. The cops concluded the so-called V most likely started the fire with fuel oil and cut herself; they secretly advised her friends of their suspicions, and suggested they have the alleged V go back to her home for their own safety. The woman was taken to a local hospital for medical treatment, with a strong suggestion that a psych consult should also be in order.

After returning to her own house, the nurse began calling the police again stating that she was still receiving death threats via notes slipped under her windows. (Does that sound familiar?) She also had the beleaguered officers respond repeatedly because of prowler(s). At this point, Vancouver PD set-up nighttime surveillance of the woman's residence in an effort to either catch the stalker, or prove the nurse was a whacko and was making up all of this stuff.

On the night in question, police communications received a 9-1-1 call from the woman: She sounded very distraught and under the influence of drugs/alcohol, or both. She told dispatchers that a man had broken-into her home and had attacked her. When police arrived, just a minute or so later, they could not get the lady to answer the door, so they broke in. They found the woman prostrate on the living room floor, unconscious and unresponsive. In addition, the first responders found a death threat note in her hand, impaled with a razor sharp stiletto, which was stuck in the floor! Paramedics revived the V and rushed her to the ER. Along with the pierced hand, the docs also found a fresh needle mark in a vein of her arm; subsequent toxicology reports proved that the V had been "mainlined" with morphine!

Needless, to say, the VPD police had some serious reservations about these incidents—which made our case seem pale by comparison: Given the set fire and forensic improbabilities in the first episode, phantom prowlers leaving death notes, and the fact that a police unit was parked down the street only a stone's throw away from the V's house, this caper wasn't ringing true. Couple that with morphine being found in the V's system causes one to ask: Who has access to morphine, other than medical personnel or some low life who might have stolen it from a hospital or pharmacy? Nevertheless, the investigators couldn't just come out and accuse the nurse of false allegations unless they could prove it. Well, they didn't have to: A few weeks later, a patrol unit found the lady's car, apparently abandoned in a secluded parking lot. The driver's door was open and the V's wallet and its contents were scattered on the pavement by the vehicle, as if a struggle ensued. When police searched the area, they found the lifeless nurse in an abandoned house; there was a fresh needle mark in her arm. She was DOA when transported to the hospital. Authorities later learned that she died of an overdose of morphine. . . So, is there any wonder why I wanted to bring our *"Bizarre Beyond Belief"* drama to a swift conclusion before it spiraled out of control like the Vancouver Debacle?

Curtain Time

Sergeant Bryan asked Princess to come to the station for a "Victimology" interview; she really bonded with the sergeant and gladly accepted his invitation. P had no idea who I was until we were introduced; she seemed very excited about this event and warmed-up to me immediately. Although I had a carefully scripted format, I digressed a lot and we chatted about other things than the topic at hand. Because of my age, I think she regarded me, perhaps, as a surrogate father figure, which I had hoped for. Once I established sufficient rapport and felt that she was comfortable with me and the inquiry, I began to slowly interject some of the so-called speculative questions such as: What should happen to the person who is doing this to you? As I previously indicated, an innocent person will almost always want punishment for the offender—to the letter of the law. But, this case was different: Although we were sure that there was no other person doing this, P might give the "law and order" response. But, instead, she exhibited sympathy for the purported suspect and thought that the person needed help. I'm certainly no shrink, but I've read about this phenomenon, which is called projection. . . As I worked through more of these theoretical questions, I began to see more and more empathy for the alleged assailant who was causing her all of this grief. Her answers defied logic, so I hit P with the big bait question that I had in my grab bag; it went something like this:

RKN: "P, you've watched police and detective shows, or perhaps even read a few books, right?"

P: "Oh yes!"

RKN: "Well then, you might know that when the police get a situation like you have been experiencing, they may set-up an undercover video camera so that they can monitor a given area with hopes of identifying a suspect(s), right?"

P: No response, but she nodded in the affirmative and displayed a quizzical look on her face.

Without telling her that we, indeed, had such a system in play, I glanced over to a VCR and TV monitor, which were sitting on an adjacent table. The monitor was on, displaying "snow" on the screen, as they do until a video cassette is inserted. I then asked:

"So, would there be *any* reason that you would be seen on that TV (pointing) placing a note on your window sill Valentine's night?"

My question was answered with that "deer in the headlights" look! My pager then went off, as planned, so I excused myself and told P that I had an emergency call to make. When I got into my office, my detectives were huddled around the TV/VCR which was recording the interview via a hidden camera and microphone. It was painful to watch this confused young woman squirm like a worm on a fish hook. She was pondering my question, all the while looking around the room as if she knew there was a camera in there—somewhere.

Time for Truth

After about 10 minutes, I returned to the interview room armed with a four inch thick folder of reports and the time lapse video tape of the note being deposited on P's window sill. I stood over the young woman, who was then shaking like a leaf in a hurricane and declared:

"Young lady, here are the results of our exhaustive investigation; this video tape is conclusive proof that you put this note (displaying the evidence) on your window sill." She then tried to speak, but I silenced her with a hand gesture indicating "Stop!" I sat down and pulled my chair very close to Princess and looked her square in the eyes and began my monologue:

"This is not a matter of who has been doing this, we already know that! This is now a matter of why this happened, and what we, you and I, have to do to bring this thing to a conclusion in a manner that will cause you the least amount of embarrassment and pain. Please work with me; we can put thing to rest right here and now, get you the help you need and deserve, so that you can get on with a productive life, OK?"

At that point, the young lady had a total meltdown, and I became a crying pillow instead of the big mean interrogator I often was. I really felt bad for this kid, despite all the grief she caused our department, the University and her parents. Within minutes, Sgt. Bryan came to the rescue and took the broken woman off my hands. W*hew*, I sighed, *I'm glad that's over with*...

Epilogue

Much to the chagrin of the DA's Office, I did not bring this case forward for prosecution. Instead, the Dean of Student Affairs Office put the woman on leave for a Quarter, and arranged for intense psychological therapy. This route turned the young lady's ship around and put her on a new and productive course. Sgt. B and I received cards from her periodically in which she thanked us for our help and reported the positive things that were happening in her life. I'm glad it turned out that way and didn't end-up like the troubled nurse in Vancouver...

SA Mary Ellen O'Toole liked the way we handled this matter and requested (and received) a copy of my interview, which she later used in training FBI recruits in the National FBI Academy in Quantico, VA. Agent O'Toole was later appointed as a member of the Bureau's elite Behavioral Analysis Unit, and has appeared on several episodes of the TV series "Criminal Minds." I similarly gave a copy of the tape to my good friend, Detective Jackie Waggoner of Garland PD, TX, which he used for many years in training his folks in *The Art of Conversation*.

CHAPTER TWENTY SEVEN

Bad Boys Bad Boys

Whatcha Gonna Do When Dey Come For You?

Author's Note: This is the chapter I absolutely hated to write: It's about people who took an oath to uphold the laws of the land and to support the United States Constitution; it's about individuals in whom we put our trust—everyday—to do the right thing and ensure that the community will be safe from criminality. Instead, the persons named herein defiled out trust: They took advantage of their positions to satisfy their selfish desires. I borrowed the theme from the popular TV program "Cops" to illustrate my disgust for the guys who screwed-up our department's honor and integrity!

Bad Boy #1: The Tupperware Bandit

It was just another day on the Farm: 10 cups of coffee, shooting the breeze with the A-Units in Cap'n Bill's office, then, upstairs for report review and telephone call returns. At about 10:00 AM, the buzzer went off; it was Cap'n Bill:

"Niemeyer, I got a problem," he boomed in his Barry White-like voice. "Can you come down Code 2 so we can talk about it?"

"Be right there, Bill!" In a flash, I was bounding down the stairs—this was in the period I call "BH"—Before Hips, as in bilateral replacements, which was to come in the early 90's.

The door to the Captain's office was closed; that meant something was up as Bill *always* had an open door! I knocked and entered and was surprised to see CSO, Clifton Clarke, our excellent Jamaican parking enforcement officer—the scourge of campus scoff-laws because Cliff took his job seriously—very seriously! He took no prisoners, that guy...

"What's up?" I queried.

"Go ahead, Clarke, you tell him," the captain deferred.

"Well, Captain," Cliff began in his inimical Kingston accent, "Mr. Crabbe (who ran the pay lot parking program) had to take his wife to the doctor for an emergency, so he left campus. The gate arm machine at the tennis lot jammed so they called me to fix it. When I opened it up, there was no lock box, only this," as he displayed a 6 inch tall by 4 inch wide Tupperware container with $7.50 cents in quarters in it. There was a black line, drawn with a felt tip pen, about 2 inches from the top. This didn't sound or look good for Mr. Crabbe—the hair on the back of my neck stood up. Clarke continued that he repaired the coin slot so it wouldn't jam, installed a lock box in the machine, and immediately reported this to his commander.

It didn't take a rocket scientist to figure out that perhaps something wasn't right here. I instructed Officer Clarke to return to the machine, remove the lock box and replace the Tupperware just as he found it. Most of all, I admonished Cliff not to breathe a word of this to anyone—even though Cap'n Bill and I were certain about this man's integrity, I wanted to ensure this case would be totally discreet.

The much hated parking program was evolving in those days. Realizing the sizable amount of revenue that could be generated by pay parking, the University delegated the DPS to run it. The best and most trusted CSOs were assigned to this program; they were put on tri-wheel Cushman scooters for routine timed parking enforcement. In addition, the department installed wooden gate arms at several big parking lots, such as TMU, the tennis courts and Stanford Medical Center. In order to gain entry, one had to drop quarters in the slot, which should cause the arm to raise and allow entry—but, this system was very unreliable due to frequent malfunctions, which in this instance, blew this whole caper sky high. The way the system was designed to work was the night CSOs were charged with installing the coin mechanisms into the gates in the early A.M. This apparatus had a lock box into which the coins would drop; only one office employee had the key to these boxes, which she would utilize at the end of the day when Mr. Crabbe brought them in. The clerk would deposit the coins into a counting machine; the take was then bagged, recorded, secured with special wire and a lead seal, and stored in the safe. An armored car service would later transport the coins to the bank at TMU. On paper, this process seemed to be bullet-proof—yeah, until somebody figured out how to game it. There will be more on that later.

I met with the Chief and Cap'n Bill and proposed a plan. The only way to solve this case was to catch the thief with his hand in the "Tupperware"—so to speak. . . I proposed a sting: I'd have my detectives (Philip Love and John McMullen) Code 5 the TMU and tennis court lots in the early A.M, before Crabbe charged the machines. After he left for an extended breakfast at TMU cafeteria (which we knew was his M.O.), our snoops would check the machines to see if anything was amiss. The biggest problem I envisioned in this operation was communications. We didn't dare use P.A. Communications, fearing eavesdropping and a tip-off. I then remembered that the S/O had special tactical radios at County Communications. I called the Director and got the OK to borrow them for a few days. I took off and headed for Carol Drive in San Jose, where County Communications was located, high up on a hill.

The next morning, the three of us met at O-Dark 30 in a Menlo Park shopping center, where we briefed. I gave the keys to the machines that Cap'n Bill had provided to the detectives. Philip and John took off and hid out. I had a leisurely breakfast and didn't go to my office at that time, so as not to raise suspicion. At approximately 6:30AM, John came on the air:

"A-2 and FC-3, the subject (Mr. Crabbe) has just opened the machine and armed the gate. I'm in the bushes and can't see exactly what he did."

"10-4, John," I replied. "Stay hidden until he leaves, and then see what kind of container is inside the machine." A few minutes later, Philip reported:

"A-2. The suspect just set the machine at TMU. He's left and believed to be at the cafeteria." Ditto was my response.

McMullen then reported that he looked into his machine, and guess what? You got it: There was no lock-box, but instead the infamous Tupperware was in its place.

The day before this operation, I employed an old trick that bar owners used to make sure their employees weren't skimming the profits from the cigarette machines: They marked quarters with red fingernail polish so when they shook-down a suspected thief and the marked coins showed-up in their possession—Case Closed! So, we did that.

Both detectives dropped a few of the marked coins into the Tupperware containers so all we had to do was wait!

Later that afternoon, my detectives staked-out our employee parking lot; we believed the culprit would drive up to his car, deposit his booty, and return the coin boxes to the Front Office's Parking clerk. Once again, we were right as rain: The man pulled up to the rear of his Mark IV Lincoln, which was about the size of an Iowa Class Battleship, popped the trunk, and was in the process of putting a bag therein when John and Philip pounced on Mr. Crabbe like hungry lions on a gazelle! After cuffing and removing the suspect to Investigations, they found a large thick paper bag (the kind you used to get ice cream in) filled with quarters. He even put some red grease rags in the bottom of the bag for reinforcement! While they were carting Crabbe off, I took the bag of quarters to the Sergeants Office and dumped them out. As I recall, there was about $125 in that bag; moreover, I found all of our bait coins! Now, all we had to do was get a confession.

As soon as the detectives placed the suspect into the interrogation room, the tape was rolling. I viewed the man for several minutes before taking him on. He apparently was rehearsing his mantra:

"I'm juss gonna tell 'um I was juss bringin' 'um in," which the thief recited over and over again. It was pathetic but I had to do my job. This man was well liked by most of the people in the department, so busting this ol' guy would not go over well with the rank and file, I figured. But, we caught him red-handed! So, when I entered to tell him that he was under arrest and read him his Miranda Rights, he continued the aforementioned mantra. When I asked him if he wanted to talk with me, he invoked Miranda, so that was the end of that. *Looks like we were going to be in for one helluva investigation to prove this case,* I mused. Little did I know...

Rebellion

As I expected, the rank and file was in an uproar over the arrest of poor Mr. Crabbe. The SPOA (Stanford Police Officer's Association) held an emergency meeting to denounce the arrest: They targeted "The Ivory Tower" (an endearing moniker the troops gave Investigations)—me in particular—as the bad guys who were just trying to make an name for ourselves by framing an old man for a crime he never committed. They had ZERO facts, yet they persisted in their diatribe. During a heated meeting, Deputy Chuck "Hardy" Kemper exploded. He got up and said, in effect: "I know Captain Niemeyer and his detectives. There is no FN way he would arrest ANYONE, let alone one of our officers, for a crime they didn't commit. Fuck you all!" He abruptly departed the meeting with his middle digit in the air! Well, at least we knew where Chuck stood on this issue. That was very comforting to us in Investigations, but we were still getting a lot of stink-eye from the rest of the troops.

As things came down from a full boil, we were developing a lot of interesting information about our Mr. Crabbe. One of the first people to contact me was the Night CSO supervisor, Mr. Leonard Screws (R.I.P.). Mr. Screws was one of the most interesting people I had ever met in the department: He was a retired Army Sergeant—a "lifer" who put in 35 years in the service of our country. Mr. Screws was recruited by Chief Davis into the Old Guard. Leonard was extremely articulate and had an edict memory. In addition, he was a Black Civil War Historian—which piqued my interest, as I was also a fledgling student of the Civil War. Mr. Screws had mapped-out battle plans of all the engagements that freed slaves participated in.

He identified all of the regiments and even knew who the commanders were. Mr. Screws was indeed unique!

When the dust cleared, Mr. Screws confided in me that he felt Mr. Crabbe was an opportunist and prone to dishonesty. Leonard, related that Crabbe was a "Club Sergeant" in the army—this had no context with me, so Mr. Screws elaborated: Club Sergeants ran the NCO (Non-Commissioned Officers) clubs and took any advantage they could devise. Skimming, theft and deception ran rampant in those operations, Leonard asserted.

In addition to Leonard's input, other disturbing information about Mr. Crabbe started to surface. Someone shared an interesting observation during one of our department BBQ's in Master's Grove: (As mentioned in a previous chapter, Chief Frank Jurian and Captain Wullschleger put on this fabulous spread once a year. As I noted, Frank was an epicurean and only bought high dollar New York strip-steaks from an exclusive meat market in Menlo Park. These Angus morsels where so tender they would melt in your mouth! The feast had everything: Beans, corn, fresh rolls, dessert, beer and soda—enough for a hungry army.) Mr. Crabbe was seen loading cases of soda and beer into his van, while the department members were engaged in a hotly contested softball game on a nearby field. This was hearsay at best, but incriminating, nonetheless. It sounded like we were on the right track, but we still had much work to do!

The Investigation

I contacted the District Attorney's Office and requested a Deputy DA who was conversant in financial investigations. Clearly, we established a prima facie case for petit theft, but I knew that where there was smoke, there would be a fire—I had no idea how big the conflagration would turn out to be. The DA came through in volumes: Not only did they assign a guy who knew about monetary inquiries, but they gave us the Guru in this field at that time. His name was Julius "Jules" Finkelstein, who had recently brought down the corrupt Mayor of the City of San Jose. Mr. Finkelstein and his lead investigator, Cecil "Cec" R. Rhodes (who also happened to be a very close friend of mine), convicted Mr. Alfredo Garza of numerous counts of felony bribery and a host of other related crimes, after an exhausting yearlong investigation. This was a huge shock and black mark on the City as Garza was the first Hispanic mayor of a major city in the United States, which was a big feather in the cap of San Jose's 20% Hispanic community. The verdict was like the guillotine. In any event, Mr. Finkelstein delved into the fray and barked out more orders than a Marine Drill Instructor. "If you bring Jules into the mix, Cec warned, be prepared to roll up your sleeves as Julius is going to drive you like a team of Alaskan Huskies." Julius was not only a motivator and mentor, but he, too, would work his tail off with you in order bring the matter to a swift victorious conclusion. Needless to say, DDA Finkelstein was one sharp cookie!

The Plot

When circumstances change, nefarious characters can often take advantage of the situation and use it to their benefit. Due to a change in personnel and policy, it didn't take this crook long to figure it out and make a plan. At some point, the coin counter machine was removed. This was important, as the former clerk got an accurate count each and every day, which was recorded. Variances in the daily count could be readily be discerned by reviewing the ledger. Some disparities could be due to inclement weather, and of course, during Quarter and Summer breaks, but for the most part, the income was fairly consistent.

Under the new system, Mr. Crabbe simply brought the parking funds into the office where they were dumped into bags, tagged, and secured later to be transported to the bank for deposit. The bank apparently weighed the bags and credited the Parking Program with the funds. There was no ledger or spread sheet kept at our office. In the meantime, the suspect wrested control of the coin boxes: Admittedly, many malfunctions of these devices occurred and they had to be sent out to the manufacturer for repair. Mr. Crabbe cleverly sweet-talked the hierarchy to send him to the manufacturer for technical training so that he could fix the boxes in-house. In theory, this was a good idea; in reality, this was a very bad idea! Next, he took the night CSOs out of the picture by asserting many of them were causing the jams by incorrectly inserting the boxes in the machine. In addition, so many lock boxes were on the fritz that the night guys sometimes didn't have any to install. (Our inquiry suggested that this sly ol' fox was intentionally sabotaging the machines.) Crabbe volunteered to come in early, thus would be responsible for the whole operation, so if there was a problem, he could address it immediately. This was like the fox guarding the chicken coop! Now, he was in total control without oversight checks in place. Having Crabbe's M.O. unraveled, we proceeded to move on to proving all of this.

Sources and Applications

This is a phrase that the FBI coined during their investigation of Alphonse "Al" Capone. After years of unsuccessful attempts to convict the infamous mobster for murder and racketeering, the Bureau scratched their collective heads and suddenly, the light went on: In those days J. Edgar Hoover required all of his men to be either lawyers or accountants. The only way to bring down this gangster, they concluded, was not with gunslingers, but with "Bean Counters". Yes, accountants! They knew that Capone had amassed hundreds of millions of dollars through illicit means. However, he failed to report this ill gotten gain to the Internal Revenue Service. The Bureau and IRS raided Alphonse's "Bookie"—in this case, his accountant—seizing Al's books and flipping the terrified bean counter. Capone's reign was over. In short, the evidence proved that "Scarface's" income shown on his tax return didn't reflect how much money this crook actually amassed.

I had been to an FBI seminar on White Collar Crime and thought this would be the method in which we could demonstrate how much Mr. C actually bilked from the parking fund. This game plan was approved by DDA Jules, and he was forthcoming with search warrants for the financial institutions where the suspect banked. Crabbe was a clever devil as he had numerous accounts in the area, which didn't make this a slam dunk, nor did it make the bankers happy campers: It had been my experience that banks disliked cooperating with the police by providing us with one of their clients' records—primarily because it's a lot of work and they didn't get paid for their efforts, so they had a tendency to drag their feet:

(In a subsequent financial case, a Palo Alto bank manager refused to turn over the records to one of my detectives until we paid for their services. Establishing a Show of Force, four of us went to the bank in Raid Jackets and I demanded to speak to the manager. She was a very unpleasant individual: There is a name for her type that starts with "B," but in the name of political correctness, I will not utter it. . . After several minutes of unsuccessful negotiation, often heated, I called the Municipal Court Judge, the Honorable Stephen Manley, known affectionately in law enforcement circles as "The One-eyed Judge Roy Bean"—he wore a pirate's patch over his damaged eye.

After explaining the situation to Judge Manley, he told me to put the manger on the phone. Everyone in the bank could hear the judge's voice:

"Madame, this is Judge Stephen Manley. I am ordering you to *immediately* hand over the documents delineated in my search warrant. If you fail to do so, I will order Captain Niemeyer to bring you forthwith to my courtroom without delay! Do you understand that Ma'am?" The judge's declaration was replied with a whimper: "Yes." You could have heard a pin drop—save for some muffled snickers by the manger's staff. I guess we weren't the only ones who thought Ms. Snooty was indeed a "B.")

We knew how much SUDPS paid Mr. Crabbe and discovered how much his army pension was. There were a few suspicious deposits, but people who knew him revealed he had received an inheritance. Actually, our game plan was faltering at this point, as we couldn't show any income out of the ordinary via his bank and credit union accounts. We need to know two things: 1) How much did Mr. C actually pilfer? And, 2) Where was it? We needed to shift gears and get back to the drawing board.

Bring on the Bean Counters

It was clear that we needed some people with computer and accounting skills. Enter stage left, Mr. Chris Cannelos, Managing Accountant and Mr. Ken Schultz, a computer whiz kid from the Computer Science Department. We had a meeting with Mr. Finkelstein presiding. He outlined the strategy and sent us on our way. Chris and Ken put their bright noggins together and labored over every piece of information on the parking program for the previous 4-5 years. In addition, they obtained Mr. Crabbe's work schedule for that period and started crunching the numbers and creating computer spread sheets which would shed light into a chasm of darkness. Within a few weeks, Mr. Cannelos and Mr. Schultz returned with an absolute masterpiece. Through the magic of computer science and just plain ol' bean counting, they put together a beautiful line graph that tracked the proceeds of the parking funds. At first glance, nothing came out and poked you in the snout. But, after their succinct explanation, the plot began to unravel:

As previously said, Mr. Crabbe was not only sly, but he was one of the sharpest knives in the drawer. During peak periods, revenues seemed to be consistent but about $125-150 dollars less than in the years when the counting machine was used. That was weird because the usage of the pay lots was always constantly high. We also learned through the suspect's worksheets that he never took a day off or a vacation during the time school was in session. However, in a couple of instances when Mr. C had to take his wife to the doctor and was replaced by Mr. Clarke, there was a marked spike in revenues. The most telling example was when Mr. C's brother died suddenly, forcing him to take bereavement leave; this event was unfortunate for the Crabbe family, but was fortuitous for our investigation. During the period when Clifton Clarke was in charge of collecting the parking funds, the graph spiked consistently during that week. And, during the following weeks when the suspect resumed work, the graph dipped and leveled off as before. This friends, is known as the "Salami Technique," wherein the embezzler takes a thin slice at a time; this is how Mr. C avoided detection for at least 3-4 years. Our financial gurus estimated that Mr. Crabbe got away with *at least* $68, 000 in quarters. So, where did they go?

The Perfect Laundry

When DDA Julius issued a search warrant for Mr. Crabbe's residence, no one was home so we forced entry; Detective McMullen opened the garage door and I was astonished to find a brand spanking new Olds 88. *Where did this come from?* I asked myself. *He never ever mentioned having another car other than his big ol' Lincoln.* Once we got into his paper files, we'd know the answer.

During a cursory search, we all were amazed at how much finery was in that place: Beautiful new furnishings, carpets and drapes, a new big screen TV, the best of cookware, utensils, dining and glassware. When we looked in the closets, we found first cabin haberdashery for Mr. C, and his wife's wardrobe and shoes rivaled Imelda Marcos'—both in quality and quantity—especially the shoes...

In rifling through his files, I learned that the new Oldsmobile was bought and paid for with cash! All of the stuff in this house was purchased with cash. I never found a single credit card account with a balance. My hunch on how this sneak thief converted all of that silver into greenbacks was confirmed when I found hotel and motel receipts from South Lake Tahoe and Reno. What better place to launder quarters—tons of them! We envisioned Mr. C making a run to the Tahoe casinos with the tail of his Mark IV dragging on the roadway like a low rider—maybe even showering some sparks when he hit a bump. It's a wonder the CHP never bagged him for being lower than rim height...

This was a brilliant scheme, culminated with a foolproof method of laundering his ill-gotten gain: All he had to do was grab a couple of those slot machine coin buckets, walk out to his car, fill them up and go to the nearest casino cashier. Knowing this man like I think I do now, he probably spread the wealth around, so to speak—never doing more than one transaction in the same gambling emporium.

What a guy! In the end, he was caught and found guilty, served minimal time in jail and was ordered restitution to the University. This caused his wife's poor health to worsen and she died shortly thereafter. Ditto for Mr. James Crabbe, who died a disgraced pauper.

Bad Boy #2: A Ghost from the Past

A Front Office clerk buzzed and advised me that there was an irate guy on the phone who claimed he was a P.I. (Private Investigator).

"So, what is his problem and what does he want?" I tersely replied, perhaps displaying my general disdain and distrust of that breed. *Most of those guys were wannabe cops, and generally didn't know their posteriors from a hole in the ground, I thought.* Having cleared my emotional slate, I told our lady to put him on.

"Captain Niemeyer, sir, how can I help you?" I faked pleasantness.

"I'm told that you are in charge of Investigations, is that true?" He barked.

"Yes," I clipped, "So, what is the problem?"

"The problem is I'm trying to conduct an investigation and one of your detectives gave me the run around," he shouted.

"Sir, calm down. What do you need me to do?" I retorted. *This guy is beginning to piss-me-off but I wasn't going to let him in on my secret,* I mused. *And, who in the hell does he think he is, Magnum P.I.?*

When the boil came to a simmer, the P.I. said he represented a client who was getting a divorce and she needed an agent to accompany her to a residence in Gilroy in order to retrieve her personal effects. The woman explained that her ex-husband was a former Stanford Police officer who had numerous guns and she was afraid for her life. En route from San Jose, the lady told the agent that her husband had a virtual museum in their house, having stolen numerous precious artifacts, rare books, art and anything he could put his hands on. When they arrived at the Gilroy home, the investigator walked around and saw a number of black statues and carvings he thought were priceless. The P.I. continued that he called our department about these items and was told by one of my detectives that he checked our files and didn't find anything.

After hearing this tale, I defended my guy:

"Sir, this man is brand new up here and wouldn't have known about past thefts; but, I have a file of old unsolved cases and will check right away and get back to you. And, oh, by the way, what is this alleged thief's name?" I quizzed.

"His wife, Mary, says his name is Stephen (Crawdad!)." I felt like I was sucker punched.

"Okay, sir, I'm on it and will get back to you ASAP. Needless to say, I want you to hold this conversation in the strictest of confidence," I asserted.

I hung-up and made a beeline for the four drawer metal cabinet in the hall near the stairway. After thumbing through the files, I found what I seemed to recall: The Archaeological Museum burglary, which occurred in early 1977. Several invaluable pieces of argillite carvings were pilfered in that caper. This collection was one of Jane Lathrop Stanford's favorites. These pieces were carved out of pitch black slate by the Haida Indians, who lived on the Queen Charlotte Islands in British Columbia. The motifs depicted tribal life and celebrated mythical characters in their culture. Seaman often traded these idols during the 19th Century; Mrs. Stanford acquired several rare specimens and fell in love with them.

Next, I called Bob Beth, Manager of the Risk Management Department—a great guy and clearly one of the most informed people in the University. When I inquired if those argillite carvings were still MIA, he got back to me in a few minutes and confirmed the artifacts *were* still at large. I informed Mr. Beth that I may be hot on the trail of them and asked if he had any photos of the pieces. He didn't but steered me to the Museum. One of the curators provided me with a pictorial catalog of argillite works, and although it was unknown if the pieces shown in the book were the same as was in Crawdad's home, I figured that perhaps the P.I.'s agent might be able to make an identification.

With that, I was on my way to the P.I.'s office. When I arrived, my inner feelings about this character were confirmed—he was arrogant and thought he WAS Magnum P.I.—Not! I wasn't enamored with this individual but had to work with him anyway. The kid who took Mary to the house in Gilroy thumbed through the little book I got from the museum and pointed out several items that looked very much like what he had seen in the residence. *Bingo,* I silently rejoiced, *I got this slimeball and he's going down!* Before that, however, I had to establish contact and some rapport with Crawdad's soon to be ex. But, she was very suspicious: She didn't trust me or the department. In her mind, Mary felt that we would support her husband because he was a Stanford Police officer, because "cops always covered-up for their kind." Boy, was she mistaken! Mary didn't realize that we despised this weasel. Crawdad might have been a sworn "peace officer" in the Old Guard, but when Chief Herrington took the helm in 1972, he downgraded most of the so-called officers to CSO. Crawdad loathed the demotion and hated all of the A-Units for that. In my view, Crawdad was an arrogant pseudo-intellectual whose self imposed importance was revolting. Moreover, when he stalled the Arlis Perry murder investigation by invoking his Miranda Rights—as you may recall in Chapter One—I knew there was something seriously wrong with this cat. I relished the opportunity to exact a chunk of flesh from his sorry ass!

Mr. P.I. arranged for me to meet Mary at the FBI Office in San Jose after two agents, whom I knew, vouched for my veracity and integrity. I took a statement from her, said I intended to obtain a search and arrest warrant for Stephen and asked if she would accompany us on the execution of the search: I made this offering so she would see for herself that everything would be above board and she could recover her belongings without interference or threat from

Crawdad. *Little did I know*... She agreed and we arranged to meet early the next morning for breakfast at a local restaurant.

In the meantime, I raced to the DA's Office for the warrants. While this was going on, my investigators were putting a game plan together, using all the assets they could muster, with the help of Patrol and the CSOs. Doug Williams, our excellent and invaluable logistics guy, ran around like a crazed man, setting-up the mobile Command Post, Evidence Vehicle and all of the accoutrements necessary to pull-off this raid at the 11th hour. We would meet at the Gilroy P.D. at 6:00AM for a final briefing.

The Take-Down

The operation was humming along like a Swiss time piece. John McMullen, my lead detective, put on his uniform and partnered up with a big strapping deputy, "Tom," and arrived at Gilroy PD in a marked unit. These two men would be our entry team: This duo would take down the scumbag, hook 'em and book 'em (*Danno.*) We arrived at 6:55AM; I hid behind the uniforms—Hey, I was an old man by then and didn't want to spend my retirement in a wheelchair... However, I wore my Raid Jacket, a bulletproof vest and clutched my Colt 1911 .45 very tightly.

BAM BAM BAM. The front door almost disintegrated! McMullen shouted:

"Stanford Police, Search Warrant, Open Up!"

After about 20 seconds of nothing, we heard some rustling around inside. John had a key provided by Mary, so he unlocked the door and threw it open! There, standing in the hallway was our prey, Stephen Crawdad, clad in a robe, shaking like a leaf and acting as if he didn't know whether he should defecate or go blind. Two big guns were leveled at him, yet he just froze-up and didn't respond to John's commands. (John later confided that he thought he was going to have to shoot that low-life.) The take-down officers rushed in and snapped the bracelets on the thief. He was speechless and looked like he was going to pee in his robe...

Once our collar was shackled, I rushed to a rear room and located an argillite statue that the P.I.'s agent pointed out to me when I showed him the museum's catalog. I then returned to the foyer, stuck the piece in Crawdad's face and declared:

"Stephen Crawdad, this was stolen from Stanford's Archeological Museum; you, my friend, are under arrest for 496 P.C., possession of stolen property. Now, get this vermin out of here!" His blank stare was not unexpected from this sociopath. This was a very defining moment in my career: Not only did we recover a valuable piece of Stanford history, but we eliminated a despicable creature who had the gall to brag that he was a police officer. The men spirited-him-out and took him to jail in San Jose! Now, we could get on with our work.

The Search

The group sprung into action like a well choreographed dance troupe: Everyone in this team knew their job and performed like people on a modern auto assembly line. Ever since I started getting our folks involved in search warrant execution, we all became more efficient and knowledgeable. Although I was taught the basics by the Narco Squad at the Old S/O back in the late '60s and early '70s, our New Guard was picking-up a good head of steam and came-up with many innovative methods and ideas. The basics were sacrosanct: One official *Finder*, usually the team leader; one *Scribe*; one *Evidence Officer*. This was done to establish a credible "Chain of Evidence" which could withstand defense challenges later on in court. Early on, I adopted a methodical system in which the team would work in a clockwise motion during the initial search. *Smurfs*—officers who initially tore the place apart and found contraband—needed to immediately contact the Finder and point out where and what evidence was to be seized. At that point, pre-numbered cards were placed next to the item(s), photographed, tagged and logged-in (time, date and initials of officer) by the Scribe. This system was crucial: In the old days, cops would race around like a bunch of saloon cowboys, throw stuff all over the place, and when the dust settled, many team members couldn't remember who found what or where. It was a nightmare! And, many cases were tossed out during 995 (P.C.) motions to suppress the evidence. Everybody just needed to slow down and do it right. I later employed a video cam for surveying the premises, but we killed the sound so that untoward comments, laughter, and typical cop banter would not make us look like buffoons in court. As Finder, I dictated every move into my trusty pocket tape recorder; this enabled me to record the event in real time, which was invaluable later on when I wrote the report. This tape was later placed into evidence so I had to be careful with my language, too.

The first piece spotted as we entered the foyer was a huge (maybe 1 foot thick) dictionary on a podium—it came from the Library's Rare Books collection. As this point, I called for a detective to see if they could get an expert to join us, as the place was like a city library, for crying out loud! Fortunately, we were able to get Ms. Maggie Kimball, Director of the Stanford Library's Rare Collection and an associate to join our happy little group—they were invaluable in pointing out dozens of rare books purloined from the University's library system.

Having been inside a few Professors' homes in the Faculty Ghetto, I could best describe Crawdad's digs as a wannabe's facsimile: His parlor was adorned with the aforementioned argillite carvings, paintings, antique furniture, elaborate throw rugs, a smoking stand and many other exquisite pieces, which escape my memory at the moment. His wife, Mary, told me that he loved to gloat about his elitist taste and possessions—even though most of the stuff was hotter than molten lava. I believe he fancied himself as a highly educated aristocrat! Mary said that he loved to sit in his high back antique chair, adorned in his satin smoking jacket, puffing on an expensive pipe, while he read or listened to highbrow music. My kinda guy. . .

As our search expanded to the patio room, all sorts of interesting items started popping-up: We located a Stanford Police badge and ID, which he obviously failed to turn in when he quit in 1977. Searchers also located a huge ring of keys typical of what CSOs were issued, which allowed them access to virtually every building on campus. We then stumbled on a gem: There, in a fancy leather case, was a Leland Stanford Junior University *sheepskin* declaring that Stephen Crawdad had earned a Bachelor of Science degree at one of the world's most prestigious institutions of higher learning. The hell you say? That scumbag wormed his way into the highly secure Registrar's Office and ripped-off a blank diploma, then had the gall to have his name printed on it! Well, when you have keys to the joint and know all the alarm codes, anything is possible. This act particularly ticked-me-off, as I had just put my daughter through Stanford at a considerable cost and sacrifice. This Crawdad guy just bypassed four years of grueling study and matriculated by his own devices. What a phony!

I.E.D.

While working in the patio room, Mary grabbed my arm and started screaming hysterically. I had no clue as to what she was trying to tell me, as she literally dragged me to the front door:

"That guy there just stole my stuff!" as she pointed to John's arrest team partner, Tom. After booking the suspect, they returned to the house to help out where needed. I assigned Tom to assist in taking the sealed evidence boxes out to the Evidence Bus, which was being guarded by a Sergeant and a CSO. When the Evidence Supervisor (in the house) was done logging the items, the evidence was put into boxes and taped shut. The boxes were then stacked near the door.

Upon hearing Mary's accusation, Tom's face turned ashen white and his eyes doubled in size.

"Tom," I bellowed, "What's going on?"

"Captain, I'm just transporting the evidence," he sheepishly returned. This sounded like a reply I had heard several years before in the Tupperware Bandit caper...

"No, he didn't," Mary screamed, "He took my case and put it in the trunk of that patrol car," she exclaimed and she dragged me out to the sidewalk. "Just to make sure, I went back to the patio room, and my case was gone. I also caught him taking my stuff before and told you about it." She then turned to Tom and pushed him toward his patrol unit.

"Open that trunk, I want my box back!" Mary roared.

"Tom, what in the hell are you doing putting evidence in your trunk? I told you that all evidence was to go in that bus!" as I pointed to the Evidence Vehicle.

All I got in return was a blank stare. I was hoping that this was all a big mistake; however, when Tom popped the trunk and removed the black case (aka "Posse Box," used by cops to carry report forms and other equipment), Mary snatched it out of his hand. At that moment, I heard a thud inside the case. When the outraged woman opened the case, I saw a Sony Watchman mini TV, which I had seen in a cardboard box of personal belongings in the patio room near a posse box; Mary said the TV belonged to her husband and the posse box was hers.

"See, I told you," she shrieked. "You are all a bunch of crooks! I'm outta here!" as she dashed to her car and sped off.

Perfect, just what I needed! Here we are busting a dirty ex-department member and one of my most trusted deputies, and a good friend, too, steals the victim's stuff while we are conducting a lawful search warrant. This is damn serious, I continued to ponder. *This is a crime committed under "color of authority," a FN FELONY—possibly a federal offense!*

I was sick to my stomach. After all of this good hard work to right a wrong and bring about justice, I felt we all had been hit by an Improvised Explosive Device (I.E.D.). Shocking!

The Aftermath

I immediately called the Chief and apprized him of this debacle. I could feel him cringe—even over the cell phone. I had ordered Tom to return to the station. Chief Herrington said he would be there and immediately relieve him of his badge and weapon and place him on suspension until the matter could be investigated.

No sooner than I got off the phone with A-1, Palo Alto Communications contacted me and said the FBI wanted me to call them Code 2. *Uh-oh,* I thought, *this cannot be good. Mary must have called them; I figured we were in deep do do...*

I called one of the Agents who facilitated the initial meeting with Mary and told him what had occurred. I assured him that I had the situation under control, that the suspected the "bad boy" was en route to Stanford and would be summarily suspended by the Chief on arrival. I urged the Agent to have Mary return so that we could secure the residence and assure her that this stupid stunt would not go unpunished. She returned shortly thereafter and I smoothed things over as best I could. Not only was our department's reputation severely tarnished, but this didn't bode well for law enforcement in general. On the way home, I dictated the events on my recorder; other motorists must have thought I was a nut job, as I was so pissed-off, hollering into the recorder and gesticulating wildly. No wonder they have outlawed DWCP—Driving While on Cell Phone—as I must have been weaving all over the roadway like a drunk driver...

Bad Boy #3: "Clepto" Tom

This misdeed by Tom was like an implosion in the department: The place literally burst at the seams, as this man was one of the most popular guys in the organization. Although there were three eye-ball witnesses to the theft—including a sergeant and a CSO who didn't think twice when they saw Tom carrying a police posse box to his patrol car—many of the rank and file couldn't conceive that Tom was a thief, and thought it was just a big mistake. What they didn't know is that Mary saw him cruising around the house with a box, picking-up little pieces of art work—her art work—and she told him to put her things back! After she informed me of this incident, I admonished Tom not to touch anything without my approval. Furthermore, the items Tom had "picked" were not on the search warrant and clearly not previously stolen from Stanford! This was a seemingly innocuous incident at the time, but stuck in my craw after

Mary caught him red-handed with her posse box, which contained Crawdad's Sony Watchman TV. This suggested motive, in my mind.

IA

Whenever alleged misconduct occurs in any law enforcement agency, a thorough IA (Internal Affairs) inquiry must be conducted. Although most IAs are handled by experienced in-house investigators, this one needed to be done by another agency. The Santa Clara County Sheriff's IA division assigned two top-notch detectives to the matter. After reviewing all reports and evidence, the investigators conducted thorough interviews with all relevant parties and witnesses. Their conclusion was that Tom, indeed, violated SUDPS policy and found that probable cause existed to charge him with petty theft; thus, the case was referred to the District Attorney's office for their review.

The Trial

The case of People of the State of California vs. Tom was held in San Jose Municipal Court; the defendant chose to have the matter heard before a jury. This was a gut-wrenching experience! Several of Tom's department friends and allies made it very uncomfortable for those of us on the prosecution's side. I made sure that our witnesses were kept well away from Tom's hostile supporters; we were holed-up in a jury room until it was our time to testify. The defense did a great job of portraying their guy as a stable, church going, good family man, who merely got confused and thought the infamous Posse Box belonged to one of our officers, thus put it in the trunk of his patrol car for safe keeping. Like my *Super Weenie* civil trial (Chapter Thirteen: The Other Shoe), Tom's lovely family was positioned in the front row of the courtroom so that they were never out of the jury's sight.

After what seemed like a month—it was actually a little over a week—the jury came to a swift conclusion: Not Guilty! Needless to say, the prosecution and those men on our team were stunned! Our ADA, a darn good man and a fierce advocate of justice, was particularly devastated: Our DA later confided in me that convicting cops in San Jose is always an uphill battle; but, given the evidence and witnesses we had, he thought we would prevail. When our prosecutor polled the jury, they admitted that Tom probably stole the items, but given the fact he would lose his job and had been publicly humiliated, they felt justice had been served—a classic case of jury nullification if I've ever seen one... What the jury failed to take into consideration was that cops have unions and associations, so terminating an individual charged with a crime who had been found not guilty is never a foregone conclusion. The fight had just begun...

SPOA vs. Stanford University

As expected, Tom and Co. were not planning to go away quietly. He had been terminated as a Deputy Sheriff at Stanford and wanted his job back. After all, a jury of his peers had found him not guilty of theft, therefore, in his mind, he should be absolved of all wrongdoing and be re-instated. The Stanford Police Officer's Association filed a labor law action on Tom's behalf. Enter stage left, Stanford's General Counsel! They assigned two of the brightest stars in the office to make sure that a crook would never be able to wear a peace officer's badge and carry a firearm on the Stanford campus again—ever! The lead attorney was Susan Hoerger, one of the smartest individuals I have ever met in my life. Mrs. Hoerger specialized in labor relations law and was always at the top of her game.

Co-counsel was a dear friend and our department's judicial advocate, Jennifer Q. Westerlind (R.I.P.), who sadly passed away in 2009. I first met Jennifer when she was a Legal Office Administrative Assistant. She later pursued her dream and became a member of the General Counsel's Office after receiving her law degree.

The Hoerger/Westerlind team attacked this case in a determined and methodical way. The first thing they wanted to know was everything about plaintiff. I hired a retired FBI agent to conduct a new background investigation on Tom. The original background inquiry, admittedly, was not as thorough as it could have been. At the time, we had part time background investigators, as I previously wrote, who had never been completely trained in the art of ferreting out negative information on prospective candidates. Many previous employers were reluctant to divulge any derogatory information for fear of being sued, thus would *shine the investigator on*—or simply refuse to cooperate. Subsequent legislation precluded candidates from suing former bosses if their information resulted in the applicant failing the process. The candidate had to sign a form, which indemnified a prior employer; still, many folks wouldn't give us the straight story. It often took some finesse to separate the wheat from the chaff—so to speak.

I noticed one red flag in Tom's original PHQ (Personal History Questionnaire) in which he admitted being terminated from a building supply company for being in possession of a stolen skill saw. He told the BGI that it was a big mix-up as "some other dude" gave him the saw. Well, the "some other dude" was part of an organized ring of employees who were stealing power tools like they were going out of style. I often wondered if our guy was more complicit than he let on. . . When our BGI tried to follow-up, the company had since gone belly-up, so the people in the know were nowhere to be found. After receiving favorable reports from his most recent employer, friends and clergymen, I gave Tom the benefit of the doubt and hired him. Shame on me. . .

The second investigation was a horse of a different color, however. Our "hired gun" found out that Tom had quite a history of questionable behavior and veracity: Inventory and random items under his control seemed to disappear into thin air. When confronted with these irregularities, the man would have no clue! There were also rumors of infidelity with clients, e.g., accepting sexual favors in exchange for merchandise and other perks. This picture was not pretty.

But, suspicion and innuendo would never be allowed into any judicial proceeding, so our legal team delved into the facts of the Gilroy search warrant, which had gone horribly wrong. This entailed hours and hours of interviews with the accusatory persons involved. Guess who was the number one target?

I was accustomed to intense scrutiny on civil cases, having been prepped by the "Dynamic Duo" of Bob Von Raesfeld and his partner, Keith Bowers, hired guns who the University employed in defending our department's lawsuits: Those attorneys once grilled me unmercifully for two (2) 10 hour sessions, over a weekend, on a case wherein the plaintiff claimed police abuse. Mr. Von Raesfeld played our defense lawyer while Keith Bowers took the role of the plaintiff's antagonist. This session was tantamount to the Spanish Inquisition: Every time I uttered a *faux pas* or misspoke, Bob kicked me in the shins with his "cock-a-roach-killer" shoes—(In Hawaii there are millions of roaches, some as big as B-29s. Someone characterized these sharp pointed shoes accordingly, as they ensured a kill when the pests tried to hide in a corner). After those sessions with Bob and Keith, jeez, my shins looked like I had been shot by a shotgun cartridge loaded with buckshot!

Save for the *cock-a-roach* killer shoes, Susan and Jennifer's interrogations mirrored Bob and Keith's inquisitions. But, when we showed-up for the hearing, all of us were ready and confident that our testimonies and recollections were 100 percent correct. We were good to go!

The hearing was convened in a small conference room on campus. The Labor Relations Board assigned a very bright lady as the Arbitrator. She seemed to be alert, very engaging and above all, fair to both sides. The worst part of this ordeal for me was sitting across the relatively small table and enduring the *stink eye* from Tom's association representative, whom I dubbed the "cue ball." We previously had some problems with this individual and forced him to go to a psychologist. I once told a close friend I hoped the "witch doctor" would shrink his bald head down to the size of a cue ball. . . To say that I didn't like this guy would be an understatement!

All personnel on our side testified as they had in Municipal Court. There were no changes in testimony or inconsistencies, to my recollection. When Tom testified, he re-iterated what he said in the criminal trial--he merely put the posse box in the trunk for safekeeping, thinking it belonged to a fellow officer. That testimony was suspect in light of Mary's earlier observation and was immediately keyed-in-on by Ms. Hoerger and Westerlind. At a recess, Susan proposed a "gotcha:" We put the Sony Watchman in the posse box and placed it on the end of the table next to the Arbitrator. When the session reconvened, Ms. Hoerger asked Tom to pick-up the box as he had on that day of infamy. Being a very congenial fellow, he eagerly complied. When he grabbed the handle of the posse box and pulled it off of the table, a loud thud was heard. The Arbitrator looked at our legal experts and me with that "You've gotta be kidding me look!" Just as all the witnesses had previously testified to, under oath, the telltale "thud" was unmistakable! All witnesses who were in earshot heard that thud when Mary snatched the posse box from Tom's hands. Game Over!

Tom's bid for reinstatement to the SUDPS was summarily denied. After the charade was over, the Arbitrator shook her head in utter disbelief that our "Bad Boy" was not convicted of criminality. I still wonder about that, too...

Bad Boy's #4 and #5: What a pair to draw to!

Once again, a couple of well respected guys, popular and well-liked by everyone in the department, suddenly derailed and went haywire. One of these individuals was a religious and seemingly principled man; he was devoted family man whose kin were deeply rooted in the University. What would possibly cause these folks to go so bad so quickly? Greed! For the almighty dollar—in this case they were pieces of silver—not 30, but tons of them...

Hmmmm: What's Wrong with this Picture?

From a vantage point in his office, an observant and curious University employee happened to notice something very odd: Like clockwork, every single morning at nearly the same time (early AM), a guy in a white van would drive-up in the large parking lot and retrieve items from a parked car. The man in the white van was highly recognizable as he wore a SUDPS CSO's uniform, and was on the dreaded parking enforcement team. Like a robot, "Frick" (I call him) would transfer various items from his vehicle and put them into the white van. Most curious was the medium size gym bag, which he would *fling* into the van. At day's end, Officer Frick would return to his mid-size pick-up with a camper shell, and transfer the items back into his car. Frick was a very slim guy and stood about 5' nothing; he couldn't have weighed more than a buck thirty-five—dripping wet. However, instead of "flinging" the gym bag back into his little pick-up, Frick would labor with the bag, as it was seemingly full of something—a very heavy something. After several days of observing this scenario, our spotter concluded that something was wrong here. He surmised that because the CSO was part of the parking meter team, the contents of the gym bag could be full of ill gotten gain, so he called the Chief.

I had been on a short vacation and was briefed when I returned. I was in the waning months of my career and was working with Captain Marvin Moore so he'd be up to speed with the Investigation's Unit once I retired. The parking enforcement Lieutenant was on the case and a team was conducting a covert surveillance detail on Frick. But, at the time, they didn't know for sure who the brain trust of this operation was, although they believed he could possibly be Frick's partner, Officer "Frack," the religious individual I told you about. Every morning, after making the rounds and collecting the parking meter proceeds, the entire parking enforcement team would gather at the Medical Center's cafeteria for coffee and nurse ogling. . . Frack was the *de facto* leader of the group and met with the crew in the cafeteria at about 9:00AM every morning. While this was going on, Frick was busily filling-up his tote bag to the brim so that even Arnold, *"Da Govenata,"* in his prime, could barely lift the damn thing! Frick would then join the group and it was business as usual. But, on D-Day, the surveillance team caught Frick with his hand in the cookie jar—so to speak—loading up his gym bag. He and his cohort were done!

So, how in the hell did these crooks have open access to the coins retrieved from the hundreds of meters around campus you might ask? It was an almost re-run the of Tupperware Bandit's scam of wresting apparatus control from the system, which, in theory, was supposed to thwart pilfering: The CSO collection detail was equipped with heavy gauge steel carts on wheels. There was a special hopper affixed to the top, which when mated with the meter, allowed the quarters to drop into the cart. When full, F&F would wheel the cart back to the van and get another one. Well, wouldn't ya know; those damn hoppers began jamming—according to F&F. And, the turn-around repair time threatened the whole operation. F&F convinced the Lt. that they needed to 86 those pesky hoppers and allow them to deposit the contents directly into the cart's slot. At first, the trap door was locked until they brought the booty into the station for bagging and tagging. But, that system soon evaporated and F&F acquired the key to the locks. This was a page out of Mr. Crabbe's playbook. Talk about dangling a carrot in front of a couple of starving rabbits? The plot was hatched.

Mop-up

My good friend, Marvin Moore, and I were like the U.S. Army in the Pacific during WWII: We were left to mop-up after the Marines took an island. By comparison, this mission was a piece of cake, as Frick and Frack were stupid beyond recognition. Unlike the clever Tupperware Bandit, these dummies deposited thousands of dollars into their Stanford Federal Credit Union accounts. It didn't take Inspector *Clouseau* to figure this one out: When a guy's average balance was only a few hundred bucks a month in the past, and it suddenly jumped to $140,000 for Frack and $120,000 for Frick, that's a *clueso* . . . The most troubling part of the mop-up was when we searched Frack's home and seized his financial records. There were religious icons all over the place; the entire home had the atmosphere of a warm, friendly domicile. I looked Frack in the eye and told him how disappointed I was in him. I told him I couldn't understand how a man with his great reputation and religious beliefs would ever have committed such a despicable crime—this lapse of sanity damaged his very being, as well as that of his endearing family. I cannot describe the look on his face. But, it was one of contrition and bewilderment. I guess many of his family members depended on him in so many ways that he was over his head in debt and desperately needed an avenue of relief, thus concocted this crime spree.

Frick, on the other hand, was a real piece of work. I later learned that he was a real operator and was smarter than the average bear: He cleverly laundered wheelbarrows of quarters at a Redwood City Safeway store, which had a coin sorting machine. The market charged an 8% fee, but I guess you might write that off to the price of doing business. . . Many of the employees at Safeway were suspicious of Frick; however, he convinced them that he owned a profitable vending company and was merely cashing-in the proceeds of his coin operated washing and snack machines.

Fortunately, this unit of "Crime Inc." wasn't in operation for more than 6 months. In the end, much of the stolen loot was recovered, and these clowns were eliminated from our organization and punished by the judicial system. I believe our department's integrity was rehabilitated because the swift and long arm of the law hammered these Bad Boys and gave them their just due! And, thank God for our observant citizen—without him, Frick and Frack might have continued to ride their gravy train for whose knows how long. . .

Chapter Twenty Eight

Typical Farm Crime

Little Stealins'

Most of the crime on the Stanford University campus was once described by my Ol' Sergeant, Everett "The Gunner" York as: "Little Stealins." He was truly a throwback; the good sergeant began his law enforcement career about a century too late. He wasn't much on "book learnin'," either, but was big on common sense: During the early '70s, prior to the establishment of the New Guard, S/O deputies had to respond to every call that involved an arrest or felony. On one occasion, a deputy was called to investigate a somewhat complicated case, which was probably embezzlement. The officer called Sgt. York for counsel, as he really didn't know what to do. After explaining the circumstances, The Gunner interrupted and barked:

"Listen, Buster! In my book, there's little stealins' *AND* big stealins', so, you figure it out!" Click!

Boy, that was inspiring. . . But, that's the way it was in those days.

When I got on the scene in late 1974, I reviewed the stats and found that most of the crimes on campus were, indeed, "Little Stealins'." But, when you did the tally, the bottom line almost always amounted to "Big Stealins'."

Bike Thefts

As I recall, the bike theft tally during the calendar year of 1974 was a whopping 874. Now, we aren't talking about Taiwan/China "knock-offs" (junk bikes); these kids came to school with high dollar, tricked-out 10-15 speed models, which, even then, cost at least $700 to a grand or more. Stanford was a virtual cherry patch, as an OG guy once coined it. Why were so many of these kids getting their transportation ripped-off? Those of you alums and current students know that without a bike on the Farm, you'd have to be a marathon runner to get around the campus, especially during class changes.

Well, it didn't take this San Jose State College graduate long to figure out that the cause of so many bike thefts was a lack of preventative security: In those days, the students simply didn't lock-up their cycles to an immovable object. If the kids locked their mount at all, it was usually to itself. I guess they figured that the crooks wouldn't simply carry it off and throw the bike into a van or pick up. This was especially the case during registration, when scores of freshman came out of Maples Pavilion only to find their brand new cycle MIA. Sophomores and upper class students had learned from their first year's experience, thus didn't lose too many of their steeds. What to do?

Initial attempts of warnings to the student populace generally fell on deaf ears as the bike thefts continued at a staggering rate. The notion that thieves were just area kids who simply wanted a nice bike was generally over exaggerated; I later learned that there was a big market for these choice cycles in the Bay Area, especially in San Francisco: The "chop shops" fenced this booty, obliterated or altered the serial numbers, and sent them out the door at an incredible profit. Bike theft at Stanford was a high dollar industry!

More had to be done. I subsequently hired a Crime Prevention Manager, Dan Smith, and we established the SSU (Stanford Student's Unit): We enlisted bright community service oriented students to develop an effective Crime Prevention program, not only to create written and visual materials, but also to interface with the students to preach our gospel. And, by God, it worked!

Gang Busters!

Despite our best efforts of bike theft awareness, the cycles continued to go away at an alarming rate. With the advent of the sturdy "Kryptonite" U-lock and the SSU's mantra of "lock your bike to an immovable object," thefts dropped a staggering 50 percent. That was encouraging. However, all of a sudden, bikes started disappearing from the racks where they were secured with the new U-locks; curiously, the locks vanished as well. How were these thieves defeating the highly touted Kryptonite, which the manufacturer claimed to be stronger than Superman! This was, indeed, a real mystery. However, one observant student called in a suspicious subject lurking around a big gaggle of bicycles near Stern Hall. When the patrol unit arrived, the deputy spotted a guy checking out the bikes as if he was a government inspector looking for unregistered units. When the subject espied the officer, he suddenly took off like a jackrabbit on his skateboard. A coordinated perimeter was quickly established and they tackled the would-be-thief after a short foot chase. When the suspect parted company with his wheeled *surfboard*, the board flipped over and revealed something interesting fastened to the undercarriage: It was small tire jack, later identified as being manufactured by Volvo. This leveraging device fit perfectly between the U-locks, and after several pumps on the handle, the so-called bulletproof lock shattered as if it was made of glass. *Who in the world thought of this,* I wondered. *Probably someone in jail or prison with way too much time on their hands,* I supposed. My detectives called several local auto wrecking yards and discovered that they couldn't keep the Volvo jacks in stock. A proprietor of one "pick 'n pull" told my investigator that he couldn't figure out why so many shady characters sought out these jacks, as none of them appeared to be members of the Volvo community...

Bones

When Dan Smith shared this startling revelation with his biker contacts, a couple of enterprising young men came up with a quick fix: They called their invention "Bones." These devices were simply hardened steel sleeves which fit over the existing U-lock shanks, thereby increasing the strength exponentially. In order to demonstrate how difficult it would be for the average thief to defeat a U-lock equipped with Bones, the inventors put on a *dog and pony show* at our department, which we videotaped. The presenters outfitted themselves with face shields and a baseball catcher's vest, as well as shin protectors. In their first attempt to break the device with a Volvo jack and the standard 12 inch lever, there was no way! The lock began to bend a little but did not crack. They then used a 3 foot lever and cranked on that jack until the U-lock resembled a big doughnut before it finally exploded and sent shrapnel flying all over the place. Fortunately, the onlookers were at a safe distance and didn't get hit by airborne shards of steel. A person without protective gear would have had to be nuts to try to break one of the Bones-reinforced locks. To my knowledge, students who availed themselves of this clever invention, for a mere ten bucks, never had their wheels stolen. Nothing like American ingenuity, I've always said.

Backpacks

Backpack thefts were a biggie on campus. Not only did students lose a bundle of very expensive books and class notes, but they usually lost their wallets or purses, which often contained varying sums of cash—But, more importantly, all of their credit and bank cards, student IDs, driver's licenses, computers and other personal information. If anyone has ever experienced this type of crime—which these days often results in identity theft—you have to sympathize with the poor victims, who certainly didn't need the additional stress. In many cases, the crooks removed wallets, purses and other valuables, then discarded the backpacks in the nearest trash can or dumpster. But, invariably, there was more to come.

Most of the backpacks were pilfered from areas where the students congregated, such as the student union, libraries and special events. Whenever high profile dignitaries or celebrities appeared, backpacks were not allowed inside of these venues. In many cases, the DPS assigned special security officers to keep an eye on the attendees' property, which proved to be a huge deterrent.

In addition to targeting student gathering sites, many adventurous criminals ventured into student dorms and university offices to ply their devious trade. Many of these characters cleverly memorized name tags on student's doors or staffer's offices. So, if they were challenged, they would quickly say: "Oh, I'm looking for Joe Blow or Sally Jones." The Velcro fingered cats who prowled the offices knew exactly where to find women's purses—right in the back portion of the lower right hand desk drawer! Most of these guys (we never caught a woman) were as slick as shucked oysters; they were rarely seen or apprehended. Needless to say, our Crime Prevention Unit was always busy trying to educate a transitioning student population, as well as our University employees.

The ATM Scam

Many naive student victims of purse and wallet thefts went for the ATM scam like a hungry fish goes for a big, fat earthworm. And, once the bait was presented, the "fish" swallowed it hook-line-and-sinker! Because the bad guys had all of the victim's personal information, it didn't take them long to find their phone number. At approximately 11:45PM, usually the day of the theft, the crook would call the unsuspecting student and purport to be either a police officer or bank official. The conversation would go something like this:

Groggy student: "Hello."

Alert Criminal: "Ms. (or) Mr. Smith?"

Victim: "Yes. Who is this?"

Criminal: "This is Sergeant (*DoWrong*) of the San Francisco Police. Sorry to bother you at this hour, but we just apprehended an individual who is in possession of your wallet (they loved to use cop talk); he says you let him borrow it; it that true?"

Shocked Student: "No. No! Of course not! My backpack was just stolen today and I reported it to the Stanford Police!"

Criminal: "Well, that's what we figured. This suspect here was intending to use your ATM card, so in order to verify that you *really* are Ms. (or) Mr. Smith, we need to know what the P.I.N. number is."

Elated Student: "Just a minute, I have it written down here. Oh, I'm so relieved that you recovered my wallet with all of my ID and stuff. Oh, My God! Here it is: 4888."

Elated Criminal: "Confirm, 4888?"

Relieved Student: "Yes, 4888."

Soon to be richer Criminal: "OK, that's great. Now, you can pick up your wallet at the Mission Station, located at 630 Valencia St. between 8 and 5, OK?"

Jubilant Student: "Oh, thank you Sergeant, thank you so much. Goodbye."

Immediately after terminating the call from a pay phone across the street from a bank ATM, the bogus "sergeant" beat feet to the ATM and withdrew the maximum cash amount—$200-$300. And, after the clock struck 12 midnight, the sneak thief reinserted the card, punched in the P.I.N. and collected another fistful of dollars. The bad "sergeant" was then, most likely, off to the nearest drug dealer...

Auto Burgs

Car break-ins were an everyday event at Stanford. I think we led the county in this category. Not only did many of the students have nice rides, but the staff, both at the University and the sprawling complex of the Stanford University Medical Center (SUMC) did, as well. When you add visitors to the campus' facilities for research, tourism and special events—most notably football—we had acres, upon acres of "pick 'n pull." At the top of the "shopping" list were high dollar stereos, which nearly all of the newer cars had. However, the damage done to the vehicles usually amounted to 4 or 5 times what the radio was actually worth: The MO of choice was to pry or smash a window. Once inside, the crooks would rip out the device with a large screwdriver, or, what I call, a "Stevie Wonder Bar,"—a short crowbar. This action would effectively destroy the dashboard! Although most folks had insurance, the deductible premiums were often excessive. So, having a fancy sound system without a loud, obnoxious alarm system was a recipe for disaster on this campus!

Most of the car burglars were juveniles or young adults, so even if we got lucky and our cops were fast enough to catch them, a slap on the wrist was about all they would get in court. However, every once in awhile an older, slower dude would arrive on the scene. . .

The Wind Wing Burglar

During the early 1970s, we experienced a rash of auto burgs wherein the suspect gained entry by smashing in the passenger side wind-wing, which was common in most cars of that period. This guy preyed on areas where joggers parked their cars, such as along Junipero Serra and Stanford Avenue; he was only after valuables, wallets and purses, which people often left out in plain sight. In many instances, the cars weren't even locked, but our moron didn't have the presence of mind to check the door handles before busting the glass. This became the man's signature, which was shared among numerous Bay Area law enforcement agencies, for this cat ranged far and wide. He was finally nabbed in the act at an East Bay Regional Park and sent to prison where he was locked up for a very long time. His name was John Morton, a serious heroin hype who fed his habit with the proceeds from his car thefts.

In the late 1980s, we began experiencing a rash of window smash burgs which were similar in nature to Mr. Morton's MO: Passenger side windows were blown out—the newer model cars didn't have wind-wings anymore, so the entire piece of glass went away. Like before, many of the victims failed to lock their doors, despite of our efforts at Crime Prevention 101. And, this thief didn't mess with stereos; he only took loose valuables. Crime scene investigations showed that, unlike in the days when the crooks broke windows by prying or hitting the glass with a blunt object, these windows shattered as if they were shot out with a scatter gun or something. Closer inspection revealed that small pieces of ceramic were located in the pile of shards. These objects turned out to be ceramic insulation used on spark plugs, which we later found out were being stolen from junkyards or wherever. Somehow, these geniuses figured out that if they broke these spark plugs into small pieces and threw them at a car's window, the pane would shatter into a million pieces. This would not only take out the window, but the glass shrapnel would do a lot of damage to the surrounding paint. Trust me, I know about this, as my car was broken into (in 2006) in this manner, which cost me over $1,000 in repairs!

Could this be the work of Ol' John Morton? I asked myself. *Naaaaa,* I replied. *That dude is still in the joint, and he's way too old to be out here smashing car windows.* Nonetheless, we set up some surveillance teams, and I put out a BOL on Morton (as a remote possibility), as well as other known burglars. Furthermore, these burglaries were occurring in some of the SUMC parking lots; John *always* hit remote areas where joggers parked their vehicles, so in my mind, this couldn't possibly be him.

Well, after only a few days, our ever observant CSO Clifton Clarke, who was in an unmarked car with a pair of binoculars, spotted a dude smashing a window and entering a vehicle in one of the medical lots. He immediately put out an alert to patrol (which I heard over the monitor in my office), and they were all over this one like ugly on ape! A short foot pursuit ensued but the suspect was in cuffs and en route to the station in short order. When I heard the 10-29R (warrant and records check) on the collar, I almost fell out of my chair. It was none other than Mr. Morton himself, who recently got out on parole. I went out to the Annex holding area to meet this legend, as I had only heard about him from my late Detective, Don Lillie, who chased this guy around for years. When I saw him, he looked like he was in his late 50s, although he was barely 40. So, I chided:

"Mr. Morton, aren't you getting a little old for this stuff? Hell, you can't out-run these young buckaroos at your age and in the shape you're in."

He merely nodded and said: "Cap'n, I just gotta do what I gotta do."

I looked at the man's arms and they sported more tracks than the Union Pacific railroad...

"You gotta get off that smack, before it kills ya, John!" I offered, as I bid him farewell and headed back to my office.

Big Stealins' #1

I barely discovered where to find the coffee and the bathrooms when I heard about a big hush-hush case that Investigations was working on. As you may recall, I was Patrol Commander during my first three years at the department. Lt. Walter "Walt" Konar and Det. Don Lillie were the only investigators at the time; they were assisted in this case by Kris Henderson, who was on loan from Patrol. Although a rookie, this young lady was a dynamo and became a very capable detective. The group was working a huge rare book theft case, which occurred over some period of time in the Special Collections Section of the Stanford Library. A young man, who had posed as a post doctoral researcher, had been smuggling very, very rare and extremely valuable books from the prestigious collection. A library staffer realized the scam and alerted his superiors who immediately called for a police inquiry.

The brazen thief, James Mole (my spot-on pseudonym), was a Palo Alto resident who lived with his mother. He hung around the libraries and various bookstores in the Palo Alto/Menlo Park area, and was well known by store proprietors as an individual who needed a shower, shave, haircut, as well as some clean clothes, and perhaps, some serious delousing—a classic "dirt bag," he was! Mole was also viewed by bookstore personnel as someone to keep a jaundiced eye on as his character was very dubious! It was a shame that our librarians weren't a bit more circumspect when it came to this charlatan, but then, hindsight is always 20/20. In the final analysis, Mr. Mole got away with a car load of prized manuscripts and books. Lt. Konar's team served several search warrants and recovered some of the books, but the pick of the litter were in the wind, along with the thief.

The S/O assigned the very smart North County Detective, Richard "Dick" Min, to oversee the operation. The FBI's Antiquities Detail was apprised of the matter and entered the suspect's information into the U.S. computerized database, once a $200,000 warrant had been issued for Mole's arrest. The FBI also put out an international BOL for this fugitive through INTERPOL,* as it was believed that Mole had absconded to Europe. Sure enough, Scotland Yard nearly nabbed Mr. Mole when he attempted to *fence* the rarest of the books at the renowned London auction house, Sotheby's. But, like his apropos *handle*, this thief somehow burrowed his way out of the trap and vanished.

Several months later, James Mole surfaced in Zurich, Switzerland. Down on his luck and nearly flat broke, Mole made the mistake of trying to run down a member of the Swiss *Polizei* with a rental car: It seems that our fugitive was holed up in a Zurich flop house and when he tried to skip out with paying his rent, the hotelier called the cops. When the first responder tried to detain Mole, he apparently panicked, attempted to flee in his vehicle and struck the officer in the process. Mr. Mole was summarily taken prisoner at gunpoint and was transported to the hoosegow by the *Gendarmes*. Like most police anywhere on the globe, the Swiss cops didn't appreciate nearly losing one of their own to a two bit punk! When the Zurich cops entered their collar's name, rank and horsepower into the INTERPOL database, our $200,000 arrest warrant popped-up like the arcade game, "Whack a Mole." The Santa Clara County Sheriff assigned Detective Sergeant Min and SUDPS' Lt. Konar to travel to retrieve the itinerant book thief. In a recent interview with the retired sergeant, Min related the following course of events:

* International Criminal Police Organization: Officially formed in 1923, this network is comprised of 189 countries, which cooperate with its members on international investigations.

Min and Konar had to fly to Washington D.C. in order to be sworn-in as "federal agents" at the U.S. Department of State. Both men flew to D.C. armed with their side arms—when it was permissible for peace officers on duty to declare and carry weapons on board airliners. Officers must now surrender all weaponry, which are locked up and secured in the cockpit. Once duly sworn as official U.S. federal agents, they flew into Switzerland. When they landed in Zurich, Dick and Walt were immediately relieved of their hardware. The *Polizei* weren't big on foreigners walking around in their country packing large caliber "cannons"...

After literally being "wined and dined" by their gracious hosts—a European custom practiced by many law enforcement officers there, although foreign to our cops from CA—they were taken to the prison to meet their quarry. When introduced to the prisoner, one would think that the inmate might be somewhat intimidated by the size of Konar, who stood over 6' and weighed nearly 200 pounds.

Who would possibly fear the diminutive Sgt. Min, who, when stretched, stood 5'6" and weighed 145 pounds—soaking wet? Ah, my friends, but looks can be deceiving, for my Honolulu "home boy" was a highly trained martial artist and could hang with the likes of Bruce Lee... An anonymous source related that on a domestic call in San Jose's infamous eastside, a burly and very intoxicated knuckle-dragging outlaw biker-type once challenged the mild mannered, soft spoken Min to "try" and take him to jail. My on--scene witness said that before you could blink an eye, the menacing combatant was immobilized when Dick flew through the air like a guided missile and took the man out with foot strike to the head!

Realizing that the lawmen from CA were going to have to escort Mr. Mole nearly 6,000 miles in an airplane, without restraints and firearms, Min admitted that he wanted to make an impression on the hippie thief. When they entered Mole's cell, the sergeant greeted the suspect with a firm hand—a grab to the scruff of the neck—whereupon he levitated the shocked inmate a foot off the floor and explained the facts of life. Sgt. Min calmly whispered: "We are going to take a long flight back to CA, so don't even think about moving an errant muscle! Are we clear?" The crook could only nod in the affirmative. Dick said that the very PC *Polizei* were shocked and amazed that a man of Min's stature could initiate such a maneuver, and although impressed, asked the sergeant to refrain from any further Old Western style justice while in Switzerland. Min recalled he smiled and agreed, and all was OK for the remainder of their one week holiday in beautiful Zurich.

The trip across the Pond was uneventful as James honored his verbal contract and never made a whimper or untoward move during the long trek. Mole was "monkey in the middle," and I believe that Dick's bit of theatrics in the lock up, indeed, made a lasting impression on the arrestee. Before the trio deplaned in D.C., Min and Konar put the shackles on their guest, to ensure that the fugitive would continue to remain in their custody. However, when they entered Customs, all the bells and whistles went off and the trio was quickly surrounded by several gun-toting agents. It seems that U.S. Customs was ahead of the airport security game by installing magnetometers. Once the feds learned that Min and Konar were duly sworn federal marshals, the green light was turned on and they proceeded to their ultimate destination, Santa Clara County, CA! Finally, the man who had a penchant for Stanford University's Special Collections' books was sent to prison; most of the manuscripts were recovered and returned to their rightful places so legitimate researchers could utilize and enjoy them.

Student Crime

Although most crime at Stanford University was committed by outside interlopers, I'm sorry to tell you that even the brightest and the best in society crossed the line once in a while. Most student indiscretions occurred in the Stanford Bookstore. When I first began my career at the DPS, perhaps only one or two shoplifters were caught a week. In that era, the Bookstore employed plainclothes security personnel who posed as shoppers and would catch thieves, if they could. Back in the day, bagging a store thief in the act was more difficult than you might imagine:

****

When I was a young S/O deputy, I moonlighted as a so-called "store detective" for Mayfair Super Markets, both in Cupertino and San Jose. That was hard work! I don't know how many miles I logged-in behind a grocery cart posing as a shopper, all the while keeping an eyeball on suspicious persons whose actions often drew attention to us shoplifting hawks. Because these stores lost a ton of expensive cosmetics, I often spent many hours in a walk-in beverage cooler, freezing my ass off, while eye-balling the shelves where the make-up, lipstick and fingernail polish was displayed. When you spotted someone secreting items on their person, you had to dash out of the cooler, follow them around and make sure they didn't toss the products before going through the cashier's station. Once the suspect(s)—almost always *teeny boppers*—went through the cashier, you'd have to confirm they didn't pay for the items, stop them outside and ask:

"Excuse me, young lady. Did you forget to pay for those items you have stashed in your bra?" While a torrent of tears and dramatic sobbing was going-on, you had to drag them back into the store in bracelets—of the cop variety. The so-called "Perp Walk" was a good deterrent to other would-be sticky finger shoppers! We would take the hysterical girl(s) to the manager's office, where a female employee (out of your presence, of course) would retrieve the ill gotten gain. You then had to call the parents, bag and tag the evidence, write a *Juvie* citation and a crime report, and book the evidence into the S/O later on. What a pain! And, all for a measly 7 bucks an hour. I didn't last very long. The decision to terminate my employment with Mayfair Inc. was a no-brainer, after a friend and colleague from San Jose PD got shot at during an aborted robbery attempt by a pair of ex-cons. My buddy thought that these dangerous individuals were merely shoplifters and tried to make a detention; one of the bandits pulled out a .45 and blasted away at him. Fortunately, the shooter couldn't hit the broadside of a barn with a blunder buss, so my partner escaped that very close call, unscathed.

****

The foregoing procedure—save for the "Perp Walk" and gun play—was essentially the same procedure that our department utilized when investigating Bookstore thefts in the early days. Several of our troops complained to me about how time-consuming these cases were, especially when the officers had to testify in court on misdemeanor cases that **were not** committed in their presence (these were essentially citizen arrests). And, the DPS had to foot the bill for overtime for cases that amounted to only ten to twenty dollar pilfering. This simply didn't make sense. And, the Bookstore security folks were getting more efficient in their craft with additional manpower and technology, so they were making arrests hand over fist. The new Security Manger was very progressive; he had video cams installed in every nook and cranny of that place. These cameras were monitored via a dozen or so TV sets in their office. If someone was bent on swiping merchandise, the chances were they would be spotted and nabbed. So, we put our collective heads together and crafted a new method of handling and processing shoplifters: After getting the green light from the DA, it was determined that when a violator was detained by security officers, a deputy would respond and monitor the arrest and processing. After making sure that the suspected thief was free of weapons and contraband, the security person would make a Citizen's Arrest and handle the matter from that point forward. Our deputy would issue an arrest citation and write a "one liner" report: "We came, we saw, we cited, we left!" The Bookstore personnel processed their evidence, wrote incident reports, and, if necessary, testified in court later on. I'm here to tell you that stealing, even a pen or pencil, was (and still IS) not a prudent thing to do in the Stanford Bookstore!

Big Stealins' #2

Often, *Little Stealins'* lead to big ones: The intricate video monitoring system that led to the arrest of many petty shoplifters in the Stanford Bookstore sometimes snagged bigger fish. As is evident from this section, most of the crooks who operated on the Farm were outsiders—non-students who were pretty good at their craft. Well, the guy I'm going to tell you about was *very good* at his craft, as well! You got it! This young man was one of the *ten percenters* who got into this prestigious university. I'll just call him Joe.

The Chief of Bookstore Security called for a meeting with me and my detectives one day. He said that he was possibly onto an insider, who was somehow making off with brand new Apple computers—right under their noses. This parley revealed that the suspect was a part-time employee, who usually worked the evening shift. Accountants discovered the thefts, about a dozen of them, when the sales receipts didn't jive with the inventory. The Chief zeroed in on Joe because they noticed that a single computer would turn up missing, periodically, the day following Joe's shift. He was smart enough not to take a bunch of them at one time, and used what I have previously described as the "salami technique:" One small slice at a time!

Security personnel reviewed the tapes that corresponded with dates Joe had worked, as well as the time frame computers had turned up missing. Security officers noticed that Joe was apparently responsible for taking empty boxes out back to the dumpster. At first, he was seen just carrying the boxes out in his hands; however, every once in awhile, Joe used a hand truck to haul the boxes to the dumpster, which was located near the freight loading dock. *Hmmmm*, we all thought. *Joe Slick was probably carting out a new computer in that stack of boxes, stashing it in the dumpster and then retrieving it later on that night.* Although this was a burglary and grand theft investigation, I sanctioned Bookstore Security to set up surveillance on the evenings when Joe worked, and to detain him when he came back and loaded a hot Mac in his vehicle. I was a bit worried about turning over this investigation to non-sworn personnel, but they figured it out in the first place, so I thought they deserved first crack at this clown! I had confidence they could pull this one off without much difficulty.

After a couple of fruitless nights, the Bookstore officers finally hit pay dirt and bagged this crook in the act of loading a brand new Apple computer into the trunk of his car. They held Ol' Joe until our patrol deputies took him forthwith to the lock up at North County, where he would be held until bail could be set at arraignment. My detectives and I hotfooted it over to the Bookstore Security office to review the videotape and take it as evidence. It was a gem: Just after closing the store, you could see Joe trucking out a stack of boxes.

When he reached the dumpster, he broke up and flattened out all of the boxes except for one, which was on the bottom of the stack on the hand cart. He looked around furtively and then hid that box by the trash container; he deposited the flattened boxes into the dumpster and wheeled the dolly back into the store. About thirty minutes later, the exterior camera captured the headlights of a car coming into the loading dock area; the vehicle pulled up to the dock, and there was Joe, bigger than life, loading the Macintosh computer box into his ride—you could even see the big Apple logo! As he was preparing to leave, several young men ran up, slapped handcuffs on the thief and escorted him into the store. One of the security guys stood by Joe's getaway car until two squad cars roared up. Game over!

While being held in the security office, one astute young Loss Prevention Officer—a more sophisticated term for "Store Dick," which is what I was called when I worked for Mayfair Markets—had the presence of mind to ask Joe where he was storing all of the computers he stole. Joe wasn't as slick as I thought he was: He quickly copped-out that he was stashing the goods in a storage unit in Woodside, CA. This was a big deal for us because we now could search his dorm room (a given), as well as the storage area, and perhaps recover some of the hot computers. The questioning by the LPO was spontaneous: They were not told, by any peace officer, to interrogate the suspect, so an admission would, and *did*, hold up in court later on! That afternoon, my detectives flew over to the DA's Office and obtained two search warrants which would be served simultaneously at first light the following morning. They asked the Presiding Judge to hold Joe without bail so we could complete our investigation without giving the thief an opportunity to get rid of crucial evidence. The good judge granted our wishes.

The Big Mac Attack

The next morning, our search teams hit the targets: Detective Sergeant Tim Hanrahan led the storage facility team, while I took the point at Joe's fraternity, affectionately known as "THE TAXI" house, a.k.a. Theta Xi. I met with the fraternity president, showed him the warrant and asked him to take me to the kid's room. The place was like entering Memorial Church. The silence was deafening. Unlike most experiences of going into frats, these young men didn't say *nada*: No wisecracks, cat calls. *oink oinks* or under the breath curses; those kids got out of our way. It was like hungry wolves entering a corral of sheep. Joe's roommate scampered out of the room like a spooked mouse. I chuckled to myself. It must have been our ominous Raid Jackets...

Sgt. Hanrahan told me via radio that they located several stolen computers and were getting ready to mount-up and head back to the barn. In the meantime, we hit the mother lode in Joe's room: His computer later proved to be a treasure trove of information as to where the Macs went and how much he got for them. We also learned that this budding entrepreneur was selling these hotcakes via the San Jose Mercury News classified ads. One of the big buyers of these sizzling Macs was a prominent attorney in the San Jose area. He was not a happy camper when another one of our strike forces, armed with yet *another* search warrant, did the *Big Mac Attack* on his office, which effectively shut him down for several days—broke my heart! A judge later issued an order which allowed someone from the lawyer's staff to download his proprietary information, which we had no interest in. The moral of this story for our "Officer of the Court" is: When a deal looks too good to be true, it probably is... Buyer Beware!

Have Pencil—Will Travel

I received information from a confidential source (CI) that a certain undergraduate student had been hiring himself out as a "Professional Exam Taker." For a fee, aspiring law or medical school wannabes could hire this genius to take the difficult LSAT (Law School Admission Test) and MCAT (Medical College Admission Test) tests for them. This young man was reputed to have a near genius IQ and could pass any exam that you threw at him! Once a deal had been solidified, the scammer, whom I'll call *Adonis,* would obtain a fraudulent identification in the name of the person who wished to game the system. He then would show up at the exam site, and in a few hours, receive a pocketful of cash. The client assuredly "passed" the brutal test with flying colors, and ostensibly would be admitted to a law or medical school down the line. Talk about WRONG!

Our CI gave us the name of the student who was the actual applicant for the LSAT exam, which would be administered one Saturday at Sacramento State (CSU Sacramento). So, I put my two *best* men on it, Sgt. Philip Love and Det. John McMullen—actually the only men I had, but you gotta play the hand that's dealt. . . The investigators reached out to the CSUS campus police investigators about this caper and collectively set-up an ambush. Love and John "Mac" buzzed up to the Capitol City's campus, met with their counterparts, and lay in wait. Like clockwork, *Adonis* showed up on time, signed in and was issued the test materials. After the first session's break, the plain clothes officers quietly approached *Adonis,* walked him out of sight, and slipped the Peerless bracelets on the cheater's wrists. The long trip back to The Farm must have been agonizing for *Adonis*. He should have realized that in the end, SUDPS, too, Have Cops—Will Travel . . .

CHAPTER TWENTY NINE

Some Good Pinches

The Great Imposter

The Front Office called and said Ms. Jennifer Westerlind, Esq., from Stanford General Counsel's Office was on line 1. I had known Jennifer ever since I set foot on campus in 1974; she was an Administrative Assistant to Chief Counsel in those days while she attended law school. She later got her JD, was hired by the Stanford Legal Office, and became the DPS' "mouth piece." Wonder what kind of trouble we are in now, I imagined?

"Captain Niemeyer. Jennifer, what sort of jam are we in now?"

"Good morning, Captain "Evil." (She gave me that handle for reasons that escape me after all of these years, but I'm sure it had something to do with some unusual tactic I employed on a crook. . .) How are you this lovely morning?" she chirped.

"Well, my dear Jennifer, I was as fine as a frog hair split four ways until you called," I rejoined. "What's up?"

"Do you remember the case that one of your detectives was working on involving a Law Student, Norman Lau? He was the Asian student that was suspected of identity theft. Whatever became of that investigation?" Ms. Westerlind asked.

"Yes, I recall that case, but frankly don't know where it stands at the moment, as the man who initially investigated it left the department. Let me check and get back to you in a bit. I have a brand new detective, "AJ"—good cop from Alameda PD—we'll get the file; this will be a good way to get his feet wet!" I announced.

"Great, as time is of the essence: He's due to graduate from the Law School soon and we have some serious concerns about him aside from the alleged identity theft you were working on," Jennifer asserted.

"Okey-dokey, we are on it, Jennifer, and I'll get back to you PDQ." I promised.

After terminating the call, I tracked-down AJ and the file. We reviewed the case and discovered that a considerable amount of follow-up was needed. Here's what alerted me to this caper: Several months before, I received a call from the Assistant Attorney General (AAG) of the State of Minnesota. He reported that when he was attending Stanford's Law School a few months before, someone had compromised his identity. The man went on to say the culprit apparently obtained several credit cards in his name, and then embarked on an all expense paid tour of Yosemite Valley's premier hotel, the Ahwahnee Lodge! The imposter racked-up over $1,000 in dining, lodging, a rental car and gas! The MN prosecutor was not a happy camper and said that he had never been to Yosemite Valley in his life.

The initial investigation indicated that the crook more than likely stole Mr. AAG's mail from the dorm's office. The postal delivery system at that house was abysmal. The US Postal delivery person deposited all of the mail into one box, which was later sorted by residence staff and put into open pigeon holes. Clearly, the "honor system" didn't work in this case, for the thief simply helped himself to other students' mail. In our matter, the perp obviously purloined the victim's credit card mail, which apparently contained applications for new credit cards. The creep filled-out applications in the victim's name and just waited for the new card(s) to arrive. And, once the postman delivered the targeted envelopes, the ID thief was off to the races with approximately $7,000 of credit at his disposal—someone else's!

To AJ and me, this was a no-brainer: We had a short, stocky Asian dude, masquerading as a 6' tall medium build Caucasian! The plan was to put together a photo array of college age Asian males, Mr. Lau's DMV mug shot included, so hopefully someone at Yosemite could identify the suspect. I then arranged to meet Ms. Westerlind so we could to find-out what new information Jennifer had on Mr. Lau.

After introductions and the usual pleasantries, we all got down to real business.

Ms. Westerlind revealed that Mr.Lau (or whatever his true name might be,) was quite the scam artist: In checking out Lau's academic file and doing some investigation, Jennifer suspected that Lau's letters of reference from his undergraduate college could be bogus! So, now, we had another mission.

Once back at the office, AJ began burning up the land lines to Lau's college in an effort to verify the documents the kid submitted when applying to our law school. The police authorities at his school checked out the "glowing" letters of reference, and ascertained they weren't worth the paper they were written on. The professors were real but they had never heard of Mr. Norman Lau. Can you believe the gall of this young fabricator?

In addition, this crafty lad somehow was able to falsify his transcripts and change a number of his grades to make him eligible for admittance to Stanford's School of Law. The irony of this imposter's skullduggery is that he sailed right through one of the toughest law schools in the world—save one assignment he failed to submit. As a result of this misstep, his sheepskin was held-up—a fortuitous slip-up for Stanford University and everyone else downstream. . .

Although there was clearly criminality in Lau's application process, these crimes occurred in another state—Detective AJ verified that the police authorities back East were very interested in pressing charges, but time was a factor in our situation. The Law School bore some responsibility for Lau's admittance and for a lack of due diligence in vetting; however, we were determined to nail this charlatan on impersonation, forgery, and fraudulent use of a credit card—all felonies! But, first things first: AJ took a quick trip to Yosemite National Park in an effort to get an identification on our suspected flim-flam man. I've always said that it's better to be good than lucky, but when you're both, how can it get any better than that? AJ got several positive IDs on Mr. Lau, proving that he, in fact, used the AAG of Minnesota's identity to entertain himself and his girlfriend. And, once we got this viper in tow, we'd get a handwriting sample and seal his fate! It didn't take long for our DDA to issue a no-bail arrest warrant (he was a flight risk) for the Law School's Great Imposter! Now, all we had to do was find this spurious snake...

We should have been at a craps table in Las Vegas as Lady Luck was on our side. A little bird told us where our fugitive lived and worked. AJ and I decided to take him out with aplomb, and drove to Sausalito, CA, where this skunk worked. When we arrived at the given address, we suddenly realized that this was a high-power financial management firm. *Uh-oh,* I alerted, *this shady character is going for the big bucks!* I conveyed my notion to AJ and he returned with his sheepish grin. I buzzed the receptionist and asked to speak to Norman Lau. She replied that Mr. Lau was on a business trip and wouldn't return to the office until the following day; she asked if anyone else could help us, and I responded by saying it was just a minor inquiry and we would return the next morning. We left the office and I got to thinking, as I was troubled about a couple of things: First, I was concerned that the receptionist might tip-off our fugitive that the cops were looking for him. And, secondly, this *scamster* might clean-out the firm and abscond to the parts unknown. Knowing my luck, we would then get blamed for not giving the firm a head's-up that Lau was a righteous fraud, capable of doing them some serious monetary damage. I decided that we should take a chance with the CEO.

When we re-entered the foyer, the receptionist looked worried, especially when I asked to speak with the boss-man. She immediately got on the phone and said:

"*Mister Enron*, (obviously, another one of my pseudonyms) there are two investigators who would like to see you. OK, I'll show them to the conference room."

The lovely Ms. ushered AJ and me to the boardroom, brought us some coffee and said that the CEO would be there in a jiffy. She wasn't kidding, for almost immediately, four men attired in Brooks Brothers Suits filed in, introduced themselves and sat on the opposite side of the enormous oak table. The man who identified himself as the CEO nervously asked what this was all about; all of the principals were ashen faced and leaned forward with great anticipation.

"Well," I began, "we have a felony no-bail arrest warrant for one of your employees, a Mr. Norman Lau."

Suddenly, color began to reappear in the faces of the men across from us, as AJ and I just looked at each other—curiously.

"Whew," Mr. Enron exclaimed! "You guys scared the hell out of us. We thought you were from the SEC..." Everyone laughed.

"No sir, not hardly," I began, "we're just deputy sheriffs trying to arrest our Great Imposter, who scammed his way into Stanford's Law School, and while he was at it, availed himself of another student's identity, who is now an Assistant Attorney General in Minnesota, and went on a lavish spending spree with the AAG's credit cards! I also wanted to alert you that if I were in your shoes, I'd have your CFO peruse your books for any irregularities that might bring the REAL SEC down on *ya* with a twenty pound sledge hammer!" More laughter. The boss promised that "Mum's the Word" so we could take the nefarious one off his hands. And, by God, he kept his word, as AJ and another deputy made a collar the minute Lau entered his office the following day. After all of his deceptive planning and thieving, our bad boy did not receive his Doctor of Juris Prudence from the prestigious Stanford School of Law. Also, he did not pass Go; he did not collect $200, and he went directly to jail!

I often wondered about that financial management bunch: They were very relieved that AJ and I weren't SEC examiners. Perhaps my pseudonym for the CEO wasn't too far off the mark. . .

In Pursuit

It was a very dark night. Deputy Henderson Q-11 was "surveilling" the area on Campus Drive near Escondido when he spotted a white compact pick-up truck hauling-ass down the thoroughfare; the mini-truck was driven by a lone subject and there were about 8-10 bicycles in the bed. *Hmmmmm,* Bob thought, *what's that dude doing, driving around campus with a bunch of bikes at this un-godly hour? I'd better check this cat out.* And, off he went, his roof-top Christmas display lighting-up the night, with the siren wailing.

"Radio, Q-11," he barked. "In pursuit of an 11-54—a small white pick-up full of bikes. I'm southbound on Campus Drive approaching Bowdoin, and he's not yielding!"

"Attention all units, Q-11 is in pursuit of a small white pick-up in the area of Campus and Bowdoin. Units to fill?"

At this point, the airways were jammed with every unit in North County attempting to force their way into the conversation;

neither Radio nor Q-11 could decipher a word. Communications then asserted itself.

"All units hold your traffic. Hold YOUR traffic. Q-11, what is your current 10-20?"

"Q-11, Q-11 (voice amplified) he turned on Bowdoin and we are now on Pine Hill. He's pulling over, he's pulling over; he just bailed-out, foot-pursuit, foot pursuit. . ."

"Q-11, what is your exact location? Q-11. Q-11, answer-up." Silence! Save for:

"Q-9 resp bzzzzzz/ 80-L-22 where's bzzzzzz/ FC-bzzzzzzz.

"Radio Q-11, Code 4, one 10-15!"

When the Patrol Sergeant arrived on the scene, he asked Henderson what had happened. Bob, matter-of-factly, related that he saw the suspect buzzing down the street at a high rate of speed with a gaggle of bicycles in the back, so he alerted and gave chase to merely check-out this dude. Upon seeing the pursing patrol unit, the suspect put the pedal-to-the-metal and tried to get away—Bob said the suspect nearly flipped the truck when he suddenly diverted left to Bowdoin Street, and again when he hooked a right on Pine Hill Road. Then, the turkey jumped-out of the vehicle at about 10 mph and took off like a gazelle into a backyard where he jumped a fence. The kid was pretty quick—about 5'7" and a Buck 50 something!

"Beep-Beep. Q-11 and all units at the scene, 10-36 traffic to follow!"

"Q-15, go ahead."

"Q-15 your suspect's vehicle is 6F-Frank, a 10851 stolen out of San Francisco. Also, we have received a couple of calls from students stating that some white guy in a little white truck just made off with their bikes. Q-15 more 10-36 traffic. . ."

"Q-15, go ahead."

"Your suspect is a PAL (parolee at large) and eligible for immediate incarceration."

After all the "high-five's" and back slaps of adulation, Deputy Henderson continued to brief the patrol boss. Bob continued that when the culprit hit the pavement, he took-off and had a good 20 yard lead. Bob closed the gap in a heartbeat and was like a tether, as the crook vaulted the barrier. This punk was toast! The perp was shell-shocked, as he probably out-ran the cops all of his former criminal life. But, little did he know that his pursuer was a Class A athlete, who was soon to win medals in track and field as well as weight-lifting in the California Police Olympics—just ask some members of the Stanford Cardinal football team about Bob's speed!

Three Strikes

After the dust settled, we learned that our "dude" was a very, very "bad-ass," recently released from "Q" (San Quentin). He had a long history of committing serious felonies, including assaults with deadly weapons, carjackings, numerous burglaries and assorted drug offenses. But, the best was yet to come: After receiving permission from the Parole Board, my detectives executed a search of the crook's San Francisco apartment. As it turns out, the man was a prolific writer. He had numerous drafts and copies of letters he had apparently sent to his "homies" (homeboys) in Q. One of the most disturbing pieces he composed was his intent to eviscerate his maid, and to perform disgusting acts of necrophilia on her corpse. In my mind, when a criminal like this maniac has such evil thoughts and then commits them to writing, you have a stick of dynamite with a lit fuse! Not only did we have one sick puppy on our hands, but this character, whom henceforth shall be known as "Stupid," was one of the scariest individuals I had ever encountered in over three decades of police work!

Stupid's most recent letters indicated that his new crime of choice was bicycle theft. Many folks scoffed at this notion, but this guy focused on high dollar cycles that would net significant rewards when sold to the various "chop shops" in "Baghdad by the Bay." In one foray, Stupid took BART (Bay Area Rapid Transit) to Berkeley and made his way to the U.C. campus, where he searched for an expensive specimen. After sitting on a prospective target for some period of time, he finally made his move. He carried implements, which could defeat most security systems, in a backpack and was confident. Who says there are no learning opportunities in prison? As he was getting ready to ride-off with his prize, a 6'5" inch 220+ pound student (volleyball player) ran-up to Stupid and said:

"Hey, what in the hell do you think you're doing? That's my bike!"

"Not anymore, Big Boy," Stupid shot back as he displayed an 8 inch Commando-type serrated trench-knife.

"Back-off, Sonny or you'll get some of this!" That, my friends, is a 211 PC—robbery by force or fear!

Although the Stanford family often teases the "Weenies" as not being the brightest bears in the woods, this kid realized Stupid meant business. He lost a nice bike, but lived to tell his grandkids that story—some day in the future.

After presenting all of our evidence to the District Attorney Office, a special prosecutor decided to try Stupid as Santa Clara County's FIRST "Three Strikes" candidate.

When the state of Washington passed a measure that imposed longer sentences for repeat offenders in 1993, Proposition 184 in California passed by an overwhelming majority—72% to 28%.

Clearly, the CA populace had spoken loudly; they were tired of habitual criminals beating the system, getting out of the joint with minimal sentences, only to pillage, rape, and murder again. Trust me, in those days, criminals had to really screw-up big-time before a judge in "Santa Claus" County ever sentenced anyone to state prison. I recall seeing hundred of inmates' records when I worked the jail in San Jose. Their rap sheets read like Russian novels but they were still doing county time. Ridiculous! In any event, our new law mandated enhanced sentences for criminals who committed a third felony, providing there were two other felony convictions that were deemed to be either violent, serious, or both. This certainly was the case with Stupid! However, when the media discovered he was going down for three-strikes, behind a vehicle and bicycle theft, they went bonkers. I was excoriated by the print and TV media for sending this "poor kid" to the bucket for a minimum of 25 years for such a CS pinch.

Unfortunately, I had to bite my tongue and absorb the shots as I could not divulge our all of evidence, nor Stupid's out of state rap sheets. This situation became a major soap opera, especially when the convict's mother got into the mix. If they had seen what we had discovered in Stupid's lair, I think most of the critics would have concurred with the DDA's assessment, buttressed by our feelings that this man was a clear and present danger to any community he ventured into. Hopefully, Stupid is still sharing crime stories with his homeboys at CDC; perhaps he'll get in better shape so he can out-run the likes of Bob Henderson (NOT) when he gets out! Officer Henderson is currently ensuring that the residents of the City of Santa Clara are safe.

The Great Stamp Caper: As recalled by Detective Tim Schreiner.

I received a call from a retired professor regarding a devastating loss he sustained during a burglary of his home. The crooks broke-in during his absence and carted off a small safe. Adding insult to injury, they used his hand truck, which he kept in his garage. The safe contained an extremely rare collection of World War II stamps valued at approximately $75,000! This was a one-of-a-kind collection which he was going to donate to a Smithsonian Museum in Washington D.C. The patrol deputies processed the scene for physical evidence, but as is the case 99 percent of the time, smart burglars wear gloves and simply don't leave any clues. And, as usual, a neighborhood canvas yielded nothing. People never seem to notice strange cars or folks, despite the best efforts of programs like Neighborhood Watch. I told the grieving man I would put my best detectives on his case.

I summoned my two best detectives at the time, Allen "AJ" James and Tim Schreiner—come to think of it they were the only two investigators at the time... I designated Detective Schreiner as the "lead" in this case. The first order of business was to re-examine the scene and neighborhood for clues and possible leads on a suspect vehicle. AJ went over the home with a fine tooth comb and beat the bushes. The results were the same: Negative. Because of our active membership in The California Burglary and Theft Investigator's Association (C.B.T.I.A.), we learned to immediately teletype a BOL to all agencies in the greater Bay Area, with special attention to investigators who were on the pawn shop detail. These detectives would routinely contact the proprietors of these establishments and give them a list of recently stolen goods—for the dealer's own good. Despite the unsavory reputation of pawn shop owners, most do not want to buy hot stuff only to have it confiscated later by the police.

In addition to notifying the local PDs, S/Os and the FBI, my nose to the grindstone detectives let their fingers do the walking in the Yellow Pages and called every stamp collector's shop in the region. This bit of old fashioned cop work really paid off, for within a week, a proprietor of a little stamp shop in Marin County called and said he recently purchased some of the stamps believed to have been purloined. Our victim zoomed up to the shop in question and immediately identified the stamps as being a page from his precious collection. The shop's owner said that the seller was a young female who said she inherited the collection; she was willing to sell more stamps if the proprietor was in the market for them. The man said he was very interested in purchasing more of the collection; the girl said she'd be back in a few days.

Further investigation revealed that the young woman was a known drug addict and prostitute; we all knew how unreliable dopers could be, so this was going to necessitate a stake-out of the premises during the shop's hours of operation. AJ and Tim contacted the Marin County police agency and made arrangements to hook-up with one of their detectives the very next morning. But, as in most cases involving surveillance, you never hit pay dirt on the first day. True to their MO, flaky addicts either never show-up when they say they will, or are always late. After two boring days of nothing, our crew became discouraged and was ready to throw in the towel—But, I wouldn't let them! I was determined to catch these crooks and get that poor man's beautiful stamp collection back. So, I directed these first-rate detectives to hang-in-there, for they would soon hit the Mother Lode.

On day three, still no luck. About 20 minutes before closing, the home town detective, who was with Schreiner in his City's unmarked car, said he really wanted call-off the detail as he was going on vacation early the next morning. Tim wasn't too keen about that so they went into the store to check with AJ, who was posing as an assistant shopkeeper. All of a sudden, the gal they were looking for came into the establishment. Tim and his counterpart were taken aback and pretended to be customers. After the proprietor surreptitiously indicated that this woman was indeed the suspect, Tim and his partner went back to their unmarked, in order to get marked patrol units headed their way.

As suddenly as the suspect blew in, she blew out and got into a white Cadillac driven by a white male. AJ soon emerged and was headed for his unmarked while Tim's partner tried to get his car started. Wouldn't you know—the damn motor wouldn't fire! They were, what I call, DIW: Dead in the Water! Tim sprinted for AJ's ride, hopped in and they took-off after the fleeing Caddie. Within a matter of minutes, AJ caught up to the suspects and directed the locals in with their patrol units to make the stop. Both suspects were arrested and taken to the local PD for questioning. These two were big time dirtbags: The male had an extensive rap sheet and was currently on parole. As previously thought, the female was a street walking heroin addict, who plied her trade for drugs. She was now assisting her boyfriend by selling the ill gotten gain from burglaries he committed all over the place. As they expected, the police found some of the professor's stamps in the getaway vehicle.

While the property was stolen from the Stanford campus, we couldn't prove a burglary offense; the crime of possession of stolen goods, however, occurred in Marin, so the locals took over the investigation at that point. Their detectives attempted to interrogate the arrestees using the old ineffectual method of "hard-assing" them. These folks were both con wise, so getting anything out of these clams was fruitless. However, being a student of "The Art of Conversation" (Chapter 26), Detective Schreiner artfully gained the confidence of the woman: Tim S. played on the female's emotions by telling her how much the elderly professor loved that collection, and that it meant the world to him. Our smooth talking detective told the woman that he really just wanted to recover the extremely rare specimen so the world could enjoy the display at a Smithsonian Museum. She caved-in like an old mine and led the officers to the house where the parolee was staying. They obtained consent to search and recovered the collection in its entirety—good thing Detective Schreiner used the gift of gab on this, as 95 percent of the collection was in that house!

Now, this is what I call a "Great Pinch;" Tim and AJ used all of the tools in their roll-away, and then some. I wish I could have given them a raise and a medal. . .

CHAPTER THIRTY
The Jogging Burglar

Squeaky Wheel

It was about 0830 and I had just returned to my office after having way too many cups of coffee. It was a relatively quiet weekend: A few DUI arrests, a couple of 14601 pinches (driving while suspended), and a party or two. But, thank God, no residential burglaries. Records buzzed and advised me that FBI Agent Mike Kelley, of the Palo Alto office, was on the phone.

"Hey, Mike, what's going on in the world of Super Sleuthing," I dug. I knew most of the Bureau guys in the region as I worked-out and played racquetball with them. The Palo Alto Resident Agency crew recruited me to be the "ringer" on their fledgling softball team because of my killer mountain ball style of pitching—with a twist—which struck-out many a batter from the San Jose R A, much to their chagrin. They were younger, bigger and faster. But, like I always said: "Youth and exuberance can always be overcome by experience, determination and treachery!"

"Morning Captain, how's your day going?"

"It was going great, Mike, but something tells me that my agenda is about to change; you never call this damn early in the morning unless something's up," I replied.

"Hey, you remember that burglar you've been trying to catch; the guy who left a bunch of rare stolen plates on consignment up in Washington?"

"You mean the guy I tried to get "FB-1" to charge so we could arrest him for the 50 some odd residential burglaries which he's committed around here? Robert Lee O'Connor, the parolee who is holed-up over the hill in La Honda and who rips us off with impunity?" I dug further.

"Well, you know I went to the U.S. Attorney about that and he rejected the case, as it didn't meet the federal monetary guideline of transporting stolen property out of the state. The property has to be in excess of $20,000, and you said that the stuff up there only amounted to about $500 to $1,000," Agent Kelley excused.

"Yeah, Mike, I know but if we could ever get into this guy's house, we are going to hit a fricking gold mine!" I asserted. "So, what's up, now?"

"Well," he sheepishly replied. "The U.S. Attorney wants us to open a case and interview the subject. Can I come over and talk to about it some more?"

"Absolutely," I enthusiastically blurted. "But, I don't get it. What made him change his mind?" I queried.

"About eight very pissed-off Stanford Professors, who pounded on his desk for about an hour! If it's OK, I'll be over there is a little while."

"Ok, Mike, I'll see you then," I got out, after nearly gagging while I choked back my laughter. *Good,* I thought, *the FBI hasn't figured-out yet that "I" sicked those outraged and equally abrasive faculty members on the U.S. Attorney, after they had pummeled "Me" for about an hour!*

As regional coordinator of this ad hoc investigative group, it was my job to ensure that all pertinent information about these serial burglaries was immediately disseminated amongst the affected Santa Clara and San Mateo County law enforcements agencies. It was also my job to take the heat—and indeed I did: Word got out in our "Faculty Ghetto," where most of our high dollar burglaries were occurring, that we had a viable suspect and knew where he lived.

Suddenly, I was confronted by several of these faculty members who simply wanted to know why I hadn't arrested this criminal and returned their precious property to them—like last week. After my succinct but pointed lecture on Constitutional Law 1A, and explaining the corpus of "probable cause," the esteemed academicians became more student-like. . . I confessed that we had tried to get the Feds to open a case on interstate transportation of stolen goods so we could coattail them and contact the person of interest—perhaps see something at his residence that might give rise to probable cause—which could possibly lead to a search warrant. I further divulged that absent the property the suspect had left on consignment in Washington, we had absolutely nothing to tie this man to the crimes that were committed at Stanford, Palo Alto, Los Altos and various jurisdictions in San Mateo County. I confided that this perpetrator was the consummate professional thief: He had many years of criminal experience and incarceration, thus had honed his craft over the years so as never to leave tell-tale evidence, never to be seen, and never to leave a trail. Well, in this case, he erred and failed to notice a receipt in the bottom of the box of dinnerware, which belonged to a burglary victim in Los Altos. He then shot himself in the foot by divulging his true name, address, and phone number to the antique dealer. The antique dealer subsequently found the invoice and notified the true owner, who, of course, called her police department.

Despite this very damaging and incriminating evidence, without a federal mandate, we were powerless to act. So, I skillfully tossed the ball into our professors' hands and showed them "the way to San Jose. . ." Clearly, there is some credence to the old adage that "The Squeaky Wheel Gets the Grease. . ."

Modus Operandi

I was perusing my binder when Agent Kelley was shown into my office. I began to assemble this ledger after it became apparent that we were experiencing a serious crime trend in the faculty/senior staff residential area. My record wasn't anything special—just a big three-ring folder in which I inserted copies of the cases, descriptions of the stolen property, and photos, if any. I also put together a crude matrix that profiled the days, dates and times of occurrences, property taken, method and point of entry, and any other pertinent information. I shared my records with Mike and gave him a synopsis of our burglaries:

I noted that after about 15 cases, we discovered that many of the homes were in close proximity of each other, and that 2 or more houses were often hit during the same time frame. Most of these crimes were committed during the twilight hours, while the inhabitants were out of the house—many of them, dining out. In addition, several of our homeowners were traveling abroad, on sabbaticals, business trips, and so on. The method of entry varied, although most of the time, the crook sought the path of least resistance and availed himself of open or unlocked doors and windows. The burglar avoided alarmed houses like the plague and seldom broke-in through glass. On the few occasions when he made entry through windowed doors, he carefully removed or broke a small pane and apparently wrapped duct tape around his free hand, applying the sticky side to the glass. We deduced that this old trick was used when we found traces of adhesive on the broken glass; rest assured he never left any of the tape behind: Long before forensic science TV shows like CSI and The New Detectives, O'Connor understood what cops would look for at a crime scene and virtually left nothing; he knew that discarding duct tape remnants at a crime scene might give investigators an opportunity to find latent prints on the smooth side and visible ridges on the sticky side. In addition, they might be lucky, get into his "crib" and find the "mother roll," which could be matched-up to the tear-off as well as all sorts of other manufacturing information. This guy learned these tricks by trial and error, and from his stints in the "school of hard knocks"—

the California Department of Corrections. Although he never spent much time in the joint, he was a quick study. Finally, Robert shied away from properties that were well-lighted. He preferred places which were heavily foliated and overgrown. Many of his targets were like rainforests—perfect concealment for this pro—an urban "Rambo!"

Initially, our *perp* was very selective: He took only the finest of Asian, Native American and Middle-Eastern rugs. He scooped-up paintings, China, silver settings, exquisite gold and silver jewelry, crystal and antique home furnishings as if they were going out of style! He never touched reprints or facsimiles of any kind! He definitely knew the art world, thus was certainly cognizant of the value of these collectables. He also had a penchant for firearms, swords, and war memorabilia—the rarer, the better. Mink coats and stoles also went into the bag...His only anomaly was that he took tennis racquets, balls and sports shoes, which he carted away by the trunk full. I surmised he was either a tennis coach or had a lot of kids! Finally, he carted his booty away utilizing the victim's luggage, duffel bags, or plastic trashbags. Something told me that if we ever got this guy, we'd have enough luggage to outfit a football team's traveling squad...

From day one, the crime analysts of our time professed that once a criminal established success with a particular M.O., he rarely deviated from those tactics. This certainly seemed to be the case with our burglar, so we decided to put together a comprehensive surveillance plan and catch this crook in the act, or shortly thereafter. Utilizing off-duty officers from other jurisdictions—many of the best in the business—I designed a cordon around the burglar's target area, the Faculty Ghetto, of roughly 2 square miles. All points of ingress and egress were monitored by undercover personnel in non-descript vehicles, motorcycles, bicycles, and mopeds. We used roving and stationary observation posts and hid in bushes and trees, so all roads within the perimeter were covered.

We knew (or thought we knew) what kind of vehicles the suspect had, and what he looked like. In order to block any counter-surveillance eavesdropping of our police radios, we rotated the tactical frequencies every night, and used code names for streets and locations, which were shuffled prior to every foray. We had approximately 22 sets of eyes and ears out there on any given night! After several weeks of nothing, the burglar finally struck! He hit four homes on a cul-de-sac, not more that a stone's throw away from a marked patrol unit that was assigned to pursue and apprehend this crook, once we had a fix on him. We were burned, Big Time. Robert basically gave us the finger! After 6 long weeks (5PM to Midnight) of fruitless Code 5's, I scrapped the project in utter frustration. The only positive fruit of our labors was that he stopped hitting US! It was a lot like the old days at the Sheriff's Office when we herded the drunks back over the railroad tracks and into the City of San Jose. . . Our colleagues in the surrounding jurisdictions were getting hammered!

Stealthy and Catlike

For over three enjoyable summer months, our campus was virtually crime free. It irritated me that our mark had gotten away, scot-free, but without cause, there was little we could legally do about it. Then, without warning, I was greeted by some of the night shift patrol guys one morning as I drove into our parking lot. They were an antsy lot, and excitedly related facts about the latest home burglary:

"So, don't tell me," I interrupted, "He's, Baaaaack?"

They didn't think so: This incident occurred in the dead of night, and the burglar came into the home while the family was sleeping *upstairs*. Clearly a different M.O., and a very scary one—*Got to be another guy*, I surmised. Besides, this burglary was weird: Instead of the valuable treasures previously stolen, this perpetrator took utilitarian household objects, such as dishes, pot and pans, cleaning supplies, brooms, mops, a vacuum cleaner and the like. He apparently loaded up the stuff in the victim's VW bus, took the key from a key rack like most people have in their kitchens, and drove off. The family didn't hear a thing—not even the vehicle starting-up. Boy, this one surely got my attention. There's nothing worse, in my estimation, than having a "Cat Burglar" creeping around your home in the middle of the night. Was he armed? What would have happened if the inhabitants awoke and confronted this criminal? *Man,* I thought, *we have GOT to get this dude, and put him out of commission—muy pronto!*

Knock and Talk

I spotted our patrol sergeant, Nick Brunot, roaming our hall so I flagged him down. Nick had been involved in this case from early on, having run several unproductive stake-outs—through no fault of his or anyone else's—as we were dealing with a cunning and very stealthy crook. Our Palo Alto counterpart, Detective Liz Morton, was also in the building, so I invited both of them to join Agent Kelly and me, as we were all going to pay Mr. O'Connor a personal visit.

A lot of information was racing through my mind as our caravan ascended the mountain range toward Skyline. I knew the road well as a result of driving it several times a month en route to my Trials motorcycle club property where we roared around on dirt bikes—scaring the hell out of ourselves, as we zoomed through the redwoods on narrow cow trails. As we passed Skylonda, I began to formulate a plan: Kelly was in his bureau car, and I was in my personal vehicle; Nick and Liz were in an unmarked bringing up the rear. Once over the hill, we lost radio contact with our communications station in Palo Alto. However, I was able to talk to the Sergeant and the PA Detective via our walkie-talkies. Just prior to our destination, we pulled over and discussed the game plan. The Sergeant had reconnoitered the suspect's pad before and was somewhat familiar with the locale. For that reason, I had him drive-by in order to see if Robert's white Saab station wagon was at the house. Nick reported that the there was an old dilapidated vehicle in the front yard and a white VW bus in the driveway—but, no Saab. He checked further up the street and there it was, parked well away from the house—the white Saab wagon that we were on the look-out for. Bob, indeed, was a *cagey bastard!* This was the same vehicle that he used in an ill-fated burglary in Menlo Park over a year before:

It was about 2300 hours on a darkened street, when an alert neighbor observed someone removing property from a neighbor's home and loading it into a white Saab station wagon. The good neighbor knew that the people who owned said house were on vacation so she called the police. Surprisingly, the officer arrived in a matter of minutes and began looking into the Saab. After seeing a volume of rugs, paintings, furniture etc., she began looking for the driver of this suspicious vehicle. Upon searching the back yard, she observed a shadowy figure hunkered down behind some bushes near the rear fence. When she hollered: "Freeze, Police!", that shadowy figure vaulted over the 6 foot fence like a gazelle and disappeared into the night, never to be seen again. The only description that the officer obtained was that the guy was a male, about 5'10", slim athletic build, with great leaping and running ability. Indeed!

In addition to recovering a load of very valuable artifacts, the cops found a wallet secreted under the front seat of the Saab. Among other things, they found a CA Driver's License in the name of: Robert Lee O'Connor, photo and all, with an address in La Honda. Detectives thought that this case would be a slam-dunk! Much to their surprise, their DA refused to bring charges against Mr. O'Connor, "for a lack of evidence. . ." A positive ID by the officer would have helped, but he was just too fast and his hooded "Ninja" suit disguised his features. Why this man was never arrested on this case is as mysterious to me now as it was 25 years ago. How a recent parolee, with a rap sheet that read like a Russian novel, managed to escape this beef is unconscionable! But not for this information, we probably never would have been able to figure out who this prolific burglar was, unless we caught him red-handed. And, that amounted to three chances: Slim, none and nonexistent...

As I drove up the street, I noticed a young, very pregnant woman walking downhill—apparently heading to the Mom and Pop store at the corner. I recognized her from a DMV photo as Robert's young wife, Maureen. She didn't seem to notice me, so I pulled over and proceeded to O'Connor's house on foot. The place was a dump: The dirt yard had a rusty old '68 Mustang in it, trash and debris was scattered about, and the structure hadn't received a coat of paint in eons. Agent Kelley and I quickly approached the front porch, with Mike in the lead. The Sergeant and PAPD Detective Morton went around the left side and headed toward the rear. As I passed the large front window, I suddenly saw a shadow move quickly from left to right—presumably heading toward the rear of the residence.

"Mike, I saw him, he's in there!"

The agent rapped on the door and announced: "FBI, come to the door, Sir!"

I added, after pounding on the wall: "Sheriff, Open-up Robert, we just want to talk to you!"

Too late! The sergeant, Nick, ran around to the front and said that the suspect had just burst out of the rear door, and was possibly hiding by some pigeon coops out back—O'Connor was an avid pigeon racer and had a squadron of birds. Nick said Robert was wearing a red shirt. As I rounded the corner and had a view of the rear yard, I heard some thrashing around those pigeon cages and caught a blur—rather, a flash: This guy busted out from behind those coops like a mad hornet leaving a nest. *I'm going to get this sucker,* I thought, and took off after him. He headed across a large meadow as if he had been shot out of cannon. In my lifetime, I had never, EVER, seen any human being run so damn fast! I was 44, overweight and out of condition—there was no way that I could ever catch this antelope, except maybe on my Yamaha—certainly not on foot. Nonetheless, I slogged on, coughing and wheezing along the way. He was approximately 50 yards ahead, and as he was about to enter the dense redwood forest, I shouted:

"STOP OR I'LL SHOOT!"

With that, I whipped out my trusty Walther PPK .380 and pointed it toward my fleet-footed target. My admonition must have had an effect because the man stopped and looked back at me for just a split second, as if to say, "You ain't gonna shoot." All of a sudden, that damn German pistol barked, with a loud crack. *Jeez, how did that happen,* I choked? *I thought the safety was on.* Then, much to my astonishment, the runner crumpled to the ground as if he were hit by a .50 caliber Sharps buffalo gun!

As I ran forward, my mind was racing like crazy: *What in the hell have I done? There's no fricking way that I could have hit that guy at that range. This is a back-up piece; I can barely put 5 out of 8 on the target at 10 yards, let alone at 50. This is the most ballistically inferior round on the planet. You'd do more damage by throwing the damn gun than firing it. Will Prop 8 save my ass? Can we now shoot fleeing career criminals? Am I going to lose my job? Or worse, go to jail? Oh, shit! The Chief is going to flip cheeseburgers. . . Maybe this is a trick; yeah he's just playing possum. I gotta be careful.*

I cautiously approached the lifeless form, prone and face down.

"Hey. Robert! Robert! Are you OK? Hey, don't mess with me, man. If you move a muscle I'll shoot your ass, again!"

There was no response. I crept even closer and nudged him with my foot. Still nothing, so I rolled him over and immediately saw a tiny hole right in the middle of his forehead.

"You've got to be shitting me," I cried. "I killed this poor bastard!"

Then, something caught my eye. *What's that scruffy stuff around his neck*, I asked myself? As I knelt down and reached for his neck, I knew exactly what that was: One of those rubberized identity change masks that the "Mission Impossible Team" used. Upon ripping that damn thing off, I broke out into a profuse sweat and felt like I was going into shock:

"This isn't Robert Lee O'Conner," I gasped, "this is a young black guy!" With that, I let out a blood curdling Yeti primal scream: "AAAAARRRRGGGGHHHHH! I've killed the wrong guy! I've killed the wrong guy!"

All of a sudden, I found myself in a darkened room, in a sweat soaked bed. My wife was shaking me:

"Honey, honey, wake up, wake up!" The kids barged into our bedroom; they were visibly shaken. "Dad, what's the matter?" my son asked.

"I guess I was having a nightmare son; go back to bed, it's OK."

This eerie dream occurred 2 days after our first encounter with Robert Lee O'Connor on November 4, 1982, after 36 sleepless hours!

What started out as a simple "Knock and Talk" deal turned out to be a horrible nightmare! And, to add insult to injury, that pesky crook disappeared into the redwoods, and eluded us once again. This encounter reminded me of the Tortoise and the Hare fable: That speedy ol' hare might have won the first leg, but this old Tortoise had "experience, determination and treachery. . ." I refused to be denied!

We searched the deep dark redwood forest for nearly a half hour and finally concluded that he was gone Johnson. *Damn, we almost had him,* I lamented, *if only we had a dog. . .* Oh, well. We dejectedly trudged back to the cottage; I could see Robert's pregnant wife coming up the road from the store. When she reached the front porch, Agent Kelley identified himself as FBI and asked if we could come in.

"Not without a warrant you can't," she sternly declared.

Boy, this young chick is very con-wise, I thought.

"Listen young lady," I asserted, "we have reason to believe that there is a lot of stolen property in this residence, so you can do it the easy way or the hard way. Let us in so we can see what's up and we'll be out of your hair. That's the easy way. Or, if you want to play games, I'll freeze this house like an iceberg. Then, I'll go to Palo Alto, obtain a search warrant, arrest you, and you'll have your child at the Women's Detention Facility at Elmwood. So, what is it?"

"Go get your warrant," she barked and slammed the door in our faces.

"Whoa, this gal is a real hard case, especially being so damn young"—She looked to be about 18 but was actually 27. "Robert trained her well," I uttered.

At this point, I told Sgt. Brunot and the Paly detective to keep an eye on her while I walked around the perimeter of this little house. As I crept around the back, I could see numerous rugs and paintings adorning the walls of one bedroom. I recognized one as being an Indian rug that had been pilfered from one of our homes on campus. Amazingly, I had a photo of the darn thing in my binder. *Awesome*—I rejoiced to myself, *that should give me enough PC to get a warrant.* As I proceeded around further, I observed at least 50 suitcases, duffel bags and gym bags under an exposed area under the house. When I made the circuit, I was near the driveway where the white VW bus was parked. Boy, that was the lousiest paint job I had ever seen. It looked like a Kragen Special—sprayed with about 20 aerosol cans of white paint! The Sergeant pointed out that there was orange paint bleeding through. On closer inspection, indeed, I noticed a hint of orange *was* bleeding through that "driveway special"—"He should've taken this bus to Earl Scheib," I chuckled. Incredibly, the door jambs had never been painted and were original VW orange. *Wasn't that an orange VW bus stolen in our cat burglary case?* At that point, I copied the VIN and license plate and was ready to speed over the hill right for the DA's Office. *This could be BIG,* I rejoiced, *REALLY BIG!*

Before departing, I gave explicit orders to keep an eye out for Robert and to not let anyone in or out of that premises. I also ordered the officers not to touch the VW bus as I felt that vehicle would be the key to getting us into that place. In my mind, I had a hunch that we would discover a treasure trove of stolen goods in Robert L's pad.

Bingo

As I got to the summit of Skyline, I initiated contact with Palo Alto Communications:

"Palo Alto, 26-A-3 10-28 on a license plate, please."

"Go ahead 26-Adam-3."

"10-28 and 29 on California plate 296 Frank Robert Zebra."

"10-4, Adam-3, standby one."

"Adam-3, Radio, your license plate comes back to a '68 Chevy. No wants.

"Confirm a Chevy? This is obviously a bogus plate as my vehicle is a 'German Roadblock'—I mean a V-Dubb bus," I snickered.

"Well, run this VIN for me: 425 002 025 114."

"Adam-3, that VIN is 6 F-Frank. It comes back to 1972 Volkswagen bus, CA plate 1ACY039, reported stolen from Stanford."

With that news I let out a blood curdling whoop—like when the Raiders *used to* score touchdowns—I almost drove off the roadway; this was one of the most joyous moments in my law enforcement career. Indeed, this was going to be BIG!

Pulling Eye Teeth

On my ride in the elevator to the 3rd floor, my mind was racing like the Indy 500. *One thing for sure,* I promised myself, *I ain't leaving this DA's office unless I have a bona-fide search warrant in my hot hands—period, end of story!*

The Assistant DA was a nice enough guy, but I had what I perceived as a raw deal from this prosecutor many years prior when I worked the Redwood Estates area in the Santa Cruz Mountains:

****

It was a cold, damp, foggy night in that maze of curved roads that typify those little mountain settlements. I got a Code Three call of a head-on collision; lucky for me, it was right off of Hwy 17 so I actually found it with ease. CHP was also responding as they were responsible for handling accident reports in county jurisdiction. When I arrived, I was happy to see that it wasn't a major crash, but a woman in the other car received a laceration in her forehead when she hit the windshield. Fire units arrived quickly and administered first-aid. Upon contacting the other driver, his breath would have torched the redwood forest had I lit a match anywhere near him. . .

Damn, he was "blitzoid!"—A good .25, I guessed. Not only that, but he was a monster—a good 6'4" weighing close to 300. He could barely stand, so I took advantage of his disorientation and unsteadiness, and whipped the cuffs on him before he realized it. Luckily, the "Chippies" showed up and helped me pour this gargantuan into my unit.

When it came time to testify in court, I learned that instead of charging this drunk with felony DUI, the DA reduced it to a misdemeanor despite injury to the other driver with a blood alcohol level of .28 (I was close). They simply let my collar off the hook! After seeing that my arrestee had several priors on his rap sheet, I confronted the prosecutor and asked why he hadn't charged the man with felony deuce? He sort of pooh-poohed me and stated that the guy was an upstanding businessman in Los Gatos and was going into a rehab program. . . That didn't seem right to me, but I kept my mouth shut and moved on.

****

So, sitting across the desk was the same prosecutor—a bit older and hopefully a lot wiser. When I excitedly ran down the case to him, he frowned and gave me the "I don't think you have enough" look. I then plopped my huge 3-ring binder on his desk and showed him all of the reports and photos I had of stolen property; of particular interest on SUDPS' crime report IR82-9866A was "a Chimayo Indian Rug with a dark maroon and an orange and white design" taken in a Faculty Ghetto burglary on July 16, 1982.

"I espied a similar looking rug hanging on a wall in the rear room of this residence while I was standing outside the house looking through a window," I asserted.

Clearly, a big game changer was the 10851 VW bus that we found parked in the La Honda driveway. This vehicle was stolen from the garage of a Stanford Professor's home, during the night of July 1-2,

1982. The sergeant saw a blue sleeping bag in the car; the victim stated in the police report that a blue sleeping bag was in his bus when it parted company from its rightful parking spot in the Stanford driveway. Finally, the dozens of duffels, luggage, and assorted bags of all shapes and sizes convinced the DA that I had sufficient probable cause to have a search warrant issued in this matter. It was like pulling eye teeth, but the DDAs good judgment prevailed in this one.

With that precious paper in hand, I dashed over to the Superior Court Judge's chambers. I called His Honor once I knew the DA would issue the warrant and I begged him to wait (it was nearly 5p.m.) for me as I had a whopper on the line; the Judge graciously said that he would be delighted to review my Affidavit in Support of Search Warrant.

As I sat across from the Judge's enormous desk, I wondered if he comprehended the content of my affidavit, as he flipped the pages like his fingers were walking through the Yellow Pages. He then asked:

"Captain, is this going to be a good one?"

"Your Honor, this is going to be the Mother Lode," I boasted.

The Honorable Justice gave me a broad smile and put pen to paper and handed me the documents.

"I'm sure you know that these have to be filed at the Court Clerk's Office within 10 days; I wouldn't do it now so the press doesn't get the scoop before you finish-up your investigation," the judge offered.

"Yes sir, I'm well aware of that and I appreciate your counsel. By the way, sir, I don't mean to be disrespectful, but did you actually read and understand my report?"

"My dear Captain, I am a graduate of the 'Evelyn Wood' speed reading course; I read and understood every word. If you have any doubts, go ahead and hit me with a question," the jurist challenged.

"No sir. Far be it for me to challenge your reading comprehension ability, but I was once badgered on the stand by an obnoxious PD (Public Defender), wherein he asked me if the judge read every page of the affidavit in question. I told the jerk to contact the judge about that..."

"Good answer, Raoul. Good Luck!"

"Thank you, your Honor, I'll keep you informed," and waved as I left his chambers.

Logistics

I sped to the police station to brief the Chief. I was in a hurry but needed some logistical support and assistance for this caper. When I told A-1 what we were working, he leaned back in his chair and rolled his eyes: *"Why me?"* I suspected he was thinking. When I reminded the Chief of the outrage on campus amongst the faculty and high level staff that this burglar was running rip-shod over our turf, A-1 came out of orbit and basically commissioned Capt. Wullscheleger, and then Lt., Marvin Moore (Patrol Commander), to provide me whatever help they could muster. The first order of business was to rent a truck—A Big Truck! Within an hour or so, one of the support guys lumbered-in with 19 foot U-Haul—the largest at the time—a good start but I was afraid we might have to make another trip or two...

One of the most important persons on my search warrant team was our Evidence/Court Liaison Officer, Sandra Bennett Mize. She came to our department in the mid-1970s. She had extensive experience as a private security officer so she melded well in our operation. She started out like the O/G Door Shakers, but soon matriculated to Parking Enforcement where she wrote more tickets than the rest of the other CSOs combined. With this apparent "focused personality," Detective Carl Gielitz, who was soon to retire, thought that Sandra would be a natural for the arduous task of being an Evidence Officer. Boy, was he right! This woman took over that job and had that disheveled evidence room whipped into shape in a heartbeat. To say that Ms. Mize was meticulous would be a grave understatement! This woman took the bull-by-the-horns and made that operation first-rate. She quickly assumed a leadership role in the CA Evidence Officer's Association and in short order was at the top of her craft. So, it was a no-brainer that I commissioned Officer Mize to be our evidence curator in this important case; any misstep could be fatal later on down the prosecutorial road.

Our convoy of vehicles, containing some 10 deputies and CSOs, trudged up Alpine Road and over the top to La Honda. When we arrived, I sensed a tremendous amount of tension among our personnel: Apparently, they had taken a lot of gas from some San Mateo County deputies who were upset that the search warrant process had taken so long. I didn't like that at all and challenged the sergeant to tell me who the complainers were so I could set them straight. He didn't want to go there. But, I immediately went berserk when I realized that one of our over-anxious people had called for a tow truck, and had moved the VW bus out of the driveway and onto the street. Ballistic, would be more apropos: I explicitly told my officers not to touch anything until I arrived with a signed search warrant. I was paranoid that this breach could scuttle our entire case, as the V-Dubb bus was our master key into this residence. There were a lot of bruised egos over my rant, but we proceeded in spite of it all.

The Search from Hell!

Per Section 844 P. C. (the Knock and Notice rule), I pounded on the front door and announced:

"Stanford Sheriff; I have a search warrant. Open up!"

Through the large front picture window, I saw the very pregnant woman, Maureen, struggle to get out of her recliner and shuffle to the door. When she opened it, I said:

"Maureen I'm Captain Niemeyer of the Stanford Department of Public Safety. I have a signed search warrant for these premises and all appurtenant structures. May I come in?"

I'll never forget the look on that poor young woman's face. She looked like she had seen Lucifer in the flesh! I helped her to her chair and she crumpled in despair. God, I felt terrible. At this point, I set out to find a single piece of stolen property so we could arrest and remove this fragile lady from this hellhole. It didn't take long. I found a .32 caliber pistol in a dresser drawer, as well as a man's driver's license (not Robert's), so I had an assistant call communications for a want check. Sure enough, both items were hotter than *luau* rocks! Not only that, but this would be an additional charge of 12020 P.C. (felon in possession of a handgun; this con was going to spend a lot of time in the pen, when and *if* we caught him.) I gently put my hand on Maureen's shoulder and whispered:

"I'm sorry to have to tell you this, Maureen, but I'm placing you under arrest for 496 P.C.—possession of stolen property. You are going to have to go with this officer." I thought that she was going to have her child right then and there! This was one of the toughest arrests I ever had to make. We held-up proceedings until she was led out of her home and transported to the Women's Detention Center where she was held in lieu of $150,000 bail.

Let's Get Ready to Rumble

Now to the part of police work which cops hate the most: Processing evidence after a pinch. And, we didn't even have the satisfaction of collaring the main crook—all we got was a scared, very pregnant young lady. Oh well, like the Bible says: "A bird in the hand is worth two in the bush..."

The sergeant came up to me with a frustrated look on his face; he asked how we were possibly going to recover and process all of this stuff. Like I told the judge, this was going to be the Mother Lode, but I didn't expect the Comstock. The walls were literally covered with Persian rugs, valuable oil paintings, antique guns and such. The front room looked like an antique store—priceless collectables everywhere. I assured the troops that I had a plan. I warned them that this would take awhile, but in the end, they would be happy with the fruits of their labor, and this evidence would stand the test of jurisprudence. This sounded like one of the half-time speeches I gave to my youth football team when we were trailing 20-zip...

I learned how to execute search warrants as a patrol deputy, flying by the seat of my pants—and with great advice from seasoned detectives, Stan Shaver and Ed Perovich, who were the S/O's night "Dicks". Both Detective Sergeants had earned their stripes over the years and developed considerable expertise, particularly with dope cases. They were good! After being on a number of narc raids as back-up, I realized that doing a search warrant without a methodical plan could be very problematic later on in court. Many of these overexuberant marauders were like a bunch of kids attacking their Christmas presents under the tree, ripping off the wrappings and throwing stuff all over the place. Then, when it came time for the lead investigator to ascertain who found what and where, the "finders" would shrug and point to the other guy. Not a way to do business these days, guys!

My evidence officer, Sandy Mize, had done a number of searches with me so she knew the drill. However, the others had not, so it was imperative that they understood the game plan. I set-up a security perimeter and utilized my best deputies for this detail. I knew that Robert was lurking out there somewhere, and I wouldn't put it past him to do something stupid, like take some pot-shots at our troopers. He had a penchant for firearms and Lord only knew where he might have some stashed around his crib. I also assigned a CSO to stand by the U-Haul truck, which was backed-up near the rear door. His job was to make sure that once evidence was put in the truck, nothing, AND I mean *nothing* was to be removed without my authority.

Next, I formed preliminary finder teams, comprised of two deputies. Their task was to look for possible evidence under every nook and granny and put a card next to, or near the piece. Being the principle finder, I would follow-up and determine whether the item(s) met the criteria specified in our search warrant. I then asked our keeper, Sandy, for an item number, which I wrote on the card and had the photographer shoot a picture where it was found. A collector would then take the evidence to Officer Mize. She would log the item(s) on her evidence sheet, bag and tag the piece and instruct the transporters to put it in the U-Haul. Because of the magnitude of this effort, I always searched in a clockwise motion. We assigned lot numbers to each wall and area: We photographed the material on the wall or area so the lot number could be readily identified. When logging in the evidence, Sandra wrote down the lot number, followed by the item designation, e.g., Lot 1—Item 1. The lot number deal was an impromptu plan, but it worked well.

While rummaging through a small dresser in the front room, I hit an unexpected bonanza—an innocuous receipt from a mini-storage facility in Redwood City, near the Bay. I had a gut feeling that Robert probably had a storage facility jammed full of booty. I made a mental note to follow up on that first thing the next day when the facility's office opened.

The first room was a bear. The crew was mulling along but they soon got into the swing of things, and after several agonizing hours, they finished that very difficult and very time consuming area. We then moved into the rest of the house. Once an area was completed, I had one of the senior deputies re-search it for missed goodies. Our preliminary finders did a pretty thorough job, as very little was overlooked—I thought . . .

It was very dark outside and bloody cold! All of a sudden, I heard a lot of commotion, with deputies running outside, guns drawn. I ran out the back, too, and asked what was going on. The excited rear security deputy blurted:

"Captain, he was out there! I saw him back by the pigeon coops. He was wearing a red shirt. I shined the light on him and he split."

"OK, guys. That fricker must want something out there. Check out those coops and be careful. This crook loves guns and he may have some."

Sure enough, a few minutes later, one of the deputies returned with a little ditty bag which contained 4 pistols and some ammo.

An Arduous Task

It was well past midnight, November 5th. The crew, as well as their leader, was bushed—and damn near frozen to death! We had been at this since dusk, the day before. It must have been close to freezing that night. Most of the troops had their winter jackets, but the cold wind cut through those things like a stiletto. We didn't turn on the heater due to all of the in and out traffic, so we just endured. In addition, we were famished: Sandy gave one of the CSOs ten bucks and sent him down to the corner store for some fruit and soft drinks early on. Other than that, there was no meal—there was no time! I promised the group a full-blown breakfast at Stickney's come morning.

A couple of other big finds were in the laundry room: Unbelievably, there was a huge white parrot in a cage. I called this beauty a "Baretta Bird," after the New Jersey PD TV detective of the time, Baretta, played by the now infamous Robert Blake, believed to have shot and killed his wife and beat the rap. The bird in Robert's home was stolen in a Menlo Park burglary some months before. I later learned the pilfered avian was a Moluccan Cockatoo. We called Animal Control and they later reunited the cockatoo with his owners.

In my estimation, the biggest nugget of the search was "Bob's Burglar Bag." I stumbled on this find in the laundry room, too. It was a small rucksack which contained very culpable evidence: A flashlight, gloves, a screw-driver, and a small pry bar; in addition, it was equipped with a climbing rope, black clothing, a watch cap and several disguises—3 wigs, a beard and several false mustaches. This was very incriminating! Here were the instrumentalities of Robert's crime spree. I was elated.

Back to the Farm

We finally got out of there at about 0700 hours. I was so tired I could barely navigate back to the campus. The U-Haul was jam-packed with every collectable under the sun. The troops skillfully packed that thing like professional movers. We backed the rig into the fire department's training yard, which could be secured. As I opened up the rear doors to show-off our find to the Chief and other curious fire and police folks, it suddenly occurred to me that there was no place, save the truck, to put this evidence. Coincidently, the first thing the Chief said was:

"So, where are you going to put all of this stuff?"

"I was thinking about that very problem, Chief. Do ya think we can rent one of those 60 foot office trailers?" I trial ballooned.

"And, who is going to pay for it?" he replied.

"We'll stick the county with the tab, boss. They are going to reap all of the benefits of this caper, anyway. We are operating under their authority, so they need to pony-up!"

Marv gave me that "yeah right" grin and said he'd have Cap'n Bill work on it.

Before he left, I approached A-1 up close and personal and said:

"This team was fantastic; they worked their asses off all night in that dark pneumonia hole without taking breaks or having anything to eat. I promised that YOU would buy them breakfast at Stickney's; is that OK?" He gave me a short punch in the arm, smiled and gave me the green light. And, without further delay we dashed over to Town and Country for a de-briefing meal and rounds of "war stories"...

"Who *is* That Guy?"

Robert Lee O'Connor was born in 1942 and raised in Pennsylvania. Bob was 39 when all of these Bay Area burglaries occurred. He enlisted in the U.S. Air Force when he was 18 years old and served an overseas assignment in Taiwan. It was there that he met his first wife, Nancy Ping Lee. Records indicate that O'Connor killed a local pedestrian with his motorcycle while riding drunk. Robert was honorably discharged in 1965. He moved to Pasadena, CA with his wife and children.

O'Connor's criminal behavior began in 1967 when he was arrested for a strong armed robbery: He tore a purse from the hands of an elderly woman who was walking down the street, minding her own business. Fortunately, Robert was caught almost immediately. O'Connor was convicted, fined and sentenced to 5 years probation. Robert violated his parole 7 months prior to completion of his term for not adhering to the rules of the agreement. A warrant for his arrest was issued, but Robert went on the lam, and remained a PAL (parolee at large) until September 1973 when he was arrested in a botched residential burglary attempt in Pasadena, CA. His first burglaries were petty, in that he mainly ripped-off bikes from open garages during the early evening. He later entered garages at night and stole tools and anything else that he could sell at flea markets. In one caper, he copped a large Craftsman roll-away tool chest, but the wheels squeaked so loudly that he brazenly went back into the garage, grabbed a can of WD-40, and sprayed the annoying wheels.

On August 27, 1973, a female victim reported that her 1971 Ford had been stolen from her garage. This lady's home had been burglarized 12 days before and among other things, the spare set of keys to her vehicle was missing. On September 3rd, Pasadena police officers responded to an attempted entry but the would-be interloper was scared-off by a neighbor. The suspect fled in a 1971 Ford with an Asian female passenger. An "eye-in-the-sky" quickly spotted the duo and a brief chase ensued. When the male suspect realized that the cops had him surrounded, he bailed out of the stolen car and tried to escape on foot, leaving his passenger in the lurch. The desperate thief tried to hide in a dumpster, but the cops ferreted-him-out. He was bagged and tagged after a brief scuffle. The man was, of course, our hero, Robert L. O'Connor. The woman in the hot car was none other than his wife, Nancy. O'Connor was subsequently imprisoned at Pilot Rock Conservation Camp in the San Bernardino Mountains for 6 to 10 months—clearly a cushy place to do some time—nothing more than a slap on the wrist. Charges against his wife were dismissed.

Prison Break

After serving only four months, RLO flew the coop and was not seen again until 4:11a.m. February 5, 1976 while he was burglarizing an Indian jewelry store in Arcadia, CA. Mr. O'Connor climbed on top of a 1 and ½ story building, cut a hole in the roof, and shimmied down a rope. Little did he know, the store was "bugged." When the officers arrived in response to the silent alarm, they saw Robert removing items from a display case; one of them hollered: "Freeze!" With that, O'Connor hopped on the rope and began ascending to the rooftop. Then, he suddenly descended and then went back up again. The sergeant at the scene told me: "He looked like a monkey on a string, going up and down like that." When Bob finally made up his mind, he muscled up the rope and *ran-off* that roof without breaking stride! Robert sprained his ankle when he hit the ground but that didn't slow him down: He ran through the cordon of police officers, crawled over an 8 foot chain link fence, and tried to limp away. The sergeant chuckled that someone's shotgun "accidentally" went-off, whereupon Mr. O'C hit the deck and capitulated without further fanfare. Arcadia cops found a bag full of necklaces, bracelets, pins and nearly 300 turquoise rings—wholesale value $48, 815!

But, this caper wasn't all he was going to be charged with. Shortly after escaping from Pilot Rock (October 11, 1974), O'Connor and a group of cohorts planned to break into a home in Glendale, CA, where they knew 94 silver bars were stashed. According to one co-conspirator, Robert used a ladder to gain entry via an open window. They made off with an estimated $18,000 in silver, plus an antique Zenith radio with wooden cabinet, and a portable color TV. Investigators dusted for latent fingerprints and lifted two readable specimens on the wall below the window.

The case remained dormant until July of 1975, when Glendale detectives developed a snitch, who admitted he took Robert O'Connor to the house in question, and that it was Robert who actually entered and removed the property. Police then compared the latent prints obtained at the scene to rolled impressions from previous arrests, and sure enough, Robert Lee O'Connor left those latent fingerprints on the wall.

Justice Denied

With all of these pending beefs, one would think that the courts would put Mr. O'Connor away so deep they would have to pump O2 to him. . . But, this man wasn't only a master burglar, he was the guru of getting out of jams by invoking sympathy and minimizing his crimes. After all, save for the strong armed robbery, which had been reduced to grand theft from a person, he maintained he had never committed a violent crime—I guess running over and killing a Taiwan citizen while drunk on a motorcycle didn't count? Unbelievable! Without the benefit of high dollar mouthpieces, Robert was able to get his offenses reduced so that they were barely eligible for imprisonment in CDC (CA Dept. of Corrections). He also cried that he had no job, no money and was simply trying to care for his family, which had grown to four dependants, plus his wife.

In the final analysis, O'Connor was sentenced to 2-counts of 2nd degree burglary concurrently, and would serve a minimum of one year. He was committed on 4/23/76 and would be eligible for parole on 2/5/77. Robert was initially incarcerated in San Quentin and then to Folsom. He sniveled that the bikers had a "contract" (death warrant) on him as he once befriended some black inmates at Pilot Rock. That is the reason he gave for escaping. O'Connor then absconded to Utah, but was lured back to do the "silver bars caper" in order to get a stake so he could return to Utah. Robert wound-up in a medium security prison, California Institution for Men, Chino, CA and was paroled 1/26/78. He moved his family—lock, stock, and barrel—to his new hide-out in La Honda. Incredibly, O'Connor was discharged from formal parole less than 9 months later. If anyone needed supervision, Robert would have been my choice.

The Easter Egg Hunt

Once the celebratory breakfast was over, I grabbed my detectives and shot over to that mini-storage facility in Redwood City. Once the office opened, we learned that O'Connor had two storage lockers—one huge 24' x 15' exterior unit, and a smaller 5' x 10' locker inside an enormous warehouse. I positioned a CSO in an unmarked car near Robert's outside locker and asked the office personnel to call us if anyone tried to access the inner unit. We then flew back to the office to prepare another affidavit for the mini-storage facility. While working on that, an investigator, who I assigned to study our crime reports, recalled that we missed several items that were listed as stolen, so I had write another re-search affidavit for the cottage. Thus, off we went again—no sleep, but determined to wrap up this case. Thanks to our logistics man, Doug Williams, who set-up a generator and lights, we could now deal with the storage facility units in the dark. When I opened-up the big one, I almost cried: That thing looked like Dagwood's Closet! So, we had to do the drill all over again, this time, totally out in the open, with the Bay's frigid winds reminding me of the first time I experienced the "Hawk" in Chicago: 10 degrees in the dead of winter on the shore of Lake Michigan, with the stiff breeze plummeting the wind chill factor to way below zero.

The team's experience last night, coupled with working on pure adrenalin, sped-up the monotonous process, and before I realized it, we were done.

"Ooops," I lamented and announced, "We still gotta do the little locker—but that's inside, gang. It'll be warmer and we'll be outta here in no time. . ." The groans were painful to my ears, but this task had to be completed. As it turned out, the best was left for last. This is where Bob stored his most precious treasures: Artifacts, antique furniture, exquisite silver settings, hundreds of gold objects, and the most valuable firearms. In a large paper shopping bag marked

"Bob's Choice," with a red felt tip pen, I found 18th and 19th Century pocket pistols: First model Colt cap and ball revolvers, 4 barrel pistols called "Pepper Boxes,"and a number of rare over and under .44 caliber Derringers. This guy was the consummate connoisseur!

When will it end?

Our investigative team found a considerable amount of missed evidence at the La Honda residence, which ultimately gave rise to more search warrants. We learned that Bob had dumped his first wife, Nancy Ping Lee O'Connor, for their 16 year old babysitter, Maureen, who was now on the verge of having his child. Ms. Lee was living in San Mateo and was believed to have a ton of stolen property in her home. So, off the gang went to recover that stuff and arrest Nancy. From there, the trail extended to Sebastopol, in Marvelous Marin County, for goods in the possession of Bob's sister, Mary. After scoring some really fine objects, Mary was arrested. Up to this point, we had initiated 5 search warrants and had 3 and 3/4 bodies in jail—3 women and the sex of the 3/4, yet to be determined...

However, the principle was in hiding, in lieu of a $250,000 arrest warrant. *Where in the hell is that dude?* I agonized. *He could be in Canada by now, for Chrissakes!*

The Louvre West

Meanwhile, back on the Farm, stolen stuff was coming in at an alarming rate—5 U-Haul truckloads all told! We had to rent a second trailer. The Plant Services carpenter shop built some nifty shelves so that the property could be displayed. Sandra Mize skillfully arranged the mass of property (10,000 items) so that when the time came, victims could be brought through the trailers and hopefully, identify their treasures. The media got onto this story like a duck on a June bug. Once all of the property was set-up, streams of television and print reporters traipsed through the gallery. That's when I dubbed our trailers "The Louvre West," and tongue-in-cheek told reporters that Evidence Officer Mize had been promoted to "Curator Emeritus". . . The biggest challenge was keeping the victims away. Our poor office staff handled hundreds of calls from every burglary victim in the Greater Bay Area who wondered if we had their stuff. We announced there would a showing forthcoming for verified victims, whom we had identified by investigators from the allied agencies who were working on this case. That held them off for awhile.

CLO Sandra B. Mize, Curator Emeritus

WSSBIA

In October 1982, I did a presentation on Robert L. O'Connor for the Western States Safe and Burglary Investigator's Association annual seminar, held at Lake Tahoe, NV. In addition to the aforementioned profile information on Robert, I had learned that our suspect had been arrested in Lovelock, NV on June 21, 1981. The police made a traffic stop on O'Connor and found the following in his vehicle: Cocaine, marijuana, prescription drugs (controlled substances) without an Rx, a 12 gauge sawed-off shotgun, two pistols—.38 and .32 calibers—tools, several chainsaws, 4 oriental ivory statues, 57 rings, 2 Canon cameras and a large amount of miscellaneous jewelry. He was criminally charged but the case was never adjudicated in the wake of our case. Lovelock police detectives developed information that Robert frequently flew to Washington D.C. and drove cars back to CA as a sideline business. Little did I know then, that in about 3 weeks, we would be the lead police agency in his capture and subsequent prosecution. During our prolonged investigation, we learned that O'Connor routinely traveled to NV, where he would have gold melted down. There was also speculation that he periodically flew to the eastern seaboard and disposed of stolen property there, however we were never able to make a definitive connection.

Two

In a task force briefing after our initial search warrants were executed, Detective Morton of Palo Alto PD offered she recalled that a rare Abyssinian cat named "Two" was taken in one of their burglaries. This was an animal worth $2,000, a tidy sum back in the day! Morton suspected that Bob may have taken the cat because of his fondness for animals. So, armed with a photo of the feline, she went back to Robert's neighborhood and canvassed. Lo and behold, kids in the area recognized the kitty, and said that O'Connor had given her to his "girlfriend," another "Nancy," who lived in the coastal town of Montara. *Maybe this is the reason O'Connor began stealing household items,* I surmised. *He was setting-up a household for his new "squeeze."*

The Take-Down

Sergeant Brunot and associates reconnoitered Nancy Burt's home in Montara, CA, which was right off the Cabrillo Highway 1, a few miles north of Half Moon Bay. The house sat on a bluff, with a gorgeous view of the Pacific Ocean. *Neat hide-away; no wonder we hadn't found him.* There was a 30 foot edifice facing the street, so most of the cops felt that was a plus, as no one in their right mind would ever jump off that cliff. I had my doubts, knowing how desperate this criminal might be, so I asked San Mateo County S/O, who were going to assist in this apprehension, to bring a K-9 unit or two, as there weren't any cops that I knew who could out-run this cat. The take-down was scheduled for O-Dark 30—Tuesday, November 9, 1982 at 0500 in the AM. I opted out of this detail as I wanted our young guys to flex their muscles. And, between you and me, I was getting too damn old for this rough stuff.

The team arrived about 0515 hours and 14 officers surrounded the 2-story house. I had insisted that our rookie Deputy, Iran White, be on the arrest team as he was quick as a leopard and strong as a bull. Iran was with Sergeant Brian Beck, one of my old buddies at the S/O; he was a mountain of a man and mean as a pit bull. If Beck got a hold of you, he would never let go! This duo was also backed-up with two San Mateo deputies and one very disagreeable German Shepard. What a five-some, loaded for bear and ready for action!

Bam-Bam-Bam. "Stanford Police, we have a warrant, open up," the sergeant bellowed.

A slim female answered the door. The sergeant told her he was looking for Bob and to have him come to the door. She balked, but through the open door, Nick saw a shadow dash across the hall and into a bedroom, which faced Hwy 1. The troops were alerted. According to Deputy White, here's how it went down:

All of a sudden, Robert came out of the second story window at a sprinter's pace. Iran tackled him in the iceplant as the fugitive was trying to make it to the cliff. They glommed onto Bob like a giant squid, and he was done. But, the pooch wasn't; he wanted part of the action and nearly bit Iran in the face. I later asked Robert what he thought of our game plan, especially the K-9: He told me it was pretty good and interjected he was trying to get away from "those gorillas," but didn't sweat the dog. Bob bragged that if he had gotten away from the arrest team, he would have been home free!

"So, what about the K-9," I asked?

"The dog wouldn't have been a problem," Bob rejoined.

"I was going to jump off the cliff! No dog would ever be stupid enough to do that!"

Post script: As suspected, the cute Abyssinian feline, *Two,* was in Nancy B's home, safe and sound. So was a pile of stolen goods; Ms. Burt was taken into custody and booked for possession of stolen property and harboring a fugitive. *Two* was taken by Animal Control and held as a "material witness." After the smoke cleared, I attempted to acquire a linguistic expert from Stanford's famed language department. After reporting to our DA, she decided to release *Two* to her rightful owners, as no one at the University was conversant in Abyssinian. . .

Twenty years later, I was asked by Rocket Productions in CO to appear in their Animal Planet production: "Busted," a TV series that featured war stories about animals who led cops to crooks. That was a fun gig. Animals Rule!

Evidentiary Hearing

The District Attorney's Office was all over this one. Our original prosecutor, Lorraine O'Keefe, a very smart (very nice, too) seasoned litigator was close to retirement, so the matter was lateraled to a veteran felony DA, Mr. Tom Hanford. He was a gem: Not only a congenial soul, but Tom was an extremely detailed and meticulous individual; however, at the same time, he was a pleasure to work with. He understood, given the enormity of the evidence, that this case would not be a cake walk, so my investigators and I worked tirelessly to get our stuff together. We boxed and flagged reports, photos, evidence, the search warrants (now up to 7) and other pertinent data so when in court, we were on our game and could produce required data in a heartbeat.

When the evidentiary hearing was about to happen—brought forth by the defense, challenging the prosecution to show cause why all of the evidence seized in the case should be allowed despite defense *claims* that the police violated the search and seizure clause of the U.S. Constitution—I was about as nervous as a hooker in church. Not about our work, but whether our initial entry, to the rear of the property, would withstand judicial scrutiny. Fortunately, the people of CA had passed a crucial piece of legislation called Proposition 8—not to be confused with 2008's Prop 8 of gay marriage fame—the 1981 amendment to CA law allowed the police wider latitude when conducting criminal investigations. In this incident, Municipal Court Judge Joseph Biafore Jr. ruled that because of O'Connor's propensity to evade arrest, our sergeant and Palo Alto's detective were allowed to go into his backyard in an effort to prevent his escape, even though he had not yet been formerly charged with any crime. The Court also opined that because I followed rules of law in obtaining and executing our search warrants, we were good to go! Robert L. O'Connor and all of his women were next scheduled for a preliminary examination in Santa Clara County Municipal court, Judge Edward J. Nelson presiding. After winning the first round, I noticed that the defendants were none too pleased: If looks could kill, I would have been dead and buried deep four times over!

Mea Culpa

On December 4, 1982, the San Jose Mercury News released portions of a letter of remorse and contrition by Bob to his children: Robert Jr. 16; Robin 14; and Frank 12. In my mind, this letter of confession came about after O'Connor was busted on November 9th in Montara. Following the arrest, four case detectives contacted the kids at their mother's (Nancy Lee) home in San Mateo, and chatted with them in earnest. . . Although their Dad had lavished the children with stolen items ranging from gold certificates (proceeds from jewelry that was sold and melted in NV) to expensive athletic shoes and sportswear, our investigators felt that Robert's offspring really didn't know where these gifts had originated. In fact, our sergeant relieved one of the boys of an Adidas jacket he was wearing when the name of another kid was found sewn on the inside! It was our gut feeling that these poor children were made victims by their father's actions. O'Connor obviously felt the same way, as his admissions reflected those very sentiments. Needless to say, Robert's remorseful epistle didn't bode well for his initial *not guilty* plea.

Capitulation

Prolonged discussions between O'Connor et al.'s attorneys, DA Tom Hanford and Presiding Judge Honorable Edward J. Nelson went on all day. Just before 5:00 p.m. on 3/21/83, Judge Nelson said that the case was close to settlement, but the attorneys needed some more time to discuss the details. The judge indicated that O'Connor, his wife, girlfriend and sister were due in court the next morning where they were expected to plead guilty to the charges. Deputy District Attorney Hanford said that RLO could be sentenced to 19 years for the 26 felonies he was charged with, and his accomplices could also receive considerable prison and/or jail time. The case was then sent to Superior Court Judge Robert M. Foley for sentencing.

Sentencing

Another significant provision of Proposition 8 was that this was the first time in California judicial history that victims of any crime could not only attend all sentencing procedures, but could testify in open court before the sentencing judge as to how the crime(s) affected them personally. Section 1191.1, in essence, allowed victims to testify, in open court, how the criminal behavior of the perpetrator(s) affected their lives following the event(s).

This break-through legislation was devastating for the defense, as a long line of well prepared, well spoken victims made their personal feelings known to the Honorable Robert Foley! One victim articulated that immeasurable psychological harm was inflicted on his 12 year old daughter as a result of O'Connor's "cat burglary" of his family residence:

"She is still afraid of being alone in our home and of coming home to an empty house—even in broad daylight. She still has nightmares about the person or persons who invaded our home. She will carry her concerns for many years..."

This victim suffered an approximate $50,000 loss, plus insurance deductibles. In addition, the household lost irreplaceable family heirlooms as well as the victim's high school and Stanford mementos! Needless to say, testimony like this must have had a tremendous impact on the Court—and it seemed as though there was an endless parade of impressive speakers who imparted similar, deep-wound stories of despair!

The Hammer

On Monday, May 24, 1983, the Honorable Robert M. Foley dropped the hammer on Robert Lee O'Connor, and his criminal enterprise came to a screeching halt! Robert, 39, was sentenced to 19 years in state prison. Judge Foley said O'Connor's "reign of terror has been legally brought to an end." Citing the "multitude of victims" who appeared in court for the sentencing, Foley said that the burglaries were "outrageous and revolting."

O'Connor's wife, Maureen, who was seeking a divorce, got the maximum sentence of 3 years for her guilty plea of receiving stolen property, and was sent to Corona. She tried to mitigate her involvement due to her love for her man. Robert's "friend", Nancy Burt, was committed to the Women's Facility at Elmwood for one year for receiving stolen property.

Show 'n Tell

At last! The time had come for Evidence Officer, Sandra Mize, to return the estimated 1.5 million dollars worth of stolen booty to the rightful owners. After 18 months of sorting, classifying, charting and escorting known, as well as possible, victims through The Louvre West, Judge Foley ordered us to abate the evidence. Hundreds of people from the Bay Area and beyond filed through the trailers in search of their precious belongings. However, most people went away sorely disappointed. Of the estimated 500 burglaries that were attributed to O'Connor and Co., only 181 actual victims were located and verified through their police agencies' crime reports. We knew that there were many more, but discovered early on during the course of this investigation that O'Connor, being an accomplished jeweler—among other things—broke-up valuable, identifiable pieces, reset many precious stones and had most of the gold melted in NV. We found photos depicting the entire family sorting through a myriad of rings, chains, broaches—every bauble imaginable—on a large table with Robert overseeing the *festa* as titular head of his band of gypsies.

After weeks of folks claiming their property, the well dried-up, as no one else could identify what was theirs. It was then that Judge Foley ordered all unclaimed property to be sold at public auction, with a portion of the proceeds going to compensate our department for operating costs. The County Administrator commissioned a highly reputable auctioneering firm, Neale and Sons, to handle the sale, which was scheduled for July 9, 1983. But, suddenly a huge fly landed in the ointment...

The San Jose Mercury headline said it all: "Burglar demands that police return his property." Robert maintained all along that a great deal of the property we confiscated was actually his. I admitted in a court hearing on this matter: "We weren't discriminatory—we took everything that wasn't nailed down." I was simply telling the truth as just about everything in Robert's house and storage lockers matched property he had pilfered during his rampage. RLO wrote me a letter to this effect. I, in turn, challenged him to prove what was his, and promised I would return any item(s) that passed muster. Being fair and balanced, Judge Foley issued a very unusual ruling (No. 87418: Order to Acceptance, Transportation and Return to Custody of Robert L. O'Connor). This order mandated Robert be released from jail custody to my heavily armed and physically imposing knuckle-dragging guard detail, and be transported to our trailers for *his* "Show 'n Tell." Bob's girlfriend, Nancy Burt, who was serving a one year term for receiving stolen property, obtained a like order from the judge, as she claimed we took her personal belongings as well.

Under an umbrella of heavy security, both convicts inspected the unclaimed property, in my presence as well as Officer Mize's. O'Connor subsequently wrote a 7 page list of property, most of which was more utilitarian in nature than the high dollar collectables he ripped-off during his spree. He also described what he believed was his, prior to 1978, with, in many cases, good specificity and backed his claims with statements from family members and friends who verified his allegations.

After reviewing the property on Robert's list, I met with Judge Foley and DA Hanford, as I had a gut feeling that Bob was telling the truth about his claim. I based my notion on the fact that none of the things on Bob's list had ever been identified by victims, and although O'Connor was an admitted and convicted thief, that didn't necessarily mean he was a bald-faced liar, as well. I also had conversations with his Mom and Dad, whom I found to be very credible. They corroborated Bob's story and independently described family heirlooms.

There was another motive for my perceived "moment of madness:" I wished to establish some rapport with this guy so that law enforcement could better understand what made this extremely adept criminal tick. He might be able to open-up a lot of doors for future investigations, which I planned to impart in my role as a trainer. Both the Judge and my friend, Tom Hanford agreed. So, on September 1, 1983, Judge Foley ordered me to release approximately 200 personal items, primarily clothes, shoes, some household things and miscellaneous "dust collectors" to O'Connor's family. This nightmare was finally nearing closure.

G-2 (Intelligence)

The belated rapport I built with Bob O'Connor was the result of me doing the right thing about his stuff; I believe this move was rather fruitful. Some feel I caved-in and gave Robert's family the fruits of his crimes, but I vehemently disagree. The amount of intelligence gleaned as a result of sitting down, up close and personal, with this celebrated crook was literally worth its weight in some of the gold he fenced. Where do I start? Here are some of Bob's "War Stories:"

Speed and Stealth: These are the attributes that Bob utilized in his trade. He was blessed with God-given athletic ability, and honed his gift by way of conditioning and competing in the rough and tumble sport of rugby, which was very popular in the Bay Area. Bob belonged to a Palo Alto club called the B.A.T.S. (Bay Area Touring Side). Bill Starbuck, one of our deputies, at various times during his early law enforcement career, not only knew Bob, but they were on the same team. Bill told me that Bob was one of the fastest and toughest dudes on the squad, and coming from a tough guy like Bill, I knew that was the case! They called O'Connor the "Mosquito," not only for his speed, but when he hit an opponent, it "stung!" Unlike football, rugby players wear no pads, whatsoever. Maybe this is why they say: "Ruggers have leather balls!" Robert was also a part-time track coach at a La Honda middle school. It was reputed that at age 39, he could still run the 100 yard dash in 11.5 seconds!

Stealth is the reason this man was never seen, except for the caper in Menlo Park: When spotted by a responding officer, he was only described as a "shadowy figure in a Ninja suit," and once he vaulted the fence, he was history. Bob confided that he went through great lengths in planning his ingress and egress to the crime scenes. He selected target areas which tended to be heavily foliated because this offered many avenues of escape. Robert said that he usually drove around beforehand in potentially "target rich" environments, and selected clusters of homes which provided concealment and cover. I once asked Bob why he never hit Los Altos Hills, where the multi-million dollar homes there would yield bountiful harvests. There were several reasons, he replied:

- The homes were too far away from each other, with virtually no foliage for concealment. If caught in the open, he would be a dead duck, despite his speed advantage over the average cop. Dogs and helicopters scared him.
- Most of these places were heavily alarmed with state of the art equipment.
- Many homeowners enlisted the service of private mobile patrols.

In one of our cases—the area of Peter Coutts Road and Stanford Avenue—Bob was in the process of collecting goods he had stolen earlier and stashed in the bushes, when a vehicle suddenly appeared on Stanford Ave. It was after midnight, so Robert suspected it was a patrol car. He was at the bridge over the creek near Bowdoin St., so he jumped from the roadway and hung onto the bridge's abutment until the car passed. Sure enough, it was one of our units—they never saw him.

The Assault: O'Connor always parked his Saab far away in areas where there were other vehicles, such as shopping centers or strip malls. He would then don his burglar backpack and ride one of this many fine 10 speed bikes (stolen, of course) to the targeted area. This typically occurred at twilight. Bob would usually rap on the door or ring the bell. If no one answered, he'd make his way around the perimeter, peer in the windows and listen for sounds therein. When he was certain that the home was unoccupied, Bob would look for evidence of an alarm system. In those days, most people only had their doors and windows bugged, if at all. The majority of the houses in our area were not alarmed. However, if there *was* a contact alarm and his visual inspection revealed an abundance of rugs, art, and precious silver, he might break or cut-out a window and crawl in. Once inside, our burglar would quickly check out the residence for people—perhaps someone asleep—which actually happened in a couple of cases. Once clear, Bob selected a route of escape and then pillaged the place using black trash bags, pillowcases, duffels etc., to cart away the loot and stash it in a blind, usually where he hid his bike. O'Connor would repeat this drill three of four times and then retreat to an observation position. Robert had an almost perverted sense of humor in that he delighted in seeing the shocked victims react to their plight.

Physical Evidence—Or Lack Thereof: O'Connor also got a kick out of watching the "dumb cops" searching the grounds with flashlights for the perpetrator and/or clues. He once said:

"You know why you cops never found me at the scene?"

"I give," I choked.

"*Cuz ya* always look at the ground and never up! A lot of times I was up in a tree or on a roof. . ." he bragged.

I hated to admit it, but he was right—for the most part. We generally followed the Sherlock Holmes' school of evidence detection. On the other hand, the only tangible piece of evidence we ever found that could ID Robert was a shoe impression in a flower bed. We later recovered the shoe that made the impression when we searched his La Honda home. This key piece of evidence allowed the DA to charge him with that particular crime. So much for bad-mouthing Sherlock and his faithful companion, Holmes. . .

Another element of amusement for O'Connor was the exhaustive search for latent prints our deputies undertook on each and every break-in. Part of this was for "PR," because if the investigating officers didn't throw some powder around areas where the perp entered or might have touched, I could bank on getting a phone call the very next day asking: "Why didn't your officers dust for prints?" Remember that burglary in Southern CA Robert got busted for, behind a couple perfect latent prints he left at the entry point? Bob learned two important lessons from that caper:

1) Never leave tell-tale prints at a crime scene, and; 2) Don't ever do crimes with associates: They are liabilities who will, more than likely, "snitch-you-off!" And, you have to share the spoils with them. That's precisely why Robert wore gloves from then on and was always a solitary criminal!

Exit Stage Left: Once the cops left and the victims turned out the lights for the night, Robert emerged from his lair, retrieved his 10-speed and rode to his car. He usually waited until the early AM, picked-up his stash and headed home. No wonder O'Connor went undetected for nearly three years.

"Marks:" One of the most interesting War Tales that Bob shared was a Palo Alto job where he got away with the bag of antique firearms he dubbed "Bob's Choice." Robert was a gun nut and frequented gun shows all over the region. At one show, he met a collector who had this incredible array of extremely rare 18th and 19th century pocket pistols. Being an affable individual, Bob quickly established rapport with the collector and expressed a sincere interest in purchasing some of those pistols. The "Mark" gave Bob a business card, which not only displayed a phone number, but it also had the collector's address printed on it. So, Bob asked when it would be convenient for him to come by and look at the guns. The totally oblivious Mark advised Mr. RLO that he was going to be vacationing in Europe for several weeks. Uh-oh: A nefarious plan was hatched in Robert's criminal mind. So, when the Mark was abroad, Bob reconnoitered the premises and laid-out his approach. Much to Bob's surprise, the residence was not alarmed, as far as his initial inspection revealed. Robert quickly jimmied a door and was in like Flynn. Upon searching the home, there was no gun safe; furthermore, a cursory search failed to locate the bag of guns he saw at the gun show.

After giving this dilemma a considerable amount of thought, he recalled that the 94K in silver bars he made away with in Glendale CA was stashed under the kitchen sink, way in the back, behind all of the cleaning supplies. As Bob sprung into action and zeroed in on the sink, he noticed a funny looking mat, strategically positioned in front of the cabinet's doors. On closer inspection, Robert recognized this mat as a pressure sensitive device that would trigger an alarm—clever victim, but no match for a smarter crook! Bob carefully slid the mat away, crawled under the sink, and *Voila*, there was "Bob's Choice!"

Because the Mark was going to be away for an extended period of time, Bob decided that he would avail himself of his cozy domicile: Hell, the Mark had a wonderful wine collection, fine cigars, a fridge full of beer and food, a library of Penthouse, Playboy and Hustler magazines—plus an inside hot tub that was fired-up to a Buck 02— What better way for Robert to decompress after a hard day at the "office:" Soaking in a spa with a glass of premium Merlot, a Cuban, and the latest edition of Playboy! Life was good for Ol' RLO!

Achilles' Heel: Clearly the mistake that brought Robert Lee O'Connor's empire down was the discovery of an invoice in a box of exclusive gold rimmed dinner plates Bob left on consignment at an antique store in Bremerton, WA. When the owner of the store found this receipt, she called the victim in Los Altos and reported her find. The victim called Detective Lee Lira of Los Altos P.D. who later reported this break to our task force. This was the straw that broke the camel's back!

Robert later told me that this was a major screw-up on his part as he meticulously checked all stolen property for owner identifiers; however, in this instance, Bob related that he had played a very physical rugby match in WA and took a major shot to his head. When he got to his motel room, his head was spinning, so he smoked a "joint" and passed-out. He maintained that he seldom used drugs, but in this case it was necessary. The next day, he took his booty to the shop and left his true name and phone number with the owner should someone want to purchase the plates. In retrospect, this was a very dumb move, Bob lamented. Oh well, hindsight is always 20-20. . . And Bob's crime episode on the Peninsula was effectively over.

The Grim Tally

Although we figured O'Connor committed an estimated 500 burglaries, our statistics said otherwise. Many of Bob's crimes may have gone unreported or previous victims may have moved away. In any event, here's what we ended up with:

- Palo Alto-70
- Los Altos-45
- Menlo Park-34
- Stanford-22
- San Mateo County-5
- Half Moon Bay-4
- Redwood City-1
  Total: 181

The Auction

After a couple of legal hiccups, Stanford's Auction of the Century went off in the Public Safety Department's parking lot on Saturday, September 17, 1983. Auctioneer extraordinaire, Doug Neale of Santa Clara's well established firm, Neale and Sons, hawked some 20,000 unclaimed articles, purloined over a three year crime spree by the "Jogging Thief," as Doug called him. Over 1,000 people attended the extravaganza.

It took three of Neale's personnel six very long days to organize the loot. My evidence officer, Sandra Mize, and her assistants, Deputies Harris Kuhn and Rick Miller, toiled for approximately two weeks categorizing and displaying the contents of six, 19-foot U-Haul trucks brimfull of stolen goods. Mize's team meticulously laid-out the property on 3-tier shelves in the two 60-foot trailers we had procured. And, that didn't count the dozen high-end bicycles and pile of automotive *trick* accessories, which they stored in our bike compound.

As indicated in the auction flyer, there were still quite a few interesting items destined to go on the block. One of the most celebrated treasures was an 18 carat gold *Patek Philippe* pocket watch, which sported an opening bid of $4,000. However, at the 11th Hour—during Friday's "show and tell"—the timepiece's rightful owner claimed it. But wait, there's more: A 17th century pirate piece of eight, a 1794 US silver dollar and 500 loose stones including diamonds, emeralds, sapphires, rubies, jade, tons of gold jewelry, rings, necklaces and the like.

It took less than six hours for Doug Neale's crusty auctioneer to dispose of O'Connor's spoils. The audience was like a bunch of kids in a candy store. Neale later commented: "There's a mystique about the stuff because O'Connor stole it." An Indian basket went for $400, and an unemployed guy bought three huge boxes of tennis rackets for $300. When asked by a reporter why he was so jubilant about his purchase, the obviously satisfied customer replied: "I'll sell them at the flea market and I think I can get my money back!" That is precisely what Bob said when I asked him how come he stole a bizillion rackets and tennis shoes—his return was "pure gravy."

Then, there was that box of 40 pornographic tapes that sold for $450 after a ferocious bidding war between a local fire station and a Bay Area cocktail lounge.

About Those Tapes...

Early on in our investigation, we discovered that Bob loved to record his escapades, both on audio as well as videotape. He also reveled in taking photos of his booty, most likely using some of the high dollar cameras he'd ripped off. In a series of evidentiary pictures, we discovered Robert featured his entire family sorting jewelry on a large table, set up on his back porch!

Prior to the preliminary examination, D.A. Tom Hanford learned about Bob's propensity to record data about his crimes, after we played several audiotapes and showed him the incriminating photos. When he heard about the supposed porn tapes, Mr. Hanford asked me if anyone had viewed them for possible evidentiary value. "No way, Tom," I asserted. "People have been fired for stuff like that!"

Once court was back in session, D.A. Hanford addressed the judge:

"Your Honor, it has been brought to my attention that defendant O'Connor often recorded his misdeeds on audio and videotapes. Here is a transcript of one such recording which I want submitted into evidence." The D.A. then handed the tape transcript to the defense counselors. The lawyers briefly scanned the transcript and told the judge, "No objection, your Honor."

Mr. Hanford rose again and said, "Your Honor, there is another matter on this topic, namely 40 videotapes, believed to be of a pornographic nature that should be viewed to see if any culpable evidence might exist. I propose that my lead investigator perform this task, without future recrimination."

The presiding jurist, then bellowed, "Captain Niemeyer, you are hereby ordered by this Court to review the tapes in question and report back to me when we reconvene in one week."

"Yes, your Honor," I replied, amidst muffled snickers and laughs from the audience.

After untold hours of "porn-o-rama," I reported back to the court, as so ordered. I passed the bar, approached the bench and declared:

"Judge Nelson, I reviewed all 40 tapes as ordered and although *they contained a mountain of "hard evidence",* nothing pertained to the People's case against Mr. O'Connor or his co-defendants!" Well, that's what I wanted to say, but thought better of it, as being way too glib before the Court could land one in the bucket...

Epilogue

I'm glad this long chapter is "almost" over—not only in this book but in my life! While I have the fondest memories of the biggest pinch in my career, it was also one of the largest, most newsworthy theft cases in Santa Clara County's history at the time. Although I managed the event which brought an end to O'Connor's crime spree, I could never have done it without the support of our department's personnel and administration. It is without reservation that I give special kudos and thanks to Ms. Sandra Bennett Mize, whose life was totally consumed by this monumental task. Who would have *thunk* that a small campus police department could have pulled this off? Many in our region thought of our fledgling department as "Security," even though we were really *sworn Sheriff's Deputies...* And, with less than 10 years under our belts as a fully trained, effective law enforcement agency, at that! But, we had some very smart, talented and determined people on board in those days, so it never, ever occurred to me that we couldn't do it.

Once all the adulation—back slapping and high-fives—was over, everyone pitched in and were focused on the task ahead. During the adjudication phase, our District Attorney's Office, with special attention to DDA, Tom Hanford, dug into this very complicated case like a badger in his burrow! No stone was left unturned and no detail was overlooked. This matter moved-along like an Olympic skater on fresh ice! Of course, all of our success was facilitated by an aggressive judiciary, who, as I like to say: "Took no prisoners!"

There was another important component of the People vs. O'Connor et al. case: Emotion! We all felt the gut-wrenching agony that hundreds of O'Connor's victims endured, once they realized their castle's walls had been breached. Prior to sentencing, there was a queue of teary-eyed folks, who made heartfelt speeches to Judge Robert Foley explaining how O'Connor's crimes affected their lives. Aside from losing treasured heirlooms, mementos—some passed down from deceased ancestors—and other cherished personal items, we all realized how traumatized these people were—as if they had been raped! The testimony of one faculty member describing how frightened his daughter was to be in their home alone after one of Robert's "cat-like" forays was riveting and put an exclamation point on this escapade. Not many in the court's gallery felt one iota of sympathy for Mr. O'Connor and company.

As strange as it may seem, this ol' grizzled cop experienced some empathy for Robert—not for him personally, but for the damage he'd done to his family. His three children, from the union with Nancy Lee, were uprooted and devastated! His current wife, Maureen, bore him another son while she was in custody; she would be incarcerated for three years and earn a badge of dishonor as a convicted felon—a black mark that would haunt Maureen for the rest of her life and prevent her from achieving career goals. Nancy Burt and Mary O'Connor got their just desserts, so I lost no sleep there. However, I really felt sorry for Mr. and Mrs. O'Connor, Bob's parents: You could just read the disappointment and remorse in their eyes throughout the ordeal.

Then, there was the man himself, RLO: Although we both loathed each other at the outset, our mutual contentiousness seemed to wane and almost thawed when I agreed to return seized property to his family that was not *hot*. After he was sent to state prison, I received a letter from Robert regarding the personal property issue. During this procedure, I tried to remain fair but firm. Above all, I employed a family maxim I learned from my dad, Irv: "Son," he often said, "if you treat people fairly and with respect, no matter what they've done, you'll feel good about yourself and your efforts will reap dividends!"—or something to that effect. *Well, Dad,* I thought, *from the day I put on the star and took the oath as a law enforcement officer, I employed your advice, and, as always, you were one hundred percent right!*

So, here is an excerpt, from Bob O'Connor's letter:

". . . Perhaps you have independently decided to return those items, as a matter of honor, and with confidence in what I feel must be your innate sense of the truth when presented with it. I hope so.

I am happy that all this is over, and I am sure that you are, too. As I said, I feel that the way in which some of the property was settled (the 'hit' method) was not a product of sanity, but I do feel that you certainly handled the situation and your part in it, with the utmost in fairness. Though my respect may not be of value to you, I feel compelled to say that you earned a large measure of it under the most trying of circumstances. Likewise, Ms. Mize."

Sincerely,

Bob O'Connor

Well, you could have knocked me over with a left jab. I was stunned, but glad this infamous burglar realized that I wouldn't kick him while he was down. Perhaps his 19 and a half year sentence (out in 8 years, for good behavior), would cause him to see the errors of his ways. Robert commented that he received more time than Angela Arvidson's killer, Donald Amos, who got 19 years (Chapter 31). In theory, Bob was right: Save for accidentally killing a man while he was DUI, and for his exploits on the rugby field, I never found any evidence that Robert was a violent man. However, he was a career criminal with a long history of felony convictions for burglary, theft and prison escapes, so the judge meted out justice accordingly. Did Robert Lee O'Connor see the errors of his ways? I believe the jury is still out on that one...

The Open-Space Burglar (circa early 1990s)?

Suddenly, my phone was ringing off the hook about this guy again, so rather than regurgitate my spiel a hundred times, I hosted a seminar at Stanford's Faculty Club. It was jam-packed with detectives from all over the Bay Area who were investigating a new series of residential burglaries. However, after hearing about this crime spree, I wasn't totally convinced that O'Connor was responsible: I learned that a task force had Robert and his new wife, Nancy Burt O'Connor, under surveillance because they felt he could be responsible for dozens of burglaries in the Bay Area. Police had busted the pair for possessing an old VCR and a Red Tail hawk's claw. Bob said, "He bought the VCR at a flea market and found the talon in a field." This was very possible on both counts, as Robert loved to shop and trade at flea markets. And, as you may recall, Bob was a huge bird lover and probably didn't know that it's unlawful to possess a talon or any other part of a federally protected species—I didn't.

As far as I know, none of the loot taken in the area wide burglaries was ever recovered in Bob's possession. I immediately discounted that O'Connor committed the Los Altos Hills jobs, for reasons previously written. Authorities dubbed the perp, "The Open Space Burglar," exactly what Bob avoided like the plague.

However, there *was* a link between Marin and San Joaquin counties, because Robert would periodically visit the child he had with Maureen: Bob lived in the San Joaquin valley while his "ex," resided in marvelous Marin, so he could have done some of those...

Another aspect of the "Open Space" guy which gave me pause was the fact that Bob never threw objects through glass in order to gain entry to a residence. Many of the crimes in Marin County began with the burglar(s) throwing large objects through sliding patio doors. O'Connor was as quiet as a cat and would never alert the neighborhood with glass breakage!

I don't recall how the open space investigation turned out, and presume Bob is enjoying his senior years as free as the homing pigeons he had a passion for—But, I could be wrong...

I am now, indeed, done with this saga, and only hope that if Mr. O'Connor ever reads my book, he doesn't attempt to hunt-me-down and burn-me-out like he once promised.

CHAPTER THIRTY ONE

Angela

A Fall?

It was another gorgeous autumn day at the Farm—October 22, 1982, approximately 2:50 PM. I was leaving the station, headed for a meeting, when the radio crackled:

"Any Stanford unit! A 10-45 injury fall at 1850 Allardice Way; Any unit to respond, Code 3?" One of our patrol units, Q-5, jumped on it. I also told Radio that I was responding. The given address was in the Faculty Ghetto—and on the street where A-1, the Chief, lived. *Jeez,* I thought, *I hope it's not HIS residence.* Within a couple of minutes, Q-5 went 10-97. Almost immediately, a shrill oscillating voice—like an off-key violin chord—shrieked over the airwaves:

"Qqqqq Fiiiivvve. Ca-ca-Code 3 ammmbulance! Female victim severely injured—blood everywhere!" I kicked that old Merc into giddy-up and weaved my way thru the minions of students on bikes, all of whom were busting stops signs with impunity. Me, too! Then the transmission that cops hate to hear:

"A-3, Q-5. This could be a 187!"

"10-4," I stoically answered. *Shit! How come murders are never dispatched as 187s? -- Always some other random designation: Man down; sick person; drunk; OD; a fall; possible suicide,* I quizzed?

As I roared down Allardice and passed A-1's home, I drew a sigh of relief: Q-5's unit was up ahead, still lit up like a Christmas tree. I skidded to a halt and saw FC-3, Sgt. Rick Enberg, across the roadway, literally vaulting from his unit. As I jumped out of my car, I asked if he had copied the 187; he grimly nodded and took off on a dead run toward this beautiful, upscale residence. As I ambled along behind, I hollered for him to check the house for suspects—he already knew that, but being the consummate crime scene micro-manager I was, I wanted to make damn sure. Pistol in hand, I waited outside, keeping an eye on the rear until Rick and Q-5 reappeared and signaled the all clear.

As I entered the foyer, I glanced to the left and eye-balled a very large pool of very dark, very fresh blood at the foot of the stairway. "What in the hell happened?" I barked.

"Captain, she's in there," Q-5 nervously replied, as he pointed to the living room, while quickly walking that way. I followed him and was aghast when I saw a young woman, lying face-up on the coach, with a huge gaping incise wound to her throat. In fact, the low-life who did this nearly decapitated the poor young woman. She was still warm to the touch. After regaining my composure, I noted that the killer apparently attacked the victim at the foot of the stairs, carried her into the living room, placed her on the coach and covered her with a comforter. The murderer apparently placed a pillow under the dead girl's head. *Who would commit such a horrific act and then apparently show some compassion,* I asked myself? But, was it compassion?

Palo Alto Paramedics arrived, took one look at our unfortunate victim and pronounced her dead at the scene. It was now time for me to go to work. I ordered the scene secured and instructed the Sergeant and Deputy to retrace their steps and to make careful notes: Exactly what they did on arrival, where they walked, what they touched, and the approximate time of their actions. Electing not to use the house phone for fear of evidence contamination, I was forced to use my hand radio—as much as I hated to—as I knew that a million media folks would be tuned in to our channel and would soon descend upon us like a Midwest swarm of locusts!

Upon reflection, it would have been nice to have a cell phone in those days, for any detective worth his salt would never put-out proprietary information over the airwaves so as not to leak crucial information to the press. We were so land-line oriented then that all deputies were expected to carry enough change in their pockets to make a pay phone call, if necessary.

I got on the air and told all personnel to switch to Frequency 2 so as to not tie-up the primary channel. I ordered all Deputized and Community Officers to our location. Over the years, our personnel became masters at crime scene and special event control. It was like a well choreographed maneuver: In just a matter of minutes, men and material streamed-in. The Patrol Sergeant set the plan in motion like a director of a symphony orchestra. All of the players knew their parts and performed them magnificently. Before I knew it, traffic controllers were in place, metal barricades were set-up to ward off gawkers and the media, and a large area around the house was cordoned-off with that yellow *Sheriff's Crime Scene* tape, that nobody—especially students and reporters—ever paid attention to. A scribe was also assigned to record everyone who was at the scene, especially those who had entered the inner perimeter: I wanted name, rank, horsepower, and time in and out. Because the homicide was committed with what we believed was a knife, we alerted all personnel to BOL for a knife, razor or any instrument that could inflict death by slashing.

In the meantime, I located the reporting party, a 16 year old boy, who found the victim. His name was Jason Williams (a pseudonym), a freshman at Gunn High School in nearby Palo Alto. He lived in the home with his parents; his father was a professor at the medical school. Jason revealed that the victim was, "Angela," a Stanford student who was their part-time housekeeper. The kid, who was ashen faced and shaking like a leaf in a gale wind, said that when he entered the home he immediately saw the large pool of blood at the foot of the stairs. Jason called-out for his Mom and Dad, but got no reply. Jason saw the vacuum cleaner in the kitchen and realized it was the day their housekeeper came. He called out for her, too, but, again got no response. Curiously, the boy glanced around and saw what appeared to be more blood on a couch pillow in the living room. Jason had an eerie feeling; he was also very frightened and wanted to bolt from the house, but he slowly advanced toward the bloody pillow. When he lifted it, Jason's eyes were drawn to a woman's hand, protruding from the under the covers; he quickly realized that it was Angela, whose throat had been severely slashed. The traumatized youth sprinted from his home and sought refuge at a neighbor's place. Confused as to what had really happened, the neighbor called 9-1-1 and reported that there was a serious injury—possibly from falling down the stairs. No one could have possibly thought that this could be a homicide—not at Stanford University—that peaceful institution of higher learning. . . So, the call went out as given: "10-45, an injury fall."

Somewhere in my "self-initiated" training, I read in an old homicide investigation book (written in the late 1930's) that the mind is like a moving picture camera as it captures sights, sounds, odors, and stores these facts deep in the brain. Often, horrific images are locked away forever, especially when the person receiving that data is traumatized. But, some data can be successfully retrieved, the sooner the better, if the investigator walks the witness through the crime scene from beginning to end. Blocked information can also come to light if the detective walks the witness backwards, from the end to the beginning, as well. Taking this old page of detective wizardry from my memory, I asked Jason to accompany me to the street and to relive every step of the way, from the time he entered the family's property: I reminded him to visualize every sound, every odor, and every object on the ground and above. We started out at the mailbox where he said he had picked-up the mail. About every 4 or 5 steps, I had Jason stop and I asked him to look up, down, all around. I also told the shaken youth to take deep breaths, in an effort to test his olfactory recall. In addition, I inquired if he had heard anything when he first entered the property. After about

10 paces into the driveway, the young man stopped dead in his tracks and said:

"Wait a minute. There was a piece of paper."

"Where," I implored?

"Right here. Right here!" as he pointed to the asphalt driveway.

"What happened to it?" I pushed.

"I put it in my Mom's car. I think it's hers; she has a home sales business," he said as he took a couple of steps forward and opened up the vehicle's door.

As his hand went toward a yellow piece of paper on the seat, I swiftly glommed onto his arm with a vice-lock grip and warned him not to touch it. I took out my handkerchief—this was before CSI so we didn't carry latex gloves in those days—and carefully retrieved the find by one of the corners. It was an invoice for some plastic trash bags, which were apparently delivered to 1850 Allardice Way, Stanford, CA 94305. According to the header, the company was based in Palo Alto, just a few miles away.

"Is this your Mom's?" I asked.

"No, sir, it's something different," Jason asserted.

"Ok, son, now, where *exactly* did you find this?" He pointed to the driveway a few feet from the entrance, next to the border of a small hedge.

"Jason, have you ever seen this invoice before, like when you went to school this morning?" I queried. The lad shook his head in the negative. *Hmmm*, I mused, *this could be a clue. A MAJOR clue! Especially when you consider who delivers this kind of stuff— solicits magazine subscriptions and other services—my experience leads me to the impression that most door-to-door people are unemployed losers, many of whom have long rap sheets, and whose elevators don't go all the way to the top floor...* As I placed the suspicious invoice where the kid indicated he had spotted it, my former lead investigator, now a Patrol Sergeant, Philip Love, aka, Philippe Crueseau, walked up the driveway.

"Perfect," I asserted. "Philippe, you are now my crime scene evidence guru. Guard this piece of paper with your life. And, detail some CSOs to take down info on every damn car on this street—and, on the adjoining blocks, too: Have them record license numbers, makes, models and colors. Also, tell them to check the grill area to see if it's hot, warm or cold. Oh, and, if there are any spare deputies, have them do a door to door canvass of every house around here—I want names, ranks and HP—phone numbers, too. We can leave no stone unturned on this one. Christ, a 187 right in the Chief's neighborhood. Damn!"

"Oui, oui, Mon Capitan, Sargent Philippe Crueseau, at yur serveese," he chided as he clicked his heels and snapped a crisp salute.

"Quick, call a comedian," I shot back. "Just GOI, good Sergeant," I snapped: GOI, as I previously mentioned, was a stern order that I learned from the Chief—and when he said "Get On It," you'd better well get to steppin.' I chuckled to myself as Philippe *got to steppin'* and I thought, *he's a good man with great organizational skills, so I had nothing to worry about.* Approximately five minutes later, Sgt. Crueseau had a small phalanx of troops down on their hands and knees, ciphering the grass on the front lawn—seeking *clue-sos*, no doubt.

The Investigation

The crime scene was secure. The Chief was on board and thoroughly briefed. He had the daunting task of dealing with the University officials as well as Angela's parents and other family members. We had to cope with several incursions by the press—

especially by an obnoxious, pushy reporter from a nearby weekly fish-wrapper. This clown skirted around the barricade and attempted to use the surrounding foliage to conceal his stealthy move, but one of our hawk-eyed, CSOs, Clifton Clark, caught him red-handed and sicced the Sergeant on him. We could always depend on Cliff to be ever vigilant and on the ball; it was pretty hard to put one over on a guy who grew up on the mean streets of Kingston, Jamaica, "Mon."

About this time, Mrs. Williams had returned from her shopping trip. She freaked-out when she saw dozens of cops and patrol cars around her barricaded home. She was given a synopsis of what had happened and was escorted to the neighbor's home, where Jason was waiting. My troops ascertained that the victim was Angela Dee Arvidson, a 20 year old human biology honor student from Portland, Oregon. Mrs. Williams said that Angela had just been hired a few weeks ago to perform household cleaning a couple of days a week. We further learned that the victim had a relative also attending Stanford. This information was passed onto the University officials so that Ms. Arvidson's family could be notified. At approximately, 3:30PM, members of the Sheriff's Homicide and Evidence team began arriving.

This was a new group of detectives, as my contemporaries (John Johnson, Ken Kahn, Dave Pascual and Tom Beck) had moved onto other assignments within the department. Although I knew all of these folks—having been involved with their hiring and initial training when I was at the S/O—I had never worked a case with them before and would soon learn that they certainly had their own focus, M.O., and clearly marched to the beat of their own drummer. . . I briefed the lead detective about what we had done thus far, and especially brought his attention to the invoice Jason and I located. I opined that I thought the killer(s) might have inadvertently dropped this invoice while fleeing the scene. Detective Sergeant Michael McCreedy (pseudonym) ordered the invoice to be photographed where it lay, bagged, tagged and transferred to his custody. This was now the Sheriff's Office investigation, but I told the detective that our personnel would assist their team in any way they deemed necessary. I also advised the Sgt. that our officers were obtaining vehicle ID information, as well as conducting door-to-door inquiries, as we spoke. The S/O crew invaded the premises and conducted a very thorough crime scene search for fingerprints, blood, and other trace evidence. They also did comprehensive interviews with the Williams family, in an effort to identify a possible motive and suspect.

Angela's ravaged body was taken to San Jose by the Coroner for an autopsy. I later learned that the poor young woman had been stabbed several times in the upper torso, as well as in the neck, before the maniac performed a *coup de grace* by slashing her throat. She never had a chance! Clearly, this was one of the most brutal murders I had ever seen, up to that point in my 18 years of service in Santa Clara County. So far, none of the S/O investigators had a clue as to who the perpetrator was, and neither did I. However, I thought, *the invoice that Jason called my attention to, kept gnawing at my brain: Call it tunnel vision but I was convinced the transaction receipt was the key that might unlock the door to this mystery.* I voiced my theory to the lead investigator, but perhaps he was on *overload* with processing the scene and interviewing friends and associates for possible leads to a motive and killer; therefore, I believe he put this piece of evidence on back-burner. I even offered to have our investigators contact the trash bag distributor, if for nothing else, to eliminate this clue from further suspicion. But, alas, my overture fell on deaf ears . . .

Days elapsed without fruitful developments. Our troopers obtained information on approximately 70-80 vehicles in the vicinity and this information was immediately given to the S/O detectives for DMV checks. Although a long-shot, you never know if a panicked suspect might have left the scene on foot, or in another car, leaving a stolen one behind. Our canvass of the neighborhood met with similar results: Nada, Zip, Zero. And, this was a Neighborhood Watch zone. But, like I always told my charges: "People just don't see Dick!" Nonetheless, we always have to go through that drill, just in case—the old CYA maneuver, widely practiced in law enforcement!

Let There Be Light

On Sunday, I got a call from Q-5 informing me that the Sheriff's investigators had possibly IDed a potential suspect.

"Wait, don't tell me," I interrupted. "It was the guy who dropped that trash bag invoice on the driveway, right?"

"Bingo," the deputy replied! He then advised me he was sitting at the suspect's house, in North San Jose, waiting for the detectives to get a search warrant.

Well, I thought, the damn light finally came on; better late than never, but I seriously doubted the murderer would still be around. The cops might be slow, but not stupid—and neither was this killer, who had probably hit the road days before.

After an all-nighter, the detectives finally arrived at the suspect's residence, search warrant in hand. There was only one problem: The bastard was MIA. The Homicide Dicks found the bloody clothes that the killer wore during the attack, a couple of guns, one of which was stolen, drug paraphernalia—but, no knife. His name was Donald John Amos, 29, a parolee with a very violent rap sheet. Neighbors told the detectives that Amos was married and had three children. A neighbor also saw Amos dash into his house Thursday afternoon. He soon reappeared in a different change of clothing and hurriedly left in his light blue Mercury Monarch. Later that evening, the same neighbor observed the family loading suitcases and other belongings into their car. When the neighbor asked Amos what was up, the murderer replied that they were going on a short vacation. And, indeed they were. . .

After learning of this, I had Palo Alto Communications *run* this creep: Amos' criminal history read like a Russian novel! He had arrests, as a juvenile, for violent acts against women and had also been busted on some minor drug offenses. In following-up with my sources in the Santa Cruz S/O, I learned that as a 16 year old, Amos and some buddies picked-up a couple of teenage girls in Santa Cruz, bought some booze and headed for the hills to party. Once in a secluded spot, they plied their quarry with alcohol and when they thought the girls were "loose enough," Amos announced that it was "show-time!" When the girls declined, that punk calmly walked over to his car and brought out a .22 rifle, which he fired repeatedly at his terrified victims' feet—just like the *guys in black* did in the old cowboy movies. After this perverse form of intimidation, the frightened girls finally submitted to being gang raped.

The records indicated that Amos had lived in Sunnyvale most of his adolescent life. A check with Sunnyvale's DPS revealed Donald and his brother had a very checkered past and were continually in hot water with that city's cops. In discussing the Santa Cruz incident with the Sunnyvale detective (who knew these jerks quite well), he stated that Donald nearly beat another girl to death with a tire iron: While driving around in Southern California, Amos picked up a female hitchhiker, and shortly thereafter, pulled-off to yet *another secluded spot,* where he attempted to sexually assault the woman. Once rebuffed, this loser suddenly produced a tire iron and savagely beat the woman about the head and neck, causing near fatal injuries. How she survived such a vicious attack is beyond medical reasoning. This time, however, after receiving his "sheepskin" from *Juvie,* he was matriculated by the State of California to a more secure environment—CYA—the California Youth Authority, where he was incarcerated for several years.

Now, he was on the loose again after committing the ultimate crime—the savage murder of a totally unsuspecting victim—a brilliant and musically gifted young woman who was simply trying to make a few bucks while going to school. *This could have been my daughter,* I recalled thinking when I looked at her lifeless body on the couch! Clearly, Angela was in the wrong place at the wrong time. But, how could she, or anyone else, for that matter, have known that the stranger at the door was a vicious animal with a very short fuse and bent on sexual assault—although there was no evidence he was successful. And, how would this 20 year old student have predicted that this menacing hulk would become so wildly assaultive if provoked in any way!

My theory on this horrific crime is, as follows: When Angela opened the door, Amos had an uncontrollable sexual urge to violate this shapely and attractive young lady. She had taken some women's self defense classes, so I believe that when the beast made a move on her, she might have tried some defensive kicks and strikes. These *katas* (moves) look good and seem to work well in the gym with an actor or dummy, but Amos was no dummy! He was big, over 6' tall and weighed more than 200 pounds. This size differential, coupled with his nasty temperament toward women, made him a formidable adversary, especially when armed with a knife. I believe he stabbed her several times in the torso while she retreated toward the stairway. Angela either turned to run upstairs, or Amos spun her around and then effectuated a classic commando execution—a near head severing incise wound to her neck which terminated her instantly. Perhaps, feeling some remorse, he then carried her to the living room couch, covered her up with a blanket and covered her face with a pillow. During his hasty escape, he inadvertently dropped the trash bag invoice in the driveway. Although the crime scene technicians located Amos' bloody fingerprints in the house, this murder could have gone unsolved for quite some time: Fingerprint automation had not yet come on-line, so in order to match a questioned fingerprint found at a crime scene, you needed a known sample e.g., the suspect's fingerprint impressions. Once the automated fingerprint system became functional, an investigator simply submitted questioned samples to a qualified examiner, and if readable, *and* if a subject had ever been fingerprinted, not only in California, but anywhere in the United States, the identity of the perp would be immediately known. In addition, CCI's (California Criminal Identification Bureau) highly skilled experts had the ability to enhance marginal prints, and quite often, made positive matches.

A classic example of this wonderful crime solving technology was demonstrated in a recent murder conviction, a crime that had actually been committed during the 1970s. For over 25 years, detectives had tried to solve a brutal robbery, rape and killing of an elderly woman in San Diego. Once the automated fingerprint system became operational, detectives periodically entered latent print specimens that had been located at the crime scene—to no avail. However, in 2005, the investigators hit pay dirt when they got a positive match on the killer. He was a man in his early 50s, who had no previous criminal history, save for a fairly recent shoplifting offense—no fingerprints, no match. Upon arrest, the detectives learned that their man had been in the Navy and was stationed in San Diego during the period when the crime had been perpetrated. He quickly shipped out to parts unknown. When his hitch was completed, he received an honorable discharge, and, thereafter, apparently led an honest, crime-free life—until he was arrested for a minor violation and was fingerprinted—Oops!

But not for the trash bag invoice dropped by Amos, this killer's identity would have been a mystery for a lot longer than it was.

On the Lam

Despite a tremendous amount of media coverage and nationwide publicity, Donald Amos and his family simply vanished from the face of the earth. Even if John Walsh's "America's Most Wanted" show was on TV in those days, I doubt very seriously that law enforcement could have found this murdering SOB. These people apparently went deep underground—much like the Centennial Olympic Park Atlanta, GA bomber (Eric Rudolph) who eluded the authorities for seven years in the Appalachian Mountains. Despite hundreds of FBI, Sheriffs and local police, who utilized some of the best southern bred hound dogs in the business, they were unable to find their killer, until a small town rookie cop caught him dumpster-diving in the middle of the night. Even with all of our modern technology, such as helicopters, heat sensors, night vision equipment—desperate fugitives can be awfully hard to find.

And, so it was with Amos, until he chose to give up the ghost: On the morning of November 14, nearly three weeks after the homicide, the fugitive suddenly appeared at the Santa Clara County jail and turned himself in. The wheels of justice were about to turn.

The Trial

Unlike most criminal cases, this one seemed to move forward rather quickly, for in short order, I received a call from a senior prosecutor, George Kennedy. Although I had never met or worked with Mr. Kennedy, word on the street was that he was one of the best in the District Attorney's Office. A man of very few words, he said that he wanted me to testify about my role in coordinating the crime scene and facilitating the find of the crucial piece of evidence, the trash bag invoice, which ultimately pointed suspicion to the defendant, Donald John Amos.

When I appeared in Superior Court, I met Mr. Kennedy for the first time. He simply allowed me to give testimony to all of the facts I had detailed in my report. Kennedy's calm and succinct demeanor when I was on direct examination was indeed impressive: He didn't beat around the bush and ask me redundant questions. He knew exactly where he was headed and never deviated from his course. Having testified in court many times during my career, I often would cringe at some of the methods employed by attorneys. Early on in my career, I used to go to court early and sometimes stay after my testimony so that I could learn from other's mistakes—cops as well as lawyers. During my time on the stand, I quickly realized that Mr. George Kennedy was a consummate pro!

Once my spiel was over with, I departed the courthouse, but kept tabs on how the case was going. Despite overwhelming physical evidence, Amos tried to play dumb and not take responsibility for his actions: He acknowledged being in the Stanford area, but had a hazy recollection of what had actually happened because he had smoked some marijuana and consumed alcohol. Amos admitted to being in the professor's home and seeing some blood on the floor; he maintained that when he got there to deliver the trash bags, the door was ajar; he called out, but there was no answer and when he entered the foyer, he saw Angela's bloody body. Amos disingenuously said that he couldn't possibly have done it. . . He lied!

The Public Defender, Mr. Randy Schneider, a formidable opponent with whom I had tangled several times in the past, mounted a vigorous defense on behalf of his loser client. Schneider made a motion to the Court to reduce the Murder 1 charge to second degree. The Honorable Judge Kennedy (no relation to the DA) ruled in favor of that motion. I can't speak for most of the officers who were intimately involved in the murder of Ms. Arvidson, but I would have liked to have seen that creep sitting in the little green room at San Quentin. I wondered if the look on his face, while those cyanide pellets were slowly lowered into the vat of H_2SO_4, would have been similar to Angela's facial reaction of being mutilated by that monster!

As the law existed in those days, it would have been very difficult to obtain a first-degree murder conviction, given the apparent lack of pre-meditation. As I previously opined, I believe that this slaying was a spontaneous crime of opportunity. Thus, Donald Amos was convicted of murder in the second degree, as well as a felon in possession of a concealable firearm and a stolen weapon. He was sentenced to a term from 8 years to life and was matriculated, this time by DOC (Department of Corrections), to DVI, Deuel Vocational Institute, in Tracy, CA—where he still remains to this day, thanks to the efforts of District Attorney George Kennedy and his staff in fighting repeated parole attempts.

Epilogue

But not for this terrible crime, I may not have been able to develop a relationship with, in my opinion, the best DA that Santa Clara County has ever had! Some years after the trial, George called me and asked if I could write something about my personal feelings when I went into that home on Allardice and became a first-hand witness to the brutality of that crime. Although now the boss, Mr. Kennedy felt so compassionate about this homicide that he personally appeared before the parole board in opposition to the murderer's release.

Using every bit of literary skill that I could muster, I composed an extremely graphic description—factual and without embellishment—of what I saw and felt. It apparently struck a nerve with the parole board when read to them by George. Once geared-up, Mr. Kennedy can deliver very powerful oratory and he convinced the parole board, on two occasions, to keep Amos behind bars! I recently learned that a successor to the DA's prosecution team foiled yet another effort by Amos' camp to spring him. Clearly, the people of the State of California are considerably safer with Donald John Amos in the slam!

CHAPTER THIRTY TWO

Tales from the Cuckoo's Nest

Ol' Charley (OC)

It didn't take me long to figure out that college campuses, in general, are huge 51-50 (mentally imbalanced) magnets, with our esteemed institution leading the pack. I might have previously mentioned that during the Arlis Perry murder investigation, I discovered there were more nuts hanging around the Quad than one would find in the largest Harry and David Christmas gift basket! Our investigative team must have reviewed hundreds of FI cards and field photos of some of the weirdest cats on the planet.

One of my favorite weirdoes was Ol' Charley, who over the years developed a bizarre relationship with yours truly. We looked at Charley for the Mem Chu homicide but quickly ruled him out. In another case in which a female was attacked near the Church, we looked really hard at Charley: The woman fought off her assailant and gave us a vague description of a slightly built, somewhat disheveled male who, one of the first responders thought, matched Charles. The would-be mugger left a beautiful imprint of a tennis shoe in the soft soil, of which our I.D. technician made an excellent plaster of Paris impression. It didn't take long for the troops to round OC up and transport him to the station for an up-close-and-personal chat with me. Charley was never hard to find: If he wasn't hanging around TMU bumming money for coffee or eyeballing the ladies, then he was temporarily MIA, but could usually be found the following day.

Charles' Mom was an alumnus of the late 1930s; I believe that our person of interest (POI—not to be confused with point of impact) was also a Stanford graduate of the late '60s. He just couldn't bear to leave his comfort zone once he received his sheepskin...

After talking with OC for about 15 minutes, I felt confident that he was *not* our man. When I compared his tennis shoes to the impression lifted at the crime scene, I was certain. However, a short time later, Charley was in our custody again—this time after bashing another nut job over the head with a tennis racquet. Over the next ten years, I periodically reviewed reports involving OC for a variety of misdeeds. The most serious involved stalking an attractive female, who happened to be an acquaintance of my daughter. The victim became very afraid of Charles after she innocently befriended him at Tresidder Union. A torrent of cards, letters and flowers in which Charley professed his affection for her then followed. When we learned OC was following this unfortunate student all over campus, the hackles rose on the back of my neck. *Did we miss the boat on this guy for the attacks and murders of young women in the '70s,* I quizzed myself. Once again, the hounds were unleashed and Ol' Charley was brought in; you guessed right—he was lurking around TMU.

My tactic was to read this guy the riot act, so to speak, and to threaten him with incarceration so deep that the jailors would have to pump O2 and H2O to him. My T/O, JJ, once told me: "Trying to reason with drunks and crazies was like talking to a stone wall!" Generally, JJ was right. But, when dealing with this grade of character, who wasn't totally *schizo* or violent, intimidation often worked. Like the law dogs of the old West used to say: "Bouy get outta ma town before sundown or I'll string ya up!" By God, it worked: And, I was only toting a paltry .380 instead of a .45 Peacemaker—Ol' Charley got on his horse and rode outta Dodge! *He left the Farm forever,* I hoped.

Several months had passed and no one had seen hide nor hair of OC. Then suddenly, penny postcards started arriving; they were all nearly identical and read:

Dear Captain Niemeyer,
When are you going to get crime on the Stanford Campus under control?

Sincerely,

Charles *****

It seemed that Ol' Charley had a new abode as all of the correspondence was sent from Yosemite National Park. *Uh-oh*, I thought, *now OC is at one of the most popular recreational places in the world, with thousands of visitors availing themselves of the stunning vistas. And, there must be a lot of unsuspecting young ladies running around who have absolutely no clue that OC's elevator doesn't go all the way to the top floor; more disturbing was that his affection toward his imagined lovers always went unrequited! I'd better give the U. S. Park Police (USPP)a heads-up.*

After giving a USPP investigator the low-down on our subject of mutual interest, I learned that OC had garnered a job as a *hasher* in the Ahwahnee Lodge's kitchen. This facility was primarily staffed by college age kids, many of whom were female. *Perfect*, I cringed. I was also informed that OC fancied himself as a world class rock climber: The investigator related that during one of the meals in the Lodge's huge dining halls, Charles climbed nearly two stories up the enormous rock fireplace. He clung near the rooftop like Spider-Man, for God's sakes, and refused to come down. It seemed to me Ol' Charley made a perfect *testicle* of himself. . . If I was in charge, I probably would have called in the fire department and had them charge a hose. . . Well, the police finally coaxed Charley down and gave him a warning. I suggested to the investigator they should have pointed OC toward *El Capitan,* bid him farewell and good luck!

Perhaps another year went by before I heard any more about OC. One morning, I received a frantic call from another USPP investigator who wanted to know everything I knew about my dear friend, Charles. When I asked what suddenly piqued their interest, the detective advised me that someone had killed a female hiker and they recalled my telephone warning about a year before. The investigator related that they had been reviewing OC's file and recalled that I had cautioned them about his appetite for beautiful young women. The victim was an attractive visitor from Sweden and was discovered brutally stabbed, just off a popular trail. Further, she said that two other Swedish women were also missing; they were last seen on a bus headed for Los Angeles. A guy resembling Charley's description was seen with the pair who had vanished. Finally, contrary to my unverified opinion that OC had never exhibited any overt violence toward women—save for the *tennis match* with the other F/W at TMU—the officer stated that he was cited for *rough dancing* at one of the nightclubs—*maybe he was trying to do the BUMP or some other crazy '70s dance,* I mused—being a "sandwich short of a picnic" doesn't necessarily make one a murderer; however, as far as I was concerned, the jury was still out on this dude.

Apparently, OC admitted to the USPP that he had been a prime suspect in the Arlis Perry murder (pure uncut BS), as well as a number of other sexually motivated incidents involving young Stanford women. Boy, those inflated admissions really got the USPP amped-up! Typical Charley: He was yanking their chains, big-time, and had a captive audience.

Like so many random, unwitnessed and clueless homicides, this one at Yosemite, sadly, went unsolved. I don't believe the two ladies who went missing were ever located—another unsolved crime. Ol' Charley was *persona non grata* at Yosemite National Park and faded into oblivion. Not! Like that dreaded horror movie, "Child's Play," starring a sadistic murderer named "Chucky"—OC was indeed back, this time with a vendetta against his Ol' buddy—me! Charles began with a litany of succinct letters which echoed his obsession over the illusion that I was incapable or unwilling to control crime on campus. After receiving a slew of idiotic messages,

I was obliged to respond in kind with one of my *Nasty Niemeyer Notes* (NNNs) in an effort to get this whacko off my tail. We verified that Charles was now residing in Sacramento. However, my usual success with bloviating diatribe obviously didn't work, as OC started calling our office staff and unmercifully harassing them. On one occasion, he even showed-up in the lobby and raised holy hell. When the hounds were called, he took-off like a scared jack rabbit!

At this point, my nefarious brain went to work—sometimes not a good thing for me—and I crafted a *doozy* of a letter, ostensibly written by a high-ranking CIA operative, but in reality. . . My clever computer gurus were able to obtain a very good facsimile of the Agency's logo and letterhead. I included a copy of my previous letter to Charles, as well. The thrust of the CIA epistle was that OC was to cease and desist with his harassment of the SUDPS in general, and Captain Niemeyer, in particular—immediately—or else! Nut cases hate when Big Brother conveys a stern warning to them, as they imagine covert surveillance, listening devices, phone taps, spy satellites and the like. As a result, these characters almost always cease and desist—end of story. My plan was to mail my work of *mass deception* to a U.S. Secret Service buddy of mine who worked at Washington D.C.'s headquarters. Agent 007 would then post the ominous letter to OC—for effect. But, at the last minute, I chickened out: All I needed on the eve of my retirement was to pick-up the Daily and read the headline:

Stanford Captain Charged with Fraudulent Intimidation!

Ol' Charley kept pushing his luck and continued his harangue over the phone. We recorded several of his tirades and after putting our very compelling case together, Det. Sergeant McMullen got our DA to issue an arrest warrant for my pal. The next day, John and I headed for Sacramento. Charles had recently rented an apartment close to CA State University at Sacramento—go figure. We made several attempts to roust him at his pad but he was MIA. John and I were truly disappointed as we wanted to bring him before our Palo Alto judge, who was familiar with the case, and wanted to get OC some much needed psychological intervention.

Before we headed back to the Farm, we stopped at the Sacramento County Sheriff's Department so I could meet with an associate who was in charge of the Warrants and Fugitive's detail. This Sergeant was a great guy: He gladly agreed to serve our warrant and would notify us when OC was in the *slam*! As we were pulling into our parking lot late that evening, PA Comm. advised that Sac S/O had Ol' Charley in their bucket and wanted to know when we would pick him up. My reply was: *"Manana!"*

And, so it was; Ol' Charley was later booked into North County Jail and was brought before the magistrate forthwith. I felt a great deal of remorse for OC's family, especially his lovely Mom, who carried a heavy burden with her misguided offspring. Charles' parents were named conservators and I never heard from Charley again. I can't say that I missed him, but I sincerely hope he received the help he needed.

Krazy Kevin (KK)

This individual was the *'60s Burn-out Poster Child!* The poison he inhaled, snorted and shot into his emaciated body reduced his brain matter to mincemeat! Kevin was the ultimate outdoorsman: He resided under the bridge at *Alameda de las Pulgas* and *San Francisquito* Creek. Save perhaps for washing his face in the creek once in a while, I don't believe he had a real bath in decades. Kevin's first booking photo looked like he had stuck a finger into a 220 volt socket: His eyes were as big as saucers and his scraggly hair stood on end, similar to Madeline Kahn's in the hysterical movie, "Young Frankenstein." Suffice it to say, Krazy Kevin was a classic dirt bag!

Residing within walking distance of TMU, Kevin was often seen loitering around, bugging students and trying to get a free lunch. Being naïve students, the kids were soft touches. But, their empathy created a huge problem for much of the community and, of course, the police, as the SUDPS was continually called to shoo away this pest. In one such encounter, one of our female deputies was forced to arrest this blight of humanity for disturbing the peace; when the officer put hands on the bum, he resisted arrest. Well, that wasn't a good idea as Krazy Kevin soon discovered he had a wild cat by the tail . . .

Deputy Kris

I knew this young lady when I was the Training Sergeant in the S/O: I was coaching candidates to pass our difficult physical agility test of the early '70s. Although slim and wiry, Kris was as tough as nails. However, like most females of that period, Kris' upper body strength was not on par with most physically fit men. The Achilles' Heel for women police candidates, as well as overweight males, was the dreaded pull-ups. At that time, there was a 5 pull-up minimum, so I attempted to get candidates past this hurdle. When Kris first began training for this event, she could barely eke out a single chin. Before long, she was doing 4, but couldn't quite get her chin over the bar for that final repetition.

Rumor has it that when Kris was engaged in her final attempt to beat this nemesis, the good sergeant threatened to *goose* her while she was struggling to gut-out that last chin. Now, I have absolutely no recollection of that *alleged* motivational *threat*, but she cleared the bar! Like most rumors, they are almost always proved to be false and just another *rumor*. . .

Kris and another young lady were actually the first known women on patrol in Northern California. Kris was, without a doubt, one of the best street officers in the department during that era. She was very observant—a self starter who followed-up on hunches and often uncovered crimes in progress or bagged wanted subjects. And, if there was a fight, she was the first one in and was no slouch! I once saw a *beef* break-out in the stands at a Stanford football game—oh really?—and her back-up, an SEP from another police agency, simply stood by while Kris dove into the pile and quashed the event until our deputies could assist. I later fired that gutless wonder!

Back on the Farm

Needless to say, Kevin wasn't much of a match for our gal: She whipped the punk into an arm lock and slapped her Peerless bracelets on him in one fluid motion. And, you know, I think he liked that; it was sort of like "love at first pinch"—from that point on, that F/W sought out Deputy Kris like a Blue Tick hound dog: Kevin would literally flag down passing patrol cars in an effort to find out if Deputy Kris was behind the wheel. In the past, he would holler obscenities and flip the bird at the cops. At one point, he pounded on the Annex door and found himself staring down the muzzle of a six inch Colt Python! The deputy, Tony Navarra, told KK to hit the road and never come back! However, the *Love Bug's* bite was infectious: The Krazy man once traveled to Santa Cruz after he discovered Kris joined that County's Sheriff's Department. I heard the jail deputies in Santa Cruz weren't amused and were somewhat harsh to KK's sudden appearance—those deputies were clearly not akin to the *Banana Slugs* of the UC Santa Cruz university campus . . .

Epilogue

Kris came back to the Farm after a spell and was promoted to sergeant. She was a great supervisor and an even better investigator. She later took a DA's investigator's position in Butte County and became the President of the CA Sexual Assault Association. She quickly rose in the DA's Office and became the Chief Investigator. She married a popular judge and is now happily retired.

Letter Writers

If you think the USPS delivers *you* a lot of junk mail, multiply that by twenty, and that would approximate what the Stanford President's Office received on a daily basis. The DPS became the ultimate repository of these unsolicited and certainly unwanted correspondence—most of it was penned by nut jobs, who delighted in nonsensical gibberish—some of it, so vile that even I would never reprint the contents of these epistles verbatim. . .

"Earl the Pearl"

As most of you know, Stanford University always attracts world renowned scholars, often with celebrity status, where they continue their advanced studies, write memoirs, and publish the results of their research and so forth. We once had a very high-profile professional woman (whose identity is Top Secret, but her pseudonym is Ms. Jones) who accomplished extraordinary feats in her career. Shortly after she arrived on campus, my detectives reconnoitered her office and provided her staff with information so she could work in relative peace without having a bunch of *celeb hounds* and *paparazzi* pestering her. One of the first suggestions was to remove Ms. Jones' nameplate from the office door; they also advised her administrative assistant to carefully screen all would-be visitors, and to call 911 immediately if *goofy* folks started seeking her out. We briefed the staff to BOL for suspicious packages and mail. Well, it didn't take long for the nutty letters to arrive. Especially troubling were the letters written by a guy I dubbed "Earl the Pearl." This character used his true name and address in Florida. His composition ability was probably at the 3rd grade level. He printed on lined note paper, usually with blue or red ink. Most peculiar was the fact that letters with tails (g, p, y, etc.) abruptly stopped at the line. One of my detectives that we called "The Father"—much to his dislike (Tim had briefly attended a Catholic seminary until he got the "calling" to cop hood), opined that Earl was using a ruler when he wrote. He further offered that the writer was possibly a stevedore, as the dock bosses taught many of the dock workers to write with rulers in order to keep their lines straight.

"So, Father," I asked. "How in the hell do you know that?" (Fr. forgive me.)

"'Cuz I worked on the docks in San Francisco when I was a kid," he explained.

But, it wasn't the style that I was concerned about; it was all about the content. This goof-ball would begin his epistles with praise and adulation for Ms. Jones. He would heap on the kudos for about one page, then quickly transition to some of the nastiest thoughts I had ever seen—in a professional capacity, that is. Without getting into the real *nitty gritty*, suffice to say that Earl's real interest in Ms. Jones was prurient in nature. Judging from his letters, Earl was clearly fixated on the oral aspects of sex. . . Letter after letter featured "The Pearl's" demented mantra. After about 10-12 of these smut grams, I decided to author a *Nasty Niemeyer Note* of my own. This was the grand-daddy of NNNs; this time from the "Commander of the Special Investigations Bureau." Fancy, ominous titles really got these *loons'* attention. The body of my message was that Ms. Jones did not want, nor did she appreciate, Mr. Earl's communication, and he needed to cease immediately or face serious consequences! But, the cc's must have gotten Ol' Earl's attention—Big Time! I cc'ed all the usual suspects: CIA, FBI, U.S. Postal Inspection, Florida State Police and so on. You can't argue with success, as we never heard from Earl the Pearl again. Good riddance, as I knew the Chief wouldn't fly me to Ft. Lauderdale for a one-on-one chat with that creep. . .

Robert L. Westham (A Pseudonym)

Speaking from a position of *some* expertise on this matter, I can assure you that Mr. Westham, aka "Bob", was the most intelligent, prolific, driven author of crazy letters on the planet! In early 1981, The President's Office received two or three of Bob's voluminous diatribes on a daily basis: In just over six weeks, I received ninety-two of Robert's works. He composed his worldwide theories on any subject known to man—possibly even God—on double sided lined paper, often ten to twelve pages each! He wrote beautifully—tiny, clearly printed fluid sentences, indicating this man was educated and quite versed on a great many subjects. There was only one problem—not even Rhodes Scholars could understand what most of this gibberish meant. On the other hand, I'm confident Robert L. knew exactly what was on his mind, however confused. After reading about twenty of these dissertations, I tried to pick-out some coherent thoughts I could comprehend and began entitling these passages. Bob was as nutty as a fruitcake, but he was extremely funny in spots. He was a fouled mouth old cuss and had many jaundiced views on women, blacks, gays, Jews, cops, governmental officials, and medical staff. You might describe Mr. Westham's personality as "an equal opportunity hater." It didn't take a "Rhodes" guy long to figure out that Ol' Bob had spent some time in a Cuckoo's Nest or two. . . Maybe three or four!

One of Bob's favorite harangues was kids; I got from his passages that he didn't hate *all* children, only ill-mannered, spoiled brats, such as the diminutive TV personality, "Arnold." This particular piece caught my eye, so here's what Bob had to say:

"Treat a child like an adult and he acts like one. This does not mean to make him like an ignorant [CS'er] like Arnold on TV, who couldn't survive in a grocery store. I can't stand children who know everything. There is nothing more hideous than the death of childish wonder, awe, and curiosity, in a brat who rules his parents. The only correction, initially, for any such child under puberty, in his or her purely muscular stage, is a sore ass. This shows the little creep he didn't know everything, and that life can strike anytime.

'You can't make me empty the garbage.'

'I can.'

'You can't.'

WHAP   WHAP   WHAP

'I'll empty the garbage.'

I figured you would. Then Arnold, you can scrub the flagstone terrace with a toothbrush. All you need, you nasty little freak, is to do some work. I normally don't hang children, but I'd really enjoy hanging you. You stink. You know less than a sparrow possessed of curiosity."

Bob then continued on with this rambling discourse about the inferiority of the black race, the structure of which made very little sense at all. But, what did make sense, in my mind, anyway, was this individual was in desperate need of some serious head shrinking! But, given the state of CA law at that time, there had to be something more ominous in content before law enforcement could seek mental health intervention. I felt it was only a matter of time before we could pursue this crazy man with a pen, so I kept on reading and re-reading some of the earlier diatribes which I had stored in an accordion folder after giving them a quick once over and thinking: *Yep, this guy's a nut case but I'm just too busy to deal with this nonsense now.* I soon found myself taking Bob's treatises home with me as there was never enough time at work to concentrate and cipher-out his inner thoughts. I knew that Bob was a hand grenade with the pin pulled; therefore, I sought a legal reason to begin a formal investigation of this loon.

Executions

After systematically perusing Bob's letter file, #31 hit me like a punch in the gut. The crazy bastard had actually written a detailed account of all the people in the world who he thought should be executed. Most were governmental, judicial, penal, religious and mental health officials. After a brief nonsensical introductory paragraph, Bob went right to the heart of the matter. Here's a verbatim account:

"As it can be arranged, the military will set up the executions. These will be conducted in Houston, at the Astrodome. Bruce* (see following page) knows what I want there. At the first session, the following will be executed.

Chief Justice

One Senator

One Congressman

One Cabinetmember (sic)

Hugh Hefner

Frank Sinatra

Sammy Davis Jr.

Chairman Federal Reserve Board

Three matrons from female prisons selected by their inmates

One Oklahoma psychiatrist

Oral Roberts and the Pope will be crucified. All executions will be broadcast over worldwide television.

I will be provided with military transportation with the following weapons:

.357 Smith & Wesson double action revolver, 6" barrel, adjustable sights, 100 rounds hollow points. This will be sighted to place the sights at the point of aim at 50 yards. Holster (Right hand) and ammo belt.

.308 Winchester Model 100 semi-automatic carbine with leather sling, Lyman receiver peepsight, (sic) with large aperture, 100 rounds 150 grain Remington bronzepoint (sic) ammunition. This will be sighted to place the slug 2" over the line of sight at 100 yards. It will be in a leather case, 100 rounds. Extra clip."

Do you get the picture? Oh, and there was a lot more, but I don't want to bore you with the minutia. In addition to the above arms, Bob called for a .270 WCF Winchester Model 70, a 12 gauge Browning semi-auto shotgun, and a 9mm semi-auto pistol, lots of ammo, extra magazine and a shoulder holster! However, being just a regular guy, Bob further ordered:

"None of these (weapons) is to be chromed or engraved fancily. All regular blued finish, walnut stocks or grips, checkering. I don't like cosmetics on weapons." Well, we all thank you for that, Robert.

Being an avid gun collector and shooter myself, this epistle really struck a nerve with me. Not only was this guy crazy, but in my opinion, he was describing his arsenal in a very detailed way. Somebody had to check-out this dude: My calls to the Secret Service, FBI and ATF (Alcohol, Tobacco and Firearms) fell on deaf ears. No one even wanted to go "knock and talk" with this character! I guess it never occurred to them that mentally ill folks aren't

---

*Bruce often appeared in Bob's scribbling. I never figured-out exactly who he was, but conjecture he was a fictional ally who was always available to lend our pen pal a hand.

supposed to posess weapons such as Bob described. Sure, he could have gotten his information from any Guns and Ammo magazine, but couldn't they just pay Westham a little visit and see if he had any weapons or not? So, it certainly looked like we were going to have to do this ourselves, even though we were sort of out of our jurisdiction...

WOW

As I guessed, Robert L. Westham was a ticking time bomb, which could go off at any moment. We learned that Bob lived in a trailer park—go figure—in Morro Bay, CA. We confirmed the address with MBPD; the local police gave us an exact location and DOB as they had some previous contacts with the man, who they aptly described as being "very 51-50 (nuts)"—*Tell me something I don't already know, guys*, I thought, but did not say.

A more detailed records profile was done and we learned way more about Mr. Westham than we ever imagined. I could tell from Bob's scriptures that he wasn't your run-of-the-mill high school drop-out; I soon learned that he had a near *genius IQ*, and at one time, had been a successful attorney, although that didn't compute, to my way of thinking... I believe after a bitter divorce, Bob began to lose it. He somehow got busted for trying to smuggle a functional bomb aboard a U.S. Air Force transport plane at Tinker AFB, in Oklahoma City. Why and how Bob was able to get on a USAF base with an explosive device and board a military plane, as a civilian, is beyond me. Maybe that's what alerted the police. In any event, Westham was convicted in Federal Court and sentenced to a long prison term. Because of his deteriorating mental condition, Robert was later confined to the prison's loony bin. After learning about this incident, it made sense that Bob included an Oklahoma shrink in his Super Bowl of executions.

After getting this background information, all sorts of horror scenarios raced through my mind: What if this guy actually started offing people and I knew about it but just sat on my hands—like the

Feds were doing? What if Bob paid an unscheduled visit to Building 10 and went-off on University President Donald Kennedy's reception staff with a verbal tirade like he did in his letters? Worse, what if, after they hit the panic button and our troops were en route, Bob suddenly opened up with some of his aforementioned firepower? I was determined that wouldn't happen on my watch, so I dispatched my aging detectives, Don Lillie and Carl Gielitz, to Morro Bay.

I especially wanted Carl (aka Captain Midnight) to go as he was a firearms aficionado and would be able to assess what kind of guns this lunatic had in his possession, if any.

All morning, I worried like an expectant father. Finally, I got a call from an excited Don: Now, that got my attention because Det. Lillie *never* got excited about *anything*!

"Captain, if we ever come down here again, we're going to need a SWAT team!"

"OK, so what's going on, Don?" I probed.

"Well, like you said, this guy is really crazy, but he's also very abusive and threatening. He seems to really know the law and refused to let us in his place. Carl got a peek into his trailer and saw several long guns in there. I'm sure glad we had Morro Bay officers with us 'cuz there's no telling what would have happened," Lillie reported.

"OK, Don. Get whatever info you can from the locals and come on back. I want a detailed report about this, and tell Morro Bay PD we'll shoot them a copy. I don't believe we've heard the last from Mr. Robert L. Westham. See ya soon," I said before signing off.

The Magic Words

On April 2, 1981, I received epistle #72, which I entitled: *"Hinkley's (sic) a Poor Shot."* Now, these were *The Magic Words* that really got the attention of the Secret Service! As most Americans recall, an equally crazy individual named John Hinckley, Jr. attempted to assassinate newly elected President, Ronald Reagan, as he was leaving a speaking engagement at Washington D. C.'s Washington Hilton Hotel. Hinckley (in his clouded mind) was trying to become a celebrity and impress actress Jodie Foster, with whom he had engaged in an obsessive (but unrequited) love fantasy. This coward staged in the crowd of well-wishers, opened-up on the President as he was about to enter his limo. Hinckley fired six rounds from a usually paltry .22 caliber pistol; however, the "Devastator" ammo was equipped with explosive projectiles which exacted horrible damage on his victims: The first shot struck Press Secretary James Brady right in the forehead. A D.C. police officer was hit in the neck; one of the President's Secret Service agents took one in the stomach. The sneaky shooter hit President Reagan with his last bullet, a lucky ricochet, as the *Man* was being jammed into the limo by his detail leader. No one knew that the President was wounded until his Agent in Charge, Jerry Parr, realized that something was wrong and ordered his driver to speed the Commander-in-Chief to George Washington Hospital. ER Docs soon learned that the President was gravely injured: That last round perforated Reagan's lung and lay very close to his heart. After a touch-and-go surgery in which the President lost half of his blood volume, the Chief survived and returned to work within one month. Mr. Brady suffered the most grievous injury which impaired his speech and later paralyzed him. Hinckley was committed to a mental institution.

Having set the context, here are some excerpts from letter #72, Westham's editorial:

"Make... (illegible) censure of Mr. Hinkley's (sic) for poor shooting. If he can't do better than that, Mother Nature will find other agents of her will, in slaying the sleazy [CSers]. He hit everything but the target. One good shot is better than a bunch of random shots. Until these queers get out of GHQ, they're going to get shot, and shot at, by natural law."

... "Back to Hinkley (sic). Please advise people that if he is not released, the entire American government structure, all criminal, will be punished even more severely in infinite program. Hinkley (sic) was only doing his duty in attacking a fascist regime practicing genocide. What do you think, Sam?"— I have no idea who Sam is.

The Assault

After relaying this letter to the RAC (Resident Assistant Agent in Charge) of the United States Secret Service in San Jose, their agents sprung into action—PDQ. I later learned that the USSS, backed-up by a SWAT team, performed a classic *pincer maneuver* on Westham's lair, by utilizing resources from their northern and central offices. This coordinated maneuver worked like a charm, and they had the nut case in handcuffs before he could utter: "John Hinckley was a . . ." After locking-up the mean spirited author for making threats to the President of the United States, they hauled off a truckload of guns from his mobile home. Some of the weapons Bob listed in his infamous "Super Bowl of Executions" manifesto were among the inventory, plus many others. Mr. Westham was later committed to the Atascadero State Hospital for some much needed mental health adjustment. To my knowledge, he never wrote a single nasty letter again. And, if he did, I am certain he never, ever said those "Magic Words!"

Axe Detail
Deputies Tony Navarra and Chuck Kemper

Oski Busted

Detective Tim Schreiner
with Oski in tow

CHAPTER THIRTY THREE

Pros and Cons

Woody: A Pro

"Radio H-1—puff. . .puff. . .puff—foot pursuit, foot pursuit, white male—huff. . . puff—medium build, light clothing, running toward ECR from Intramural Field!"

"Attention all units, H-1 is chasing a subject from the stadium area toward the ECR; units to fill?"

"Buzzzzzz, bzzzzzzz, Rad. . . bzzzzzzzz"—everyone talking over one another making the two-way radio system totally useless. . .

"H-1, I got 'em, I have him in custody"—between deep breaths—have Stanford units respond."

"10-4, H-1 are you near the ECR? What is the nature of your arrest?" the dispatcher inquired.

"Radio, I have several SEPs with me now, and I'm near the fence. This subject broke into a motor home and maced a pregnant woman. Advise A-2," Agent James Coffman of Palo Alto PD replied.

Coffman was a team leader "moonlighting" for the Special Events Patrol security force we utilized for big events. This was always a spirited and contentious football game between Stanford and my Alma mater, San Jose State University. (Although my heart was with my overmatched college, Stanford paid my salary so I had to go for the Cardinal!) The SJSU students were actually pretty good—definitely not on the order of the University of Spoiled Children or the demonic Cal Weenies—SJSU occasionally beat the Stanford squad and their loyal fans let us know about it, too.

When I got to the Compound headquarters/booking trailer, I met with Jim and gave him a *high five*, and teased:

"Pretty damn good pinch for a Paly cop," I dug, "but looks like you need to spend a little more time on the treadmill, Agent Coffman." *I should talk,* I thought, but Jim was all smiles.

"So, what in the hell happened?" I quizzed.

According to Jim, he was on foot patrol amongst the hundreds of motorhomes all around the stadium near Gate 11, when he spotted some sort of a disturbance; he jogged to the scene and espied a guy apparently fighting with several citizens, and using a form of pepper spray on them. The low-life then "beat feet" with Coffman and his partner in hot pursuit. Despite the heavy jumpsuit, boots, duty belt, baton, radio and other cop gear, Jim slowly closed the gap on the fleeing man; Coffman took the creep to the ground and applied his Peerless bracelets on the suspect's wrists. Game over! The man identified himself as David Keith Smith and was being processed under that handle.

When our deputies arrived at the scene, they learned that a *very* pregnant woman had come back to her RV for something and found the man rummaging around in the vehicle. When she asked him what he was doing and tried to stop his hasty retreat, the bum blasted her in the face with mace. The commotion alerted some folks who were tailgating nearby and they came to the woman's aid, only to be sprayed themselves. Enter stage left, H-1 and his partner, and the chase was on. The victim of the burglary said that the burglar was rifling through her purse, but her cursory look failed to find anything missing.

In the meantime, I learned that the group of citizens and SEPs who were chasing the jerk found a bag containing 31 credit cards in the names of various people from all over the country, as well as a ring of keys that had been filed down. At this point, I was certain in my mind that all things aren't always as they appear: If this dude was really David Keith Smith, then I was George Washington! By this time, my lead detective, John McMullen, came into the facility and I had a special assignment for him: First, I wanted a good set of prints rolled on this guy (Sandra Mize was an excellent finger printer, so she accomplished this task); then, we would use our brand new, high dollar, high quality Fax machine—I had to pull eye-teeth to get that gadget—to send "Mr. Smith's" prints to the FBI, *PDQ*. We needed to find out the true identity of this coward!

Second, I wanted our collar to be booked-in as a "John Doe" so he wouldn't be able to obtain a get-out-of-jail-free card before FBI got back to us. Done!

Third, I instructed one of the deputies to run the credit cards we found in "Mr. Smith's" burglar bag. As I suspected, "Smith's" plastic was hotter than molten lava. Needless to say, many of the cards that were entered in the stolen property system were stolen in burglaries all over the US of A: As I recall, we got hits from Maryland, North Carolina, Oklahoma, Nebraska, Reno NV, and Provo UT. It appears that Mr. Smith had been a very fortuitous traveler to have "found" all of this plastic...

Nailed!

I was watching the 10 O'clock news on Channel 2 when the phone rang:

"Yeah, John (I guessed) and you better not tell me that Mr. Smith is clear," I snorted.

"Heh-Heh," that devil chuckled. "No, actually you were right on, A-2, this guy is like Jesse James was; he's wanted all over the place. His true name is Garry David Woody, 39, and he has a million *akas*. There's a federal parole warrant and several from Louisiana for fraud, check writing, burglary, auto theft—you name it, he's done it, pal," John boasted. "But, let me tell you, getting the "Feeb's" fingerprint unit to analyze our prints was like getting an elephant into the back seat of my Jetta!"

"Whaddya mean, John?"

"After I faxed the prints, I called the FBI's ID Section to confirm they received them. A lady said that our prints would have to go to the bottom of the pile as they had a ton of much bigger and more important cases to deal with. Using my great charm," the cocky kid bragged, "I told her that we had a really bad guy here and needed to ID him so he wouldn't assault any more pregnant women! She asked me what happened and when I told her what the creep did, she said: 'Well, that's a different story. I'll get right on this now and have the results within an hour'—well, sure enough!"

"Good job, 'Weed' (his other nickname)—that was good thinking to put the pregnant woman angle in this!" In modern jargon: He played the Pregnant Woman Card... *This kid was going to go far,* I thought. *He's just a natural cop!* Something I could never take credit for.

"OK. Looks like we have a lot of work to do come Monday, John, so I'll see ya then; have a good weekend..."

Illumination

It didn't take long for the phone to start ringing off the hook, especially after we sent out a nationwide bulletin advising law enforcement agencies of Woody's arrest on our serene "Campus of Oz."

"Good Morning, this is Captain Niemeyer."

"Mornin' Captain, this is Inspector William Cartwright from the Nevada Gaming Commission; I hear y'all got Garry David Woody, eh? You know who this ol' bouy is?" he drawled.

"Not exactly, William, but judging from all of the arrest warrants on him, I figure a lot of folks want to get their paws on him," I remarked.

"Well, Sir, and you can call me Bill, let me tell you about this varmint—I've known him for many, many years and he's a clever one, he is."

I was all ears: Inspector Cartwright, "Bill," first ran into Woody in the Reno/Carson City area nearly 15 years before—it was October 4, 1990 when we bagged Woody. According to Bill, Garry was a genius; a first-rate slot machine technician. He also dabbled in gaming, only he didn't like the "House Odds" so he endeavored to level the playing field, if you will. . . He crafted a small battery powered drill which could be concealed in his fist and while he was cranking away on the old slots of yesteryear, he surreptitiously bored a tiny hole in the side of the case. Woody then fished-in a small wire into the box and manipulated the spindle so that a jackpot was hit! When the bell went off, he quickly secreted his equipment, patched the small pinhole with putty, and waited to collect his spoils.

Needless to say, Woody wasn't playing nickel machines! He perpetrated this scam for some period of time until the gaming sleuths were tipped-off by machine slot mechanics that a lot of their "one armed bandits" had holes drilled into their cases. It didn't take the investigators long to figure out who their "two armed bandit" was, so they 86ed Woody from all casinos in their area. However, that didn't deter ol' Garry as he moved around in northern Nevada hitting every Mom and Pop store, gas station and truck stop, to pursue his craft. Garry preferred Northern Nevada as, according to Inspector Bill, going to Las Vegas was not a good idea for: "Those ol' bouys play rough down there" . . .

By this time, the gaming industry became extremely sophisticated; not only were all the slot machines electronic, but

Vegas security was state of the art, with a *bizillion* cameras installed in nearly every casino.

I had the opportunity to see one of the security camera rooms at one of the top casinos on the Strip and was amazed at how good their systems were. Some of those high powered lenses could zoom-in and actually read inscriptions on college rings, for crying out loud. So, spotting cheats was now a piece of cake, if you knew what to look for.

Our hero quickly eschewed his archaic method of slot machine skullduggery and modernized his MO with a new device he invented, which would actually hypnotize the slot and allow Woody to manipulate the outcome of the wager. In order to pull-off this clever scam, Garry employed 10-15 associates (Smurfs) to assist him in this sleight-of-hand venture: Once a high dollar machine was targeted (many might pay-out up to $10,000), the group would crowd around, almost like a football huddle, while Garry employed his wizardry. When the bell went off, the group would disperse to another casino, leaving one Smurf behind to collect the spoils. The Smurf then went to the cashier, received the jackpot and later met up with Woody and Co. As specified in the agreement, the Smurf received $1,000 in hard, cold cash and hit the road. Not a bad payday for Mr. Woody as his 9K was free and clear. This operation went on for many months until the entire house of cards came crashing down: What ol' Garry didn't tell his Smurfs is that whenever one benefits from a wager, the IRS requires the winner to sign an affidavit acknowledging that they are liable for taxes for their "good fortune." So, when the "Tax Man Cometh," Woody's associates, who probably weren't the sharpest knives in the drawer, caved-in and unraveled the entire ball of yarn. . . . Without casting aspersions on our law enforcement authorities or the so-called Vegas mob, Garry was immediately *persona non grata* in Sin City! And, get outta Dodge, he did. I'm guessing that no one in that town wanted to reveal how they were hoodwinked but Woody is damn lucky that his bones weren't the subject of a "Forensic Files" episode . . .

Bill concluded his biography on Garry Woody by saying that the last he heard, Woody absconded to the Principality of Monaco and continued to game the system in that Mecca's ostentatious casinos. But, as in most cases, all good things come to an end. Woody met his match with the Crown's *gendarmes*. He was incarcerated for cheating and sent to prison for several years. Once he completed his sentence, the authorities gave him a one-way ticket back to the States with an emphatic edict: Don't ever come back!

Entrepreneur

During the week, we received several more calls from law enforcement agencies in the Gulf States; Woody was originally from Texas, I was told. Once back on American soil, he wasted no time conjuring-up an ingenious plan to make money—lots of it! One such phone call, and perhaps the most interesting, went something like this:

"Good morning, this is Capt. Niemeyer, may I help you?"

"*Mournin' to you suh.* This *hea* is *Share-riff* Bobby-Wayne Taylor from Mason County, down *hea* in the Texas, and I *hea* you have an *ol' bouy* called Garry David Woody?"

"Yes, Sheriff Taylor, we sure do; we have a ton of local felony charges pending and a drawer full of arrest warrants from all over the country. You want him, too, eh?"

"I *shore*, do *Cap'n, ann ya'll* can call me Bobby-Wayne. *We-all have been a-huntin' that thar polecat ever since he conned some folks down hea, ann I wann-um so bad, I can taste-um!*"

"Well, don't feel like the Lone Ranger—no pun intended (but I lied)—Bobby-Wayne there are a lot of coppers all over the country who want to get their hands around Woody's throat. I personally would like to see that crook locked away so deep that they'd have to pump air into his cell!"

"Well, let me tell ya something," Bobby-Wayne asserted, *"If ya'all ship his sorry-ass down hea to me, gar-un-tee, I'll put-um in a pink tee shirt ann skivvies, ann he'll neva see sunshine a-gain— ya'll can take that to the bank!"* After picking myself off the floor, and between chuckles, I replied:

"Sheriff Bobby-Wayne, you're my kind of guy; I wish we had more like you out here. I'll have my detective keep tabs on this case and let you know when we are done with him. Take care, Bobby-Wayne, and great talking with you!"

Damn, I thought, *wish I had recorded that*—Ol' Bobby-Wayne nearly killed me!! Years later, when Arizona's tough Sheriff, Joe Arpaio, came to the forefront, I mused that he must have learned his *hard-ass* craft from Texas Sheriff, Ol' Bobby-Wayne Taylor. . .

While in Louisiana, Woody took out a classified ad in the local newspapers announcing that he was going to create a new start-up electronic company and hire a bunch of folks. The ad specified that all applicants needed to come to an office he had rented for face-to-face interviews. All prospective employees must have valid birth certificates or driver's licenses and social security cards in their possession. If the "human resources" people gave a candidate the thumbs up, they were required to fill out a standard employment form and allow the staff to copy the birth certificates, DLs and SS cards. I was told that many *were* called and *ALL* were chosen. . .

In the interim, our budding CEO had not only opened an account with a reputable banking institution in town, but he deposited a considerable sum as collateral. Are you following my drift here? Just a couple more loose ends and Woody would soon be a very rich man again. Garry purchased a check protector, designed checks with a fancy logo and started issuing payroll checks to his "employees." His new group of Smurfs created bogus DLs and SS cards, utilizing the duped candidate's personal information, and simply cashed the bogus paper wherever they could. Once all of Woody's team had cash in their hot little hands, they blew out of town like a Texas cyclone. But, not before the mastermind claimed his considerable salary from his stooges and withdrew his "collateral" from the "Company's Bank!" Neat scam, huh? Woody pulled-off this sting in at least two southern cities that I know of and quickly went on the lam, as the heat in the kitchen became unbearable...

With cops from hell looking for him, Garry hit the road and went into a new form of stealth and trickery—this time by his lonesome, as partners are, more often than not, a huge liability. No one knew where this cat was until Stanford's Finest (of course, with the help of Paly cop, Coffman) caught him with his hand in the cookie jar, so to speak.

In tracing Woody's adventures from the Eastern Seaboard to the West Coast, it was pretty clear in my mind that he targeted big special events: NASCAR races, college and pro-football games, and he zeroed in on RVs while the fans were in the venues. With his ring of custom keys, there weren't too many motor homes or travel trailers this sneaky thief couldn't get into. Once inside, he would look for women's purses and remove the credit cards. Garry would then replace the stolen cards with "hot" cards that he had stolen at previous events. He never took cash or anything but credit cards. This guy had way too much time in that Monaco prison, I think, in order to come up with this scheme. Most people wouldn't realize that they had been ripped-off until they tried to use their John Jones Visa credit card, only to find out from the piercing eyes of the store clerk that the card presented belonged to Mr. Jim Smith... Bummer!

Needless to say, our switchboard was lit-up 24-7. We learned that Mr. Woody had visited the following venues: BYU vs. WSU football game in Provo, UT, the Reno Air Races in Reno, NV, the San Francisco 49er game the weekend before, then us.

This criminal was the classic, consummate pro! He must have been a student of Darwin: Unlike most stupid lawbreakers who overload our prison system, this guy figured out that if one is to be a successful crook, one has to adapt and change. We saw this in the "Jogging Burglar" case. Plodding along with the same old methods and course will give those criminals a reserved berth in "stir." Why do you think there are very few beds available in our nation's prisons?

I often wonder what happened to this clever dude—as you all know by now, I abhor criminals, but admire some of the innovative methods employed by the good ones; but they are few and far between...

Hennigan: A Con and Computer Thief, *Par excellence*

Suddenly, in early 1990, computers started walking away from the campus at an alarming rate. The burglaries began in the Quad's academic office. The crook(s) hit in the late evening to early morning hours, usually by prying the doors and getting away with PCs, Macs and printers—often as many as two or three at a crack. As usual in this environment, there were no witnesses or physical evidence left at the scene. Of course, many folks thought that the perps were none other than the poor janitors, who were just trying to do their job and provide for their families. It seemed that every time there was a nighttime break-in on campus, the custodial staff was unjustly accused. My detectives interviewed all of the workers and supervisors, and despite the language barrier (most were Hispanic, but we utilized an in-house interpreter), we were convinced that the clean-up crew had no part in these crimes. Despite heightened awareness on the part of our CSOs and Patrol staff, no persons of interest were developed in the Quadrangle computer thefts.

On April 16th, three Next Inc. computers were stolen from a temporary trailer which housed the Center for Computer Research in Music and Acoustics, located clear on the other side of campus, behind the Music Knoll. These, then state of the art machines valued at $15,000 each, stored volumes of research material. A graduate student exclaimed in despair: "I've lost most of my dissertation. They stole my backups and all the writing [for the dissertation] is gone!" Our hearts went out to this poor student, but again, the criminal(s) who did this left us nothing to work with in trying to ascertain his identity and when he was going to hit again. This guy(s) was beginning to really piss me off!

By mid July, the total dollar figure of lost computers and related equipment approached 155K. How these thefts could occur with such regularity and the perp(s) were never heard or seen was baffling beyond belief. My Crime Prevention Unit came up with a novel program called STOPP (Stanford Office Protection Project). In exchange for adopting some basic crime prevention options, like installing a security alarm system—many clever innovations were out there such as fiber optic cables which were secured to the computers/printers and would alert if tampered with; magnetic interior alarms, heavy duty, locked tower mounts, etc.—And, engraving identifiers on your machine, you would qualify for an insurance program through Stanford's Risk Management Office. Given the cost of Mac SE ($2,000) and Mac II (4k) in that era, a $1,000 deductable per incident was an attractive offer, especially when a slew of the machines were ripped-off. Many departments availed themselves of our program and a number of computers were engraved and the serial numbers recorded.

A Sighting!

Shortly after the rash of thefts at Sweet Hall and the other computer labs in the area, a grad student reported the theft of a high dollar printer at one of the labs he was working in, one morning in the wee hours. Shortly after midnight after many hours of work on a project, the student hit the print button, waited a few minutes then headed down to the printer room. As he was approaching the area, the young man spotted a "technician" coming out of the room with the printer on a wheeled cart. The kid objected and said: "Hey, where are you going with that printer? I just sent some work to it."

"Sorry," the "technician" replied, "I have to take it in for service," as he hastily wheeled the machine away down the hall. As the man was leaving, the student hollered: "So, where's my stuff?" The guy looked back quickly, shrugged his shoulders (I don't know) and was soon out of sight. That didn't set well with our frustrated victim for he not only didn't have the work he needed for class that morning, but the damn printer was history.

Obviously, this student didn't get into Stanford's Computer Science Program because he was dumb, so he quickly called 9-1-1. Our Patrol units raced to the scene but the so-called technician was long gone. The cops and the kid soon realized that this individual wasn't a repairman but probably our serial computer thief! Although the witness got a great view of the crook, no usable physical evidence which would ID this cat was gleaned, so like the infamous "Jogging Burglar," we were just going to have to catch this merciless sucker in the act—and I hoped it would be sooner than later.

That morning, the flustered victim showed up at Investigations eager to assist in nailing this pesky purloiner of computer equipment, the life's blood of this institution of higher learning. One of our budding detectives, Keith Viveiros, had taken some classes in creating composites on the Macintosh computer via a program called Mac-a-Mug. We thought we'd give Keith a shot as this student seemed like a good witness and described the suspect to a tee: The man in question was an older man, perhaps in his mid 50s, clean shaven, about 5'10" tall, and nearly 200 pounds. He was dressed in a long sleeve grey uniform type shirt, dark blue pants and sported a distinctive tan Ben Hogan type cap, similar to what the Chicago thugs of the 30s and 40s wore. Another peculiarity was that this character walked with a noticeable limp. We checked with our Plant Services and computer service vendors but nobody fit the suspect's description.

After about an hour or so, our computer guru printed what the witness thought was a pretty good likeness of the guy he saw wheeling away the lab's computer and his work. Our Special Services Unit plastered the campus with this poster and soon the calls started coming in. Typically, they were: "Hey, we see that guy all the time at night and in the early AM—all over the place." All we had to do now was to nab this thief red-handed with some stolen goods and then we'd have something. After about a week or so, an observant student called in and reported that the suspect was in one of the buildings where crimes had previously occurred. Several units raced to the area and detained the individual. He was questioned and identified himself as the night shift janitorial supervisor who worked for a contract company. Not wishing to let the cat out of the bag, the deputies initiated an FI card and told him to report to the station in the morning as Investigations wished to speak to him. He was waiting for the front office to open-up and an early bird detective already had him in the Annex lock-up and was questioning him, when I arrived for work. As per protocol, the covert video camera was rolling and I had a peek at our quarry on a monitor in another office. The poor guy, I'll name Salvatore (Sal for short), was as nervous as a treed raccoon. Boy, if this wasn't our suspect then he must have a twin, judging from our Mac-a-Mug sketch. A tan Ben

Hogan cap covered his bald head and he wore a grayish uniform. There were a couple of discrepancies, however: Sal was considerably shorter than the man seen by the student and he didn't seem to have a limp. In addition, he said he had been employed by the janitorial service at Stanford for many years, so it seemed implausible to me that Sal would suddenly become a serial computer thief. But, one never knows. . . We released this man, but he surely seemed like someone we needed to check-out and keep an eye on.

My detectives tried to locate the grad student who got this ball rolling so we might present him with a photo spread; however, after releasing Sal, who became very agitated and uncooperative that we were looking at him as a possible suspect, it was realized that, in our excitement, we neglected to get a photo of him. What to do? *Well, I thought, why not put together a video line-up?* And, so we did! We dragged in a bunch of middle aged gentlemen including fire Captain, Pat Cady, our Captain, Bill Wullschleger, a contractor who was doing some work around the place, yours truly, and posed them before the hidden camera. The tape was edited to show each individual for about 30 seconds. When we finally located our witness, he immediately identified Sal as "possibly" being the person who swiped the printer. Although "possibly" isn't usually good enough for the DA, I thought it might be worth a shot and perhaps we could get a search warrant for Sal's home in nearby Mountain View. I detailed Sgt. Philip Love to stake-out Sal's residence while newly promoted Sgt. John McMullen flew over to the DA's Office with our video line-up. I knew that this form of ID would be considered somewhat unconventional, but I figured it would probably pass legal muster. Hell, if you don't think out of the box once in awhile, life would be awfully boring, now wouldn't it?

Shortly thereafter, John returned from the DA's Office in hysterics: When he showed our video to DDA Lance Beizer, the prosecutor went into a spontaneous laughing jag and nearly fell on the floor. Beizer thought it was the most hilarious photo spread that he'd ever seen as a prosecutor and choked out: "Where'd you find all of those old guys, John?" *Thanks for including me in that stereotype, Lance...* But, the important thing was that the legal eagle thought the line-up was ok and told John to get cracking on an affidavit for a search warrant. In the meantime, Sgt. Love called me on the radio and reported that the Person of Interest (POI), Sal, had just pulled up in his driveway and was suspiciously unloading stuff from his car; one of the items was covered with a towel or something and the other thing appeared to be a vacuum cleaner.

Knock 'n Talk

After receiving Sgt. Love's message, Sgt. McMullen and I sped to the scene. Once in place, I called the POI on my new-fangled mobile car phone—we're talking a prehistoric forerunner of the "I-Phone"—and told the man we had a search warrant (I fibbed) and intended to storm his home in a few minutes. Within a minute, Sal bolted out the front door dragging a vacuum cleaner behind him, which he quickly stashed in the trunk of his car. Once this now very suspicious character retreated into his house, we donned our Raid jackets and approached the residence. I didn't even have to knock on the door for Sal threw it open and invited us to check everywhere. He was really steamed: Gesticulating with his arms, cursing us in broken English with several Italian invectives tossed in. The minute I crossed the threshold, I realized that this man, however furtive and evasive, was not our guy! This home was a virtual shrine—almost like a small chapel, adorned with Catholic statues, paintings, shrouds and votive candles. Then, we found his elderly mother, who was dressed like a nun: The poor woman was very aged and frail; she wore an ornate crocheted shawl and was trembling while reciting prayers in Italian, all the while fumbling with a rosary. Broke my heart that we had to scare this woman, but her son was acting like the proverbial cat that just swallowed a canary!

After a cursory, non-productive search, Sgt. McMullen asked him what the deal was with the vacuum cleaner that he hid in his trunk. Salvatore sheepishly admitted that he had just borrowed it to clean his home because his machine was on the fritz. John scolded him for taking University property without permission and told him to return it when he reported to work that night. We got out of there, shaking our heads, for we just struck out, *big time*, on this one...

Macris Sketch

Because our Mac-a-Mug composite was so rudimentary, we concluded that San Jose Police Department's professional artist, Tom Macris, should be enlisted to draw a more accurate sketch of our computer thief. Tom, a really good guy, agreed to help us out. The grad student was amenable to working with Macris and, together, a very remarkable composite was rendered. We tore down all of the computer generated composites and replaced them with copies of our "Macris Sketches," which looked more like photographs than drawings. In addition to campus postings, we got the Stanford Daily, Times Tribune and San Jose Mercury News to publish this thief's mug. Despite these efforts, the computers continued to walk at an alarming rate. To add more flies to the ointment, several of our stolen machines were recovered in Phoenix, AZ, thanks to the engraving program. Clearly, our crook was ripping-off our stuff and shipping it to other areas. Who was this criminal, and how was he accomplishing this? He must have a network—at least some henchmen who were lending a hand in this endeavor. This was truly baffling, to say the least.

Bingo

It was early Saturday afternoon and I was relaxing around the house when I got a call from an unusually excited Sgt. McMullen, who was back in uniform and on patrol:

"Hey, A-2, it's me. What are you doing?"

"Well, John, I *was* enjoying my day off until you rudely interrupted me. What's up?" I answered.

"We got 'em, Man. We got 'em!" John blurted. He seemed like he couldn't contain himself.

"Got who, John?" I cluelessly asked.

"Kenneth Hennigan! The computer thief! He's a PAL (parolee at large) and has a ton of warrants out on him. Doug Kuffel spotted him getting off a Marguerite (campus shuttle bus) and busted his ass at the Palo Alto bus station. The guy had a little cart with a computer on it, which was covered with a trash bag. We have him locked down now and wondered if you want to try to flip him; he's in total denial right now."

"OK, let me throw on some clothes and I'll be there within an hour; tell Doug, good job." I gleefully exclaimed. *Hopefully, this won't be another false alarm,* I worried.

The Non-Interrogation

When I arrived at the Annex, Deputy Kuffel was busily getting the mounds of paperwork in order. He told me that while on routine patrol, he received a radio transmission from Communications that a person called 9-1-1 and said that a subject matching the Macris Sketch had just boarded the shuttle at the top of the Palm Oval. The caller related that the man walked with a limp, was wearing khaki pants, a blue windbreaker, *that* tan golfer's cap, and was dragging what appeared to be a covered computer tower on a small telescoping luggage carrier. Kuffel, who was formerly in the Silicon Valley's high tech industry, didn't need a computer to figure out that the bus was headed for the Palo Alto bus/rail depot, so he made a beeline for that location. Sgt. McMullen copied the traffic and zoomed in for the "fill." When they got to the train station, the suspect was sitting on a park bench. Kuffel asked this POI what he was doing with the computer. The crafty individual said that he was a contract computer repairman and was waiting for a bus to San Mateo to take the machine to his shop. When asked, "So, where's your vehicle?" he, of course, replied that it was inoperable. As this point, Sgt. McMullen had heard enough of this bull, so he ordered the man to be arrested.

Upon checking-out this cat, John and Doug learned that their collar was Kenneth Hennigan, a career criminal who had spent much of his adult life in jail and prison. When the Sergeant advised the arrestee of his Miranda Rights, the congenial "conman" politely declined to make any statements. I figured that the chances were slim that I would be able to get any information out of this very experienced career criminal, but took a stab at it anyway.

I entered the holding room, introduced myself and asked Ken if he would be willing to chat with me for a bit. Hennigan looked up from the bench he was shackled to and politely replied: "Captain, I respect you as a man, but I'm sorry that I will not be able to tell you anything you want to know!" Well, so much for that. . . After giving the "Book 'em Danno" order, I headed home.

Chasing Wild Geese

About an hour later, John called me again and said that one of the jail deputies called him and related that Hennigan phoned someone in Daly City to inform that person he was incarcerated; the crook also made a reference to some "other stuff." In my mind, the person who Ken called might very well be the guy who was fencing all of our hot computer equipment. Palo Alto Communications pinpointed the residence that Hennigan contacted, so McMullen and I were off to chat with this man.

Hennigan's "associate" was a naturalized Filipino citizen (Eduardo), who at first, denied even knowing the con. However, this dubious character later admitted that Ken *had* done "odd" jobs for him at his small appliance store in Daly City. Judging from the high dollar digs where this gentleman and his family resided, ol' Ed must have been fixing a helluva lot of sewing machines, typewriters and vacuum cleaners. . . . I didn't buy it. I surmised that Hennigan was a *mule* and that this budding entrepreneur was shipping those computers somewhere. But, now we had to prove that theory, which I knew was going to be a very tall order.

We did a drive-by on Eduardo's alleged business and found that it was a tiny store front in the industrial area; there was a large shipping container to the rear of the small building, which certainly piqued my interest. John and I went to the Daly City Police Department, told them what we had, and asked for their assistance. The Watch Commander was extremely cooperative and rolled-out the "Welcome Mat" and basically told us: *"Mi Casa Su Casa!"* A patrol unit went to the target's store and sat on it until our personnel arrived. We didn't want to risk losing any evidence out the back door and sure enough, that sly owner came down to the shop and tried to enter; the Daly City coppers told him to hit the road as a search warrant was in the offing.

Judicial Technology

Well, sort of. . . As you may recall from my writing about the Jogging Burglar case, obtaining a search warrant was akin to pulling eye teeth: The investigator had to, first, convince a DA why the police should be allowed to violate someone's Fourth Amendment Rights. If successful, the DA would call in a stenographer who would record an "Affidavit in Support of Search Warrant" in short hand, then laboriously type out the document. The detective would then find a friendly jurist, ask the judge to review and sign said document, and, if fortunate, we were good to go. But, what happened if you needed a warrant at night or on the weekend? Well, in the olden days, you just had to drum your fingers on your desk and wait until the DA's doors opened for business the next day.

Certainly, this was not a good way to run an airline, so we all complained, especially when drugs and associated violent crime began during the 60s and continued to gain momentum. Too much valuable evidence was being lost and criminals were getting off the hook because of it.

So, in an attempt to streamline the often cumbersome search warrant procedure, the courts began to allow officers to obtain warrants at night and on weekends via an old invention, Alexander Graham Bell's telephone. This new and improved procedure had just been sanctioned in Santa Clara County, so I thought I'd give it a shot. The Daly City PD's Lt. set-me-up in an office, so I called County Communications and asked them to have the on-call Deputy DA contact me. Within a few minutes, a familiar voice was on the line. It was my old friend, DDA Tom Hanford, who prosecuted the O'Connor cabal in the Jogging Burglar matter. After exchanging pleasantries, we got to the business at hand. Tom admitted that this was going to be his inaugural telephonic search warrant and possibly, the first one their office had processed. So, it was basically going to be one of those "flying by the seat of our pants" deals. The telephone company set up a three-way line which now included a DA's stenographer who lived in Cupertino. After what seemed like an eternity, the affidavit and search warrant was dictated and the transcriber told me that we could pick it up in about an hour. John and I broke several land speed records getting to the steno's home. From there, we zoomed to Palo Alto and got the on-call jurist out of bed. It was just after midnight, but Judge Navarro was good natured about our intrusion and put his *John Hancock* on the documents.

When we got back to the suspected honey-hole, the owner was there and let us in—that saved his chintzy glass door, for sure, because we were tired and a bit cranky! Our team went through the place with a fine tooth comb and didn't find a single computer or related equipment; lots of junk old appliances, ancient typewriters and vacuums, but none of the items we were looking for. We *did* find some interesting invoices, however, which recorded the sale and shipping of computers to Manila, P.I., but that was like chasing the geese after they flew the coop. Once done with the shop, we cut the lock on the shipping container. I held my breath as I opened the large steel doors for I knew that we'd find a million stolen computers in there. To our surprise, all we found was a huge pile of old typewriters—many obsolete IBM Selectrics, some old Royals and Underwoods, but not even a computer cord! Well, at least we got the con, Kenneth Hennigan, and perhaps the parade of computers marching down Palm Drive would come to a grinding halt.

When Mr. Hennigan's arrest hit the papers the next morning, the first guy waiting for the PD to open up was none other than Sal, the janitorial supervisor who we focused on as a POI early in the investigation. He was madder than a wet hen and demanded to see me, all the while gesticulating wildly and cursing (under his breath) in his native tongue. My detectives and I promptly met with him and profusely apologized for zeroing-in on him as a possible suspect. Sal was not moved; he asserted that we ruined his life! I showed the distraught man a booking photo of Hennigan alongside the Macris sketch of the "suspect" and asked: "Now, Sal, look at these; as anyone can see, you two could be twins, right? As we said before, several times, we are very sorry that we had to investigate you, an innocent man, but that happens sometimes. Thank God you weren't arrested and convicted. So, please understand that we were just doing our job, and in this case, we were wrong." Sal abruptly got up and stormed out of the room as he shouted invectives at us—surely to get him a stiff penance next time he went to Confession.

Epilogue

Mr. Hennigan pleaded guilty to one count of burglary and possession of stolen property and was sent back to prison for a spell. I thought we had seen the last of Kenneth Hennigan, but like our ill fated search of the Daly City fence's store, I was wrong: In 1993, one of our patrol units spotted this con walking around the campus and recognized him as our infamous computer thief from a few years before. The dummy was still wearing his tell-tale Ben Hogan cap and repairman's uniform. When asked what he was doing, Ken told the deputy that he was working with a Stanford professor in developing an electronic instrument that would kill and eradicate the dreaded Fire Ants, so ubiquitous in Arizona. He couldn't recall the professor's name or where his office was, and further spun that he was involved in this joint venture with the Engineering Department at Arizona State University in Tempe. The guy had most of the answers down pat except the important ones. However, the wily ol' cop didn't buy his yarn and ran a records/warrant check on Mr. H. Within short order, Radio advised that, once again, Mr. Hennigan was a wanted PAL; the idiot violated his parole from our *beef* after he promised a gullible panel he would never, ever offend again. . . Perfect! Criminals rarely become rehabilitated and Parole Boards often don't believe that pie in the sky notion.

McMullen, now back in Investigations, and I visited our buddy in the Santa Clara County Main Jail. As in our first chat, after he was busted with a freshly purloined computer, Ken reiterated: "Captain, I respect you, but don't have anything to say." And, so it was. As for this chapter, *I respect you (my readers) and don't have anything more to say.*

CHAPTER THIRTY FOUR

Honorable Mention

Hardy: A DPS Icon

The most notable and recognizable of the New Guard's characters was Charles "Chuck" Hardy Kemper (R.I.P.). He came to us from the Sunnyvale Department of Public Safety. Chuck was forced to retire from the D.P.S. due to a neck injury he sustained while fighting a huge conflagration in the City of Sunnyvale. He had undergone a successful laminectomy, but the City held that he would be unfit for fire duty. We used to chide that "Funnyvale's" personnel were half cop/half fireman and didn't know if they should go for their gun or spanner wrench...

I was familiar with the laminectomy procedure as my Dad had undergone that surgery in the early 1950s (then, in its infancy and very experimental), and he carried on without any side effects. Nonetheless, Chuck's condition was a liability question and viewed by some as a risk. However, after going through a complete medical examination and review by our Orthopedist, he was given a clean bill of health. Besides, he wasn't going to fight fires anytime soon in our department...

Right from the get-go, I loved this guy. He was a cop's cop: Salty as a Dubuque ham, would be the first guy in there during a fight, and could swear like a China Sea sailor. I worried that his foul mouth would get him into trouble someday, but he was an equal opportunity potty mouth: Chuck cussed at and around students, faculty and staff and never once got a complaint! And, it's not that he was inconspicuous either, for Kemper was in his mid to late 40s, medium frame, well built and wiry, well tanned and he sported light brown tightly curled hair—dyed in the wool, so to speak. When he arrived at a police action scene, he wasn't large, but he *was* in charge! I think he developed that swagger and confidence when he was an Arizona Highway Patrolman.

While at a training seminar at Sunnyvale, I had the occasion to meet the D.P.S. Chief when we were working out in their gym. After introductions, the chief asked:

"So, how's my good friend Hardy these days?"

"Hardy? Hardy who?" I replied in bewilderment.

"Kemper. Hardy Kemper" the chief said.

"Oh, you mean Chuck; I never heard Hardy before; everybody calls him 'Chuck,'" I advised. "Boy that guy is something else; but we love him!"

"Yeah, it's not the same around here without him, but as chief I don't miss wondering everyday what Hardy was going to get us into," he snickered.

At that point we started exchanging some anecdotes involving Chuck.

"Did you ever hear the one about the time he stopped a car full of Samoans after a near riot at one of our clubs?" the boss asked. He then related the following tale:

"So, it's pretty near bar closing time when we get a panic call from one of our club owners who reported a humongous fight involving a large number of Pacific Islanders. He tells the dispatcher that the assailants took off in a large American sedan and were last seen heading toward the El Camino. Perfect, as the last thing we wanted to do was get embroiled in a knock-down-drag-out with a group of drunken Samoans, right? So, within a couple of minutes, Hardy puts out traffic that he's stopping a possible suspect vehicle at ECR and Wolfe. I was patrol supervisor then, so I flew to the scene.

When I get there, I see a big Pontiac that looks like it's lowered all the way around; hell, the frame is almost dragging on the roadway. All I can see via the spotlight is huge bodies in the car, with Hardy approaching the driver's side. All of a sudden, the door pops open, and the driver slowly gets out—and, he never stopped getting out—all 6'5" of him, three hundred and 45, at least! So, Hardy gets the guy's DL, shines his flashlight on the photo, then illuminates the hulk's face and says:"

"Is this you?" as he points to the picture on the license.

"Yeah, daass me," the monster replies.

Hardy looks at the license again, shines the light back in the Islander's face and declares:

"How in the hell does an ugly M...Fer like you get a name like George Washington?"

"As I was reaching for my club, for I knew the fight was just about to start," the chief continued, "the big Samoan put his arm around Hardy and laughingly said:"

"You funny guy! I like you. Ha Ha Ha."

"The other three gargantuans in the car began laughing hysterically. Situation diffused!"

Later that day, I got to thinking about that story involving those Pacific Islanders, and couldn't help recalling a major incident that occurred in Lakewood Village (we called it "Snakewood Village") about 10 years before, when I was working a beat in Cupertino:

****

Right about midnight, County Comm. put out a Code 20, (officers need help, desperately!) in Lakewood Village, in the City of Sunnyvale. Dozens of police units were screaming toward the scene, Code Three! I was cancelled by my sergeant as a sufficient number of officers were already there. Someone put out a Code 4 (no further assistance needed). As it turned out, a fight is never over until it's over, and the last participant is in cuffs and en route booking—and, that wasn't the case, as a number of combatants were arrested after a prolonged physical battle. Quite a few cops had to check into area hospitals for treatment of injuries—if you ever had to tangle with these guys, then you'd know what I'm talking about!

I later learned that a lone Sunnyvale cop was initially dispatched to a 415 party—no big deal as cops routinely respond to dozens of these calls everyday and twice on weekends. So, here's what happened in this melee: The cop hears a lot of racket emanating from this house and pounds of the door. A rather large, very inebriated Pacific Islander throws open the door and immediately goes into choreography of Karate moves *(katas)*, all the while screaming:

"Hi-Yaaaa. *Kata-tay*! Me black belt *Kaa-rrate*!"

Somewhat stunned, the officer took a couple of steps back, put his hand on his gun and responded:

"Hi-Yaaaa. Me black belt .38!"

And, the fight was on. The Samoans, Tongans and countless others never stopped coming through the door. It took nearly 50 officers to quell this "misunderstanding. . ."

That lone cop *had to be* our most "notable character," Charles Hardy Kemper.

****

Detective McMullen and I were monitoring a protest rally at Building 10 (the President's Office) sponsored by SOSA (Stanford out of South Africa) and BSU (Black Student Union). This was an old tune played by a new orchestra: As you previously read, students demanding that Stanford divest their South Africa portfolio dates back to 1977 when 294 students were arrested for occupying and refusing to leave the Old Union. Unlike that peaceful event, a sit-in at the same venue on October 11, 1985 became more difficult when five of the nine protestors decided to go limp. Our arrest teams tried to coax the interlopers into walking on their own to our temporary booking site down the hallway, but they refused. The teams employed reverse wrist-locks on the resistors known as "compliance/pain" holds, which usually work: If you comply you get no pain; if you don't comply, you get pain. Once applied, most arrestees tiptoe to the desired location rather quickly. However, one of the main protesters, Bobby Beekins from Chapter 14 fame, was double jointed, so his wrists, although large, were like rubber. Consequently, the hold had little or no effect. He put on a good show for his colleagues by screaming like a banshee and bawling like a baby—Bobby adamantly refused to walk or cooperate in any way, thus, had to be dragged.

John and I were observing Mr. Beekins, who apparently had assumed a leadership role within these groups. He had a number of students huddled around him as he was preparing to address the crowd of about 300, detailing how the Stanford Police had brutalized him and his cohorts the week before. Suddenly, out of the corner of my eye, I spotted an older man with a very angry look on his face. We knew this character as Jack Testa, a "loosely wrapped" individual who had been hanging around the fire station and our office. Our Front Office staff had mentioned this man's presence, as he had showed up on more than one occasion, flirting with and trying to get dates with the women. Det. McMullen knew about him, too, nonetheless, I told my detective to keep an eye on this cat. I no sooner finished voicing my concerns to McMullen when Ol' Jack ran up to Bobby and began hurling racial epitaphs, all the while flailing his arms in a feeble attempt to strike the young man. John and I sprung into action: We snared Mr. Testa and pulled him away. We took him around the corner and put him up against the wall where I commenced to pat-down this troublemaker. I pulled his coat back and immediately found a large sheathed hunting knife on his belt. Out came my bracelets and while applying same, I advised:

"You're under arrest Jack!" He began to fight like hell whereupon McMullen and I gently implanted his visage into a crevice of the classic Stanford limestone wall, while I once again recited my mantra:

"Stop fighting, Sir, you're hurting yourself, you're hurting yourself, you're hurting yourself. . ."

In return, John and I received a litany of invectives and threats that would make a sailor blush. . . McMullen called for a patrol car as this dude was going downtown for 12020 P.C., feloniously carrying a concealed knife, as well as disturbing the peace, and resisting arrest—as frosting. We marched the recalcitrant arrestee down Lasuen Mall toward the waiting patrol car. Timing was not on our side as classes had just let-out for lunch, so the mall was awash with kids on bikes streaming toward their dorms. All of a sudden, our deputy jumped out of his unit and loudly lambasted the arrestee:

"Testa, you dumb M. . . Fer! You're a no good piece of . . . I warned your sorry ass that we'd bust you sooner or later. You stupid S.O.B.," Deputy Hardy "Chuckie" Kemper boomed invectively—and, within earshot of a million students, faculty, staff, God, and, oh damn, my tape recorder, too! Well, so much for this tape as evidence, I lamented as I gave it the "Watergate" *cleansing*. . .Hardy "Chuck" Kemper was clearly one of the most interesting and unconventional deputies we ever had, but he was a great cop!

Tone: An Unsung Hero!

Anthony "Tony" Navarra (later known as Tone) was one of the first deputies I met when I was appointed as Patrol Captain at SUDPS. I went on a ride-along with Tony early on, for a couple of reasons: Although I was no stranger to the workings of a squad car and the rudiments of police patrol, I could barely find my way to the bathroom, let alone navigate myself anywhere on campus. I found the place a virtual cornfield maze! Even with a map, locating specific locations was no easy task. I also wanted to get acquainted with the personnel and share my philosophy with them: As I understood my mission, I was to transform the newly re-organized department into a viable modern police force. I had heard rumors that my intended course of action was viewed by some as a bit Draconian. . . And, I certainly got that impression after my first day on the beat with DPO Navarra.

Tony struck me as being an extremely congenial man. He was also very bright, having received a BA from the University of California's School of Business in 1972. Navarra said that he was drawn to campus policing by a desire to help people and was recruited by my predecessor, who was big on "community policing," with heavy emphasis on PR and low priority on crime fighting. That, of course, created a difference of opinion between us. Although I was acutely aware that maintaining positive relations with the community you served was paramount, I also knew that, given the high crime stats at Stanford, a blend of both schools of thought would be necessary. I recall that there were over 800 bike thefts in 1974, not to mention hundreds of burglaries and other thefts on The Farm. One of the Old Guard Sergeants called campus a "cherry patch," with most of the criminals from the surrounding areas, raiding and pillaging like the Goths who sacked Rome.

But, as it turned-out, Tony Navarra was one of the most conscientious and reliable deputies we had during the "Growing Pains" era of our development. He was a good trainer, an excellent report writer, and did everything by the book. His leadership qualities made him a role model, which eventually rubbed-off on the recruits and started the ball rolling toward our goal of excellence! Tone was also the first guy to roll-up his sleeves and help his fellow deputies with whatever needed to be done—no matter how mundane or tedious the task may be! I can remember how hard that man worked and encouraged others during that "all-nighter" we pulled at the Jogging Burglar's freezing house, while we were confiscating a truck load of stolen booty.

Our First Pre-Dawn Raid

At about 6'3" and weighing over 200 pounds, Tony could be a fearless, imposing figure. That is precisely why I selected him to be my entry man on an early morning raid we effectuated on an Escondido Village apartment. We were after a wanted convicted felon, who was shacking-up with a graduate student. The man's Parole Agent designated the convict as a PAL (Parolee at Large), and warned that the guy could be armed with a .45 and might use it in order to evade arrest. I obtained a WWII ballistic vest—the type used by B-17 waist gunners during their bombardment of Germany—these shields were literally bulletproof for a .30 caliber projectile—and outfitted it on Tone during our briefing. I recall that one of our first female recruits gave me grief for not assigning her to be on the entry team. I curtly reminded the young lady that she was a recruit in training and I was the Captain, thus would make the assignments for this dangerous detail! Plus, she only had about 2 weeks in the FTO program and was a diminutive five foot nothing, whereas, Navarra was built like a Sherman tank! Who would you choose as your point person? End of discussion. . .

We had a "No-Knock" warrant, which legally allowed us to make forceful entry without prior notice; this con was reputed to be a bad-ass, armed drug dealer, so we didn't want to give him an opportunity to get to his piece and do us damage. At about 0430 hours, I kicked-in the front door. Deputy Navarra charged-in like a Brahma Bull with the other entrants close behind, using Tony as an armored shield. The suspect and his girlfriend must have thought they were having a nightmare! We quickly took both into custody without a whimper. Our team located a small quantity of drugs, but no firearm; we all heaved a huge sigh of relief.

The Fire

During an afternoon on March 19, 2001, Deputy Anthony Navarra was on routine patrol in the Faculty Ghetto, in the area of Frenchman's Road, when he heard a 9-1-1 call come over the airways—a 904 (house fire) on Gerona Road. Tony was right around the corner so he zipped over to the scene and pulled-up just in time to see a young male struggling with a wheelchair bound elderly woman on an upstairs balcony. Smoke was pouring from the residence. The deputy ran to the area below the balcony and urged the man to drop the woman in his arms; being a big, strong guy, Tony had confidence that he could catch the frail lady without hurting her. However, the young fellow (the woman's caregiver) freaked-out, cried hysterically and refused to heed Navarra's commands. Sensing imminent danger for the stranded occupants, Tony charged through the overpowering smoke in the home and sprinted up the stairway to where the victims were. Deputy Navarra then picked the woman out of the wheelchair—amidst her protestations and some physical resistance—and headed toward the stairs, with the caregiver also in tow. However, Navarra encountered a huge impediment in his rescue attempt: There was a banister chair lift at the top of the stairs, which forced Tony to muscle the poor woman over the obstacle; in doing this, she almost separated from the deputy's grasp, but he held onto her and scampered down the steps and out into the fresh air.

By that time, the firefighters from Station 6 had arrived and began giving the woman and her so-called "caregiver," oxygen. I guess the FD was short on O2 that day as they never offered Tony any, despite the fact he was nearly overcome by smoke inhalation and was gasping for air. Instead, the Battalion Chief gave our hero a dressing down for A): Blocking the driveway with his patrol car, despite the fact that there was a huge open lawn, so any piece of apparatus could have easily been driven around to the house. And, B): For risking his life by dashing into a smoke-filled home without proper equipment.

Following this unwarranted and unwanted ass-chewing, the whacko caregiver continued on with his histrionics, and told Tony that someone else was in the house. Without regard for his own safety, Deputy Navarra again raced back into the home but was driven back due to the intense smoke. As it turned out, the pseudo (nurse?) who was literally on drugs, was hallucinating for nobody else was ever in the home. Sensing that this doper was heavily under the influence of a controlled substance(s), he ordered a Crime Lab Technician to the scene for a sample of the guy's blood.

As it turned out, this "brain surgeon" was free-basing cocaine, ala Richard Pryor, save for the facial and hair conflagration the comedian was awarded for his stupidity. . . Tony's crack-head apparently left his smoldering materials unattended (he said that everything was contained in an ashtray—but, we all know how drug addicts lie) when he went upstairs to look-in on his patient. Then, suddenly, *dung happened,* and the place caught fire. Tony charged the charlatan with several controlled substance violations, as well as Elder Abuse—all felonies, so he was summarily booked into North County Jail. The idiot later pled guilty.

Medal of Valor?

Based on my research of the Stanford Police, no officer had ever demonstrated more heroics in the line of duty than Deputy Anthony N. Navarra. He put his life on the line to save two human beings from certain death. Sure, some folks might believe that Navarra risked his life unnecessarily by going into a burning house without proper training and equipment. Tell that to some of the many WWII heroes who were awarded the Congressional Medal of Honor: All of those men might have had proper training but they *certainly* didn't have the proper equipment when they put their lives on the line while charging fortified machine gun nests under withering fire, wearing only their cotton uniforms. In the heat of battle, many individuals just step-up and accomplish extraordinary feats because they feel they have to! Tony Navarra, like the WWII folks I alluded to, weren't *born* heroes; they just put duty and honor above their personal safety, thus spontaneously attained that accolade!

Then Chief, Marvin N. Moore, awarded Deputy Navarra with the highest award that any law enforcement officer can receive—The Medal of Valor! Chief Moore presented this coveted prize to Tony in a ceremony that was covered by the Bay Area media. The medal and State of California certificate were to be displayed in the lobby of the DPS. Unfortunately, Chief Moore tragically passed away one month later, and the official paperwork was never submitted to the State. Tony's heroic act soon faded, and the "official" meritorious award was swept under the rug. So, in effect, Deputy Navarra's event on Gerona Road that night became just another day on the Farm. Now, this is what I call a travesty of justice and morality, and Tony became just another "Unsung Hero!"

Anthony N. Navarra retired in 2002 and was honored by his true friends at a gala party in the Faculty Club. He's happily retired and lives in his San Jose home, where he has the Medal of Valor and certificate, which he rightly earned, displayed on his wall of memories.

Jeff Bell

There were many good men and women in the SUDPS's New Guard during my 25 year stint, most of whom I have mentioned in the previous pages of this saga. Officers like John McMullen, Philip Love, Bob Henderson, Kris (Henderson) McNellis, Allen James, Tim Schreiner and others, who got the most ink in this effort, were people with whom I had worked on many significant cases. But, one of the most dedicated and hard working deputies in the department, who I never really got to work with on an ongoing basis was Jeff Bell. He was one of the unsung troopers who worked the midnight shift. Jeff was smart, soft spoken and could always be counted on to be on the job and on time; Jeff's uniform and equipment was always perfectly appointed, and when called upon to act, he was *Johnny on the Spot* and could always be counted on to do the right thing. I don't ever remember anyone saying a bad word about Deputy Bell. You might say that if his first name was Edward, we'd call him "Steady Eddie!"

Jeff Bell was the consummate Midnight Marauder: He was always prowling around the campus in a very visible way thus personified what we termed "preventative patrol." There is no way to measure how many crimes this man deterred, but his almost obsessive patrolling and detentions of suspicious persons, in my mind, certainly kept many would-be-intruders away. In one case, he nabbed a couple of suspicious characters in the early A.M. near the Corporation Yard and recovered a truckload of sound equipment that belonged to the Athletic Department. There were many, many other good pinches that Jeff made and although they didn't make media headlines, they nonetheless made an impact in keeping our campus safe. I tried on numerous occasions to recruit Bell into

Investigations, but he respectfully declined stating that his calling in police work was being a patrolman. And, indeed he was.

In early 2002, Bell was involved in the first officer involved shooting in our department's history: One of our CSOs reported that a suspicious person was apparently trying to break-in-to cars on Stanford Avenue near Junipero Serra. When Jeff arrived, he saw a Palo Alto PD officer talking to a subject in a parked vehicle. Bell got out of his cruiser and as he approached to back-up the other officer, the car suddenly roared to life and took-off with the officer's body being dragged along like a ragdoll. The PAPD officer had apparently reached in to turn off the ignition, but became entangled and couldn't get loose. The driver made a sudden U-turn, and attempted to dislodge the officer by literally scraping her off on the line of parked cars. Acting instinctively, Deputy Bell fired several shots into the vehicle's engine compartment in an effort to disable the car; but, realizing that shooting any more rounds might endanger his colleague, Jeff ceased fire. The imperiled cop drew her weapon and dispatched the maniac, who was literally trying to kill her! Paramedics responded immediately, but it was too late—the crook was DOA.

The deceased car thief belonged to a Redwood City chapter of the notorious prison gang known as *Nortenos*. This was not a good omen! The family of the man who was killed during the commission of multiple felonies was outraged by the police action and promised reprisals. These threats were echoed by other gang members. Chief Herrington was so concerned about the threats to Jeff and his family that he put Bell on administrative leave and relocated them to a secret location, where they remained until his retirement in November that year.

After Jeff left his calling for good, the family moved to Northern Nevada. In 2006, I heard that Jeff had contracted terminal cancer and had very little time left. Because of some medical issues that I was dealing with at the time, I was unable to join a group of department folks who had planned a tribute event in NV, so I sent him a heartfelt message basically stating what I have written here. Deputy Bell responded with an upbeat return vowing to fight his disease with all the vim and vigor that he displayed during his 25 years as one of Stanford's most dedicated and relentless Midnight Marauders! Sadly, Jeff passed away peacefully in late 2007. R.I.P. good buddy!

Doug Williams

When I began my sojourn at the newly reorganized DPS in 1974, Doug Williams was the Communications supervisor of that bunch of misfits, whom I described in some detail in Chapter Five. Try as he might, there was little Doug could do to untangle this sack of rattlesnakes; despite over one hundred documented complaints, the union made it impossible to turn this operation into a viable, functional new age communications department. So, when we opted to contract for police radio service with the City of Palo Alto in June of 1977, Chief Herrington appointed Doug Williams as our Communications and Safety Coordinator. This position soon evolved from being a mere paper-pusher to a hands-on guy, of which Williams had considerable experience: Doug was an excellent hot rod and motorcycle mechanic and soon learned nearly everything there was to know about police communications and patrol unit electronic applications. He ensured that all of our new cop cars received the state-of-the-art equipment and truly brought us out of the Neolithic Age. When I arrived, the department's patrol cars looked more like taxicabs than real police units: They were a God awful brown color, sported yellow lights and had stick-on letters on the doors: SHERIFF PATROL (sic). After several back flips, I had the cars painted white, put Sheriff's seals on the doors and grammatically added 'S. . . I also 86ed the yellow flashers for old school red "bubble gum" rotating lights on the roof. Most of the OG cars had the "old school" sirens which were driven by an engine belt. I recall my first Code 3 run back in the day at the S/O: Every time I stepped on the floor mounted siren switch, the damn car slowed down to about 15 MPH and all of the lights dimmed. This was not good! So, the primitive sirens, radios and emergency equipment controls went bye-bye. Doug soon changed all of that and brought us from the 50s into the New Age!

In addition to outfitting and maintaining our department's police equipment, Williams also ran the University's complicated alarm program. This place had more alarms than Fort Knox and it seemed that there was always some issue with them. Somehow, Doug was able to sort out the myriad of problems and still maintain his sanity and great sense of humor.

Logistics, Logistics, Logistics

As the demand for more and more services from our relatively small operation occurred, the need for a Logistics Manager was apparent, so Doug Williams was "Knighted". . . One of our biggest challenges was the deluge of Special Events that seemed to envelope us—often reaching flood stage! We needed hundreds of steel interlocking barricades for football games, other sporting events, dignitary visits, demonstrations and the like. On more than one occasion, we needed generators and floodlights to accomplish extensive, long duration search warrant operations. Doug and his crew were always up to the challenge. He developed mobile command and control operations centers, using an old RV and modular trailers. All of these centers contained communications, copiers, fax machines and other related equipment needed in the field when managing a big event. Because of a tight budget, Doug usually begged, borrowed and stole—well, not exactly—whatever he needed to get the job done. Whether it was a stake-out, search warrant, protest or head-of-state visit, Williams and company always took care of the hungry and thirsty troops—often numbering upwards of 100 personnel. Doug always made sure the troops were nourished and well hydrated. In fact, outside and allied agencies often commented that they loved coming to Stanford, if nothing else, for the great lunches and refreshments we provided. As I said before: "No dry, green baloney or peanut butter and jelly sandwiches for our troops."

Ranger Williams

In the late 1990s, Doug became Ranger Williams and was responsible for supervising the University's lands in the foothills, which we commonly referred to as "the Field Sites." Because of crime and environmental damage done to the vast area above the campus, restrictions and access to the property by non-Stanford people was put into place. The Ranger, along with other members of the DPS, vigorously patrolled this area and attempted to exact some semblance of order up there. Overall, I believe these efforts were successful as I never heard of any more murders or rapes—like we experienced in the 70s and 80s—after Doug became the ramrod of this operation. Aside from being a hard working go-to-guy, Doug Williams always comported himself in a very professional manner and was such an asset to our department that, without him, we would not have been able to accomplish some of the feats we did. Oh, and did I mention that Doug is one helluva nice guy? Doug is now enjoying his retirement with his loving wife and family, still on the beautiful Stanford campus.

Sandra Bennett Mize—Gal Friday

On the eve of his retirement, after 33 years of service to the Stanford community, Detective Carl Gielitz, a.k.a. Captain Midnight, approached me one morning and asked if I had thought about who was going to replace him. After telling Carl that nobody could ever "replace" him, I replied that we were considering the possibility of creating a non-sworn Evidence Officer's position in lieu of assigning another deputy to handle the workload Gielitz was performing. At that point, Carl's eyes lit up and announced that he had just the person: Her name was CSO Sandra Bennett Mize.

I listened intently as the detective made his sales pitch for Ms. Mize. She had quite an impressive quasi law enforcement background when she came to our department as a DPO candidate: Ms. Mize had been a Special Deputy Sheriff in San Mateo County; she later became a Redwood City Police Reserve and worked as a security officer for the Port of Redwood City. After we took Sandy on board, she successfully completed the Basic Peace Officer's Academy. However, during that period when women were first being admitted to sworn peace officer jobs, the culture made it very difficult for their success—I'm sorry to say. So, Sandra opted out of the Field Training program and accepted a CSOs position. Ms. Mize made a name for herself as the first female (CSO) on the dreaded Graveyard security shift. In that position, she excelled by continually observing numerous suspicious characters, which often resulted in apprehensions of criminals who were caught in the act of wrongdoing—by a woman, no less! Sandra was clearly one of the most proactive officers out there, and as a reward for her good work, she was transferred to the light of day as our first female Parking Enforcement Officer. I personally question whether that was a promotion or demotion, given the amount of abuse that our parking enforcement personnel endured—but that's yet another debate. . . Parking Enforcement Supervisor, Mr. Leonard Screws, assigned Mize to the worst section on campus—the medical center's lots which were always jam-packed with flagrant violators. Sandy took care of that problem in short order when she set a record for busting scofflaws, the old way, in which each citation had to be meticulously written by hand—not like today's computerized ticket dispensers. . .

After reviewing Ms. Mize's personnel file and receiving numerous accolades about her work ethic, she was appointed as

Investigation's Evidence Officer as well as Patrol's Equipment Officer. Like the CA Highway Patrol professes, she worked "all roads—all codes!" When wearing her Patrol equipment hat, she was responsible for all vehicle necessities such as first aid boxes, flares, evidence collection kits and the like. She also had to order all forms and in many cases, revised and created new ones. But, that was only part of her day.

While in her evidence realm, Sandy had to maintain the Evidence room which, over the years, had turned into a hoarder's paradise. But, Mize dove into this quagmire with all the determination of a "White Tornado:" She worked on that storage trash bin for weeks, abating crap that had been accumulating for eons. She dumped so much stale beer and booze that if the inhabitants of the Ol' Drunk Tank would have witnessed this Prohibition tactic, they surely would have gone into a total meltdown. Prior to Sandy's purge, the evidence cubby smelled like some of the fraternity houses my son worked on during the summers; however, after the "white tornado" touched-down, the little room was tolerable again.

Another nightmare Sandra had to deal with was the *bizillion* lost/stolen and abandoned bicycles that were jammed and piled high in a compound behind the Annex. One of the cases Det. Gielitz had worked on involved a creative entrepreneur who took availed himself of hundreds of bikes left for the summer by the students. This clown clipped locks and hauled the bikes off to his house, cleaned them up and offered his ill gotten gain for sale in the Fall via ads on kiosks around the campus. So, when Carl finally nabbed this thief, we were stuck with a huge gaggle of cycles, which had to be stored in the already crowded compound. Sandy untangled the mess and made some order out of the chaos. This is what can be accomplished when people work their tails off!

Because of an increase in crime, in general, our department really needed a crime scene technician (CSI) who could go into the field to collect and preserve evidence on significant cases. In addition, Crime Technicians had to be able to provide expert testimony later on in court. I sent Ms. Mize to the CA Department of Justice's prestigious Evidence Officer's school, where she was taught contemporary methods of evidence collection, preservation and the legalities of one of the most crucial aspects of modern police work. Sandra, who always took copious notes, brought back a plethora of current information from her training and schooled some of us dinosaurs—yours truly included—on some of the new and improved techniques in crime scene evidence such as: Fingerprint collection (often utilizing the Super Glue technique), ninhydrin (iodine) fuming for raising latent prints on documents, ALS (Alternative Light Source) for evidence location, and many other crime detection methods you can see on any of the television cop shows featuring Hollywood's CSI darlings.

Sandra's first example of creativity in an old evidence collection method was when I called her out to the scene of an attempted rape. The attacker left a beautiful shoe impression in the soft dirt near the location, and although we took some good 35mm photos of the print, I wanted a plaster cast. When Sandy arrived, she had assembled an impressive suitcase of needed implements of the trade. Mize mixed-up some plaster of Paris and slowly poured the slurry into the cavity, taking care not to slosh the goop into the void which could disturb the tread marks. I watched as she went into her bag of tricks and pulled out a wire coat hanger and bent it into a rectangular U shape.

"So ,why are you doing that, Sandy," I asked.

She inserted the wire into the hardening mixture and said, "So I'll have a handle when the cast solidifies." "I learned this in the school you sent me to, Captain," she retorted, thus putting me in my place. All I could do was smile, nod and shut my big mouth!

CLO/EO (Court Liaison/Evidence Officer)

Within short order, the administration realized that the department needed to expand the scope of the Evidence Technician's job description due to considerable growth in services and the level of performance by patrol personnel, which resulted in a marked increase in criminal apprehensions and prosecutions. It wasn't that crime was spiraling out of control; it was the fact that our cops were becoming very adept at catching bad guys, often before or during their criminality. I had a detective assigned to court liaison, which essentially entailed a lot of running paperwork to the Courts and S/O, thus cutting into that person's time for doing detective work and following-up on cases. With the help of my investigators and Sandy, we brainstormed a new job description which would relieve a detective of those duties and effectively put the person who got this job into a hamster's treadmill—so to speak!

Because of the SPOA (union), this job had to be offered to all bargaining members who met the minimum qualifications. And, in good faith, we interviewed several CSOs, but no one came close to Ms. Mize's resume, so she got this torturous position by default. In my biased view, there wasn't anyone around who could match Sandy's training and proven experience, so she earned that job. As I have mentioned in the "Jogging Burglar" piece, after the thrill of the arrest was over, Sandra became one of the most important hubs (not spokes or cogs) in this wheel. In addition to her evidence collection and subsequent investigation—latent fingerprint identification with the CA Department of Justice and often San Jose PD, who had an excellent analyst—Sandra managed all booking and processing operations at major special and sporting events, as well as the all important processing center during mass arrests. Ms. Mize was always there, on time and prepared! I rarely had to give her instruction because she knew what was expected and continually pushed for extra mileage. She was truly one of the department's star performers! She was not only our "Gal Friday," but our Gal

Monday-Friday, 24-7! Chief Herrington recognized Sandra's worth when, in 1999, he elevated her position to "exempt" and compensated her accordingly. Sadly, Sandy's career was cut short in the early 2000s due to a nagging back injury. She retired and relocated to the arid Southwest where she now lives with her Yorkie, "Nigel."

CHAPTER THIRTY FIVE

Bitter Rivals

Sporting Events

It's clear to me that sporting competition is the root cause of the bitter rivalry between Stanford and Cal—especially football. But, the "Great American Pastime" was a factor in the early years, too, as the Stanford baseball team clubbed Cal repeatedly from 1892-1896. Cal finally won the grudge game in 1897.

The first Big Game was played on a field in "The Haight" (Ashbury) in San Francisco, March 19, 1892. The Cardinal squad, formed in 1891, was a rag-tag bunch of kids, most of whom had never seen a football game, let alone played in one! They had zero equipment—no uniforms, and they were coach-less; these *gridders* practiced on a rock hard grass/dirt field next to Encina Hall and sometimes ran plays and drills in the dorm's hallways—probably during inclement weather. They recruited a volunteer coach, a local high school teacher, who had played some football at Lehigh during his college years.

When the motley Stanford crew arrived at the field, they were greeted to a Cal chorus of boos and chants: "Jordan's Boys. We're going to kick your asses. . ." (I made that part up, but I'd bet my guess is close to spot on!) The overmatched and relatively green Stanford football team somehow eked-out a 14-10 victory over the cocky UCB bunch. I'm sure the Cal team and their cohorts boarded the ferry and cried all the way home.

In my mind, the events that spawned this intense and tumultuous relationship, at least on the *Good-Guy's* side, was the provocative "Axe Yell," created by Will Irwin and Chris Bradley in 1896. You remember? . . . "Give 'em the axe, the axe, the axe! Where? In the neck, the neck, the neck. . ." Now, this is what I call a REAL call to arms: Nothing like threatening the opposition with beheading! Some of the greatest warriors in military history intimidated the other army with chants, yells and provocative theatre. Even today, the Fresno State Bulldogs are trying to get the NCAA to outlaw the Hawaii Warrior's Samoan war chant before kick-off; their routine is pretty scary. Being a former University of Hawaii student, I was elated when they 86ed the "Rainbows" from the team's name—how wimpy was that? Adding Warrior to their handle was more Hawaiian-like, as the original *Kanakas* were, indeed, fierce battle hardened combatants.

Now, let's take a gander at Berkeley's "Oski Yell" which was allegedly first performed around 1900:

Oski ! Wow-Wow!

Whiskey! Wee-Wee!

Olee! Munchie-eye!

Olee! Berkeley-eye!

California! Wow!

Oh, wow! Aren't you just terrified? The wimpy guys who came up with this cheer needed to be strung-up on the Campanile! No wonder the Stanford faithful call them Weenies. . .

As previously described: At the Stanford-Cal baseball game in San Francisco on April 14, 1899, an over-exuberant cheerleader, Bill Erb, did exactly what the rooting section exhorted him to do: The guy went berserk on the Golden Bear effigy with a huge lumberman's axe and reduced the mascot to confetti. The Stanford fans roared with glee; the Cal rooters were not amused. But, as I've always said: "Don't get mad, get even!" And, indeed, they did get even. The Weenies later pulled-off one of the most historic thefts in the history of this acrimonious co-existence. Following the Big Game of 1899, in which the Stanford *Kidlets* were thoroughly taken to school by Cal's mainstays (22-zip), the triumphant ones took advantage of an opportunity that curiously presented itself: The obviously dejected Farm rooters failed to secure Billy's instrument of debasement, so the victors availed themselves of the spoils, and *The Axe* was MIA for 31 years! The fervor over this trophy has never been surpassed by any idol in the history of mankind—save, perhaps, the Holy Grail. . .

After the turn of the 20th Century, both teams annually slugged-it-out on the gridiron. These contests were often described as pitched battles. The first Big Game on the Stanford Campus was played November 11, 1905 on a field near Encina Hall, which surprisingly featured a grandstand that accommodated 4,500 spectators. By all reports, this was a very *down 'n dirty* game. This was also the last Stanford-Cal Big Game for 15 years! Shortly thereafter, Stanford and UC presidents, Jordan and Wheeler, as well as faculty from both universities, decided to *axe* American rules football in favor of Australian/New Zealand rugby. They opined that rugby's fast pace and wide open style of running and passing the ball around highlighted the participant's individual skill, rather that a coached form of gladiator-like combat. Most spectators initially favored the mud, blood, and tears of the contest so Cal went back to the American way in 1912. However, Stanford fans began to fall in love with rugby and continued playing it until 1919, when they decided to go with the flow and return to the *Coliseum-like* spectacle. . . It was interesting to learn from A Chronology of Stanford and its Founders that Stanford played Big Games (rugby) versus the University of Santa Clara from 1915-1917, and took on Army in 1918.

Farm Mascots

From what I have learned, the mascot issue didn't become a significant huckleberry until *The Tree* came on the scene in 1975. Although Stanford maintained its Cardinal color from day one, they didn't have a mascot until they adopted the *Indian* in 1923. This was on the heels of a highly charged pep rally with an Indian theme prior to the Big Game that year. That, coupled with the recent unearthing of Indian burial grounds on campus sort of provided the catalyst, so the ASSU Executive Committee declared that the Native American would be Stanford's mascot. Most folks regard Indians as brave, proud people, whose warriors and hunters could easily overwhelm bears—that was a good thing—and other animals, which many college sports teams chose as their idols. However, in 1937, the stoic, imposing brave acquired a little brother: A Daily contributor created the "Lil' Injun," a caricature, which later appeared in the Daily's cartoons. While many students and alums loved the little guy, others wondered if a cartoon character was a proper rendition of the original intent of the Stanford Indian: I remember the tee shirts of the 1960s displaying a gangly little guy apparently stalking his prey, with a tomahawk in hand. He had an angular face and a disproportionately large nose, long skinny neck with a large protruding Adam's Apple; he was bare from the waist up and his skin was prominently red. It's no wonder that as the climate in the 1970s moved toward political correctness, the administration *axed* the Indian and went without a mascot until *The Tree* emerged as the odds on favorite in 1975.

When I was hired in 1974, one of Chief Herrington's main pre-game briefing points was about the Indian issue: The Big Boss in Building 10 had been getting a lot of heat from both sides. Native American groups were adamant about eliminating the Indian, while many alums were desperately trying to resurrect their fallen hero. Many pro-Indian folks sold *Lil' Injun* tee shirts and trinkets at the football tailgate parties, all the while trying to build support for their cause. A lot of these old codgers were nice fellows and would often try to engage us cops in friendly conversation about their beloved *Injun*. I avoided them like the plague as I liked my job too much... SOP (Standard Operating Procedures) at all home games was not to allow *any* Indian supporter(s) down on the field, under any circumstances—most of the rebels proudly wore their *Lil' Injun* tee shirts with unabashed fervor.

He's Baaack!

At one of the low-key games in the 80s, I was foot patrolling the area near the old stadium's ramp, when I suddenly heard a ruckus and turned around just in time to see an Indian, in full headdress and regalia, galloping down that ramp on a beautiful Paint. He charged onto the track, spear upraised while exhorting the throng. The fans went nuts! So did the Chief! He barked orders over the radio to get that damn horse off the field. At that moment, I knew exactly how Custer felt! Here we had Chief Lightfoot (Tim Williams, a Yurok Indian) prancing around on that marvelous high-stepping steed, while our Chief, I guess, wanted my foot soldiers to engage this mounted warrior. As a deputy sheriff years before, I worked some rural beats and learned that trying to make a big skittish horse do *anything* is next to impossible—especially when you don't know a damn thing about equines! I chickened out! After one circuit around the track, Chief Lightfoot made his point and as suddenly as he rode in, he rode out. We later learned the breech in security was pinned on a couple of gate tenders who were in on the plot. Pretty exciting, but we made sure this spectacle never occurred again—at least not on my watch.

What a Pair: Oski vs. the Tree

Prior to Stanford-Cal basketball games, Bay Area television stations often play a classic ESPN clip of the knock-down-drag-out *beef* between Oski and the Tree—both idiots were duking-it-out, center court, at a spirited basketball game at Maples Pavilion, Stanford. Now, this wasn't just a choreographed, staged, dramatic WWE routine—this was the real deal, as both clowns in their ridiculous suits were trying to hurt one another. It took SUDPS' big, strapping young Detective, Tim Schreiner, in uniform for that event, to pull the pugilists apart. Good thing the combatants were heavily padded and the Tree didn't get any of his limbs torn off. . .(Oski busted: See photo page 641.) But, let's go back a few years, to the summer of 1986.

All Right Now

I heard a news flash that the UC Berkeley news bureau had just reported their enormous 6-foot, 200 pound stuffed Grizzly bear was MIA from its display case in the ASUC Student Union. We later received a BOL from UC Police. *Hmmmm, I wonder who did this?* I mused.

Shortly thereafter, I received my daily call from daughter, Nina, who was working at the Conference Office. After a little chit-chat, I gleefully said:

"Hey, Nina, did you hear that person(s) unknown ripped-off the Weenie's Golden Bear sometime last night?"

"No, I didn't," Dad. "Hey, wait. Theresa (her roomie) and I heard The Band playing their theme song ("All Right Now") last night and we both wondered why The Band was on campus during summer break. I'll bet those guys did it."

"That's exactly what I was thinking." I confirmed. "Well, I think we are going to be in for it this fall when those *Bezerkeley* numbskulls finally figure out this one."

In researching this event, it seemed evident to this now retired investigator that the LSJUMB was the culprit—Now, understand that I don't have a shred of evidence nor one iota of proof—just call it an educated guess, or maybe my God gifted Sixth Sense...

According to Daily Californian reports, the hostage takers of the Golden Bear, who, in ransom demand notes, referred to their prize as "Oskie" (sic—with emphasis on the "e," intimating ignorance of the *bear-nappers*—as if everyone should have known that the bear's name is spelled OSKI)—Just call me stupid, I didn't know that! Actually, the Grizzly bear that the stealthy interlopers *rescued* had been at the university when the institution was first organized. Although Oski, the goofy looking mascot, came on the scene in 1941, the so-called "Oski Yell" was first performed around 1900.

The Play

Nearly every year, as college football dominates TV programming, you have undoubtedly seen that disgusting "Play" clip, in which Stanford lost the Big Game at Cal in 1982, 25-20, with only 4 seconds left in regulation play. All experts have concluded that a Bear player's knee was clearly down when he received one of many laterals; the video confirmed that a referee signaled the play was over. However, victory for Stanford was snatched from their grasp because the gutless *Zebras* didn't make the call. And, when LSJUMB rushed onto the field (and that caused me to stick another pin in my Band's *Macumba* doll), the lily-livered refs refused to stop the game due to fan interference. In my view, this event was the greatest travesty of justice in the history of American sports. The only gratifying moment in that fiasco, for me, was when the trombone player got knocked on his posterior. I could write a book on the final minute of that game and then you'd know how I *really* feel. This debacle subsequently cost a great guy (Coach Paul Wiggins), former Stanford All-American and NFL standout, his coaching career on the Farm. The team was so traumatized by "The Play," their fire was extinguished and they went 1 and 10 the next season. I'll never forget hearing the Cal chorus during the 1983 Big Game at Stanford: "One and Ten, Try it Again!" That hurt. And, the UCB team won their second Big Game in a row, which stung like a yellow jacket... Too bad the Band didn't resurrect the taunt they used in the Big Game of 1967:

"*The dirty golden bear did something quite unfair.*"

"*The cops were lax; He stole the Axe.*"

"*Now no one knows where it's at.*"

"*The theft showed no real class.*"

"*And Axe Committee called it crass.*"

"*So let's give 'em the goddamn axe; And shove it up his . . .*"

The only redeeming factor after *The Play* debacle was the clever sting put on the Weenies by some very bright staffers at the Stanford Daily. Working tirelessly, day and night immediately after that travesty, the Daily concocted an unprecedented scam, in my view, never, ever surpassed in the annals of "PAYBACK'S A BITCH!"

The following Monday, as Cal students flocked to the locations where their "fish wrapper," The Daily Californian, was deposited. Many of the readers were eager to delve into their copy in order to relive the moment when their invincible Bears outwitted those hoity-toity, spoiled rich kids from across the Bay. But, after glancing at page one, the Weenies writhed, gritted their teeth, convulsed—some even hurled:

EXTRA

THE DAILY

CALIFORNIAN

SERVING THE CAMPUS COMMUNITY SINCE 1892

VOLUME XIV, NO.51 WEDNESDAY, NOVEMBER 24, 1982
BERKELEY, CALIFORNIA

Three days later, it's 20-19

NCAA awards Big Game to Stanford

Bears shocked, and appalled

Decision stuns Joe Kapp

[Photo of Coach Kapp]

Joe Kapp: "Life isn't fair—I swear to God it isn't"

See Page 4

This unprecedented stunt was huge—the Weenies were stung by a swarm of African Killer Bees! Oh, by the way, as in the Stanford Daily's annual April Fools' edition, there is NO page 4!

El Palo Alto: The Tree

The real *Tree* is still alive and well on the banks of the San Francisquito Creek near the ECR. Thanks to the efforts of the City of Palo Alto, a concrete berm was recently constructed around its base, so "The Tall Tree" wouldn't suffer the same fate as its sister, who slipped into the creek many years ago due to severe erosion. When first spotted in 1769 by adventurer Gaspar de Portola, the twin redwoods were a landmark that could be seen from miles away; the trees were believed to be 1,000 years young. Stanford University adopted the towering redwood on their seal in 1908 and in the 1920s, made it the centerpiece of their corporate seal. Later, the green tree was embossed in the big block S of sports attire. The SUDPS similarly featured this icon on the officers' shoulder patches. Several of these department patches were designed by the late Captain Bill Wullschleger's widow, Crystal, who worked in the office for many years.

While the Stanford Family reveres *The Tree* symbol, its detractors abhor not only the symbol, but its handcrafted 11 1/2 foot replication, worn at most sporting events. It seems like all of the PAC-12 schools delight in peppering this mascot with great regularity. If I was paid a dollar for every instance *The Tree* was attacked and pummeled during my 25 year tenure, I could probably send my granddaughter to the finest university on the planet, without dipping into my reserve. In a clever article written by Edwin Garcia, a staff writer for the San Jose Mercury News, the attack by *U-Dubb* band members on November 8, 1994 illustrates what happened to *The Tree* more often than not. I couldn't have written this piece better and I was an eyewitness, so here it is in its entirety:

Stanford Tree felled again

Jumped by Husky band members, the plucky mascot fought back

The Stanford Tree, that wild and wacky mascot with the university's irreverent band, now does more than a dance-and-cheer routine for thousands of football fans – it defends itself from predators.

The 11 ½ foot, cone-shaped evergreen was uprooted once again this time by a pack of Huskies, 15 to 20 University of Washington band members, during the halftime at Stanford Stadium on Saturday.

You'd think the student-in-the-tree-suit was ready for the saw mill. He was beaten by Cal fans last year, beaten in a parking lot at Northwestern University in September, and he expects another bruising later this month when Stanford plays Cal.

But this tree is made of sturdier stuff.

"I do it because I love Stanford and I feel it's the best expression of the way I feel about the university," said Ari Mervis, 19, whose trunk was quite sore on Monday as he repaired the huge costume."

"Not only did they tackle me, but they were throwing punches, kicking and grabbing at the costume, pulling pieces of it off," said Mervis, of Chicago. "I fought them off as best I could."—which must have been hard with a dozen attackers all over his bark. And his hands were sticking out among strips of green fabric that resemble pine needles.

"They were trying to rip off his limbs!" said Stanford Police Capt. Raoul Niemeyer.

A student from Redmond Wash., Alexander Soriano Balente, was arrested on suspicion of misdemeanor battery. Last year, five Cal fans were arrested for beating the tree.

Saturday's attack angered Stanford's assistant band manager, Chris Quaintance: "The tree costume was trashed, and we're sending a bill for that to the athletic department at the University of Washington," said Quaintance, 20. "Repairs will top $100,"he said.

"Stanford's last home game is Saturday against the University of Oregon, whose fans and band aren't expected to harm the tree."

But, a week later, Stanford plays its last game of the year at Cal, its archrival. LSJUMB members are certain to BOL (be on the lookout) for lumberjacks among the Berkeley fans.

"We're going out there with the knowledge that we'll likely be attacked and there's really nothing we can do," said Mervis. "We have to take that risk because we're the Stanford band."

Hostage

Beaten repeatedly and stolen several times—now, our beloved Tree has been burgled and held hostage by those pesky ruffians from across the Bay! In late October, one month before the upcoming Big Game of 1998, person(s) unknown broke into the LSJUMB Shak in the early AM. Shortly thereafter, one of our alert coppers espied a suspicious vehicle driving around (at about 0430 Oct. 17), and the deputy lit-up the night. Subsequent inquiry revealed the occupants were a bunch of Cal students who were shaking like leaves on *El Palo Alto* in a windstorm. . .When asked what they were doing, the driver gulped and said they were looking for a party. Yeah, I believe that: Five UCB kids looking for a party at Stanford at O-Dark 30? Gimme a break, guys! They were FIed and released as there was no evidence of the purloined Stanford mascot's costume in their car. It was later determined that these five dudes and their car had been seen poking around the Shak.

The scene of the crime revealed that the Shak was entered by force; the burglars broke a window, entered and then broke down a door, and busted through a sheetrock wall in order to access the costume.

Initially, I called UC Berkeley and offered the *perps* total amnesty if the mascot was returned unharmed. The UCB cops said they'd pass the word on to the hierarchy and to the student body. Kudos to UC Chancellor Robert Berdahl, for he announced that if the Tree was not returned by midnight Wednesday, Oski would be benched for that weekend's game. I thought that we were *golden*, but I was fooled. That very Wednesday, a group who called themselves the "Phoenix Five" assembled local media, including TV station KTVU Channel 2, and put on a dog and pony show; the *Five* paraded the blindfolded Tree and a character in a Grim Reaper's suit in front of the camera. There was also some dialogue that the Tree was happy to be rid of the Farm and lauded the wonderful UCB hostage-takers for their humane treatment and for rescuing the foliated mascot. *Hmmmm*, I figured, *they must have watched the confessions of our downed airmen in the Hanoi Hilton!* The Tree-nappers further stated they simply wanted the public to know their captive was in good hands, would not be injured and would be repatriated before the Big Game on November 21st.

Like most deadlines, "they just come and go," so I decided to ratchet-up the rhetoric and play some *hardball* with these Cal hucksters. After identifying (DL Photo) the driver of the vehicle that was stopped possibly minutes after the Tree was ripped-off, I sent a couple of detectives to Cal to have a *friendly chat* with him. Accompanied by uniformed UCB cops, our guys showed the flag and stormed into the kid's Frat. Of course, this suspect denied any complicity in the crime, but looked like he was about to soil his shorts... That tactic served its purpose as it put the *Phoenix Five* on notice that we were hot on their trail.

In news releases with the media, I really poured it on. I sternly defined the element of the crime as:

459 P.C. of the CA Penal Code states that: Every person who enters any house, room apartment—bla bla bla—building. . . . with the intent to commit grand or petit larceny or any other felony is guilty of burglary.

461 P.C. Burglary is punishable as follows:

1. Burglary in the first degree: By imprisonment in the state prison for a term for two, four, or six years.

2. Burglary in the second degree: By imprisonment in the county jail not exceeding one year or in state prison.

I kept the *Five's* feet to the fire by trumpeting to the press in a series of statements: "First," I said, "we were tired of being 'jacked around.' Our initial effort to get the Tree back was to grant amnesty. This is now null and void! There is nothing about this that is a joke! If you do the crime, you'll do the time! We've IDed one of the burglars, got his DMV photo, and have witnesses who saw this guy lurking around the Band Shak. Once we get an arrest warrant for this individual, I'm confident that he'll flip and we'll know who the rest of the *Phoenix Five* are."

Needless to say, my comments were a tad ominous. A long time celebrity at KTVU thought I was a bit heavy-handed and admonished "Captain Ogre" on the air: "After all, this was a prank and these were just college kids," he announced. I suspect that my nemesis was a Cal sympathizer—maybe even a Weenie!

Well, after the press releases, we got a call that our mascot would be returned ASAP, if I called-off the pit bulls. Agreed! And, at about 6:00 PM on Nov. 1st, a UCB patrol unit pulled into our police parking lot. An older gentleman, obviously not a member of the *Phoenix Five*—unless he was a perennial grad student—returned Stanford's cherished mascot. Although Chris Henderson, the kid behind the mask, wasn't there, I know he was pleased. All's well that ends well.

P.S. In my 35 years as a cop, this was one of my finest hours: If the truth be known, I didn't have one shred of evidence to charge anyone in this caper! That's right, kids, I pulled-off the ultimate bluff. . . Cracks-me-up, to this day! Those Weenies swallowed the bait like a Louisiana gator. I guess that was predictable as the

Phoenix Five clearly weren't the "Brightest Bears in the Woods." I wish I had been in a poker game with them—my winnings might have paid for my daughter's medical school.

LSJUMB

The Leland Stanford Junior University Marching Band may be a lot of things, but a marching band they are NOT! Our bitter rivals across the Bay have a marching band; the obnoxious University of "Spoiled Children" have a marching band, albeit led by a pompous, arrogant leader; the Huskies of U-Dubb have a pretty good marching band, too; but the best marching band in the USA—if not the world—is the high stepping group from Grambling—They ARE *The Incomparable MARCHING BAND!* While the rag-tag bunch from Stanford can't march, they can surely render entertaining halftime shows, however controversial...

While the Band's halftime routines are always a mystery until they unfold, their pre-game activity is as predictable as sunrise: After throwing down a *few* eye-opening toddies—more, not less—they suit-up, grab their instruments and straggle over to Chuck Taylor Grove, where the *crème de la crème* alums party. Now, my idea of tailgating is having a few brews, squatting down over a hibachi and burning some dogs and burgers. Not this set, who actually conceived the Cardinal's favorite pastime, way back when motorcars first started crawling around the Farm. Later on, the alums utilized the tailgates of their 20s-30s Caddies, Lincolns, Buicks, and maybe a Deusy* or two, to haul their exquisite cuisine, choice nectar of the vine and accoutrements: Antique tables and chairs, candelabras, fine china, exquisite silverware, crystal wine goblets—oh, and let's not forget the red and white table cloths and napkins... Let the party begin. This group was later coined the "wine and cheese crowd."

*Duesenbergs were high-end luxury cars built between 1917-1937 in Auburn, IN.

Save for the automobiles—Escalades and Navigators now being the rides of choice—the spread is identical to when the Indian reigned. Enter LSJUMB: At this point in their pre-game warm-up, they break-up into smaller groups and become roving *Mariachis,* playing tunes for food and libation. And, if you've been to a Cardinal football game, with kick-off slated for 1:05 PM, you will have undoubtedly noted that the *Mariachis* are entertaining tailgaters as early as 10:00 AM: They play a few tunes, eat and imbibe—mostly imbibe—until they have to line-up at the Band Gate at about 12:00 Noon. So, is there any doubt in your mind why Stanford's musicians are often a tad off-key by game time?

Once herded just inside the gate, the goons from SUDPS and the SEP shook-down this bunch as if they were being booked into the County's Main Jail. Once in a while, a few cans of beer were confiscated from the *newbies,* but more often than not, the cops found *NADA.*

BTW, in 1978, Constitutional Amendment XVIII, took effect at Stanford Stadium, much to the chagrin of students and some alums. During my first four years at Stanford, there were countless fights, rock throwing incidents and general unruliness, clearly due to alcohol abuse. In the olden days, fans were allowed to bring large coolers of beer, wine and booze with impunity.

After numerous fights, many resulting in injuries and subsequent lawsuits, the astute Assistant Athletic Director, Ray Young, convinced the Administration that we needed to stop allowing alcohol into the stadium. Cooler heads prevailed and the ban was put into effect and proved its worth in gold! It cost a few more bucks to enforce the ban as we had to hire more and better security officers, but it kept most of the contraband out. More on this short-lived ban later...

Based on what I have written so far about the Band, one might get the notion that I disliked the LSJUMB; not at all. In fact, I really got a kick out of those zany, rebellious and creative kids. They always seemed to pull the wool over our eyes: Shortly after the ban on booze began and the members were searched, I was glassing the group from our Command Center high up in the Press Box when I spotted a guy handing out beverages—certainly not soda! A closer look revealed they actually had a blender on their band box and were churning out *Margaritas*!

And, to add insult to injury, they brought an extension cord and were running their machine with University power. Well, in retrospect, with what their parents had to pay, even then, I guess they were entitled to a few amps...

Deep Do-Do

You know it always seemed that the band was like that proverbial guy in Hell who was placed in a vat of raw sewage; he was standing on his tiptoes and the level was at his bottom lip. All he could say was: "Please, don't make waves!" But, they always did. I generally loved their halftime shows as the skits clearly showed that these kids didn't just dream-up the routine the night before, like many students do on term papers... I was almost always in the Command Center for halftime so I'd have a bird's-eye-view of the extravaganza. Then, over the very loud public address system, a commanding baritone voice boomed:

"And, Now! The One—The Only—The Incomparable— Leland Stanford Junior University Marching Band!"

From the sideline, a herd of kids in a variety of *uniforms* and costumes scrambled onto the playing field with their instruments and assumed their positions—whatever they were, indiscernible to the fans until the announcer clued-us-in. Katy Bar the Door! *What would they do now,* cringed the University President and Athletic Director? LSJUMB, the Band Director and only God knew. . .

Major Spankings

While most of the Band's routines were comical and directed at other teams and current events, they often crossed the line—Big Time, and received several well deserved corporal punishments for their indiscretions.

F-up #1: At a 1990 Oregon University game at the "Quackers" stadium, our Band teased the OU fans with a show that lampooned the very sensitive controversy over the Spotted Owl. This was a major hot button in the Northwest, as the "Tree Huggers" wanted a moratorium on logging old growth forests where the endangered owl resided. But, the foresters' livelihood was in play here. Not a bright idea to go to someone's backyard and harass them about an issue that had economic as well as environmental consequences!

F-up #2: In 1991 at a home game vs. Notre Dame, some morons got the bright idea to dress-up a band member like a Maryknoll nun: I knew that order of nuns well as I got my knuckles rapped with a ruler on more than one occasion by those hard-nosed sisters when I was in St. Augustine's Elementary School, HI. The pseudo nun then conducted the band with a large crucifix. Later on, the imposter gallivanted around the track until a group of Irish supporters charged onto the field and gang slapped the irreverent one. Notre Dame banished the LSJUMB from their venue, indefinitely.

F-up #3: There's an old saying, "Once Burned, Twice Learned." Not this group, however: After receiving a huge Administration flogging following the heretical behavior at the Notre Dame game in 1991, the wild bunch continued on their errant ways in 1997 when The Fighting Irish came back to the Farm. Their tasteless show was a spoof on Ireland's Great Potato Famine of 1845, in which over a million people perished and another million emigrated to America. What didn't the Band understand about religious and ethnic bigotry?

F-up #4: Another religious poke in the eye occurred at the 2004 Brigham Young University game in Provo, UT. Five knuckleheads, the Band's dancers, traipsed around during the intermission wearing bridal veils. . . Boy, I'll bet Joseph Smith and Brigham Young thought that one was about as funny as a heart attack!

The Devil Within

After a cry for improved crime prevention and safety awareness on campus, I created the SSU, Special Services Unit. Comprised of Stanford students, we essentially force-fed safety and security concerns to the students in their own environment: We learned a long time before that brochures and pamphlets about making a student's life safe and secure was like shoveling sand against the tide. My manager, Dan Smith, and his charges developed an outreach program, wherein the SSU kids literally brought "the mountain to Mohammed!" I gave Dan free reign in running the program, as he understood the elements of crime prevention, having performed that function for several years at another department. More importantly, Smith worked well with the community, especially the students. Over the years, we had dozens of energetic young men and women cycle through our unit. I frequently met with Dan and the SSU group to discuss upcoming efforts and always met new members after they were hired. At one such gathering, Dan introduced me to a very attractive young woman; she seemed very cordial and of course, being a Stanford student, she was as bright as the sun. The only problem I had with this newbie was her purple hair. So, after the meeting, I had a *pow-wow* with Mr. Smith and asked him:

"Dan, what's the deal with the hair?

Dan smiled and said: "Captain, she's a really nice person and smart, too!"

"Oh, I'm sure your judgment is correct, but I'm concerned how the Chief is going react to a purple-headed SSU member representing the department," I opined.

"Well, Captain," Dan continued, "I guess her hair is part of her persona: She's a member of the Band!" I swear to God, I almost fell out of my chair.

Dan then admitted that most of the best kids in SSU were, in fact Band members. *You've got to be kidding me,* I mused. *The LSJUMB has infiltrated our department; they'll know all our secrets! This is how the CIA operates.* After my BP returned to 125/70, I realized that these kids had done an excellent job with our program. And, if I had micro-managed the SSU, we might never have achieved our goals without the diverse talent Dan recruited. The young woman in question later dyed her hair black and asked me if I could teach her to ride a motorcycle. After only one short lesson in a school parking lot, the gal was zooming around on her Ninja 500! She scared the hell outta me! I saw her the following summer and her hair was green. Well, at least there weren't any spikes!

I realized then that first impressions and stereotypes are often dead wrong!

Before I go onto the final chapters of my three and a half decades in law enforcement, I wanted to mention that after two years on the lam, Cal's beloved 6-foot stuffed Grizzly, *Oski,* suddenly appeared on the streets of San Francisco, none the worse for wear, save for a badly broken left paw. The night after the 1988 Big Game, which was knotted 19 all—the rivalry's last tie—the "trophy" was found chained to the Vaillancourt Fountain at Justin Herman Plaza, sporting a Stanford tank top. So, is there any question who was responsible for this whodunnit? Well, it's "All Right Now!"

CHAPTER THIRTY SIX

Football & My Last Big Game

Prologue

The August 20, 2011 NFL pre-season game between the Oakland Raiders and San Francisco Forty-Niners sparked the writing of this chapter today, although my thoughts about the nightmare of policing football games at Stanford had been stowed away in my brain for decades. The debacle at Candlestick Park this weekend not only resulted in a beat-down of the Raiders on the field, but this intense rivalry permeated the entire stadium during and after the contest: As seen on TV newscasts, vicious fights broke out in the stands throughout the game, with gangs of thugs—judging from their jerseys, both 9er and Raider "fans"—raining blows on one another, while a circle of losers cheered them on! A twenty-six year old man was found unconscious in a restroom, the victim of a savage beating by unknown perpetrators; last heard, he was in guarded condition at a Bay Area Trauma Center. This pummeling is reminiscent of a similar event that occurred after a S.F. Giants/L.A. Dodger baseball game at the Dodger ballpark: The victim was a young father of two and was beaten senseless by two gang-banger Dodger "fans" who put their "adversary" into a comatose state for many weeks. Although now awake, the poor guy suffered irreparable brain damage—the long term effects of this drubbing still remain undetermined. (On October 11, 2011, this poor man was finally released from intensive care and transferred to a rehab center, where he will undergo treatment until he can rejoin society in some capacity).

While many of the fans enjoyed post game tailgate parties, one unknown assailant entertained himself by blasting two apparent Raider supporters with a firearm; the lucky one only sustained superficial face wounds, while the dude who was wearing a "Fuck Niners" shirt, suffered four life threatening gunshots to his abdomen. This was the absolute worst display of violence I have ever heard of or seen at any sporting event—and I policed a lot of them during my 25 years on the Farm.

For the Love of the Game

In 1975, I became an assistant coach with the Campbell "Pee-Wee" football team (90-110 lbs), sponsored by the San Jose Police Activities League (PAL). My son, Kirk, then a mere 8 years old, was knocking heads with some pretty big, tough kids. He didn't play much that year, but learned the fundamentals of the game which aided his later successes. After winning the Northern California Championship, the Head Coach stepped down and handed me the reigns. This was going to be a daunting task as I was right in the middle of rebuilding the Stanford DPS. Whenever I had a spare moment, I dove into the stacks of Green Library searching for books on how to coach football. I read everything written by every famous coach, starting with Stanford's greatest mentor, Glenn Scobey "Pop" Warner (see page 707)*, Vince Lombardi, and perhaps one of the best teachers of the game, George Allen.

My first playbook featured a lot of Pop Warner's novel formations and plays—this drove the competing coaches nuts, as they had no idea how to counter some of those plays of yesteryear. One coach even complained to the PAL officials about my unorthodox formations and plays. I subsequently told the man that he needed to do more research and less sniveling. . . Although our main formations were contemporary, I had fun throwing in what I called: "The Wrinkle of the Week." The kids loved it, much to the chagrin of our opponents. I coached PAL for five years until Kirk went to high school. I later became a Defensive Coordinator at Gunn High School (Palo Alto) for two years and loved the kids, the game and my contribution to youth in the community. But, as you will soon see, there is one helluva difference between loving, playing and coaching football *and policing* the often volatile college games.

*Coach Warner was a Cornell alum and guard on their football team. He coached at many universities beginning with Georgia in 1885. From there he taught the game at Iowa State, Cornell (twice), Carlisle Indian, Pittsburgh, Stanford, Temple, and even at my alma mater, San Jose State, as an associate. This College Football Hall of Fame coach took Pittsburgh to three national championships from 1915-1918. In 1926, Warner swept the nation with Stanford's squad after only two seasons on the Farm. Among his achievements are:

- The screen pass
- Spiral punt
- Single and double-wing formations
- Shoulder and thigh pads
- Designated helmets: Backs wore red, ends white.

While at Stanford, Warner took Cardinal teams to three Rose Bowl games. The most notable contest was against Notre Dame's vaunted coach, Knute Rockne, and his Four Horsemen—and that was in Pop's first year! Although the Cardinal lost 27-10 (primarily due to turnovers), they actually outplayed the Irish, thanks to the effort of the entire team and outstanding play of All-American, Ernie Nevers, who was named co-Rose Bowl Player of the game. This accolade was proclaimed retroactively in 1953, when the award was first created. Coach Warner is widely known for his contribution to youth sports, hence the Pop Warner League honors the memory of his innovations in American football.

****

Football on the Farm

My first experience in policing a Stanford football game occurred in 1968 when the Cardinal was hosting the U.S. Air Force Academy. I was a member of the Sheriff's Crowd Control Unit at that time. At first glance, this should have been a ho-hum event because neither team was a barn burner at that point in time. However, the protest over the Vietnam War was picking-up a full head of steam: With our B-52s bombing the *Ho Chi Minh* Trail, guess who the target was? A contingent of nearly 200 motley dissidents from San Francisco was creating quite a ruckus in the area adjacent to the Stanford alum section. Despite efforts by gate security, the protesters managed to smuggle-in banners, signs and sticks, which was outlawed by the university—not because it was a political issue, but for the safety and comfort of other fans who didn't want to have to look through signs and banners, or be beaten over the head by a clown with a stick. This rule also applied to umbrellas. So, our Sergeant came up to me and my partner Dick Cabral (a husky tough dude who later eschewed the gun and badge for a coach's clipboard and a whistle) and said:

"Niemeyer, you and Cabral go in there and get those sticks and signs from those protesters!" *Yeah, right,* I thought. *Easy for you to say; just go in there and get that stuff. We are going to need a whole squad of guys...*

But, alas, we didn't have a squad. Dick and I were it! The other Sheriff's teams were spread out all over the stadium when they were really needed here, where the trouble was. But, being good soldiers, we waded into the mob of Haight-Ashbury "Flower Children." Luckily, the main troublemaker wasn't too far in from the aisle. For those of you who remember the Old Stanford Stadium, you might recall how treacherous those stands and stairs were—steep, rickety and very well worn wooden stairs (built in 1921); the bleachers were long, with passageways barely wide enough to shuffle along empty, let alone when fans were packed in there like sardines and had large ice chests crammed in there, too. I approached the dude in question and said:

"Ok, buddy, sticks and signs are not allowed in the stadium; hand it over!"

The kid gave me the middle finger and said something unkind about my mother, whereupon I snatched the stick out of his hand before he could blink an eyelash. The guy stood up and made an aggressive move toward me so I countered with a reverse wrist lock and walked him out (he was on his tippie-toes, which is what that hold tends to cause a resister do) and up the stairs. This caused a very negative audience reaction and we immediately took "incoming:" rocks (there were plenty of them under the seats—big ones, too), soda cans, spit, liquids, ice—you name it, they pelted us with it—even from so-called neutral or just random fans, for Chrissakes! This scenario repeated itself several more times for Deputy Cabral and I before the final gun. At the end of our shift, I remember commenting to my partner: "You know Dick, this is bullshit! I'd rather go break-up a big fight in a cowboy bar than to go into that stadium ever again. I can't believe I volunteered for this crappy detail!"

****

USC vs. Stanford (1974)

I had obviously forgotten about what I told Deputy Cabral way back in 1968, for I had just been hired as Stanford's Patrol Captain, and among many other duties, I was in charge of football policing. In retrospect, I must have been suffering from amnesia. I was very worried about our final home game vs. USC (thankfully, the Big Game was scheduled to be played in Berkeley), as we only had 8 uniformed deputies in the stadium, plus the Chief, Cap'n Bill and myself. We could really be in for it if something major occurred, although we still had "Elton's Raiders"—many off duty Sheriff's deputies in red Security blazers (Red Coats), who could be called on as a last resort. And, next to Cal, the "University of Second Choice" was #2 on Stanford's hate list. . . Plus, we had nearly sold-out the place with over 80,000 boisterous fans in attendance. Our cops had a number of disturbance calls but the incidents were all resolved amicably. The order of the day was to avoid making arrests unless an officer or public safety was in jeopardy.

After the game ended and the crowd was streaming out of the stadium, we got a call from a Red Coat reporting gunfire in a parking lot near Master's Grove. All hands hustled over there. When I arrived, both suspected shooters were already in handcuffs. The intended "victims," about four of them, were also being detained. As the story unfolded, there was a helluva lot more to the situation than what met the original eye: As it turned out, the so-called victims had been harassing the two arrestees throughout the game. Our officers responded twice to the scene of this disturbance and finally relocated the two USC fans who had been targeted for unwarranted bullyragging. The men were from Los Angeles, and were, by all accounts, merely minding their own business when the bullies behind them began dousing them with beer, ice, hotdog mustard, etc., all the while hurling insults about their race and choice of teams. After the game was over, the four thugs spotted the two black men, followed them into the parking lot and threatened to "kick their asses."

When the two men reached their vehicle, the group of guys continued to threaten these fellows, whereupon, one of the tormented guys produced a small caliber handgun and popped a couple of caps at the foursome. Luckily, no one was hit, and an off-duty S/O deputy witnessed the fray and took the shooter into custody. This stupidity, on both sides, nearly got someone killed or injured—much like the Raider/Niner debacle described in the

Prologue. While I kind of felt sorry for the men who were harassed, I lectured them about taking the law into their own hands, before they took the short ride to North County Jail.

The Zoo

The Oakland Raiders have an end zone called The Black Hole; back in the day, we called our North end zone "The Zoo!" These were the cheap seats, occupied by all sorts of people who weren't necessarily football fans per se, but they sure loved a good fight—and there were plenty of them.

One of the chief contributors to the melees was the PATs: In the old days, the ball was kicked straight-on; even when the rules allowed the kickers to use tees, the resultant kick was never a gimme, so *if* the ball cleared the uprights, it almost *never* went into the stands. The exception to this style of PAT kicking was the world record field goal kicker, Tom Dempsey. Although Tom had a deformed foot (he was born without toes on his right foot as well as a fingerless right hand), he wore a specially reinforced square tip shoe, which many critics felt gave him a huge advantage over those who kicked with conventional round toe shoes*. Prior to being drafted into the NFL, Dempsey kicked for a semi-pro team called the San Jose Apaches, who played their home games at San Jose City College. I used to go to those games and marveled at how far this man could boot that pigskin: He'd kick that thing out of the end zone on nearly every kick-off! A number of times, I also saw him kick field goals of over fifty-yards in practice.

*Wikipedia: The NFL later created the so-called "Tom Dempsey Rule" in 1977, which mandated that "any shoe that is worn by a player with an artificial limb on his kicking leg must have a kicking surface that conforms to that of a normal kicking shoe."

On November 8, 1970, while playing for the hapless New Orleans Saints—known by their disgruntled fans as the "Aints:" Many of the "unfaithful" even wore paper bags over their heads with eye and breathing holes, of course—Tom Dempsey was called into the game with a mere 2 seconds left in regulation, trailing the Detroit Lions 17-16. The ball was placed down on the Saint's 37 yard line. Former Lion's player, Alex Karras, best described the event as "a cannon going off" when Dempsey booted the ball. No one in that stadium could believe their eyes when the ball cleared the bar with only a few feet to spare—a 63 yard game winner, which shattered the 17 year record of 56 yards. Prior to 1974, the uprights were positioned on the goal line. (Field goals are measured from "line to gain" to the upright's crossbar.) The NFL's 1974 rule placed the goal posts on the end line of the end zone, so you must now add 10 yards to any field goal attempt. Jason Elam, the Denver Bronco's kicker, later equaled Dempsey's feat, but that was at Mile High Stadium, so the altitude gave Elam the edge. And, then on Monday Night Football, September 13, 2011, Oakland Raider's place kicker, Sebastian Janikowski—The Polish Cannon—tied Dempsey and Elam's efforts, albeit at Denver, but it *was* during a rain squall.

By the late 1970s, nearly all kickers adopted the soccer style of striking the ball with the side of their foot. This phenomenon not only created great distances, but also caused the pigskin to fly higher. Herein was the problem at Stanford Stadium: Although the lower wall around the perimeter of the stadium had a 6' wire mesh fence on top of it, the PATs soared into the stands. Dozens of juveniles swarmed to the ball, wanting a brand new souvenir and they fought tooth and nail for the prize. At first, we decided not to intervene as the wrestling matches for the ball were usually of short duration and the situations often stabilized within a few minutes. However, when the fights for the spoils became more aggressive and kids were getting hurt after being pummeled by bigger, stronger youths (many in their late teens and twenties), the deputies were forced to break-up the fracases. This, of course, brought forth an uproar of boos and hisses from the crowd and the officers were summarily showered with cans, rocks, liquid and ice. This was simply a no-win situation due to complaints from alums when we didn't act and displeasure from rabble-rousers when we did. Clearly, going into the Zoo for any reason was not something our cops relished...

Being the liaison with DAPER (Department of Athletics, Physical Education, and Recreation), I begged the grounds staff to install a catch net similar to what the NFL and other NCAA schools employed. Their first attempt was paltry at best: They put up a couple of flag poles and a net, but it was too short so the balls kept sailing into the stands. Thanks to the efforts of Assistant Director, Ray Young, taller poles and a *real* net solved the problem. This not only saved our department a lot of grief, but the Athletic Department benefitted by not losing all of those new footballs!

The Trojan Marching Band

It was another superb Fall day on the Farm. Unfortunately, our entire department and our contingent of 100 SEPs (Special Event Patrol) had our hands full with over 85,000 exuberant fans at Stanford Stadium. The first half didn't go well for the Cardinal footballers or Stanford's finest public safety officers, either: On our front, the police teams had responded to numerous disturbance calls and had to make several arrests for drunken, disorderly behavior. While that was going on, our field deputies were contending with the USC marching band—especially their pompous-ass band director: The USC band had been admonished by our field supervisor not to venture over to the Stanford rooting section under any circumstance. The director gave the sergeant a lot of lip but reluctantly agreed to keep his legions in the middle of the field. But, as soon as the halftime show began, that idiot led his large group straight over to the Stanford sideline and played a few bars of the home team's theme song: "All Right Now!" Talk about rubbing salt into a gaping wound! Predictably, the Cardinal faithful responded with a barrage of rotten fruit, which thoroughly pelted the intruders. Shortly after the barrage, the Spoiled Children's musicians (I have to admit that they are pretty good) retreated out of range—to the middle of the playing field where they were supposed to be in the first place. Then, the condescending ass of a leader came up to me and complained that had we been doing our job, his precious darlings wouldn't have been assaulted by the Stanford hooligans. While I was telling the maestro basically to get off his high "Trojan" horse, a Stanford band member snuck-up on an unsuspecting flute player, purloined his helmet and disappeared into the throng. The band director went berserk and demanded that we not only retrieve the "souvenir," but that we apprehend the culprit and bring the thief to justice. *Yeah, right,* I thought, but dutifully replied that we would do our best to recover that stupid USC helmet—*Maybe,* I mused further, *and in due time. . .*

"John L. Sullivan"

Suddenly, my attention was diverted to a huge fight that was going on in the Zoo: There must have been a half dozen people pushing and shoving in the middle of the end zone seats. One of the dudes was shirtless and was raining serious blows on his opponents. About four of our deputies fought their way through the mob and tried to subdue this maniac—without much success. As the melee continued, then Lt. Marvin Moore weighed into the fray and received a swift kick in the groin by the "Roid Monster." It took about 6 deputies to drag this pugilist out of the stands and down onto the track, but they simply could not get this mad man cuffed, as he was extremely strong and grabbed his inner thighs—an old wrestler's trick to avoid the opponent from getting his arms back.

I ran up to the scrum and hollered at the man: "Stop fighting, you're hurting yourself." But, this guy was so intoxicated and powerful that, in his mind, he wasn't going to be taken—dead or alive! So, reverting back to my defensive tactics training, I gave the guy a short chop to the left scapula (shoulder blade) with my baton and screamed at him to stop fighting. By God he did, momentarily, and the officers got him into handcuffs, onto a golf cart and out of there. My tactic was not appreciated by the crowd who pelted us with a shower of rocks. My feeling was I had to do what was necessary to get control of this animal, and it worked, thanks to the mentoring of the famous LAPD martial arts instructor, Bert Koga.

Master Koga was a "million" degree Black Belt in a number of martial art disciplines: Koga was a world class expert in Karate, *Judo* and *Jiu-Jitsu.* He was the master of using distraction as a method of bringing recalcitrant suspects under control. Some of the most effective techniques in getting a subject out of a car when the resister is holding firmly on the steering wheel and refusing to budge includes: Thumping the guy in an eye with your finger, firmly inserting the knuckle behind the suspect's ear (the mastoid bone), a short judo chop to the collar bone, and grasping the mule by the upper lip, twisting and pulling him out—very much like the nuns did with my ear when they led me to the Mother Superior's office for misbehaving in class. . .

None of these *katas* (moves) are debilitating and they almost always work. However, when you employ one of these tricks before a multitude of irate fans, you are going to pay the price! And, I did: I was vilified and lambasted in the press for weeks, which didn't make my Chief very happy. But, when the media discovered what this troublemaker did, not only to our officers but to the fans around him, I eventually got a pass.

I dubbed this man "John L. Sullivan" because, not only was he as tough as the famed boxer of yesteryear, but he was as solid and chiseled as a marble statue—a carpenter by day and a two fisted boozer at night: This guy had serious anger management issues and beat-up a lot of bar patrons in and around the San Francisco Bay Area. He had a four page rap sheet for drunken, out of control incidents, where he continually battered whoever crossed his path. Like they used to say in the Old West: "This was one bad *hombre!*" This fracas started when Sullivan noticed that the man sitting in front of him was wearing a USC shirt; John L. apparently hated USC fans, so the more he drank, the madder he got. John's chiding soon turned into angry insults and threats. The issue came to a head when the bar battler urinated on the man. As we profane cops say: "This really pissed-off the victim and a lot of people around him!" When our coppers arrived, he vigorously resisted, assaulted them, and committed a felony battery on a police officer, by kicking my good friend, Marvin Moore, in the balls—and that really pissed *me* off! Little did our fighter from the City know at the time was that, in addition to all of the other charges, he violated an officer of the judiciary, a Municipal court Judge from L.A., by urinating on him! Needless to say, severe justice was meted out on this one.

Elder Abuse

As usual, it was another absolutely gorgeous Autumn Saturday on the Farm. The only thing that could have made it better was if I was lounging around poolside at home sipping cocktails, instead of being Field Commander at the WASU vs. Cardinal football game. The crowd was estimated at about 50,000—not bad for this so-so contest—and the radio was unusually quiet. Then, it began:

"Beep, Beep, Beat 1 and FC-6; An irate Stanford Alum reports 415 subjects in Section TT, drinking beer, splashing it around and using foul language."

"Ah, 10-4, Beat 1, responding."

How in the hell did they get that alcohol through the gates? I wondered. We fought like hell to make Stanford Stadium a "Booze Free Zone!"

Sergeant John McMullen (FC-6) and I were partnered up, strolling around the lower perimeter of the stadium. I think he was actually trying to keep me out of trouble. We watched the deputies and their SEP partners contact a group of subjects—about 20 of them, approximately 30 rows up, right in the middle of the Reserved Section. I wondered how they got those seats as they didn't appear to be alums or members of the Chuck Taylor Grove crowd. This was a gang of young adults, some shirtless, some in tank tops and a few wearing "Do-Rags." *Hmmmm, this could be interesting,* I thought. After a few minutes, our troopers cleared the call and advised that the situation was under control.

About 15 minutes later, radio dispatched Beat 1 again to the same group having received several more complaints of drunken, rowdy behavior. I then told FC-6 to go up there and see what was going on. From my safe vantage point—after all, I was being paid to lead, not fight—I could see that the situation was escalating, especially when I heard FC-6 shout over the radio:

"FC-6, get some more units over here Code 2 and have the transportation units respond to the field gate; we're going to have some 10-15s (arrestees) coming at ya very shortly!"

Almost immediately, there was a swarm of activity in that section with bodies flying all over the place.

"Radio, A-2, we have a major 415 up there, where *are* those fill-units?" I barked.

"They are en route, A-2," the dispatcher replied—undoubtedly thinking, *Jeez, Captain, chill out!* But, this kind of situation could go off like a powder keg—I learned that after working these games for well over 20 years, so I wanted to nip this problem in the bud, ASAP.

Well, that got their attention. In a heartbeat, we had a gang of cops on the problem. Then, the procession began: Several rowdies were under tow, being muscled down those treacherous stairs. As the troops dragged their quarries to the field gate, I assumed a "doorman's" role by opening up the gate as the deputies had their hands full—and I didn't mind. One of my last cops to drag an arrestee down the stairs was my hero, John, FC-6—and his pinch was a real hand grenade—definitely not going along with the program. As John was struggling with this wildcat, another dude came-up on the fly, in an effort to rescue his buddy from taking the short ride in the golf cart. I pulled the gate shut and initiated the classic "Halt" sign; however, this punk whacked my hand away, ripped open the gate and started to run down onto the field. *Not so fast Buster*, flashed on my internal screen, as I simultaneously whipped a Hulk Hogan neck lock on this brash young man; the inertia flung both of us some 4 feet to the turf, luckily, with my catch on the bottom! *I had 'em*, I thought, until a huge mass of humanity came crashing down on us. Could this be the other guys from *their* group? It seemed like a classic football pile-on and I was hoping that a ref would blow a whistle and throw a flag or something. All the while, the poor bastard I had affectionately attached to my right bicep was screaming:

"OK, I give, I give, I give!"

"All right, man, but stop fighting! You're hurting yourself," was my refrain!

He and all of the others were hurting me, too. When they finally un-piled, it wasn't the bad guys or the football team. Damn! It was MY guys—about 4 of them, led by my favorite deputy, of CPR fame, none other than Harris Kuhn—all 250 pounds of him—maybe more with all of that battle gear he carried! As I dusted myself off and hitched a ride to our compound, I clearly knew that I was getting way too damn old for this rough stuff...

At the lock-up, the real work began: Photos, prints, collecting the arrestees' property and filling out reams of paperwork. I went to the report writing section of this modular building and perused the Penal Code. *Aha, there it is,* I mused while snickering. I'm going to have some fun with this homeboy. When it was time for my collar to be processed, I borrowed a pair of mirrored glasses worn by those southern Sheriffs and made famous in the great flick "Cool Hand Luke." I entered the room and upon seeing me, my pinch inquired:

"So, Sir, what have I been arrested for?"

Like the old Sheriff in Smokey and the Bandit used to say, I drawled:

"Bouy, you in a heap a trouble! I'm a throwin' the book at ya! We gonna start off with drunk in public, disorderly conduct, assaulting an Executive Officer, a felony, resisting arrest, AND: Section: 11174.4 P.C!!!"

"What is that, Sir?" he sheepishly asked.

"Son, that would be ELDER ABUSE!"

"Elder Abuse? I might've done them other things you said, but I damn sure didn't do no elder abuse!" he shrieked.

"Young man," I quietly replied, "You assaulted me—I'm an old man!"

"Sheet, you ain't THAT old. You kicked ma ass!" he countered.

I simply could not hold back and spontaneously burst into laughter.

"Naaaaa, I was just bullshittin' ya!" and I patted him on the back. The entire room broke up, including his homies, who chided him unmercifully—not only for being "whupped" by an old man, but for swallowing the bait—hook, line and sinker!

Before leaving, I learned that this group came up from Salinas to cheer-on their buddy, a former star player at their high school. Their "Hero" was the speedy tailback for WASU—and they had a lot to root for that afternoon, as that kid really put a hurt on Stanford's "D." It was too bad they had fouled-up their day at the Farm, but I promised to put in a good word with the DA if they didn't cause us any more grief.

The next week, I went to the Sheriff's Staff meeting and got the business from Sheriff "Chuck" (Gillingham), who, after describing the scenario, said: "Captain, you aren't working the Burbank or the Drunk Tank anymore. Aren't you getting a little too old for that stuff?" *Go ahead Chuck, rub it in,* I thought, but just laughed at myself along with the rest of the staff. . .

Finale

John and I were on our way to the DA's Office in the North County Court House one day when we saw our Salinas buddies in the lobby. We exchanged pleasantries and learned that our "good word" to the DA apparently worked as the guys were being allowed to plead-out to 647f (intoxication), pay a small fine, and do a year of summary probation. My collar thanked me for not charging him with that dreaded crime: "Elder Abuse". . . We all had a good laugh.

"Trouble Brews at the Farm"

This was the headline in the Peninsula Times Tribune on October 18, 1981; it was written by Richard Hanner whose subtitle read: *"Violence at stadium fueled by alcohol."* Ya think? After several years of intolerable behavior by inebriated fans, our department lobbied then Assistant Athletic Director, Ray Young, for a moratorium on alcoholic beverages within the confines of the stadium. In 1978, DAPER outlawed all booze, cans, bottles and containers that were larger than 15"X 12"X 9." Needless to say, this was a very unpopular and controversial rule: For years, spectators had hauled-in huge ice chests—even beer kegs in tubs of ice—which made it nearly impossible for fans to walk through the very narrow passageways between the bleachers. This caused folks to grumble, which often led to fights. Students took the alcohol ban very personal—obviously, because they were the ones who brought in most of the humongous coolers and kegs—however, Mr. Young candidly countered that the rule was for everyone, pointing out that the students were a small minority of the total 70-80,000 plus fans who attended the games. Needless to say, it was "game-on" with our very clever students who tried a million ways to smuggle "Demon Rum" into the games. I put some of my best SEPs at the student gate and got maybe 80% of the alcohol, but like the War on Drugs, some always seemed to get through—especially via the LSJUMB...

For that season, disturbances, fights and drunk-related arrests plummeted. But, unlike Prohibition in the 1920's, Stanford's Temperance Movement was short lived: The new Athletic Director and his staff caved in to student pressure and rescinded the ban on booze but retained the container size mandate. Almost immediately, it was like Old Tombstone again—save for the gunfights... This resurgence in violence and drunken antics prompted Mr. Hanner to pen his article in the Times. He told me that he had been to a number of games, so the following excerpts are from an eyeball witness:

"As the game proceeds, some fans will be splattered with beer sloshed by their hard drinking neighbors. Others will be struck by a can or ice cream container, hurled from the upper reaches of the stadium. A number of spectators will be treated to the sight of drunken men pulling down their trousers and urinating against the upper rim of the stadium." I commented on this issue:

"These are guys who are blitzed out of their gourds. They have openly displayed themselves to everybody—women and children included. We will not tolerate that!" In fact, we didn't: We cited numerous young men—come to think of it, there *was* one woman whose defense was 'the line was too long!'—and charged the violators with 374b of the Penal Code, littering or dumping noxious waste in public—for lack of a better section.

Reporter Hanner continued:

"As spectators leave the stadium, they may witness a fight or some other unsavory incident, perhaps besotted pranksters tipping over chemical toilets."

"Another problem that concerns security officials is what Niemeyer calls the 'senseless throwing of hard objects.' Some fans, many of them youngsters, try to pelt television crew members and other prominent targets on the playing field. The missiles include bottles, cans, and rocks. Last year, Niemeyer was the target of such an attack."

"A can of chewing tobacco came out of the stands and flew within a few inches of my head," the Captain recalled. "We put plainclothes personnel throughout the stands and pinpointed missile hurlers, who were immediately arrested and charged with felony assaults. I once bagged a couple of kids, quite by accident, while patrolling the South end zone. These two were trying to nail a photographer, who was taking pictures in the prone position on the field, and had no idea he was a target. The stone thrown by one of the culprits was about the size of a papaya! Once the stories about numerous arrests for throwing stuff got out in the press, that miscreant behavior came to a screeching halt!"

I think this account by an outside observer gives one an *undistorted view* of what the SUDPS went through during football season back in the day. To the man and woman, we hated working these games: One could only hope that at shift's end, you weren't in the ER; at the end of the season, everyone would heave a sigh of relief—providing you weren't subpoenaed for a deposition in a pending lawsuit. I remember Chief Herrington always saying: "Whew. Well, we got through another one." Indeed, and very soon, I was going to experience my last Stanford/Cal home game—I never "volunteered" to work that melee at Memorial Stadium in Berkeley, for the chance of getting hurt up there was quite good, especially if you were with the white and red team: The stadium at UC held about 75,000 screaming folks, most clad in blue and gold. Worse, there was no perimeter fence around the stands, so when the game was over, win or lose, the frenzied crowd would pour over the wall and spill onto the field like a Tsunami. Everything in their way was inundated and if you wore red or a police uniform, you were fair game for a beat down! One of my colleagues, a Lt. with UCB Police, nearly lost an eye in the fray after a Big Game: Some coward threw a brick that hit him right in the face. Luckily, he was adjusting his eyeglasses at the very moment the brick hit its mark; he received a broken hand and severe cuts to his face; however, it could have been a lot worse.

Last Home Big Game

As I reported in the Hell Week chapter, hosting the Big Game at Stanford was pure HELL! It didn't take me long to figure out that in order to protect our beloved campus from serious damage from marauding Cal vandals, we needed extra security 24-7. In the old days, the Huns from across the Bay used to begin showing-up in the wee hours Thursday or Friday before the event. But, as time went on, the wanton damage to buildings, fountains, and sculptures began as early as one week before the game. Dye in Mem Aud's fountain and bear paws all over the place became routine. But, when the culprits started pouring black motor oil on the brick walkways, painting the Rodin statues with blue and gold oil paint, and writing "CAL" on the 50 yard line on the stadium's turf with acid, those stunts clearly crossed the line. Although putting our SEPs on alert around the clock was going to be costly, it was effective in preventing serious vandalism and we apprehended a number of would-be damage doers in the process. The media helped scare away the miscreants by publicizing our "blanket" security plan of having a cop behind every bush—highly exaggerated, of course, as well as the number of the Weenies we nabbed.

One of the most guarded sites was that huge ancient stadium. We had token coverage during the day, but assigned numerous security officers in and around the venue during the night, starting Wednesday. Because of the gauntlet we established, the Cal culprits avoided the place like the plague, but we caught several of our SU students trying to smuggle-in booze: One crafty crew was caught red-handed way up on the berm, burying a huge ice chest packed with ice and Corona. Nice try guys, and because they were minors, they lost about 75 bucks worth of beer to our evidence room; we offered to give them their expensive cooler back, though. Perhaps the most extraordinary pinch involved a couple who was literally caught with their pants down, carrying the "Moonlight Kiss in the Quad" tradition to the next level—on the 50 yard line, no less. . .

It was 1997. I had already decided that I was going to pull the plug and retire in about a year. At this point in my waning career, although I was in full uniform, I had virtually no involvement in game operations, except to advise and ensure that arrests were proper and that all of the bases were covered for prosecution. I recall trudging up the flight of 80 plus stairs and then another 3 flights up in the Press Box to our Communications/Command Post. Being in my late 50s with bilateral hip replacements and carrying way too much weight, 30 pounds of which was attributed to the gun belt, cuffs, baton, ammo, radio and all of the other cop paraphernalia, the ascent was all the more difficult. After having my Cheese House sandwich and "Monday Morning Quarterbacking" the Cardinal's performance, I went down to the field and took up a position near the North end zone, aka., the Zoo. I loved to watch the game from that vantage point, especially when that little Stanford scatback, Darrin Nelson, ran back kick-offs and punts. That young man was incredible: Once the ball was in the air, the sound of 21 players running down the field was like a thundering herd of bison. The resultant clash of plastic helmets and shoulder pads was indescribable! In spite of the horrendous collisions, Nelson always managed to make the catch, elude most of his pursuers—many of whom left their "equipment" lying on the field—and weave his way through that mass of humanity for TDs or substantial gains. Experiencing those runbacks was a sight to behold and certainly worth the price of admission.

In addition to seeing the tactics of the game unfold up close and personal, another perk of working the field was occasionally bumping into legends of the game. Although I was never a big autograph hound, I once spotted the iconic Alabama coach, Paul William "Bear" Bryant standing by the South goalpost during an East/West Shrine Game. I approached the old coach and asked if I could shake his hand. He replied in his inimical southern accent: "It would be a *pleasha, Suh!*" The great coach sadly passed on a few years later.

As in all Big Games, the place was packed—standing room only. While officials claimed that the old Stanford Stadium's capacity was approximately 85,000, I figured they were wrong. My guess was there were no less that 90,000 souls jammed into every nook and cranny of that house. It was virtually impossible to walk through the narrow concourse which was designed to facilitate Model T Ford pick-ups; they used "Ts" to supply the make-shift hotdog/drink stands that were wedged-in under the bleachers. Need to go the bathroom? Forget it, especially if you were female. The lines were as long as those at the student gate before game time! Our deputies literally needed to push and elbow through the mass of humanity in order to get anywhere; we ran into a lot of blockades and got some angry looks from the fans when "excuse me" fell on deaf ears and we had to gently muscle our way through the crowd. We always got the feeling that people at the games didn't like us much—even the

Stanford faithful, unless we came to their rescue when they were being hassled or pummeled.

I must say that the Stanford student section seldom posed any real problems: Virtually no fights, unless outsiders started them, and only an occasional call of other minor disturbances. The troops often had to wade into the sea of red to confiscate a keg, but other than that, our kids weren't unruly. Even the Band, once seated in the stands, behaved rather well!

Medieval Warfare

Now, the people in blue and gold were a horse of a very different color. Our biggest headache was Cal's ancient mastery of the catapult, e.g., home grown slingshots. I am told that the kids from UCB resurrected this archaic method of warfare many decades before: Using 3 to 4 foot long double lengths of surgical tubes, the teams attached the large rubber bands to a bra, usually one B-size cup—perfect for their projectiles of choice, mostly apples and oranges, but an occasional grapefruit, too. The fusiliers smuggled-in the weapons under their clothing so it was almost impossible for the gate security officers to keep those things out. Once the game was in full swing, the Berkeley crews would work with the efficiency of Civil War cannoneers: Two sturdy lads seated about 4 feet from each other would thrust their arms into the air, firmly gripping the slingshot's surgical tubes; a big guy about two rows back would pull back on the rubbers, while a loader would drop a missile into the chamber and the launcher would *let her fly* toward the Stanford rooting section. Unbelievably, these Cal shooters could pick-off targets all the way across the field—some 80 to 100 yards— especially when the LSJUMB was assembling on the track. But, those who got into Stanford University were accepted for a good reason: Having experienced these bombardments in the past, the brainy ones brought forth Stanford's Lacrosse team to the rescue;

these guys were very adept at snagging the airborne fruit in their snares, thus thwarting most of their adversary's mischief.

While Cal's sharpshooters were busy at their craft, our spotters in the press box were zeroing-in on them with high powered binoculars. Once the slingshot teams were pinpointed, our squads of deputies, usually led by the fearless Marvin Moore, charged into the sea of blue and gold, nabbed the culprits and confiscated the catapults. After a couple of detentions and ejections from the game, the Weenies kept their weapons in their holsters, never to emerge again in this game, anyway. . .

Breakout

As the game raged into the Fourth Quarter, both sides on the gridiron were trading blows like punch drunk boxers on the Friday Night Fights. Meanwhile, the "natives were restless" in the Cal rooting section: A lot of the kids were out of their seats and many congregated down by the perimeter fence and started shaking the barrier fence. We didn't like the looks of this and moved a number of deputies and SEPs that way. On arrival, the troops were greeted with a barrage of rocks, cans, and cups filled with ice. The only safe place was close to the fence; deputies reported that things were getting very ugly. Suddenly, a couple of Weenies climbed over the fence and began running around on the field. Figuring that our cops didn't have time to arrest and transport these troublemakers, the order from HQs was to put them back into the stands. So, our gate keepers tossed them back in. I muttered to myself: *That's a big mistake!* Had I been at the helm, I would have put the plastic cuffs (hands and feet) on the rabble-rousers and laid them out on the field as a warning to the rest of the dung disturbers: In 1984, LAPD used this tactic in the Coliseum when the, then, LA Raiders, won the Championship game and were headed to Tampa Bay and Super Bowl XVIII. After the 1984 play-off game in LA, hundreds of fans stormed the field, so the coppers snagged as many as they could and trussed them up like roped steers. Once the revelers saw that, discretion overcame the urge to valor and they got out of Dodge, post haste! Alas . . .

Back to my last Big Game: When the final gun sounded, the scoreboard read 21-20 and the Axe Trophy would remain in the hands of the victor—The Stanford Cardinal. Then, to add insult to injury, some Stanford team members, backed-up by the entire squad, headed over to the Cal side and flaunted the coveted prized—talk about rubbing one's nose in it. . .

The Weenies went nuts, broke down one section of the fence, forced open the field gate and rumbled onto the field like an avalanche. The Cardinal team hightailed it for their locker room with Axe in tow and knocked over anyone in their path, including the old "peg-legged" Captain. Talk about "Getting No Respect."

Not to be outdone, the Stanford students streamed on the field and formed a huge scrum near Cal's mob. They faced off about 20 yards apart, apparently trying to muster enough courage to engage one another; however, our troops got between them, in an effort to dissuade the groups from coming to blows. In my opinion, it was much like two grade school kids who didn't like each other and were feigning a fight, but were relieved when school officials pulled them apart. Both groups seemed equally scared and didn't appear to have the guts to get into a knock-down-drag-out battle. I was headed that way until the players and other maniacs tried to knock me on my ass, so, for once, I used some common sense and took a seat on the Stanford bench, all the while thinking: *The last thing I need is to get a hip dislocated over this nonsense; and, on the eve of my golden years, no less. Let those idiots fight it out!*

After the Cal hooligans tore down one of the goal posts, the grounds crew quickly disassembled the other one before someone got hurt or killed. After about 20 minutes of people running around on the turf like stampeding cattle, they suddenly left. As the Chief would later remark: "Whew, we got through another one!" *Barely,* I reflected, as I made my way back to the station. During my trek home I thought: *One more football season without the Big Game here, and you're home free, big guy! May God be with me...*

CHAPTER THIRTY SEVEN

Aloha 'Oe

Exit, Stage Left

After nearly six months of serious soul searching, I finally made-up my mind to hang-up my gun belt and turn in my badge. This was an agonizing decision, for I truly loved my job. Clearly, my medical issues with bilateral hip replacements was a big factor: Although I was primarily a desk jockey, my position required me to get out into the field on major crime scenes, walk marathon dignitary visit venues while doing advance recon, as well as working the big events, such as the Gorby and President Clinton extravaganzas—just two examples of the 250 VIP visits Stanford hosted during my tenure. In addition, during football season and numerous other special events, I had to don my Sheriff's regalia, with about 30 pounds of equipment around my waist, which really raised holy-hell with my after-market joints. However, one of the primary reasons for my decision was that my mission was pretty well completed: When hired by Chief Herrington in 1974, my charge was to recruit, hire and train a fresh cadre of deputized officers to meet the new challenges facing campus law enforcement in the twilight of the 20th Century and into the new millennium. In my opinion, those goals had been met and the department was functioning quite well without my guidance; like the proverbial old bull, I was ready for the green pasture of retirement. So, I tendered my resignation to be effective on January 31, 1999.

After receiving my letter, the Chief and I had a meaningful chat and reminisced about the good ol'days, which included innumerable very difficult and stressful periods, as well as some positive recollections, which were numerous, as well. My final request from the Chief was that I be allowed to host an exit party. I loved parties!

This wish was granted and my generous boss agreed to augment any addition expenses, not covered by tickets sold to family, friends and colleagues, which was traditional in organizing law enforcement retirement *soirées*. I asked for our Office Manager, Ramona Kelley, to help in organizing this event—something she was very good at. The theme I selected was to return to my roots—a full blown Hawaiian *luau* (with all of the traditional food), slack key music, hula dancers, knife/torch jugglers and all! We hired a Hawaiian catering group which would take care of the myriad of details involved in putting on a bash for an estimated 100 plus attendees. Naperdak Hall, in north San Jose, was chosen because of its long history of facilitating successful parties: This venue afforded easy access and ample parking, and had a first-rate kitchen as well as a huge banquet hall. The only thing that Ramona and I underestimated was the attendance. As the event date neared, Ramona was besieged with dozens of last minute folks (typical cops) who wanted to join the celebration. We ended up with about 200 people, most from the numerous local, state and federal agencies with whom I worked for over three decades. I was humbled and frankly blown away by the response!

When the time arrived, I was delighted to have my chosen Master of Ceremony, Captain Marvin Moore, take control of this high spirited group, especially after a couple of *mai tais*—well, maybe more than a couple. . . As expected, I knew I was going to be roasted. However, I didn't anticipate ending up as the main *entre* instead of those *kalua* pigs, which had spent 6 over hours in an i*mu* (underground oven lined with white hot rocks)! All of the speakers torched me, but none like my good friend, Deputy Chief Tom Wheatley (San Jose PD), for whom I once procured Stanford student credentials so he could infiltrate a dissident group. Tom excoriated me for being an Oakland Raider fan after the Stanford Police Officers Association presented me with a beautiful high dollar leather team jacket. Wheatley literally "mugged" the audience when he demonstrated how the police photograph Raider arrestees—full face and profile! Although at my expense, Tom's theatrics were hilarious and brought down the house.

As planned, my farewell tribute was fantastic: Lovely music, great food, libation, fellowship, and a full-blown Hawaiian/Tahitian floor show which was incomparable. Everyone seemed to enjoy themselves, which is exactly what I intended. But, like my career, my retirement *luau* was over in a flash. Where did all the time go, I asked myself the following morning? The whole gig—a 35 year stint as a cop was a lot like the roller coaster ride on the old Santa Cruz Boardwalk. Unlike the days when I rode that thriller over and over again, I wasn't going to be able to get another ticket—not in this lifetime, anyway. . . I took me several days to realize that my exit was truly an *Aloha 'Oe* (Farewell to Thee) to the friends and colleagues I had associated with for over three decades.

Captain Marvin Moore, Master of Ceremonies.

Marvin and me, with Ramona Kelley and teary-eyed, daughter, Nina, in the background.

Epilogue

Despite a year of travel to NASCAR races all over the U.S. and a couple of cruises, it took me nearly that long to get over the fact that my life long career in law enforcement was truly over—*Pau*, as we say in the Islands. I tried to keep busy by learning how to use a computer (even put one together) and puttering around my Campbell home. I wrote and published a short history booklet about the California Safe and Burglary Investigator's Association, which would be celebrating its 50th Anniversary in 2000. I later spoke at that Conference in Las Vegas. I also attended a number of luncheons and events of groups I had been involved with for many years. But, after a while, the attendees seemed to get younger and younger, while I got older and older. Plus, I didn't know many of the *Old Breed's* successors, so I went on to other pursuits. This was a difficult transition, but I "toughed-it-out" and decided to relocate to another area with my fiancée, Pennie. That move was an important game changer for it forced me to re-focus. We had a new home built and were totally immersed in landscaping and setting-up the new digs, so there was little time to lament my life change. I still maintain many police contacts via the Internet and keep abreast of the job through interaction with my son, Kirk, who is going on his 17th year with the San Jose Police Department. But, after watching the news several hours a day, and a million cop/murder mystery shows on TV, I'm glad I'm not out there on the streets anymore. Almost every day in the Sacramento/San Joaquin County area, there are several brutal murders, shoot-outs, high-speed car chases, kidnappings, rapes and way too many other unimaginable crimes to cite here. So, I have concluded that much like the military, police work in this day and age is for youngsters—not for seniors!

Finally, writing this book has been an incredible experience for me. I learned volumes, not only about myself, but about Stanford University's fascinating history and traditions. When I first set foot on that campus as a young man back in the 1950s, I had no idea what that vast institution was all about, other than it was a big, very expensive college. Incredulously, I never imagined—not in my wildest dreams—that I would ever be a cop, let alone one at Stanford University! That transformation from a 20 year old kid to a 60 year old SUDPS Captain (when I retired) still overwhelms me to this day.

Chapter Thirty Eight

Marvin Nathaniel Moore
Chief of Police

The Ascension

It all happened so suddenly: Marvin N. Moore, a product of an East Palo Alto neighborhood, excelled in academics as well as in sports. He was a college graduate and the first African American appointed as a Deputized Patrol Officer at the newly reorganized (NG) Stanford University Department of Public Safety—Marvin was a rising star! Moore established himself as a leader and role model for his peers, always accepting challenges and seeing them through to fruition; he was quickly promoted to Sergeant, Lieutenant and after a few years, Marvin's lovely wife, Marie, pinned on his gold Captain's bars—Marvin N. Moore was our Patrol Commander.

When Chief Herrington finally decided to retire, a committee of University human resources (personnel) and law enforcement officials cast their lots for Stanford D.P.S.'s first minority Director of Public Safety, Marvin N. Moore—Stanford's fifth Chief of Police. And, I can attest that after more than 25 years of personal interaction with this man, race had nothing to do with Marvin's appointment: He was simply the best man for the job, period! As I commented to a friend after his promotion, there just wasn't anyone out there who knew more about the department, the job, the institution, and the community than Chief Moore N. Moore!

After a little more than a year on the job, Marvin was playing "hoops" with his beloved sons and some friends when a medical episode sidelined him. Shortly thereafter, God's Angels took him aloft! Needless to say, everyone who knew this man was stunned. "How could this happen?" many asked. Here was a guy in seemingly excellent physical condition, in the prime of his life with the whole world ahead of him, and the Lord took him away in an instant. This tragic event was more than mere mortals could comprehend, that's for sure...

Way Back When...

I first learned about Marvin Moore when I was the Training Sergeant at the S/O: Captain Frank Beasley—then, the Captain at the fledgling SUDPS called me and wondered if I could lobby the Sheriff for a candidate of his, Marvin Moore. The story was that while in an Oregon College, Marvin got into a little jam with the local police. The situation, in essence, was a very minor banking issue which all of us have made at one time or another. Apparently, the cops up there were pretty hard-nosed and wanted to make a federal case out of a small check that bounced. Our S/O's background investigators—equally as hard-nosed in those days—indicated they wouldn't deputize Marvin for this indiscretion. In my humble opinion, this situation was a pretty "Mickey Mouse" deal, so I went to bat for him.

After hearing the circumstances and reviewing the file, I went to my Captain and pleaded Moore's case. Fortunately, my boss was Captain Bill Miller (R.I.P.)—my mentor and supporter. After explaining that Marvin made a mistake, owned up to it, and made restitution (the case was never adjudicated), I vigorously opined that we should give this man a second chance. By all accounts, Mr. Moore had been an outstanding citizen, save for this one faint blemish on his record. I also argued that if we were ever going to achieve diversity in law enforcement, we needed to get off of our current mind-set that cop candidates needed be "Altar Boys," for God's sake! After a huge dog-fight in Sheriff's Staff meeting, Captain Bill prevailed and Marvin received his commission. I was elated, even though I had never met the man.

It was nearly two years hence when I finally shook the massive hand of DPO Moore, the day after I was appointed Captain at Stanford. It was during my first assignment, a "citation writing 1A class" that I spoke about at the beginning of this treatise, that I first met the men and women of the New Guard. I immediately knew Deputy Moore was going to be the inspirational leader of this reconstituted group of rookies, as he seemed to "buy into" the transition and was eager to make the new program work. Many others had doubts. . . So, it wasn't a surprise that Marvin excelled in every challenge along the road to excellence—and solidified my notion when he was the only deputy who aced the "final exam"— the Field Operations course I described in the "Growing Pains" chapter. Marvin was a true believer—not a blind follower, but a visionary who knew that in order for the DPS to evolve, he needed to be a positive force in achieving that goal. And, indeed he was!

A Friend and Fierce Competitor

Right from the get go, I realized that Marvin and I might have been cut from a similar bolt of cloth: We both were diehard competitors who always wanted to be number one; losing or coming in second was not an option for either of us. Unfortunately for me, Marvin was a very quick study, and I soon felt him nipping at my heels. I quickly learned that Moore had superior physicality and hand-eye coordination—something I struggled with all my life. But, when it came to shooting, I figured this upstart had a long way to go to beat his Ol' Captain, for I was literally born with a gun in my hand! I was pretty good with a rifle and very good with a handgun. However, I soon found that this young whipper-snapper, Marvin, who had never fired a pistol until he got into police work, was like he was on a downhill freight train with a handgun! As I said earlier, I formed a pistol team and we surprised the CA police shooting community by placing 12th in the state. Marvin and I traded shot for shot in every match, trying to win that coveted "Top Gun" trophy within our team. We were almost neck and neck during our first season, but I think he beat me a few more times, which he frequently needled me about. It was all in fun, but, damn, I sure hated losing to that guy; however, I often used the "old man" excuse when I lost. . .

The Supreme Court

About twice a week, Marvin and I would check-out of the office during our lunch hour and tell the Office Staff that we'd be at the "Supreme Court." One of our Records ladies once told a colleague that Captains Niemeyer and Moore must be great cops because they were *always* in Court. . . However, this wasn't a judicial venue we were off to: It was a health club and racquetball court. Marvin was a superb athlete, standing about 6'3" and weighing-in at about 220 pounds. He looked like a stylized Greek statue, sporting maybe 5% body fat. On the racquetball court, he moved around like a leopard and seemed to have arms as long as Shaq O'Neal as he rarely missed a shot. I, on the other hand, am built like a lowland gorilla; despite my bulk and lack of flexibility, I used to be fairly quick on my feet and could move around the court fairly well. Although I played gallantly and put my body on the floor and into the walls, I never could beat that guy. Over the years, we played over a hundred matches: Every game was an absolute dogfight, but in the end, I always came up a point or two short. Boy, that ticked me off, especially since I am a very sore loser. However, just before my left hip started to go away, Marvin and I engaged in a tooth and nail battle, in which I finally bested my nemesis by *one* measly point! While we were on our way back to the office, I probed:

"So, Marvin, did you throw that last game and let me win?" He looked at me sternly and replied:

"*Kalani*, I never let *anyone* win at *anything!*" And, so it was—I finally beat Marvin, fair and square!

Farewell

Marvin N. Moore's farewell was an extremely somber event. Hundreds of family, friends and colleagues flocked to Memorial Church. I know that the eulogies were intended to be uplifting, but for me, the shock of my good friend's passing cut deep. I still couldn't come to grips with the fact that the young man who I mentored, competed with, and who later became an invaluable colleague, was suddenly taken from us in the prime of his career. This was a tough one. Chief Moore left an important historical legacy at Stanford University, as well. I never heard anyone, of any worth, utter a bad word about Marvin. Needless to say, my heart poured out to his beloved family, who he talked about endlessly. We all lost a very good man! And, I shall never forget that young man who pulled himself up from humble beginnings, received an education on his own dime, fought hard to get a deputized officer's position at Stanford, and achieved unimaginable goals, thus setting a very high bar in his wake. In many ways, Chief Marvin Nathaniel Moore reminded me of Stanford's first African American employee, Sam McDonald (featured in Chapter Two), who was a trailblazer in his own right, during the dawn of the 20th Century. In any event, I hope you like what I wrote about you, Marvin.

Aloha 'oe and R.I.P., buddy.

Kalani

CHIEF MARVIN N. MOORE

Sunrise: July 23, 1950
Sunset: February 10, 2002

SERVICES:
Memorial Church
Stanford University
Stanford, California

Friday, February 15, 2002 ~11:00 A.M.

OFFICIATING:
Reverend J.R. Cooksey, Pastor
True Light Missionary Church

POST SCRIPT

Laura Wilson, Public Safety Director

Stanford's sixth Chief

After Chief Moore's sudden passing, retired Chief Marvin Herrington assumed the department's controls until a permanent appointment could be made. A panel of campus luminaries, as well as Santa Clara County Sheriff, Laurie Smith, convened in an effort to select Stanford's sixth Police Chief. Lt. Laura Wilson was the odds-on favorite among the finalists due to her decade of tenure with the DPS. She was also a Stanford alumnus, having received her bachelor's degree in 1991. Ms. Wilson moved-up through the ranks quickly during her ten years of service to the Stanford community. Of note, Laura was a team member of the United States Secret Service when Chelsea Clinton first came to the Farm and indoctrinated Chelsea's protection detail to life on the Farm. Wilson was selected as the new Chief in May 2002. Following the precedent of "Firsts" set by Marvin Moore, Chief Wilson was not only Stanford's first woman C.O.P., but she was also the University's first graduate to be elevated to that position! Laura Wilson continues to be Director of Public Safety as I conclude this book in 2014.

Acknowledgements

There have been so many people who have contributed to this book in so many ways that I just don't know where to begin, and hope I don't inadvertently miss anyone. Way back in the day, when I was a Deputy Sheriff by night and college student by day, an old friend suggested I write a "good book," someday, about the unusual events I experienced as a cop. Well, after nearly five decades, I finally put pen to paper, so to speak, and wrote *that* book. But, whether this book is *good* or not remains to be seen. When I began at Stanford, I met Karen Bartholomew, then a writer with the Campus Report and Stanford Historical Society, who encouraged me to write about the Stanford Police Department's history. I thank Karen for nudging me along, all the while providing me with her Stanford historical work and counsel.

My first editor and guru was Tom Conger, a high school football teammate, who then lived on Maui, HI. T/C provided a great deal of inspiration for this project and encouraged me to get my thoughts on paper when they came to mind—often in the middle of the night! Tom's game plan was spot-on and he helped in sorting out a lot of issues, which provided direction to the right track. For that, I am eternally grateful.

Having only rudimentary typing skills—at 30-40 wpm—there was never a need for a stand-by bucket of water near my keyboard. . . I am prone to being a typo-maniac, thus needed folks to eyeball my drafts. I thank Diana McLaughlin and Valerie Smith for their help.

The major player in reviewing and editing my work is my daughter, Nina L. Niemeyer D.O., who not only has an eagle eye, but knew the stories very well, because she lived them—not only as my dear friend and confidant, but as a Stanford student, as well. Nina is blessed with an edict memory and often cleared-up the fog that developed in my memory over the years. She painstakingly poured-over my material despite having a torturous schedule as a physician in the E.R. at Nellis AFB, and later as the Emergency Department's boss of the new Veteran's hospital in Las Vegas, NV. I'll never be able to repay her for her labor of love!

And, to my son, City of San Jose Police Officer, Kirk J. Niemeyer #3452, whose knowledge of contemporary policing was invaluable in reviewing various cop-related subjects. He also did some detective work (on his own time) researching public information at the courts. Because of Kirk's efforts, I'm confident that most of the law enforcement issues herein are factually correct.

A shout-out is in order for my good buddy, and positively the best man I ever worked with, Inspector John McMullen (Santa Clara County DA's Office Ret.), formerly, my faithful Detective. Like Nina, John has a memory like a steel trap! I called him dozens of times about cases we worked on and he remembered nearly every detail, including the names of the players. John was like my SUDPS "Google." So, my hat's off to him for his contribution.

Other friends and department colleagues (all retired) who came up with some interesting stories are Sgt. Philip Love, Deputies Anthony Navarra and Tim Schreiner. Tim, originally a very shy reserved young man, turned into to a darn good investigator and offered some good insights into a major burglary case he and Allen James solved. Thanks, guys!

Without the training, experience and association with so many colleagues and friends at the Santa Clara County Sheriff's Office, my career and this book would not have been possible. I've mentioned most of them throughout this saga, but still would like to acknowledge their contributions: Lt. John "JJ" Johnson, my Training Officer. Lt. Howard DeSart, one of my Patrol Sergeants, and the "collection of physical evidence" guru; Howard was also a tremendous resource for the chapter on homicides. Much thanks to Sgts. Dave Pascual, Ken Kahn, and Tom Beck, who were the primary detectives on the Arlis Perry homicide. Also, hats off to my good friend and beat partner, Dave LaDuca, who provided me with a lot of insight into undercover work. Last, but not least, Captain Bill Miller (R.I.P.), who helped shape my destiny. As my patrol supervisor, Bill Miller liked my work ethic and reinforced that by taking time to write-up some of my early accomplishments, which helped my resume. When I was promoted to Sergeant, Miller appointed me the S/O's first Training Officer under his tutelage. Capt. Miller began chronicling the history of the Sheriff's Office and identified the Sheriffs from the department's inception in 1850. Much of Miller's work is featured in the <u>Santa Clara County Sheriff's Office Commemorative History Book</u>, which was compiled and edited by Sgt. Rick Sprain (Ret.). As Training Officer, Miller encouraged me to continue on with a department periodical, "The Sheriff's Journal," of which I later became editor. Most importantly, when I was offered the position of Captain at Stanford, Bill urged me to give it a shot and he thought—despite all of the challenges there—I could make it work. Whether it worked or not is debatable, but I surely gave it my best shot!

I also wish to recognize Mrs. Fred-a Jurian, a wonderful lady and widow of Stanford's Finest Fire Chief, Frank Jurian. Fred-a provided me with a plethora of information and photos which enabled me to expand on Chief Jurian's splendid career on the Farm. Doug Williams, who worked closely with Chief Jurian over the years, also gave me a lot of insider information about the Chief's pet project, the old hand pumper called "The Leland." Doug was a crew member of that award winning team and knew all of the players. Williams' contribution is greatly appreciated.

And, immeasurable thanks to wife, Pennie and her daughter, Melissa Lyons, for their assistance when it came to this darn fickle typing contraption called a computer. I had my share of frustrations with this damn thing—mostly because my big fingers hit a wrong key or something which would put my hard copy into Purgatory for an eternity, thereby causing a bit of a rant, which often elevated my BP to alarming levels. Pen would order me out of my lair and calmly fix the problem. "How did you do that?" I would implore. But, she would simply tell me, in effect, the solution was way above my knowledge and capability and to call her when I messed-up again. . . Melissa came to my rescue in the waning moments of this project by showing me how to scan and store the photos I suddenly decided to add. And, out of the blue, her friend, Sami Zmander, sorted out all of my photo issues; he enhanced the resolution, sized the shots, and professionally inserted them into the text. That saved me hours of frustration, so thanks, Sami.

I want to express a special thanks to Pennie's nephew, Thomas Dangerfield, of Cincinnati, OH who designed the cover of this book. This clever young advertizing designer put forth a lot of effort in making his creation an "eye catcher," so I'm very indebted to Tommy and his unique artistic talent.

Office Manager Ramona Kelley and I were almost always like minded and worked together very closely in making our department a first class operation. Ramona, who had an extensive background in Human Resources (formerly known as Personnel), worked tirelessly with me in honing our recruitment, selection and hiring process. Together, we greatly streamlined the procedure and fought "City Hall" in order to assimilate the polygraph into our vetting/background investigation for sworn personnel—a last ditch effort to ferret-out bad apples. RK was also my main go-to-person when we began hosting law enforcement related conferences such as the Western States Safe and Burglary Investigators, among others. Finally, my biggest tribute to Ramona was all of the effort she put into my retirement *soirée*; I'll never forget that experience and thank RK profusely for making my swan song the best party, ever!

Another shining star was our Department Secretary, Mary Jane Tralongo. During her career, MJ cranked-out more documents than the old mimeograph of the day—some of you youngsters may have to look that one up! During the period before computers, the women in the Front Office typed everything because most handwritten reports were illegible—and most of us men couldn't type a lick! I can remember when I first walked into the office in 1974 and saw the staff plunking away on old—and, I mean *OLD*—manual machines! The breakthrough came when IBM came out with the Selectric II, on which Mary Jane could spit-out over 130 wpm. However, the greatest benefit of having MJ prepare my drafts, especially when I was steamed about something, was that she often held-off finalizing the document for a day or so. When I hadn't heard from her and barked: "Are you done with that letter yet?" she'd reply, "Are you sure you want to send this?" Most of the time, Ms. Tralongo was right and I appreciate her for not allowing me to dig myself in deeper. . . Thanks for all of your dedicated service, Mary Jane.

Recently, Stanford University Philosophy Professor, Christopher Bobonich, and I crossed paths: Chris and his Dad, retired Professor Harry M. Bobonich, were writing a book on unsolved murders on university/college campuses, and reached out to me regarding some of the homicides I had investigated at Stanford. After exchanging some articles on this gruesome topic, we all became e-mail/phone pals. Professor Chris encouraged me to finish this book and "get it out there," as he put it. That bit of advice invigorated me and got me out of one of the many doldrums I experienced over the past 10 years. Chris' father, Prof. Harry, an accomplished author in his own right having written several paperbacks, has been very, very helpful in pointing me in the right direction as I approached the goal line. Both professors suggested that I self publish my story, which is exactly what I have done. I really appreciate the information and guidance I received from the professors, and I am extremely grateful for their insights and expertise. The Bobonich's book, Bloody Ivy, is now in print and is also available on Kindle. Check it out—it is a good read!

I would like to thank Chief Marvin L. Herrington for giving me the opportunity to work in one of the most interesting and challenging venues in America. I don't know where my career would have taken me had I remained at the Santa Clara County Sheriff's Office, but I am certain that I would have never experienced the variety of people, events and adventures I described herein. Although an experienced law enforcement officer in the urban and rural theater, I was clearly a neophyte in the realm of campus policing. I appreciate the guidance and backing Marv Herrington afforded me throughout my tenure on the Farm. It would have been a tough slog without him.

Finally, I credit my late Dad, Irving "Irv" Niemeyer, for instilling in me an interest in writing and history. At an early age, my Dad encouraged me to formulate my thoughts on paper. Irv was a rebellious Chicago teenager who ran away from home when he was fifteen, and pursued his education via the "School of Hard Knocks." He developed a penchant for travel—on the cheap, by hopping freight trains, which took him to every state in the lower 48. During these sojourns, Dad became a voracious reader and gained knowledge about the world, politics and life, thus achieved what he called: "Native Intelligence." After a couple of run-ins with the law, Irv saw the error of his ways and straightened himself out by enlisting in the U.S Army; he eventually became one of the last of the "Pony Soldiers," in Ol' General John "Black Jack" Pershing's outfit, the First Cavalry Division. He was later transferred to Ft. Ruger, Honolulu, T.H. (Territory of Hawaii) where he met my Mother, Gladys Pilares—hence, my emergence later on.

My Dad worked at Pearl Harbor after his discharge from the Army and was damn lucky to be home with Mom and me during the December 7th attack. And, we were extremely fortunate not to be hit by that errant bomb which disintegrated a home and its inhabitants nearby; I was on our balcony and saw the Zero zoom overheard after the explosion. During the WWII years, Irv became a "liquor cop" with the Honolulu Liquor Commission. After receiving his much belated high school diploma, Irv went up through the ranks and subsequently became Chief Investigator. It was during this time that he assisted me with my writing, which aside from "Shop", was the best grade I received in high school. . . So, I owe a lot to my Dad and have fond memories of how patient he was with his "difficult" pupil. It is for this reason that I have dedicated this book to his memory.

Dad and Daughter

Author and Editor-in-Chief

About the Author

Although born in CA, Raoul *Kalani* Niemeyer, grew-up in Hawaii—positively the best place to be, even during the WWII years. *Kalani* swam, surfed and fished in the warm, beautiful waters of Waikiki Beach when there were only three major hotels!

Raoul was fortunate to receive a solid primary education in Catholic Schools. In his junior year, *Kalani* was accepted to Punahou School, established in 1841, one of the oldest (and best) schools in America. It was there that Niemeyer lettered in football, and in the classroom, honed his penchant for writing under the tutelage of excellent mentors, as well as from his Dad, Irv. When he graduated in 1956, *Kalani* enlisted in the U.S. Air Force and was trained as a jet engine mechanic. Airman 1st Class Niemeyer was assigned to the Strategic Air Command where he worked on long range B-36 and B-52 bombers, which often carried nuclear ordnance. When discharged from the service, he had his sights set on being an aircraft mechanic for a major airline, but had to settle for building armored personnel vehicles (M-113s) at FMC, in San Jose, CA. It was there that he met a colleague, Dan Montgomery, who was about to be hired as a police officer in the City of Los Gatos, CA. (Dan later relocated to Westminster, CO where he was Chief of Police until he retired in 2007 after 47 years of service!) Dan suggested that Niemeyer become an officer, too, because he was "big, tough, and had the gift of gab"—apparently, the primary prerequisites back in the day... Being a cop was the last thing *Kalani* thought he'd ever be...

After a year of study and testing, the Santa Clara County Sheriff's Office swore-in Raoul K. Niemeyer, pinned a badge on him and sent him out to police the mean streets of San Jose. Deputy Niemeyer worked in patrol at night and attended San Jose State College during the day; he received a Bachelor's Degree and continued post graduate studies in Public Administration. When promoted, Sergeant Niemeyer became the department's first Training Officer. As an editor, he wrote many historical police-related articles for the *Sheriff's Journal*. Raoul also authored a booklet to celebrate the 50 year history of the California Safe and Burglary Association.

Raoul K. Niemeyer was hired as a Captain for the Stanford University Department of Public Safety in 1974; his mandate was to recruit, hire and train a cadre of deputized officers. This is partially what this book is about; however, Stanford University itself is very rich in history and tradition, which he has woven into this work. Captain Niemeyer retired in 1999, and now lives in Northern California with his wife, Pennie, and their beloved Bichon Frises, "BeBe" and "Harley."

Cop Jargon

290: Sex offender required by **Penal Code Section 290** to register with the local police or sheriff.

509: Driving with one's head in their rectum.

5150: Welfare and Institutions Code definition of a person who is a danger to himself or others.

6-F (Frank): Wanted for a felony.

86ed: Cop term to cancel or eliminate; derived from bar slang to stop serving alcohol to an inebriated patron.

ADA: Assistant District Attorney.

AH: Adam Henry: An anatomical description of Jerk!

AKA: Alias; Also Known As.

A.N.N.E.T: Allied Narcotic Network Enforcement Team— a Santa Clara County Task Force.

Beef: A criminal charge; also can be a fight.

Billy Club: A short wooden club, developed in England, 1848.

Buzzed: Displaying law enforcement badge/credentials.

BOL: An alert—be on the lookout for wanted subjects/vehicles; aka, **BOLO.**

Burned: When cops are identified by criminals.

Bushwhacked: Ambushed.

C.A.T.: Counter Assault Team (snipers).

CCI: Criminal ID Bureau, Department of Justice, Sacramento, CA.

CI: Confidential Informant.

CDC: CA Department of Corrections.

Code 2: Urgent response: Proceed quickly but safely.

Code 3: Emergency: Proceed with red lights and siren.

Code 4: Situation stabilized, no further assistance needed.

Code 5: Covert stake-out; surveillance.

Code 7: Mealtime.

Code 10: Bomb Threat.

Code 20: Urgent, Officer needs assistance.

Code 30: Emergency, Officer is in imminent danger of being hurt or killed.

Code 1000: Plane Crash.

Collar: Arrest.

Con-Wise: A street wise criminal who is adept at thwarting a Police interrogation.

C.O.P.: Chief of Police.

Cop: Old English acronym: Constable on Patrol.

Cop-out: Confess or admit to a criminal offense.

CP: Command Post.

CS: An insignificant arrest or citation, aka., "Chicken Poop."

C.Y.A.: CA Youth Authority (youth prison) aka, "YA".

CYA: Cover your ass!

DA: District Attorney.

DDA: Deputy District Attorney.

Dicks: Detectives—in this context.

Dirt Bag: Nasty, disheveled drug/alcohol ridden individual.

Dog Watch: Midnight patrol shift, so named due to the stray dogs (cats, too) running around.

Doing the Chicken: A resister thrashing around when the carotid hold is effectively applied.

DPS: Department of Public Safety.

Deuce: Driving while intoxicated; derived from old Penal Code Section 502.

ECR: El Camino Real.

Fat Pills: Doughnuts.

Fence: Unsavory buyer of stolen goods.

Fill: Back-up police units.

Foot-Sweep: Judo move wherein an aggressor's feet are swept out causing a sudden introduction to Terra Firma!

Flatfoot: Term used in the 19th Century when most policemen patrolled on foot which often resulted in fallen arches, hence, "flatfoot."

FNG: FN New Guy or Gal—a rookie.

FTO: Field Training Officer.

FUBAR: F—Up Beyond All Recognition!

G-Unit: Non-sworn Community Service Officers.

FW: Fricking Weirdo: A pervert, whacko or strange individual e.g., "one can short"—of a six-pack.

Gut Busters: See Fat Pills.

High Chest Hold: Euphemism for the carotid restraint aka, the dreaded "Japanese Sleeper Hold."

Hip-Pocketing: Withholding investigative information (in a detective's notebook, traditionally kept in the hip pocket) from colleagues so that all praise and adulation would be solely bestowed on the hoarder.

J. Serra: Junipero Serra Blvd.

Juice: Influence; pull, with the ability to gain favors; also used to describe steroids.

Made: Same as burned.

Magged: Checking people for weapons via a Magnetometer.

Mule: A criminal who transports drugs or other illicit goods.

Narc: Undercover narcotics officers, often in heavy disguise such as: Drug Dealers/Outlaw Bikers.

Off: To kill or eliminate.

O.P.: Observation Post.

Paddy Wagon: Panel trucks and vans used to transport inebriates to jail. Derived from the derogatory reference to New York's Irish immigrants (Paddies), who had a tendency to become intoxicated, thus had to be removed from public places via horse drawn wagons.

P.A.L.: Parolee at Large.

P.C.: Probable Cause for arrest. Also, **Penal Code**.

PC: "Politically Correct."

PDQ: Pretty Damn Quick.

Perp: Perpetrator of a crime.

Pinch: An arrest.

Peerless Bracelets: Handcuffs made by the Peerless Co.; Cuffs are also made by Smith &Wesson.

Podunk PD/S/O: Rural, often small police/sheriff agencies who are sometimes unprofessional.

POI: Person of Interest; also Point of Impact in collision cases.

Pop Knot: A swollen contusion.

P.O.S.T.: Peace Officer's Standards and Training. The CA state agency that enforces a minimum standard of training for all sworn law enforcement officers.

PPD: U.S. Secret Service's Presidential Protection Detail.

QOA: Quiet on arrival.

QOD: Quiet on departure.

Rabbit: One who runs from the police.

Raid Jacket: Lightweight jackets, emblazoned in large letters "**SHERIFF, POLICE, FBI, DEA,**" etc. worn by cops during dangerous situations.

Rap Sheet: Arrest and Conviction record.

Red Coats: Aka, "Elton's Raiders:" Old S/O Lt. Elton Heck's red jacketed group who provided football security at Stanford Stadium before 1975.

Rescue: To forcibly take a prisoner from police custody.

R/P: Reporting Party.

S&R: Security and Receiving for prisoners at San Jose's main jail.

S.N.A.F.U.: Same as FUBAR.

S/O: Sheriff's Office.

Score: Purchase drugs.

Scumbag: Same as Dirt Bag.

Schrooms: Psilocybin "psychedelic" mushrooms.

Skell: A criminal.

Slam: The "slammer;" jail or prison.

Smurfs (Crooks): An organized team of low level criminals who follow the lead of their crime boss.

Smurfs (Cops): A team of officers who initially seek evidence during a search warrant.

Snitch: Police informant.

SOP: Standard Operating Procedure.

Street Urchin: A homeless person you wouldn't bring home for Thanksgiving dinner!

Snubby: A short barreled revolver carried by "Dicks" back in the day.

The Bucket/*El Cubo*: The Jail/*El Carcel.*

T/A: Traffic Accident/collision.

T/O: Training Officer.

VMC: Valley Medical Center: Santa Clara County Hospital, San Jose, CA.

Made in the USA
Las Vegas, NV
24 August 2022